Contemporary Issues in the Psychology of Education

Aoife M. Lynam
Trinity College Dublin, Ireland

Conor Mc Guckin
Trinity College Dublin, Ireland

IGI Global
Scientific Publishing
Publishing Tomorrow's Research Today

Vice President of Editorial Melissa Wagner
Director of Acquisitions Mikaela Felty
Director of Book Development Jocelynn Hessler
Production Manager Mike Brehm
Cover Design Jose Rosado

Published in the United States of America by
IGI Global Scientific Publishing
701 East Chocolate Avenue
Hershey, PA, 17033, USA
Tel: 717-533-8845 | Fax: 717-533-7115
Website: https://www.igi-global.com E-mail: cust@igi-global.com

Library of Congress Cataloging-in-Publication Data

Names: Lynam, Aoife M., DATE- editor
http://id.loc.gov/rwo/agents/n2025020494 | Mc Guckin, Conor editor
http://id.loc.gov/rwo/agents/nb2014024091
Title: Contemporary issues in the psychology of education / edited by Aoife M. Lynam and Conor Mc Guckin.
Description: Hershey, PA : IGI Global Scientific Publishing, [2026] | Includes bibliographical references and index. | Summary: "This book is divided into three sections to create a strong narrative that gradually builds upon foundational psychological topics, explores practices for improving teaching and learning, and culminates in discussions about the future of contemporary education"-- Provided by publisher.
Identifiers: LCCN 2025016749 (print) | LCCN 2025016750 (ebook) | ISBN 9798369312933 hardcover | ISBN 9798369349083 paperback | ISBN 9798369312940 ebook
Subjects: LCSH: Educational psychology
http://id.loc.gov/authorities/subjects/sh85041141
Classification: LCC LB1051 .C678135 2025 (print) | LCC LB1051 (ebook) | DDC 370.15--dc23/eng/20250513
LC record available at https://lccn.loc.gov/2025016749
LC ebook record available at https://lccn.loc.gov/2025016750

British Cataloguing in Publication Data
A Cataloguing in Publication record for this book is available from the British Library.

Table of Contents

Detailed Table of Contents

This book and this chapter are about psychology of education – what we mean by it and how psychology is applied to education, and the ways in which psychology and education are interdependent. As we shall see, psychology contributes to an understanding of every facet of the educational process. This chapter will provide an overview of the conceptual foundation of the chapter and psychology of education, including the different sub-disciplines and the big debates in psychology of education. The authors then explore the dominant frameworks from psychology – its schools of thought – and how they inform and enable the process of education. Finally, this chapter concludes with some cautionary notes for a psychology of education. As will become clear, psychology's contributions to education are considerable, but there is also a need to be critical and apply psychological principles and practices with an appreciation for their limitations. So, the authors delve into critical psychology, considering some of the issues within a psychology of education.

This chapter explores how we should unlearn colonial narratives in the field of psychology of education. We know that psychology has historically been shaped by ethnocentric and Western perspectives, which has often excluded the voices and experiences of non-Western, female, and marginalised groups. This exclusion continues to reinforce a biased understanding of human development and behaviour, perpetuating and contributing to exclusionary practices. This chapter discusses how we can integrate diverse perspectives into academic knowledge and highlights the importance of reflexivity and "unlearning" of entrenched biases as part of a broader decolonising effort, encouraging both educators and students to critically examine their own positionality. This chapter advocates for a broader psychology of education

Schools are at the forefront of attempts to integrate an increasingly multicultural population, build an inclusive society for disabled people, and tackle persistent socioeconomic inequality. This chapter assesses recent evidence on the success of policy in supporting inclusion within and beyond Irish schools and looks at how students are faring in the midst of wider societal changes. The discussion draws on combined psychological and sociological theories understanding inclusion and exclusion at different institutional levels. Focusing on recent evidence from Ireland, the chapter provides unique insights into understanding inclusion and how it is best achieved, highlighting policy priorities for the period ahead.

This chapter explores and examines the possibilities that Universal Design (UD) and Universal Design for Learning (UDL) offer the psychology community in education. The chapter will first outline Universal Design (UD) and Universal Design for Learning (UDL) approaches that focus on the design of learning environments for inclusion. It will then share the models of disability, and how the shift from segregated learner to included learning, shapes thinking in relation to inclusion and exclusion in education. The different psychological theories and how they, when informed by these approaches, will then be explored. The chapter will in essence develop its argument by way of sharing what the combined learning from these theories can offer resulting in a N*UDE approach; that is a new approach for universal design in education in that it invites all professionals to adopt inclusive philosophies and redesign to include to meet the challenges set in the United Nations Sustainable Development Goals, particularly SDG4 Quality Education.

An understanding of stress and coping is important for all educators. Understanding the stress experienced by students, for example, in relation to teaching, assessment, and coping, is important if education is to be optimized, and it helps educators understand their own stress experience and potentially cope better, making them more effective in their relations with students. This chapter opens by outlining what is meant by stress and how it has been studied from a historical perspective. Stress has tended to be conceived as synonymous with distress, and most empirical studies use measures that construe it in this way. An overview will be offered of some of the key research that has explored the adverse consequences of stress, along with the research efforts that have explored stress as a necessary ingredient to achieve. Stress is both the physiological and psychological response to demands, and stress also refers to those demands that trigger that response. Sections will be offered on those stimuli demands or sources of stress and on their effect on students.

In schools today, many children carry the invisible weight of adversity and trauma, affecting their ability to learn and thrive. Through the use of vignettes, specifically the story of Bobby, a young boy grappling with significant trauma, the authors explore how trauma manifests in the classroom and how educators can respond with compassion and understanding. Bobby's journey is emblematic of the countless children who bring their personal histories of violence, neglect, or instability into school, often resulting in behavioural and emotional challenges. By examining both individual-level interventions and systemic changes, this chapter emphasizes the potential of TIC to foster healing. The authors also critique traditional methods that overly focus on individual change while neglecting the trauma-inducing environments many children face. Trauma-informed practice, as explored through frameworks like EMBRACE, demonstrates how schools can shift from managing symptoms to addressing root causes, nurturing both students and staff alike.

Most school-age children experience the death of a close family member or friend. This chapter summarizes the range of common adjustment reactions and the factors that may complicate or prolong children's grief. In addition, this chapter offers practical strategies for school professionals on how to start the conversation with children about primary and secondary losses, adapt academic requirements, develop coping responses when grief responses are activated in the classroom, develop school-based memorial and commemorative activities, conduct outreach to grieving families, and mobilize peer support for the grieving student.

cognitive, and ethical one. Drawing on foundational theories from educational psychology, it explores how technology mediates not only how students learn, but how they experience autonomy, construct identity, and navigate emotion and motivation in increasingly digital environments. The discussion traces how these experiences are shaped by deeper systemic factors such as inequitable access, ethical tensions around data use and surveillance, and the emergence of generative AI. Throughout, the chapter argues for a move beyond either enthusiasm or resistance, advocating instead for a human-centred, augmentation-oriented approach to technology, one that respects learners' psychological needs, supports equity, and prepares students for critically engaged digital citizenship in a rapidly changing world.

Educational policymaking has always been complex and contested but has become even more so in recent years. Education policy faces a range of challenges, many of which have heightened since the pandemic. These include growing and more complex needs of children and young people, especially in relation to SEN and mental health; increasing contestation and politicisation of education among a variety of stakeholders; growing international competition; and growing societal inequality in many countries. This chapter provides an overview of these developments and how they may shape and be shaped by educational psychologists.

Throughout this book, a range of factors have been explored that impact on educators and on students. Chapter 7 puts the spotlight on the student experience of stress. What is critical, of course, is how well one copes and this is the focus of this final chapter. In trying to create a structure to see the key influences that relate to student stress, the author separated the sources of stress from their effects and from how students cope. This is an over-simplification of course. The sources and effects of stress and how students cope are all inter-related and bi-directional. The significance of a source of stress depends on one's current wellbeing, and this is affected by how well one has and is coping. It was mentioned in Chapter 7, for example, that responses to stress can become new stressors, such as loneliness as a response to stress and this response interacts with other stressors, such as the student's experience of academic stress leading to a greater impact on academic outcome. Moreover, students with an earlier history of childhood trauma were more likely to experience more adverse outcomes on wellbeing, health, and academic performance compared with students

Preface

We saw a need for this book as a way to bridge essential psychological theories with the real, evolving challenges educators, students, and policymakers face in contemporary education today. Education is becoming increasingly complex, with new demands around mental health, trauma, inclusion, and the effects of rapid technological and societal change continuing to permeate the school environment. We know that children come to school with more than the bags on their backs, yet navigating these demands for educators can feel overwhelming without a solid psychological foundation. This book offers a framework that starts with key psychological principles and then addresses practical issues, like supporting student mental health, fostering belonging, addressing trauma, and preparing for the effects of climate change and technology on learning. Our goal was to create a resource that not only deepens understanding of these concepts but also connects them to everyday educational practices. The book helps readers reflect on how psychology informs teaching and learning, from the classroom environment to the policy level. We hope it will be a go-to guide for those seeking to understand how psychology can make education more inclusive, compassionate, and impactful, ensuring that students are equipped, not just academically, but emotionally and socially for the future.

The chapters are organised into six sections, each addressing key dimensions where psychology informs educational practices. Naturally, it begins by establishing a theoretical and historical foundation before progressing to the exploration of practical issues such as inclusion, mental health, and trauma, and concludes with discussions on future developments, including the role of technology and climate change education. The first section, *Psychology of Education: Looking Back to Move Forward*, sets the groundwork by examining the historical and theoretical underpinnings of psychology in education. *Chapter 1: Do We Need Psychology of Education?* explores the relevance of psychological principles in modern educational environments, laying a foundation for the discussions that follow. *Chapter 2: Unlearning Colonial Narratives in Psychology of Education* critically evaluates the ways in which traditional psychological models have been shaped by colonial and Eurocentric paradigms, and advocates for the adoption of more inclusive and culturally responsive approaches.

The second section, *Values and Motivation in Education*, focuses on the significance of values, ethics, and teacher beliefs in shaping student outcomes. *Chapter 3: Values and Social Conscience in Education* discusses the necessity of embedding ethical and social values within educational systems to nurture socially responsible and reflective learners. *Chapter 4: Contemporary Classrooms: The Role of Motivation and Teachers' Beliefs* examines the impact of teachers' beliefs and expectations on student motivation and performance, offering insights into how educators' perceptions influence learning.

The third section, *Fostering Identity, Belonging, and Inclusion*, shifts attention to the creation of inclusive educational environments that support the development of identity and belonging. *Chapter 5: Equality, Diversity, and Inclusion: The Journey Ahead* addresses the progress and challenges associated with implementing Equality, Diversity, and Inclusion (EDI) in education, with a particular focus on the systemic transformations required to promote equity. *Chapter 6: Adopting a New Universal Design for Education (N*UDE) Approach: Universal Design for Learning (UDL) Aligned With Psychological Theories* explores how the UDL framework can facilitate inclusive educational practices, ensuring that all students, regardless of background or ability, have access to meaningful learning opportunities.

The fourth section, *Mental Health, Stress, and Wellbeing in Education*, turns to the critical importance of mental health and emotional well-being in student success. *Chapter 7: Understanding and Managing Student Stress* identifies the various sources of stress that affect students and outlines strategies for managing it to support academic performance.

The fifth section, *Trauma and Empathy in Educational Settings*, considers the psychological impact of trauma and the role of empathy in supporting students through difficult experiences. *Chapter 8: EMBRACE the Healing: Cultivating Compassion in Trauma-Informed Schools* discusses how trauma affects student learning and offers practical strategies for implementing trauma-informed educational practices. *Chapter 9: Supporting Students Through Grief* explores the ways in which educators can provide emotional support to students dealing with grief and loss. *Chapter 10: Mainstream Education for Children and Young People With Acquired Brain Injury: Enabling a Supportive Return to Education* focuses on the specific challenges faced by students with brain injuries and outlines the support structures necessary to facilitate their academic success.

The final section, *The Future of Education: Technology, Climate, and Policy*, addresses emerging challenges that are reshaping education. *Chapter 11: Climate Emotions and Climate Change Education* examines the psychological impact of climate change on students and the role of education in addressing climate-related emotional responses. *Chapter 12: Embracing the Digital Age in Contemporary Classrooms* explores the implications of the increasing use of digital tools in education, focusing on both the opportunities and challenges they present for teaching and learning. *Chapter 13: Educational Policy: A Complex Landscape* concludes the volume by analysing the complexities of educational policy and governance, highlighting how decisions made at the policy level influence classroom dynamics and learning outcomes. *Chapter 14: Promoting Wellbeing and Coping Skills in Higher Education* expands this discussion in the context of higher education, examining the unique stressors faced by university students and offering approaches to promote well-being in these settings.

Together, these chapters offer a timely exploration of the intersections between psychology and education, addressing both historical foundations and contemporary challenges. Each section builds upon the last, encouraging readers to critically reflect on past practices, engage with present issues, and consider how psychology can continue to shape educational experiences for future generations. This book is designed to serve as a valuable resource for educators, researchers, and policymakers seeking to deepen their understanding of the psychological principles that underpin modern educational practices.

Chapter 1
Do We Need a Psychology of Education?

Kate Carr-Fanning
https://orcid.org/0000-0003-4434-7260
University College Dublin, Ireland

ABSTRACT

This book and this chapter are about psychology of education – what we mean by it and how psychology is applied to education, and the ways in which psychology and education are interdependent. As we shall see, psychology contributes to an understanding of every facet of the educational process. This chapter will provide an overview of the conceptual foundation of the chapter and psychology of education, including the different sub-disciplines and the big debates in psychology of education. The authors then explore the dominant frameworks from psychology – its schools of thought – and how they inform and enable the process of education. Finally, this chapter concludes with some cautionary notes for a psychology of education. As will become clear, psychology's contributions to education are considerable, but there is also a need to be critical and apply psychological principles and practices with an appreciation for their limitations. So, the authors delve into critical psychology, considering some of the issues within a psychology of education.

1. WHAT IS PSYCHOLOGY OF EDUCATION?

Part 1 will consider how psychology and education are inextricably linked by considering the nature of each and their relationship to each other. It explores what unites the fields of psychology, and the subtle, but important, differences in paradigms and sub-disciplines, and their role in a psychology of education. To be able to critically engage with the psychology of education literature (and the other

DOI: 10.4018/979-8-3693-1293-3.ch001

chapters in this book) we will also explore the big debates in psychology and the role of critical psychology.

1.1 What We Share and What Sets Us Apart?

To understand the field of psychology of education, we must first consider what we mean by a psychology of education. We need to be clear that psychology is not a unitary concept, it might be more appropriate to think about the *psychologies* as different sub-disciplines and Schools of Thought, each with their own important contribution to make to education. Despite differences, there are also ideological and methodological underpinnings of psychology, and so we will begin by exploring what unites the field, before we set out the big debates and critiques..

A Psychology of Education

The field of a psychology of education exists because psychology and education are interdependent. Education is an active ongoing lifelong process, it takes many forms (formal and informal) and traverses all of life's contexts (e.g., home, school, community). As John Dewey (1938) put it, education is a 'social process' dependent on people and relationships. Education aims to educe (like the Greek notion of educere) which means to 'bring out' that which is within the person and other people. Psychology, in turn, is about people – it's the scientific study of behaviour and mental processes (American Psychological Association, 2022), its relationship to education, therefore, is inextricable. Psychology is a diverse scientific discipline that explores different aspects of or factors affecting learning and development (e.g., biological, cognitive, emotional, personal, and social processes), and people are the core of the process of education – as educators and/or learners.

Another significant contribution of psychology to education is the field's emphasis on 'scientific study'. In a psychology of education, research and practice is closely aligned. The emphasis is on using psychological knowledge (especially evidence-based / research-informed practice) to understand and promote mental, emotional, physical, and/or social learning and development. Psychology provides the tools, developed through scientific research, to understand learners and their educational contexts, so as to design educational activities and promote learning and development.

Evidence-based programmes are educational practices or programs that have evidence to show that they are effective for the specific group of learners in a particular setting; they're usually applied in a uniformed (standardised) way. In a somewhat similar (but also distinct) way, research-informed practice is educational experiences that are designed based on the best available evidence, however, there is more flexibility in how that knowledge is applied, it allows for more creativity and allows the context / learners' needs to inform the approach developed.

The Psychologies

A psychology of education is a dynamic process where many different psychological frameworks and research are used within the process of education. A psychology of education supports an understanding of learners, environments, social processes, and enables us to develop approaches that are respectful, appropriate, and effective. When we talk about *psychology*, we might consider it a unified field and there are many things all psychologists have in common. However, in other ways we can think of psychology more as the *psychologies*. As we shall see below, there are distinct Schools of Thought (or dominant frameworks or paradigms), and there are also distinct sub-disciplines within the discipline of psychology, and most if not all can be applied to different aspects within the process of education.

When we say a psychology of education, you might immediately think of *educational psychology*, and this area is the scientific study of how people learn, in practice, there is a particular focus on learning difficulties. However, psychology's application to education goes beyond individual differences in learners to consider all aspects of the process of education, including teaching, learning, and assessment. A psychology of education draws on a range of sub-disciplines within psychology. For example, we draw on a range of psychologies to understand learners – to understand their learning needs, know what works to motivate and engage them, and how we could promote their social and emotional wellbeing, resilience, and also to support those struggling with difficulties (e.g., learning or mental health). For example, we also draw on *developmental psychology*, which seeks to understand how people grow intellectual, emotional, social and moral development of human beings. *Clinical psychologists* and *abnormal psycholog*y provide insights into individual differences in psychological distress (e.g., mental health difficulties) which can inform the subject matter and/or help us to understand and support learners with additional needs. We draw on *social psychology* to understand social networks and group dynamics, because educational contexts involve social relationships.

A psychology of education also goes beyond individuals and groups of learners, the educational process, and the context of learning. Psychology can also inform educational initiatives developed by educators or policy makers. For example, *forensic psychology's* focus on anti-social or criminal behaviour has informed educational policy maker's approach to behaviour management in schools and preventive programmes in disadvantaged communities. We draw on *organisational psychology*, because places of education (e.g., children centres and schools) are also workplaces. We can also acknowledge that many psychologists have educational components to their roles. For example, clinical psychologists often engage in psychoeducation (e.g., teaching an adolescent about their depression) or when a health psychologist works with young people to promote their health or prevent illness using education.

In this way, we can see that psychology of education is for everyone – for learners, educators, families, leaders, policy makers, and for psychologists. As *research* or *experimental psychologists*, we do the research that supports the rest. An understanding of psychology and the knowledge, understanding, and practices that emerge from it can be used to create better strong educational systems, schools, and classrooms.

1.2 Debates in Psychology of Education

There are many debates within a psychology of education, should we conduct research on or with children (ethics), is there such thing as consciousness or free will, or should we use labels? There is often no 'the answer' to these questions, there are different theoretical perspectives and studies proffered, and a part of being a critical reflective educator is to engage with that evidence and develop your own practice and response. However, in psychology of education there are five major debates, that traverse many areas of research and practice. In Part 2, we will explore the Schools of Thought. These psychological frameworks often adopt specific positions on these debates and/or these debates can be used to critique theory/research. Therefore, we will explore these now, and you can use them later to critically engage with the literature.

Nature vs Nurture

Probably the best known is nature-nurture debate. This debate questions the degree to which learning, and development is down to inherited biological factors (nature) or our experiences growing up (nurture). Parents who achieve well (academically and occupationally) tend to have children who perform well academically (e.g., Tesfagiorgis et al., 2020) – why is this? We might assume these children's success is down to the genes (intelligence) they inherited from their parents (nature) – or – we might consider that parents who valued and understood education might provide the type of environment and support that is conducive to academic achievement (nurture).

Materialism vs Constructionism

Some psychologists focus on the physical (material) underpinnings of learning and development. They argue that behaviour is nothing more than the result of firing neurons, hormones, and cortical structures. In contrast, constructivists focus on psychological reality, or the meaning people give to phenomenon and social contexts. Leaper's (2011) review of gender differences in academic skills, suggested that boys tend to score better on measures of spatial and mathematical skills, while girls perform better verbally. The materialist would attribute this to differences in the structure and functioning of their brains. Whereas the constructivists might think about gender norms, what was valued and encouraged within their community.

Person (Trait) vs Situation (State)

A state is more temporary, a more temporary way of thinking, feeling, or behaving, for example, a person may act aggressively when they feel threatened. Whereas traits are more stable and enduring characteristics or patterns of behaviour; and so, you might say a person's temperament was more aggressive. The question of whether someone's behaviour is down to something within the person (trait) or within the situation (state) affects education in all sorts of ways. For example, psychological testing often aims to identify traits to support learners (e.g., ability testing for school placement or guidance counselling).

This argument is also involved in the assumptions we make about learners based on snap shots of behaviour. Educators design educational experiences and build student-teacher relationships informed by their perceptions of the learners' ability, engagement, suitability for an educational programme, or their prospects. From social psychology's attribution theory, we know there is a tendency for people (e.g., educators) tend to attribute their own behaviour more to situational effects, whereas they attribute the behaviour of other people to personal traits / characteristics (Malle & Korman, 2013). If a war refugee doesn't show up to a life skills class, we can attribute this to a lack of motivation to integrate or find a job (personal trait), or we might think about the fact that the class is held next to a government building with armed guards outside, which trigger traumatic memories when fleeing their country (situation).

Continuity vs Discontinuity

Developmental psychology and the question of whether and how people can change across a lifespan is obviously an important one for education. Discontinuous theories suggest development progresses through distinct stages based on genetic predispositions, and often development shifts (often abruptly) in distinct phases or stages. Think about theorists like Jean Piaget's theory of cognitive development. It claims that there are four stages, with distinct shifts in cognitive abilities (which he assumed was based in part on brain development), for example, children exist in the sensorimotor stages from birth until 2years, where they explore sensorily and they develop many of the foundations needed for the next phase, but it isn't until they transition into the preoperational stages (2-7 years) where they can think symbolically and develop language, but remain quite concrete in their thinking. While continuous theories view development as a slow continuous process, with development slowly emerging building on what came before. For example, social learning theory focuses on how children develop through what we pick up from those around us (e.g., teachers, siblings, peers, family members) and this type of learning and development is likely to be more fluid and occur over time (Hergenhahn & Olson, 1999).

Culture

Some people will argue that there are some cultural universals, that people are the same wherever you go. There does appear to be universals, a smile conveys happiness everywhere in the world. Others have argued there are big variations. Eye contact, for example, varies – in the West it's a sign of confidence, good social skills, and respect, whereas in some parts of the middle and far east it's considered disrespectful in some or all situations. Understanding these cultural nuances is an important part of multicultural educational settings.

The role of culture variation is important for psychology of education; because we do need to think critically about the knowledge we use and apply in practice. This is particularly true when we think of furthering anti-racist / Equality, Diversity, and Inclusion (EDI) educational practices. The question is *to what degree* can we apply knowledge developed in and for a particular culture (usually in the developed west, by middle class White people) be applied to educational practices within or with members of different cultures, different races/ethnicities, social class, etcetera.

Greenfield (1997) suggested that psychological tests are based upon the values and behavioural expectations of western societies in which they were developed, thus do not easily cross cultures. The Cultural Test Bias Hypothesis emerged out of the well documented racial differences in IQ scores in the USA attributed to biases against Black and Latinx learners, in high stakes tests, that are used to make important decisions (Ford, 2021). Cultural bias is not only built into psychological tools. One meta-analysis by Tenenbaum and Ruck (2007) found that, when compared to White and Asian American learners, teachers referred African American and Latinx learners for tests of gifted less and special needs more, and teachers use less positive or neutral language when speaking with African / Latinx learners. For the most part, these biases are assumed to be unconscious, however, they have significant consequences impacting important decisions, micro-aggression, stereotyping, and affecting students' self-esteem and self-identity.

1.3 A Critical Psychology of Education

In Part 2, we will explore the contributions of the dominant psychological frameworks to the field of education. However, while traversing the intellectual terrain we need to do so cautiously. Therefore, before Part 2, we need to think critically about psychology, and critical psychology provides a paradigm to do so.

What Is Critical Psychology?

Critical psychology, as Parker (2007) suggests, "… turns the gaze of the psychologist back on the discipline …" (pg. 1) it examines how some psychologies action and experiences are privileged over others and how psychology operates to reinforce systems of power and inequality, and the status quo. Critical psychology asks challenging questions of psychological knowledge and practice. Let us take research into gender differences, such as Leaper's (2011) systematic review that concluded that boys have better at spatial and math's skills, while girls do better in verbal skills. A critical approach would ask to what extent this research assumes and reinforces notions that we are biologically unchangeable or that gender is a binary construct. As we explore the frameworks below, I suggest you continue to ask these challenging questions.

Normative and Non-Normative Development

A great strength of psychology is its emphasis on science. However, when we mention 'evidence-base' we need to recognise the limitations of science. While science has its contributions, there will always be limitations to the knowledge it generates. Psychology tends to focus on normative models of development and values 'big data' or large representative samples. When we think of big samples and norms, we are embracing and valuing normative models of development or normative assumptions about learning. In doing so, we marginalise the experiences of people and groups who do not fit into that norm, that is, minoritized learners. For example, certain psychological frameworks explored below, such as psychoanalytic psychology, pathologizes people in the LGBTQI+ communities by trying to apply normative stages of development to unique experiences. As discussed in the previous section, we may need to question the use of intelligence testing, which may reinforce underlying differences between ethnic groups or disadvantage neurodivergent learners.

Positionality

Sabnis and Proctor (2021) argued that knowledge is an extension of those who produce it, and actions and beliefs are bound to group interests, ideological affinities, and social positions. Thus, we must consider the positionality of psychology and psychologists. Psychology is ethno-centric as a profession and a science it is predominantly White middle class and Western and includes large representative sample from within these dominant groups within society. Take for example parenting styles. While it is normatively understood that authoritative styles are associated with negative outcomes, this has not been found to be the case across ethnic groups. In his now seminar work, Spencer (2006) criticised universal notions of parenting styles, which positioned African American Young People (AAYP) as 'at risk' and reinforced Eurocentric norms by including predominately White American (WA) samples in research, in developing notions of parenting styles and exploring developmental outcomes. Spencer demonstrated that AAYP engage pro-socially at similar rates than their WA peers and argued for the need to consider adolescent's affective evaluation of a parent's behaviour.

Systemic Marginalisation

In their call to psychologists working in education, Sabnis and Proctor (2021) asked them to fundamentally rethink psychological research and practice. They claimed that many educational institutions are oppressive and marginalise learners, citing the following examples:

1. how racially and ethnically minoritized learners are overrepresented in special education;
2. how minoritized learners are more likely to receive disciplinary approaches that push them out of school;
3. how experiences of oppression outside of school affect these learners' psycho-emotional states which negatively effects their academic performance.

Educational institutions are often informed by psychological research and practice, particularly in the field of special education. Before we move on, pause and reflect:

- *Why do you think these phenomenon happen?*
- *What factors external to the students themselves might contribute to these phenomenon?*

The above examples could be viewed as evidence of systemic marginalization and oppression in education. That is, deep-routed institutional structures and practices that disadvantage particular groups based on certain characteristics, such as race/ethnicity, class, socio-economic status (SES), gender, disability, language, or sexual orientation. These can include or reinforce individual acts or biases, which have positive and negative consequences. For example, unconscious biases exist where white male students experience higher expectations in maths (privilege) while minoritized learners' are placed in lower ability reading groups (oppression). However, systemic marginalisation goes beyond individual acts; they are built into the design of educational systems and include a range of biases and social oppressions. Minoritized students experiencing bullying and microaggressions, inaccessible environments, and other forms of sexism, ableism, and/or racism in their everyday interactions with staff and other students (see also Section 1.2). Other examples of systemic oppression in education include:

- Funding disparities exist between disadvantaged and wealthier schools.
- Curriculum and testing biases privilege the language and cultural norms of the powerful (see Section 1.2).
- Discriminatory disciplinary practices exist where low-SES and minoritized students experience exclusions more than their peers due to educational policies and practices (see Welsh & Little, 2018).
- Ability grouping biases whereby low-SES and minoritized students are underrepresented in gifted programmes and over-represented in special education (e.g., Peters & Engerrand, 2016).

Marginalisation is often considered singularly, but many learners experience multiple marginalisations. We can understand their impact using the concept of 'intersectionality', because as Crenshaw (1995, pg. 3) observed, "we are simultaneously members of many groups", and it is these "complex identities" that shape experiences of bias. In this way, we understand learners based on their complex and layered experiences of privilege and marginalisation. For example, a learner who identifies as disabled and Black experiences both racism and disablism. This learner is more likely to be misdiagnosed, placed in restrictive environments, and disciplined (rather than accommodated). Their cultural background is often misunderstood or ignored during assessment and intervention (Frederick & Shifrer, 2019). Intersectionality provides a lens to understand social oppression, particularly its impact on identity, more fully.

A problem with psychology (and its dominance in education) is it is the study of people. It sometimes neglects the social systems that people interact with and are affected by. Reducing complex (socio-culturally embedded) problems to problems within the learner, ignoring socio-environmental contexts.

Scientism

We can understand advocating for a complex and nuanced understanding of development and a need to question the ideological assumptions underpinning psychology, as a need to be critical of the methods applied in some types of psychological research. Several of the Schools of Thought (e.g., positive psychology and cognitive psychology) have been accused of *scientism*. That is, that psychology applies the scientific method, which seeks to reduce and control specific variables or attributes and study them in unusual conditions (like labs or children knowing they are observed in a classroom). In this way, psychology discovers 'truths' about behaviour and mental processes. However, the scientific method can be reductivist, that is, it can reduce very complex phenomena (e.g., like behaviour in a learning environment) to the point that it becomes meaningless; or, as discussed above, consider them free from context. This is not true of all Schools; indeed, humanistic psychology and systemic models are so complex / holistic that they do not easily lend themselves to empirical evaluation. We must also be careful about how we interpret and apply psychology; and avoid overgeneralising or oversimplifying. For example, while we can say that children who experience trauma are more at risk for poor mental health (see Section 2.1), we cannot say all children who experience trauma have poor mental health. Learning and development is extremely complex. Good quality research is very specific, it shines a light on a particular phenomenon, it cannot definitively predict behaviour.

Pseudo-Psychology

A final cautionary note on the psychologies would not be considered psychology in the truest sense of the world, which is pseudo-psychology. Psychology as a science and a practice has permeated every aspect of education. Some entrenched beliefs and practices in education are based on myth, like the neuromyth that people have different learning styles. Be a critical consumer of psychology when applying it to your educational practice, consider questions, such as:

1. Who or what is the source (how reliable are they)?
2. What methods did they use to obtain it, and what did they actually find (i.e., what is the nature of the evidence they are using to support their claims,)?
3. Are they applying that evidence appropriately and ethically?

1.4 Review and Reflect

At the end of Part 1, pause and reflect, *what do you think about the role of psychology in education?*

Part 1 provides us with the tools to critically engage with Part 2. We explored the contributions psychology can make to education, in terms of different disciplines and its emphasis on science and research-informed educational practice. We discussed the big debates within psychology (nature-nurture, state-trait, continuity-discontinuity, and culture). These debates advocate different approaches to research and practice, and suggest caution in how we interpret and apply psychological knowledge. Finally, we explored critical psychology - the need to challenge psychological knowledge, particularly when it comes to marginalised learners and the nature of science. Use these concepts to challenge the theory and research within the different frameworks in Part 2.

2. PSYCHOLOGICAL FRAMEWORKS IN EDUCATION

Part 2 will explore psychology's contributions to education through the lens of its dominant Schools of Thought (psychological frameworks). These different frameworks provide different lenses to the scientific study of behaviour and/or mental processes:

- Psychodynamic and Attachment
- Behaviourism
- Humanistic Psychology
- Cognitive Psychology and Cognitive Neuroscience
- Social Cognitive Approaches
- Positive Psychology
- Holistic approaches: Bio-ecological and Bio-psychosocial Models

Each framework will be explored theoretically to demonstrate their contributions to education. To demonstrate both the theory and the role of science (and research-informed practice), we will draw on specific psychological research studies, and apply them to important educational issues. We cannot cover all important educational issues nor can we describe all the various contributions from each framework, because there are too many. We will include a few examples for illustrative purposes only.

These frameworks are explored separately. However, it's considered good practice in education to adopt what is known as an *integrated approach.* An integrated approach means you draw on different frameworks depending on what is needed, for example, you might draw on one to better understand the learner, another to make sense of a group dynamic, while another perspective helps to design learning outcomes or an educational environment.

As we consider each framework, remember the issues raised in Part 1 (i.e., the big debates and critical psychology) to challenge the ideas set out. Chapter 1 provides you with the foundations for the rest of this book. Subsequent chapters delve into specific educational issues; you can use the below frameworks, with a critical lens, to probe and to challenge the psychology of education literature (within this book and beyond).

2.1 Psychodynamic, Attachment, and Trauma-Informed Education

While the 'father' of psychology was William James, perhaps one of the most famous psychologists of all time – Sigmund Freud - founded a School of Thought within psychology that permeates education to this day. Psychodynamic perspectives, originating with the work of Freud, place significance on early childhood experiences, in particular, relationships with primary caregivers. The effects of these early experiences reside within the unconscious mind and inform behaviours, including how the individual views themselves and how they relate to others (e.g., teachers). While psychoanalysis has not been particularly influential in most educational contexts, it has influenced a range of ideas and practice which are.

Attachment

Drawing on the work of Freud, Bowlby (1977) introduced notions of Attachment which was originally defined as the 'psychological connectedness' between a child and their primary carer, usually their mother in Bowlby's post-war days. Once restricted to other people, it is now understood that children can also form attachments with institutions (e.g., schools or religious communities). Attachments have significant outcomes, forming an important part of the learning process. Attachment to school means the learner trusts teachers and peers, they feel safe to make mistakes and to learn and grow, and they believe that education is worthwhile. As such, it is central to resiliency and learner engagement (Center on the Developing Child at Harvard University 2015; Cooper & Jacobs 2011; Bomber 2007).

The principles of psychodynamic (especially attachment) have informed the nurture approach. This approach is a school-based intervention, to small groups of students or within the whole school, which aims to address gaps in early experiences by developing positive relationships and supporting emotional development.

Figure 1. Principles of the Nurture Group

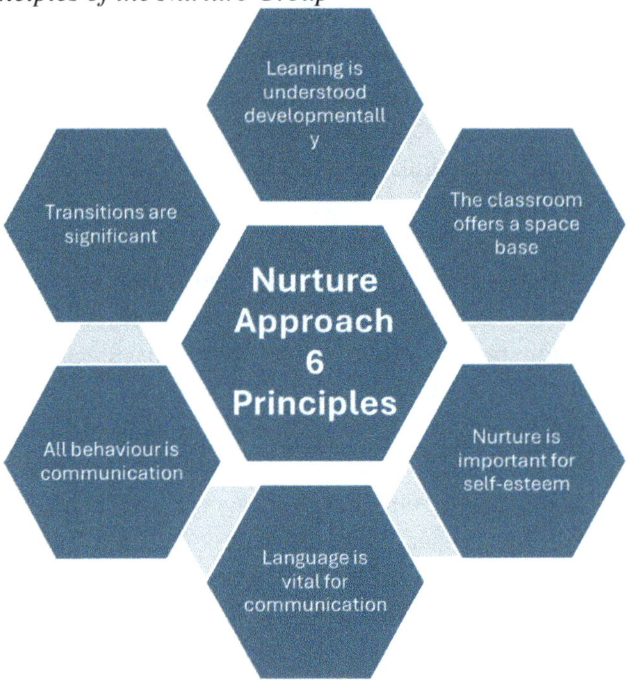

While attachment to school is important for all learners, it may be important to another group of learners and area of practice strongly informed by psychodynamic principles, which is trauma-informed education.

Trauma-Informed Education

An emergent area of practice, informed by principles from psychodynamic school and attachment theory, is known as trauma-informed or trauma-sensitive education. While all children will experience risk and stress, the experience of toxic stress and trauma is distinct. Toxic stress occurs when children experience too much stress/risk without sufficient social buffering. Trauma is 'an emotional response to a terrible event' (American Psychiatric Association, 2000). Trauma is more common than once thought. One longitudinal study of 2,232 children born in England and Wales in 1994-1995 found that by the age of 18, about 31% have experienced at least one trauma (Lewis et al., 2019). Trauma can be simple trauma, the result of a single event, or it can be complex trauma, usually occurring within an important interpersonal relationship over a prolonged period of time (van der Kolk 2014). While both are associated with negative (and some similar) outcomes, simple trauma tends to have more immediate effects, while complex trauma has the potential to be more devastating, with long-lasting physical, emotional, and cognitive effects.

Many children experience trauma – including developmental trauma - through Adverse Childhood Experiences (ACEs), which are highly stressful or traumatic events that occur within childhood/adolescence. In their landmark study, Felitti et al. (1998) demonstrated the links between ten categories of abuse, neglect, and household dysfunction and a range of negative outcomes (e.g., physical and mental health, educational / occupational outcomes, and risky behaviours). Subsequent research with more representative samples, have added to the categories of ACE beyond the family home, these so-called community-level ACEs, include chronic bullying / victimisation, racism, witnessing violence, unsafe neighbourhoods, and experience in foster care (Cronholm et al., 2015).

Trauma-informed education, while not a clearly defined or unified approach, has really helped educators to understand the behaviours of some children and young people, such as avoidance, aggression, and disengagement. In their systematic review, Thomas, Crosby, and Vanderhaar (2019) suggested that one of its contributions is when challenging behaviours happen, that educators shift away from asking, 'what's wrong with you' to considering 'what's happening to you' – enabling educators to approach their learners more sensitively. The approach emphasises educational contexts that focus on building positive relationships, providing learners with consistency, safety, and security, and the need for a community response. In their systematic review, Hobfoll et al. (2007) identified five essential elements to trauma-informed practice: providing learners with safety, calmness, and connectedness, while also promoting learners' sense of self-efficacy and hopefulness.

Pause and reflect:

Think back to critical psychology (Section 1.3): how might this shift in focus from problems within individual learners, to an understanding of the effects of their socio-environmental context support anti-oppressive educational practices?

2.2 Behaviourism

Based on the work of Pavlov, Watson, and Skinner, behavioural approaches focus on objective behaviours that can be observed. They are not concerned with internal processes, such as thoughts and feelings. This School emerged in reaction to the dominance of psychodynamic approaches, with its focus on unconscious forces and early childhood experiences. Behaviourism claims that what we can see and measure objectively is overt behaviour.

Behaviour Is Learnt

The assumption is that behaviour is 'learnt' through experiences in the child's environment, and so if one changes the immediate environment, they can change behaviours or develop entirely new ones. In understanding all development and behaviour, the emphasis is on what features within the environment develop/maintain it and then adjusting these. One cannot underestimate the impact of behaviourism on education generally, but particularly schools, – from behaviour management through pedagogy to the very understanding of what it means to have learnt.

Skinner's (2019) work on operant conditioning or 'contingency management' has been particularly influential. This approach suggests that behaviour is motivated by consequences, positive (e.g., praise) and negative ones (e.g., punishment) that are commonly used. Behaviourism dominates school behaviour policies (Maguire, Ball, & Braun 2010) and practices (Armstrong, 2018), such as Positive Behaviour Support. The reason for this in part is due to the efficacy for the approach for the majority of learners who respond well.

Pause and Reflect:

What would the critical psychologist say about this approach to the study of learning and development?

Criticism of Behaviour Modification

According to Coombes at al. (2016), these methods might control or promote behaviour in the short-term in a particular context, they do not necessarily lead to lasting effects. The approach is also reductive, due to the focus on controlling overt behaviours, it may ignore other essential factors, often involved in the development and maintenance of psychosocial difficulties. The use of punishment, while purported to have fallen out of favour, is alive and well in many institutions. The critical psychologists (see Section 1.3) are deeply sceptical about the use of these disciplinary approaches. They cite problems including higher rates of exclusion of minoritized learners, and biases in how behaviour is interpreted and responded to without consideration for cultural background. Similarly, Armstrong (2018) argued that learners with psychosocial difficulties experience 'disadvantage, suspension or exclusion' (aka punishment) as a direct result of the application of this model in practice. He further argued for a need to reject 'wholeheartedly' ineffective approaches based on behavioural management and discipline, support teachers who are at risk of burnout, incentivise schools to keep (i.e., not exclude) these learners, and to base educational responses on research (especially developmental psychology).

Educational Design

It is not just about behaviour management; behaviourism has influenced how we think about and approach learning itself. As Woollard (2010) explained, behaviourism in the classroom advocates educators break down behaviour and then sequencing, shaping, or chaining them to achieve the desired result. The child is viewed as the 'blank slate' where the educator writes upon them. Wherever you are drawing on the National Curriculum, a university degree, or the UK's National Youth Agency's curriculum you will find learning outcomes or learning objectives. This is a direct result of behaviourism – you objectively define the behaviours you want the learner to demonstrate, you break them down and shape those behaviours across time. A typical behavioural lesson would include rote learning and positive reinforcement (e.g., positive feedback). It is learning, which is highly structured, sequenced, didactic, efficient, and effective; the way we know it's effective is through precise assessment. We could also then ask how appropriate it is for humanitarian organisations from the Global North, with Eurocentric notions and structures about the educational process, to work within communities in the Global South who might approach learning more dynamically (see Section 1.2 and 1.3).

2.3 Humanistic Psychology

In response to the (often) negative and reductive approaches of psychodynamic and behavioural schools, which often compare humans to animals, a new school emerged – Humanistic Psychology - as psychology's *Third Force*.

Humanistic Education

Driven by theorists such as Rogers and Maslow, Humanistic psychologists believe that all human beings are inherently good, and that underpinning human behaviours are basic needs and, according to Maslow, a drive towards self-actualisation. This respect for the person is where student-centred learning comes from, the idea that we must trust and follow the child. The learner is viewed as the authority on their learning, and provided they have their needs met (including that they are placed in the right environment), they will be self-directed towards optimal learning and development.

Humanistic psychology's view of learners as inherently good and that education should focus on discovering rational ways of educating the 'whole' child (e.g., socially, academically, artistically, emotionally, self-esteem, practical life). At its core, humanistic education would emphasise learner control and autonomy, to self-direct their own learning and self-evaluation (rather than assessment). They view emotional and academic learning as inextricable and equally important, and emphasise feelings of safety within the learning environment.

Relational Practices

Carl Rogers (1951) believed in the power of the relationship – when they're genuine, non-judgmental, unconditional, and full of empathy. Relationships are at the heart of education, to Dewey it was the essence of education. It is also central to healthy human development. Resiliency research is about 50 years old, and the most significant predictor of resiliency (or bouncing back in the face of adversity) is positive relationships (Masten, 2014). One authentic meaningful relationship with someone who cares about you, even a brief one, can significantly impact someone's life for the better. In some educational settings, we call these 'turn around teachers' (National Scientific Council on the Developing Child, 2015).

When things go wrong – sometimes called challenging behaviour or mental health difficulties – we often ask the question what is 'wrong' with the individual, and how can we help (aka fix) them. We seem to forget that learners exist within social networks; within educational contexts and beyond them. The power of these social, systemic, and relational influences are, at times, less recognised and less mobilised. However, a growing interest in *relational practices* has been emerging, with discourse on culturally responsive, restorative, narrative, and solution-focused practices in education.

Relational practices acknowledge systems of power and the interconnected social nature of learning and development. What do you think the critical psychologist would have to say about humanism and relational practices? Humanism recognises the complexities involved and the uniqueness of individual development, which makes it difficult to research (and so validate) empirically.

When we say relational practice, this is at its core about relationships, but it's also about meaning, the meaning we co-construct with others (Vasilic, 2022). Gergen's (2009) relational theory proposes that all meaning grows from coordinated action, or what he calls 'co-action'. All that we hold dear – everything we view as 'real', rational, and valuable depends on the well-being of our relationships. For example, if I nod my head, you might interpret it as a greeting (and so you might smile) or you might view it as a sign of aggression (and so flee). All behaviour and events depend upon the meaning the individual (on the receiving end of those behaviours or events) gives to those behaviours / events. So, relational practice depends on meaning that is respectfully co-produced. An understanding of different systems of meaning (and being open to these) is at the core of relationship practice.

Pause and Reflect:

What would the critiques (see Section 1.2 and 1.3) say about relational practice? Given that it provides space for different identities (e.g., different cultural/ethnic backgrounds) and their inclusion in education.

One area of relational practice that has been gaining ground more recently is restorative practice (RP). RP is an educational approach that encourages behaviour that is supportive and respectful. RP aims for the individual to be held accountable (by others and themselves) for the harm they have caused and provides them with the opportunity to learn and grow and repair the harm they have caused. At its core, restorative practice is based on relationships, which include an ethos that builds and maintains healthy relationships. This framework includes strategies, beliefs, and languages that are underpinned by specific values; these are applied in any situation when 'something' needs to be restored. The approach varies depending on context, but it includes effective communication, positive relationships, empathy, perspective taking, respect, psychological safety, affective language, self-awareness, and repairing the damage done. It's characterised by high levels of structure, boundaries, accountability, and support. It can be contrasted with punitive approaches, with their focus on retribution and punishment; which are similarly high in structure, but low in terms of support and relationships. While often adopted as a complimentarily strategy, alongside behavioural approaches (Section 2.2), among the issues involved in its implementation is it conflicts with these traditional power structures (McCluskey et al., 2008).

2.4 Cognitive Psychology and Cognitive Neuroscience

This section will consider cognitive psychology and cognitive neuroscience, what these areas of study are, and how they provide a science of learning. Cognitive developmental psychology will be briefly considered given its dominance in education.

Cognitive Psychology

The cognitive School of Thought within psychology focuses on mental processes, it seeks to explain learning in terms of all the workings inside your mind (and for the neurocognitive psychologists, your brain) – this includes perception, thinking, memory, attention, language, and problem-solving. Cognitive psychology - the study of how people think and process information – provides education with a science of learning.

Cognitive psychology focuses on the individual cognitive processes involved in learning, which can be applied to the design of educational experiences. For example, cognitive load theory explains how people learn in terms of their ability to process the content being presented, it refers to the amount of working memory (or short-term memory) resources are used (and available) within the process of learning. Working memory has a limited capacity, and it's used to move information into long-term memory. In response to the use of technology as an emergent issue in education, Brame (2016) drew on this theory and reviewed psychological experiments to explain to educators how to develop the most effective educational videos to maximise learning without overwhelming or creating passive learners. He suggests they should keep videos brief, using audio and visual elements, be conversational and enthusiastic to enhance engagement, and embed active learning (e.g., questions, homework assignments).

Cognitive Developmental Psychology

Some of the most influential psychologists in education were cognitive psychologists. Jean Piaget's (1952) theory of cognitive development from birth to adolescence emphasises language, memory, reasoning, and morals. He believed that development was down to biological maturation and interaction with the environment, where the child acts like a 'little scientist' exploring their environment and developing understanding. Ideas like active learning or exploratory learning are based on these ideas, as are the ideas that we build on previous knowledge (in the way you must understand how to add and subtract, before you move on to multiplication). He proffered a staged approach to cognitive development from just using their senses to process the world (sensory motor) to being able to engage in hypothetical and analytic thinking (formal operational). His theory has informed many educational approaches, such as child-centred and active learning, matching teaching strategy to stages of development, and the importance of play. However, the critical psychologist would argue that his normative theory does not account for disability or SEN (see Section 1.3).

Similarly embracing the active nature of learning, other cognitive psychologists within the social constructivist camp, such as Vygotsky (1978) and Bruner (1966), placed more of an emphasis on the social and cultural context where the child develops. This emphasis on social interaction and the co-construction of knowledge between learner and others is why the field is known as *social* constructivism. As Bruner (1966) claimed:

We teach a subject not to produce little living libraries on that subject, but rather to get a student to think...for himself, to consider matters...to take part in the process of knowledge-getting. Knowing is a process, not a product (p. 72).

Vygotsky (1978) particularly emphasised the role of the more knowledgeable others (e.g., educators or peers) in enhancing development, he also provided information about techniques like scaffolding learning with this type of support. These ideas lead to the development of approaches such as inquiry-based or discovery learning, which are more student-centred, giving learners more control over the educational process. Working in the USA, Witt and Ulmer (2010) were concerned about the impact of high stakes testing (and teaching to the test). So, they explored the efficacy of inquiry-based learning in middle school classrooms, and found that it resulted in higher academic achievement, when compared with traditionalism (more didactic methods).

Cognitive Neuroscience

In the 1990s, an interest in the science of learning really took off, along with a desire to understand and develop educational programmes that were 'brain-based'. This was often unscientific and led to many so-called *neuromyths*, like that learning styles exit or people use either their left or their right brain (Howard-Jones, 2014). Neuroscience and cognitive neuroscience have made many advances in understanding and enhancing teaching and learning drawing on insights from the mind and brain. A range of terms have been proffered to encapsulate this area, such as 'neuroeducation', 'educational neuroscience', 'mind, brain, and education', or a 'science of learning', which as summed up by Howard-Jones (2018) explores the neurocognitive processes and structures underlying how the mind engages, consolidates, and builds knowledge, as well as barriers to these essential learning processes. For example, a recent study demonstrated increased activity in reward systems, while learners answered educational questions in certain (engagement promoting) conditions (Howard-Jones, et al., 2016). While others (e.g., Young et al, 2012) have shown subcortical activity - such as activation of the amygdala (the emotion centre of the brain) - are involved in math anxiety and negative emotions towards other areas of learning. Or explored how the prefrontal cortex (located at the front of your brain) is involved in effortful reflective processes, such as attending to and the manipulation of new information as it is consolidated into knowledge by the learner (Kane & Engle, 2002). We might need to be a bit critical here, in terms of the conclusions we draw from this type of research. We could critique this approach for many reasons, including being too reductivist and potentially over-simplifying complex problems like math anxiety (see Section 1.2 and 1.3).

For many years, aspects of your psychology, like intelligence and the structure and functioning of one's brain, was assumed to be (particularly after childhood) relatively fixed. However, the 90s interest in the science of learning saw the emergence of a new concept and set of practices to harness its ability. For example, neuroplasticity refers to your brain's ability to restructure or 'rewire' based on experience across the lifespan. You can play video games, learn a different language, exercise, play sudoku, do something creative (e.g., make music), or travel to improve your brain. For example, Stein et al. (2012) studied the brains of 10 English speaking students studying German in Switzerland across five months, as their proficiency in German developed so too did the density of their grey matter. Others have developed cognitive training or (when applied to neurodiversity or disorders) neuro-retaining exercises, curriculum, or games to develop specific cognitive skills, such as attention, working memory, and planning. However, despite early enthusiasm for these approaches, their efficacy remains questionable (e.g., Cortese et al., 2015; Sala & Gobet, 2019). Less effortful approaches have also been proposed, for example, transcranial direct current stimulation has been applied to brain regions involved in learning, with some showing improvements in children's maths ability (Cohen Kadosh et al., 2012). These approaches raise all sorts of ethical questions, such as whether anatomy is destiny, or what are the long-term outcomes for children (Cohen Kadosh et al., 2012) and indeed the world - do we want designer brains?

2.5 Social Cognitive Approaches

The social constructivism were not the only ones to emphasise the social nature of learning. Social Cognitive Theory (SCT), drawing on the work of two people Michael and Bandura (working independently) emphasised the social nature of learning. SCT straddles both 'cognitive' and 'behavioural' psychology, as it focuses on how behaviour is learnt and it acknowledges the role of internal mental processes, such as observational learning and beliefs (e.g., self-efficacy).

Modelling and Self-efficacy

In his now seminar Bobo doll experiment, Bandura (1977) demonstrated that children don't need to have direct experience to learn, as the behaviourists claimed, they can learn observationally. Children watched a video of an adult interacting with a blow-up doll (Bobo) and when given the chance to do so themselves they produced the same behaviour as the model. The concept of modelling the behaviour, the learning activity, or the correct response has been applied by educators and educational initiatives for decades. For example, gender disparities in STEM education and occupations is well documented. In explaining this phenomenon and suggesting interventions, United Nations Children's Fund (UNICEF, 2020) advocates the need for more female role models (at home, in school, and in society). Drawing on this idea, in Colombia, a STEM intervention *Pequeñas Aventureras* (Little Adventurers), found gender differences between caregivers' preference for STEM vs non-STEM toys. Drawing heavily on the concept of modelling, they developed a community education program to address gender stereotypes in schools (teacher training, guidelines, and session plans) and at home (texting households which promoted gender equality and STEM career and learning). Findings showed an increase in girl's math skills and reduced gender stereotypes in caregivers and teachers.

However, it is not only specific pedagogical approaches that are included from SCT, it's about psychological processes underpinning learning, such as Bandura's (1986) concept of self-efficacy. Self-efficacy is the *perceived* ability to perform the required behaviour. In essence, you do not only need knowledge and skills, you also need to believe that you are capable (e.g., of completing homework, doing math, learning to drive, or resolving conflict). Artino's (2012) systematic review synthesised a decade of research to provide instructional strategies to promote learners' self-efficacy suggest the following:

- Help students set clear and specific goals.
- Encourage the use of challenging and proximal goals.
- Provide honest, explicit feedback to increase students' efficacy beliefs.
- Facilitate accurate calibration of self-efficacy.
- Use peer modelling to build self-efficacy.

Social and Emotional Learning (SEL)

Social Cognitive Approaches have also informed programmes and pedagogical practices for Social and Emotional Learning (SEL), promoting resilience or wellbeing, and/or interventions targeting challenging behaviour or mental health difficulties within schools, family centres, and clinics. For example, the Why Try! Program is a school-based intervention programme for learners (often those with challenging behaviours). It engages, motivates, and builds resilience in students through the development of social and emotional skills that aim to change how learners think, feel, and behave.

The concept and educational practice of developing SEL refers to the process whereby learners develop and use the knowledge and skills to support healthy development and relationships. SEL is an umbrella term for a range of skills with numerous models being proposed. According to the CASEL (2015) model, SEL encompasses self-awareness, self-management, responsible decision-making, relationship skills, and social awareness. While SEL is beneficial for all. Social and emotional skills are reportedly deterministic of children's academic attainment (more than IQ scores: Duckworth & Seligman, 2005) and their adult mental health (Richards & Huppert, 2011). SEL may be particularly important for those who struggle or have social, emotional, and/or mental health difficulties. For example, one meta-analysis by Durlak et al. (2011) which included a sample of 270,034 learners found that universal SEL programs enhanced behavioural adjustment, increased prosocial behaviours, and reduced conduct and internalizing problems. Given these outcomes, many (Domitrovich et al., 2017; Elias, 2019; Elias et al., 2015) argue that all children should have access to explicit SEL opportunities.

2.6 Positive Psychology and Positive Education

This section will explore the evolution of positive psychology, what it is, and how it applies to education.

What Is Positive Psychology and Positive Education?

In the beginning, psychology focused on studying the good life as much as the difficulties, problems, and risks. However, after two world wars with many soldiers returning from battle with post-traumatic problems, research funding and practice became consumed with a deficit-perspective. A deficit-perspective is a focus on finding and solving problems in people or trying to understand disorder and deviance, this is a problem that continues to this day. However, when Martin Seligman become the President of the American Psychological Association in 2000, he made it his mission to shift this focus to a more positively strengths-based one.

According to Seligman and Csikszentmihalyi (2000, pg. 5), psychology needed to move away from, '. . . repairing the worst things in life . . .' towards the study of positive experiences, personal strengths, and positive institutions. Of these so-called three pillars of positive psychology, the latter (positive institutions) are probably the least well researched. While Humanistic psychology (Section 2.3) did emphasise the positives, what positive psychology included was a focus on science – the scientific study of what makes life and people better. Positive psychology has had an extensive impact beyond formal education, including personal and professional development from childhood to old age. For example, discourses on doing yoga for your mental health, practice self-care, gratitude, or journaling, and focusing on your personal development, while ensuring a work-life balance, and developing flourishing organisations have all been influenced by the field.

The application of positive psychology to schools and other educational endeavours has become known as positive education, which Gable and Haidt (2005: 104) defined as, '. . . the study of the conditions and processes that contribute to the flourishing or optimal functioning of people, groups, and institutions . . .'. It focuses on developing the whole learner (e.g., social, emotional, moral, and academic learning: Waters, 2011) and a range of educational approaches, such as preventative interventions, wellbeing and resiliency promotion programmes, strengths-based assessment and development, and collaborative practices (Wright & Lopez, 2009).

Positive Education Initiatives

One of the most significant contributions of positive psychology to education is its applied value; and its emphasis on evidence-based practices within schools.

A core concept within positive psychology is notions of psychological well-being. While there are many models of psychological well-being, Seligman's (2011) PERMA model, which consists of five characteristics which can be enhanced and are intrinsically motivating: (a) Positive emotions; (b) Engagement; (c) Relationships; (d) Meaning; and (e) Achievement. Seligman worked with the Geelong Grammar School in Australia to apply this model to formal education, embedding these principles within the curriculum and practices using a whole school approach. For example, they embedded it within the curriculum by discussing character strengths in English literature, they adopted a programme called *Giving for A Better World* where older student mentor young ones to make meaningful contributions to their community (enhancing positive purpose and meaning). They trained staff in Active Constructive Responding, which is a communication technique used when someone shares positive experiences or information. Rather than passively saying 'well done' the receiver actively responds in a manner that boosts wellbeing in all involved in the conversation, promoting positive emotions and positive relationships (Lambert et al, 2013).

The influence of positive psychology on education has been enormous from thinking about teachers' wellbeing (Hascher & Waber, 2021), to the development of school-based programmes for primary and secondary students like BOUNCE BACK (Noble & McGrath, 2016), to general wellbeing curriculum in Irish primary schools (Department of Education, 2019), through to individual interventions like mindfulness, social support, wellbeing programmes and psychoeducation for teachers (Cann et al., 2024) and for students (Seligman et al., 2009); and whole school climates and practices, such as developing a safe and collaborative environment where teachers and students can thrive (Kangas-Dick & O'Shaughnessy, 2020).

Early Days

The field of positive psychology is still very much in its infancy. 20 years of research has yielded much scientific understanding, however, two decades is not a long time in science. Certain theoretical frameworks and statistical analysis originally considered the foundations of the field have been criticised, amended, and/or ultimately discarded. For example, Fredrickson and Losada's (2005) critical positivity ratio, which claimed we needed 3:1 positive to negative ratio in terms of emotions was based on statistical evidence that was not only criticised, but extensively disproved (Nickerson, 2018). However, the great thing about science is that it is never an endpoint, it endlessly endeavours to develop better knowledge and understanding. So, positive psychology is certainly a one to watch in a psychology of education.

2.7 Holistic Approaches

A holistic and systemic approach is often considered best practice to understanding and responding to any area of development. Adopting a holistic perspective, we can understand an individual's learning and development to be shaped through a dynamic interactive process with other people (e.g., parents, teachers, peers) in different contexts (e.g., school and home) across their lifetime. Therefore, while some Schools of Thought take a narrow perspective on one aspect of learning or development, there are others that consider the educational and developmental process within its entirety.To understand learning and development holistically we must understand the reciprocal interactions between a range of factors (e.g., biological, psychological, social, cultural, political, and environmental). Adopting systemic perspectives, Bronfenbrenner's (2005) Bio-ecological Model and Engel's (1977) Biopsychosocial Model provide good frameworks for the complexities involved in people and educational practices. In this way, learning and development can be understood to emerge from complex interactions between biology, psychology, and the social and environmental and cultural context. These frameworks are essentially integrated approaches, which consider the factors present within other models and how they interact to produce learning.

Bio-Ecological Model

According to Bronfenbrenner's (2005) Bioecological Model, learning and development can be understood as emerging from *interactions* within and between multiple nested ecological systems or environments wherein the individual interacts, with processes that are influenced at distal and proximal levels. For example, a child has direct interactions with people and objects in their immediate environment, like home and school, but these interactions are influenced by the processes between these environments (e.g., home-school communication). The child's experiences will also be influenced by wider social structures, like a school's funding for extracurricular activities, a parent's degree of stress at work, mass media, or government policies (within the ecosystem). All of these systems are nested within the macro-system or the wider socio-cultural context, with various attitudes and ideologies within a given culture. We also must think about time (chronosystem) which is (a) time since the child has been alive (and all their lived experiences that they bring to any interaction) and (b) socio-political-cultural time (e.g., modern schools are influenced by an older Prussian model of education from the 19th century).

Biopsychosocial Model

Engel's (1977) Biopsychosocial Model suggests that development cannot be fully understood by considering any one factors. Instead, it involves a complex interplay of biological, psychological, and social elements. For example, a young person with ADHD may smoke cigarettes due to the personality trait extraversion, a tendency towards risk taking and impulsivity, media portrays of smoking as 'cool', a desire to fit in with their social group, and they might have a parent who smokes. We cannot assume their behaviour is entirely attributable to risk taking or their social world.

These frameworks do provide us with a more comprehensive understanding of learning and development, and while they have been criticised for being too complex, to not be directly testable. However, their applied value is still considerable. Educators can draw on them in any number of ways. They would also subsume all the factors discussed previously within the different Schools of Thought; and so provide a framework to apply that integrated approach discussed at the outset of this section.

CHAPTER SUMMARY AND CONCLUSION

This chapter considered the question, do we need a psychology of education? Part 1 explored the inextricable relationship between a psychology of education. We considered the different sub-disciplines within psychology and the role of science and research-informed educational practice. Education is complex – we need to understand educational contexts, individual learners, groups of learners (group dynamics), organisational development, etcetera. We need psychology to understand and promote the many different facets within the educational process. However, psychology is not united on all fronts, the big demonstrates conflict standpoints within the field, such as whether learning and development is down to genetics (nature) or the impact of our environment (nurture), or whether development happens in fixed stages (continuity) or more fluidly (discontinuity), and whether psychological knowledge can be applied across all cultures. Clearly, we need a psychology of education. However, nothing can ever be considered definitive - no field, no study, and no theory provides us with all the answers. So, as you traverse the intellectual terrain, be sure to do so cautiously, as critical psychologists would. There are issues with the evidence-based, that seek to standardise and develop normative models for learning and development; because we live in a diverse world which requires nuance to ensure all learners are included and recognised for their uniqueness.

Part 2 considered the breadth of psychology by exploring the main frameworks (or Schools of Thought) within psychology. It applied these frameworks using specific research studies as examples. However, we need to recognise that their breadth and implications go well beyond the examples included here. We explored the psychodynamic school, in terms of its insights from attachments and trauma-informed practices. The dominance of behavioural approaches was explored and critiqued in its application to behaviour management and educational design. Humanistic education's holistic approach provides techniques, such as relational practices, which are respectful and nuanced. Cognitive psychology and cognitive neuroscience provides us with a science of learning. Social and cognitive approaches combine insights from behaviour and cognitivism, informing pedagogical practices and educational initiatives (e.g.., SEL). Positive education's provides us with insights into the role of wellbeing, strengths, and flourishing educational institutions. It contributes a range of educational initiatives, which are evidence-based. More holistic systemic models provide us with insights into the complexities involved in learning, involving multiple personal and socio-environmental factors interacting over time. Each framework provides unique and important insights into the process of learning, and supports educational practice.

As is apparent within this chapter and will be within subsequent chapters, we need a psychology of education. We have begun the journey into a psychology of education, take the tools from this chapter, and apply them as you read.

Discussion Questions to Consider

1. How does the interdependence between psychology and education influence the way we design and implement educational practices?
2. In what ways do different sub-disciplines of psychology (e.g., developmental, cognitive, social) contribute to understanding diverse learner needs and improving educational outcomes?
3. How can educators critically engage with evidence-based practices while ensuring they do not marginalise minoritised or non-normative learners?
4. What are the implications of key debates, such as nature vs. nurture or continuity vs. discontinuity, for how we understand learning and development in educational settings?
5. How can an integrated approach, drawing from multiple psychological frameworks, enhance both the learning experience and the well-being of students in educational environments?

REFERENCES

American Psychiatric Association. (2000). Diagnostic and statistical manual of mental disorders (4th ed., text rev.; DSM-IV-TR). American Psychiatric Publishing.

American Psychological Association. (2022). Definition of Psychology. https://dictionary.apa.org/psychology

Armstrong, D. (2018). Addressing the wicked problem of behaviour in schools. *International Journal of Inclusive Education*, *22*(9), 997–1013. DOI: 10.1080/13603116.2017.1413732

Artino, A. R. (2012). Academic self-efficacy: From educational theory to instructional practice. *Perspectives on Medical Education*, *1*, 76–85. DOI: 10.1007/s40037-012-0012-5

Bandura, A. (1977). *Social learning theory*. Prentice Hall.

Bandura, A. (1986). *Social foundations of thought and action: A social cognitive theory*. Prentice Hall.

Bombèr, L. M. (2007). *Inside I'm hurting: practical strategies for supporting children with attachment difficulties in schools*. Worth.

Bowlby, J. (1977). The making and breaking of affectional bonds: I. Aetiology and psychopathology in the light of attachment theory. *The British Journal of Psychiatry*, *130*(3), 201–210. DOI: 10.1192/bjp.130.3.201

Brame, C. J. (2016). Effective educational videos: Principles and guidelines for maximizing student learning from video content. *CBE Life Sciences Education*, *15*(4), es6. Advance online publication. DOI: 10.1187/cbe.16-03-0125

Bronfenbrenner, U. (2005). Making human beings human: Bioecological perspectives on human development. *Sage (Atlanta, Ga.)*.

Bruner, J. S. (1966). *Toward a theory of instruction*. Norton.

Cann, R., Sinnema, C., & Rodway, J. (2024). What do we know about interventions to improve educator wellbeing? A systematic literature review. *Journal of Educational Change*, *25*, 231–270. DOI: 10.1007/s10833-023-09490-w

Center on the Developing Child at Harvard University. (2015). *Supportive relationships and active skill building strengthen the foundations of resilience* (Working Paper No. 13). https://developingchild.harvard.edu/wp-content/uploads/2024/10/The-Science-of-Resilience2.pdf

Cohen Kadosh, R., Levy, N., & O'Shea, J. (2012). The neuroethics of non-invasive brain stimulation. *Current Biology, 22*(4), R108–R111.

Coombes, L., Chan, G., Allen, D., & Foxcroft, D. R. (2016). Mixed-methods evaluation of the good behaviour game in English primary schools. *Journal of Community & Applied Social Psychology, 26*(5), 369–387. DOI: 10.1002/casp.2268

Cooper, P., & Jacobs, B. (2011). *Evidence of best practice models and outcomes in the education of children with emotional disturbance/behavioural difficulties. An International Review*. NCSE.

Cortese, S., Ferrin, M., Brandeis, D., Buitelaar, J., Daley, D., & Dittmann, R. W.European ADHD Guidelines Group. (2015). Cognitive training for attention-deficit/hyperactivity disorder: Meta-analysis of clinical and neuropsychological outcomes from randomized controlled trials. *Journal of the American Academy of Child and Adolescent Psychiatry, 54*(3), 164–174. DOI: 10.1016/j.jaac.2014.12.010

Crenshaw, K. W. (1995). Mapping the margins: Intersectionality, identity politics, and violence against women of color. In Crenshaw, K., Gotanda, N., Peller, G., & Thomas, K. (Eds.), *Critical race theory: The key writings that formed the movement* (pp. 357–383). The New Press.

Cronholm, P. F., Forke, C. M., Wade, R., Bair-Merritt, M. H., Davis, M., Harkins-Schwarz, M., & Fein, J. A. (2015). Adverse childhood experiences: Expanding the concept of adversity. *American Journal of Preventive Medicine, 49*(3), 354–361. DOI: 10.1016/j.amepre.2015.02.001

Department of Education. (2019). *Wellbeing Policy Statement and Framework for Practice*. Government of Ireland.

Dewey, J. (1938/1963). *Experience and education*. Collier Books.

Domitrovich, C. E., Durlak, J. A., Staley, K. C., & Weissberg, R. P. (2017). Social-emotional competence: An essential factor for promoting positive adjustment and reducing risk in school children. *Child Development, 88*(2), 408–416. DOI: 10.1111/cdev.12739

Duckworth, A. L., & Seligman, M. E. (2005). Self-discipline outdoes IQ in predicting academic performance of adolescents. *Psychological Science, 16*(12), 939–944. DOI: 10.1111/j.1467-9280.2005.0164

Durlak, J. A., Weissberg, R. P., Dymnicki, A. B., Taylor, R. D., & Schellinger, K. B. (2011). The impact of enhancing students' social and emotional learning: A meta-analysis of school-based universal interventions. *Child Development, 82*(1), 405–432. DOI: 10.1111/j.1467-8624.2010.01564.x

Elias, M. J. (2019). What if the doors of every schoolhouse opened to social-emotional learning tomorrow: Reflections on how to feasibly scale up high-quality SEL. *Educational Psychologist, 54*(3), 233–245. DOI: 10.1080/00461520.2019.1636655

Elias, M. J., Leverett, L., Duffell, J. C., Humphrey, N., Stepney, C., & Ferrito, J. (2015). Integrating SEL with related prevention and youth development approaches. In Durlak, J. A., Domitrovich, C. E., Weissberg, R. P., & Gullotta, T. P. (Eds.), *Handbook of social and emotional learning: Research and practice* (pp. 33–49). Guilford Press.

Engel, G. L. (1977). The need for a new medical model: A challenge for biomedicine. *Science, 196*(4286), 129–136. DOI: 10.1126/science.847460

Felitti, V. J., Anda, R. F., Nordenberg, D., Williamson, D. F., Spitz, A. M., Edwards, V., & Marks, J. S. (1998). Relationship of childhood abuse and household dysfunction to many of the leading causes of death in adults: The Adverse Childhood Experiences (ACE) Study. *American Journal of Preventive Medicine, 14*(4), 245–258. DOI: 10.1016/S0749-3797(98)00017-8

Ford, D. Y. (2021). Intelligence testing and cultural diversity: The need for alternative instruments, policies, and procedures. In *Alternative assessments with gifted and talented students* (pp. 107–128). Routledge.

Frederick, A., & Shifrer, D. (2019). Race and disability: From analogy to intersectionality. *Sociology of Race and Ethnicity (Thousand Oaks, Calif.), 5*(2), 200–214. DOI: 10.1177/2332649218783

Fredrickson, B. L., & Losada, M. F. (2005). Positive affect and the complex dynamics of human flourishing. *The American Psychologist, 60*(7), 678. DOI: 10.1037/0003-066X.60.7.678

Gable, S. L., & Haidt, J. (2005). What (and why) is positive psychology? *Review of General Psychology, 9*(2), 103–110. DOI: 10.1037/1089-2680.9.2.103

Gergen, K. J. (2009). *Relational being: Beyond self and community*. Oxford University Press.

Greenfield, P. M. (1997). You can't take it with you: Why ability assessments don't cross cultures. *The American Psychologist, 52*(10), 11–15. DOI: 10.1037/0003-066X.52.10.1115

Hascher, T., & Waber, J. (2021). Teacher well-being: A systematic review of the research literature from the year 2000–2019. *Educational Research Review, 34*, 100411. DOI: 10.1016/j.edurev.2021.100411

Hergenhahn, B. R., & Olson, M. H. (1999). *An introduction to theories of personality*. Prentice-Hall, Inc.

Hobfoll, S. E., Watson, P., Bell, C. C., Bryant, R. A., Brymer, M. J., Friedman, M. J., & Ursano, R. J. (2007). Five essential elements of immediate and mid–term mass trauma intervention: Empirical evidence. *Psychiatry*, *70*(4), 283–315. DOI: 10.1521/psyc.2007.70.4.283

Howard-Jones, P. (2014). Neuroscience and education: Myths and messages. *Nature Reviews. Neuroscience*, *15*(12), 817–824. DOI: 10.1038/nrn3817

Kane, M., & Engle, R. (2002). The role of prefrontal cortex in working-memory capacity, executive attention, and general fluid intelligence: An individual difference perspective. *Psychonomic Bulletin & Review*, *9*(4), 637–671. DOI: 10.3758/BF03196323

Kangas-Dick, K., & O'Shaughnessy, E. (2020). Interventions that promote resilience among teachers: A systematic review of the literature. *International Journal of School & Educational Psychology*, *8*(2), 131–146. DOI: 10.1080/21683603.2020.1734125

Lambert, N. M., Gwinn, A. M., Baumeister, R. F., Strachman, A., Washburn, I. J., Gable, S. L., & Fincham, F. D. (2013). A boost of positive affect: The perks of sharing positive experiences. *Journal of Social and Personal Relationships*, *30*(1), 24–43. DOI: 10.1177/026540751244940

Leaper, C. (2011). Research in developmental psychology on gender and relationships: Reflections on the past and looking into the future. *British Journal of Developmental Psychology*, *29*(2), 347–356. DOI: 10.1111/j.2044-835X.2011.02035.x

Lewis, S. J., Arseneault, L., Caspi, A., Fisher, H. L., Matthews, T., Moffitt, T. E., & Danese, A. (2019). The epidemiology of trauma and post-traumatic stress disorder in a representative cohort of young people in England and Wales. *The Lancet. Psychiatry*, *6*(3), 247–256. https://www.thelancet.com/action/showPdf?pii=S2215-0366%2819%2930031-8

Maguire, M., Ball, S., & Braun, A. (2010). Behaviour, classroom management and student 'control': Enacting policy in the English secondary school. *International Studies in Sociology of Education*, *20*(2), 153–170. DOI: 10.1080/09620214.2010.503066

Malle, B. F., & Korman, J. (2013). *Attribution theory*. Oxford University Press.

Masten, A. S. (2014). *Ordinary magic: Resilience in development*. Guilford Press.

McCluskey, G., Lloyd, G., Kane, J., Riddell, S., Stead, J., & Weedon, E. (2008). Can restorative practices in schools make a difference? *Educational Review*, *60*(4), 405–417. DOI: 10.1080/00131910802393456

National Scientific Council on the Developing Child. (2015*). Supportive Relationships and Active Skill-Building Strengthen the Foundations of Resilience: Working Paper No. 13*. Retrieved from www.developingchild.harvard.edu

Nickerson, C. A. (2018). There is no empirical evidence for critical positivity ratios: Comment on Fredrickson (2013). *Journal of Humanistic Psychology*, *58*(3), 284–312. DOI: 10.1177/0022167817740468

Noble, T., & McGrath, H. (2016). *Bounce back! A wellbeing & resilience program* (3rd ed.). Pearson Australia.

Parker, I. (2007). Critical psychology: What it is and what it is not. *Social and Personality Psychology Compass*, *1*(1), 1–15. DOI: 10.1111/j.1751-9004.2007.00008.x

Peters, S. J., & Engerrand, K. G. (2016). Equity and excellence: Proactive efforts in the identification of underrepresented students for gifted and talented services. *Gifted Child Quarterly*, *60*, 159–171. DOI: 10.1177/0016986216643165

Piaget, J. (1952). Jean Piaget. In Boring, E. G., Werner, H., Langfeld, H. S., & Yerkes, R. M. (Eds.), *A History of Psychology in Autobiography* (Vol. 4, pp. 237–256). Clark University Press. DOI: 10.1037/11154-011

Richards, M., & Huppert, F. A. (2011). Do positive children become positive adults? Evidence from a longitudinal birth cohort study. *The Journal of Positive Psychology*, *6*(1), 75–87. DOI: 10.1080/17439760.2011.536655

Rogers, C. R. (1951). *Client-Centred Therapy: It's Current Practice, Implications and Theory*. Houghton Mifflin.

Sabnis, S. V., & Proctor, S. L. (2021). Use of critical theory to develop a conceptual framework for critical school psychology. *School Psychology Review*. Advance online publication. DOI: 10.1080/2372966X.2021.1949248

Sala, G., & Gobet, F. (2019). Cognitive training does not enhance general cognition. *Trends in Cognitive Sciences*, *23*(1), 9–20. DOI: 10.1016/j.tics.2018.10.004

Seligman, M. (2011). *Flourish*. Random House.

Seligman, M. E., Ernst, R. M., Gillham, J., Reivich, K., & Linkins, M. (2009). Positive education: Positive psychology and classroom interventions. *Oxford Review of Education*, *35*(3), 293–311. DOI: 10.1080/03054980902934563

Skinner, B. F. (2019). *The behavior of organisms: An experimental analysis.* BF Skinner Foundation.

Spencer, M. B. (2006). Phenomenology and ecological systems theory: Development of diverse groups. In Damon, W., & Lerner, R. (Eds.), Handbook of child psychology: Vol. 1. *Theoretical models of human development* (6th ed., pp. 829–893). Wiley.

Stein, M., Federspiel, A., Koenig, T., Wirth, M., Strik, W., Wiest, R., & Dierks, T. (2012). Structural plasticity in the language system related to increased second language proficiency. *Cortex, 48*(4), 458–465. DOI: 10.1016/j.cortex.2010.10.007

Tenenbaum, H. R., & Ruck, M. D. (2007). Are teachers' expectations different for racial minority than for European American students? A meta-analysis. *Journal of Educational Psychology, 99*(2), 253. DOI: 10.1037/0022-0663.99.2.253

Tesfagiorgis, M., Tsegai, S., Mengesha, T., Craft, J., & Tessema, M. (2020). The correlation between parental socioeconomic status (SES) and children's academic achievement: The case of Eritrea. *Children and Youth Services Review, 116*, 105242. DOI: 10.1016/j.childyouth.2020.105242

Thomas, M. S., Crosby, S., & Vanderhaar, J. (2019). Trauma-informed practices in schools across two decades: An interdisciplinary review of research. *Review of Research in Education, 43*(1), 422–452. DOI: 10.3102/0091732X1882112

United Nations Children's Fund (UNICEF). (2020). *Towards an equal future: Re-imagining girls' education through STEM.* UNICEF.

Van der Kolk, B. A. (2014). *The body keeps the score: Brain, mind, and body in the healing of trauma.* Viking.

Vasilic, B. (2022). Behaviour as relational process: Linking theory to practice. *Educational Psychology in Practice, 38*(4), 379–391. DOI: 10.1080/02667363.2022.2098257

Vygotsky, L. S. (1978). *Mind in society: The development of higher psychological processes* (Cole, M., John-Steiner, V., Scribner, S., & Souberman, E., Eds.). Harvard University Press.

Waters, L. (2011). A review of school-based positive psychology interventions. *The Australian Educational and Developmental Psychologist, 28*(2), 75-90.

Welsh, R. O., & Little, S. (2018). The school discipline dilemma: A comprehensive review of disparities and alternative approaches. *Review of Educational Research, 88*(5), 752–794. DOI: 10.3102/0034654318791582

Witt, C., & Ulmer, J. (2010). The impact of inquiry-based learning on the academic achievement of middle school students. In *Proceedings of the 29th Annual Western Region AAAE Research Conference* (Vol. 269, p. 282).

Woollard, J. (2010). *Psychology for the classroom: Behaviourism.* Routledge.

Wright, B. A., & Lopez, S. J. (2009). Widening the diagnostic focus: A case for including human strengths and environmental resources. In Lopez, S. J., & Snyder, C. R. (Eds.), *Oxford handbook of positive psychology* (pp. 71–87). Oxford University Press.

Young, C. B., Wu, S. S., & Menon, V. (2012). The neurodevelopmental basis of math anxiety. *Psychological Science, 23*(5), 492–501. DOI: 10.1177/095679761142913

Chapter 2
Unlearning Colonial Perspectives in Psychology of Education

Aoife M. Lynam
https://orcid.org/0000-0002-5984-8941
Trinity College Dublin, Ireland

Lucie Ehiwe
Trinity College Dublin, Ireland

Conor Mc Guckin
http://orcid.org/0009-0001-1090-3057
Trinity College Dublin, Ireland

Patricia McCarthy
Trinity College Dublin, Ireland

Geraldine Fitzgerald
Trinity College Dublin, Ireland

ABSTRACT

This chapter explores how we should unlearn colonial narratives in the field of psychology of education. We know that psychology has historically been shaped by ethnocentric and Western perspectives, which has often excluded the voices and experiences of non-Western, female, and marginalised groups. This exclusion continues to reinforce a biased understanding of human development and behaviour, perpetuating and contributing to exclusionary practices. This chapter discusses how we can integrate diverse perspectives into academic knowledge and highlights the importance of reflexivity and "unlearning" of entrenched biases as part of a

DOI: 10.4018/979-8-3693-1293-3.ch002

broader decolonising effort, encouraging both educators and students to critically examine their own positionality. This chapter advocates for a broader psychology of education curriculum to create a learning environment where all students feel represented and have a sense of belonging and equity.

INTRODUCTION

Decolonisation is a complex and multifaceted process, and its meaning can vary depending on the context. Decolonisation does not have a single meaning, highlighting the need for a nuanced understanding of what it means in different educational settings. In the context of education, decolonising the curriculum involves more than just expanding reading lists or including token non-Western voices. It requires a fundamental transformation of how knowledge is constructed, presented, and valued within academic disciplines. The legacy of colonialism continues to shape education, particularly within the field of Psychology of Education. Historically, psychological theories and practices have been developed predominantly from Western perspectives, reflecting the experiences of a narrow, privileged demographic; primarily white, Western men, while marginalising or ignoring the voices of non-Western and minority communities (MacDonald, 2006). This chapter explores the critical importance of reflection on one's positionality, critical examination of colonial narratives in Psychology of Education, and potentially, unlearning of preconceived biases. A focus on reflexive exercises for all members of the higher education environment, as well as critical review of curricula, reading lists, and teaching practices can contribute to a more inclusive and equitable learning environment.

Drawing from international perspectives on decolonisation in education, this chapter outlines how we can reflect as educators to consider dismantling the colonial legacies and practices within our Psychology of Education programmes. The chapter argues for a transformative and holistic approach to decolonisation, which goes beyond mere diversification and aims to reframe the ways in which knowledge is constructed and presented in educational spaces.

WHITE SAVIOURISM AND FRAGILITY

Aronson (2017) critically examines the concept of *White Saviourism* in education, drawing from Teju Cole's (2012) framing of the White Savior Industrial Complex (WSIC). Aronson (2017) argues that WSIC emerges when well-meaning white individuals, particularly teachers, assume a heroic role in "saving" non-white or marginalised students from perceived deficits. Aronson (2017) argues that this narrative, while often driven by good intentions, reinforces white privilege and perpetuates systemic inequalities. White saviours are emotionally rewarded by these acts of "saving" but fail to confront the broader, structural causes of the social issues they aim to address. In educational settings, this mentality undermines the agency of students of colour by viewing them as passive recipients of help rather than active participants in their own learning and transformation. Furthermore, WSIC fails to acknowledge how systemic factors, such as white supremacy and colonial legacies, contribute to the very challenges these students face. The concept of white saviourism has important implications for how we approach teaching, learning, and curricular content in Psychology of Education. We know that Psychology has historically been shaped by Western, ethnocentric perspectives, which frequently disregard non-Western or marginalised voices. Educators, particularly in the context of decolonising Psychology of Education curricula, must avoid reproducing "white saviourist" narratives when attempting to address the gaps in representation of diverse perspectives. This involves moving beyond surface-level inclusion of non-Western scholars and engaging in a deeper critique of the colonial and racial dynamics that underpin traditional psychological theories. Additionally, educators must critically reflect on their own positionality and biases to ensure they are not positioning themselves as saviours but rather as facilitators of a more equitable and inclusive learning environment. This shift is essential in Psychology of Education, a field where the lived experiences of diverse cultural groups must be acknowledged to avoid perpetuating harmful hierarchies and reinforcing the marginalisation of those already underrepresented in psychological research and practice.

It is important to consider alternative perspectives on Aronson's (2017) white saviour concept. For example, Lemalu-Sankale (2023) discusses Mr. Beast's building of wells in Kenya. Mr. Beast is a white American Internet personality who has used his wealth to contribute to a number of humanitarian causes, including feeding needy Americans, planting millions of trees, and building wells to provide people in Kenya, Cameroon, and Zimbabwe with clean drinking water. He has received criticism from some who suggest that his actions perpetuate the idea that Africans need a handout, or that he is ultimately profiting from the attention gained with these humanitarian efforts (Miltimore, 2023). Lemalu-Sankale (2023) suggests that such criticism often comes from those who are removed from the hardship being addressed. For the communities involved the impact and its domino effect can be profound. "These wells represent a path to a different future. With access to clean water, children can and do spend more time in school, their health improves with a decrease in waterborne diseases, and agricultural productivity increases, enhancing the economic stability of the communities" (Lemalu-Sankale, 2023). This perspective reminds us that this issue is complex and contains many perspectives. Focusing on this phenomenon in an educational context in the USA, Brown (2013) explores the subtle ways in which teacher bias can impact in the classroom.

Brown (2013) critically reviews the trope of the white female teacher as saviour in the context of a New York public school which focuses on college readiness. Introducing the concept of the saviour mentality, she describes a white educator's assumption that she is "responsible for students' success, and problematically constructs students and their families through a deficit lens; they can only be 'saved' with the school's help"(Brown, 2013, p. 124). She argues that the saviour mentality is evident in the educator's attempts at the social justice work of supporting students to become more attractive or acceptable to, what she considers, an inequitable social and economic system. An alternative, Brown (2013) suggests, would be to critique or challenge the system itself. Focusing her argument on the cultural context of America, Brown (2013) refers to the typical media portrayal (e.g., the movie Dangerous Minds) of white, female teachers saving students of colour from themselves and their communities in order that they might achieve academic success. She proposes that this representation is reflected in the tendency for white females to enter the teaching profession in the United States of America (USA). Moreover, Brown (2013) believes that racist attitudes are perpetuated, not only by media representations, but also by teacher training, professional development, and policy debates. Brown (2013) states that much racism in the urban American classroom manifests as unintentional, passive, or 'dysconscious' behaviour. Brown (2013) gives an example of a teacher (a composite composed of two teachers she had observed and given the name 'Ms. Joseph') lacking in self-awareness and displaying cultural bias during a grammar lesson:

> *Ms. Joseph elevates her own raced and classed discourse ... without explicit social critique or self-reflexivity ... she does not ... demonstrate an awareness of herself as a racial actor in that setting who elevates her own experience to normalcy and correctness without a critique of the constructed and problematic nature of this hierarchy (p. 141).*

This example contrasts with another composite of two teachers interviewed and observed in the same study. 'Ms Easton' is also white but grew up and was schooled (for the most part) in a multi-cultural and ethnically diverse community. She is quick to advocate and defend student perspectives among other staff and "She views students' communities and experiences through an asset-based lens, and does not normalize her own experience through her pedagogy or praxis" (Brown, 2013, p. 146). Furthermore, Ms. Easton would like to see more involvement of parents and more holistic education, as opposed to focusing entirely on preparation for college. In undertaking a student cultural exchange with predominantly white working class students from Maine, Ms. Easton shifted the focus and objective away from a colourblind perspective, and instead asked the students to explore the differences between themselves and their counterparts. This embracing of, and curiosity regarding difference, provides a useful example of how positionality can be explored and methods of reflexivity developed.

REFLEXIVITY AND UNLEARNING: KEY STEPS IN DECOLONISATION

A key aspect of decolonising Psychology of Education is fostering reflexivity among educators and students. Reflexivity involves a continuous process of self-examination and critical reflection on one's positionality, biases, and assumptions. Pinar (1975, 2011) highlight the importance of *currere*, an autobiographical method that encourages educators and students to critically engage with their own educational experiences and examine how these experiences are shaped by colonial narratives.

Unlearning colonial biases requires educators and students to interrogate their own assumptions about knowledge, power, and identity. This process is not only about identifying and addressing explicit biases but also about recognising the more subtle, implicit ways in which colonial ideologies continue to shape educational content and practices. By fostering reflexivity and encouraging open, critical dialogue, educators can help students develop a deeper understanding of how colonialism has shaped the field of psychology and work towards a more inclusive, global perspective.

"Elaborated awareness of past experience, when faced with contrast, challenges embedded assumptions. Then these assumptions can be theorized rather than dismissed as idiosyncratic" (Okely, 2012, p. 36). Okely (2012) describes how the anthropologist in the field unlearns what he/she has taken for granted (sometimes) since infancy. Furthermore, she suggests that it is by making mistakes or breaking rules in a different cultural context that one comes to understand the mistaken assumptions. "Unlearning, by definition, entails confronting what has already been learned, whether enforced or naively absorbed, so that it may later be problematised" (Okely, 2012, p. 37). "Unlearning" is regarded by Okely (2012) as an important factor contributing to creativity and originality. One might ask, how can such unlearning be supported in an educational context. Finefter-Rosenbluh (2017) describes how social perspective taking can allow an individual to remove oneself from one's own frame of reference and the relevant constraints and biases of perspective. Researchers engaging in qualitative research often apply reflexivity as a means to better understand one's own position and bias. Harding (as cited by Okely, 2012) refers to positionality as awareness of aspects of oneself (e.g., gender, ethnicity, class, age) and how these things have shaped learning from early life. Considering one's positionality requires looking outwards and reflexivity can lead to greater understanding of difference and "others". Holland (1999) defines reflexivity as “that which turns back upon (or takes account of) itself or the person’s self” (p. 464). Finefter-Rosenbluh (2017) cites both Pillow, and Mauthner and Doucet to define reflexivity as a “... continual internal dialogue and critical self-evaluation of the researcher's positionality … which leaves the researcher changed in its wake” (p. 2). Reflexivity is typically used to refer to the critical self-reflection engaged in by a researcher but can also refer to a practitioner's approach.

Finefter-Rosenbluh (2017) describes her approach to perspective taking in three steps. Although she is describing a process of self-reflection for research purposes, a similar approach could be adapted for trainee teachers. In step one, Finefter-Rosenbluh (2017) undertook to activate the mental process of perspective taking. Realising that she had reached very different conclusions from an 'outside' researcher who had conducted a similar study, she adopted the 'outsider' perspective. She recognised the shared elements of the two studies. Step two involved anchoring her own 'insider' perspective and dissecting the other researcher’s “outsider” perspective. For example, Finefter-Rosenbluh (2017) describes how she had a dual relationship with the research sample in that she was both colleague and researcher which sometimes called for discernment about ethical challenges. Step three required consideration of different ways of understanding without imposition of commonly shared meaning. Upon exploring the complex perspective of the outsider-researcher, Finefter-Rosenbluh (2017) reflected on her own methodological processes, biases, and ethical dilemmas with critical awareness. This approach is related to research, but could be adapted as a useful cognitive exercise for trainee educators. Okely (2012) describes more experiential approaches to interrogating different cultural positions.

Okely (2012) explains how social anthropology exposes one to all cultural possibilities. Describing her early university experiences and introduction into work in education, she discusses how examination of one's own positionality can expand one's understanding of cultural difference. An example of working with students' subjective and lived experiences is described by Okely (2012) in relation to a movement which allowed trade unionists to study at Oxford. The culture of the university could have been intimidating for these students, however, she describes how tradesmen were encouraged to share their specialism and grounded experience as a means to enhance awareness of their own position in history (they were studying history at the time). “Lived experience was not incompatible with theoretical knowledge, generalizing or holistic contexts” (Okely, 2012, p. 39). Okely (2012) describes her own approach to supporting Jamaican students in examining their positionality during the 1960s as part of Social and Economic History studies. Rather than repeat the narrow and racist teaching she had received when learning about slavery and its economical relevance, she embraced the multiculturalism in her classroom and approached the task of allowing both white and Caribbean students to examine their positionality with subtlety. She used art to facilitate this process with music such as Billie Holiday's 'Strange Fruit' and the movie 'In the Heat of the Night' as means to examine the legacy of slavery and racism. “The intention was to encourage lateral identification among the Jamaicans and deconstruction of stereotypes among the white students” (Okely, 2012, p. 41). In another example Okely (2012) explains how she requested that first year students reflect on their subjective positionality, by considering a time in which they were in an unfamiliar cultural context, and how they made mistakes and were surprised. This led to sharing of personal vulnerability and learning about difference. The students realised that they had wrongly assumed some “rules” or experiences to be universal. They came to better understand the lived experience of ethnocentricity when they transgressed other cultural rules. Okely (2012) discusses the advantage that students of mixed heritage (nationality or ethnicity) enjoy as they have 'bifocal vision'; that is to say, they may have experienced different languages or lived in different cultures and therefore already knew that one culture cannot be superior to another. This perspective was much appreciated by one of her mixed heritage students (born in Hull but with Ukrainian roots) who had always been denigrated for not being 'real Hull'. This unlearning had allowed the young woman to experience her positionality with pride. Ultimately Okely (2012) proposes that “New learning can be inspired by building on the student's prior knowledge and identity as a means of fostering both commonality and contrast” (p. 42).

DECOLONISING THE EARLY CHILDHOOD AND SCHOOL YEARS

Tembo and Bateson (2024) examine how racial discrimination and colonial legacies shape early childhood education and development, arguing that race and racism are embedded in children's play and relational habits long before explicit acts of racism emerge. They critique traditional anti-racist approaches in early education, which focus on surface-level interventions, such as diverse books and discussions about race, but fail to address deeper colonial norms that shape children's interactions. Drawing on the concept of “coloniality” Tembo and Bateson (2024) argue that many early childhood settings perpetuate colonial power structures through neoliberal values like individualism and competition, which reinforce racialisation. Tembo and Bateson's (2024) work highlights how colonial legacies shape children's interactions and relational habits before explicit racism emerges, showing the importance of addressing these deep-rooted norms within psychology of education. By critiquing neoliberal and individualistic values that reinforce racialisation, they argue for pedagogies that prioritise relational learning and free play, such as Froebelian methods, which allow children to explore their identities outside colonial frameworks (Tembo & Bateson, 2024). For psychology of education, this means we need to rethink developmental models that often implicitly reinforce colonial ideologies. Decolonising this field requires moving beyond surface-level diversity initiatives to address the deeper, often unconscious, colonial structures that shape children's socialisation and learning. Tembo and Bateson's (2024) approach encourages a re-examination of how psychology of education conceptualises child development, identity, and learning within decolonial frameworks.

Neville (2023) proposed an approach to language teaching advocating for the empowerment of student teachers as agents of change within their post-primary classrooms with pupils aged between 12-18 years. This model encouraged teachers and local curriculum leaders to challenge the dominant, canonical narratives embedded in the education system. Teachers need to be empowered with the critical skills necessary to interrogate their teaching practice, classroom environment, institutional contexts, and the broader educational system. Neville (2023) argued that teachers could continually deconstruct and renegotiate their identities, positioning themselves in what was referred to as a "Third Space", a dynamic area of professional reflection where they could act as agents of transformative change, promoting greater equity, diversity, and inclusion within their classrooms. Neville (2023) introduced the concept of Critical Decolonial Reflection (CDR), building upon the foundational idea of Critical Decolonial Awareness (CDA). CDR encourages teachers to critically reflect on their practice in a participant-centred manner which should occur throughout teachers professional careers through ongoing dialogue and reflection among teachers, focusing on key aspects of subject knowledge, pedagogy, and classroom practice (Neville, 2023). One key aspect of CDR, as outlined by Neville (2023), involved student teachers reflecting on their own Language Teacher Identities (LTIs) and examining whether their teaching practices perpetuated traditional, Eurocentric approaches or embraced a decolonial perspective. Neville (2023) stressed the importance of recognising the plurality of knowledge systems. Student teachers were urged to reflect on their own subject knowledge and consider whether their teaching included peripheral epistemologies, particularly those from the Global South. Neville's (2023) CDA-CDR model was piloted with a small group of student language teachers (N=7) at University College Cork (UCC) and the results indicated that the model enhanced the participants' awareness of decolonial issues and encouraged them to engage with diverse content in their teaching. However, there were challenges, particularly in relation to workload and a lack of autonomy during school placements. Neville (2023) argued that while the CDA-CDR model made a valuable contribution to the decolonisation of language education, more research is required to understand how such approaches could be embedded in post-primary education. This research highlights the need for collaboration between teachers, curriculum leaders, publishers, and policymakers to support the ongoing development of culturally responsive pedagogy that will permeate through all aspects of education from early childhood through to higher education and beyond.

COLONIAL LEGACIES IN HIGHER EDUCATION

We know that Psychology, as a discipline, has been historically shaped by colonial and ethnocentric frameworks. Literature (MacDonald, 2006; Henrich et al., 2010) has shown that much of psychological research and theory has relied on WEIRD (Western, Educated, Industrialised, Rich, Democratic) populations, which limits its international applicability. This over-reliance on Western perspectives has created a narrow understanding of human development and behaviour; which is often reflected in university curricula and reading lists. As a result, we may continue to perpetuate colonial biases and legacies by exposing students to a curriculum that prioritises Western, male scholars, marginalising the perspectives of women, minority ethnic groups, and those from non-Western cultures.

O'Neill (2024) highlights the "epistemological ignorance" present in United Kingdom (UK) Politics curricula, shaped by whiteness and Western-centrism. O'Neill (2024) draws on the lived experiences of racially minoritised students to argue that the curriculum is narrow and biased toward Western, white perspectives, thus failing to acknowledge alternative epistemologies and the legacies of colonialism. The key findings of the study are that students experience the curriculum as lacking in diversity, particularly in how it presented political theory through a predominantly white, male lens, often omitting or marginalising non-Western perspectives. This "narrowness" can lead to a lack of engagement with colonialism's role in shaping political thought, treating it as an isolated historical issue rather than an ongoing influence. O'Neill (2024) acknowledges the constraints faced by educators, noting that while individual lecturers can push for change, institutional structures and traditional norms often hinder more radical transformation. This offers critical insights into how whiteness and Western-centrism can shape academic disciplines, including Psychology of Education. It is important to recognise how these biases affect curriculum content, and highlights the need to pluralise educational materials by integrating non-Western perspectives. Just as in Politics, Psychology of Education curricula could benefit from including diverse epistemologies, engaging with the global contexts of psychological theories, and addressing the historical role of colonialism in shaping the field. Moreover, the idea of "epistemological ignorance" can be applied to critique how traditional psychological theories have often ignored or marginalised non-Western forms of knowledge. In practice, O'Neill's (2024) work suggests that decolonising the Psychology of Education curriculum should not be limited to diversifying reading lists; it must involve a deeper transformation of how knowledge is framed and taught, ensuring that students from diverse backgrounds feel represented, included, and that critical perspectives on race, colonialism, and power are embedded into the core of the curriculum.

In order to decolonise the Psychology of Education curriculum, we must recognise and address these biases. Phiri et al. (2023) argue that decolonisation seeks to reverse the harmful impact of colonisation on marginalised groups by ensuring that educational spaces reflect diverse voices and experiences. In this context, unlearning colonial narratives involves critically examining the historical and ongoing influence of colonialism on the construction of psychological knowledge and its dissemination in higher education.

Phiri et al. (2023) emphasise that surface-level efforts, such as adding a few non-Western authors to a reading list, are insufficient to address the deep-rooted colonial biases present in academic curricula. Instead, they argue for a comprehensive re-examination of the underlying frameworks that shape educational content, ensuring that the perspectives of those who have been historically marginalised are given equal legitimacy and representation. This process involves critically engaging with both the "hidden curriculum", the implicit norms and values that shape the academic environment, and the "null curriculum", the content that is excluded or ignored (O'Neill, 2024).

Chikoko (2021) discusses how re-visiting the decolonisation of higher education in South Africa has become a critical focus since the #FeesMustFall movement, revealing a range of approaches to addressing colonial legacies. Chikoko (2021) categorises these into three broad strategies: (a) soft reform; (b) radical reform; and (c) beyond-reform. Soft reform refers to surface-level changes, such as improving access or supplementing curricula with non-Western content, without challenging the deeper power structures that sustain coloniality (Zembylas, 2018). These changes maintain the status quo and fall short of meaningful transformation, as they fail to disrupt the Eurocentric foundations of higher education. Chikoko (2021) describes such efforts, which target isolated aspects of the system like qualifications or individual programmes, as "sub-soft reforms", unable to address the entrenchment of colonial values. Radical reform, in contrast, aims to dismantle these entrenched colonial values. This approach calls for transforming the entire curriculum, leadership, and research practices to empower historically marginalised groups (Zembylas, 2018). However, Chikoko (2021) notes that while these reforms address the curriculum, universities are broader institutions, and focusing solely on curriculum change may still fall short of the necessary transformation. The notion of beyond-reform goes further, recognising that higher education institutions are fundamentally tied to coloniality. Zembylas (2018) suggests that decolonisation should encompass all aspects of the university, including administration, pedagogy, and student life. Chikoko (2021) argues that universities cannot fully decolonise in isolation from the broader colonial context of society, and therefore must simultaneously act as agents of societal decolonisation. Thus, while progress has been made towards decolonising South African higher education, meaningful transformation requires a more holistic approach that extends beyond curricular changes to challenge the underlying colonial structures of the institution and society. This could be said for many aspects of education.

Pierre du Plessis (2021) discussed leadership in post-colonial educational contexts, particularly in South Africa, by examining the challenges university heads face in leading within a decolonised education framework. The research aligns with findings by Moncrieffe, Race, and Harris (2020), who also underscore the need for educational leadership to critically engage with the legacy of colonialism and work toward social justice in curriculum design. Du Plessis (2021) highlights how educational leaders in South Africa must develop contextually relevant leadership practices that are responsive to the unique socio-political and historical challenges of the region. Like the findings in Moncrieffe, Race, and Harris (2020), Du Plessis identifies tensions in practice between the ideals of decolonised leadership and the realities of social issues within universities. Similarly, Manathunga (2020) addresses the importance of recognising diverse knowledge systems and the psychological impact of epistemic dominance on learners. In Psychology of Education, understanding how students' cognitive and social development is influenced by the cultural relevance of the curriculum is critically important. The continued dominance of Northern knowledge systems within higher education can contribute to a sense of alienation and marginalisation for students from Southern, Indigenous, and other non-Western backgrounds. This reflects broader psychological issues related to identity formation, self-efficacy, and motivation, as learners may struggle to see their cultural and epistemological perspectives reflected in what they are taught. By advocating for the inclusion of Southern knowledge systems, Manathunga (2020) highlights the need for educational environments to support the cognitive and emotional well-being of students from diverse backgrounds. Decolonising education, therefore, aligns with key principles in the psychology of education that stress the importance of culturally responsive teaching, which fosters a sense of belonging and engagement. Such approaches can contribute to more effective learning outcomes by validating students' identities and experiences, enhancing their intrinsic motivation, and promoting psychological well-being. This shift also encourages more inclusive, democratic ways of learning that recognise and accommodate diverse ways of knowing, thinking, and being in the world.

GRASSROOTS DECOLONISATION INITIATIVES

Shain et al. (2021) explored the evolution of decolonisation within UK higher education (from 2014 to 2021), with a particular focus on its shifting discourse and institutional responses. The study identifies three overlapping phases of decolonisation efforts. The first phase, initiated in 2014, was predominantly student-led, driven by campaigns such as "Why Is My Curriculum White?" and "Liberate My Degree", which sought to challenge the Eurocentric dominance of university curricula and advocate for greater inclusivity (Shain et al., 2021). These movements highlighted the grassroots origins of the decolonisation agenda, as students and student officers spearheaded initiatives to raise awareness of structural inequalities within higher education. In response to student-led campaigns, several educational institutions have adopted decolonisation agendas, raising critical questions such as, "Why isn't my Professor Black?" and "Why is my Curriculum White?" (Peters, 2015). Shain et al. (2021) note how in 2018, industrial action led by the University College Union (UCU) over pension reforms witnessed a broader critique of the neoliberal policies shaping UK universities, where the slogan "We are the university" became a rallying cry for those resisting market-driven models of higher education (Shain et al., 2021). Decolonisation was increasingly incorporated into these critiques, reflecting growing discontent with the commodification of education and the marginalisation of diverse epistemologies. The third and final phase in 2020, following the Black Lives Matter (BLM) protests, marked a shift towards institutional-led decolonisation. Universities began to adopt top-down approaches, publicly committing to decolonising curricula in response to external pressures, such as heightened scrutiny on racial justice and the need to appear progressive in the face of global movements (Shain et al., 2021). However, participants in the Shain et al. (2021) study expressed concerns about the superficiality of these efforts, which were often perceived as performative and motivated by reputational gains rather than a genuine commitment to anti-racism. The mainstreaming of decolonisation therefore saw little impact on the deeper structures of inequality within higher education (Shain et al., 2021). This highlights the tensions between grassroots decolonisation initiatives and institutional progress. While universities have increasingly engaged with decolonisation discourse, the risk of "tokenism" or "superficial" reform remains. Thus, a more critical and sustained engagement with decolonisation that resists its commodification and ensures that it leads to meaningful structural change is needed (Shain et al., 2021).

In Ireland, Trinity College Dublin (TCD) renamed its main library, previously called the Berkeley Library, in honour of renowned Irish poet and Trinity alumna Eavan Boland, making the Eavan Boland Library the first building on TCD's campus named after a woman (Sloane, 2024). The renaming follows TCD's removal of George Berkeley's name due to his associations with slavery, which the university deemed inconsistent with its values of inclusivity and equality (Sloane, 2024). The decision, endorsed by the University Board, follows research, public consultation, and analysis led by the Trinity Legacies Review Working Group who are working toward decolonising higher education. The gender imbalance can be seen historically, but continues to permeate present day in different and often invisible guises. Churchland and Davatolhagh (2024) highlighted the ongoing issue of gender citation bias in neuroscience, where women are consistently under-cited compared to men in academic papers, even as the number of female researchers rises. Male authors tend to over-cite other men, perpetuating gender imbalances that affect academic recognition and career advancement. Tools like *cleanBib* and *anneslist* help analyse reference lists for citation diversity, encouraging researchers to cite more equitably across gender and race. Their findings highlight the need to address not only racial and cultural biases but also gender and demographic imbalances. Utilising tools like *cleanBib* could ensure that reading lists and course materials reflect a diverse range of voices, actively promoting inclusivity and representation in academia, which is central to the decolonisation effort (Churchland & Davatolhagh, 2024).

THE CHALLENGE OF DECOLONISATION

A major challenge in decolonising the Psychology of Education curriculum is the pervasive influence of whiteness and Western-centrism. Whiteness refers to the racialised power structures that privilege white perspectives and experiences, while Western-centrism elevates Western knowledge systems as the universal standard, marginalising or dismissing non-Western forms of knowledge. This creates a narrow and exclusionary framework within the curriculum, as ideas and perspectives that originate from Western, typically white scholars are deemed authoritative, while contributions from non-Western, Indigenous, or historically marginalised communities are overlooked or undervalued. These biases not only limit the diversity of perspectives taught but also maintain existing hierarchies of power, reinforcing a colonial legacy that continues to shape the educational landscape (O'Neill, 2024). O'Neill (2024) highlights the ways in which curricula are shaped by both whiteness, which refers to racialised power structures, and Western-centrism, which privileges Western knowledge systems as the standard against which all other perspectives are measured. These biases not only narrow the scope of what is considered legitimate knowledge but also reinforce existing power imbalances, marginalising non-Western voices and perspectives (O'Neill, 2024).

In many educational settings, particularly in psychology, Enlightenment thinkers such as John Locke, Immanuel Kant, and René Descartes are often central to the curriculum. While these figures have undoubtedly contributed significantly to modern psychology, their work is intertwined with colonialist and racial ideologies that must be critically examined. For example, many Enlightenment thinkers upheld ideas of racial superiority and Eurocentrism, which have long influenced the way psychological theories are framed. O'Neill (2024) stresses that decolonising the curriculum is not about discarding these thinkers entirely but about situating their ideas within the broader context of colonialism and race. By doing so, educators can challenge the implicit assumptions of superiority tied to these figures and encourage students to engage with psychological knowledge in a more critical and inclusive manner. This approach seeks to broaden the scope of what is considered legitimate knowledge, ensuring that the contributions of non-Western scholars and perspectives are given equal weight and that students are exposed to an international understanding of psychology.

DECOLONISING TEACHER EDUCATION: INTERNATIONAL IMPLICATIONS

The process of decolonising Psychology of Education must begin with teacher training. As Phiri et al. (2023) argue, change should start early in the education system, with teacher training programmes playing a critical role in shaping future generations of educators. Drawing on examples from Bolivia's teacher training reforms (Lopes Cardozo, 2012), this section explores how decolonisation efforts in other contexts can inform global strategies for transforming Psychology of Education. Bolivia's reforms, which sought to address the denial of indigenous culture and knowledge within education, serve as a powerful example of how teacher training can act as a foundation for broader decolonisation efforts. These reforms were not simply about adding indigenous perspectives to the curriculum but about fundamentally restructuring the frameworks that govern education. For Psychology of Education, this means rethinking how psychological knowledge is taught, ensuring that diverse perspectives are integrated into the curriculum from the beginning of a teacher's training.

Moncrieffe et al. (2020) discuss the efforts to challenge the Eurocentric nature of educational curricula and the barriers this movement has faced. The decolonisation of the curriculum, which seeks to integrate the experiences and histories of Black and minority ethnic (BME) communities, is part of a broader epistemological struggle to dismantle dominant discourses that have historically excluded non-Western perspectives. While this movement has long-standing roots, dating back to the 1960s and 1970s when Black parents in the UK established supplementary schools to teach African-Caribbean histories, recent campaigns have brought renewed attention to the issue. Moncrieffe et al. (2020) argue that decolonising the curriculum goes beyond mere inclusion of diverse voices. It involves rethinking how knowledge is constructed and disseminated in schools and universities. Rather than "tokenistic" approaches (e.g., isolated celebration of Black History Month) decolonisation calls for a fundamental change in the content and pedagogical methods being used. This process encourages educators to question and reshape the monocultural, often Anglocentric or Eurocentric narratives that dominate curricula and to introduce a more inclusive worldview that represents marginalised groups. A significant challenge, highlighted by Moncrieffe et al. (2020), is that of *"white fragility"* which is the defensive reactions by those in positions of privilege when confronted with the realities of racial inequality and colonial legacies. This fragility can result in, for example, discomfort, resistance, and even the reluctance to engage with the necessary but often difficult conversations surrounding race, privilege, and historical power imbalances. However, Moncrieffe et al. (2020) assert that it is critical to push through this discomfort if we want to dismantle systemic racism in educational practices. Moncrieffe et al. (2020) emphasise that the decolonisation of the curriculum is not just about what is taught, but how it is taught. It requires educators to adopt critical approaches that validate the lived experiences of all students, create space for collaborative learning, and ensure that diverse perspectives are not marginalised. This, in turn, fosters greater engagement, a sense of belonging, and critical thinking skills in learners from all backgrounds, contributing to a more equitable and inclusive educational environment, which is what we will discuss in the next section.

THE ROLE OF UNIVERSAL DESIGN FOR LEARNING (UDL) IN DECOLONISING PSYCHOLOGY OF EDUCATION

Universal Design for Learning (UDL) offers a progressive framework that supports decolonisation efforts within psychology of education by prioritising inclusivity and accessibility. UDL's foundational goal of creating curricula that cater to all learners aligns with decolonial approaches, as it seeks to dismantle entrenched biases in educational content and practice. As highlighted by Quirke, McGuckin, and McCarthy (2022, 2023), UDL promotes the design of curricula that are inclusive "from the get-go," ensuring that learners of all backgrounds have equitable opportunities to engage with educational material. This reflexive approach enables educators to critique their teaching practices, exposing and mitigating colonial influences embedded in the curriculum. UDL's flexibility and focus on accessibility thus provide a means of integrating diverse, culturally responsive perspectives in psychology of education, creating an environment where students feel represented and valued.

However, critiques of inclusive education, particularly from a Global South perspective, suggest a need for caution when applying Western-centric models such as

UDL. Walton (2018) analyses the use of inclusive education in post-colonial contexts like South Africa and argues that if such frameworks are applied uncritically, they risk perpetuating neo-colonialism. Walton (2018) identifies three key dimensions of this coloniality; the coloniality of knowledge, power, and being. Eurocentric models often dominate inclusive education, marginalising local knowledge systems and presenting Western pedagogical frameworks as universal (Walton, 2018). Furthermore, external pressures from international agencies may compel countries like South Africa to adopt resource-intensive policies, often misaligned with local needs. Walton (2018) critiques the value of integrating learners into educational systems that continue to perpetuate colonial hierarchies, even under the guise of inclusivity. However, Walton (2018) suggests that inclusive education, if adapted to local contexts, could play a transformative role in supporting decolonial efforts.

Kamenopoulou's (2020) findings revealed similar critiques regarding the "transplanting" of Northern educational models to the Global South, but emphasised different aspects of this issue. Walton (2018) and Kamenopoulou (2020) highlight the risks of perpetuating neo-colonialism through the uncritical adoption of Western models, but Kamenopoulou (2020) focuses on the socio-cultural and economic conditions of Colombia, illustrating how the intersection of poverty, displacement, and cultural diversity complicates inclusive education efforts. Kamenopoulou (2020) further explores the marginalisation of special education in favour of mainstream inclusion, despite the vital role it plays in practice. Walton (2018) argues that decolonising inclusive education requires challenging the epistemological foundations of Western psychology that underpin much of the educational framework. Thus, we should reconsider psychological approaches to education in postcolonial contexts to foster more culturally relevant and equitable practices.

Castillo-Montoya and Madriaga (2024) explored the decolonisation of assessment in higher education which links to a UDL approach. Drawing on Shahjahan et al.'s (2022) work on decolonising curricula and pedagogy, they argue that traditional assessment practices, rooted in colonial and Eurocentric frameworks, perpetuate epistemic violence by marginalising non-Western ways of knowing. They highlight that decolonising assessments involves challenging the dominance of standardised exams and other forms of summative evaluation, but often fail to recognise the diverse knowledge systems and experiences of racially and minority ethnic students. Castillo-Montoya and Madriaga (2024) suggest disrupting the colonial legacies embedded in assessment by creating more inclusive and humanising approach which would allow students to draw on their own lived experiences and prior knowledge. The article further critiques deficit-oriented, individualised assessment methods that pathologise students who deviate from normative standards, such as disabled students, and calls for broader, universal design principles that minimise the need for accommodations while promoting equity (Castillo-Montoya & Madriaga, 2024). In addition to addressing the inclusivity of assessments, Castillo-Montoya and Madriaga (2024) emphasise the importance of relational teaching and learning, advocating for an ethic of care in classroom environments that centres students' emotional and intellectual well-being. They argue that decolonising assessment requires recognising and valuing community knowledge, and suggest that universities must engage with local communities as co-creators of knowledge, ensuring that their perspectives are integrated into the learning and assessment process (Castillo-Montoya & Madriaga, 2024). We should try to move towards culturally sensitive and contextually grounded approaches in psychology of education. While UDL offers a promising framework for inclusivity, its success in decolonising education depends on its adaptation to local contexts, addressing not only academic achievement but also the emotional, cognitive, and social development of learners.

CONCLUSION

Decolonising the Psychology of Education curriculum, and education more broadly, requires an approach that addresses both structural and epistemological legacies of colonialism. As discussed in this chapter, critical reflexivity and unlearning is essential for educators, enabling them to examine their own positionality and biases, while dismantling the dominance of whiteness and Western-centrism narratives. Curriculum reform must move beyond tokenistic inclusion of non-Western perspectives, demanding a fundamental restructuring of how knowledge is produced, with an emphasis on integrating diverse epistemologies, particularly from the Global South and Indigenous cultures. Taking a collaborative approach to learning and knowledge production, which values the lived experiences of marginalised communities, should be central to this process. We can see from the grassroots movements discussed in this chapter that institutional commitment is crucial for enacting meaningful change, including reforms in hiring, leadership, and policy to support diversity and inclusion. To begin, we need to start with teacher training programmes to embed culturally responsive pedagogies to ensure future educators are prepared to challenge colonial legacies in the classroom and critical thinking amongst students to advocate for change. Inclusive frameworks such as Universal Design for Learning (UDL) must be adapted to local contexts to avoid perpetuating Western-centric models. Ultimately, decolonising Psychology of Education requires a sustained and transformative approach that reshapes knowledge and fosters equitable and culturally responsive education. Decolonisation is a complex process with no 'quick-fix' solution. It demands time, patience, and ongoing reflexivity, with deliberate, thoughtful steps toward meaningful progress.

REFERENCES

Aronson, B. A. (2017). The White Savior Industrial Complex: A Cultural Studies Analysis of a Teacher Educator, Savior Film, and Future Teachers. *Journal of Critical Thought and Praxis*, *6*(3).

Brown, A. (2013). Waiting for Superwoman: White female teachers and the construction of the" neoliberal savior"" in a New York City public school. *The Journal for Critical Education Policy Studies*, *11*(2).

Burgstahler, S. (2007). Who needs an accessible classroom? *Academe*, *93*(3), 37–39. Retrieved September 24, 2024, from https://www.jstor.org/stable/40253051

Chikoko, V. (2021). Re-visiting the decolonising of South African higher education question: A systematic literature review. *South African Journal of Higher Education*, *35*(1), 21–36.

Churchland, A., & Savatolhagh, F. (2024). Women are systematically under-cited in neuroscience. New tools can change that. https://www.thetransmitter.org/publishing/women-are-systematically-under-cited-in-neuroscience-new-tools-can-change-that/

Cole, T. (2012). The white savior industrial complex. *The Atlantic (Boston, Mass.)*, *21*(March). https://www.theatlantic.com/international/archive/2012/03/the-white-savior-

Lemalu-Sankale, N. (2023, November 21). *Beyond the 'White Saviour': A grateful African's view on Mr. Beast's wells.* Medium. https://medium.com/@gratefulafrican/beyond-the-white-savior-a-grateful-african-s-view-on-mr-beast-s-wells-19935aa7e648

Lopes Cardozo, M.T. (2012). Transforming pre-service teacher education in Bolivia: From indigenous denial to decolonisation? *Compare: A Journal of Comparative and International Education, 42*(5), 751-772.

MacDonald, K. (2006). Psychology and white ethnocentrism. *The Occidental Quarterly*, *6*(4), 2007.

Manathunga, C. (2020). Decolonising higher education: Creating space for Southern knowledge systems. *Scholarship of Teaching and Learning in the South*, *4*(1), 4–25.

Meyer, A., & Rose, D. (1998). Learning to read in the computer age. In *From reading research to practice*. Cambridge, MA: Brookline Books.

Miltimore, J. (2023, November 15). *Why Mr. Beast is under fire for bringing clean water to 500,000 Africans*. American Institute for Economic Research. https://aier.org/article/why-mr-beast-is-under-fire-for-bringing-clean-water-to-500000-africans/

Moncrieffe, M., Race, R., Harris, R., Chetty, D., Riaz, N., Ayling, P., & Steinburg, S. (2020). Decolonising the curriculum. *Research Intelligence, 142*(9).

Neville, C. (2023). Developing critical decolonial awareness and reflection in language teachers at post-primary level: Empowering student language teachers as agents of change. *Irish Educational Studies*, 1–21.

O'Neill, S. (2024). *Decolonising politics curricula: Exploring the experiences and views of racially minoritised students*. Learning and Teaching in Politics and International Studies. DOI: 10.1177/02633957241276065

Peters, M. A. (2015). Why is my curriculum white? *Educational Philosophy and Theory*, *47*(7), 641–646.

Phiri, P., Sajid, S., & Delanerolle, G. (2023). Decolonising the psychology curriculum: A perspective. *Frontiers in Psychology*, *14*, 1–6. DOI: 10.3389/fpsyg.2023.1193241 PMID: 37388662

Pinar, W. F. (1975) *The method of currere*. Paper presented at the annual meeting of the American Educational Research Association, Washington, DC.

Pinar, W. F. (2011). *The Character of Curriculum Studies: Bildung, Currere, and the Recurring Question of the Subject*. Palgrave Macmillan.

Quirke, M., Mc Guckin, C., & Mc Carthy, P. (2023). *Adopting a UDL attitude within academia: Understanding and practicing inclusion across higher education*. Routledge.

Quirke, M., Mc Guckin, C., & McCarthy, P. (2022). How to adopt an "inclusion as process" approach and navigate ethical challenges in research. In *SAGE Research Methods Cases*. SAGE Publications, Ltd. DOI: 10.4135/9781529605341

Shahjahan, R. A., Estera, A. L., Surla, K. L., & Edwards, K. T. (2022). "Decolonizing" curriculum and pedagogy: A comparative review across disciplines and global higher education contexts. *Review of Educational Research*, *92*(1), 73–113.

Shain, F., Yıldız, Ü. K., Poku, V., & Gokay, B. (2021). From silence to 'strategic advancement': Institutional responses to 'decolonising' in higher education in England. *Teaching in Higher Education*, *26*(7–8), 920–936. https://doi-org.elib.tcd.ie/10.1080/13562517.2021.1976749

Sloane, E. (2024). Trinity College Dublin renames former Berkeley Library after poet Eavan Boland. https://www.irishtimes.com/ireland/education/2024/10/09/trinity-college-dublin-renames-former-berkeley-library-after-poet-eavan-boland/

Tembo, S., & Bateson, S. (2024). Before race: A literature review on de/colonial habits in play within early childhood. *Journal of Early Childhood Research*, *0*(0). Advance online publication. DOI: 10.1177/1476718X241241142

Walton, E. (2018). Decolonising (Through) Inclusive Education? *Educational Research for Social Change*, *7*(0), 31–45. DOI: 10.17159/2221-4070/2018/v7i0a3

Zembylas, M. (2018). Reinventing critical pedagogy as decolonizing pedagogy: The educationof empathy. *Review of Education, Pedagogy & Cultural Studies*, *40*(5), 404–421.

Chapter 3
Values and Social Conscience in Education

Noel Purdy
Stranmillis University College, UK

Conor Galvin
University College Dublin, Ireland

ABSTRACT

In this chapter, the authors outline the importance of values and social conscience in education, arguing that values represent a foundation for beliefs, attitudes, and ultimately, behaviours in a society where we are interconnected in a complex web of relationships. Drawing on the ideas of leading thinkers in psychology, philosophy, and sociology, they present a case for re-valorising values and social conscience in education, arguing that it is more important today than ever before. While acknowledging the many challenges that face such a shift in thinking and practice, they present evidence of encouraging shoots of new growth, where values-based, relational education has the potential to transform individual lives and to create a kinder, fairer, and more equitable society.

INTRODUCTION

In the ever-shifting landscapes of contemporary life and education, the cultivation of values, ethos, and ethics and how these intertwine to foster *social conscience* is always going to be a matter of discussion and debate. In this chapter we explore the intricate interplay between education and the development of social conscience and argue for an education that contributes to nurturing the holistic and ethically grounded learning experiences that we believe necessary to form and sustain a

DOI: 10.4018/979-8-3693-1293-3.ch003

values-based social conscience. If educational psychology is centred on deepening our understanding of learning and learners within a social context, then we assert that an awareness of the importance of values and social conscience is a fundamental prerequisite in this endeavour.

The chapter opens with a discussion of the nature and the importance of "values" as a type of personal warranting system that, arguably, constitutes the foundational framework of beliefs, principles, and ethical standards that guide an individual's attitudes, decisions, and actions; and as such profoundly influence that individual's character, choices, and overall life trajectory. Such a system embodies the core convictions and priorities that shape how someone perceives the world, evaluates situations, and makes choices. But as people are best understood as fundamentally ecological and interconnected, any discussion of values needs to reflect the understanding that individuals are intricately linked to and influenced by their environment and the broader web of relationships within society (Moran, 2016). As such, the discussion must also address how, as social beings, we craft and exercise shared, social conscience shaping value systems that represent a broader collective set of beliefs, principles, and ethical standards embraced within a community or society.

This involves examining a number of constructions relating to "values" that can be traced to the seminal work of Milton Rokeach (1973), a social theorist and psychologist, who drew widely from across a wide range of disciplines and fields to argue that "the value concept, perhaps more than any other in the social sciences, is meaningful at all levels of social analysis" (p.1) while acknowledging the contingent and ever-shifting nature of value bases that inevitable result from "the ever changing salience of societal issues" (p.137). We work particularly with the issues raised by Rokeach's observations on the relations of *enduring belief* to values at both a personal and societal level (and some of the implications of this for education) as well as his formative detailing of the characteristics and interrelations of what he termed *end-states* (terminal values), and *modes of behaviour* (instrumental values) (Rokeach 1967; Rokeach 1973; Rokeach & Regan, 1980). Our purpose in doing this is not to validate that, or indeed any, particular modelling of values, *per se*, or Rokeach's particular way of thinking about their potential; rather, it is to allow us a way to draw out and explore heuristically the sometimes idiosyncratic construction of values and ethics that can characterise the ethos and work of contemporary schools and other institutions of education as they try to navigate the multiple and often contradictory demands placed on them by systems premising how social capital can be captured from embedded resources within their offerings.

In the second part of the chapter, we turn to the concepts of kindness, fairness, and equity and what these could mean practically in an education system that premises social conscience and social justice. In this discussion, we highlight education's potential for addressing social injustice and promoting fairness, drawing particularly on insights from Paulo Freire and Amartya Sen. In so doing, we advocate for an education system that fosters critical thinking, challenges oppression, abandons traditional models of schools and schooling, where necessary, and emphasises the interconnectedness of ethics, the economy, education, and well-being.

In the final part of our discussion we turn to the implications of an education based on understandings of *care* and *being care-full*, as articulated by Lynch (2020, 2021) and how such a values-centred education offers a way for schools and schooling to contest "the logics and ethics of neoliberal capitalism that dominate public discourses and politics in the early twenty-first century" which "morally endorse and institutionalize forms of competitive self-interest that jettison social justice values"(2021, p.196). In its place Lynch proposes an education centred on care and solidarity, premised on the defining shift to educate in and through "affective relations in structural social justice terms" (Lynch, 2020, p.118).

In an era marked by rapid technological advancements, cultural diversity and global interconnectedness, the role of education extends beyond the transmission of knowledge; it must actively engage in shaping individuals with a profound sense of agency, optimism, and social responsibility. Our belief is that current systems of schooling and education are by and large unable to meet this challenge and thwarted from such endeavours; although it is a matter of existential importance that they begin to do so. By examining and re-thinking the conceptual underpinnings of values in education and considering ways in which educational institutions can be permitted and facilitated to evolve into nurturing spaces for ethical decision-making and the cultivation of a robust social conscience, we hope to contribute to moving this discussion forward.

1. THE NATURE AND THE IMPORTANCE OF HUMAN VALUES

Personal value systems are centrally important to gaining an understanding of the outworking of psychology in real-world educational contexts. These personal value systems are deeply individualistic and subjective, reflecting a unique amalgamation of experiences, cultural influences, and internalized beliefs (Brewer & Roccas 2015) and serve as a fundamental framework guiding individuals in their decision-making processes. They are stable yet adaptable, and are hierarchically organised (Sagiv et al., 2017) with some values, or sets of values, taking precedence over others, helping individuals navigate situations where conflicting principles may arise. Additionally, while some values may be widely shared within a cultural or social context, others are highly individualistic and reflect the balance between adhering to societal norms and expressing one's unique identity. The emotional significance attached to personal values underscores this profound impact on an individual's identity, so contributing to a sense of meaning and purpose in life. In short, they act to warrant or provide dispensation for action.

Personal values not only serve as a moral and ethical compass but also play a vital role in guiding behaviour. They provide individuals with a sense of direction, helping them make choices that align with their core beliefs. Indeed, the enduring and influential nature of values in shaping personal and collective conduct is frequently noted in the literature as is the reach of a given value. Life experiences, both positive and negative, have long been recognised to further shape and refine value systems with personal growth often accompanied by a re-evaluation and adaptation of values (Mok, 2002; Farley et al., 2021). In essence, personal value bases can be described as rather stable but potentially dynamic, multifaceted constructs that contribute significantly to self-awareness, identity, and the decision-making processes of individuals in their journey through life (Rokeach 1973; Schwartz 1992).

Consideration must however be given to influences beyond the individual, for cultural and societal influences also play a crucial role in shaping such personal value bases, with norms, traditions and societal expectations contributing to these. The internalization of such societal values runs deep, making them an integral part of an individual's identity and influencing how they perceive themselves and their role in the broader societal context. However, as Pelling et al. (2014) note, values at the societal level, although usually held relatively constant, are far from immutable and when they change, this can take several forms, including "radical shifts, directional turns or step changes in normative and technical aspects of culture, [personal] development or risk management" (p. 113).

The duality of operating within personal and more broadly vested societal value systems challenges narrow, simplistic assumptions about the nature of the psychology of education in contemporary society and raises some interesting and complex challenges for educators, especially those who work with and teach the young. Values are not innate: they need to be inculcated in the learner and, ideally, generated through processes of deliberation and learning. The very act of educating engages both the personal and the social dimensions of a learner's value base. In addition, the educator's part in this is rooted perhaps incontestably in their own value frameworks so that any learning activity with learners is guided by these core values and beliefs, even if these are modulated or restrained.

It is helpful to turn at this point to the work of Milton Rokeach and Shalom H. Schwartz who remain two seminal figures in the field of human values. Both Rokeach and Schwartz worked on the defining nature of basic human values and the features and concerns that are common to all such values as well as what distinguishes one from another. Their respective theoretical positions are outlined below and summarised in Table 1.

Firstly, Milton Rokeach's distinction between *terminal* and *instrumental* values is helpful in gaining a better understanding of individual and societal value systems. Introduced in his seminal work "The Nature of Human Values" (1973), *terminal* values represent the desired end-states or ultimate goals that individuals aspire to achieve in their lives. These values are seen to encapsulate what individuals consider to be the most important and meaningful outcomes of their activities. The identification of such terminal values can offer insights into an individual's long-term aspirations, life purpose and the overarching principles that guide their decisions and actions. Examples of terminal values, as detailed by Rokeach, include happiness, inner harmony, wisdom, social recognition, and a sense of accomplishment. By contrast, *instrumental* values refer to the means or modes of behaviour that individuals believe are necessary to achieve their terminal values. Rokeach proposes that these values guide behaviour and actions on a day-to-day basis. Understanding instrumental values is therefore helpful for comprehending the strategies individuals employ to realize their ultimate goals. These shape the ethical and behavioural frameworks people adopt in pursuit of their aspirations. Examples of instrumental values, as outlined by Rokeach, include traits such as honesty, responsibility, perseverance, and cooperation, which are viewed as essential in the journey toward achieving terminal values.

The significance of Rokeach's distinction lies in its clarity in the analysis of complex value systems. It allows researchers, psychologists, and classroom educators to categorise and understand the hierarchical structure of their values. Additionally, it can help identify whether disagreements arise from differences in ultimate goals or merely in the methods to achieve shared objectives. Furthermore, the framework offers useful intercultural insights by revealing how different cultures may prioritize certain terminal or instrumental values and how these may influence their specific societal norms and behaviours. However, it is also important to acknowledge some limitations and critiques of Rokeach's work. Critics argue that his binary classification oversimplifies the complexity of human values, and some values may possess both terminal and instrumental attributes. Moreover, the applicability of his distinction might be context-dependent, and the significance of certain values may vary considerably across cultures, situations, and individual life stages.

Secondly, Shalom H. Schwartz made a further significant contribution to the understanding of human values by expanding Rokeach's dual-factor model. Schwartz introduced a circular model that identifies ten basic human values categorized into four higher-order groups: openness to change, self-transcendence, conservation, and self-enhancement. To measure individual value priorities, Schwartz developed the *Portrait Values Questionnaire* (PVQ) which enabled a detailed analysis of value systems. Unlike Rokeach's dichotomy, Schwartz's model provides a more nuanced understanding of the complex interrelations among values. It emphasizes the motivational structures that underpin values-led action and highlights how individuals prioritize values based on compatibility or conflict rather than treating them as independent factors (Schwartz, 1992).

Schwartz's *Theory of Basic Human Values* has found extensive application in cross-cultural research. Global studies utilizing the framework have explored variations in value priorities across different cultures, revealing cultural differences in the importance assigned to values. The theory suggests a set of universal values that transcend cultural boundaries, offering insights into shared human motivations and aspirations.

Furthermore, Schwartz's values theory has been integrated into interdisciplinary research, particularly in psychology, sociology, organizational behaviour, and education. Scholars employ the framework to investigate how values influence individual behaviours, decision-making processes, and societal norms. In organizational studies, researchers use Schwartz's values theory to examine workplace dynamics, employee motivation and the alignment of organizational values with individual values. Still viewed by many as a work in progress, Schwartz's frameworks have provided a robust foundation for understanding the intricate role of values in diverse aspects of human life, including the classroom learning context.

Table 1. Comparison of Rokeach and Schwartz on Human Values

Aspect	Milton Rokeach	Shalom H. Schwartz
Main Contribution	Distinguished between terminal (end goals) and instrumental (means to ends) values	Developed a circular model of ten basic human values, grouped into four higher-order categories
Conceptual Focus	Emphasises a hierarchical structure—values as goals vs. behavioural guides	Emphasises motivational interrelations, including compatibility and conflict between values
Key Value Types	- Terminal: happiness, wisdom, social recognition - Instrumental: honesty, perseverance	- Ten basic values (e.g. benevolence, achievement) - Grouped into: Openness to Change, Self-Transcendence, Conservation, Self-Enhancement
Measurement Tool	Rokeach Value Survey (RVS)	Portrait Values Questionnaire (PVQ)
Application Contexts	Education, ethical reasoning, intercultural comparison	Cross-cultural psychology, sociology, organisational studies, education
View of Values	Values shaped by culture, society, personality; guide behaviour and decision-making	Values reflect universal motivational goals underlying attitudes and actions across cultures
Strengths	Clarity, practical distinction between goals and strategies	Nuanced, flexible, globally validated, applicable across disciplines
Limitations / Critiques	May oversimplify value complexity; binary distinction not always adequate	Still evolving; conceptually rich, but may require specialised tools for applied contexts

We would therefore emphasise at the outset the foundational significance of human values and their relations to both human action and intention. We would also argue that values transcend mere behavioural guidance functioning instead as integral, principled components that define preferred objectives in life and so shape human activities profoundly. In essence, values are not only the compass directing actions but also help significantly in forming and outlining the aspirations behind those actions. This broader reading aligns with the wider discourse on values in the education literature and helps emphasise the enduring and influential nature of values in shaping personal and collective conduct. As we navigate the dynamic landscape of contemporary educational practice, it is helpful to pay close attention to the power and possibility of a values-based approach. As Rokeach (1973) notes, culture, society, and personality are the major antecedents of values, while attitudes and behaviour are their major consequences. These are the determinants of any meaningful education in and for the contemporary world, and arguably underpin the nature of all learning relationships. We turn now to consider the implications of educating for moral and ethical aspects of living in ways that are fair and respectful of contemporary equality / equity imperatives.

2. EDUCATION FOR KINDNESS, FAIRNESS, AND EQUITY

It is argued that while values are deeply held beliefs, ethics goes further in representing a set of principles that set out to govern behaviour within specific contexts. As such, ethics wrestles with real-world applications of principles in complex and contested environments. In this section we consider how education has the potential to promote ethical living in ways that promote kindness, fairness, and equity.

The foundation of education for kindness, fairness and equity is a realisation that we live in relation to others within community, and that we have a responsibility towards others with whom we are interconnected. Once again it is useful to look beyond the discipline of psychology to inform our understanding of this interconnectedness. Within philosophy, for instance, this can be seen in the shift from the highly *individual* focus of A.J. Ayer's logical positivism to the *inter-personal* focus of Ayer's successor as Grote Professor of Logic at University College London, John Macmurray (Pring, 2023). In his 1958 public lecture at Moray House, Edinburgh, Macmurray expounded his conviction that education was at its core a process of learning to be human within a community. Here he set out his belief that the first principle of human nature is mutuality and that "a person is always one term in a relation of persons" (Macmurray, 2012, p.670). Consequently, the priority in education must be learning to live in personal relation to other people or living in community. Macmurray believed further that the task of the teacher is therefore in "helping other people to learn to be human" which requires the teacher themselves to be able to "enter into positive relations with each individual among his pupils" for "no person who doesn't really care for children should ever teach" (p.673). As such, education is more than a technical activity or the mastery of what might be referred to as "competences" or "standards" in today's policy context. Macmurray wrote that "The attempt to turn would-be teachers into technicians by teaching them classroom tricks is as stupid as it is ineffective" (p.673), for teaching "is not an engineering job. It is personal and human" (p.674). Moreover, the purpose of education is practical wisdom and action, rather than the accumulation of technical knowledge or facts for their own sake. Values are central to this vision. Macmurray argued that children must be given the opportunity through education to learn "the values and understandings which rest upon a common humanity" (p.668) where children can learn to live "the good life" together in freedom and equality within a context of kindness and care. As Fielding (2012) summarises, Macmurray's writings (dating mostly from the 1930s to the 1950s) are equally relevant today in a world "where bewilderment and hope, deep disillusionment and passionate commitment to the creation of a more just and fulfilling society zig-zag their way to a precarious future" (p.676).

Macmurray's espousal of the importance of education as being relational, values-based, and fundamentally human find later resonance in the Ruskin College, Oxford speech of UK Prime Minister James Callaghan in 1976. Here Callaghan argues that education in the past wrongly aimed to prepare children solely for the world of work, and that henceforth in a changing and more complex society there should be a realization that education should also "cater for a child's personality to let it flower in its fullest possible way", equipping children for a "lively, constructive place in society" (Callaghan, 1976). Callaghan argued that children require not just knowledge and skills, but "lively inquiring minds and an appetite for further knowledge that will last a lifetime" but, importantly, Callaghan argued that education should aim to mitigate as far as possible the "disadvantages that may be suffered through poor home conditions or physical or mental handicap". Callaghan posed the question to his Ruskin College audience "Are we aiming in the right direction in these matters?". As well as offering a defence of the English comprehensive model of schooling (Silverwood & Wolstencroft, 2023), the Ruskin speech is often cited as a watershed moment in UK education, sparking a great debate in education (attacking progressive teaching methods and advocating a common curriculum in schools) and confirming a new age of state interest in and control over schools, the beginning of the age of accountability (Brighouse & Waters, 2022). However, there is also an often-overlooked emphasis in Callaghan's speech on how education should focus on the *personal* and *interpersonal* qualities required for living in a changing and challenging world where social interaction and cooperation are of much greater importance than in the past and are to be valued in addition to more industrial notions of education as a preparation for the workplace.

If living a "good life" is thus inherently relational, then it is argued that education should be aimed at encouraging the responsible, agentic, action-focused living within community (as advocated by Macmurray). This can be realised in several ways, but in this chapter, we will briefly consider, first, education to promote kindness and, second, education to promote fairness or equity.

2.1 Education to Promote Kindness

That schools should aim to be caring, kind institutions seems self-evident today, but much is owed to the influence of the pioneering headmaster and author, Michael Marland, whose writings half a century ago served to introduce pastoral structures to large post-primary comprehensive schools across England and sought to validate the positioning of the pastoral alongside the academic in terms of importance. Marland (1974) wrote that school is essentially "a community concerned with the total welfare of the young person - a caring community" (p.5) and that "what we have come to call pastoral care is the essence of a school" (p.204). In similar vein, another pioneering writer on pastoral care in education, Douglas Hamblin (1978) called for a "carefully planned integration of the pastoral and the curricular aspects" of the school and warned against reactive pastoral care as "emotional first aid for adolescent tensions in a complex society" (p.1). Where pastoral care is effective, children thrive; where children do not "learn to be human" and fail to learn how to live in "community" (Macmurray), conversely, aggression, bullying and violence flourish.

Even then (in the 1970s), this was not a new realisation. In Hughes' Victorian novel *Tom Brown's Schooldays,* first published in 1857, Tom Brown and other younger boys in Rugby School are victimised by older fifth and sixth-form boys, led by the brutish character of 'Flashman the School House bully'. And yet the true hero of the novel is in fact the reforming headmaster, Dr Arnold, who works to eradicate bullying and who effectively transforms the school climate, restoring order and promoting care and kindness. Tom Brown describes Dr Arnold as a "true sort of captain" (p.103) but also as a "fellow-soldier" who was forever "striving against whatever was mean and unmanly and unrighteous in our little world" (p.103). In transforming the school, Dr Arnold epitomises the school leader committed to values, ethos, and ethics, and who can relate to the boys, despite his position of authority. As Tom Brown recounts in his description of Dr Arnold:

> *"It was not the cold clear voice of one giving advice and warning from serene heights to those who were struggling and sinning below, but the warm, living*

voice of one who was fighting for us and by our sides, and calling on us to help him and ourselves and one another" (p.103).

More recently, as Trotman et al. (2023) have argued in their review of 40 years of the UK's National Association for Pastoral Care in Education, much has changed over the years in terms of the contemporary condition for children and young people, and yet the appetite for effective pastoral care in education, and the need for strong pastoral leaders like Dr Arnold to create that caring ethos within educational settings, is more compelling today than ever before. Indeed, this "whole education approach" has been adopted in the recently published national Action Plan on Bullying in Ireland (DE, 2022) which emphasises a collaborative responsibility to create an inclusive, respectful, and caring educational community. It is therefore very fitting that the new action plan has been entitled "Cineáltas" (Irish for "kindness") and that every school in Ireland has been given a Cineáltas flag to demonstrate their commitment to creating and maintaining a community characterised by kindness.

Any contemporary review of education today must also acknowledge how our values are increasingly shaped and influenced by online social media. Many recent studies have highlighted the positive benefits but also the dangers of inappropriate, harmful, radicalising and/or abusive online material accessed by children and young people through a range of devices (see, for instance, Livingstone & Blum-Ross, 2020; Scheithauer et al., 2021; Purdy et al., 2023). There has also been a particular focus on the potential for social media "influencers" to promote misogyny over recent months, in light of the highly acclaimed Netflix four-part series Adolescence, first broadcast on 13th March 2025, which tells the story of the arrest of a 13-year-old schoolboy, Jamie Miller, for the murder of one of his classmates, Katie Leonard, stabbed seven times in a car park, following Jamie's radicalisation by the online influence of "incel" (involuntarily celibate) culture, the "red pill" world and the "manosphere" – a collection of (now mainstream) online platforms and messages promoting 'toxic' masculinity, misogyny and vehement opposition to feminism. The impact of the series on the UK was very significant. Within days of the drama airing, UK Prime Minister, Sir Keir Starmer, reported that he had watched the drama with his teenage son and daughter, later inviting the makers of the series to meet him at Downing Street. Netflix also announced that all secondary schools across the UK (though sadly not in other jurisdictions) would be able to stream the series free of charge, supported by guides and resources created by the healthy relationships charity Tender. As co-writer Jack Thorne explained: "We made this show to provoke a conversation. We wanted to pose the question - how do we help stop this growing crisis? So, to have the opportunity to take this into schools is beyond our expectations. We hope it'll lead to teachers talking to the students, but what we really hope is it'll lead to students talking amongst themselves." (Prime Minister's Office, 2025).

2.2 Education to Promote Social Justice, Fairness, and Equity

Education also holds the potential as a powerful tool to address social injustice and to promote fairness and equity, and we can draw on the thinking of Paulo Freire and Amartya Sen to offer insights into how education can become a catalyst for change. In *Pedagogy of the Oppressed* Freire advocates for an education system that encourages critical thinking and where learners are empowered to challenge oppression, to question societal norms, to escape conformity and to participate actively in building a fairer and more equitable society:

> *"Education either functions as an instrument which is used to facilitate integration of the younger generation into the logic of the present system and bring about conformity or it becomes the practice of freedom, the means by which men and women deal critically and creatively with reality and discover how to participate in the transformation of their world." (Freire, 1972, p.67).*

Freire thus argues for the abandonment of the "banking" or "deposit-making" model of education (simply amassing information or knowledge) and replacing it with "the posing of the problems of men [sic] in their relations with the world" (1972, p.52). Within this approach, education aims to empower learners to reach out to their world and liberate it from the oppression of powerful forces. Moreover, literacy is seen not just in terms of *reading words* but in terms of *reading the world* through a profound and critical understanding of the socio-political context and a readiness to question the structures that have created and perpetuated inequality. Education thus becomes a vehicle for transformation and for liberation, breaking cycles, and patterns of inequality through the development of empathy and criticality, and by means of a sustained commitment to social justice and to the creation of a fairer and more ethical society.

Through his capability approach, the Indian economist, Amartya Sen also argued that education should be about more than the acquisition of knowledge or the development of individual skills aiming towards economic productivity. For Sen, education has an empowering role in addressing injustice through, for instance, giving opportunities to women and girls (in developing nations) and to the disadvantaged and marginalised (in all nations), but also in allowing individuals to use the benefits of education to help others. For Sen, justice is not just about the distribution of resources, but also about ensuring fairness and equal opportunities for all individuals, irrespective of social or cultural background and across both developing and developed countries. Social progress is therefore inherently linked to the protection and promotion of the rights of marginalised and vulnerable groups and to the promotion of their wellbeing. While Sen does not focus directly on the educational impact of his capability approach, Saito (2003) nonetheless presents a reading of Sen in which education systems must allow children to be autonomous in expanding their capabilities, realising their potential and in exercising their freedom to choose their future path. For Saito, this must apply even in highly regulated examination-focused education systems. As such, Sen's work echoes the earlier calls of political philosopher John Rawls (1971) for education to play a role in realising equality of opportunity, acting to overturn any inequalities created by children's social backgrounds through targeting additional resources towards those coming into the education system from disadvantaged backgrounds. In so doing, Rawls believes that education can work to equalise life chances for all.

Such a realisation of the interrelatedness of ethics, the economy, education and wellbeing is an encouragement to policy-makers from across government departments to work more closely together, realising the transformative power of education and striving towards a fairer and more equitable society.

Many challenges remain however in realising such a vision, not least intractable structural inequities within and across communities which effectively limit the transformative potential of education. The following case study details the difficulties in implementing one recent policy innovation to address educational disadvantage and underachievement in Northern Ireland.

Case Study: *A Fair Start*

In Northern Ireland an expert panel was established in 2020 by the Education Minister to examine the links between persistent educational underachievement and socio-economic background and to draw up a costed action plan to address the challenges. The resulting action plan, entitled *A Fair Start* (Purdy et al., 2021) was published on 1 June 2021 and was endorsed by all five main political parties in Northern Ireland. *A Fair Start* proposed 47 costed actions across 8 key areas: Redirecting the focus to Early Years; Championing Emotional Health and Wellbeing; Ensuring the relevance and appropriateness of Curriculum and Assessment; Promoting a whole community approach to education; Maximising boys' potential; Driving forward Teachers' Professional Learning (TPL); Supporting the professional learning and wellbeing of school leadership; and, Ensuring Interdepartmental collaboration and delivery. In the Foreword to the Action Plan, the authors note the "magnitude of the challenge in addressing the underlying causes of social disadvantage, the intractability of many of the issues facing families living in disadvantaged circumstances and the need for systemic change in education" (p.v). Despite the realisation of such challenges, *A Fair* Start sets out a practical, ethically-informed vision for how equity can be fostered, how greater inter-departmental collaboration can be facilitated, and, ultimately, how all children can be given a fair start in life. *A Fair Start* thus represents a concerted effort to use education in an ethical way to promote fairness and equity. At the time of writing, the implementation of the actions proposed in *A*

Fair Start has begun, but significant funding cuts imposed on the Department of Education for the 2023-24 financial year have severely curtailed budget spend. For instance, the Department of Education allocated just £2.5m to *A Fair Start* in the 2023-24 financial year instead of the £21m scheduled in the costed action plan (see Fitzpatrick et al., 2023), highlighting the significance of resource constraints and collective societal commitment to change within a fractious macro-political context.

Furthermore, education has the potential to empower and to democratise through giving a voice to children and young people. The Lundy Model of student voice (Lundy, 2007), provides a rights-based framework for engaging children meaningfully in decision-making processes, grounded in Article 12 of the UN Convention on the Rights of the Child (UN, 1989). The model highlights four key, interrelated elements: Space (providing opportunities to express views), Voice (facilitating the expression of views), Audience (ensuring views are listened to), and Influence (ensuring views are acted upon, where appropriate). When applied effectively, the model promotes the democratisation of schooling by positioning children as active participants rather than passive recipients within the educational system. It encourages schools to reframe power dynamics, foster inclusive dialogue, and create structures that respect and respond to pupil input. This, in turn, can lead to more equitable, responsive, and participatory school cultures, where pupils feel a sense of ownership and responsibility - key foundations for democratic citizenship and lifelong civic engagement.

Such an approach has become increasingly influential across the globe, and is exemplified, for instance, in the co-development and co-creation of the South Australian Charter for Children and Young People through a two-year interactive process with children and young people (Purdy & Spears, 2023). While student voice can at times be tokenistic and meaningless and while the many challenges of co-participatory work must be acknowledged (Purdy & Spears, 2020), this example from South Australia is significant in that it adopted a "closing-the-circle" approach whereby the adults fed back to the children and young people and were committed to demonstrating how exactly the children's views had been taken into account in the composition of the final Charter.

Such initiatives reflect a willingness to wrestle with the challenges of engaging meaningfully and democratically with children and young people not just in policy debates but in real-life school and classroom contexts, all of which necessitates a shift in power that some educators find uncomfortable. The importance of a values-rich foundational approach is however crucial, and must be evidenced and modelled first and foremost by the leadership of the school. In a recently completed qualitative exploration of the leadership approaches of highly successful post-primary schools in disadvantaged urban communities in Belfast and Derry/Londonderry in Northern Ireland, Purdy et al. (2025) found that the school leaders spoke of the importance of values and of their commitment to helping the children in their schools to overcome the significant challenges of their disadvantaged backgrounds and to work to achieve their potential within a caring, supportive, respectful learning environment. As one principal explained, "I work hard every day to demonstrate those [values]… compassion, caring, forgiveness. I know I can set the tone of things… Even the way I dress, the way I phrase emails, the way I speak to staff."

Both examples above, from across the globe, help to illustrate how values-rich education can, given commitment and determination, be enacted successfully in everyday educational contexts, despite the challenges.

3. THE ETHICAL, SOCIAL, AND INTERSUBJECTIVE NATURE OF VALUES

In his contribution to recent discussion of culture, values, and identities, Fahmy (2020) makes a case for reinvigorating the notion of *social conscience* in ways that imbue the idea with a greater sense of collectiveness. He proposes this to provide a more comprehensive basis from which to address "a growing failure of public orders within the global community" (17641), particularly in relation to understandings of the common good and the connected need to address marginalisation and inequality. In this, Fahmy echoes the centrality of the collective to any discussion of values, drawing we suggest on the concept developed originally by Emile Durkheim of the collective as a way of understanding the commonly shared beliefs, values and ways of thinking that create and sustain *social cohesion* and particularly on Durkheim's articulation of the role of *collective social conscience* in this.

While acknowledging that collective social conscience is difficult to create and/or sustain given the increased diversity evident in any contemporary setting and the fragmentation that "diversities in religion, beliefs, values and identities" can have on "collective forms of solidarity and identity" (Back et al., 2012, p. xiii), we still see value in trying to do so. The *relational self* is at the core of all social conscience, and, as Kittay (1999) has argued, "to miss the significance of the relational self is to miss a *"whole dimension of moral life" (p.51).*

Earlier in this chapter, we proposed that the foundation of education for kindness, fairness and equity is a realization that we live in relation to others within community in ways that require responsibility towards those with whom we are connected. To this we now add the observation that collective social conscience and the relational self on which it is premised can usefully be seen in analogy to this connectivity. Of course, the ethics and lived-out realities of this observation require further attention. Consequently, in this section we bring applicable insights from the work of Kathleen Lynch, social theorist and activist, to a discussion of this proposition.

Lynch (2020, 2021) offers a thoughtful and thorough reading of why the relational self – that part of human being which rests primarily on concepts of collective love, care, and solidarity – matters in terms of equality and human rights. Through her work in the field of social justice, particularly in the context of education, Lynch articulates a profound view of collective social conscience and its ineluctable connection to an ethical life. To paraphrase from the preface of her latest book, this is what binds us affectively and morally to others, even to unknown others, in and through the cares, loves and solidarity relationships within which people are engaged and which give direction and purpose in daily lives (Lynch, 2021).

For Lynch (2020), there is a major failing in the way that contemporary societies see and treat the affective domain in human life as, at best, secondary to its economic and political aspects. She argues that the emotional and affective forces at work in contexts of collective love, care, and solidarity form a distinct social realm, equally valid and valuable, but systematically and deliberately overlooked in ways that lead to injustices in human development. As she states:

> *"Affective relations are not social derivatives ... subordinate to economic, political, or cultural relations in matters of social justice. Rather, they are productive, materialist human relations that constitute people mentally, emotionally, physically, and socially." (Lynch, 2020, p. 118)*

Drawing on a life-time's work and that of others (such as Cantillon & Lynch 2017; Ivancheva, Lynch & Keating 2019; Lynch, Baker & Lyons 2009; Lolich & Lynch, 2016; 2017: Lynch & Kalaitzake 2020), Lynch (2020) proposes a framework for understanding these relations in the context of structural social justice. She advocates for *relational justice* as a fourth dimension within the broader discourse on social justice in addition to those of redistribution, recognition, representation. Her framework takes a sociological perspective, emphasizing in a novel way the structural inequalities that impact access to and experience of love, care, and solidarity in nurturing senses. This line is extended in her subsequent work: for instance, Lynch (2021) is concerned with the intellectual and political project of reclaiming the language of care and solidarity, in a way that is intended to help "unseat capital at the gravitational centre of meaning making and value" and create "care, love and solidarity-led logics and ethical priorities for politics" (Gibson-Graham et al., 2016, p.194).

From Lynch's work, it would seem clear that we live in a world where "an unforgiving care-lessness"[1] and its associated cultures of "24/7 availability" and "unbounded work" (2010, p.63) combine to derail the forms of education for kindness, fairness and equity that contest the more normative, human capital narratives of neoliberalism. Rooted in competitive individualism, neoliberalism by its nature contradicts the values of care and care-work in and through education and indeed society in general. To counter its impact, there is a pressing need for a new educational narrative that acknowledges human morality and values. Happily, Lynch's work also suggests that promoting such an alternative and transformative ethic through education is both possible and desirable.

We see evidence of this in the subtle but increasingly apparent move towards more socially sympathetic constructions of education and its purposes, particularly in relation to the challenges emergent regarding sustainability, the climate crisis, and the just transition to a fairer and more equitable society. A recent paper on educating for a just transition articulates this shift particularly well when the authors suggest that:

> *"...education for the just transition must affirm the importance of teachers and students as agents of transformation and promote critical educational practices and approaches which support the transition to a low-carbon economy, and which value the characteristics of justice (which include equity, equality, fairness, and inclusiveness) to build a curriculum that advocates sustainable growth and a societal just transition." (Droubi et al 2023, p.1)*

That particular call comes from a social science perspective. Similar calls come also from within the education community itself. Scalabrino et al. (2022), for instance, offer a curriculum framework built on a critical and constructivist perspective "intended as a basis for the reflection on current ES [environmental studies] practices and to inspire the realisation of the full potential of ES in formal, non-formal and informal settings, from early childhood to old age learning" (p. 735). And the policy importance of the idea can be seen in both the global pursuit of education for a more sustainable way of life (particularly through work towards UN SDG 4.7[2]) and more regional actions such as the EU Working Group on *Schools: Learning for Sustainability*, now in its third year of activity.[3]

In these and similar calls we can detect a shift towards an understanding of education and educating that is dynamic, adaptable, and focused on equipping learners with the capabilities and mindset to thrive in a rapidly changing and interconnected world – one that fosters critical thinking, autonomy, agency, and action among learners. As this shift assumes normative power within education, it has the potential to fundamentally remake practice in ways that can reshape educational discourse and emphasise the ethical and political power embedded in relational values such as those put forward by Lynch and others. Recognizing the significance of affective relations and the articulation of *relational justice* these values represent will be crucial for fostering a more equitable global order, addressing gender equality issues, and contributing to the broader politics of justice and education for fairness. In short, we argue for an ethics, as advocated by Lynch, rooted more in collective social conscience, and eschewing the privileged individualism of a neoliberal ideology.

Additionally, it is important to note, as Byrne (2022) observes, that based on a life-time's work in public education, community activism, adult education and local development, Lynch believes profoundly in the emancipatory power of education and that "transformatory positive change is possible" (p. 572). This, we suggest, is the context against which to read the invitation extended by Lynch (2021) "to live out care, equality and social justice as social practices" (p. 212) and a validation of the arguments she offers for the need to educate in relation to that vision.

CONCLUSION

This brief discussion of the ethical, social, and intersubjective nature of values in contemporary education has underscored the need for an education that celebrates dispositions of mutuality and human behaviours which embody respect for human dignity and social justice.

Fahmy's (2020) call for a reinvigorated social conscience, grounded in collectiveness, emphasises the affordances of fostering shared beliefs and social cohesion. Lynch's (2020, 2021) profound insights into the relational self, collective love, care, and solidarity, emphasise the significance of affective relations too often overlooked in contemporary education. Additionally, her framework for relational justice adds a crucial dimension to the discourse on social justice, challenging the prevailing neglect of emotional and affective forces in shaping human experiences. Increasing concerns for a more socially sympathetic construction of education, particularly evident in calls for a just transition and sustainable education, aligns with Lynch's vision of education rooted in care, love, and solidarity; what we have termed educating for kindness, fairness, and equity.

In our reading for this chapter, we detect encouraging glimpses of a slow but increasing narrative shift towards a more dynamic, adaptable, and values-focused education. We see this reflected in recent policy developments, curriculum frameworks, school leadership characteristics and global initiatives that hold promise for reshaping educational discourse and practice at every level. The emphasis this transitional, more prosocial turn places on critical thinking, autonomy, and ethical considerations echoes Lynch's (2020, 2021) advocacy for an alternative ethic rooted in collective social conscience. As the world grapples with what has been described as a deepening sense of "permacrisis" (Fabbrini et al., 2023), characterised by biodiversity loss, sustainability issues, and climate crisis, education emerges as the engine of hope; the transformative force capable of fostering positive change and shaping a more equitable global order.

In the face of neoliberal challenges and the "hypercapitalism" (Vujnovic, 2017) that undermine values of care and equity, Lynch's work provides a compelling argument for the transformative power of education. Her call to live-out care, equality, and social justice as social practices reinforces the belief that education can be an emancipatory project, capable of creating a more just and compassionate world. As we seek to navigate the complexities of contemporary society through gaining a more profound understanding of psychology of education, Lynch's vision offers a beacon for educators and policymakers, urging us to engage a relational, values-based education that embodies and embeds the collective social conscience necessary to lead to positive and fair societal transformations.

Discussion Questions

1. To what extent do you think the importance of values in and through education has been overlooked in favour of other priorities such as attainment outcomes, standards and accountability?
2. How do you think education can become more 'personal and human' (Macmurray) to promote kindness, fairness and equity in the contemporary world?
3. To what extent do you agree with Kathleen Lynch's assertion that we live in a world where "an unforgiving care-lessness" and its associated cultures of "24/7 availability" and "unbounded work" (2010, p.63) combine to derail the forms of education for kindness, fairness and equity?
4. How can the study of educational psychology contribute towards these goals?

REFERENCES

Back, L., Bennett, A., Edles, L. D., Gibson, M., Inglis, D., Jacobs, R., & Woodward, I. (2012). *Cultural sociology: an introduction*. Wiley-Blackwell.

Brewer, M. B., & Roccas, S. (2015). Individual values, social identity, and optimal distinctiveness. In *Individual self, relational self, collective self* (pp. 219–237). Psychology Press.

Brighouse, T., & Waters, M. (2022). *About Our Schools: Improving on Previous Best*. Crown House Publishing.

Byrne, A. (2022). Care and Capitalism: Why Affective Equality Matters for Social Justice. *Journal of Political Power, 15*(3), 572–576. DOI: 10.1080/2158379X.2022.2105496

Callaghan, J. (1976). Ruskin College Speech. https://education- uk.org/documents/speeches/1976ruskin.html

Cantillon, S., & Lynch, K. (2017). Affective equality: Love matters. *Hypatia, 32*(1), 169–186.

Department of Education. (2022) *Cineáltas Action Plan on Bullying*. Department of Education (Ireland). https://www.gov.ie/en/publication/52aaf-cinealtas-action-plan-on-bullying/

Droubi, S., Galamba, A., Fernandes, F. L., de Mendonça, A. A., & Heffron, R. J. (2023). Transforming education for the just transition. *Energy Research & Social Science, 100*, 103090.

Durkheim, E. (1952). *Suicide: a study in sociology* [Le suicide: étude de sociologie]. Routledge & Kegan Paul. (Original publication 1897)

Fabbrini, F., Bokhorst, D., Sabato, S., Theodoropoulou, S., Spasova, S., Marenco, M., Debusscher, P., Atanasova, A., Rasnača, Z., Vanhercke, B., & Moja, F. (2023). Social Policy in the European Union: State of Play 2022. Brussels: ETUI: European Trade Union Institute Belgium.

Fahmy, M. N. (2020). The Need for a Collective Social Conscience. *Global Perspectives, 1*(1), 17641. DOI: 10.1525/gp.2020.17641

Farley, S. B., Yoon, H. J., & Padilla, C. (2021). What Values Will Define and Guide OD in the Future? *Inspirations for the Future of OD & the Reality of Our Work*, 27.

Fielding, M. (2012). Education as if people matter: John MacMurray, community and the struggle for democracy. *Oxford Review of Education*, *38*(6), 675–692. DOI: 10.1080/03054985.2012.745044

Fitzpatrick, C., Loader, R., McCartney, S., McConnell, B., McMullen, J., Murray, C., Orr, K., Purdy, N., & Simms, V. (2023). *The Consequences of the Cuts to Education for Children and Young People in Northern Ireland.* Ulster University, Stranmillis University College, Queen's University, Belfast, Newcastle University.

Friere, P. (1972). *Pedagogy of the Oppressed*. Penguin.

Gibson-Graham, J. K., Cameron, J., & Healy, S. (2016). Commoning as a postcapitalist politics. In Amin, A., & Howell, P. (Eds.), *Releasing the Commons: Rethinking the futures of the commons* (pp. 205–225). Routledge.

Hamblin, D. (1978). *The Teacher and Pastoral Care*. Basil Blackwell.

Hughes, T. (1993). *Tom Brown's Schooldays and Tom Brown at Oxford*. Wordsworth Classics. (Original work published 1857)

Ivancheva, M., Lynch, K., & Keating, K. (2019). Precarity, gender and care in the neoliberal academy. *Gender, Work and Organization*, *26*(4), 448–462.

Kittay, E. F. (1999). *Love's Labor*. Routledge.

Livingstone, S., & Blum-Ross, A. (2020). *Parenting for a Digital Future: How Hopes and Fears about Technology Shape Children's Lives*. Oxford University Press.

Lolich, L., & Lynch, K. (2016). The affective imaginary: Students as affective consumers of risk. *Higher Education Research & Development*, *35*(1), 17–30.

Lolich, L., & Lynch, K. (2017). No choice without care: Palliative care as a relational matter, the case of Ireland. *Soundings: An Interdisciplinary Journal*, *100*(4), 353–374.

Lundy, L. (2007). 'Voice' is not enough: Conceptualising Article 12 of the United Nations Convention on the Rights of the Child. *British Educational Research Journal*, *33*(6), 927–942. DOI: 10.1080/01411920701657033

Lynch, K. (2010). Carelessness: A hidden doxa of higher education. *Arts and Humanities in Higher Education*, *9*(1), 54–67.

Lynch, K. (2020). Affective Equality and Social Justice. In Celentano, D., & Caranti, L. (Eds.), *Paradigms of Justice: Redistribution, Recognition, and Beyond* (pp. 118–139). Routledge.

Lynch, K. (2021). *Care and Capitalism*. Polity Press.

Lynch, K., Baker, J., & Lyons, M. (Eds.). (2009). *Affective equality: Love, care, and injustice*. Palgrave Macmillan.

Lynch, K., & Kalaitzake, M. (2020). Affective and calculative solidarity: The impact of individualism and neoliberal capitalism. *European Journal of Social Theory, 23*(2), 238–257.

Macmurray, J. (2012). Learning to be Human. *Oxford Review of Education, 38*(6), 661–674.

Marland, M. (1974). *Pastoral Care*. Heinemann Educational Books.

Mok, Y. F. (2002). Teacher growth: The formation and pursuit of personal values. *Interchange, 33*, 115–138.

Moran, E. F. (2016). *People and nature: an introduction to Human Ecological Relations*. John Wiley & Sons.

Pelling, M., O'Brien, K., & Matyas, D. (2015). Adaptation and transformation. *Climatic Change, 133*, 113–127. DOI: 10.1007/s10584-014-1303-0

Prime Minister's Office. (2025). Downing Street opens doors to Adolescence creators for vital discussion on protecting our children. Press Release. https://www.gov.uk/government/news/downing-street-opens-doors-to-adolescence-creators-for-vital-discussion-on-protecting-our-children#:~:text=Jack%20Thorne%2C%20Adolescence%20Co%2DWriter,schools%20is%20beyond%20our%20expectations

Pring, R. (2023). Pastoral Care in Education: On Being and Developing as a Person. In D. Trotman, P. Jones, N. Purdy & S. Tucker (Eds.), *Pastoral Care in Education: New Directions for New Times* (pp.32-39). Cambridge Scholars.

Purdy, N., Ballentine, M., Lyle, H., Orr, K., Symington, E., Webster, D., & York, L. (2023). *Growing up Online: Children's online activities, harm and safety in Northern Ireland – an Evidence Report*. Stranmillis University College/Safeguarding Board for Northern Ireland. Available at https://www.stran.ac.uk/growing-up-online-in-ni/

Purdy, N., Logue, J., Montgomery, M., O'Hare, K., & Redpath, J. (2021). *A Fair Start: Final Report and Action Plan*. Department of Education for Northern Ireland.

Purdy, N., & Spears, B. (2020). Co-participatory approaches to research with children and young people. *Pastoral Care in Education, 38*(3), 187–190. DOI: 10.1080/02643944.2020.1788816

Purdy, N., & Spears, B. (2023). Co-participatory Research Methods in Pastoral Care: Lessons from two case studies. In Trotman, D., Purdy, N., & Jones, P. (Eds.), *Pastoral Care in Education: Time for Change*. Cambridge Scholars.

Purdy, N., Symington, E., Ballentine, M., Orr, K., Walsh, G., & Tate, K. (2025). *Effective School Leadership in Disadvantaged Communities*. Centre for Research in Educational Underachievement, Stranmillis University College.

Rawls, J. (1971). *A Theory of Justice*. Harvard University Press.

Rokeach, M. (1967). *Rokeach Value Survey*. DOI: 10.1037/t01381-000

Rokeach, M. (1973). *The Nature of Human Values*. Free Press.

Rokeach, M., & Regan, J. F. (1980). The Role of Values in the Counselling Situation. *The Personnel and Guidance Journal*, *58*, 576–582. DOI: 10.1002/j.2164-4918.1980.tb00454.x

Sagiv, L., Roccas, S., Cieciuch, J., & Schwartz, S. H. (2017). Personal values in human life. *Nature Human Behaviour*, *1*(9), 630–639. PMID: 31024134

Saito, M. (2003). Amartya Sen's Capability Approach to Education: A Critical Exploration. *Journal of Philosophy of Education*, *37*(1), 17–33. DOI: 10.1111/1467-9752.3701002

Scalabrino, C., Navarrete Salvador, A., & Oliva Martínez, J. M. (2022). A theoretical framework to address education for sustainability for an earlier transition to a just, low carbon and circular economy. *Environmental Education Research*, *28*(5), 735–766.

Scheithauer, H., Schultze-Krumbholz, A., Pfetsch, J., & Hess, M. (2021). Types of Cyberbullying. In *The Wiley Blackwell Handbook of Bullying: A Comprehensive and International Review of Research and Intervention.* Wiley Blackwell.

Schwartz, S. H. (1992). Universals in the content and structure of values: Theoretical advances and empirical tests in 20 countries. In Zanna, M. P. (Ed.), (pp. 1–65). Advances in experimental social psychology. Academic Press.

Sen, A. (2001). *Development as Freedom*. Oxford University Press.

Silverwood, J., & Wolstencroft, P. (2023). The Ruskin Speech and Great Debate in English education, 1976–1979: A study of motivation. *British Educational Research Journal*, *49*(4), 766–781.

Trotman, D., Jones, P., Purdy, N., & Tucker, S. (2023). Concluding Remarks. In D. Trotman, P. Jones, N. Purdy & S. Tucker (Eds.), *Pastoral Care in Education: New Directions for New Times* (pp. 336-338). Cambridge Scholars.

United Nations. (1989). Convention on the Rights of the Child. Treaty no. 27531. United Nations Treaty Series. Available at: https://treaties.un.org/doc/Treaties/1990/09/19900902%2003-14%20AM/Ch_IV_11p.pdf

Vujnovic, M. (2017). *Hypercapitalism*. The Wiley-Blackwell Encyclopaedia of Globalization. DOI: 10.1002/9780470670590.wbeog278.pub2

ADDITIONAL READING

Lynch, K. (2021). *Care and Capitalism*. Polity Press.

Purdy, N., Hall, K., Khanolainen, D., & Galvin, C. (2023). Reframing Teacher Competencies around Inclusion, Equity, and Social Justice: Towards an alternative values-centred model of Teacher Education. *European Journal of Teacher Education*, (Special Issue). Advance online publication. DOI: 10.1080/02619768.2023.2288556

Purdy, N., Logue, J., Montgomery, M., O'Hare, K., & Redpath, J. (2021). *A Fair Start: Final Report and Action Plan*. Department of Education for Northern Ireland.

ENDNOTES

1 Best understood as the neglect or deliberate devaluation of care-related activities, responsibilities, and values within a society which in the interest of capital too often drives people to ignore, or engage minimally with, the care needs of those to whom they are related or connected. See Lynch (2010) for a detailed discussion of this in the context of higher education.

2 "By 2030, ensure that all learners acquire the knowledge and skills needed to promote sustainable development, including, among others, through education for sustainable development and sustainable lifestyles, human rights, gender equality, promotion of a culture of peace and non-violence, global citizenship and appreciation of cultural diversity and of culture's contribution to sustainable development."

3 See https://wikis.ec.europa.eu/display/EAC/Learning+for+Sustainability

[illegible]

ADDITIONAL READING

[illegible]

[illegible]

ENDNOTES

[illegible]

Chapter 4
Contemporary Classrooms:
The Role of Motivation and Teachers' Beliefs

Kieron Sheehy
https://orcid.org/0000-0001-7623-8400
The Open University, UK

Andrew J. Holliman
University College London, UK

ABSTRACT

This chapter examines why motivation and teachers' beliefs are an important part of contemporary and future educational practice. It starts with a focus on motivation, drawing from self-determination theory (SDT) and considers the positive influence this may have on students' learning, psychological functioning, and wellbeing. It also briefly considers the potential importance of teachers' motivation. It then considers the implications of teachers' epistemological beliefs for inclusive education as well as their responses to climate-change related disaster education. The authors argue that, in the context of contemporary classrooms, the motivational climate and teachers' epistemological beliefs shape and underpin the wellbeing of the whole class community. Conclusions are made regarding the need to support teachers' agency within the classroom and curriculum and to facilitate pedagogies that foreground social engagement in order to move towards healthier, more inclusive classrooms, that work well for teachers and pupils alike.

DOI: 10.4018/979-8-3693-1293-3.ch004

INTRODUCTION

There is a tendency for predictions and recommendations regarding the development of future classroom practices, and the key issues therein, to emphasise technologies and technological solutions for pedagogical challenges. This is clearly an important issue for educators and researchers to address. The physical environment of the classroom is increasingly challenged by the educational affordances of virtual and augmented spaces (Quintero et al., 2019). These technologies are able to extend learners interactions and perceptions of their current environment, providing information in new, more accessible and engaging ways (Sheehy et al., 2019). The technological tools available to educators and learners potentially transform the expectations of what education should look like in practice. These practices are situated within and influenced by a multitude of layered and interacting systematic factors, such as policy mandates, assessment and curriculum regimes, school leadership structures, and cultural and historical developments (Rix, 2015, Rix, 2013). Numerous publications and reports have considered the diversity and differences of these policies, inter- and intra-nationally, suggesting that there is not a sense of a coherent and unified approach to inclusive practice at these levels (Rix, 2015). In contrast, this chapter chooses to focus on the influence of human factors. As new classroom practices develop their use and success will be predicated on human, not technological factors. If we are to understand how to make our educational practices effective, engaging, and inclusive for learners, it is essential not to lose sight of these human factors that shape and drive our pedagogical approaches and experiences. Specifically, this chapter examines two factors, which research has shown to have profound effects within the classroom and on learning outcomes, expectations, and experiences.

WHAT IS MOTIVATION?

Motivation is derived from the Latin term 'movere', which means 'to move'. In education contexts, it can refer to students' inclination, energy, and drive to learn, to work effectively, and to achieve their potential (Martin, 2007).

In education systems around the world, a long-standing (and key) priority for educators/teachers is to help optimise students' learning. This priority is often reflected in the implementation of national high-stakes assessment (Suto & Oates, 2021). However, it is argued (see Hallum, 2005), that in order to sustain the time and effort needed to optimise learning, psychological factors such as motivation and personal commitment are of importance. Indeed, results from a meta-analysis of 12 studies (including 25 effect sizes) found significant differences in test performance between 'motivated' and 'unmotivated' students (see Wise & DeMars, 2005). Another, more recent, priority for educators/teachers is to help optimise students' psychological functioning. This encompasses the promotion of wellbeing and reduction of the incidence of mental ill-health, which is viewed as a global concern, (WHO, 2022). There is evidence that motivation has influence on these important academic and wellbeing outcomes (Deci & Ryan, 2000). Taken together, it appears that motivation, and an understanding of effective strategies to help optimise motivation, would be of great value to all key stakeholders, in contemporary classrooms.

So far, motivation has been considered as a broad, holistic concept, but there exist several distinct theoretical perspectives within the motivation literature, that help explain its relationship with educational outcomes. As summarised by Martin (2013), there are theories relating to 'self-efficacy' (that is, a person's belief in their ability to accomplish specific tasks) and 'expectancy-value' (linked to self-efficacy, but also reflecting the value individuals assign to tasks)—these theories hold that individuals who believe in their abilities and value their tasks are more likely to be motivated and engaged to do them. Theories relating to 'need achievement and self-worth' distinguish between ones motivation to succeed or avoid failure. It follows that success-oriented students tend to exhibit higher self-efficacy and resilience whereas fear of failure is associated with anxiety, disengagement, and self-sabotaging behaviours. Moreover, 'attribution and control' theories focus on the extent to which individuals believe they have control over their learning/behaviours. It has been found that those with higher sense of perceived control (internal locus of control) tend to do better in a range of educational outcomes. Finally, theories relating to 'goals, self-regulation, and self-determination' have likely received most attention in the field. Goal theory explains motivation through the lens of what an individual strives to achieve, whereby a 'mastery orientation' (focused on learning and improvement) is positively linked with persistence and self-regulation whereas a 'performance orientation' (which focuses on outperforming others), tends to correlate negatively with educational outcomes. Among these perspectives, self-determination theory (SDT; Ryan & Deci, 2017) is especially compelling and is the primary focus of this chapter. SDT not only integrates aspects of the aforementioned theories but also offers a comprehensive framework by distinguishing between intrinsic and extrinsic motivation and emphasizing the fulfilment of three core psychological needs: autonomy, competence, and relatedness. When these needs are supported, students are more likely to experience sustained motivation, deeper engagement, and improved educational outcomes.

In the sections that follow, we draw from self-determination theory (SDT; Ryan & Deci, 2017) to consider why motivation is important and offer guidance on what contemporary classrooms might look like, in order to help optimise motivation and in turn, facilitate a positive impact on students' learning, psychological functioning, and wellbeing.

SELF-DETERMINATION THEORY

SDT (Ryan & Deci, 2017) is a psychological framework that has relevance for understanding the implications of motivational processes underpinning student functioning (e.g., students' learning and wellbeing in education contexts). According to SDT, individuals have three basic psychological needs that are considered essential for one's self-determination and optimal functioning (Deci & Ryan 1985): the need for '*autonomy*', to feel free from external constraints and in control of one's own actions and choices; the need for '*competence*', to feel effective and capable (to have mastery) in one's interactions with the environment; and the need for '*relatedness*', to feel connected and involved with others and to experience a sense of belonging. According to SDT, when a student in a classroom feels that these three needs are met, they are more likely to perceive their actions as 'self-determined' and 'intrinsically motivated'. Consequently, they engage in an activity for its own inherent interest, satisfaction, enjoyment, and challenge, rather than for external factors, such as rewards, grades, or money. The research literature has shown that intrinsic motivation and a greater sense of self-determination, is positively associated with effort and persistence (Dille & Mezack, 1991) and academic achievement (Chow & Yong, 2013). Indeed, a recent meta-analysis across 344 samples (Howard et al., 2021), found that intrinsic (rather than extrinsic) motivation was positively associated with student success and wellbeing (see also Ntoumanis et al., 2020, for a meta-analysis that demonstrates the effectiveness of SDT-based interventions for promoting physical and psychological health outcomes). However, many education policies and practices do not adequately account for students' and teachers' needs in this respect (see Ryan & Deci, 2020), with very real constraints on action in contemporary classrooms such as learning from a set curriculum or having to adhere with behavioural expectations in the classroom. The question is therefore raised as to how best to help students to 'perceive' that their basic psychological needs are being met (e.g., experiencing a degree of autonomy and choice – see Patall et al., 2008), in order to feel optimally motivated. How might contemporary classrooms bring about optimal motivation of their students?

HOW TO OPTIMISE MOTIVATION IN CONTEMPORARY CLASSROOMS

In this section, we harness SDT to consider how educators/teachers in contemporary classrooms might help optimise motivation, specifically intrinsic motivation, and thus support students' functioning by fostering a perceived sense of autonomy, competence, and relatedness.

Autonomy and Sense of Control

A major part of supporting autonomy is to create classrooms that allow students to make choices, express opinions, and ultimately have a heightened sense of control over the environment (Ryan & Deci, 2017). Although challenging, educators/teachers might consider what 'must' be controlled and restricted (i.e., where there are more immovable constraints on provision and practice), but also what opportunities there might be for students to operate in a more 'self-determined' fashion as agents of their actions and influencers of their environment. This might include minimising external (extrinsic) rewards, such as grades and comparative performance with peers, and a focus more on students' personal goals, and efforts to support those goals. Having these improved perception of autonomy-support in the classroom is predictive of academic outcomes (e.g., Howard et al., 2017), and student functioning benefits more from autonomy-supportive environments (e.g., Deci & Ryan, 2002; Johansen et al., 2023). Contemporary classrooms would therefore need to deviate from current prescriptive models, which can be highly controlled, to practices that allow students more choice (Patall et al., 2008) and more voice, wherever possible. By listening to and involving students (see also 'Relatedness and Sense of belonging', below), educators can better understand their students' interests and needs, creating conditions in which students' intrinsic motivations are acknowledged and can become better aligned with learning tasks and activities.

Competence and Mastery

A major part of supporting students' needs for competence/mastery is to create classroom learning tasks and activities that provide an appropriate level of challenge and in which constructive feedback is offered as immediately as possible. This can be complementing associated opportunities for targeted skills development. The outcomes of this change would not be only academic. In terms of psychological functioning, Ramakrishnan and Masten (2020) found positive associations between mastery and students social and emotional functioning. Moreover, in a recent meta-analysis of over 144 studies (Bureau et al., 2022), competence emerged as the strongest positive predictor of intrinsic/self-determined motivation. It therefore follows, that students who believe in their capability to succeed in a task or activity, are more likely to persist in it. This is somewhat akin to Vygotskian approaches, whereby educators/teachers are encouraged to consider classroom tasks and activities that are challenging but nonetheless situated at an appropriate level of challenge for the student learner (Elliott et al., 2004; Rodger et al., 2014). This would of course, involve careful consideration of the learning level of the student and the difficulty level of the task/activity, which can be challenging when teaching to a large group; but even the selection or design of tasks and activities might incorporate student perspectives so they are perceived as being, and are, co-created. Contemporary classrooms might therefore benefit from more personalised and co-constructed (or at least, consulted) learning provision (tasks, activities) to reduce the likelihood of external locus of control and subsequent disengagement.

Relatedness and Sense of Belonging

A major part of supporting students' needs for relatedness is to create a positive and supportive social environment where students feel a sense of connectedness and belonging with their peer group, but also with their teachers and the wider community environment. In this type of social environment students are more likely to engage with and enjoy the learning process. For example, a recent meta-analysis, which included 82 studies between 2000 and 2018 (Korpershoek et al., 2020), found that students' sense of 'school belonging' was positively associated with a range of academic and non-academic outcomes including traditional academic achievement and social-emotional measures. An implication of these findings, for teachers, is a need to reflect on the development and provision of activities that require students to work together in a mutually supportive way. This is likely to facilitate a shared sense of identity and personal belonging. As we see later, teaching approaches that foreground social relationships within their pedagogy are also found to support inclusive classrooms, producing positive outcomes for children with special educational needs and disabilities (Sheehy et al., 2009). Beyond the immediate classroom, student relationships to the wider school community also impact, as might be expected, on their sense of school belonging (see Uslu & Gizir, 2017) and a growing literature underlines the importance of school belonging in students' school lives.

WHAT ABOUT TEACHERS?

A major concern in the teaching profession is 'burnout', which is above-average relative to other professions (Kyriacou, 2015). This has often been attributed to a lack of autonomy within highly controlled administrative conditions, inflexible curricula, and a lack of managerial support. In a recent study of 502 Australian teachers, Collie (2023) found that perceived autonomy-supportive leaderships (teacher perceptions of their principal) rather than autonomy-thwarting leadership, was positively associated with their global self-determined motivation which, in turn, was associated with outcomes relating to extra-role behaviour, positive and negative affect, and turnover intentions (a correlate of burnout). Other research has also supported the hypothesis that frustration of teachers' basic psychological needs mediated the observed association between job pressures and teacher burnout (Bartholomew et al., 2014). Moreover, Collie et al. (2016) found that teachers' sense of autonomy-support from principals was positively associated with their workplace empowerment, organizational trust, workplace motivation and engagement, and a greater sense of school commitment (and therefore a reduced risk of burnout).

So far the focus has been largely on how educators/teachers might optimise intrinsic (self-determined) motivation among students. However, if we move beyond seeing teachers as pedagogic 'delivery' agents then we need to acknowledge and value their own psychological needs (i.e., autonomy, competence, and relatedness). These factors can impact not only upon their own outcomes (e.g., wellbeing, performance, and burnout) but also on those of their students (although the literature here is more mixed). In this way it can be argued that the wellbeing of the teacher is related to the health of their students. This connection has been noted in comparative research regarding cultural differences in the conceptualisations and of happiness and wellbeing, and non-western examples in which the social emotional networks of classrooms are seen as important for all members of the class community (Budiyanto et al., 2017). These transfer effects and interrelationships have been found in empirical evidence that meeting teachers' basic needs may also help to satisfy students' needs and their subsequent functioning. For example, Roth et al. (2007) found that teachers' higher in autonomy were also perceived as higher in autonomy by their students and this, in turn, made students feel more autonomously motivated to learn. Further, in Collie and Martin (2017), teachers' perceived autonomy-support was found to be positively associated with their organisational commitment and psychological wellbeing, and indirectly associated with students' numeracy achievement (via their psychological wellbeing). Although the issue of 'how much autonomy' should be afforded to educators/teachers has been hotly debated (see Timberlake et al., 2017) and there exists some contrary evidence on the link between teacher autonomy and student outcomes (Jerrim et al., 2023), the general findings suggest that in contemporary schools, organisations, principals, managers, and others in positions of authority, should consider carefully perceived autonomy-support among their teachers and other schools staff, as this is regularly associated with important outcomes, such as engagement, commitment, and psychological wellbeing for both themselves and their students.

LIMITATIONS OF APPLYING SDT IN CONTEMPORARY CLASSROOMS

SDT, as a framework in education, is theoretically and empirically grounded, offering mechanisms by which educators/teachers might optimise student functioning (e.g., learning and wellbeing) via intrinsic motivation by supporting their basic psychological needs for autonomy, competence, and relatedness. It aligns well with other theories, has clear practical implications, and while disputed in terms of generalisability in non-Western and collectivist cultures, is often regarded as universal in application, and there is some empirical support for this (see Nalipay et al., 2020). There are, however, some inherent limitations of using SDT to inform contemporary classroom practices; for example, it is not sufficiently understood 'just how much' autonomy should be offered to optimise learning with too much autonomy sometimes having more adverse consequences such as heightened feelings of uncertainty and discomfort (Schwartz, 2004). Moreover, SDT is not the only option. There exist other theoretical perspectives in the field including, but not limited to, self-efficacy and expectancy value; goal, self-regulation; need achievement and self-worth; attribution and control (not exhaustive, see also Martin, 2013). Therefore, there may be other mechanisms by which contemporary classrooms might support learning and psychological functioning e.g., through other forms of motivation. Indeed, the next section considers epistemological beliefs, about knowledge and learning (Hofer and Pintrich, 2002), and such beliefs have the potential to influence the motivation of both teachers and students (Buehl & Alexander, 2005; Aslan, 2023). Finally, there is the age-old and inescapable issue of educational resourcing, that often hampers the fruition of innovative ideas for example, around personalised support for students and increased student (and teacher) autonomy (see Reeve & Cheon, 2021, for further discussion of the potential barriers to the implementation of autonomy-supportive teaching).

SUMMARY

This section advocates that contemporary classrooms should consider (more strongly) motivational factors as a means for addressing important priorities in education systems around the world, such as optimising students' learning and achievement as well as their psychological functioning (e.g., their wellbeing and mental health). Focusing on SDT as one psychological framework, it argues that contemporary schools should reflect on existing policies and practices and ascertain whether they are optimal for the advancement of student learning and psychological functioning. The evidence presented here would suggest that, despite inherent constraints and shortcomings that have been acknowledged, contemporary schools should endeavour to create a positive motivational climate (e.g., via SDT principles, such as autonomy, competence, and relatedness) that supports students' (and teachers') basic psychological needs to help optimise outcomes relating to learning and psychological functioning.

THE IMPORTANCE OF TEACHERS' EPISTEMOLOGICAL BELIEFS

We have established the position that contemporary schools should endeavour to create a positive motivational climate, yet the political and social demands on the classroom are likely to change. However, one trend which has persisted over the last three decades has been an international agreement to develop inclusive education. We will now look at the context of inclusive education and examine how its implementation is affected by teacher beliefs, and how this influences their motivation and ability to engage with inclusive education.

Inclusive education can be seen as being inspired and validated by Universal Declaration of Human Rights (Lindahl, 2006). This has been signed up to by 192 member states of the United Nations and aims to create a situation of 'education for all' (Heung & Grossman, 2007). Numerous countries are signatories to the subsequent United Nations Convention on the Rights of Persons with Disabilities, in which they make a commitment to developing an inclusive education system (Rieser, 2014). Inclusive education might be very broadly defined as children with special educational needs having not only a to right education with their peers, but an education in which they can flourish alongside their peers in mainstream settings (Sheehy et al., 2017; UNICEF, 2023).

Although the enactment of inclusive education differs between and within countries (Rix, 2015) policy makers, around the world, have presented teachers with the challenge of being able to teach effectively in diverse classrooms, including children with special educational needs and disabilities (Rix, 2015). Whilst there have been a variety of technological and policy responses to this situation, there has been relatively little focus on factors that would facilitate effective learning for all within-classroom practices. One noticeable gap in relation to this has been understanding the relationship between teachers' epistemological beliefs and pedagogies that work for inclusive classrooms. Teachers' epistemological beliefs are "the very heart of teaching" (Kagan, 1992, p. 85) and have profound impact on what teachers do in the classroom (Jordan & Stanovich, 2003). Epistemological beliefs refer to an individual's beliefs and attitudes about knowledge, how it is acquired, and the nature of knowledge itself. They include "assumptions, attitudes, and beliefs about the nature of ability, and beliefs about knowledge, knowing and how knowing proceeds" (Jordan et al., 2010, p. 262).

There is long established research to show that these beliefs underpin how teachers plan and implement their work (Pajares, 1992), their interactions with learners, and consequently children's experiences of learning (Brownlee et al., 2012; Schwartz & Jordan, 2011). As one would expect these beliefs vary between individuals and cultures (Hofer, 2010, Sheehy, 2017). An illustrative example of these differences can be seen in a classic study by Wu and Rao (Wu & Rao, 2011), who examined the beliefs and practices of early years teachers in Hong Kong and Germany with regard to the value of 'free play' activities in learning. Their findings revealed significant differences between these two groups. The Hong Kongese teachers perceived learning as synonymous with explicit teacher-led instruction, and so free play time was not prioritised. In contrast the German teachers believed that free play was a valuable learning experience. They therefore planned their classrooms and curricula to create opportunities for free play activities to occur. The beliefs of the teachers might be broadly framed in terms two epistemological conceptions: traditional and social constructivist. The traditional conception sees teaching as a direct transfer and absorption of knowledge, whereas the constructivist conception see knowledge as built through facilitation of learner activity (Lee et al., 2013). Large scale comparative international research has identified similar, reliable, differences between teachers who hold transmission (i.e., 'traditional') beliefs and constructivist beliefs (Organisation for Economic Cooperation and Development, OECD, 2009). Differences in students' epistemological beliefs have been identified, which influence their study strategies and success (Hofer & Pintrich, 1997).

Having identified that particular epistemological beliefs are associated with different classroom practices by teachers, the next step is to consider which classroom practices are inclusive, or are likely to be inclusive, i.e., producing positive outcomes for all members of the class. An early examination of this issue was a series of three international systematic research reviews. These sought to extract insights into 'what works' by looking at 'pedagogical approaches with reported outcomes for the academic and social inclusion of pupils with special educational needs' (Nind et al., 2004; Sheehy et al., 2009). The findings suggested that pedagogies that give importance to social interaction as a means of developing learner knowledge, along with the use of different modalities in teaching activities to make the subject knowledge accessible to, and understandable for, a diverse range of learners. This complements the findings above, in relation to motivation, of the positive impact of socially grounded pedagogies. Other, classroom-based, research has also supported this perspective and shown, for example, that teaching that reflects a social constructivist underpinning can produce significant improvements in children's subject knowledge and their individual reasoning abilities (Howe & Mercer, 2007; Vrikki et al., 2019). There is also some evidence that pedagogy which reflects social constructivism can have positive effects on children's social behaviours and their attitudes towards education (Hattie, 2003), which again complements the research we have seen from the field of motivation.

So far, within this section, we have argued a) that teachers epistemological beliefs can influence how they teach and b) that teaching informed by a social constructivist pedagogy appears to have advantages for inclusive education. The next point to consider is the key question of whether teachers' epistemological beliefs influence what they do in inclusive classrooms.

Pioneering research in this field has been carried by Anne Jordan and her colleagues (Jordan et al., 2010; Jordan & Stanovich, 2003; Schwartz & Jordan, 2011). Her research revealed a significant interaction between teachers' epistemological beliefs and their beliefs about disability and the quality of their classroom teaching (Jordan et al., 2010). Teachers who saw learning primarily as a social process, tended to be aware of environmental barriers that were faced by their disabled students and saw teaching disabled students as their (the teachers) responsibly. This contrasted with those who held more passive (traditional) epistemological beliefs and saw teaching disabled students as the role of other support staff.

When looking at what teachers did in the classroom, Jordan found that the more 'inclusive' teachers were also the more effective teachers for the *whole class* and engaging at higher levels of thinking and responding with all their students (Jordan, et al., 2010), in ways that reflected a social constructivist perspective (Sheehy, 2017). Taken together, this suggests that teachers' epistemological beliefs are an important, and typically overlooked, factor in the international drive to create inclusive classrooms. Teachers' epistemological beliefs affect how they teach, which can support whether or not their teaching supports a diverse learner group, but also their motivation to engage with inclusive education. These beliefs should therefore be borne in mind in the development of inclusive practice within contemporary classrooms. It is important that research on this issue is conducted outside of North America and Europe (Hofer, 2010) and a striking example of this concerns the impact of teachers' epistemological beliefs on their motivation to engage with inclusive disaster risk reduction in Indonesia.

DISASTER RISK REDUCTION EDUCATION

The incidence of climate-related natural disasters has tripled in the last 30 years (Oxfam, 2021). It is likely that educational responses to this issue, in varying ways, will affect all classes in the future and there is large-scale, global, evidence that this issue is already a significant concern for young people across the world (Hickman et al., 2021). This issue and the role of classroom practice are highlighted in Indonesia, which experiences one of the highest incidences of natural disasters, such as floods, landslides, volcanic eruptions, and earthquakes, in the world (Mercy Corps, 2020). The group most at risk of injury and death are children with special educational needs and disabilities (SEND (Indriasari et al., 2018). Internationally, disaster risk reduction education (DRRE) in schools has been shown to have a positive impact and has been a mandated topic in Indonesian schools (Amri et al., 2017). However, the implementation of DRRE remains very low, and is largely absent for children with SEND (Sheehy et al., 2022).

Seeking to understand this entrenched issue has needed to go beyond creating accessible resources, policy mandates, and curriculum initiatives, and explore the motivations and beliefs of teachers. At a general level this research has found that teachers who hold social constructivist beliefs are more likely to hold positive beliefs about inclusive education and be more likely to use teaching approaches that will make learning more accessible and inclusive (Sheehy & Budiyanto, 2015), and this will also impact in their use of DRRE. The frequency with which teachers use DREE materials, and the likelihood of changing their teaching practices to accommodate DRRE, is associated with beliefs regarding their own agency in relation to disaster events (Sheehy et al., 2023). Teachers who believe they have the agency and competence to teach this topic, are more likely to do so, in comparison to teachers in the same situation who believe they have less agency and competence. The classroom experience of children with SEND is therefore influenced by the beliefs that teachers hold about the nature of knowledge, and also their own psychological needs (as reflected in SDT). In the context of DRRE within the classroom, the consequences of these psychological constructs for the lives of children can be profound.

The role of teachers' epistemological beliefs and motivations in shaping classroom teaching is significant, often overshadowing the influence of policy mandates, assessment regimes, and school leadership (Uztemur et al., 2020). There is also some evidence that their beliefs, which evolve over time, may be more influential on practice than the policies and leadership structures in place (Markic & Eilks, 2013). This type of research has implications for teacher training. Teacher education programs should provide structured opportunities for teachers to reflect on and develop epistemological beliefs that are most facilitative of inclusive pedagogies (Hart, 2004; Florian & Rouse, 2009), such as those aligned with social-constructivist or sociocultural models of learning. Furthermore, teachers from different disciplinary backgrounds may hold conflicting epistemological beliefs (Sheehy, 2017), therefore cross-curriculum pedagogic communities, formed during pre-service teacher training (Floran and Rouse, 2009), could help address this issue.

CONCLUDING REMARKS

This chapter has proposed that teachers' beliefs, about themselves and the nature of learning, have a significant influence that goes beyond academic outcomes. Insights from a diverse range of research, in the fields of teacher motivation and epistemological beliefs, suggest that they shape and underpin the wellbeing of the whole class community. The implications of this include a need to support teacher agency within the classroom and curriculum and facilitate pedagogies that foreground social engagement in order to move towards healthier, more inclusive classrooms, that work well for teachers and pupils alike in changing and challenging times.

DISCUSSION POINTS

1. Is self-determination theory generalizable across cultures? For example, do positive associations between the need for "autonomy" and academic achievement apply equally across Western cultures, such as the United States, and Eastern cultures, such as China? The available evidence would suggest that autonomy is positively associated with psychological wellbeing universally, irrespective of where people live; however, it is important to note, that autonomy can manifest differently across cultures. Indeed, a recent study (Nalipay et al., 2020) suggested that while autonomy and relatedness were equally important for student achievement, competence was found to be more important to students in Western cultures relative to Eastern cultures.
2. What would an intervention, informed by self-determination theory, look like, and have such interventions produced positive changes in SDT constructs and in psychological wellbeing? SDT-based interventions would typically focus on supporting one or more of the core SDT constructs (i.e., autonomy, competence, and relatedness); for example, an instructor or learner, might be provided with a more autonomy-supportive educational environment, with a heightened sense of freedom, choice, and control. A recent meta-analysis (Ntoumanis et al., 2020) found that SDT-based interventions produced small-to-medium changes in most SDT constructs, and in health behaviours, as well as physical and psychological health, at the end of the intervention period.

3. What barriers are there to implementing autonomy-supportive teaching practices? This could be considered at a systemic level i.e., resource and curricular constraints or perhaps the extent to which teachers feel they have autonomy-support from their managers or employers. However, the work of Reeve and Cheon (2021) suggest there are some personal (teacher) factors that might also reduce the perceived effectiveness (and uptake) of autonomy-supportive teaching practices; namely, personality and culture.
4. Reflect on the nature of your own epistemological beliefs. How does this influence the way in which you like to learn and what you see as a good way of learning? Research suggests that a match between the epistemological beliefs of a learner and their teacher is important for learners to best succeed with their studies (O'Siuchru & Norton, 2014). Can you recall situations in your educational life where you felt a match between how you were taught and your own preference?
5. Some teachers' epistemological beliefs appear to be better suited to supporting inclusive classroom practice. What do you think are the implications of this finding for developing successful inclusive classrooms. For example, would it be ethical to identify and seek to change the beliefs of some teachers?

REFERENCES

Amri, A., Bird, D. K., Ronan, K., Haynes, K., & Towers, B. (2017). Disaster risk reduction education in Indonesia: Challenges and recommendations for scaling up. *Natural Hazards and Earth System Sciences, 17*(4), 595–612. DOI: 10.5194/nhess-17-595-2017

Aslan, C. (2017). Examining Epistemological Beliefs of Teacher Candidates According to Various Variables'. *Eurasian Journal of Educational Research, 17*(67), 37–50. DOI: 10.14689/ejer.2017.67.3

Bartholomew, K. J., Ntoumanis, N., Cuevas, R., & Lonsdale, C. (2014). Job pressure and ill-health in physical education teachers: The mediating role of psychological need thwarting. *Teaching and Teacher Education, 37*, 101–107. DOI: 10.1016/j.tate.2013.10.006

Brownlee, J., Schraw, G., & Berthelsen, D. (2012). *Personal epistemology and teacher education*. Routledge.

Budiyanto, , Sheehy, K., Kaye, H., & Rofiah, K. (2017). Developing Signalong Indonesia: Issues of happiness and pedagogy, training and stigmatisation. *International Journal of Inclusive Education*. Advance online publication. DOI: 10.1080/13603116.2017.1390000

Buehl, M. M., & Alexander, P. A. (2005). 'Motivation and Performance Differences in Students' Domain-Specific Epistemological Belief Profiles'. *American Educational Research Journal, 42*(4), 697–726. DOI: 10.3102/00028312042004697

Bureau, J. S., Howard, J. L., Chong, J. X. Y., & Guay, F. (2022). Pathways to student motivation: A meta-analysis of antecedents of autonomous and controlled motivations. *Review of Educational Research, 92*(1), 46–72. DOI: 10.3102/00346543211042426

Chow, S. J., & Yong, B. C. S. (2013). Secondary school students' motivation and achievement in combined science. *US-China Education Review B, 3*(4), 213–228.

Collie, R. J. (2023). Teachers' work motivation: Examining perceived leadership practices and salient outcomes. *Teaching and Teacher Education, 135*, 104348. DOI: 10.1016/j.tate.2023.104348

Collie, R. J., & Martin, A. J. (2017). Teachers' sense of adaptability: Examining links with perceived autonomy support, teachers' psychological functioning, and students' numeracy achievement. *Learning and Individual Differences, 55*, 29–39. DOI: 10.1016/j.lindif.2017.03.003

Collie, R. J., Shapka, J. D., Perry, N. E., & Martin, A. J. (2016). Teachers' psychological functioning in the workplace: Exploring the roles of contextual beliefs, need satisfaction, and personal characteristics. *Journal of Educational Psychology*, *108*, 788–799. DOI: 10.1037/edu0000088

Deci, E. L., & Ryan, R. M. (1985). *Intrinsic motivation and self-determination in human behavior*. Plenum Press.

Deci, E. L., & Ryan, R. M. (2000). The "what" and "why" of goal pursuits: Human needs and the self-determination of behavior. *Psychological Inquiry*, *11*(4), 227–268.

Deci, E. L., & Ryan, R. M. (2002). The paradox of achievement: The harder you push, the worse it gets. In Aronson, J. (Ed.), *Improving academic achievement: Impact of psychology factors on education* (pp. 61–87). Academic Press.

Dille, B., & Mezack, M. (1991). Identifying predictors of high risk among community college telecourse students. *American Journal of Distance Education*, *5*(1), 24–35.

Elliott, A., McGregor, H., & Thrash, T. (2004). The need for competence. In Deci, E., & Ryan, R. (Eds.), *Handbook of self-determination research* (pp. 361–388). University of Rochester Press.

Florian, L., & Rouse, M. (2009). The inclusive practice project in Scotland: Teacher education for inclusive education. [Online]. *Teaching and Teacher Education*, *25*(4), 594–601.

Hallam, S. (2005). *Enhancing motivation and learning throughout the lifespan*. Institute of Education.

Hart, S. (2004). *Learning without limits*. Open University Press.

Hattie, J. (2003). Teachers Make a Difference What is the research evidence ? *Lloydia Cincinnati*, 12(2002), 1–17. DOI: 10.1177/002221949002300106

Heung, V., & Grossman, D. (2007). Inclusive Education as a Strategy for Achieving Education for All: Perspectives from Three Asian Societies. In *International Perspectives on Education and Society* (Vol. 8, Issue 6, pp. 155–180). DOI: 10.1016/S1479-3679(06)08005-4

Hickman, C. E., Pihkala, P., Clayton, S., Lewandowski, E., Mayall, E. E., Wray, B., Mellor, C., & Van Susteren, L. (2021). Climate anxiety in children and young people and their beliefs about government responses to climate change: a global survey. In *Articles Lancet Planet Health* (Vol. 5). www.thelancet.com/

Hofer, B. K. (2010). Personal Epistemology in Asia: Burgeoning Research and Future Directions. *The Asia-Pacific Education Researcher, 19*(1), 179–184. DOI: 10.3860/taper.v19i1.1516

Hofer, B. K., & Pintrich, P. R. (1997). *The Development of Epistemological Theories: Beliefs About Knowledge and Knowing and Their Relation to Learning. Review of Educational Research, 67*(1), 88–140. DOI: 10.3102/00346543067001088

Howard, J. L., Bureau, J. S., Guay, F., Chong, J. X. Y., & Ryan, R. M. (2021). Student Motivation and Associated Outcomes: A Meta-Analysis From Self-Determination Theory. *Perspectives on Psychological Science, 16*(6), 1300–1323. DOI: 10.1177/1745691620966789

Howard, J. L., Gagné, M., & Bureau, J. S. (2017). Testing a continuum structure of self-determined motivation: A meta-analysis. *Psychological Bulletin, 143*(12), 1346–1377. DOI: 10.1037/bul0000125

Howe, C., & Mercer, N. (2007). Children's social development, peer interaction and classroom learning. *Primary* Review Research Survey.

Indriasari, F. N., Widyarani, L., & Kusuma, P. D. (2018). Emergency Preparedness for Children with Autism Spectrum Disorder (ASD) in Yogyakarta. *Jurnal Keperawatan Soedirman, 13*(3), 155. DOI: 10.20884/1.jks.2018.13.3.747

Jerrim, J., Morgan, A., & Sims, S. (2023). (in press). Teacher autonomy: Good for pupils? Good for teachers? *British Educational Research Journal*. Advance online publication. DOI: 10.1002/berj.3892

Johansen, M. O., Elissen, S., & Jeno, L. M. (2023). The bright and dark side of autonomy: How autonomy support and thwarting relate to student motivation and academic functioning. *Frontiers in Education, 8*, 1153647. DOI: 10.3389/feduc.2023.1153647

Jordan, A., Glenn, C., & McGhie-Richmond, D. (2010). The Supporting Effective Teaching (SET) project: The relationship of inclusive teaching practices to teachers' beliefs about disability and ability, and about their roles as teachers. *Teaching and Teacher Education, 26*(2), 259–266. DOI: 10.1016/j.tate.2009.03.005

Jordan, A., & Stanovich, P. (2003). Teachers' personal epistemological beliefs about students with disabilities as indicators of effective teaching practices. *Journal of Research in Special Educational Needs, 3*(1), 1–14. DOI: 10.1111/j.1471-3802.2003.00184.x

Kagan, D. M. (1992). Implications of Research on Teacher Belief. *Educational Psychologist, 27*(1), 65–90.

Korpershoek, H., Canrinus, E. T., Fokkens-Bruinsma, M., & de Boer, H. (2020). The relationships between school belonging and students' motivational, social-emotional, behavioural, and academic outcomes in secondary education: A meta-analytic review. *Research Papers in Education*, *35*(6), 641–680. DOI: 10.1080/02671522.2019.1615116

Kyriacou, C. (2015). Teacher stress and burnout: Methodological perspectives. In Wright, J. D. (Ed.), *International Encyclopedia of the Social & Behavioral Sciences* (pp. 72–74). Elsevier. DOI: 10.1016/B978-0-08-097086-8.92087-7

Lee, J., Zhang, Z., Song, H., & Huang, X. (2013). Effects of Epistemological and Pedagogical Beliefs on the Instructional Practices of Teachers: A Chinese Perspective. *The Australian Journal of Teacher Education*, *38*(12), 119–146. https://ro.ecu.edu.au/ajte/vol38/iss12/8/

Lindahl, R. (2006). The Right to Education in a Globalized World. *Journal of Studies in International Education*, *10*(1), 5–26. DOI: 10.1177/1028315305283308

Markic, S., & Eilks, I. (2013). 'Potential changes in prospective chemistry teachers beliefs about teaching and learning a cross level study. *International Journal of Science and Mathematics Education*, *11*(4), 979–998. DOI: 10.1007/s10763-013-9417-9

Martin, A. J. (2007). Examining a multidimensional model of student motivation and engagement using a construct validation approach. *The British Journal of Educational Psychology*, *77*, 413–440.

Martin, A. J. (2013). Motivation to learn. In Holliman, A. J. (Ed.), *The Routledge International Companion to Educational Psychology*. Routledge.

Mercy Corps. (2020). *The facts: Indonesia earthquakes, tsunamis and other natural disasters*. Mercy Corps. https://reliefweb.int/report/indonesia/facts-indonesia-earthquakes-tsunamis-and-other-natural-disasters

Nalipay, M. J. N., King, R. B., & Cai, Y. (2020). Autonomy is equally important across East and West: Testing the cross-cultural universality of self-determination theory. *Journal of Adolescence*, *78*, 67–72. DOI: 10.1016/j.adolescence.2019.12.009

Nind, M., Wearmouth, J., Collins, J., Hall, K., Rix, J., & Sheehy, K. (2004). *A systematic review of pedagogical approaches that can effectively include children with special educational needs in mainstream classrooms*. https://oro.open.ac.uk/15231/

Ntoumanis, N., Ng, J. Y. Y., Prestwich, A., Quested, E., Hancox, J. E., Thøgersen-Ntoumani, C., Deci, E. L., Ryan, R. M., Lonsdale, C., & Williams, G. C. (2020). A meta-analysis of self-determination theory-informed intervention studies in the health domain: Effects on motivation, health behavior, physical, and psychological health. *Health Psychology Review*, *15*(2), 214–244. DOI: 10.1080/17437199.2020.1718529

O'Siochru, C., & Norton, L. (2014). Epistemic match: A pedagogical concept for understanding how students fit into the chosen subject. *Innovations in Education and Teaching International*, *51*(2), 195–206.

Organisation for Economic Cooperation and Development (OECD). (2009). OECD Teaching and Learning International Survey (TALIS) Teacher Questionnaire Main Study Version (MS-12-01). In *OECD Teaching and Learning International Survey* (TALIS). DOI: 10.1111/j.1469-7610.1984.tb00150.x

Oxfam. (2021). *5 natural disasters that beg for climate action*. Oxfam International. https://www.oxfam.org/en/5-natural-disasters-beg-climate-action

Pajares, M. F. (1992). Teachers' Beliefs and Educational Research: Cleaning up a Messy Construct. *Review of Educational Research*, *62*(3), 307–332.

Patall, E. A., Cooper, H., & Robinson, J. C. (2008). The effects of choice on intrinsic motivation and related outcomes: A meta-analysis of research findings. *Psychological Bulletin*, *134*(2), 270–300. DOI: 10.1037/0033-2909.134.2.270

Quintero, J., Baldiris, S., Rubira, R., Cerón, J., & Velez, G. (2019). Augmented reality in educational inclusion. A systematic review on the last decade. In *Frontiers in Psychology* (Vol. 10, Issue AUG, pp. 0–14). DOI: 10.3389/fpsyg.2019.01835

Ramakrishnan, J. L., & Masten, A. S. (2020). Mastery motivation and school readiness among young children experiencing homelessness. *The American Journal of Orthopsychiatry*, *90*(2), 223–235. DOI: 10.1037/ort0000428

Reeve, J., & Cheon, S. H. (2021). Autonomy-supportive teaching: Its malleability, benefits, and potential to improve educational practice. *Educational Psychologist*, *56*(1), 54–77. DOI: 10.1080/00461520.2020.1862657

Rieser, R. (2014). What's Happening with Inclusive Education Around the World. World of Inclusion. http://worldofinclusion.com/whats-happening-with-inclusive-education-around-the-world/

Rix, J. (2015). Must inclusion be special? Rethinking educational support within a community of provision. Routledge. DOI: 10.4324/9781315713748

Rix, J. (2013). *Continuum of Education Provision for Children with Special Educational Needs: Review of International Policies and Practices.* National Council for Special Education.

Rodger, S., Thomas, Y., Greber, C., Broadbridge, J., Edwards, A., Newton, J., & Lyons, M. (2014). Attributes of excellence in practice educators: The perspectives of Australian occupational therapy. *Australian Occupational Therapy Journal, 61*(3), 159–167.

Roth, G., Assor, A., Kanat-Maymon, Y., & Kaplan, H. (2007). Autonomous motivation for teaching: How self- determined teaching may lead to self-determined learning. *Journal of Educational Psychology, 99*(4), 761–774. DOI: 10.1037/0022-0663.99.4.761

Ryan, R. M., & Deci, E. L. (2017). *Self-determination theory: Basic psychological needs in motivation, development, and wellness.* Guilford Publications.

Ryan, R. M., & Deci, E. L. (2020). Intrinsic and extrinsic motivation from a self-determination theory perspective: Definitions, theory, practices, and future directions. *Contemporary Educational Psychology, 61*, 1–11.

Schwartz, B. (2004). *The paradox of choice: Why more is less.* Ecco/Harper Collins.

Schwartz, E., & Jordan, A. (2011). Teachers epistemological beliefs and practices with students with disabilities and at-risk in Inclusive classrooms. Implications for teacher development. In Brownlee, J., Schraw, G., & Berthelsen, D. (Eds.), *Personal Epistemology and Teacher Education* (pp. 210–226). Routledge.

Sheehy, K., & Budiyanto. (2015). The Pedagogic Beliefs of Indonesian Teachers in Inclusive Schools. *International Journal of Disability Development and Education, 62*(5), 469–485. DOI: 10.1080/1034912X.2015.1061109

Sheehy, K. (2017). Ethics, epistemologies, and inclusive pedagogy. *International Perspectives on Inclusive Education, 9*, 59–78. DOI: 10.1108/S1479-363620170000009003

Sheehy, K., Budiyanto, Kaye, H., & Rofiah, K. (2017). Indonesian teachers' epistemological beliefs and inclusive education. *Journal of Intellectual Disabilities.* Advance online publication. DOI: 10.1177/1744629517717613

Sheehy, K., Budiyanto, & Rofiah, K. (2023). *Inclusive disaster-risk reduction education*, Best poster award: Relevant global challenge to be explored in education. Green Forum Network International Conference March, Milton Keynes, UK.

Sheehy, K., Garcia-Carrizosa, H., Rix, J., Seale, J., & Hayhoe, S. (2019). Inclusive museums and augmented reality: Affordances, participation, ethics, and fun. *The International Journal of the Inclusive Museum, 12*(4). Advance online publication. DOI: 10.18848/1835-2014/CGP/v12i04/67-85

Sheehy, K., Rix, J., Collins, J., Hall, K., Nind, M., & Wearmouth, J. (2009). *A systematic review of whole class, subject- based pedagogies with reported outcomes for the academic and social inclusion of pupils with special educational needs.* https://oro.open.ac.uk/10735/

Sheehy, K., Vackova, P., van Manen, S., Saragih Turnip, S., Rofiah, K., & Twiner, A. (2022). Inclusive disaster risk reduction education for Indonesian children. *International Journal of Inclusive Education.* Advance online publication. DOI: 10.1080/13603116.2022.2115156

Suto, I., & Oates, T. (2021). High-Stakes Testing after Basic Secondary Education: How and Why Is It Done in *High- Performing Education Systems? Research Report.* http://www.cambridgeassessment.org.uk

Timberlake, M. T., Thomas, A. B., & Barrett, B. (2017). The allure of simplicity: Scripted curricula and equity. *Teaching and Teacher Education, 67*, 46–52.

UNICEF. (2023). Inclusive education. Every Child Has the Right to Quality Education and Learning. https://www.unicef.org/education/inclusive-education

Uslu, F., & Gizir, S. (2017). School belonging of adolescents: The role of teacher–student relationships, peer relationships and family involvement. *Educational Sciences: Theory & Practice, 17*(1), 63–82.

Uztemur, S. (2020). 'The Relationships between Middle School Teachers' Epistemological Beliefs and Learner Autonomy Support Behaviours: The Role of Teaching-Learning Conceptions as the Mediating Variable'. *Egitim ve Bilim, 45*(202), 211–239. DOI: 10.15390/EB.2020.8272

Vrikki, M., Wheatley, L., Howe, C., Hennessy, S., & Mercer, N. (2019). Dialogic practices in primary school classrooms. *Language and Education, 33*(1), 85–100. DOI: 10.1080/09500782.2018.1509988

Wise, S. L., & DeMars, C. E. (2005). Low examinee effort in low-stakes assessment: Problems and potential solutions. *Educational Assessment, 10*(1), 1–17.

World Health Organization. (2022). *Mental health.* Retrieved from: https://www.who.int/news-room/fact- sheets/detail/mental-health-strengthening-our-response

Wu, S., & Rao, N. (2011). Chinese and German teachers' conceptions of play and learning and children's play behaviour. *European Early Childhood Education Research, 19*(4), 469–481. DOI: 10.1080/1350293X.2011.623511

Wu, S., & Rao, N. (2011). Chinese and German teachers' conceptions of play and learning and children's play behaviour. *European Early Childhood Education Research, 19*(4), 469–481. DOI: 10.1080/1350293X.2011.623511

Chapter 5
Equality, Diversity, and Inclusion: The Journey Ahead

Selina McCoy
https://orcid.org/0000-0001-8774-4018
Economic and Social Research Institute, Ireland

ABSTRACT

Schools are at the forefront of attempts to integrate an increasingly multicultural population, build an inclusive society for disabled people, and tackle persistent socioeconomic inequality. This chapter assesses recent evidence on the success of policy in supporting inclusion within and beyond Irish schools and looks at how students are faring in the midst of wider societal changes. The discussion draws on combined psychological and sociological theories understanding inclusion and exclusion at different institutional levels. Focusing on recent evidence from Ireland, the chapter provides unique insights into understanding inclusion and how it is best achieved, highlighting policy priorities for the period ahead.

INTRODUCTION

The education system in Ireland is experiencing a period of significant change and reflection as it navigates a diversity of questions and challenges. Schools are central in Ireland's efforts to support the inclusion of an increasingly culturally diverse population, meet the needs of disabled people and address enduring social inequality. What does the latest evidence tell us about the success of policy in supporting inclusion and how are students faring in the midst of these wider societal changes? Before assessing the evidence, it is useful to ask what we mean by 'inclu-

DOI: 10.4018/979-8-3693-1293-3.ch005

sion', a widely used but rarely defined term. How inclusion is conceptualised differs widely across countries and contexts. This makes research on inclusive practices of profound importance in understanding what inclusion should look like and it can be realised (Hernández-Torrano, Somerton, and Helmer 2020). A key question is whether inclusion concerns specific groups of people or all people (Nilholm and Göransson 2017). In this chapter, inclusion is conceptualised not only in relation to diversity through ability or need, but concerns other key dimensions including social, economic and cultural background and the school processes that reinforce or address these differences (Sturm 2019, Rapp et al., 2021). In reviewing this wide literature, Rapp et al. (2021) reflect that inclusion is intricately related to diversity (Burner, Nodeland, and Aamaas, 2018), equity (Shaeffer, 2019), equality (Lundahl 2016), citizenship (McAnelly and Gaffney 2019), and the fundamental right to appropriate and adapted education (Gran 2017).

In developing a theoretical understanding for inclusive education and inclusive student experience, Rapp et al. (2021) propose a complex conceptual model drawing on three theoretical approaches and conceptual frameworks from each. They interweave Luhmann's theory of inclusion and exclusion (Luhmann and Rasch 2002) with an institutional framework on the social construction of reality (Berger and Luckmann 1966; Meyer 2010) to understand the role of policy, school leadership, teaching and learning and interpersonal relations, and the broader connections and communications within the context of education which serve to reinforce systems that form exclusion for certain students. Within these perspectives, there are distinct processes and mechanisms reinforcing inclusion and exclusion in schools across institutional layers. This approach further exposes mechanisms across subsystems for the inclusion and exclusion of students and the criteria applying to the access and rejection of a system. This is a useful lens for assessing how the evidence on inclusion in Ireland can be understood. The focus is on experiences of inequality by socio-economic, ethnic and disability status. While there are nine equality grounds in discrimination legislation, including gender, sexual orientation and family status, the focus in this chapter is on three groups where there is a strong education policy history and evidence base.

Policy Context

Before moving to the evidence, it is important to note that while the UNCRC (1991) and Salamanca Statement (UNESCO, 1994) have profoundly shaped approaches to inclusion in schools, many countries continue to face difficulties in achieving inclusive provision. These include difficulties in ensuring funding allocation systems counter exclusionary practices, supporting bottom-up, contextually responsive approaches to support real inclusion, understanding the ways to support learning environments that are innovative and responsive to individual need, and developing mechanisms to ensure effective transparency and accountability in inclusive education provision (EASNIE 2018, Kenny et al., 2020).

Ireland operates a priority funding programme (PFP), Delivering Equality of Opportunity in Schools (DEIS), which targets additional resources towards schools serving families experiencing socio-economic inequality (Department of Education and Skills, 2017a). Despite stated policy goals, there continues to be a 'multi-track' system to meet the needs of students with additional needs, with a diversity of structural arrangements and services across the special and mainstream school settings (Kenny et al. 2020). Increasing numbers of children and young people are enrolled in special class settings within mainstream schools, typically designated for one type of impairment or disability, while the remainder are enrolled in mainstream class settings, some in receipt of supplementary teaching and/or special needs assistant (SNA) support (McCoy et al. 2014). One central agency oversees special education policy in Ireland, the National Council for Special Education (NCSE), and the National Educational Psychological Service (NEPS) is responsible for psychological assessments and some specialised supports. A range of approaches are taken at government and school level to support the learning needs of migrant students, including English language supports, Regional Education and Language Teams (REALT[1]) to ensure good co-ordination and alignment of supports for Ukrainian and other children, and programmes to support intercultural education, including cross-cultural projects and anti-racism workshops that foster empathy and understanding (Devine, 2017; Horgan et al., 2022). Supporting the wellbeing of migrant and refugee children is a key requirement for their success; school wellbeing initiatives, trauma-informed care and specialised mental health supports are all central (Zheng, et al., 2024; Dempsey and McCoy, forthcoming).

Within this theoretical and policy context, the chapter begins by considering recent evidence on inclusion in Ireland – firstly how students with special educational needs (SEN) in mainstream and special schools experience school today . The second section considers the specific area of transition preparation for students with SEN. Educational supports for economically vulnerable children and young people and the adequacy of efforts to mitigate generational inequality are then assessed. The experiences of migrant and refugee children are also considered, given the large influx over the last decade in the context of the war in Ukraine and other global events. Finally, evidence on the enduring impact of COVID-19 on these groups of students is considered. The chapter concludes with an assessment of recent policy and its impact in addressing longstanding and emerging issues and ultimately supporting those experiencing inequality in our school system.

INCLUSION IN SCHOOLS

Ireland is a valuable case study with wide-ranging policy changes in the area of SEN resourcing and provision embedding alongside curricular and assessment reforms intended to change student engagement with learning, particularly at lower secondary level. Schools now have greater levels of autonomy, and responsibility, in terms of the allocation of special education supports, stemming from new resource allocation systems. But many aspects of the school system remain traditional, and reforms are being introduced to a school system centred on a curriculum which is highly prescriptive and students are assessed in a standardised way at key stages, which serves to audit and profile schools (Department of Education and Skills 2017b, Kenny et al., 2020).

Recent research as part of two large scale mixed method studies (McCoy et al., 2025; Carroll et al., 2024) provides a valuable lens on how students with SEN in mainstream and special schools experience school today. These and other studies show how everyone within and beyond the school community points to the importance of inclusion in schools, albeit through different perspectives. Across a diversity of school contexts, students report that their school embodies an ethos that supports inclusion and inclusive values. But fundamental questions remain as to how inclusion should look and how students with different types of learning needs are best supported within an inclusive vision. Commentators have suggested that the proliferation of special classes, for example, creates a tension with policy objectives around inclusion (Kenny et al., 2020; McCoy et al., 2016). Elsewhere commentators suggest that children and young people should be placed, received, or allowed to participate in a regular school setting, and the school, as much as possible, should realise the whole set of its objectives for all groups of students (Raff et al., 2021 citing Caspersen et al. 2020).

The evidence in Ireland supports this contention. Students reflect much more positively on receiving flexible support in small groups, and less positively on separate, larger groupings which often typify special class settings. Where students receive additional support, the vast majority are satisfied with that support (Figure 1). Support that takes the form of individual one-to-one tuition or small group sessions outside of regular class time is seen as more beneficial compared to support provided to larger whole class groups. Support which takes the form of peer mentoring is also viewed positively, with over three-quarters of students rating these supports as (very) helpful.

Figure 1. The Extent To Which Students See Different Types Of Extra Subject Support As Helpful

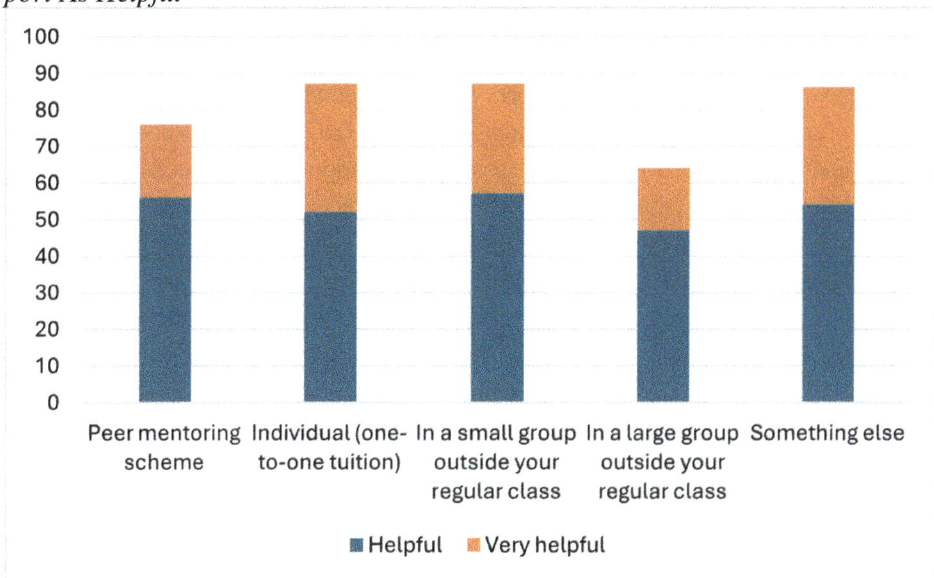

Source: Carroll, McCoy and Ye., 2024.

The organisation of additional supports, and responsiveness to individual need, repeatedly emerge as key factors in understanding student experience and outcomes. In terms of the mode of support, some school personnel feel an intensive programme spanning several weeks would provide a more inclusive support system as compared to ongoing support which involves the withdrawal of students during certain class periods. This reflects earlier research (McCoy et al., 2014) which emphasised the importance of minimising the physical separation of students; such separation highlighted as one potentially adverse impact of placement in rigid special class groupings.

> *'I don't think that taking students out of Irish and MFL [modern foreign languages] is the best way to do it for a whole year. I think the school should move towards a kind of six-week intervention model. Take the kids out of their classes for six weeks, give them the intervention...rather than keeping them withdrawn and segregated in this resource class that they're alone in. I think it's kind of isolationist almost.' (Special Education Co-ordinator, Non-DEIS School, Carroll et al., 2024).*
>
> *'Respecting the individual needs of students, knowing they're best placed with their mainstream teacher and having the individual supports to support them, that drives inclusion... having the supports in place for the boys who would be*

accessing a little bit of withdrawal but making sure the rest of their timetable is with their peers.' (Special Education Co-ordinator, Non-DEIS School, Carroll et al., 2024).

In line with our systems framework, the evidence shows that schools develop their own unique systems and structures to support diverse student need. The systems typically stem from a core team tasked with supporting the needs of students with additional needs, which in many schools includes Chaplain (or similar roles), Guidance Counsellors, as well as the key roles of teachers and SNAs. However, many schools are noting (considerable) growth in the prevalence and complexity of need, in many cases at least partly reflecting the impact of Covid-19. This is placing a pressure on support services in schools, with wide-ranging implications.

'Since Covid we are certainly seeing a huge rise in anxiety, as well as a huge rise in students qualifying for spelling and grammar [accommodations] in the state exams. I was speaking to a student yesterday and they said they didn't write for the two years over COVID-19. I think with technology as well, we have all got lazy about our spelling and grammar.' (Special education co-ordinator, Non-DEIS School, Carroll et al., 2024).

Overall, students with additional needs reflect positively on their school experiences and their engagement at school, with reasons ranging from enjoyment of the social and academic aspects of school to a sense of being a valued and respected member of the school. However, the evidence also very clearly shows that access to *effective* supports is vital to students' positive engagement with their schools, with students lacking such support reporting less positive attitudes towards school, weaker sense of belonging, less enjoyment of schoolwork, and even lower overall well-being and self-concept. There is no disputing the profound impact of effective and ineffective supports for student psychological wellbeing and educational success, which are interlinked. In this context, it is important to ask what are the key challenges children and young adults face in accessing supports?

Key challenges in providing and accessing support

Where students in mainstream schools are unhappy with the preparation their school gave them, this was typically related to having their individual need or disability recognised and accessing suitable supports (McCoy et al., 2025). Parents and students alike praise support which is proactive in meeting students' needs rather than waiting for issues to arise to react, student-centred rather than prescriptive and tailored to students' specific needs. 'Bad support', on the other hand, is that which is reliant on formal diagnosis (which in some cases is not available or very late in coming), which emphasises or even creates difference from peers rather than fostering inclusion or which could not be accessed without 'a fight'. Ensuring school supports for young people with SEN are adequate, individualised and responsive to their wishes is therefore of paramount importance in preparing students for life (McCoy et al., 2025).

Evidence across many recent studies points to shortfalls in the availability of psychological supports for students across the country (Mitchell et al., 2023; Dempsey and McCoy, 2025a). Stakeholders repeatedly highlight frustration with the availability of specialised supports like occupational therapy, speech and language therapy and socio-emotional supports, as children and young people move through school, a situation that has been exacerbated in the context of Covid-19 (McCoy et al., 2025). Questions over the adequacy of resources available to schools to meet the diversity of student need emerges regularly in contact with schools, with the available resources considered insufficient to meet the diversity and complexity of needs presented.

> *'Social media, COVID, all these things, teenagers are dealing with a huge amount ...There is a need for more supports. It's a pity that there isn't more external support- like CAMHS [Child and Adolescent Mental Health Services]. Children are waiting a year to be assessed or access supports. And it's falling to teachers.' (Home-School-Community Liaison Officer, DEIS School, McCoy et al., 2025)*

Delays in accessing assessments are repeatedly cited across research studies and by parent and advocacy groups. These Special Education Co-ordinators point to the lengthy waiting lists to access assessments and the inflexibility in the system to address fluctuations in need:

> *'This year we are only allowed 2 assessments-but there is a waiting list for next year of 5 students. ...There is no recognition of exceptional circumstances. ... with our school we would have financially vulnerable families as well who aren't in a position to get those [private] assessments done.' (Special education co-ordinator, Non-DEIS School, McCoy et al., 2025)*
>
> *'We have a list of referrals to NEPS, but our issue here is that there's just not enough availability in NEPS. This year they offered us two referrals. We have a list with ten students for referral on there. ... we have guys with extremely high needs, undiagnosed, and the parents might not have the money to do it privately.' (Special Education Co-ordinator, Non-DEIS School, McCoy et al., 2025).*

Critical shortfalls in the accessibility and availability of professional therapeutic supports and excessive waiting times for many essential services have been raised by stakeholders across schools, including among special education co-ordinators:

> *'I would love to see a whole raft of supports for SEN- SLT [Speech and Language Therapy], OT [Occupational Therapy], psychologists. There was talk each school would have access- fiction is what I call that…there's loads of kids going through while we're waiting for all these things to be put in place, putting them at a disadvantage.' (Special education co-ordinator, Non-DEIS School, McCoy et al., 2025)*

With the policy shift towards school autonomy and resource allocation decisions being made at the school level, the evidence points to increasing demands being placed on schools, and school leaders, in meeting, often increasingly complex, student need (particularly in the post-Covid era):

> *'We are now responsible for doing the Irish exemptions, it was sold that the school have the autonomy, but we are now responsible solely for that. We are now responsible for allocating the hours for the SNAs…Our NEPS psychologist is fantastic, but her role has changed hugely and it's a more supervisory role, the same testing and assessment is not done…We would find that the NCSE don't engage with schools unless it is to audit, that supportive role seems to have gone.' (Special education co-ordinator, Non-DEIS School, McCoy et al., 2025).*

Curricular developments, particularly at lower secondary level, have also had implications for students with SEN, for whom provision needs to be more flexible and tailored to their particular needs. While the introduction of Level 1 and 2 programmes as part of the new Junior Cycle Framework (NCCA 2015) has provided schools and young people with inclusive curricular pathways at lower secondary, the lack of follow-on provision at upper secondary remains a serious weakness. Also, the move to common level papers at lower secondary is seen as creating accessibility barriers. Where available, the Leaving Certificate Applied [vocational] programme provides valuable learning and skill development opportunities, and support from the support services was particularly appreciated. However, notable challenges in providing appropriate and challenging curriculum for young adults in special schools are being highlighted (McCoy et al., 2025) and point to significant policy issues around school organisation and design, their classification as primary schools, teacher allocation, funding, insurance and programme/curricular provision and guidance.

A third, and not unrelated challenge, concerns weaknesses in professional development and shortfalls in the number of staff and levels of expertise to support students with different types of needs. These challenges relate to both specialist teacher roles and wider teacher skills and competencies which are increasingly important in a whole-school approach to inclusion (Kenny et al., 2023).

'But the problem is getting staff with a Higher Diploma in Special Needs, it is really difficult…so I will have to train them all up. You can obviously sign up to NCSE courses, but there's very little about how to read a psychological report, to understand psychological reports… So we get people who are training to be a teacher and don't know anything about SEN because it's not covered.' (Special Education Co-ordinator, DEIS School, McCoy et al., 2025)

'I'd love to see all the PME teachers come out with a higher level of special educational needs training. … a lot of teachers, as it stands, don't understand the kind of behind the scenes work that happens for AEN and all the kind of interactions that happen. I'd like for teachers in the PME to experience that, to kind of get a feel of what actually happens in the AEN department.' (Special education co-ordinator, Non-DEIS School, McCoy et al., 2025)

Transition Preparation for Students with SEN

Regarding post-school education and training, in Ireland as elsewhere attention has been heavily focused on the impact of family resources/social class at school level; only in recent years are studies examining the post-school educational pathways of young people from different backgrounds (Carroll et al., 2022). Scanlon and Doyle (2021) provide useful evidence on levels of progression to further education and training programmes, through the work of the National Learning Network (NLN) and key employment preparation and skills development programmes as part of adult days services provision and rehabilitation services to support young adults with intellectual disabilities. Carroll et al. (2022) highlight greater challenges being experienced by young adults with socio-emotional or psychological difficulties – they have lower levels of progression to higher education, and the patterns are not fully explained by their earlier academic achievement, family resources and other key characteristics. Across national contexts, the evidence repeatedly points to a complexity of barriers faced by disabled young adults, reflecting physical, bureaucratic, educational and cultural constraints, which impede their access to and progression through higher education (González et al. 2021).

For students with SEN, transition preparation is critically important in terms of both preparedness for the future and optimum decision-making. Students in mainstream schools largely reflect positively on transition preparation, particularly in terms of developing interpersonal and practical skills. Similar positive reflections on school preparation and transition support were echoed by students and their parents within special school settings (McCoy et al., 2025).

In general, young adults express a high level of satisfaction with school-based guidance, with considerable diversity in their preferences for guidance. These preferences range from providing school leavers with adequate and relevant information, logistical supports, and space to reflect to make their own decisions. Students appreciate guidance counsellors going above and beyond to help them access their desired pathway. Personal factors are also important in young peoples' decision-making, from excitement over starting something new to financial concerns to implicit or explicit family pressure to enter a specific pathway. While schools may have limited direct impact on these factors, being alert to them and tailoring support and guidance accordingly can benefit young people in balancing all of the factors involved in the decision (McCoy et al., 2025).

Young adults and parents, especially those in special schools, generally appreciate the Health Service Executive (HSE) system for identifying the needs and interest of young adults, a programme in place for nearly a decade, although with changes over time. However, weaknesses relate to communication with post-school settings and application forms for adult day service/programme placements, highlighting the need for improved access, visits, and comprehensive support throughout the process. Regarding transition preparation in special schools, many schools reflected on the absence of a standard or template transition programme for special schools, leaving them needing to develop their own without any overall guidance from the Department of Education. In terms of readiness to leave school, the findings reflect rigidity within the system and the lack of flexibility where a young person is considered not ready to leave school – such flexibility needs to be available in all schools, special and mainstream. The absence of formal guidance provision was an issue for some, but not all special schools, suggesting a flexible approach is again needed. Across mainstream and special schools, the importance of high expectations for all students is clear and young adults point to SEN labels unfairly impacting on the expectations others held for them (McCoy et al., 2025).

When exploring students' experiences with their postschool settings, positive responses emerged from across higher education, further education and adult services. Students in these settings reflected positively on their chosen pathways, emphasising personal enjoyment, high teaching quality, and opportunities for exploration. Despite these positive experiences, difficulties relating to balancing various commitments, meeting deadlines, and adapting to the difficulty level of the programme were apparent.

Challenges also emerged in specialised settings. Overall, among school personnel there was a recognition that the goal is to find the most appropriate placement from what is available and within the resources available, which may fall short of the best placement to meet the needs and interests of that young adult. While many were successful in progressing to preferred learning programmes or services, some young adults reported difficulties in their transition. Across a diversity of school settings, school staff pointed to ongoing difficulties in relation to levels of staff turnover in adult day service settings, which had a profound impact on their capacity to enrol young adults as planned and on the nature of programme offered to those who did successfully enrol. There were also difficulties in relation to the range of programmes available to young people across different areas of the country, a postcode lottery in essence. Additionally, transport support and the continuity of key supports remained two major challenges for many young people in accessing programmes (McCoy et al., 2025). The issues need urgent attention at HSE level, given the impact on cohorts of young adults endeavouring to progress in their learning and skills development as they move towards meaningful adult lives. There is a particular pressing need to ensure transport support is in place where needed, and greater coordination between the Department of Education, Department of Transport and HSE may be the first step in achieving this.

Ensuring Educational Opportunities for Marginalised Groups

Research has been consistent in documenting persistent social inequality in educational access and outcomes – students from less well-resourced families and those experiencing additional needs typically fare less well than their peers across a range of benchmarks and indicators. However, students attending schools participating in the DEIS programme report generally positive experiences, including a clear emphasis on literacy skill development, engagement in extra-curricular activities (girls faring particularly well), a strong emphasis on student democracy and a positive school climate. However, two challenges have been observed. Schools serving populations experiencing socio-economic inequality but not targeted under the DEIS programme, often reflecting changing enrolment over time, can face difficulties meeting high levels of student and family need. Secondly, some schools within the DEIS programme report particularly high and growing levels of student need, and a lack of responsiveness to meet such needs within the current programme design (Carroll et al., 2024; OECD 2024).

Recent research provides rich evidence on the challenges school leaders and key school personnel face in supporting high levels of need in a context of insufficient resources:

> *'Educational Welfare Officers (EWOs) will tell you that referrals coming in, 60% are from non-DEIS schools because they don't have the resources. The*

needs are huge, the profile is changing, but there are no supports. ...but in my mind wouldn't it be lovely to have a Home School Community Liaison Officer and a School Completion Programme (SCP) in every school.' (Home-School-Community Liaison Officer, DEIS School, Carroll et al., 2023)

'We have a DEIS cohort in non-DEIS school- it's difficult within the town-competing against an ETB [Education and Training Board] school that has DEIS status-they have breakfast clubs, free book scheme, after school study, homework clubs, anything like that. We can't compete.' (Principal, Non-DEIS School, Carroll et al., 2024)

On the ground experience in school communities across the country again points to fragmentation in the provision of key supports for students and families and the need for a more joined-up approach:

'So the problem is that they all fall under different categories. So [name of agency] does some of it, but only for the kids with the more moderate needs. Then you have to go through your primary care for the others. So you're dealing with loads of different agencies, and nobody talks to each other.' (Teacher, Non-DEIS School, Carroll et al., 2024)

'There is a breakdown between education and health- they don't really talk to each other. ...We need a much more integrated support. You see it in other European countries, not here. CAMHS don't talk to us, can't refer. Health not understanding how education works ... There is a lack of understanding across sectors, and a need for a multi-agency structure.' (Principal, DEIS School, Carroll et al., 2024)

Again, the need for professional psychological support, located within as well as outside schools, has been emphasised consistently over recent years (Carroll et al., 2024; McCoy et al., 2025):

'All secondary schools should have access to somebody on site for those kids ... The traumas, really scary traumas for some children. Even as stopgap, it can be a large gap. Somebody with the appropriate skills- we as year heads try, we try so hard but sometimes you need the professional expertise that we can't offer.' (Teacher, Non-DEIS School, McCoy et al., 2025)

In an attempt to address such needs, some schools have arranged/contracted socio-emotional and psychological supports for their students, often drawing on funding allocated elsewhere, but this response is relatively recent and is not a feasible option for many schools.

> *'We have a psychotherapist in on Fridays (funded by school)- providing specialised high-level care to children that need it. That has worked extremely well. Schools do need an onsite psychologist…Schools are floundering trying to support those students and it's just unfair.' (Principal, DEIS School, Carroll et al., 2024)*

Two recent developments are likely to be important in addressing these gaps in provision. A new DEIS-plus group of schools are currently being identified, who will receive additional funding to reflect high need levels. The Minister is considering enhanced funding, staffing supports and priority access to wellbeing supports as part of the scheme (O'Brien, 2025). The Department of Education has also introduced one-to-one counselling support as a pilot programme in primary and post-primary schools in select locations around the country, to support children and young people experiencing the highest levels of socio-economic inequality (Department of Education, 2023a). These two developments address critical pinch-points in the system and could prove instrumental in supporting greater equality and inclusion in schools.

Migrant Inclusion in Schools

Supporting the academic and social inclusion of migrant and refugee children in Ireland's school system has been a strong policy focus over the last decade in the wake of a large influx of new migrants. While social support and solidarity appeared strong initially, particularly for refugees coming from the Ukraine, the lack of resolution to the housing supply crisis and a perceived strain on public services have provoked anti-immigration demonstrations across the country (Zheng et al., 2024). Placing their work in the context of theories of intergroup threat and social contact, Laurence et al. (2025) reveal poorer attitudes towards immigrants in less well-resourced communities, which is not fully explained by the financial situation of the population. The patterns are stronger where there has been a growth in the proportion of migrants since 2011. The research is notable in examining innovative measures of pressures on local services (which includes schools, but also housing and GP services), and the presence of Ukrainian refugees or asylum seekers in the local area, and the extent to which these are related to attitudes towards immigration and immigrants. Contrary to expectations, where demand for schools is higher, calculated as the ratio of and demand for primary school places, this is linked to more positive attitudes. The results suggest that *perceived* rather than actual demands on services can shape attitudes towards immigration.

There is evidence of policy success in supporting inclusion and integration in Irish schools. In terms of PISA, for example, there is no difference in reading, maths or science scores between migrants from an English-speaking background and Irish-origin students (McGinnity et al., 2023). Over 18,000 children and young people from Ukraine have been supported in Irish schools, representing one of the highest school enrolment rates across Europe (Carroll et al., 2024). The inspectorate has assessed the relative experience of Ukrainian students, with overall positive (good or very good) teaching and learning engagement for the majority reported. Among the schools inspected, almost all provided evidence of supports to ensure that children, young people and family communities experience a welcoming environment and a strong sense of belonging (Department of Education, 2024a).

Experts highlight the importance of English-language skills, underlining the importance of English-language tuition in schools (Zheng et al., 2024). It is welcome to see that specific inspections are now being implemented in relation to English as an Additional Language (EAL), providing both evidence of strengths in provision for children and young people learning English as an additional language, and acknowledging areas for improvement. Evidence from the inspectorate shows that schools are found to celebrate the diversity of their community and work hard to ensure that all children and young people feel a sense of connection and belonging to their school. The report also notes the need for stronger whole-school systems to support provision for EAL, and the need to embed such provision within the wider Continuum of Support framework. Finally, appropriate assessment methods and responsive teaching practices are important to support strong EAL learning outcomes (Department of Education, 2024b).

To enhance the engagement and learning of children and young people from Ukraine, the inspectorate make additional recommendations. These relate to supporting the parents of pre-school children to access high-quality early years education and care provision, boosting the levels of school attendance and providing accessible signposting of the diversity of post school pathways available to school leavers (Department of Education, 2024b).

The growing provision of intercultural education programmes in Irish schools is particularly welcome, with a diversity of cross-cultural projects and anti-racism workshops evident across schools, designed to support greater empathy and understanding (Devine, 2017; Horgan et al., 2022). However, wellbeing supports are also paramount, given lower levels of happiness among migrant and refugee children. Supporting students' sense of belonging and opportunities to be recognised and respected at school are also closely tied to wellbeing, particularly for students experiencing economic disadvantage, pointing to the importance of promoting these in wellbeing policies and more broadly in school ethos (Dempsey et al., 2025).

Enduring Impact of Covid-19

The evidence provides a vivid picture of how the pandemic has shaped inclusion in Irish schools and the impact of policy efforts to mitigate inequalities. When the one relative constant across all students' experiences, the classroom, was removed during the pandemic, inequalities in families' resources became much more apparent, shaping their capacity to respond, compensate and support their children's learning (Mohan et al., 2021). The home learning environments of students were more likely than the school learning environment to reproduce social inequalities. Several reasons underpinned this, such as the immediate cost implications of providing additional home learning supports, and problems that could not be solved in the short term like the need for space conducive to learning in the home and the quality of broadband connection (Carroll and McCoy, 2021).

While Ireland has lagged other countries in terms of assessing the continuing impact of Covid-19, recent evidence suggests an enduring impact, at least for secondary students (Carroll, et al., 2024). In Spring/Summer 2023, students reported that the pandemic was continuing to adversely impact their wellbeing (51%), their learning at school (62%), and their academic progress (57%), while 40% reported that the pandemic is impacting on their future plans and just half note an ongoing impact on their social lives or leisure activities. What is perhaps more interesting is the way in which these impacts vary across different groups of students and across different school settings. Across the 21 diverse school settings, the percentage of students reporting that COVID-19 is strongly impacting their learning ranged from 5% in one school to 25% in another. Levels of variation were also notable in terms of perceived impact on academic progress, ranging from 4% to 24%, impact on their social lives and leisure pursuits, ranging from 0% to 23% and on their post-school plans, ranging from 3% to 16%. Variation was widest in relation to the impact on wellbeing, with just 4% of students in one school indicating an ongoing impact, relative to 31% in another school. The results suggest that schools vary widely in the extent to which wellbeing supports are counteracting the notable impact of COVID-19 on young people's socio-emotional wellbeing (Mohan et al., 2021; Ross et al., 2021).

Figure 2. Student Views on Whether COVID-19 is Still Impacting on Their Lives and Learning

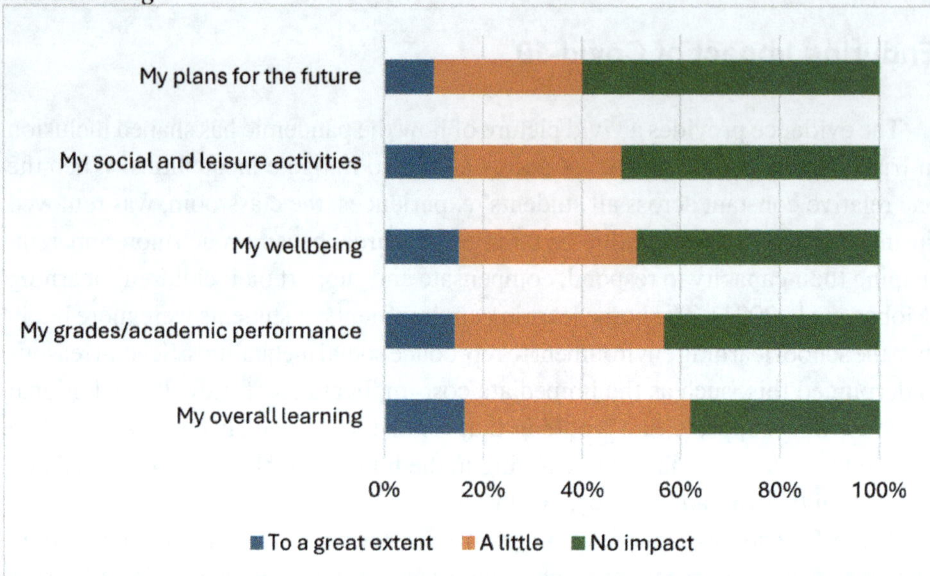

Source: Carroll et al., 2024

Notable disparities were observed in relation to student gender, stage, parental education level, and SEN status. Girls, fifth-year students, those with degree-educated parents, and students with SEN are more likely to report enduring effects of COVID-19 on their overall learning experience compared to their peers (see Figure 3). Similar patterns are also evident when we consider student reflections on their academic performance, wellbeing, social lives and post-school plans.

Figure 3. The Extent to Which Students Feel COVID-19 Continues to Impact on Their Learning

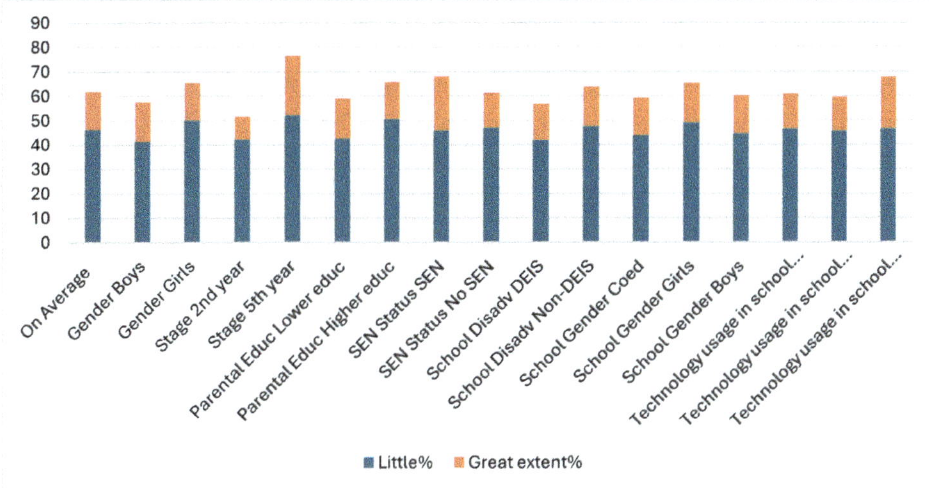

Source: Carroll et al., 2024

The result also show that learning engagement and social participation during COVID-19 is key in understanding the enduring impact on students' academic development today. Young people who reported missing their friends, having insufficient internet resources, struggling to access support from their teachers and disengaging from their studies during the pandemic are more likely to report longer-term academic and social impacts. There is less evidence of family background or school characteristics shaping the level of impact of COVID-19 today, although SEN status and educational stage do matter for longer-term impacts.

At noted in wider public discourse, mental wellbeing among young adults was negatively impacted by COVID-19. Experts observe that there was 'a general trend of less psychological well-being and more mental health problems, such as heightened stress, and depressive and anxiety symptoms during the pandemic' (Wolf & Schmitz, 2023, p. 1). There is also strong evidence that growing numbers of young people are engaging in 'school refusal' reflecting high levels of social anxiety, making reintegration into school life challenging.

> *'The long-lasting impact would be the anxiety amongst students. We have noticed a sharp increase for some students and there are still some effects on them. ... It was obviously hard to engage students when they were at home rather than*

in the classroom. It was challenging to reintegrate students into school life.' (Principal, DEIS School; Carroll et al., 2024)

'The most common problem I feel that that gets landed on our doorstep in regard to attendance is social anxiety. School refusal just based on social anxiety. There's umpteen cases of that' (Teacher, DEIS School; Carroll et al., 2024)

The phenomenon of learning losses has attracted a good deal of attention internationally, and equally in Ireland where school personnel observe significant learning gaps, as well as an adverse impact on student motivation and autonomous learning.

'COVID has a profound impact on the kids. I'd see them as 2 years behind where you'd expect them to be. There's a learned helplessness that's shocking- more and more of our time taken up doing parental jobs.' (Principal, DEIS School; Carroll et al., 2024)

Given rising mental ill health and poorer wellbeing, demand for supports at school and community levels has risen, with growth in demand for one-to-one personal counselling. Students are presenting with a diversity of challenges, including self-harm, social anxiety and phobia, school avoidance and interpersonal conflict. The evidence again raises the need for specialist and accessible supports, which address individual and family need.

'COVID has had massive effect. Students who would never cross our door in terms of personal counselling previously, they need that support now.' (Guidance Counsellor, Fee-Charging School; Carroll et al., 2024)
'Personal counselling going particularly since COVID- [We] wouldn't have seen many [going for personal counselling] pre-COVID, [and there are] loads now. There are more junior students [coming for counselling service]. [Issues include] anxiety, mental health, panic, distress in school.' (Guidance Counsellor, Fee-Charging School; Carroll et al. 2024)

'Anxiety is huge. Self-harm is huge. There's school refusal. Anxiety, you could kind of break it down into social anxiety and then just kind of educational-based anxiety, like not being able to do something ...[There is massive] anger. ... I definitely would see conflict. I would deal with conflict, not from a discipline perspective but from a kind of a mediation or a restorative-practice perspective. It's endless. I would say I know a certain percentage of it and that there's way more that I'm not even aware of'. (Guidance Counsellor, Non-DEIS School; Carroll et al., 2024)

Thus the latest evidence further highlights that the COVID-19 pandemic has, and continues to have, a significant impact on the lives of young people. Notable increases in the numbers being referred to Child and Adolescent Mental Services (CAMHS) provides further evidence of impact. While the government has increased resources to support mental health services in recent years, the level of funding to support preventative and therapy supports will need to increase considerably to address unmet need.

DISCUSSION: IMPLICATIONS OF THE EVIDENCE FOR POLICY

Over the last two decades, or in the space of a single generation, there have been notable developments in efforts to ensure students experiencing socio-economic and other inequalities are supported in their learning and social engagement at school and beyond. As the review of the EPSEN act is published, there is renewed commitment to ensuring the Act is implemented, including a roadmap for delivering necessary changes, ensuring that the policy and legislative framework supports students in accessing the education they deserve (Department of Education and Youth, 2025). Ireland has made great strides, with notable progress across a range of areas. However, several policy priorities are key if stated objectives are to be realised. These strengths and key priorities for future policy development provide timely reflections for the upcoming Education Convention in 2026, intended to inform a new long-term strategy for education in Ireland.

Strengths of Irish System

The Irish school system has made significant strides in promoting student wellbeing and engagement and creating environments where students, regardless of background or need, want to be (Dempsey and McCoy, forthcoming; Carroll et al., 2024). There is a strong emphasis on supporting the most vulnerable children and young people, a focus on successful transitions, inclusive curriculum models and evidence of student voice becoming increasingly embedded in policy and practice. This is underpinned by a responsive and supportive inspectorate focused on building the capacity of school and setting leaders and teachers and engaging with other agencies and sections of the Department to support a cohesive approach to improvement. There is also an increasing move towards cross-departmental and cross-sectoral collaborations more generally, which further strengthens policy coherence and impact.

Developments in relation to Universal Design for Learning (UDL) are also notable, where barriers to learning are seen to relate to the environment, curriculum, and context, not the student. Within this approach, there is a move away from labelling students by their disability, family circumstances, gender identity, ethnic group and so on. UDL principles are founded on the idea that provision is not 'just for' the student with particular needs, it is for all students. The approach is gaining momentum, notably as part of learning outcomes across educational sectors and in the new programme for the Junior Cycle (Department of Education, 2015), which has created flexible pathways and embedded classroom-based assessment approaches in teaching and learning (Flood, 2021). The NCSE Relate framework is also illustrative, designed to support school staff in understanding and managing student behaviour through a relationship-centered approach, emphasising regulation and practical strategies. It is a recent example of the UDL framework being employed, in the context of relational and playful pedagogy, so that teachers can design learning environments and activities that best support learners to access and participate in meaningful, challenging learning opportunities (NCSE, 2025).

While there has been notable progress, there are also a number of areas requiring continued policy innovation and development.

Areas for Development: Teacher Professional Development

One area that will need ongoing policy focus and investment relates to professional development for teachers and others working in schools. Overall, the evidence puts a spotlight on schools as workplaces, with ongoing challenges in relation to teacher recruitment and retention and work overload and burnout increasingly reported across schools. There has also been growing focus on the nature of the school system and its reliance of teacher volunteerism to provide many of the extra- and cross-curricular activities so essential to student development and wellbeing, with genuine concerns over the sustainability of this model (Carroll et al., 2024).

A common theme underpinning many of the current challenges relates to aspects of teacher professional development. The capacity of initial teacher education providers to respond to new policy directions and initiatives can be constrained by staff levels and complexity around programme accreditation (Department of Education, 2023b). Areas identified through this consultation process as requiring closer attention include keeping pace with curricular reform and preparedness to teach in increasingly diverse classrooms, themes to the fore in research. It was suggested that higher education institutions should provide evidence-based content accredited by relevant expert stakeholders in the area of supporting learners with SEN. There is evidence that this area has been given insufficient focus within current teacher education programmes and there have been calls for compulsory modules to equip teachers with the skills to support students with different types of learning difficulties (Department of Education 2023b). The report has also highlighted a gap around assessment literacy among teachers and their levels of preparedness to support the rollout of new subject specifications at both primary and post-primary levels (Carroll et al., 2024). Experts also suggest that teachers and school staff should receive comprehensive training in trauma-informed care, to support the care needs of refugee and migrant students, and others (Miller et al., 2019; Zheng et al., 2024).

It is important to acknowledge that the Teaching Council has reviewed the standards for Initial Teacher Education and produced new standards. These provide for a greater emphasis on literacy and numeracy, school placement opportunities, engagement in reflective learning and enhancing research-based practice. All teacher education programmes at both primary and post-primary levels are required to meet these new standards, as detailed in Céim (Teaching Council, 2020), and all existing programmes were required to have met these new standards since 2022. Among the key features of the standards are 7 core components, relating to areas like inclusive education, digital skills and global citizenship. It remains to be seen if these new standards will adequately address the noted gaps in teacher skills and responsiveness. An evaluation of the implementation of the Céím standards will be central in understanding the impact of these reforms and in shaping further policy development.

Resourcing Schools to Meet Diverse Needs

Equity funding programmes (EFP), like the DEIS programme, have been a core policy instrument to support schools meeting greater student need. A notable area of criticism regarding EFPs internationally, and highly relevant in Ireland, is that they can lack clear objectives and priorities have often been set without specific targets (Nicaise et al., 2024). Another criticism relates to the area of evaluation; there is a lack of rigorous and systematic evidence, limiting the conclusions that can be drawn in assessing impact (European Commission Directorate-General for Education Youth Sport and Culture, 2022). Focusing on key outcome measures, namely examination performance and second level retention, recent analysis using national-level data from 2007 to 2016, finds little effect of the DEIS programme (Gilleece et al., 2025). However, qualitative evidence provides more nuanced insights and points to positive impacts across areas like student autonomy, student-teacher relationships and extracurricular participation (Carroll et al. 2024).

Evidence also highlights growing levels of material and social deprivation and greater levels and complexity of additional needs within the DEIS urban band 1 schools at primary level and among the schools serving the most deprived communities at post-primary level. Over time, government Budgets have made modest improvements in the staffing schedule for DEIS urban band 1 schools, additional resources for senior and middle management provision, as well as a new DEIS identification model. For schools dealing with high levels of student and family need, the recent announcement of a DEIS-plus category of schools to receive additional funding is particularly welcome. Insufficient funding to meaningfully address inequalities has been repeatedly raised at EU level (European Commission Directorate-General for Education Youth Sport and Culture, 2022), so additional resources for schools facing greatest need is essential. It raises the question for us as a society, is this the amount of funding we are prepared to commit to tackling educational disadvantage in schools and, by extension, is this the level of inequality we are prepared to accept? (Carroll and McCoy, 2021).

The difficulties created, and magnified, during the pandemic have shown more than anything that deep educational and social inequality cannot be fixed by the education system alone. Schools are dealing with complex student difficulties manifesting in their engagement in learning, but stemming from wider interconnected challenges relating to their physical and mental wellbeing, housing circumstances, and experience of poverty, issues beyond the scope of schools to solve. For students waiting long periods on waiting lists to access much-needed support from NEPS or CAMHS, or who come to school hungry or experiencing unsuitable housing, what happens in the classroom is unlikely to overcome what happens outside it. Gaps in the provision of these and other core services during the pandemic, from TUSLA social work to school-provided meals, was highlighted as directly and indirectly impacting on vulnerable students' ability to engage with school (Carroll and McCoy, 2021).

Taking a Joined Up and Life Course Approach to Supporting Needs

Targeted, responsive supports within school and beyond, across the diversity of post-school settings, are paramount to ensuring disabled young adults, young adults with SEN and those experiencing economic vulnerability are meaningfully included. Given that having a physical or sensory disability at 9 years does not significantly reduce higher education progression in Ireland is evidence that inclusion can work (Carroll et al., 2022).

It is welcome that EU and Irish policy at further and higher education has placed a strong emphasis on widening access for under-represented groups, including disabled people. The fourth National Access Plan, A Strategic Action Plan for Equity of Access, Participation and Success in Higher Education 2022-2028, was published in 2022 (HEA, 2022). It is interesting to note the Plan extends the focus beyond merely access to higher education, including a new emphasis on participation and student outcomes. It includes specific targets for new entrants to higher education with a disability, including students who have intellectual disabilities.

A range of other policy measures are also important. Under Action 1.5 of the Community Employment Strategy, the Department of Education introduced a new pilot initiative to provide improved transition supports for disabled young people intended to improve access to, and opportunities for, post-school options[2]. The programme seeks to enable students to identify skill gaps and supports that they require, leading to the development of individual transition plans by schools. Clusters of schools located in two areas (Galway and Dublin) will work with key project staff over a two-year period. More recently, in February 2024, Minister Simon Harris announced support for higher education programmes across 10 higher education institutions designated for students with an intellectual disability. Finally, an allocation of €1.8 million has been provided for a diversity of inclusion measures, including to roll out sensory maps of college campuses to support autistic learners and for anti-racism measures.

The Progressing Disability Services for Children and Young People Programme (PDS)[3] is also being rolled out nationally by the HSE to provide therapeutic services for children and young people from birth to 18 years old with a disability or developmental delay. The PDS programme aims are ambitious and highly important in light of the shortfalls in current provision highlighted in this chapter and elsewhere. One final development will also be critically important. Children's Disability Network Teams (CDNTs), comprising inter-disciplinary teams of health and social care professionals, have been set up to pool resources, to help the child and family with their planning, decision-making and goal setting. Services across 96 Community Healthcare Networks will be provided by the team covering the designated geographical area (CDNT, 2022). Importantly and in line with international trends, the programme is shifting the provision of services from diagnosis-based to needs-based with the aim that all children with a disability or developmental delay have access to the most appropriate service based on their needs (CDNT, 2022).

CONCLUSION

Drawing on combined psychological and sociological theories, framing inclusion and exclusion at different institutional levels, this chapter has assessed recent evidence on inclusion in schools in Ireland. Taking an intersectional approach, inclusion is conceptualised not only in relation to diversity in the form of ability or need but also includes socio-economic and cultural diversity. The chapter provides insights from recent evidence into understanding inclusion, how children and young people are faring and concluding with strengths of the Irish system and policy priorities for the period ahead. While there has been significant policy progress over recent years, the evidence highlights that the process of translating policy into practice is far from straightforward (Azorín and Ainscow, 2020). Listening to all voices in the system, particularly the newly arrived, those experiencing SEN and/or socio-economic inequalities, is paramount in developing an effective, responsive educational system that supports everyone to flourish.

DISCUSSION QUESTIONS

1. How is inclusion in education best defined in the Irish context?
2. What does the evidence say in terms of supporting inclusion for all?
3. What are the strengths of the Irish education system in supporting inclusion?
4. To what extent is policy mitigating and addressing disadvantages in educational access and outcomes?
5. What are the key priorities for future policy development in addressing short-coming in provision evident from research?

REFERENCES

Azorín, C., & Ainscow, M. (2020). Guiding Schools on Their Journey Towards Inclusion. *International Journal of Inclusive Education*, *24*(1), 58–76.

Berger, P. L., & Luckmann, T. (1966). The Social Construction of Reality: A Treatise in the Sociology of Knowledge. Academic Press.

Burner, Nodeland, & Aamaas. (2018). Critical Perspectives on Perceptions and Practices of Diversity in Education. Academic Press.

Carroll, E., & McCoy, S. (2021). All in This Together? New and enduring forms of inequality post-pandemic. Ireland's Education Yearbook 2021. https://irelandseducationyearbook.ie/downloads/IEYB2021/YB2021-Second-Level-08.pdf

Carroll, E., McCoy, S., & Mihut, G. (2022, December). Exploring cumulative disadvantage in early school leaving and planned post-school pathways among those identified with special educational needs in Irish primary schools. *British Educational Research Journal*, *48*(6), 1065–1082. DOI: 10.1002/berj.3815

Carroll, E., McCoy, S., & Ye, K. (2024). *'Embracing diversity in all its forms': The voluntary secondary sector in Irish education, ESRI Research Series 182*. ESRI. DOI: 10.26504/rs182

Carroll, E., Ye, K., & McCoy, S. (2022). Educationally maintained inequality? The role of risk factors and resilience at 9, 13 and 17 in disabled young people's post-school pathways at 20. *Irish Educational Studies*, *41*(3), 573–594. DOI: 10.1080/03323315.2022.2093257

Caspersen, Buland, Hermstad, & Røe. (2020). På vei mot Inkludering? Sluttrapport fra evalueringen av modellutprøvingen Inkludering på alvor. Trondheim: NTNU Samfunnsforskning Mangfold og inkludering.

Children's Disability Network Team (CDNT). (2022). Policy framework for service delivery of children's disability network teams. https://www.hse.ie/eng/services/list/4/disability/progressing-disability/pds-programme/documents/policy-framework-for-children-s-disability-network-teams.pdf

Dempsey, C., Farrell, E., & McCoy, S. (2025). Understanding the role of school experiences in the wellbeing of girls, SEN and low SES students: A self-determination theory approach. *Studies in Educational Evaluation*, *86*, 101489. DOI: 10.1016/j.stueduc.2025.101489

Dempsey, C., & McCoy, S. (2025). The role of academic self-concepts, parent expectations, and teacher-student interactions in socio-economic gaps in attainment. *The British Journal of Educational Psychology*. PMID: 40913327

Dempsey, C., S. McCoy. (forthcoming). Literature Review on Wellbeing Promotion in Schools. Dublin: Economic and Social Research Institute.

Department of Education. (2015) Framework for Junior Cycle. www.education.ie/en/Publications/Policy-reports/Framework-for-Junior-Cycle-2015.pdf

Department of Education. (2023a) Counselling in Primary Schools-Pilot (CPS-P) 2023-2025, Dublin: Department of Education. https://www.gov.ie/en/department-of-education/publications/counselling-in-primary-schools-pilot-cps-p-2023-2025/

Department of Education. (2023b). Initial Teacher Education Policy Statement, Dublin Department of Education. https://www.gov.ie/en/publication/926b4-ite-policy-statement/

Department of Education. (2024a). The Quality of Education for Children and Young People from Ukraine, Dublin: Department of Education. https://assets.gov.ie/static/documents/quality-of-education-for-children-and-young-people-from-ukraine.pdf

Department of Education. (2024b). *Additional Language Needs – Whole-school and Classroom Approaches for Inclusive Language Learning: Findings from Primary and Post-primary school inspections of English as an Additional Language.* Department of Education.

Department of Education and Skills. (2017a). DEIS plan 2017: Delivering Equality of Opportunity in Schools. Retrieved from https://www.gov.ie/en/publication/0fea7-deis-plan-2017/

Department of Education and Skills. (2017b). Guidelines for Primary Schools Supporting Pupils with Special Educational Needs in Mainstream Schools. https://www.education.ie/en/The-Education-System/Special-Education/Guidelines-for-Primary-Schools-Supporting-Pupils-with-Special-Educational-Needs-in-Mainstream-Schools.pdf

Department of Education and Youth. (2025). Review of The Education for Persons with Special Educational Needs (EPSEN) Act 2004, Dublin: Department of Education and Youth. https://assets.gov.ie/static/documents/Report_on_the_Review_of_Education_for_Persons_with_Special_Educational_Needs_EPSEN_Act.pdf

Devine, D. (2017). Migrant children in urban schools in Ireland. In Pink, W. T., & Noblit, G. W. (Eds.), *Second International Handbook of Urban Education* (pp. 1103–1124). Springer. DOI: 10.1007/978-3-319-40317-5

European Agency for Development in Special Needs Education (EADSNE). (2003). *Thematic Education.*

European Agency for Development in Special Needs Education (EADSNE). (2018). Financing Policies for Inclusive Education Systems. Resourcing Levers to Reduce Disparity in Education. Brussels: EASNIE. https://www.european-agency.org/sites/default/files/fpies-synthesis-report.pdf

European Commission Directorate-General for Education Youth Sport and Culture. (2022). Investing in our future: Quality investment in education and training. Publications Office of the European Union. Retrieved from https://data.europa.eu/doi/10.2766/45896

Flood, M. (2021). An Introduction to Universal Design for Learning (UDL). Ireland's Education Yearbook 2021. https://irelandseducationyearbook.ie/downloads/IEYB2021/YB2021-Second-Level-05.pdf

Gilleece, L., A. Clerkin, D. Flannery. (2025). Reducing educational disadvantage across post-primary schools: Evidence from the first decade of the DEIS plan in Ireland, Studies in Educational Evaluation, 86. DOI: 10.1016/j.stueduc.2025.101466

Government of Ireland. (2019). Healthy Ireland Framework 2019–2025. Dublin: Government publications. www.gov.ie/en/publication/e8f9b1-healthy-ireland framework-2019-2025/

Government of Ireland. (2020). Migrant Integration Strategy. Dublin: Government publications. www.gov.ie/en/publication/5a86da-the-migrant-integration-strategy-2017-2020/

Gran, B. K. (2017). An International Framework of Children's Rights. *Annual Review of Law and Social Science*, *13*, 79–100. DOI: 10.1146/annurev-lawsocsci-110615-084638

Hernández-Torrano, D., Somerton, M., & Helmer, J. (2020). Mapping Research on Inclusive Education Since Salamanca Statement: A Bibliometric Review of the Literature Over 25 Years. *International Journal of Inclusive Education*, 1–20. DOI: 10.1080/13603116.2020.1747555

Higher Education Authority (HEA). (2022). *National Access Plan: A Strategic Action Plan for Equity of Access, Participation and Success in Higher Education 2022-2028*. HEA.

Horgan, D., Martin, S., O'Riordan, J., & Maier, R. (2022). Supporting languages: The socio-educational integration of migrant and refugee children and young people. *Children & Society*, *36*(3), 369–385. DOI: 10.1111/chso.12525

Kenny, N., McCoy, S., & Mihut, G. (2020, September). Special Education Reforms in Ireland: Changing Systems, Changing Schools, International Journal of Inclusive Education. *Online (Bergheim), 23*. https://www.tandfonline.com/doi/full/10.1080/13603116.2020.1821447

Kenny, N., McCoy, S., & O'Higgins Noman, J. (2023). A Whole Education Approach to Inclusive Education: An Integrated Model to Guide Planning, Policy, and Provision. *Education Sciences, 13*(9). Advance online publication. DOI: 10.3390/educsci13090959

Laurence, J., & McGinnity, F. (2025). F. and K. Murphy. (2025). Community-level drivers of attitudes towards immigration in Ireland. *Journal of Ethnic and Migration Studies, 51*(11). Advance online publication. DOI: 10.1080/1369183X.2025.2487198

Luhmann, N., & Rasch, W. (2002). *Theories of Distinction: Redescribing the Descriptions of Modernity*. Stanford University Press.

Lundahl, L. (2016). Equality, Inclusion and Marketization of Nordic Education: Introductory Notes. Research in Comparative and International Education, 11, 3–12. doi:.DOI: 10.1177/1745499916631059

Mac Domhnaill, C., Lyons, S., & McCoy, S. (2020). *Specialist support for persons with disabilities living in the community: Review of international practice*. ESRI. www.esri.ie/system/files/publications/SUSTAT97_0.pdf

McAnelly, K., & Gaffney, M. (2019). Rights, Inclusion and Citizenship: A Good News Story About Learning in the Early Years. *International Journal of Inclusive Education, 23*(10), 1081–1094.

McCoy, S., Banks, J., Frawley, D., Watson, D., & Shevlin, M. (2014). *Understanding Special Class Provision in Ireland: Findings from a National Survey of Schools*. ESRI and National Council for Special Education. https://www.esri.ie/publications/understanding-special-class-provision-in-ireland-findings-from-a-national-survey-of

McCoy, S., & Marcus-Quinn, A. (2025). Navigating youth, smartphones, and policy: A balanced perspective on digital wellbeing. *Pediatric Research*. Advance online publication. DOI: 10.1038/s41390-025-04288-3 PMID: 40731095

McCoy, S., Ye, K., & Carroll, E. (2025) Paths, Tracks, Gaps and Cliffs: Tracking the post-school pathways of students with special education needs. Dublin: NCSE. https://www.esri.ie/publications/paths-tracks-gaps-and-cliffs-the-post-school-transitions-of-students-with-special

McGinnity, F., Laurence, J., & Cunniffe, E. (2023). *Comparing Migrant Integration in Ireland and Northern Ireland, ESRI Research Series 158.* Economic and Social Research Institute.

Meyer, J. W. (2010). World Society, Institutional Theories, and the Actor. *Annual Review of Sociology, 36*, 1–20.

Miller, K. K., Brown, C. R., Shramko, M., & Svetaz, M. V. (2019). Applying trauma-informed practices to the care of refugee and immigrant youth: 10 clinical pearls. *Children (Basel, Switzerland), 6*(8), 94. DOI: 10.3390/children6080094 PMID: 31434278

Mitchell, G., Murphy, E., Bojarcz, S., & Cohen, S. (2023) Is an EU-Wide Approach to the Mental Health Crisis Necessary? Dublin: FEPS Policy Study. https://feps-europe.eu/wp-content/uploads/2023/03/PS-Is-an-EU-wide-approach-to-the-mental-health-crisis-necessary.pdf

Mohan, G., Carroll, E., McCoy, S., Mac Domhnaill, C., & Mihut, G. (2021). Magnifying inequality? Home learning environments and social reproduction during school closures in Ireland. *Irish Educational Studies, 40*(2), 265–274. www.tandfonline.com/doi/full/10.1080/03323315.2021.1915841

National Council for Curriculum and Assessment (NCCA). (2015). Framework for Junior Cycle 2015. Dublin: NCCA. https://ncca.ie/media/3249/framework-for-junior-cycle-2015-en.pdf

National Council for Special Education. (2017). NCSE Press Release 18th January 2017 NCSE Welcomes a Better and More Equitable Way of Allocating Teaching Resources for Special Needs. Trim: NCSE. https://www.sess.ie/sites/default/files/inline-files/NCSE_Press_Release_New%20Model_18.01.17.pdf

National Council for Special Education. (2025). NCSE Relate Framework, Trim: NCSE. https://ncse.ie/relate

Nicaise, I., Vandevoort, L., & Verelst, S. (2024). The effectiveness of equity funding in schools. In Downes, P., Li, G., Van Praag, L., & Lamb, S. (Eds.), *The Routledge international handbook of equity and inclusion in education* (1st ed., pp. 103–124). Routledge. DOI: 10.4324/9781003282921

Nilholm, C., & Göransson, K. (2017). What is Meant by Inclusion? An Analysis of European and North American Journal Articles with High Impact. *European Journal of Special Needs Education, 32*(3), 437–451.

O'Brien, C. (2025, March). Schools in poorest areas to get extra support under 'Deis-plus' scheme. *The Irish Times, 3*. https://www.irishtimes.com/ireland/education/2025/03/03/schools-in-poorest-areas-to-get-extra-support-under-deis-plus-scheme/

OECD. (2024). Review of Resourcing Schools to Address Educational Disadvantage in Ireland. Paris: OECD. https://www.oecd.org/en/publications/oecd-review-of-resourcing-schools-to-address-educational-disadvantage-in-ireland_3433784c-en.html

Owens, J., & de St Croix, T. (2020). Engines of Social Mobility? Navigating Meritocratic Education Discourse in an Unequal Society. *British Journal of Educational Studies, 68*(4), 403–424. DOI: 10.1080/00071005.2019.1708863

Peace-Hughes, T. (2021). Exploring how performativity influences the culture of secondary schooling in Scotland. *British Journal of Educational Studies, 69*(3), 267–286. DOI: 10.1080/00071005.2020.1801986

Rapp, A. C., & Corral-Granados, A. (2021). Understanding inclusive education – a theoretical contribution from system theory and the constructionist perspective. *International Journal of Inclusive Education, 28*(4), 423–439. DOI: 10.1080/13603116.2021.1946725

Richter, A., Sjunnestrand, M., Romare Strandh, M., & Hasson, H. (2022). Implementing school-based mental health services: A scoping review of the literature summarizing the factors that affect implementation. *International Journal of Environmental Research and Public Health, 19*(6), 3489. DOI: 10.3390/ijerph19063489 PMID: 35329175

Ross, C., Kennedy, M., & Devitt, A. (2021). Home School Community Liaison Coordinators (HSCL) perspectives on supporting family wellbeing and learning during the COVID-19 school closures: Critical needs and lessons learned. *Irish Educational Studies, 40*(2), 311–318. DOI: 10.1080/03323315.2021.1915842

Scanlon, G., Barnes-Holmes, Y., Shevlin, M., & McGuckin, C. (2020). *Transition for pupils with special educational needs*. Peter Lang Ltd.

Scanlon, G., & Doyle, A. (2021). Transition Stories: Voices of School Leavers with Intellectual Disabilities. *Special Issue: Education as a Catalyst for the Social Inclusion of People with Learning Disabilities, 49*, 4. DOI: 10.1111/bld.12433

Shaeffer, S. (2019). Inclusive Education: A Prerequisite for Equity and Social Justice. *Asia Pacific Education Review, 20*(2), 181–192.

Sturm, T. (2019). "Constructing and Addressing Differences in Inclusive Schooling–Comparing Cases from Germany." Norway and the United States. *International Journal of Inclusive Education*, *23*(6), 656–669.

Teaching Council. (2020). Céim: Standards for Initial Teacher Education. https://www.teachingcouncil.ie/assets/uploads/2023/08/ceim-standards-for-initial-teacher-education.pdf

UNESCO. (1994). The Salamanca Statement and Framework for action on special needs education: Adopted by the World Congress on Special Needs Education, Access and Quality. Salamanca, Spain.

Wolf, K., & Schmitz, J. (2023, April 21). Scoping review: Longitudinal effects of the COVID-19 pandemic on child and adolescent mental health. *European Child & Adolescent Psychiatry*, 1–56. DOI: 10.1007/s00787-023-02206-8 PMID: 37081139

Zheng, B., Lynam, A., & McGuckin, C. (2024) Creating Inclusive Schools: Enhancing Educational Opportunities for Migrant and Refugee Children in Ireland, Ireland's Education Yearbook 2024. https://irelandseducationyearbook.ie/downloads/IEYB2024/Irelands-Yearbook-of-Education-2024-Research-9.pdf

ADDITIONAL READING

Carroll, E., Ye, K., & McCoy, S. (2022). Educationally maintained inequality? The role of risk factors and resilience at 9, 13 and 17 in disabled young people's post-school pathways at 20. *Irish Educational Studies*, *41*(3), 573–594. DOI: 10.1080/03323315.2022.2093257

McCoy, S., Ye, K., & Carroll, E. (2025) Paths, Tracks, Gaps and Cliffs: Tracking the post-school pathways of students with special education needs. Dublin: NCSE. https://www.esri.ie/publications/paths-tracks-gaps-and-cliffs-the-post-school-transitions-of-students-with-special

Rapp, A. C., & Corral-Granados, A. (2021). Understanding inclusive education – a theoretical contribution from system theory and the constructionist perspective. *International Journal of Inclusive Education*, *28*(4), 423–439. DOI: 10.1080/13603116.2021.1946725

ENDNOTES

1 https://www.gov.ie/en/department-of-education/publications/information-for-schools-ukraine/#regional-education-and-language-teams-realt

2 Department of Education https://www.gov.ie/en/press-release/58fb9-ministers-foley-and-madigan-announce-pilot-project-to-support-young-school-leavers-with-disabilities/

3 Progressing Disability Services for Children and Young People https://www.hse.ie/progressingdisabilityservices/

Chapter 6
Adopting a New Universal Design for Education (N*UDE) Approach:
Universal Design for Learning (UDL) Aligned With Psychological Theories

Mary Quirke
https://orcid.org/0000-0002-8118-7270
Trinity College Dublin, Ireland

Patricia McCarthy
Trinity College Dublin, Ireland

ABSTRACT

*This chapter explores and examines the possibilities that Universal Design (UD) and Universal Design for Learning (UDL) offer the psychology community in education. The chapter will first outline Universal Design (UD) and Universal Design for Learning (UDL) approaches that focus on the design of learning environments for inclusion. It will then share the models of disability, and how the shift from segregated learner to included learning, shapes thinking in relation to inclusion and exclusion in education. The different psychological theories and how they, when informed by these approaches, will then be explored. The chapter will in essence develop its argument by way of sharing what the combined learning from these theories can offer resulting in a N*UDE approach; that is a new approach for universal design*

DOI: 10.4018/979-8-3693-1293-3.ch006

in education in that it invites all professionals to adopt inclusive philosophies and redesign to include to meet the challenges set in the United Nations Sustainable Development Goals, particularly SDG4 Quality Education.

INTRODUCTION

Learning matters, and that is why it is emotional; learners want to feel the range of feelings – curiosity, challenge, achievement and hope. Our relationships with our learners are central to this, as we shape the context and substance of the environment, curriculum and assessment for learners. We as professionals in education don't just direct the learning experience; how we think and feel also matters. Frenzel, et al. in 2009 identified how the relationship between the teacher and learner can influence emotions in the classroom, highlighting the impact of emotional connections on learning. Furthermore, they acknowledged that teacher enjoyment can influence learner enjoyment, suggesting that emotions can be transferred between people through subtle social cues. The researchers posited that when teachers display enjoyment and enthusiasm in their teaching, students are likely to pick up on that emotion, leading to greater engagement and enjoyment in the classroom. The findings prompt us to consider, not just the cognitive aspect of learning, but our emotional engagement with learners and how this can enhance their learning. The study highlights the powerful role that emotions play in learning and how interactions go beyond cognitive processes. Psychological theory has long focused on the development of people; it also appreciates the relationships we have with ourselves and others, and the influence of the world we find ourselves in on our development, emotions and behaviours amongst other factors.

Emotional engagement, particularly our ability to understand, welcome and engage with a diversity of learner, while also sharing enthusiasm, can be a positive influence for the emotional state of students. Fostering productive and enjoyable learning experiences while also seeking to actively include a learner's additional challenges prompts us to consider our own thinking, knowledge and experience of inclusion. Therefore, a key focus of this chapter will be on the value of our professional relationships, as non-traditional learners become more the norm than the exception; how do we engage and make the most challenged learners feel that they are a part of the wider learning experience? How do we include all learners, while appreciating their unique position as part of the community?

If we are to reframe our practice to include, this involves a reconsideration of the relationships we have with our learners when engaging in inclusive practice. Engaging with a design approach and aligning them with the psychological theories we employ allows us to reframe our work and build a foundation for going forward.

This unique focus places both the learner and you, the professional - that is your relationship - at the centre of inclusive practice.

Universal Design and the Evolution of Inclusion

Universal Design (UD) (Mace, 1985, 1997) is a useful framework to engage with when reframing our work in this regard. Quite simply, Universal Design (UD) is about thoughtful intentional design to include everyone rather than reactively considering add-on or support needs, which can leave people feeling excluded or ignored. Asking a learner to leave their classroom to avail of additional support or proposing that they do not have to engage in a subject due to challenges accessing the curriculum (McCarthy, 2013) can have a negative impact. It is now broadly accepted that reasonable accommodations to include students with disabilities can be made across the curriculum, assessment, and broader learning experiences, with the aim of ensuring equity of access and positive learning experience. Universal Design for Learning (UDL) (Meyer & Rose 2000, Rose & Meyers, 2002) has gained traction in recent decades and shifted Universal Design (UD) into educational settings, it is a framework that was developed for pedagogical practices to include a diversity of learners. While originally the focus was on including those with disability, it is not exclusive to disability and there is a recognition now that many of the pedagogical practices that ensure inclusion for those with a disability also ensure inclusion for many other diverse groups of learners. Rose and Meyers (2002) shared how Universal Design for Learning (UDL) can offer flexibility in learning experiences, thus embracing the design thinking and principles that Mace advanced for accessible environments. Universal Design for Learning (UDL) focuses on the design of engagement, curriculum and assessment and while it was originally focused for the most part on teachers and teaching relationships, across education (Ewe & Galvin 2023), other professionals are increasingly recognising the opportunity it offers (Quirke, 2024). This opportunity was identified as a *N**UDE approach (Quirke, McGuckin, & McCarthy, 2023) – a new approach for universal design in education, in that all professionals can adopt the philosophies enshrined in Universal Design (UD) and Universal Design for Learning (UDL) and redesign to include in the context of their work. Universal Design (UD and Universal Design for Learning (UDL) will be explored further later in the chapter.

Psychology, Exclusion and the Path to Inclusion

Of particular interest when considering psychology in education are the relationships that support the application of inclusive approaches in education and the influence of psychology theory in this regard. Universal Design (UD) and Universal

Design for Learning (UDL) are based on taking a more considered approach, an intentional and informed approach that allows for positive engagement. Such philosophies also appreciate the past, present and future possibilities, the relationships and experience of all engaged.

While Universal Design (UD) and Universal Design for Learning (UDL) had their origins in design thinking, they also were influenced by the experience of exclusion and segregation for learners with disabilities. An appreciation of the evolution of inclusion in education, with particular regard for the disability models allows us to understand exclusion and the development of the wider inclusive education agenda. While these approaches are informed by disability, they are not exclusive to disability in that the emphasis is on inclusivity, accessibility, and flexibility. The aim to create environments that are welcoming and effective for **all** learners from the outset. Realising inclusion in this regard is important and can be informed with a "greater sense" of both the past and moreover an appreciation of where such developments can go. As with any design approach, a deep understanding of the challenge, informs the solution, and can assist us as we reframe our thinking and own professional practice. This will be shared when the disability models and their challenge for exclusion is set out later in the chapter.

As we consider the evolution of past exclusionary practices into the more inclusionary approaches in contemporary learning environments, an appreciation of how much more we must think about arises. It can be overwhelming. It is all changing and continually changing as we respond to new learners, different curriculum and evolving demands on learning environments. Moreover, an appreciation of how many more professionals need to consider their professional practice in this regard is increasingly evident, and so the responsibility moves beyond "just" the teacher or those engaged in disability services. If the target is to achieve Quality Education SDG 04 lending to Quality work SDG 09 as enshrined in the sustainable development goals (United Nations, 2015), others must also be included in conversations about inclusive education. The necessary shift that becomes apparent is the need to move beyond an inclusive education approach that is dependent on teachers, towards a context where we can all support inclusive relationships across education. How we each think about our role and that of others matters.

Chapter Structure and Aim

While there are many factors at play, we have some very useful theories to assist us with our work. This chapter will first introduce Universal Design (UD) followed by Universal Design for Learning (UDL) by way of sharing what these approaches can offer; they are a new way of looking at what we do. We will next revisit inclusion in education and the experience of people with disabilities and use this experience to challenge each of us to think about our assumptions. We will conclude by sharing how such theories can together with psychological theory be used to reframe our work where the central tenet is our relations across education. This shift will enable us to consider adopting a N*UDE approach as set out in the latter stages of the chapter. Meeting the ambition espoused in the United Sustainable Development Goals is a target we all need to reach on.

The aim of this chapter is to deepen the readers understanding of Universal Design for Learning (UDL) in the context of psychology to support their own professional practice and therefore does not attempt to offer a comprehensive overview of all UDL applications. Furthermore, while an emphasis is placed on learners with disabilities throughout the chapter.

FOUNDATIONS AND EVERYDAY APPLICATIONS OF UNIVERSAL DESIGN

Mace was an architect with a physical disability, who had a vision to create environments, products, and services that would be usable by everyone, regardless of their abilities, and so developed Universal Design (UD). Universal Design is fundamentally a design approach that seeks to make change from the very beginning – that is at the inception stage of any idea. The approach "designs for a majority of need" resulting in greater independence and sense of belonging, not just for people with a disability, but for all of us that make up humankind.

Think about a time when you adopted some design thinking in everyday life. Planning an outfit for an evening out. What did you do? You considered where you were going; was it formal, semiformal or more casual? The occasion; was it a dinner, a concert or a night at the opera? What was happening; would you be having a meal or attending a concert venue where you might be seated or standing? Who else would be there with you perhaps, did you want to impress anyone in particular?! You also considered what you had already in your wardrobe I'm sure – was it ready to go, did it need changing up, or did you need something new? Perhaps you considered the weather, how long you would be out for, what you might be doing. The point of this reflection is to recognise that we all design and redesign, every, single, day! This is nothing new. So, what Universal Design (UD) thinking offers us is the opportunity to not just design for ourselves, but to design for the universality that is everyone.

Universal Design (UD) has its origins in architectural thinking, and has its influence in engineering, product design and assistive technology. Now think about the last time you entered a new building by way of an automated door, well-lit and spacious lobby and an environment that was pleasing to the eye – a space that made you feel welcome. Or the last time you used an electric can opener, or a remote control with ease. So many new public buildings and daily appliances seek to adopt Universal Design (UD) principles because they work for the majority of people – ensuring greater accessibility, usability and a better experience.

It is important to share that while Universal Design (UD) does not seek to negate the need for add-on accommodations for people with a disability it does diminish the need significantly. Universal Design (UD) UD is particularly evident when we consider the difference designing for a majority makes for those who would have once been disregarded. Thus, Universal Design (UD) results in inclusion and greater engagement and feeling of belonging.

Applying the Seven Principles of Universal Design in Education

Universal Design, is based on seven key principles "(1) equitable use; (2) flexibility in use; (3) simple and intuitive use; (4) perceptible information; (5) tolerance for error; (6) low physical effort; and (7) size and space for approach and use." (Storey, Mueller & Mace, 1998. P. 1).

Mace's vision was to initiate the design of spaces and settings, usable by everyone. Mace's work in physical environments and assistive technology was a direct precursor to the strategies employed in learning environments to design for inclusion. To have a greater appreciation of Universal Design (UD) it is worth considering each of the principles and how they can be applied in education and how some of these principles can be utilised when creating inclusive and accessible learning environments that can benefit all learners.

Principle 1: Equitable Use - within our education environments this means that learning materials and assessment methods are designed to be fair and accessible to learners regardless of background or disability. That a text or book can be accessible to all learners by way of example.

Principle 2: Flexibility in Use – when this principle is implemented in education, educators offer multiple means of engagement, representation and action and expression allowing learners to approach learning in a variety of ways. It is recognised that we each engage with learning in a different way; therefore, educators need to appreciate this for all learners regardless of their background or disability. How long it takes one learner to complete an assessment might be different to another – but does it mean that they know less?

Principle 3: Simple and Intuitive Use – when this principle is implemented materials should be easy to understand regardless of the learner's experience, knowledge, language, or concentration level. Therefore, within education settings this could help to reduce cognitive overload and allow learners to engage more easily.

Principle 4: Perceptible Information – within the education system this would mean that educators provide information, learning materials and assessment resources in multiple formats to support the diversity of learners in the education system. Technology and its role in education can be considered in this regard, particularly with the development of virtual realities and how they lend themselves to learning.

Principle 5: Tolerance for Error – this principle encourages creating a supporting environment where mistakes are recognised as part of the learning process which in turn fosters a growth mindset. This principle also recognises that as we ourselves implement Universal Design (UD) or Universal Design for Learning (UDL), we too are learning and therefore may not always get everything correct. It prompts us to recognise that Universal Design (UD) or Universal Design for Learning (UDL) are not checklists, but are dynamic processes and something that we must continually develop and evaluate.

Principle 6: Low Physical Effort – this principle is also relevant to education as it asks us to consider the physical environment such as the classroom within which our learners engage and interact with others. Therefore, we need to consider things such as classroom layout and how accessible this is for all learners – can they move about easily, engage with learning materials and other learners? Is it a welcoming environment?

Principle 7: Size and Space for Approach and Use – When we consider this principle within education settings it might be beneficial to think about whether practical subjects such as woodwork or Physical Education can be accessed by all learners and if not what needs to change to ensure their participation. This principle can be considered not just in terms of the environment but also how the environment support is aligned with the curriculum and assessments we employ.

By having a familiarity with and knowledge of these principles learners of Psychology will better understand the need to consider the diversity of all learners within our education system. The principles offer an opportunity to appreciate the number of different factors that need to be considered when developing inclusive and accessible environments. It is important to recognise that design thinking aligned with an inclusive philosophy is the driver for "Universal Design thinking" (Quirke, McCarthy & McGuckin, 2023) as "Universal design respects human diversity and promotes inclusion of all people in all activities of life". (Storey, Mueller & Mace, 1998. P. 11).

What do you think now? Had you considered learning and learning environments in this way. Consider your won early learning experience – how might you use these principles to redesign this experience?

Having shared UD and the seven principles, the next section will set out Universal Design for Learning (UDL) and how the design principles were reframed for education and pedagogical approaches.

CORE PRINCIPLES OF UNIVERSAL DESIGN FOR LEARNING

Mace's work with Universal Design (UD) was a direct precursor to the strategies employed in Universal Design for Learning (UDL) (Meyer & Rose, 2000), an approach that promotes flexibility and choice in how learning happens and how learner express what they know. Both approaches emphasize inclusivity, accessibility, and flexibility, and aim to create welcoming and effective learning situations for **all** learners from the outset.

The core idea of Universal Design for Learning (UDL) is to design flexible learning environments that meet the needs of all learners from the outset and is rooted in Mace's philosophy of creating environments that are usable by everyone, regardless of their abilities or disabilities. UDL (Universal Design for Learning) is credited to David Rose and Anne Meyer, who co-founded CAST (Center for Applied Special Technology) in the USA in the 1980s. Universal Design for Learning (UDL) is grounded in the principles of neuroscience and pedagogical theories, particularly in how the brain processes learning. It was originally framed round three brain networks involved in learning:

1. **Recognition Networks** (the "What" of learning): How students understand information.
2. **Strategic Networks** (the "How" of learning): How students express what they know.
3. **Affective Networks** (the "Why" of learning): How students engage in learning.

Considering learning in this manner in terms of designing for inclusion made it easily understood and a beneficial approach for a wider diversity of learners. Thus while the concept recognised that learning takes place in a community, it is rooted in the belief that every learner is unique, each with their own natural strengths, challenges, and preferences. Therefore, the learning experience should be flexible enough to work with and engage these differences. Universal Design for Learning (UDL) recognizes that learning is complex, multifaceted and very individual with learning environments continuously evolving. The focus is predominantly on those employed in education facilitating learner success.

The primary objective of Universal Design for Learning (UDL) is to improve and optimize teaching and learning for all learners by designing engagement, curriculum and assessment with this diversity of need considered from the get-go. Universal Design for Learning has three key principles

- Multiple Means of Engagement: This focuses on different approaches being employed to motivate and engage learners; it is about recognising that learners are motivated by different interests.
- Multiple Means of Representation: This principle focuses on presenting information in different formats to address the diverse ways learners learn.
- Multiple Means of Action and Expression: Universal Design for Learning (UDL) encourages allowing learners to demonstrate their knowledge and skills in a variety of ways. Learners could be assessed through presentations, projects, or digital media, recognising ability in different ways.

UDL in Practice: Designing for Diversity and Inclusion

As we consider these principles it can be useful to consider some examples in practice in education. Each principle works to overcome barriers, and while the focus can be on disability, considering what works for someone with a disability, as well as someone with language challenges or learners from different cultural or socioeconomic backgrounds is also useful. King-Sears (2009) clarifies a common misconception by emphasising that Universal Design for Learning (UDL) is not solely about technology; rather, it is equally about pedagogy—intentional instructional design that works in tandem with digital tools to create inclusive and flexible learning environments. While technology plays a significant role in facilitating access, the focus of Universal Design for Learning (UDL) must remain predominantly on how students learn best—highlighting that effective pedagogy, not technology alone, is what determines meaningful comprehension and learning outcomes (King-Sears, 2009).

When designing engaging learning experiences, offering learners choice in **how** they engage with curriculum or express their learning can be powerful. Interactive learning platforms, applying learning to real world experiences can make learning fun. Offering clear instruction, allowing learners to engage at different levels of difficulty, and allowing learners to use adaptive technologies that respond to their needs can all offer opportunities to access learning material in a different way. Offering flexible assessments while maintaining a focus on learning outcomes also provides many other learners the opportunity to succeed. Can you think of a time when one change in a classroom made a difference for that learner, and when that change also worked for others?

All these actions require a renewed focus on accessibility, language and approach which calls for some considerations. Planning is key, knowing your learners, their learning needs, the curriculum and the learning environment all necessitate careful attention. This takes time but the reward is more inclusive and engaging learning experiences for all. Resources and professional development are also key, as this approach calls for change and redesign of what professionals in education already know and do.

While there can appear to be many considerations for practice when considering applying Universal Design for Learning (UDL), it is important to not get overwhelmed. Central to the approach are the goals of equity and inclusion, proactive design and learner empowerment. In summary, Universal Design for Learning (UDL) is about making learning accessible and aims to work for most learners; it recognises diversity while it is important to remember that it never negates the need for add-on supports for those that need it. The difference is that less learners need the add-on supports when the learning environment is considered in this way from the outset.

Universal Design for Learning (UDL) continues to develop with the most recent guidelines UDL 3.0 prioritising inclusivity for all learners by shifting it from a consideration of disability to an approach aligned with equity diversity and inclusive thinking. The new guidelines also appreciate the application across the education system and adopt a renewed focus on lifelong learning skills.

Universal Design for Learning (UDL) having been informed by Universal Design (UD) share the importance of an appreciation of equity and inclusion; both also have their origins in an understanding of and appreciation of the exclusion experienced by those with a disability from education. This exclusion was a consequence of the thinking about disability in relation to assumptions about capability and vulnerability with the models of disability setting out the evolution of lived experience and thinking in this regard. These will be shared in the next section so that your approach can also be informed by disability theory, just as Universal Design (UD) and Universal Design for Learning (UDL) has been.

UNDERSTANDING MODELS OF DISABILITY AND THEIR ROLE IN INCLUSIVE EDUCATION

Inclusion in education is about ensuring that all students, including those with a disability, have access to meaningful learning opportunities. The way disability is and has been understood has a significant impact on how inclusive education is theorized and practiced today. There are several models of disability that influence inclusion in education. An understanding of these models lends a perspective on disability in relation to inclusion; consequently, an appreciation of the experience of disability in education is an important perspective when designing for inclusion.

This section will outline some of the dominant models of disability and their relevance to inclusion in education. We will ask you to reflect on your thinking in this regard – what influences your assumptions in relation to disability? This is a question we will revisit at the end of this section.

Medical, Social, and Rights-Based Models: Shifting Perspectives.

The medical or individual model of disability views disability as a medical condition requiring diagnosis, treatment and ultimately cure. This model focuses on the individual's impairments and limitations leading to a "fixing" mentality that often overlooks the social and environmental barriers that contribute to disability. This deficit model sees people with disabilities as dependent and more often thought to mean "less-ability" and can transform a description of a condition into a description of people (McCarthy, 2013) resulting in exclusion from many aspects of society. The medical model of disability has been the predominant model used in policy documents across education, that is primary, post-primary vocational and higher education. Oliver argues that these definitions both medicalise and individualise the problems of disability as well as the solutions (policies) that are applied resulting in services that ". . . are based upon an individualised and medicalised view of disability and are designed by able-bodied people through a process over which disabled people have had little or no control" (1990, p. 6). While Shakespeare and Watson, (1998, p. 14) maintain that the implementation of the medical model of disability "results in services and research aimed at the individual level" where the emphasis is on altering the individual rather than wider social processes. In essence, do we seek to fix a learner with a disability so that they work with what we do and have always done in a classroom rather than consider their needs or what needs to change within the system?

The social model of disability emerged in the late 1970s and was based on a negation of the medical model (Thomas, 2004). This model was advanced by people with disabilities - predominantly those with physical disabilities. While there are in effect two social models of disability - one originating from the UK with a materialist focus on oppression, and the other originating in the US with a minority group focus we are primarily focusing on the UK view of the social model of disability for the purposes of this discussion. Advocates of the social model argue that the medical model over-emphasised the focus on impairment, cure, and rehabilitation. Social model proponents assert that disability is an artificial creation of society and that it would ". . . vanish almost over-night if social organisation and social attitudes were transformed" (Borsay, 2006, p. 154). Therefore, the social model is concerned with the societal barriers that are placed on disabled people (Söder, 2009). Consequently, disability needs to be understood as a complex collection of conditions, many of which are created by the social environment and that ". . . it is society's collective responsibility to make the environmental modifications necessary for the full participation of people with disabilities in all areas of social life." (Duggan &

Byrne, 2013, p. 10). This would result in people with disabilities experiencing a better quality of life and more equality of opportunity (Goodley & Tregaskis, 2006).

Many criticise the social model of disability for a variety of reasons with one criticism being that it obscures or excludes the realities of impairment (Priestley, 1998). Crow (2014) reminds us that impairment is often an ongoing fact of life for many people with disabilities and therefore cannot be completely omitted from any model of disability. While criticisms exist regarding the social model of disability, it must be recognised that the shift towards a social model of disability was the start of a rights approach (Barton, 1996, 2002).

The social model prompted the redesign of places and spaces so that those with a disability could engage in a meaningful manner. By way of example, it prompted the idea that an add-on ramp at the back door of a building was the solution prompting front doors to be made more accessible and welcoming. The social model also promoted the idea that people with disabilities could be educated with their peers rather than sent to a separate school and engage in a different curriculum.

In more recent times there has been a move towards a rights-based view of disability. This rights-based view recognises that people with disabilities are experts in their own lives and, therefore, need to be appreciated as vital stakeholders in all aspects of their lives. This model centres on the inherent dignity of people with disabilities (Degener, 2016) and encompasses civil, political, economic, social and cultural rights that recognises the various realms within which people with disabilities can be excluded from society. This model of disability also recognises the intersectionality of people with disability rather than just seeing them as a homogenous group. It shifts the thinking that one solution will work for all blind people, or another will work for all Deaf people, irrespective of their unique demographics.

Disability, Society and Educational Inclusion.

There continues to be a debate regarding the models of disabilities as theories and the influence of cultures and society on these definitions with Barnes (2018) exploring the relationships between disability, economics and cultures and how economic changes influence thinking. Therefore, it can be argued that how disability is viewed in many contexts can influence the broader discourse within society. This prompts a consideration as to how we think about disability in different contexts – education, work and health by way of example.

Disability theories also prompt us to reconsider how we refer to learners and reflect on how we as professionals engage with vulnerability, disability and exclusion. Social categorisation is often used in modern society to refer to people. Definitions and models of disability that are and were used in society reflect how disability and disabled people are viewed within that society. Goffman (1990, p. 11) asserts that "Society establishes the means of categorizing persons, and the complement of attributes felt to be ordinary and natural for members of each of these categories". Furthermore, Barton acknowledges that "Disability is a significant means of social differentiation in modern societies" (1996, p. 13). While Michalko acknowledges that "How disability is made to appear to and for us influences greatly how disability will participate in our individual and collective lives" (2009, p. 66). It has been argued that "The medical model of disability has been the legitimate conceptual paradigm for understanding disability throughout the history of modernity..." (Donoghue, 2003, p. 207).

Towards a Holistic and Inclusive Educational Approach.

It is apparent that medical model thinking can lead to a deficit-based view of learners with disabilities, placing the emphasis on their limitations rather than their potential. This approach can lend itself to perspectives that are less conducive to fostering an inclusive culture in education. The debate is that while the social model highlights important social factors, it can sometimes be perceived as downplaying the real difficulties faced by learners with disabilities, particularly those with significant challenges who may require specific therapeutic support. Models that adopt a more holistic approach and consider personal health, mental well-being, and other factors that acknowledge both individual factors (e.g., personal needs) and external factors (e.g., barriers) can be complex as they necessitate a multifaceted approach that takes all aspects of the individual's life circumstances into account. Approaches that engage with personalized education planning can play a role for those learners that experience significant challenges in that they seek to remove environmental and attitudinal barriers, while also addressing the individual needs of students in an inclusive education setting.

The challenge often arises when reconsidering the more integrated approaches that take account of both individual needs and societal factors, in line with a Universally Designed system. Ultimately, a truly inclusive education system needs to draw from all the models of disability if we are to appreciate the experience while also addressing the complex and diverse needs of all learners. While the medical model focuses on correction and remediation, the social model and other models focus on removing barriers and embracing diversity. The different models of disability provide us with different lenses through which to understand the nature of disability and, consequently, how to approach our practice and our role in relation to inclusion in education.

Having explored the shift to design for inclusion and followed with the shift in thinking in relation to disability and exclusion we next move our focus to theories of psychology in education. They offer an added appreciation of the inclusion exclusion discourse in relation to the challenges for learners in education and moreover our role in this regard.

Key Psychological Theories and Their Impact on Learning

Having shared Universal Design (UD), Universal Design for Learning (UDL) and models of disability, this chapter will next explore some psychological theories and share how they can also reframe inclusion in the contemporary world of inclusive learning. It will focus on some of the key thinkers in developmental psychology and show how a basic understanding of their work, together with some emerging research can be beneficial in our work as educators.

Some seminal research in the field of education, psychology, and learning, supports the idea that how people feel about their learning is multifaceted, and can depend on individual difference, the learning environment and the context of the learning. As identified earlier in the chapter our role and how we think and feel as professionals can also contribute to the emotions, motivation, engagement, mind-set of learners, and the learning environment overall. Psychological theory can be particularly useful as it does not simply focus our thinking on the learner and their development but also considers the relationships learners engage with across education. Relationships are key.

Jean Piaget's theory of cognitive development (Piaget, 1952, 1972, 2001) remains one of the most influential and widely studied frameworks in the field of education, psychology, and developmental science. Piaget provided us with an understanding as to how we develop our thinking and cognition across various developmental stages – being capable of increasing complexity in cognition as we grow from babies through childhood and into early adolescence. Piaget's insights about children's cognitive development had a profound impact on educational practices and how teachers understand student learning, shaping constructivist teaching strategies, which focus on student-centred, hands-on, and inquiry-based learning. A challenge for the work of Piaget is that much of his research was carried out in a western context and therefore it could be argued that his conclusions may not be universally applicable to all cultures and educational settings.

Vygotsky (1978), a more contemporary theorist provided a different perspective on cognitive development, and emphasised the social interaction and scaffolding, complimenting Piaget's more individualistic view. When one considers the learning environment as a more social environment in relation to learner autonomy, support and collaboration, the education setting can be further considered in terms of the relationships that support learning.

In 1993, Skinner and Belmont, shared how teacher support and responsiveness contributed to motivated learners and positive engagement, lending to more favourable learning emotions. Deci and Ryan (2000) explored how learner autonomy promotes intrinsic motivation, which in turn fosters positive emotions like satisfaction and interest. Johnson, and Johnson (2002) identified the emotional benefits of collaborative learning, including the sense of belonging and shared achievement for learners and stated that this also enhances learning outcomes and emotional well-being.

Erik Erikson also a key thinker, proffered us a very good understanding as to how we develop "psycho-socially" – i.e., how the people around us helps us to develop a sense of who we are. Albert Bandura's research (1997) on self-efficacy shared how learners' belief in their ability to succeed can positively influence their emotional response to learning challenges. Bandura shared that learners who believe they can succeed in their learning tasks are more likely to experience positive emotions like confidence and pride, even when the learning is difficult.

Carol Dweck's concept of growth mindset (2006) added to this thinking in that it shows that learners who view their abilities as improvable and who embrace challenges tend to feel more resilience, determination, and satisfaction in the learning process, even when faced with failure.

How we think about learning and learning relationships has an impact on the learning environment. Research highlights the importance of supportive, safe learning environments in promoting positive emotions. Learners who feel supported by teachers, other professionals, peers, and technology tend to report higher levels of satisfaction, motivation, and engagement. Learners feel more positive emotions when they have autonomy over their learning choices. That is when they can set their own goals, choose their learning strategies, or explore areas of interest, they subsequently tend to feel more intrinsically motivated.

Seligman, and Maier, (1967) introduced the concept of learned helplessness, explaining how repeated failure can lead to feelings of helplessness in learners. Assessment and competition are key features of learning and while some learners thrive in competitive environments, others may feel pressure, insecurity, or fear of failure. The impact of competition on emotions depends on the individual and the framing of the assessment. Pekrun, et al., (2002) explored how negative emotions like frustration and anxiety affect students' performance and engagement in learning sharing that while anxiety was identified as the most common emotion in learning environments, positive emotions were found to be as evident as negative emotions. They concluded that emotional diversity, that is the full range of emotions experienced by learners at school needs to be appreciated more. Friedman, and Martin, (2011) advanced this when they identified how negative emotions including frustration and anxiety affect students' performance and engagement in learning.

As social interaction in learning evolves and context continues to change, we see the importance of Bowlby's Attachment Theory in educational settings – i.e., that the quality, strength, and consistency of our attachments and relationships with others are important for the healthy psychological development of the learner. For example, how do we engage and relate to our learners? Are we warm, stable, and consistent? Or cold, detached, and not predictable.

Social interaction and collaborative learning in particular, is associated with feelings of belonging and community. Hofstede's (2001) work on cultural dimensions and how other cultures value learning, helps explain how cultural contexts influence emotions and attitudes toward learning. People's feelings about learning can be shaped by their cultural background. For instance, in some cultures, there is a strong emphasis on performance and achievement, which may lead to higher levels of stress or pressure. In others, learning may be framed as a more collaborative or personal endeavour, leading to different emotional responses.

Bronfenbrenner (1979) developed his bio-ecological approach identified the importance of appreciating the symbiotic relationships between children and their "ecologies" – i.e., the very real situations and influences that they encounter in daily life. Bronfenbrenner offers us a concept whereby we can consider a learners environment, or ecology, as a multi-layered set of interconnected systems, where each influence the other, with varying degrees of directness. Considering the ecology of learning, where the learner is central, and the impact of all relationships whether directly or indirectly is helpful. It allows us to appreciate how learning is social, is based on relationships, and most importantly, how we relate to ourselves as a learner and to others.

Take a moment to think about your learning ecology; what influences you directly and indirectly? Perhaps your teacher, friends, family or where you live or perhaps the cost as set by the governing authority. Compare this to someone else you know and develop an awareness as to the different influences for different people. Having used Bronfenbrenner to consider the different influences – now reflect on your culture. Does it have an influence on your learning experience?

The theories of psychology share a picture of how learners' emotional responses to learning are influenced by their prior experiences, their identity, and the learning environment. The psychology theories share how emotions impact on learning with the research positing that learners experience a complex mix of positive and negative emotions based on how they perceive their learning environments, the degree of support they receive, and their own mindset. As we have seen a combined understanding of the theories and research provide a foundation for understanding how emotions impact learning processes. It is evident that learners experience a complex mix of positive and negative emotions based on how they perceive their learning environments, the degree of support they receive, and their own mindset.

Reflecting on Inclusive Education Through Psychological Insights

As we conclude this section think about a time that you engaged in learning, with your colleagues perhaps, how you worked with others, exchanged ideas, and discussed topics and how this enhanced your understanding and made your learning more enjoyable. Also consider how your input contributed to their experience. It is important to consider that it is the uniqueness that we each bring that adds to the learning experience.

Having at this point in the chapter, shared the different theories in relation to Universal Design (UD), Universal Design for Learning (UD), disability and psychology theories and thinking, we will now consider how they relate to each other and can inform our practice. The need to change is evident as we reflect on the increased recognition worldwide of the importance of human rights, the changing world we live and learn in ànd the need to make education genuinely inclusive. While there is a lot going on it is important to stop and reflect on what needs to be done, how we can use what we know and what our role is.

Inclusive education has the goal of removing obstacles to learning and enhancing authentic opportunities for real participation for those who are often marginalised from our education systems. In achieving this, we must all recognise that inclusion is no longer someone else's business but something that we are all obliged to adopt and implement on a continual basis. Learners are not homogenous just because they fall into the category of learner therefore, we need to recognise the diversity that exists across all stages of our education system. To have an appreciation of inclusion and inclusive education it is worthwhile remembering it is the one learner that we need to make a change for, a change that will impact positively on our practice. And that learner will remember the one that made a difference.

RECONSIDERING OUR ROLE IN INCLUSIVE EDUCATION

Having considered the different theories of psychology that inform our understanding of development alongside Universal Design (UD) and Universal Design for Learning (UDL) approaches that seek to influence our inclusive practice, this section will offer a lens so that those of us engaged in psychology in education roles can adopt what this thinking is offering in terms of a *N**UDE approach (Quirke et al, 2023). The shift we need to make is to reconsider the relationships we engage in within the learning environment, with each of us accepting responsibility for the part we play. This has significance when we consider our engagement and relationships with our learners, our work in multidisciplinary teams and how we relate to and support other professional colleagues.

Exploring the psychology theories allowed us to appreciate and understand the learner, with Universal Design (UD) and Universal Design for Learning (UDL) (Quirke & McCarthy, 2020), encouraging us to redesign our more traditional approaches for inclusion while the disability models provided a deeper understanding as to the history of exclusionary approaches.

Adopting a *N**UDE approach invites you, having considered these theories with their combined learning, to reconsider your professional role in terms of inclusion an inclusive practice, particularly in light of the call from the United Nations Sustainable Development Goals (2015). The United Nations Sustainable Development Goals (SDGs), adopted in 2015, set out a global framework to address a wide range of challenges facing the world today, including poverty, inequality, climate change, peace, and justice. Education is a crucial pillar within the SDGs, and its role in promoting inclusive education is explicitly stated in Goal 4,"Ensure inclusive and equitable quality education and promote lifelong learning opportunities for all." This goal, alongside other SDGs, highlights the importance of education as a key driver of sustainable development and social inclusion.

The Global Imperative of Inclusive Education

Inclusion is embedded in SDG 4 in recognition of the barriers to education, whether they are physical, social, or cultural and why they must be dismantled in order to give every individual a fair chance to participate in and benefit from quality education. The focus on inclusion extends beyond traditional concepts of "special education" and incorporates broader social dimensions, such as gender equality, accessibility for persons with disabilities, and recognition of marginalized groups such as Indigenous peoples and refugees.

Education serves as both a right and a means for promoting inclusion and reducing inequalities. Inclusive education is therefore linked to social justice, economic empowerment and values of equity and equality. This means that we all have a role to play in ensuring all learners have access to high-quality education regardless of background or ability, that learners will be equipped with the necessary skills and knowledge needed for economic self-sufficiency and participation in society and most importantly that learning environments help eliminate disparities between marginalised groups and the general population. This focus is about ensuring that no one is left behind, which is a considerable shift from historical thinking about capability and entitlement to education.

SDG4, is an ambitious goal with several challenges to achieving inclusive education. In many countries, schools are not equipped to accommodate students with disabilities, and this limits access and participation in education. In some regions, girls face cultural and societal barriers to education, and gender-based violence is a concern. Poverty and unequal distribution of resources means that many learners, including refugees and displaced persons, are left out of the education system and marginalised. Ethnic minorities, and migrant populations continue to face discrimination in education systems, which may be poorly adapted to their cultural contexts. While it is apparent that addressing these challenges requires systemic reforms and the concerted efforts of governments, international organizations, and local communities to create inclusive educational systems, we all play a part. How you relate to your learners, clients, other professionals in terms of your own work also matters. When you explore this, you will recognise the power you hold to reframe inclusion and inclusive practice. You are the one.

The Power of One; Embracing Your Role in Inclusive Education

Thus, the *N**UDE approach calls for intentional change, responsibility and accountability, building on the philosophies espoused in Universal Design (UD) and Universal Design for Learning (UDL). It asks that you consider inclusion in the context of your own work and the theories and practices you engage with. Reflect on the diversity of learners and people you engage with, consider how you work, the tools you use and what the ultimate goal of your work is.

This is a useful exercise for any of us engaged in education

- if you are a teacher adopting a Universal Design for Learning (UDL) approach, take the time to consider how others support your inclusive practice.
- if you are another professional take the time to consider your own work and how you can use these philosophies to redesign your approach just as Quirke (2024) did for career guidance and developed Universal Design for Guidance.

Having considered your own professional position in relation to how you can implement these philosophies in your own practice now recognise the role you can play to ensure more inclusive practices in every interaction you partake in.

CONCLUSION

This chapter introduced Universal Design (UD), Universal Design for Learning (UDL), models of disability, and psychological theories and research, sharing how the combined learning can influence our own professional practice in education as we respond to the United Nations Sustainable Development Goals, particularly

SDG4: Quality Education. When considered collectively, these theoretical frameworks offer valuable insights not only for our practice but also for the increasing diversity of learners in contemporary learning environments and the professionals who support them.

Importantly, the impact of Universal Design for Learning (UDL) significantly depends on how educators conceptualise inclusion and approach inclusive practice. Embracing a flexible, equity-driven mindset is vital to unlocking Universal Design for Learning's (UDL) full potential to effectively support diverse learners. This aligns closely with Quirke, McGuckin, and McCarthy's (2023) call for professionals to adopt a New Universal Design for Education (N*UDE) approach, which centres on intentional reflection, responsibility, and accountability in inclusive practice. Similarly, King-Sears (2009) and Ewes and Galvin (2021) highlight that creating truly inclusive learning environments requires not only systemic and structural changes but also a fundamental shift in educators' attitudes and beliefs about learner diversity and inclusion. Together, these perspectives affirm that how we, as professionals, think about Universal Design for Learning (UDL) matters profoundly and is key to fostering meaningful inclusion in education.

The strong relationship between inclusive education and the emergence of more nuanced disability theories resulted in transformative change in classrooms. These theories have long advocated for innovations in inclusion, leading to legislative and policy reforms that are shaping our learning environments today and into the future—for all learners, not just those with disabilities.

When we consider psychological theories as applied in education, we gain valuable insights into how educators can support learners in a more holistic and responsive manner. These theories not only deepen our understanding of individual learner needs but also help us reflect critically on our professional roles in fostering inclusion. By applying this knowledge within real-world educational contexts, we are better positioned to respond to the evolving needs of both learners and professionals, and to contribute meaningfully to systemic change through the implementation of inclusive practices that benefit all.

In conclusion, we hope that this chapter has helped to develop your thinking about theory in relation to professional practice and the wider system — the beginning of a N*UDE approach for psychology in education. It illustrates the importance of considering not just psychological theories in isolation but how combining these with a greater knowledge and understanding of Universal Design (UD), Universal Design for Learning (UDL), and models of disability can enable you to create more inclusive practices in every aspect of your work environment.

DISCUSSION POINT QUESTIONS

1. Having engaged with this chapter we invite you to reflect on your work and your emotional transmission. Do you enjoy what you do? Is it evident? Frenzel et al., (2009) when exploring how emotions between teachers and learners are interconnected, particularly how teacher enjoyment can influence student enjoyment found that emotions can be transferred. The learners you engage are likely to catch your emotion, leading to greater engagement.
2. Having engaged with this chapter, think of a situation that you believe is challenging for a learner, something that may also challenge you? Where do you seek your advice and learning from when exploring solutions? Who do you engage with? A community of practice such as that shared in Quirke, McGuckin and McCarthy (2023) is useful as you engage in reframing your practice.
3. How does your engagement with learners support how you work? Interestingly, Frenzel et al., (2009) also found that the quality of the teacher-student relationship played an important role. Universal Design (UD) and Universal Design for Learning (UDL) both ask us to reflect on how we do things. Do you allow time to explore your approaches in an authentic way? Take the time to explore your engagement and approaches.
4. One of the greatest challenges for the Sustainable Development Goals is the legacy of past approaches, whereby there is an assumption built on "If it's not broken, don't fix it". What do you do in the context of your work, that you believe needs to change to support more sustainable approaches for inclusion in the future?
5. Map out who and what you believe matters most in the learning environment. Use Bronfenbrenner's theory to consider the ecologies and microsystems that impact and cause change in this regard.

REFERENCES

Bandura, A. (1997). *Self-efficacy: The exercise of control.* Freeman.

Barnes, C. (2018). Theories of disability and the origins of the oppression of disabled people in western society. In *Disability and society* (pp. 43–60). Routledge.

Barton, L. (1996). Sociology and disability: some emerging issues. In Barton, L. (Ed.), *Disability and Society: emerging issues and insights*. Longman.

Barton, L. (2002). Inclusive Education and the Management of Change in Britain. *Exceptionality Education Canada, 12*, 169–185.

Borsay, A. (2006). Personal trouble or public issue? Towards a model of policy for people with physical and mental disabilities. In Barton, L. (Ed.), *Overcoming disabling barriers: 18 years of Disability & society*. Routledge.

Bronfenbrenner, U. (1979). *The ecology of human development.* Harvard university press.

Crow, L. (2014). Scroungers and superhumans: Images of disability from the summer of 2012: A visual inquiry. *Journal of Visual Culture, 13*(2), 168–181. DOI: 10.1177/1470412914534812

Deci, E. L., & Ryan, R. M. (2000). The "what" and "why" of goal pursuits: Human needs and the self-determination of behavior. *Psychological Inquiry, 11*(4), 227–268. DOI: 10.1207/S15327965PLI1104_01

Degener, T. (2016). A human rights model of disability. In *Routledge handbook of disability law and human rights* (pp. 31–49). Routledge.

Donoghue, C. (2003). Challenging the Authority of the Medical Definition of Disability: An analysis of the resistance to the social constructionist paradigm. *Disability & Society, 18*(2), 199–208. DOI: 10.1080/0968759032000052833

Duggan, C., & Byrne, M. (2013). *What works in the provision of higher, further and continuing education, training and rehabilitation for adults with disabilities. A Review of the Literature. Trim, IRL.* National Council for Special Education.

Dweck, C. S. (2006). *Mindset: The new psychology of success.* Random House.

Ewe, L. P., & Galvin, T. (2023). Universal Design for Learning across Formal School Structures in Europe—A Systematic Review. *Education Sciences, 13*(9), 867. DOI: 10.3390/educsci13090867

Frenzel, A. C., Goetz, T., Lüdtke, O., Pekrun, R., & Sutton, R. E. (2009). Emotional transmission in the classroom: Exploring the relationship between teacher and student enjoyment. *Journal of Educational Psychology, 101*(3), 707–719. DOI: 10.1037/a0014695

Friedman, H. S., & Martin, L. R. (2011). Does childhood personality predict longevity? *Journal of Personality and Social Psychology, 101*(1), 1–18. DOI: 10.1037//0022-3514.65.1.176

Goffman, E. (1990). *Stigma: notes on the management of spoiled identity*. Penguin.

Goodley, D., & Tregaskis, C. (2006). Storying disability and impairment: Retrospective accounts of disabled family life. *Qualitative Health Research, 16*(5), 630–646. DOI: 10.1177/1049732305285840

Johnson, D. W., & Johnson, R. T. (2002). *Learning together and alone: Cooperative, competitive, and individualistic learning*. Pearson.

King-Sears, M. E. (2009). Universal design for learning: Technology and pedagogy. *Learning Disability Quarterly, 32*(4), 199–201. DOI: 10.2307/27740372

Mace, R. (1985). Universal design: Barrier-free environments for everyone. In Stein, B. S., & Shoemaker, R. H. (Eds.), *Designing for accessibility: An architectural agenda for the 80's*. Van Nostrand Reinhold.

Mace, R. (1997). Universal Design: A collaborative approach. *Journal of Design and Technology Education, 2*(2), 86–94.

McCarthy, P. (2013) Expectations You Encounter: The Educational Experiences and Transition Choices/Opportunities of Blind/Vision Impaired People in the Republic of Ireland [Unpublished PhD thesis]. Trinity College Dublin.

Meyer, A., & Rose, D. H. (2000). The universality of universal design: Educational implications of principles of universal design. *Journal of Learning Disabilities, 33*(6), 505–515.

Michalko, R. (2009). The excessive appearance of disability. *International Journal of Qualitative Studies in Education : QSE, 22*(1), 65–74. DOI: 10.1080/09518390802581885

Oliver, M. (1990). *Politics of disablement*. Macmillan International Higher Education.

Pekrun, R., Goetz, T., Titz, W., & Perry, R. P. (2002). Academic emotions in students' self- regulated learning and achievement: A program of qualitative and quantitative research. *Educational Psychologist, 37*(2), 91–105. DOI: 10.1207/S15326985EP3702_4

Piaget, J. (1952). *The origins of intelligence in children* (Cook, M., Trans.). International Universities Press.

Piaget, J. (1972). *The psychology of the child* (Weaver, H., Trans.). Basic Books.

Piaget, J. (2001). *The child's conception of the world* (2nd ed.). (Grieve, J. B., Trans.). Routledge.

Postman, N. (2011). *Technopoly: The surrender of culture to technology*. Vintage.

Priestley, M. (1998). Constructions and creations: Idealism, materialism and disability theory. *Disability & Society, 13*(1), 75–94.

Quirke, M., Mc Guckin, C., & McCarthy, P. (2023). *Adopting a UDL Attitude Within Academia: Understanding and Practicing Inclusion Across Higher Education*. Routledge. DOI: 10.4324/9781003137672

Quirke, M., & McCarthy, P. (2020). *A Conceptual Framework of Universal Design for Learning (UDL) for the Irish Further Education and Training Sector Where Inclusion is Everybody's Business*. SOLAS.

Quirke, M. C. (2024). *There Has to be More Than One Way-How the Learning Experience of People with Disabilities Can Inform Career Guidance* (Doctoral dissertation, University of Dublin).

Rose, D. H., & Meyer, A. (2002). Teaching Every Student in the Digital Age: Universal Design for Learning. Alexandria, VA: Association for Supervision and Curriculum Development (ASCD).

Seligman, M. E. P., & Maier, S. F. (1967). Failure to escape traumatic shock. *Journal of Experimental Psychology, 74*(1), 1–9. DOI: 10.1037/h0024514

Shakespeare, T., & Watson, N. (1998). Theoretical Perspectives on Research. *Growing up with disability, 34*, 13.

Skinner, E. A., & Belmont, M. J. (1993). Motivation in the classroom: Reciprocal effects of teacher behavior and student engagement across the school year. *Journal of Educational Psychology, 85*(3), 571–581. DOI: 10.1037/0022-0663.85.4.571

Söder, M. (2009). Tensions, perspectives and themes in disability studies. *Scandinavian Journal of Disability Research, 11*(2), 67–81. DOI: 10.1080/15017410902830496

Thomas, C. (2004). Disability and Impairment. In Swain, J., French, S., Barnes, C., & Thomas, C. (Eds.), *Disabling barriers - enabling environments*. SAGE.

United Nations. (2015). *Transforming our world: The 2030 Agenda for Sustainable Development.* A/RES/70/1.

United Nations Educational Scientific Cultural Organisation. (1994). *The Salamanca statement and framework for action on special needs education*. UNESCO.

Vygotsky, L. S. (1978). *Mind in society: The development of higher psychological processes*. Harvard University Press.

ADDITIONAL READING

Ewe, L. P., & Galvin, T. (2023). Universal Design for Learning across Formal School Structures in Europe—A Systematic Review. *Education Sciences, 13*(9), 867.

Frenzel, A. C., Goetz, T., Lüdtke, O., Pekrun, R., & Sutton, R. E. (2009). Emotional transmission in the classroom: Exploring the relationship between teacher and student enjoyment. *Journal of Educational Psychology, 101*(3), 707–719.

Quirke, M., Mc Guckin, C., & McCarthy, P. (2023). *Adopting a UDL Attitude Within Academia: Understanding and Practicing Inclusion Across Higher Education*. Routledge.

Chapter 7
Understanding and Managing Student Stress

Chris Gibbons
https://orcid.org/0000-0001-6631-721X
Queen's University Belfast, UK

ABSTRACT

An understanding of stress and coping is important for all educators. Understanding the stress experienced by students, for example, in relation to teaching, assessment, and coping, is important if education is to be optimized, and it helps educators understand their own stress experience and potentially cope better, making them more effective in their relations with students. This chapter opens by outlining what is meant by stress and how it has been studied from a historical perspective. Stress has tended to be conceived as synonymous with distress, and most empirical studies use measures that construe it in this way. An overview will be offered of some of the key research that has explored the adverse consequences of stress, along with the research efforts that have explored stress as a necessary ingredient to achieve. Stress is both the physiological and psychological response to demands, and stress also refers to those demands that trigger that response. Sections will be offered on those stimuli demands or sources of stress and on their effect on students.

INTRODUCTION

Stress has been defined as the reaction of the body and the mind to the demands made upon it (Selye, 1956). It is a consequence of a demand that has led to 'too much or too little arousal resulting in harm to mind and body' (Schafer, 1992, p.14). From this perspective, stress is a biological reaction with the focus on the role of neurons and hormones in initiating and maintaining that fight or flight reaction. Heart rate,

DOI: 10.4018/979-8-3693-1293-3.ch007

blood pressure and respiration increase because we have adapted to respond to acute stress through a fight or flight reaction.

From an evolutionary perspective, heightened anxiety is experienced when we perceive change. It is called anticipatory anxiety (Seligman, 1971). To our early ancestors, a movement in the shadow or an unusual sound might represent a change that could be a threat and it was more adaptive for this to prompt a swift increase in anxiety to energise the body in anticipation of the potential threat. This means that most of us tend not to like change. However, to grow, we have to be willing to experience change and the transition to university and the journey towards achievement is one involving many changes.

This evolved, adaptive response, for both students and non-students, is inappropriate for most stress demands today. Most Western lifestyles mean we are exposed to frequent, non-threatening stress demands – from relationship issues and financial worries to workload and assignment deadlines. The consequence, over time, of this physiological reaction to stress increases diastolic load, wear and tear on the body, muscular-skeletal issues, immune suppression and stress-related illnesses. This is the impact on the body. The effect on the mind is felt psychologically, through changes in mood, mental health and subjective wellbeing.

Stress has also been defined as the stimuli or demands that cause or trigger that psychological and physiological reaction. The first definition represents the Response model of stress, pioneered by Cannon (1932) and Selye (1956) and the 'demands' definition, the Stimulus or Engineering model, was pioneered by Holmes and Rahe's (1967) life events research.

This chapter will explore stress in students from each of these perspectives – from the demands or sources of stress in students and from the effect or response of stress on the mind and body. Both models give little regard to the role of psychology in managing stress: From the Response model perspective, for example, when physiologically stressed, we tend to be more impatient, more emotional and concentration and cognitive functioning suffer (Eysenck, Derakshan, Santos & Calvo, 2007). These are some of the psychological *consequences* of stress, but the role of psychology is much more than the mere consequence of biological stress, it plays a critical role in how successfully we cope with those demands.

Life events research or the Stimulus model has been criticised too. It assumes that most people tend to rate external stress stimuli to similar degrees. However, the assessment or appraisal of stress is heavily influenced by our psychology. We might all see the same stress stimuli but we *perceive* it differently depending, for example, on our age, gender, personality, past experience, on our coping resources and on our histories of past coping (Gibbons, 2022, 2023a, 2023b, 2024).

One of the most cited models of stress, the Transactional model, attempts to redress some of the shortcomings of these earlier models (Lazarus & Folkman,

1987, Figure 1). It incorporates the perception and assessment of stress demands (the primary appraisal) and the factors affecting coping (the secondary appraisal), along with their influence on behaviour and health. The primary appraisal of demands equates to the Stimulus model of stress and the different outcomes that follow a stress experience – such as changes in mood, in health and performance, the Response model. However, this model places the role of psychology front and centre, not just through the different *perspectives* individuals adopt to the same stress demand (the primary appraisal) – remember, *perception* is a mental process, but in terms of the secondary appraisal too. This appraisal refers to our coping resources – the formal and informal support you are able to offer your students, for example, as well as that available across your institution and the support you as an educator are able to draw on. Other coping resources include our sense of control, our coping style, and those factors influencing coping, such as age, gender, confidence or self-efficacy and personality. In this model, psychology is not relegated to a consequence of being stressed, it represents the different ways we rate a stress demand, and that judgment is affected by all those secondary appraisal ingredients, and most of these are psychological factors. This can lead to a judgment that a stress demand is irrelevant, a challenge or a threat, and those factors or ingredients – coping style, past coping experiences, personality etc., are called upon a second time to try and manage the stress demand. That is why the arrow goes both ways in the model.

Figure 1. The transactional model of stress

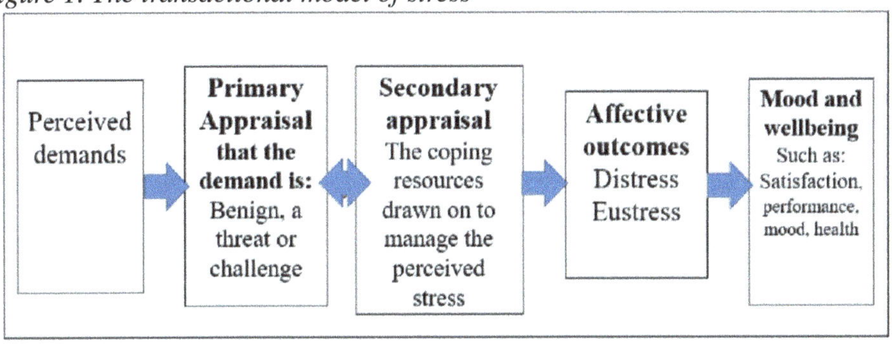

(Lazarus & Folkman, 1987)

This model incorporates a recognition that stress is not, by default, distress. Rather, that a certain level of stress is needed for a stressor or demand to be perceived as a 'challenge' that one can achieve in. The stress that enhances your performance is called eustress and, historically, there has been a paucity of research that has explored the association between stress and improved performance and wellbeing in students (Gibbons, 2008). The model should be viewed in conjunction with Figure

2, where the stress demands associated with optimal performance i.e., challenges one can achieve in, are called sources of eustress (B). Those that are perceived as associated with apathy or boredom (A) or, more often, as exceeding one's capacity to cope (C), are sources of distress (Gibbons, 2008). Our challenge, as educators, is to help our students not avoid stress but to utilise stress to help them achieve.

Figure 2. The curvilinear relationship between stress and student performance

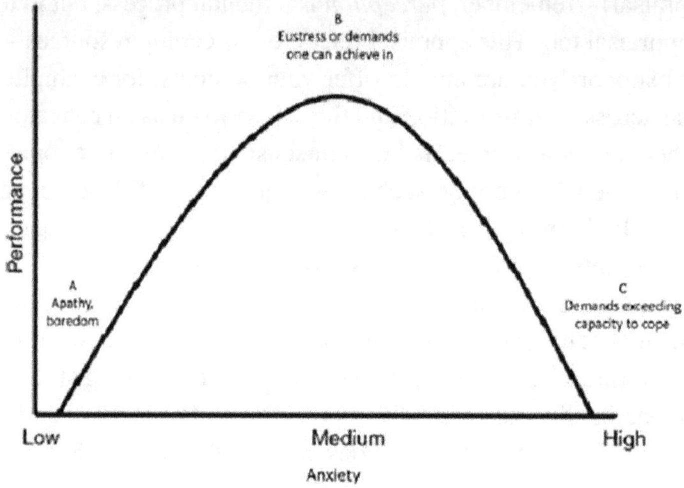

(Gibbons, 2008)

Illustrating the Curvilinear Relationship Between Stress and Student Performance

Imagine a student who knows he has an assignment due but not for several weeks. He is in his first year of study and, while he attends most classes, he does little private study. He knows he should be preparing but he is procrastinating, and he lacks the motivation and, yes, he's probably partying too much! He has some anxiety but not enough to make him that productive. He is at point 'A' in the curvilinear curve.

The same student might find that it is only when the deadline is imminent that he begins, somewhat frantically and probably superficially, to piece together the assignment and because he has not allowed enough time, he has carried out only a superficial search, putting key words into search engines, reading a few abstracts and maybe he has read one chapter or relevant article. He pulls out points that sound relevant but, because it is all last minute, the paragraphs lack structure and because he has not done enough background research and reading and note-taking, he is not sure how relevant his points are, and he can't find critical comment. His references are short and incomplete and he only gets time to skim over his assignment before submitting just a few minutes before the deadline. This student is at point 'C' on our curve.

You can also picture a student who might be better on her time and task management but who is a perfectionist and who is anxious by nature and because she places a high bar on how well she expects to do, her anxiety is higher and because she is a perfectionist, she works long hours outside class. Like a car been driven too hard for too long, without the necessary maintenance checks, the chance of problems increase, and, similarly, for our student, she is at risk of early burnout. Someone working too hard without striking the right work-life balance and/or someone who always expects a high bar of success, runs the risk that their anxiety level goes beyond the optimum to point 'C' on our curve.

The goal, of course, is not to avoid stress but to find that sweet-spot – where we experience some stress, such that study demands are more readily perceived as something one can achieve in. The student who is more proactive in her time management is likely to start planning and to tackle parts of an assignment with time on her side. She will be proactive in searching for relevant information, she will be better at summarising information from class and in her own reading. She'll realise that there is a formula to doing well and while she may not have perfected this formula, she gives herself the best chance by keeping ahead of the curve. Good time management and some discipline helps enormously with this, not least because by completing drafts of assignments ahead of the submission date, it buys time to reflect and to go over and make improvements in the coverage offered on relevant theory, research findings, critical analysis etc. And as one makes in-roads into an assignment, one begins to understand it better, to know what the question is really driving at and to know the more meaningful points and questions one should address and when you are on top of things with time on your side, you know you are coping well. This may not translate into good grades at the start. One has still to master the topic and the skill-set needed to achieve in higher education, but good results and achievement are likely to follow with this formula.

It is important to remember that the experience of stress that equates to eustress is not always or, indeed, often uplifting or enjoyable. Those with reasonable to good time management do still feel the pressure of deadlines and that's not pleasant but it is necessary. So, demands that are a challenge might not always be perceived that way!

Operationalising Stress

Research into stress usually operationalises it in terms of degrees of distress and there will be ample coverage on 'distress' in students in this chapter because it remains dominant in published research. However, there are a growing number of studies that adopt a positive psychology framework and that attempt to measure stress as demands necessary to achieve rather than as only and ever associated with adverse consequences. This is characterised, for example, by the efforts to measure stress demands as hassles (that hold the potential to have an adverse effect on wellbeing) and again as uplifts (that hold the potential to enhance performance and wellbeing and which may buffer against stress-related illness). This work was pioneered by Kanner, Coyne, Schaefer and Lazarus (1981), who designed and validated the daily hassles and uplifting scale. DeLongis, Coyne, Dakof, Folkman and Lazarus (1982), found, for example, in a longitudinal analysis, that daily hassles were predictive of adverse wellbeing and that uplifting ratings had a buffering effect. Such results suggest that stress should be measured not just in terms of major events or chronic stressors but through ratings of more frequent and often daily stressors that can have *both* positive as well as adverse consequences on health. There have been some attempts to measure and incorporate this distress and eustress perspective towards student demands in higher education (e.g. Gibbons, 2008, 2009, 2022, 2023a, 2023b, 2024; Maybery et al., 2002; Wolf, Elston, & Kissling, 1989). These hassle and uplifting ratings attempt to capture the 'threat' and 'challenge' components in the primary appraisal in the Transactional model. However, it is important to remember the earlier caveat – that the stress experiences that may equate to a challenge may often be perceived as stressful and unpleasant. We none of us like deadlines but we would struggle to achieve without them! They are necessary and it is often worth reminding our students of the value of stress in helping them achieve. The next section will consider this primary appraisal side, or the common sources of stress experienced by students.

SOURCES OF STUDENT STRESS

Studying During a Developmental Period

Most students enter university during their adolescence and this developmental period is one characterized by experiences of stress. A survey across 72 countries and sampling 540,000 students, carried out by the Organisation for the Economic Co-operation and Development (OECD), found that 59% reported significant test anxiety, even when they felt well prepared; 66% reported stress associated with poor grades and 37% felt tense and anxious in relation to their efforts to study, indicating high state anxiety and this was compounded, for some, by a tendency towards perfectionism and neuroticism. Females suffered most too, reporting higher anxiety compared to males (OECD, 2017). This survey was with fifteen and sixteen-year old students but the pattern continues for those who go on to higher education.

This is not just because adolescence is continuing but because going to university represents a major life event.

Holmes and Rahe (1967) pioneered the research into stimuli associated with physiological and psychological stress effects, such as increased blood pressure, a suppressed immune response, lowered concentration and changes in mood and illness. Key life events are not just 'events' one would want to avoid, such as a major illness, a break-up in a relationship or a bereavement, but also events experienced as positive and even welcomed, such as going on holiday, starting a new job, a new relationship or going to college. Starting university holds the potential for new friendships, new positive experiences and growth and adventure as well as, of course, uncertainties about the academic challenge. What makes an event stressful is less to do with any obvious positive and negative element and more to do with the amount of change or adjustment the event entails.

For most students, university is a period of change. They are learning to live independently, meet new people, negotiate changes in lifestyle and relationships; adjust to new accommodation arrangements; manage their own finances and all along with the challenges posed by a course that may leave them feeling overwhelmed (Bayram & Bilgel, 2008; Denovan & Macaskill, 2017; Denovan et al., 2019; Ibrahim et al., 2013; Lenz, 2001; Steptoe, Tsud a, & Tanaka, 2007). They are developing new skills and knowledge and will have some, may be frequent, experiences where they find it difficult, and for some, too difficult to achieve their learning goals. It is not unsurprising then that major life events, like attending university during adolescence, are strongly predictive of mood change and the onset of depression (Lewinsohn, Allen, Seeley, & Gotlib, 1999). It is worth reminding students, during their induction, that embarking on their studies is both an adventure and an opportunity to grow but it is one where uncertainty and apprehension, and because of this, some anxiety, is common and, indeed, is necessary.

Academic and Personal Stressors

Sources of stress for students in higher education include academic demands, such as coursework and exams; fear of failure, lack of timely feedback and critical feedback; the quality of teaching and work-life balance (El Ansari, Oskrochi & Haghgoo, 2014, Gibbons, 2022). Gibbons (2022) found that teaching and course demands, along with a range of support – from peers, tutors, the wider university and one's partner, when rated as a hassle, were higher in those 'at risk' of a stress-related illness. Support rated as a hassle was also associated with lower motivation and higher anxiety (Gibbons, 2022, 2023a). Personal sources of stress include financial concerns, managing free time, working part-time while studying, and future concerns (McCloud & Bann, 2019; Gibbons, 2015). The changes students experience as they transition to university are frequently a source of acute stress.

Identity and Stress

While transitioning to university is an opportunity to make new friends, to act in new ways and ways one may have wanted to but did not because of the pressure from friends and peers in the past, it has also been described as a 'loss experience' for students as earlier friendship ties weaken and as they move on from their former identities and former social networks (Scanlon, Rowling, and Weber 2007; Herpen et al., 2020). Critical to a successful transition is for students to establish a new identity. In the same way a young professional identifies with their career, as a 'doctor', a 'teacher', a 'manager' or a 'nurse', for example, students need to establish a 'learner identity'. That means they need to know what it means to learn effectively in higher education. This is as important to their wellbeing and sense of competence as it is for a teacher to know how to teach. The student also has to establish a 'social identity' through new relationships. To identify with a new group or community, for example, with others on one's course or through clubs and societies, by playing sports, and through social connections with new friends. A sense of identity in both these areas has been associated with improved student retention and success (Bowles et al. 2014; Meehan & Howells 2018; Wrench, Garrett & King 2014, Thomas 2012, 2016).

University Expansion and Stress

The numbers of students attending university across north America and Europe has increased year on year since the millennium. This means class sizes are often larger and it means the numbers registering with additional neurodiverse needs has also increased. This places an increased load on the university system, not just in the sheer numbers but in the capacity of faculty and the wider university to meet their statutory requirement to accommodate the needs of students registered with additional learning needs. This has meant that increasing students have found the academic demands more challenging (Andrews & Wilding, 2004).

Stress Responses Creating New Stressors

Research findings suggest that students face, in addition to the academic challenges, significant stressors felt at the individual level, for example in confidence and through interactions with others; and at the social level, in the new people they meet in new living arrangements, in class and in new part-time work. How one responds to these stressors can manifest as new stress demands too, for example through experiences of isolation and loneliness (McIntyre et al. 2018; Richardson, Elliott & Roberts 2017) and while these experiences are not new, it is likely that the experience of loneliness has a greater detrimental effect for students post-pandemic because of the experience of enforced isolation students faced earlier in their lives during the Covid-19 pandemic (Gubric, Badovinac, & Johri 2020).

In the Student Academic Experience Survey (SAES, Neves & Hewitt, 2020) (n=10,227), taken in March 2020, after most students had stopped face-to-face teaching, there was a marked increase in loneliness and decline in mood compared to pre-pandemic levels. McIntyre et al., (2018) identified academic and non-academic predictors of distress in 1135 UK university students. Loneliness was the strongest overall predictor and this replicated earlier results in the UK (Richardson, Elliot & Roberts, 2017) and in the US (Hefner & Eisenberg, 2009). Loneliness is not inevitable, but it is common and letting your students know that it is not unusual is important, along with the different ways it can be countered.

Perceptions of Support

Support is one coping ingredient and is covered in the chapter on coping, but its absence can also pose as a source of stress. The academic demands of most programmes increase as the course progresses, not just in terms of the weighting of assignments towards final year degree classifications but in students' experience of support (Tett, Cree & Christie, 2017). In a longitudinal study in Scotland, Tett et al., (2017) found that, while students felt they had a better understanding of the academic demands required of them as their course progressed, they felt there was less academic support. This is likely to reflect the expectation on students as independent learners i.e., the support is still there but students are expected to be more proactive compared to when they are transitioning in their first year.

Assessment and Feedback

Jones et al (2021) thematically analysed the results from a number of focus groups with separate groups of staff (n=33) and students (n=32) in groups of 6-13 participants from universities in the north of England and in Northern Ireland. They sought to explore the impact of pedagogy, curriculum and assessment design as sources of stress with both positive and negative effects on student mental health.

Course assessments are a necessity to test the rigour of a course, its learning outcomes and to award qualifications appropriate to university standards and any related accrediting body. However, the potential and experience of failure can impact on self-esteem and mental health, and while disappointing results are inevitable if not necessary to grow in knowledge and skills, the challenge is how best to support students. Student participants commented that being assessed meant one felt part of a 'competition' where, even if you achieved relative to the baseline of earlier successes, you might still feel disappointment because of comparisons made with others. Module co-ordinators briefing students in lieu of assessments and guiding them on how to reframe and not catastrophise results and to put the focus on learning goals, rather than 'perceived' competition, could help. Both faculty and students questioned the value of numeric grades based on norm-based referencing when criterion, competence-based referencing might be an acceptable alternative for some assessments. This could limit the stress associated with the 'competitive' element of assessment.

The traditional exam and essay-based assessment, especially where exams were closed-book and time-restricted and multiple choice, were often perceived as stressful, not just because of associated pressure but because they were perceived as often an inaccurate reflection of content understanding. There is an educational argument for the value of the different types of assessment, but other, more novel and inventive methods of assessment are increasingly offered, such as leaflet design and commentary, creating an academic poster, reviewing a website or a policy outline or an interview or a podcast, or creating one, as well as an array of problem-based learning. Often courses will include modules that draw on a range of assessments. This left respondents in the student focus groups asking why students could not be given a choice on assessment or even to propose designing their own. While the logistics of such a move are considerable, they are not insurmountable, and it gives students the power to choose a method that matches their preferences, and which might have more practical application in terms of employability. Both student and staff panels recognised that the nature of assessments had to be mapped and scaffolded around the broader learning objectives related to the skills and knowledge students were expected to develop across their course, but varying the nature of assessments and involving students in their design might help students better manage associated stress as well as being more valid to the types of work one might do in graduate employment.

The nature of assessments can pose an additional stress to the increasing number of students entering higher education with additional neurodiverse needs. Most countries, in the West at least, make it a statutory requirement that universities support learners with additional needs. In the UK, for example, the Equality Act 2010, means universities have a legal duty to make 'reasonable adjustments' for students with protected characteristics (including 'mental impairment'). In practice, this means that a register is made of students with additional needs and attempts are made to address these on a case-by-case basis i.e., these students face the same assessments presented to the course cohort and which they will perceive as more difficult because they are not catered to their additional needs and then accommodations are made on a case-by-case basis. Offering more diverse, alternative assessments and by involving students in their design and doing this earlier in the process, could help these students manage the stress associated with their assessment. It is important too that any process adopted for accommodating students with additional needs is transparent to all students to avoid the perception of unfairness or favouritism.

Interestingly, students from all the universities sampled, experienced traditional assessments [essays, reports and exams] with assessment deadlines bunched together. This timing issue seems widespread and can adversely impact individual performance. It is an issue that is entirely avoidable. With forward planning, educators and course designers can avoid this unnecessary bunching of assessments and the stress it causes students. Of course, it is possible for students to impose their own internal deadlines to stagger their workload, but they will find this no easier than you or I would! The nature of feedback was a related issue with students commenting that feedback was often critical but not always meaningful and learning from feedback is only possible if there is sufficient time to receive and learn from it before the next assignment is due.

Even with the kinds of accommodations proposed to current assessments, the respondents in Jones et al., (2021) study acknowledged that assessments, by necessity, involve stress and at a level that may impact wellbeing, but which is still needed to learn and is therefore beneficial in the longer term. It is necessary, as students move from the more teacher-directed learning approach common in schools and colleges, to becoming a more independent learner in university, just as it is to develop independence in one's adult life and success relies on this kind of autonomy. Student wellbeing and mental health has traditionally been seen as the focus of staff involved with pastoral and welfare issues. The Jones et al., (2021) study highlights the importance to educators to also consider the structure of a course, its assessments, their planning and delivery and the nature of feedback, not just from a learning and education perspective but as sources of stress that can impact student wellbeing.

Social Media and Learning – Vice or Virtue

Using social media is all Gen Z have known and the majority of university students today fall into this category. Hartnup, Dong and Eisingerich (2018) carried out in-depth interviews with 78 UK university students. They thematically analysed the results and found that social media platforms (e.g. Snapchat, Instagram, Facebook, WhatsApp, YouTube etc) were both a source of stress and a powerful source of coping. They offered a medium through which to keep in contact with family and existing friends and to contact and build new friendships with other students.

However, establishing an online persona for different audiences can also be stressful, especially in relation to the norms about how to fit in.

They found that social media was used to work with student peers e.g. through WhatsApps tutorial groups. However, the authors reported that this was associated with a sense of potential competition as students can sometimes be reluctant to share insights they might later want to use in their assignments. They also reported that students may use social media to engage with learning passively, for example, by searching and watching brief related content on YouTube.

Using social media to network, to relax and to nurture new friendships are all positive outcomes and YouTube offers a plethora of excellent education resources, together with the ever-growing number of free education related Apps. Fani and Ghaemi (2011) illustrate how Vygotsky's zone of proximal development is relevant here. This zone refers the proportion of learning that can occur with 'assistance', that could be in the form of a teacher, a peer or from online resources. I recommend my students to tap into the range of apps, podcasts and YouTube clips that dumb down areas of their learning and then that progressively tackle more complex learning. This is a critical part of the learning journey. I emphasise that they must never cite these in the reference section of their assignment but social media, if used strategically, can be a useful set of tools to ground oneself in related learning and to understand some of the more complex areas, not as an alternatively to the academic sources students are directed to but as a bridge to help them make better sense of those sources when they do tackle them.

THE IMPORTANCE OF STAFF WELLBEING

Brewster et al., (2022) drew on data gathered from a series of focus groups drawing on university staff and students from across the UK who attended a series of day-long 'roadshow' events designed to promote and shape the formation of the Student Minds University Mental Health Charter. This is a Charter established by the UK charity – Student Minds, whose mission is to promote the mental health of all students.

Data was drawn from six staff and student wellbeing focus groups (n= 3-7) who responded to research questions on the factors affecting student mental health. Themes were identified related to staff and student wellbeing. The consensus was that most university policies explicitly or implicitly put a priority on student mental wellbeing over staff wellbeing. It was reported that university cultures often left staff with the impression that their wellbeing was, not just less important, but often in opposition to the focus on student mental health. For example, staff workload models make explicit reference to expectations in research, grants and publications and hours of teaching i.e., to competitive performance-based metrics (Lynch, 2010) and with many staff on temporary or precarious academic contracts. Few universities give acknowledgement to the pastoral academic role of staff in workload models or in promotion applications. The quality of teaching, pedagogy and pastoral support available to students will suffer, and increase as sources of stress, if staff are overworked, if they perceive their important work is undervalued and if they run the risk of burn-out.

National policies to widen participation need to be matched too with additional staff support and training to best support the mental health of an ever more diverse student population. In sum, optimising student mental health cannot be done without successfully catering to the needs of staff too. It was acknowledged that a change in culture and practice to enhance staff wellbeing is ongoing across many universities but the shift in culture is unlikely to be achieved quickly and can only be done through a whole university approach. The evidence suggests that student wellbeing is impacted by their experience in class and in their pastoral experience, and managing the wellbeing of teaching staff is important in its own right, as well as in its benefits to nurture student wellbeing.

TRYING TO CAPTURE THE EUSTRESS AND DISTRESS ELEMENTS OF STRESS DEMANDS

Across several studies, with different populations of students, Gibbons (2010, 2022a, 2023, 2024) has adopted a positive psychology framework to measure student stress experiences using a hassle and uplifting scale. This allows for the sources of stress to be identified associated with both positive, eustress experiences as well as measuring those sources of stress associated with distress.

Gibbons, (2008) developed a scale (Index of Sources of Stress in Nursing-students, ISSN) to measure sources of stress in nursing students and which incorporated a hassles and uplifting response scale. Following focus group interviews with final year nursing students, three clusters of stressors were identified – those related to learning and teaching; to placement experiences and to how the course was organized. In validating the ISSN scale, Gibbons, Dempster and Moutray, (2009) compared and hassle and uplifting ratings between those 'at risk' of a stress-related illness and those 'not at risk'. Taking the traditional approach to stress, one would expect that, as hassle ratings increase, so do the risks of developing a stress-related illness but the results reported no difference in the hassle ratings between those 'at risk' and 'not at risk'. Where there was a difference, it was in the perception of uplifting opportunities, with those 'at risk' perceiving fewer opportunities to achieve. As these students were on the same course, at the same point in their studies, facing broadly similar demands, it is likely that the difference can be attributed, not to any variation in the demands they faced but to the perspective the student adopted towards those stress demands. Those who reframed challenges as an opportunity to achieve or who successfully construed demands as less threatening, had better mental health. This illustrates both the power of an optimistic outlook or reframing as an effective cognitive coping strategy and it is a research finding that would have been missed had not both eustress and distress demands been measured. Typically, module evaluations use only a Likert scale (from 'strongly agree' through to 'strongly disagree') response scale. This fails to capture how learning demands can be experienced as *both* a help and hinderance to learning. There is scope, for you as an educator, to at least verbally seek both in your formal or informal review sessions with your students.

To illustrate, in a survey of psychology students (n=162) during the pandemic, Gibbons (2023a) modified the National Student Survey (NSS), used nationally and annually across the UK, to measure student satisfaction. The Likert response scale on the NSS was replaced with a hassles and uplifting scale. The results reported that support rated as a hassle was associated with lower course satisfaction. This referred to peer support and the broader infrastructure of support provided by the university. Interestingly, support as an uplift did not feature. Neves and Hewitt (2020) and Gibbons (2015) found positive ratings of student support, pre-pandemic, to be a key predictor of satisfaction. The significance of support as a hassle, but not an uplift, suggested it functioned differently during the pandemic. During a period where most students were literally isolated at home, with their only contact with others via a computer screen, support opportunities through online peer learning activities, for example, in seminars and tutorials and through one-to-one pastoral support, took on a new importance. The ratings given to support as a source of stress could also have reflected the broader disappointment students felt during the pandemic where most experienced prolonged isolation (Gibbons, 2023a).

In this same study, where course resources were rated as stimulating learning motivation, anxiety *increased*. This appears counterintuitive, but some anxiety, like some stress, is needed to perform well and, where students rate resources 'as stimulating their enthusiasm for further learning' (an item that measured learning motivation), it suggested the anxiety reported enhanced performance and this supports the role of anxiety in states of eustress (Eysenck et al., 2007; Gibbons, 2008, 2015).

Identifying the sources and experience of stress that are likely to enhance performance and are thereby uplifting as opposed to a hinderance or hassle, is a key challenge for those who explore this aspect of positive psychology. The stress that helps you achieve may be experienced as unpleasant and unwanted at the time and, because of that, be more likely to be rated as a hassle. It is a challenge for researchers to discriminate between these different types of stress, not least, because it is a challenge for students and indeed for any of us when facing the stress and pressure to deliver. It is usually not pleasant, but it is usually necessary. If you do carry out teaching or module reviews, it is worth drawing your students' attention to this distinction.

Jones et al., (2021) identified the nature of assessments and feedback as sources of stress. Gibbons (2024) explored this from a positive psychology 'distress and eustress' perspective. He found that where students (n=184) rated assessment and feedback as an uplift it was predictive of learning motivation. This survey was carried out with a psychology cohort where the course had changed aspects of assessment and feedback that corresponded to some of the recommendations linked to the Jones et al., (2021) study outlined earlier. For example, the course moved to standardising how feedback was given, with a focus on 'strengths'; 'areas to improve' and 'how'. Assessment deadlines were closely monitored to ensure deadlines were staggered and students, in this cohort, benefitted from the introduction of a two-week, non-teaching assessment period midway through each semester to focus solely on assignments, rather than running the risk of missing classes to meet imminent deadlines.

Students met their tutors fortnightly to engage in small group teaching and they met them individually, once per semester, to monitor progress, with a focus on reflecting on feedback in relation to upcoming assessments. These initiatives helped students in their time-management, in their organisation and in learning from feedback.

Another factor measured on the NSS is 'learning opportunities' and when rated as a hassle, it was negatively related to learning motivation. Items that measure this referred to the opportunity to explore ideas and concepts and the extent to which the course built on what a student already knew. Any programme of study is a work in progress and there may be a legitimate perception that some aspects of delivery could be improved. However, both hassle and uplifting ratings should be interpreted through the lens of positive psychology: That is, to grow, one has to move out of one's comfort zone. This means learning will, at times, be hard, may be perceived as 'too hard'. Maftei, Dumitriu and Holman, (2021), found, for example, that most students who succeed in university, reported experiencing imposter syndrome at different periods during their studies. These hassle ratings may reflect the necessary stress, often perceived as distressing, associated with growth and these findings offer another example of the difficulty in distinguishing between the stress that helps and the stress that hinders learning.

This section considered the various demands or sources of stress students experience. The next considers the different ways students respond to these demands, or, put simply, to the impact stress has on wellbeing, mental health and functioning.

THE EFFECTS OF STRESS ON STUDENTS

Lazarus and Folkman's (1987) Transactional model interprets stress as an interaction between the person and the environment – the focus is on individual appraisals of environmental demands. Secondary appraisal, 'coping' resources, are called upon in making the initial judgement that a stressor is benign or irrelevant, a threat or a challenge and it is drawn on again to help manage the perceived stress. Where the individual appraises a stress demand as exceeding their capacity to cope, then the individual is exposed to the effects of stress. This is frequently reported in terms of its effect on wellbeing.

Defining Wellbeing

This is defined as: '…a state of complete physical, mental and social wellbeing and not merely the absence of disease and infirmity' (World Health Organization, 2006, p.100). While critics question the assumption of 'completeness' as integral to wellbeing, the definition highlights the critical role of psychology in wellbeing. This is reflected in Hughes and Spanner (2019), definition of wellbeing – they put the emphasis on a student's capacity to 'fully exercise their cognitive, emotional, physical and social powers, leading to flourishing' (Hughes & Spanner, 2019, p9). The mental and social elements have been operationalised through a range of outcomes, including mental health, mood, loneliness, motivation satisfaction and subjective wellbeing or happiness.

Psychological Distress, Mood and Mental Health

Sarker et al., (2017) undertook a systematic review of stress and the associated symptoms of stress and anxiety in medical students (n=9922) in India. The studies varied dramatically in the prevalence of depression (from 8.7% to 71.3%) and anxiety (from 34.5% to 51.3%), and with rates of stress at 51.3% for the studies reviewed, with female students scoring higher than males on all on all outcomes. The authors point to the need to support students more in placement and to the need to encourage students to utilise more the support structures available. These rates are comparable with findings in the West. The demand for university counselling services, for example, in universities in the UK, Europe, the USA and Australia, have grown year on year, suggesting that students are reporting increasing levels of psychological distress (Broglia, Millings & Barkham 2017; Thorley 2017; Storrie, Ahern, and Tuckett 2010). Stallman (2010), in a study of almost 6500 university students in Australia, reported levels of generalised psychological distress (as measured by the Kessler 10 scale, Kessler et al., 2010) at 84%, almost three times higher than the 29%

reported in the non-student populations. Larcombe, et al., (2016) surveyed over 5000 students in Australia and measured anxiety and depression, the two outcomes most commonly used to operationalise mood. They found that 13% reported depression and 18% anxiety symptoms rated as severe or extremely severe and this compared with an incidence rate of 5% in the non-student population.

Such findings parallel the higher prevalence of mental health issues found in students compared to non-students in the UK (Kerr, 2013; Gibbons, 2022; Royal College of Psychiatrists, 2011), in Europe and in the USA (Dyrbye, Thomas, & Shanafelt, 2006; Eisenberg et al., 2013). In America, for example, the Healthy Minds Survey (HMS), a survey routinely carried in the US since 2005, has reported a year-on-year increase in the prevalence of mental health issues in university students and, notably, an increased reporting in anxiety among female students; in students from lower socioeconomic backgrounds and in students from sexual minority groups (Eisenberg et al., 2013).

Research across western student populations and those in China, Japan, India the Asia-Pacific nations and Africa, all report student examination stress is associated with a range of mental health issues, such as depression, anxiety and reduced happiness; along with burnout, panic attacks and even suicidal thinking (Zhang *et al.*, 2012; Sarker et al., 2017; Ribeiro *et al.*, 2018; Pascoe, Hetrick & Parker, 2019; Murray-Gibbons & Gibbons, 2023). The range of stresses students experience can also lead to a range of physical effects and behaviours, including sleep disturbance, loss of appetite and poor physical health, an increased sedentary lifestyle and substance misuse (Curcio, Ferrara, & De 2006; Simic & Manenica 2012; Stults-Kolehmainen & Sinha 2014).

A widely used measure of mental health is the General Health Questionnaire (GHQ). Approximately, 15–19% of the general (non-student) population are categorised as 'at risk' of developing a stress-related illness based on this measure (Morris, Earl & Neave, 2016). This refers, not to life-threatening illnesses, but to complaints ranging from mouth ulcers, cold sores, digestive and intestinal problems, to tension headaches, back problems, irritability and mood swings. Among student populations, this can range from 30% to over 60%, depending on the study and on the discipline the student follows, with health professional students tending to be at higher risk (Gibbons, 2010, 2022; Turner, Bartlett, Andiappan & Cabot, 2015). These stress effects have been observed in students in the UK; in North America (Adlaf, Demers & Gilksman, 2004; Blanco et al., 2008); Australia (Stallman, 2010) and Sweden (Vaez, Kristenson & Laflamme, 2004) and the experience of stress has been directly linked to student attrition and retention issues (Chemers & Garcia, 2001).

The Impact of Mental Health on Other Functioning

Gibbons (2022) carried out a one sample t-test, comparing the mental health of students (n=162) studying during the pandemic against pre-pandemic normative data from a cohort of UK medical students (n=251) (James, Yates & Ferguson, 2013). Those studying during the pandemic had much higher scores on the GHQ, with a large effect size reported and 68.5% of the pandemic sample 'at risk' of a stress-related illness. While the pandemic is behind us, its effect on student wellbeing is likely to be long lasting, as illustrated by Gubric et al., (2020) findings, outlined earlier.

The effects of psychological distress impact on wellbeing and, in turn, key cognitive processes, such as information-processing, attention, memory, problem-solving, along with motivation and emotional regulation (American Psychiatric Association, 2013; Maslach, Schaufeli, & Leiter, 2001; Marin et al., 2011). Lipson and Eisenberg's (2018) analysed data from the Healthy Minds Study from four universities across the US and found that mental health issues were predictive of lower self-efficacy and motivation and increased academic dissatisfaction. This is consistent with the findings that adverse wellbeing and emotional reasons are commonly cited by students who consider deferring or giving up their studies (Baik, Naylor, & Arkoudis,2015).

Some Positive Effects of Stress

Becoming a student holds the potential for new friendships, new positive experiences, and growth. Some insight into the adverse effects of stress have been reported but the coverage would be incomplete without referencing some of the findings on the positive effects of stress and it is important that you as educators are able to convey this more complete picture of the stress experience to your students. Toyama and Sakurai (1999) explored the relationship between hassle and uplifting ratings as predictors of health in Japanese college students. The scale they used was a new one and their exploratory factor analysis revealed six factors. The scale was also valid when the different factors were totaled, and they found that the collective measure on daily hassles was associated with poorer mental health and the collective measure of uplifts was associated with positive mental health.

Gibbons (2010) surveyed a sample of final year nursing students (n=171) and found that uplifting ratings on teaching and learning (compared to ratings on placement experiences and course organisation experiences) were predictors of students' sense of personal achievement (a component of Maslach and Jackson's burnout scale, 1986). Gibbons (2010) used this measure of burn-out as an outcome measure because it included not just emotional exhaustion and depersonalisation as outcomes but personal achievement as a positive effect too.

In a survey of psychology students in Northern Ireland, Gibbons (2015) found that the more learning resources – from course specific to the wider library and university infrastructure of support, were rated as uplifting, the more students felt part of a learning community. In the same study, the more teaching experience was rated as uplifting and the more students felt able to utilize the social opportunities on the course and more broadly (through clubs and societies and social events for example), the higher was course satisfaction.

Interestingly, in a survey of second year psychology students (n=162), during the pandemic, Gibbons (2022) found that uplifting ratings for learning and teaching were associated with improved mental health; and the more teaching resources were rated as 'intellectually stimulating' (for example through pre-recorded lectures, live seminars and tutorials and through online quizzes), the higher was course satisfaction; and uplifting ratings for social opportunities predicted higher learning motivation. These results are offered to illustrate that the stress effects for students should not be construed just in terms of their adverse impact on mental health, mood, and wellbeing but on their positive effects too. Even during the pandemic, different aspects of the university experience were associated with improved mental health, mood, satisfaction, and motivation.

The Validity of Positive Effects Using Hassles and Uplifting Measures

You may be involved in developing or reviewing the measures used to evaluate student experience and research has shown that it is important to consider the order in which the items are asked on hassle and uplifting scales. Maybery et al., (2002) found that, in a study of university students (n=123), where they were asked to rate 143 events as hassles and then as uplifts, the uplifting ratings were lower if participants had been asked to do the hassle rating first. The same authors replicated this finding with a middle-aged sample (n=104) but there was no suppression of the hassle ratings if participants completed the uplifting ratings first. The authors suggest that the hassle evaluation was more often associated with negative mood, and this carried over and impacted the appraisal on uplifting ratings. Given this pattern was not observed when reversed, they suggest hassle and uplifting ratings should begin with the uplifting scale first. The hassle ratings are likely to prompt an anticipatory threat response, and it is adaptive for this to trigger a stronger stress reaction than an uplifting rating would trigger an equivalent positive affect. The same criticism could be levelled at Gibbons (2015, 2022, 2023a) efforts to measure hassles and uplifts in students – students rate each item on the NSS as a hassle and then as an uplift. The effect may not be as great because each item is rated as a hassle and then as an uplift before moving on to the next item, rather than rate all the items as hassles and then, a second time, as uplifts. If hassle ratings tend to suppress-uplifting ratings, the findings offered here on their association with improved wellbeing and learning outcomes, such as motivation and course satisfaction, may be an under-estimate of the degree to which students experience eustress and an under-estimate of the strength of the association between uplifting ratings and these positive stress effects.

Future Directions in Measuring Student Stress

Brown (2018), in reviewing the research on mental health in university students, makes two important observations. First, most research is cross-sectional and usually tests participants once. There is a paucity of longitudinal research on the sources of stress, their effects and on how students cope. Second, most research targets mental health distress or, more simply, the adverse consequences of stress. Not enough is done to explore the positive conceptions of stress, for example through uplifting ratings of demands experienced by students, and in the positive effects, through improved mental health, flourishing or performing optimally and through measures of eudaumonic as opposed to just hedonistic wellbeing. The latter refers to individual-centred benefits, captured by measures of life satisfaction, enjoyment, and subjective happiness, for example. Eudaumonic welbeing refers to the benefits derived from one's connection with others, through virtuous acts, through creativity and achievement. A redress is needed in the focus of research into student stress if students are to be better served in their experience at university. These same factors should be considered by educators who wish to assess the student experience as part of module evaluations and wider student experience surveys.

CONCLUSION

As an educator, I would encourage you to incorporate some of the key take-aways from this chapter into the guidance you offer your students – In summary, attending university represents an opportunity to grow and develop. To expand one's identity and to develop new skills, new interests and new relationships. For most students, it occurs during adolescence, and this is a developmental period often associated with mood changes. Attending university is also a period of change, and anxiety is an adaptive response to change. Specific demands include those that relate to academic factors, such as course work and exams and fear of failure, and personal sources of stress, such as relationship issues, accommodation arrangements and work-life balance, and how to utilize social media to your advantage as a learner.

Students, to achieve, must develop a new learner and social identity. In transitioning to university, it is likely that old friendship ties weaken, and new ones evolve, and this has been associated with a 'loss' experience and students have to adapt to this. In the same way teachers need to learn how to teach to establish their 'teacher identity', students need to develop their higher education skill set to develop a 'learner identity'. And they need to navigate and establish new friendships and working relationships to establish their new 'social identity'.

As university enrolments grow, so too do the demands on faculty, not just in student numbers but in the diversity of student need and catering effectively to these demands can only be successful done when consideration is given to the workload and wellbeing of faculty, as well as for students. The next chapter on coping is framed around how students cope but I would ask you to reflect on your own coping on the points raised.

Students face different demands across their studies. Early in their studies they are transitioning from the more directive approach experienced in school and college to one where they are required to become more independent. They are learning new ways of studying and for the majority, who leave home, new ways of living. This can lead to new friendships and a new meaning in life, but it is often associated with increased anxiety, and it can also lead to isolation and loneliness or through a greater identification with the expectation from peers and this peer influence can have positive and negative effects on wellbeing.

The academic pressure increases on students as their course progresses, not least in the greater weight given to assessments but often in the changing perceptions towards support and in the perceived competition over results. Educators can play an important role in briefing students ahead of assessments on how to reframe potential results, with the spotlight on learning goals rather than perceived competition, for example, and there may be scope to offer more inventive assessments and even to involve students in their design, as well as adopting criterion-based rather than norm-based referencing for some assessments.

Most research construes stress as distress but some stress is needed to achieve, and this has been operationalized using hassle and uplifting scales. The advantage of this approach is that it allows one to capture not just the adverse impacts of stress but to identify the stress associated with optimal performance and wellbeing. The approach is not without its limitations. While an inspiring lecture that enthuses a student with new learning and motivation might easily be construed as 'uplifting', so the stress of a deadline and working hard to understand complex points is needed to achieve but is unlikely to be experienced as 'uplifting'. Such stress demands are unpleasant and distressing but necessary and attempts to square this circle come by allowing for interpretations of hassle ratings as both, potentially, sources of stress needed to achieve and sources of stress that have an adverse effect. The counterintuitive finding that it was not necessarily hassle ratings that were the predictor of adverse wellbeing but the absence of uplifting opportunities, suggests that there is merit in pursuing this positive psychology interpretation of stress (Gibbons et al., 2009). Understanding the sources of stress and their effects would not be complete without also considering how students cope, and it is the influences on coping that is the focus of the next chapter.

DISCUSSION POINTS

1. How does the distinction between distress and eustress contribute to our understanding of stress in educational settings, and what implications does this have for designing interventions that enhance student well-being and performance?
2. In what ways can educators critically assess their teaching methods, assessment designs, and classroom environments to minimise distress while promoting optimal levels of challenge for students' growth and achievement?
3. How does the Transactional Model of Stress advance our understanding of individual differences in stress perception and response, and what are the practical applications of this model for educators to support students?
4. How can higher education institutions create systemic approaches that support the mental health of both students and educators?

REFERENCES

Adlaf, E. M., Demers, A., & Gliksman, L. (2000). *Canadian campus survey 2004.* Centre for Addiction and Mental Health.

Andrews, B., & Wilding, J. M. (2004). The relation of depression and anxiety to life-stress and achievement in students. *British Journal of Psychology, 95*(Pt 4), 509–521.

Baik, C., Naylor, R., & Arkoudis, S. (2015). *The first year experience in Australian universities: Findings from two decades.* Melbourne Centre for the Study of Education.

Bayram, N., & Bilgel, N. (2008). The prevalence and socio-demographic correlations of depression, anxiety and stress among a group of university students. *Social Psychiatry and Psychiatric Epidemiology, 43*(8), 667–672. PMID: 18398558

Blanco, C., Okuda, M., Wright, C., Hasin, D. S., Grant, B. F., Liu, S. M., & Olfson, M. (2008). Mental health of college students and their non–college-attending peers: Results from the national epidemiologic study on alcohol and related conditions. *Archives of General Psychiatry, 65*(12), 1429–1437. DOI: 10.1001/archpsyc.65.12.1429 PMID: 19047530

Bowles, A., Fisher, R., McPhail, R., Rosenstreich, D., & Dobson, A. (2014). Staying the Distance: Students' Perceptions of Enablers of Transition to Higher Education. *Higher Education Research & Development, 33*(2), 212–225. DOI: 10.1080/07294360.2013.832157

Brewster, L., Jones, E., Priestley, M., Wilbraham, S. J., Spanner, L., & Hughes, G. (2022). 'Look after the staff and they would look after the students' cultures of wellbeing and mental health in the university setting. *Journal of Further and Higher Education, 46*(4), 548–560. DOI: 10.1080/0309877X.2021.1986473

Broglia, E., Millings, A., & Barkham, M. (2017). Challenges to Addressing Student Mental Health in Embedded Counselling Services: A Survey of UK Higher and Further Education Institutions. *British Journal of Guidance & Counselling, 46*(4), 441–445. DOI: 10.1080/03069885.2017.1370695

Brown, J. S. (2018). Student mental health: Some answers and more questions. *Journal of Mental Health (Abingdon, England), 27*(3), 193–196. DOI: 10.1080/09638237.2018.1470319 PMID: 29768071

Cannon, W. B. (1932). *The Wisdom of the Body.* Norton.

Chemers, M. M., Hu, L. T., & Garcia, B. F. (2001). Academic self-efficacy and first year college student performance and adjustment. *Journal of Educational Psychology, 93*(1), 55.

Curcio, G., Ferrara, M., & De Gennaro, L. (2006). Sleep loss, learning capacity and academic performance. *Sleep Medicine Reviews, 10*(5), 323-337. .DOI: 10.1016/j.smrv.2005.11.001

DeLongis, A., Coyne, J. C., Dakof, G., Folkman, S., & Lazarus, R. S. (1982). Relationship of daily hassles, uplifts, and major life events to health status. *Health Psychology, 1*, 119–136.

Denovan, A., Dagnall, N., Dhingra, K., & Grogan, S. (2019). Evaluating the Perceived Stress Scale among UK university students: Implications for stress measurement and management. *Studies in Higher Education, 44*(1), 120–133.

Denovan, A., & Macaskill, A. (2017). Stress and subjective wellbeing among first year UK undergraduate students. *Journal of Happiness Studies, 18*(2), 505–525. DOI: 10.1007/s10902-016-9736-y

Dyrbye, L. N., Thomas, M. R., & Shanafelt, T. D. (2006). Systematic review of Depression, anxiety, and other indicators of psychological distress among U.S. and Canadian medical students. *Academic Medicine, 81*(4), 354–373. PMID: 16565188

Eisenberg, D., Hunt, J., & Speer, N. (2013). Mental health in American colleges and universities: Variation across student subgroups and across campuses. *The Journal of Nervous and Mental Disease, 201*(1), 60–67. PMID: 23274298

El Ansari, W., Oskrochi, R., & Haghgoo, G. (2014). Are students' symptoms and health complaints associated with perceived stress at university? Perspectives from the United Kingdom and Egypt. *International Journal of Environmental Research and Public Health, 11*(10), 9981–10002. PMID: 25264677

Eysenck, M. W., Derakshan, N., Santos, R., & Calvo, M. G. (2007). Anxiety and cognitive performance: Attentional control theory. *Emotion (Washington, D.C.), 7*(2), 336. DOI: 10.1037/1528-3542.7.2.336 PMID: 17516812

Fani, T., & Ghaemi, F. (2011). Implications of Vygotsky's zone of proximal development (ZPD) in teacher education: ZPTD and self-scaffolding. *Procedia: Social and Behavioral Sciences, 29*, 1549–1554.

Gibbons, C. (2008). *Measuring Stress and Eustress in Nursing Students* (Doctoral dissertation, Queen's University Belfast). https://ethos.bl.uk/OrderDetails.do?uin=uk.bl.ethos.501265

Gibbons, C. (2009). The two sides of stress. *Nursing Standard*, *23*(44), 61.

Gibbons, C. (2010). Stress, coping and burn-out in nursing students. *International Journal of Nursing Studies*, (47), 1299–1309. PMID: 20359710

Gibbons, C. (2015) Stress, eustress and the National Student Survey, *Psychology Teaching Review, 21*(2), 86-92. https://eric.ed.gov/?id=EJ1146635

Gibbons, C. (2022). Understanding the role of stress, personality and coping on learning motivation and mental health in university students during a pandemic. *BMC Psychology*, *10*(1), 261. DOI: 10.1186/s40359-022-00971-w PMID: 36357950

Gibbons, C. (2023a). Untangling the role of optimism, pessimism and coping influences on student mood, motivation and satisfaction. *Innovations in Education and Teaching International*. Advance online publication. DOI: 10.1080/14703297.2023.2260780

Gibbons, C. (2023b). Surviving a pandemic - Understanding the role of student stress, personality and coping on course satisfaction and anxiety during lockdown. *Innovations in Education and Teaching International*, *60*, 463–475. https://www.tandfonline.com/doi/full/10.1080/14703297.2022.2064326

Gibbons, C. (2024). Not just surviving, but flourishing – insights into student coping, anxiety and motivation. *Research Square*. DOI: 10.21203/rs.3.rs-4177097/v1

Gibbons, C., Dempster, M., & Moutray, M. (2009). Surveying nursing students on their sources of stress: A validation study. *Nurse Education Today*, *29*(8), 867–872. PMID: 19501429

Gubric, N., Badovinac, S., & Johri, A. M. (2020). Student Mental Health in the Midst of the COVID-19 Pandemic: A Call for Further Research and Immediate Solutions. *The International Journal of Social Psychiatry*, *66*(5), 517–518. DOI: 10.1177/0020764020925108 PMID: 32364039

Hartnup, B., Dong, L., & Eisingerich, A. B. (2018). How an environment of stress and social risk shapes student engagement with social media as potential digital learning platforms: Qualitative study. *JMIR Medical Education*, *4*(2), e10069. PMID: 30006324

Hefner, J. L., & Eisenberg, D. (2009). Social support and mental health among college students. *The American Journal of Orthopsychiatry*, *79*, 491–499. PMID: 20099940

Herpen, , Hofman, & Severiens. (2020). A Head Start in Higher Education: The Effect of A Transition Intervention on Interaction, Sense of Belonging, and Academic Performance. *Studies in Higher Education*, *45*(4), 862–877. DOI: 10.1080/03075079.2019.1572088

Holmes, T. H., & Rahe, R. H. (1967). The social readjustment rating scale. *Psychosomatic Medicine*, *11*, 213–218. PMID: 6059863

Hughes, G., & Spanner, L. (2019). *The University Mental Health Charter*. Student Minds.

Ibrahim, A. K., Kelly, S. J., Adams, C. E., & Glazebrook, C. (2013). A systematic review of studies of depression prevalence in university students. *Journal of Psychiatric Research*, *47*(3), 391–400. PMID: 23260171

James, D., Yates, J., & Ferguson, E. (2013). Can the 12-item general health questionnaire be used to identify medical students who might 'struggle'on the medical course? A prospective study on two cohorts. *BMC Medical Education*, *13*, 1–8. PMID: 23548161

Jones, E., Priestley, M., Brewster, E., Wilbraham, S. J., Hughes, G., & Spanner, L. (2021). Student wellbeing and assessment in higher education: The balancing act. *Assessment & Evaluation in Higher Education*, *46*(3), 438–450. DOI: 10.1080/02602938.2020.1782344

Kanner, A. D., Coyne, J. C., Schaefer, C., & Lazarus, R. S. (1981). Comparison of two modes of stress measurement: Daily hassles and uplifts versus major life events. *Journal of Behavioral Medicine*, *4*, 1–25. PMID: 7288876

Kerr, H. (2013). Mental distress survey overview. *MRS Evidence Matters*: United Kingdom. Retrieved from https://www.nus.org.uk/Global/Campaigns/20130517%20Mental%20Distress%20Survey%20%20Overview.pdf

Kessler, R. C., Green, J. G., Gruber, M. J., Sampson, N. A., Bromet, E., Cuitan, M., Furukawa, T. A., Gureje, O., Hinkov, H., Hu, C.-Y., Lara, C., Lee, S., Mneimneh, Z., Myer, L., Oakley-Browne, M., Posada-Villa, J., Sagar, R., Viana, M. C., & Zaslavsky, A. M. (2010). Screening for serious mental illness in the general population with the K6 screening scale: Results from the WHO World Mental Health (WMH) survey initiative. *International Journal of Methods in Psychiatric Research*, *19*(Suppl 1), 4–22. PMID: 20527002

Larcombe, W., Finch, S., Sore, R., Murray, C. M., Kentish, S., Mulder, R. A., & Williams, D. (2016). Prevalence and socio-demographic correlates of psychological distress among students at an Australian university. *Studies in Higher Education*, *41*, 1074–1091.

Lazarus, R. S., & Folkman, S. (1987). Transactional theory and research on emotions and coping. *European Journal of Personality*, *1*(3), 141–169. DOI: 10.1002/per.2410010304

Lenz, B. (2001). The transition from adolescence to young adulthood: A theoretical perspective. The Journal of School Meehan, C., and K. Howells. 2018. "What Really Matters to Freshers?": Evaluation of First Year Student Experience of Transition into University. *Journal of Further and Higher Education, 42*(7), 893–907. DOI: 10.1080/0309877X.2017.1323194

Lewinsohn, P. M., Allen, N. B., Seeley, J. R., & Gotlib, I. H. (1999). First onset versus recurrence of depression: Differential processes of psychosocial risk. *Journal of Abnormal Psychology, 108*, 483–489. PMID: 10466272

Lipson, S., & Eisenberg, D. (2018). Mental health and academic attitudes and expectations in university populations: Results from the healthy minds study. *Journal of Mental Health (Abingdon, England), 27*(3), 205–213. DOI: 10.1080/09638237.2017.1417567 PMID: 29265935

Lynch, K. (2010). Carelessness: A Hidden Doxa of Higher Education. *Arts and Humanities in Higher Education, 9*(1), 54–67. DOI: 10.1177/1474022209350104

Maftei, A., Dumitriu, A., & Holman, A. C. (2021). They will discover I'm a fraud!" The Imposter Syndrome Among Psychology Students. *Studia Psychologica, 63*(4), 337–351.

Marin, M. F., Lord, C., Andrews, J., Juster, R. P., Sindi, S., Arsenault-Lapierre, G., & Lupien, S. J. (2011). Chronic stress, cognitive functioning and mental health. *Neurobiology of Learning and Memory, 96*(4), 583–595. PMID: 21376129

Maslach, C., & Jackson, S. E. (1986). *Maslach Burnout Inventory manual* (2nd ed.). Consulting Psychologists Press.

Maslach, C., Schaufeli, W. B., & Leiter, M. P. (2001). Job burnout. *Annual Review of Psychology, 52*(1), 397–422. PMID: 11148311

Maybery, D., Maybery, M., Bresnan, R., Croft, B., Graham, R., Macaulay, J., & Szakacs, E. (2002). Responding to daily event questionnaires: The influence of the order of hassle and uplift scales. *Stress and Health, 18*(1), 19–26. DOI: 10.1002/smi.915

McCloud, T., & Bann, D. (2019). Financial stress and mental health among higher education students in the UK up to 2018: Rapid review of evidence. *Journal of Epidemiology and Community Health, 73*(10), 977–984. PMID: 31406015

McIntyre, , Worsley, Corcoran, Woods, & Bentall. (2018). Academic and Non-Academic Predictors of Student Psychological Distress: The Role of Social Identity and Loneliness. *Journal of Mental Health (Abingdon, England), 27*(3), 230–239. DOI: 10.1080/09638237.2018.1437608 PMID: 29436883

Meehan, C., & Howells, K. (2018). 'What really matters to freshers?': Evaluation of first year student experience of transition into university. *Journal of Further and Higher Education, 42*(7), 893–907.

Morris, S., Earl, K., & Neave, A. (2017). Health survey for England 2016 well-being and mental health. *Health and Social Care Information Centre.*

Murray-Gibbons, S., & Gibbons, C. (2023). Revealing the Complex Relationship between Social Media use, Social Comparison Orientation and Optimism on Health Outcomes. *Psychology & Behavioral Sciences International Journal, 21*(2), 556057. DOI: 10.19080/PBSIJ.2023.20.556057

Neves, J., & Hewitt, R. (2020). *Student academic experience survey.* Higher Education Policy Institute.

OECD. (2017). *PISA 2015 Results* (Volume III). OECD.

Pascoe, M., Hetrick, S., & Parker, A. (2019). The Impact of Stress on Students in Secondary School and Higher Education. *International Journal of Adolescence and Youth, 25*(1), 104–112. DOI: 10.1080/02673843.2019.1596823

Pennebaker, J. W. (2004). Theories, therapies, and taxpayers: On the complexities of the expressive writing paradigm. *Clinical Psychology : a Publication of the Division of Clinical Psychology of the American Psychological Association, 11*(2), 138–142.

Ribeiro, I., Pereira, R., Freire, I., de Oliveira, B., Casotti, C., & Boery, E. (2018). Stress and Quality of Life among University Students: A Systematic Literature Review. *Health Profession Education, 4*(2), 70–77. DOI: 10.1016/j.hpe.2017.03.002

Richardson, T., Elliott, P., & Roberts, R. (2017). Relationship between loneliness and mental health in students. *Journal of Public Mental Health, 16*, 48–54.

Royal College of Psychiatrists. (2011). *Mental health of students in higher education. (College report CR166).* Author.

Sarkar, S., Gupta, R., & Menon, V. (2017). A systematic review of depression, anxiety, and stress among medical students in India. *Journal of Mental Health and Human Behaviour, 22*(2), 88–96.

Scanlon, D. L., Rowling, L., & Weber, Z. (2007). "You Don't Have like an Identity . . . You are Just Lost in a Crowd": Forming a Student Identity in the First-Year Transition to University. *Journal of Youth Studies, 10*(2), 223–241. DOI: 10.1080/13676260600983684

Schafer, W. (1992). *Stress management for wellness* (2nd ed.). Harcourt Brace Janovich.

Seligman, M. E. (1971). Phobias and preparedness. *Behavior Therapy, 2*(3), 307–320. PMID: 27816071

Selye, H. (1956). *The Stress of Life*. McGraw-Hill.

Simic, N., & Manenica, I. (2012). Exam Experience and Some Reactions to Exam Stress. *Human Physiology, 38*(1), 67–72. DOI: 10.1134/S0362119712010161 PMID: 22567840

Stallman, H. M. (2010). Psychological distress in university students: A comparison with general population data. *Australian Psychologist, 45*(4), 249–257.

Steptoe, A., Tsuda, A., & Tanaka, Y. (2007). Depressive symptoms, socio-economic background, sense of control, and cultural factors in university students from 23 countries. *International Journal of Behavioral Medicine, 14*, 97–107. PMID: 17926438

Storrie, K., Ahern, K., & Tuckett, A. (2010). A Systematic Review: Students with Mental Health Problems -A Growing Problem. *International Journal of Nursing Practice, 16*(1), 1–6. DOI: 10.1111/j.1440-172X.2009.01813.x PMID: 20158541

Stults-Kolehmainen, M. A., & Sinha, R. (2014). The effects of stress on physical activity and exercise. *Sports Medicine (Auckland, N.Z.), 44*, 81–121. PMID: 24030837

Tett, L., Cree, V. E., & Christie, H. (2017). From further to higher education: Transition as an on-going process. *Higher Education, 73*, 389–406. DOI: 10.1007/s10734-016-0101-1

Thomas, L. (2012). Building Student Engagement and Belonging in Higher Education at a Time of Change. *Paul Hamlyn Foundation, 100*, 1–99.

Thomas, L. (2016). Chapter 9 - Developing Inclusive Learning to Improve the Engagement, Belonging, Retention, and Success of Students from Diverse Groups. In *Widening Higher Education Participation A Global Perspective*. Chandos Publishing.

Thorley, C. (2017). Not By Degrees: Not by degrees: Improving student mental health in the UK's universities. IPPR. www.ippr.org/publications/not-by-degrees

Toyama, M., & Sakurai, S. (1999). Daily hassles and uplifts, and college students' health: Focusing on daily uplifts. *Japanese Journal of Educational Psychology*. Advance online publication. DOI: 10.5926/jjep1953.47.3_374

Turner, J., Bartlett, D., Andiappan, M., & Cabot, L. (2015). Students' perceived stress and perception of barriers to effective study: Impact on academic performance in examinations. *British Dental Journal, 219*(9), 453–458. DOI: 10.1038/sj.bdj.2015.850 PMID: 26564362

Vaez, M., Kristenson, M., & Laflamme, L. (2004). Perceived quality of life and self-rated health among first-year university students. *Social Indicators Research*, *68*, 221–234.

Wolf, T. M., Elston, R. C., & Kissling, G. E. (1989). Relationship of Hassles, Uplifts, and Life Events to Psychological Weil-Being of Freshman Medical Students. *Behavioral Medicine (Washington, D.C.)*, *15*(1), 37–45. DOI: 10.1080/08964289.1989.9935150 PMID: 2923991

World Health Organization. (2006). A state of complete physical mental and social wellbeing and not merely the absence of disease or infirmity. *Constitution of the World Health Organization basic documents, 45*, 1-20.

Wrench, A., Garrett, R., & King, S. (2014). Managing health and well-being: Student experiences in transitioning to higher education. *Asia-Pacific Journal of Health, Sport and Physical Education*, *5*(2), 151–166.

Zhang, Y., Qu, B., Lun, S., Wang, D., Guo, Y., & Liu, J. (2012). Quality of life of medical students in China: A study using the WHOQOL-BREF. *PLoS One*, *7*(11), e49714. PMID: 23209595

ADDITIONAL READING

Brown, J. S. (2018). Student mental health: Some answers and more questions. *Journal of Mental Health (Abingdon, England)*, *27*(3), 193–196. DOI: 10.1080/09638237.2018.1470319 PMID: 29768071

Pascoe, M., Hetrick, S., & Parker, A. (2019). The Impact of Stress on Students in Secondary School and Higher Education. *International Journal of Adolescence and Youth*, *25*(1), 104–112. DOI: 10.1080/02673843.2019.1596823

ENDNOTES

1 I would recommend you make it part of your routine to check the Staff Educational Development Association blog (thesedablog.wordpress.com). It is packed with evidence-based ideas and findings on helping and supporting educators and students in higher education and while it is a UK based organisation, it has a global reach and draws on international findings. The '53 powerful ideas

all teachers should know', as well as the range of individual blogs on student stress, wellbeing and coping are all worth exploring.

2 Michaela Pascoe and colleagues undertook a narrative review, exploring the impact of stress on students. Some of its findings were referenced in this chapter. More exhaustive reviews are available, but this paper offers an informed and easy to understand review. It can be sourced open access and it draws out some important points that will help educators in their work.

Chapter 8

EMBRACE the Healing: Cultivating Compassion in Trauma-Informed Schools

Ruth McKernan
https://orcid.org/0009-0006-1006-3170
Maynooth University, Ireland

Catriona O'Toole
https://orcid.org/0000-0003-4721-3903
Maynooth University, Ireland

ABSTRACT

In schools today, many children carry the invisible weight of adversity and trauma, affecting their ability to learn and thrive. Through the use of vignettes, specifically the story of Bobby, a young boy grappling with significant trauma, the authors explore how trauma manifests in the classroom and how educators can respond with compassion and understanding. Bobby's journey is emblematic of the countless children who bring their personal histories of violence, neglect, or instability into school, often resulting in behavioural and emotional challenges. By examining both individual-level interventions and systemic changes, this chapter emphasizes the potential of TIC to foster healing. The authors also critique traditional methods that overly focus on individual change while neglecting the trauma-inducing environments many children face. Trauma-informed practice, as explored through frameworks like EMBRACE, demonstrates how schools can shift from managing symptoms to addressing root causes, nurturing both students and staff alike.

DOI: 10.4018/979-8-3693-1293-3.ch008

INTRODUCTION

In schools today, many children carry the invisible weight of adversity and trauma, affecting their ability to learn and thrive. Through the use of vignettes, specifically the story of Bobby, a young boy grappling with significant trauma, we explore how trauma manifests in the classroom and how educators can respond with compassion and understanding. Bobby's journey is emblematic of the countless children who bring their personal histories of violence, neglect, or instability into school, often resulting in (frequently misunderstood) behavioural and emotional challenges. By examining both individual-level interventions and systemic changes, this chapter emphasizes the potential of TIC to foster healing. We also critique traditional approaches that overly focus on individual change while neglecting the trauma-inducing environments many children face. Trauma-informed practice, as explored through frameworks like EMBRACE, demonstrates how schools can shift from managing symptoms to addressing root causes, nurturing both students and staff alike. This chapter not only offers a theoretical understanding of trauma-informed education but also equips readers with practical strategies to integrate TIC principles into school systems.

Bobby, a five-year-old boy, struggled significantly with the everyday demands of the classroom. He couldn't stay seated for more than a few minutes, found it hard to focus on lessons, and was frequently distracted—looking around the room or gazing out the window. Making and keeping friends was also a challenge. When his teacher tried to redirect him, Bobby became visibly agitated, resorting to repeatedly banging his head on the classroom's wooden floor. This behaviour was not only distressing for Bobby but also upsetting for his peers and difficult for the teacher to manage.
What the teacher didn't know was that Bobby was witnessing nightly violence at home, where his father frequently abused his mother. Bobby, too, was a target of violence from his older brother. His mother, struggling with a worsening drug addiction, was becoming increasingly emotionally unavailable. As a result, Bobby lived in a constant state of fear and unpredictability.

Bobby, while a fictitious child, is representative of many children attending our schools today. Their life circumstances may not be identical, but many children come to school feeling afraid, fearing what they have witnessed, or experienced directly, the night before, or on the way to school, what they may come home from school to (will father have hurt mother again? Or worse?) and what may happen to themselves. This living on a knife's edge would take a toll on an adult's body, but has a more significant impact on a child's, as it lays down patterns of responding that a child will have difficulty overcoming especially if not supported by their community. Judith Herman (1992/2015) points out that "*psychological trauma is an affliction of the powerless*" (p. 33) and who could be less powerful than a small child?

ADVERSE CHILDHOOD EXPERIENCES – THE ACE STUDY AND ITS SHORTCOMINGS

The existence of trauma and adversity during childhood has been recognised for generations (e.g. Rutter, 1981, Freud & Breuer, 1895, Tardieu, 1857, 1860, 1862 (cited in Labbé 2005)). However, it is a topic that falls in and out of public consciousness, as it touches on deep, unsettling truths about power, victimization, and the structures that perpetuate silence and denial (Herman, 1992/2015). In the late nineteenth century, neurologists such as Jean-Martin Charcot, Pierre Janet, and Sigmund Freud significantly advanced understanding of psychological trauma—then often discussed under the term "*hysteria*". As recounted by Judith Herman (1992), Freud initially identified childhood sexual abuse as a central cause of "hysteria" in women but later revised this position, attributing symptoms instead to unconscious fantasies. This shift, shaped in part by societal resistance to confronting the prevalence of abuse, contributed to a waning interest in trauma as a legitimate field of inquiry. Trauma re-emerged in public and clinical consciousness after World War I, when returning soldiers exhibited what was known as "shell shock" or "war neurosis"—patterns of distress that closely resembled those observed in Freud's earlier clinical work. In recent decades, trauma has once again entered mainstream discourse, with the term now part of everyday language. Contemporary research on trauma and trauma-informed practice has flourished, driven in part by and civil rights movements, campaigns such as #MeToo and #BlackLivesMatter, and the widespread impacts of war, genocide, displacement, and global upheaval. However, it was the publication of the Adverse Childhood Experiences study (ACEs; Felitti, et al.,1998) that sparked a significant and renewed interest in the topic, as evidenced in the increased number of research papers published over the last two decades, from less than ten papers a year in the dying years of the 20th century to almost two hundred papers a year in 2017 and 2018 (Struck, et al., 2021).

The ACE Study probed the occurrence of adverse life experiences prior to the age of 18. Participants were mostly White and middle-class adults, accessible to the researchers because they had private health insurance. The adversities probed fell under three broad categories: abuse (physical, sexual and emotional), neglect (physical, emotional) and so-called, household dysfunction (parental mental health or substance abuse issues, parental incarceration, intimate partner violence). Respondents were not asked to divulge details regarding the extent of their experiences of adversity, merely to indicate whether it had occurred or not. The outcome of this study surprised the researchers for two reasons: (1) it was found that the experience of adversity during childhood was commonplace, with over 50% of the respondents indicating that they had experienced at least one adverse event, and 25% indicating that they had experienced two or more, and (2) as the level of reported adversity increased, so too did the risk of numerous poor physical and mental health outcomes, including ischemic heart disease, cancer, chronic lung disease, increased risk of attempting suicide, engaging in substance abuse, perpetrating intimate partner violence, experiencing rape (Felitti, et al., 1998), experiencing economic difficulty (Henry, et al., 2018), poor educational outcomes (Burke, et al., 2011), and mental health difficulties (Hughes, et al., 2019).

Why did the ACEs study set this immense body of work on childhood adversity in motion, when other studies had not sparked the imagination of researchers quite so much? Was it simply the right study, at the right time? Prior work in the fields of *Developmental Psychopathology* (e.g. Belsky, 1984, Sroufe and Rutter, 1984) or *Cumulative Risk* (e.g. Rutter, 1979) may not have gained quite the same level of public awareness; they were not backed by the funding of a health insurance company (Kaiser Permanente) or the Center for Disease Control (CDC); they also considered populations that were marginalised in some way. The ACEs study demonstrated starkly the impacts of childhood adversity on later adult mental and physical health in a largely *middle class, White* population. It could be argued that middle class, White researchers were suddenly confronted with the notion that experiences that they, and their kin, had in their childhood could come back to haunt them in later life. Adversity and trauma were no longer only the province of the "Other".

The prevalence of ACEs found in the original study has been replicated in multiple other studies, with a population study in the USA finding that approximately 62% of the population has a history of experiencing at least one adverse event (Merrick, et al., 2018). Internationally, there have been some differences in rates of ACEs reported, for instance respondents reporting one adverse event during childhood in Ireland was 65.2% (McCutchen, et al., 2022), in Poland 76.6% (WHO, 2018), Denmark 34% (Dahl, et al., 2017). However, the different prevalence rates may not indicate differences in populations but rather differences in what was measured. Consequently, based on the prevalence rates suggested, the average teacher will probably have between 8 and 10 children in class who have experienced or are experiencing ongoing adversity and trauma of one kind. Of these children, there could be six who have experienced more than one type of adversity.

A meta-analysis by Bellis et al. (2019) estimated that across Europe and North America, over 500 million adolescents and adults are living with the effects of at least one adverse childhood experience (ACE), with approximately 245 million affected by multiple ACEs. The World Health Organization (WHO, 2024) reports that in

Europe alone, 55 million children are impacted by emotional abuse, 44 million by physical abuse, and 18 million by sexual abuse. It has called for increased investment in evidence-based prevention programmes targeted at children and families identified as being at elevated risk (WHO, 2018). Failure to act has been criticised as a form of "short-termism in the thinking of governments and society at large," given that ACE-related healthcare costs are estimated to exceed $13 billion annually across North America and Europe (Bellis et al., 2019).

These statistics illustrate why the ACE Study was instrumental in bringing childhood adversity into public policy discussions. However, several researchers (including the Study authors themselves) have since raised concerns about how the ACE questionnaire has been applied in practice (Anda, Porter & Brown, 2020; Finkelhor, 2018). Originally intended for use at the population level, the ACE questionnaire is sometimes misused to assess individuals, despite not being designed to capture personal experiences or predict individual outcomes. Furthermore, the study's focus on adversity within the family overlooks wider social, structural, and institutional forces that often shape and intensify such experiences (Kelly-Irving & Delpierre, 2019).

This limited framing risks creating deterministic narratives in which people view their ACE score as a fixed indicator of their future. Such self-labelling can restrict opportunities for healing and reinforce deficit-based views, particularly for those from historically marginalised communities. In addition, critics argue that ACE research does not sufficiently account for the deeply emotional and subjective nature of trauma. For educators and practitioners, it is crucial to understand that childhood trauma is not merely a statistical phenomenon—it is a lived reality that shapes how children understand themselves, form relationships, and navigate the world around them (O'Toole, 2022).

TRAUMA AND HOW IT MANIFESTS IN CLASSROOM CONTEXTS

The term "trauma" originates from the Greek word τρα μα (traûma), meaning "wound." In contemporary literature trauma is defined and understood in different ways. For example, a common distinction is made between single-incident trauma, which results from a specific event (such as a car accident or a natural disaster), and complex trauma, which involves repeated or ongoing interpersonal threats, including various forms of abuse, violence, and violation. Most childhood trauma falls into the latter category (Courtois & Ford, 2009). However, trauma can be covert as well as overt; is not just about what happens to a child, but equally what should have happened, but did not; such as the absence of an attuned, responsive attachment relationship in early life (Maté and Maté, 2022). We could also consider a more expansive concept of 'everyday trauma' to include threats or challenges arising from 'normal' cultural practices, often in media and advertising, but also in schools (Thomas, 2014), which create social pressure and encourage comparison with other children or with an ideal standard, especially in relation to appearance or achievement (Johnstone & Boyle, 2018).

In addition to expanding definitions of trauma, it is vital to recognise how experiences of harm are shaped by broader systems of power and identity. An intersectional lens (Crenshaw, 1989) reveals how children positioned at the margins due to race, class, disability, gender identity, or migration status may be disproportionately exposed to structural and relational forms of trauma—including racism, ableism, or poverty—and yet have their distress minimised or pathologised rather than understood. For instance, a Black child repeatedly subjected to racial microaggressions at school may internalise a sense of shame or hypervigilance, which can deeply affect their development and sense of self. Similarly, a disabled child who is consistently excluded from full participation may experience a chronic sense of unworthiness or invisibility that is rarely acknowledged as traumatic within dominant frameworks.

This connects to the notion of epistemic injustice (Fricker, 2007), where children's testimonies and meaning-making are discredited or dismissed, particularly when they challenge dominant social narratives or emerge from marginalised identities. When a child's emotional or behavioural responses to adversity are interpreted solely through diagnostic or disciplinary lenses, without attending to their lived context, a form of testimonial injustice occurs—silencing the knowledge they hold about their own experiences. For example, a Traveller girl expressing distress in school may be framed as 'disruptive' rather than as responding to chronic cultural stigmatisation or educational exclusion. This prompts us to not only consider the nature of the threat or absence, but also whose trauma is recognised, whose stories are believed, and whose needs are met. Recognising these layers of injustice calls for an expanded, socially attuned understanding of trauma that challenges dominant norms and centres the voices of those most affected.

The Substance Abuse and Mental Health Services Administration (SAMHSA, 2014, pg. 7) define trauma in relation to three Es (event, experience and effect), as follows: "Trauma results from an event, series of *events*, or set of circumstances that is *experienced* by an individual as physically or emotionally harmful or life threatening and that has lasting adverse *effects* on the individual's functioning and mental, physical, social, emotional or spiritual wellbeing". This is a helpful definition in the sense that it acknowledges not just the external event or circumstances that causes harm, but also the subjective nature of how such events are experienced. However, it falls short in accounting for the structural dimensions of trauma—particularly the power imbalances that shape children's lives, the realities of epistemic injustice, and the intersecting impacts of race, class, gender, disability, and other social identities (Frehill & Booker, 2025; O'Toole, 2022). Without this critical framing, there is a risk that trauma is understood primarily through an individualised, decontextualised lens—one that overlooks the broader social conditions that produce and perpetuate harm.

Each child's response to trauma is unique; some may appear outwardly unaffected, while others struggle in visible or hidden ways. There are some factors that make adversities harder for children to cope with, such as having no one to confide in, no one who believed or supported them, experiencing threats that are physically invasive, repeated or ongoing, and experiencing threats at a younger age (Johnstone & Boyle, 2018). Children also filter these adversities through their own unique lens, which may include temperament, intelligence, and prior experiences, with consequent differences in how they make sense of their situations, and ultimately how adversities impact both immediately and in later life. These factors influence how they interpret and make sense of what has happened, and in turn, how the adversity affects them both immediately and in the long term. As a result, it is difficult to predict any individual's response to what may, on the surface, appear to be the same traumatic event. Indeed, given the complex interplay between the nature of the adversity and personal and environmental factors, some individuals emerge from significant childhood adversity with strong physical and emotional wellbeing, while others may experience ongoing distress. There are also those who channel their experiences into personal insight, empathy, and resilience, demonstrating what is often referred to as post-traumatic growth (Tedeschi & Calhoun, 1995).

Trauma is also a deeply embodied and visceral experience. When a child is exposed to a perceived threat or adversity, the body's stress response system is activated, triggering a cascade of physiological, hormonal, and neurochemical reactions designed to ensure survival—commonly known as the fight, flight, or freeze response (Perry et al., 1995; Porges, 2011; van der Kolk, 2014). Under normal conditions, once the threat has passed, the body returns to homeostasis—a state of balance. However, children who grow up in threatening or relationally impoverished environments may become stuck in patterns of chronic dysregulation, overwhelmed by distressing sensations, implicit body memories, and emotional reactivity. These trauma responses can be triggered even in settings that appear safe to others, such as classrooms. As a result, a teacher may perceive a child as "overreacting" to a situation that seems minor or innocuous, leading to misinterpretations and labels such as "impulsive" or "unpredictable." Trauma-experienced children often have a narrow window of tolerance (Siegel, 1999), meaning they are more easily pushed into states of hyper-arousal (e.g., panic, rage) or hypo-arousal (e.g., dissociation, withdrawal). These states undermine their ability to self-regulate, focus attention, process information, and retain learning—abilities that are essential for school success.

Unfortunately, when trauma responses are not recognised, they are often misread as laziness, apathy, deliberate defiance, or disrespect. These misinterpretations can become self-fulfilling prophecies, as teacher expectations and responses shape the child's behaviour over time (Fullerton et al., 2009). Thus, without the support of regulated, attuned adults, children's trauma-related behaviours are frequently misunderstood and met with punitive measures, which can further entrench the cycle of dysregulation and disconnection (O'Toole, 2022).

This misinterpretation is particularly common for children from marginalized or underrepresented communities, who frequently experience higher levels of discrimination and oppression. An intersectional lens helps us understand how children's social identities can intensify exposure to systemic harm and limit access to support. Trauma often affects entire groups and can be passed down through generations. The root causes of this collective trauma lie in historical and ongoing social inequities such as poverty, racism, sexism, and other forms of systemic oppression and power imbalances (Falkenburger, et al., 2018). In Bobby's case, both his parents grew up in marginalized and under-resourced communities. Decades of systemic neglect and underinvestment had contributed to high levels of poverty, unemployment, crime, and substance abuse in their environment. The lack of access to essential services, along with deteriorating infrastructure, compounded these challenges. The conditions in which Bobby's parents were raised profoundly affected their physical and mental health, limiting their opportunities and shaping their life paths. His mother struggled with addiction and mental health challenges, while his father became involved in crime and violence. These difficult circumstances understandably impacted their capacity to provide the emotional and physical support that Bobby needed. From an intersectional perspective, Bobby's class identity further complicates how he is perceived and treated within the school system. Children from low-income backgrounds are often subject to implicit bias, with their struggles dismissed as poor choices or family dysfunction rather than symptoms of broader structural inequality. Staff may view Bobby's behaviours through a deficit lens—labelling him as 'disruptive' or 'unmotivated'—rather than considering the cumulative impact of intergenerational poverty and trauma.

At seven years old, Bobby was finally referred for special educational services. By this time, his coping mechanisms had shifted dramatically. Instead of banging his head on the floor, Bobby's immediate response to any demand from his teacher was to flee the classroom. His body would tense, his heart pounding in his chest, overwhelmed by a wave of panic that pushed him into flight. Each request felt like a threat beyond his capacity to manage, pushing him beyond his window of tolerance. When he ran, it wasn't just to avoid the task—it was a desperate attempt to escape the crushing fear and helplessness flooding his senses. He sought refuge in corners of the school, sometimes climbing to the roof, seeking a space where the walls wouldn't close in on him.

The support Bobby received focused primarily on controlling his behaviour. A Special Needs Assistant was assigned to reward him for good behaviour and enforce consequences for non-compliance. But for Bobby, this system only deepened his confusion. Each reward felt meaningless, unable to penetrate the storm of emotions that consumed him. What could a sticker or a point system offer him when he felt like he was drowning? When the adult escorted him out of the room after an outburst, Bobby felt even more isolated—further proof, in his mind, that he didn't belong. Shame washed over him in those moments, his stomach twisting with the belief that he was failing at school, just as he seemed to be failing at life.

What the school staff didn't know was the deep emotional turmoil Bobby was battling. His father had been arrested and imprisoned and while the direct threat to his mother was gone, Bobby still lived in constant fear at home. His older brother's bullying left him feeling powerless and exposed, both at home and at school. His mother's ongoing drug dependency only added to the instability, leaving Bobby in a constant state of hypervigilance. Every interaction felt like a potential threat, every demand an impossible task. School wasn't a place of learning—it had become another battleground where his sense of inadequacy and fear overwhelmed him, flooding his mind and body with the visceral pain of not being safe anywhere.

Children, like Bobby, carry an 'invisible backpack' to school the weight of which may cause them difficulties in learning, socialising, and conforming to the rules and expectations that are common in most schools. As noted above, children growing up in chronically stressful environments have an overactive stress responses, which can cause them to present as being "aggressive, impulsive or needy" (Perry and Szalavits, 2017, pg. 273). Research also shows that children who have been exposed to three or more ACEs have been found to have a higher likelihood to need to repeat a grade, score lower than peers on standardised tests, have discipline issues that result in suspensions and expulsion, and be referred for special educational intervention (Grevstad, 2007, cited in Hertel and Johnson, 2020). Burke et al. (2011) found that the proportion of children with no ACEs who were reported as having behaviour or learning problems at school was only three percent, but that this increased to 21% when the child had one-three ACEs, and to 52% for those with four or more ACEs. In addition, children with higher numbers of ACEs have also been found to be more likely to be diagnosed with a mental health condition and to be referred to special education settings or services (Porche, et al., 2016).

These patterns have contributed to debates about the intersections of trauma, mental health, and special educational needs, including neurodevelopmental differences like Attention Deficit Hyperactivity Disorder (ADHD) and autism. Children, in particular, may not have the words to convey emotional pain, and so distress is frequently expressed through behaviours, emotional and relational patterns, and somatic complaints. Their distress may manifest as very low mood, worry, irritability, or anger - patterns associated with various mental health difficulties. Behavioural responses may also mirror patterns typically associated with ADHD, such as inattention, hyperactivity, or impulsivity (Jabour, 2015). For children exposed to chronic trauma, like Bobby, survival is the immediate priority and they typically have few remaining resources for striving for academic success. If and when they fall behind academically, they are often labelled as having learning difficulties or special educational needs. Unsurprisingly then, concerns have emerged about the limitations of the medical model (Johnstone & Boyle, 2018), and the risk of misdiagnosis, which may lead to inappropriate use of medications or ineffective therapeutic interventions with trauma-exposed children (Al-Attar & Worthington, 2024). This underscores the importance of clinicians taking a comprehensive social history, exploring the potential contribution of trauma in the assessment and formulation with children and young people (McDonald, et al., 2001), as well as greater collaboration with families, schools, and community organisations around trauma-informed care (Cole, 2023; Jabour, 2015). For schools, whether or not a child has a formal diagnosis, they are uniquely positioned to observe behavioural patterns, foster safety, and respond with compassion. School staff do not need to question the legitimacy of a child's diagnosis, but by adopting trauma-informed principles, schools can become spaces of recognition and care—irrespective of any diagnosis or lack thereof.

TRAUMA INFORMED CARE IN SCHOOLS

Trauma-Informed Care (TIC) is an approach that recognizes the widespread impact of trauma and seeks to create environments that promote healing and resilience. Pioneered by Harris and Fallot (2001), TIC emphasizes understanding trauma's effects on individuals' behaviours, relationships, and coping mechanisms. It advocates for a shift from asking "What's wrong with you?" to "What happened to you?" (Bloom, 2013). SAMHSA (2014) further developed this framework by outlining six key principles: safety, trustworthiness, peer support, collaboration, empowerment, and cultural sensitivity. These core principles can be embedded in all human service organizations to foster supportive environments that minimize re-traumatization and address both the individual and collective effects of trauma.

The provision of interventions to support children who have experienced adversity and trauma has been undertaken in both clinical and school settings, with schools being the most frequent delivery site (Dorsey et al., 2017). These interventions are typically targeted at individual children known to have experienced trauma, and offered by specially trained staff – they include Cognitive Behavioural Intervention for Trauma in Schools (CBITS; Jaycox, et al., 2012) and Trauma-Focused Cognitive Behavioural Therapy (TF-CBT; Cohen, et al., 2006). While such interventions are often shown to benefit children who participate, they do little to address the trauma inducing environment or upskill school staff who have everyday interactions with children. In addition, it is clear that given the numbers of children who experience adversity and trauma, most do not find their way to such specialist services or intervention programmes (Blaustein and Kinniburgh 2019, p.35).

In contrast to targeted interventions, a whole-school trauma-informed approach aims to embed key principles across all aspects of school life, creating environments that are safe, supportive, and empowering for everyone. Whilst a whole-school approach may include targeted supports as part of a Multi-Tiered System of Support (MTSS), the emphasis is on building knowledge and capacity at a universal level to cultivate a relationally attuned, emotionally safe school climate for all students and staff. The implementation of whole school (or school-wide) trauma-informed approaches has gained traction in many jurisdictions. For example, in the United States, 29 out of 50 states have incorporated trauma-informed principles into their educational policies (Simon et al., 2020). In most cases, this includes a requirement for teachers to undertake professional development in trauma awareness. While these developments are promising, research into the impact of whole-school trauma-informed care remains limited. The existing body of evidence consists of a small number of studies employing varied frameworks and methodologies, making it difficult to compare findings or draw generalisable conclusions (Avery et al., 2021).

Furthermore, the limitations of targeted interventions can still be reproduced within whole-school models. Chafouleas and colleagues (2001) describe the translation of ACE findings into school settings as the "first wave" of trauma-informed practice. Much like the ACE framework itself, this initial wave has been criticised for adopting an individualistic and decontextualised lens that overlooks the broader social, cultural, and structural conditions in which trauma occurs and persists (Becker-Blease, 2017). As a result, such approaches may inadvertently reinforce deficit-based perspectives, positioning trauma-affected students as problems to be fixed, rather than recognising their inherent strengths and capacities for healing and growth (O'Toole, 2022). In response to these shortcomings, the remaining sections of this chapter describe the EMBRACE Framework, which calls for a "second wave" of trauma-informed research and practice in education—one that is grounded in a relational and embodied ontology. This perspective recognises that human experience, including trauma, cannot be fully understood apart from the body, nor from the web of relationships and social contexts in which we are all embedded (O'Toole, under submission).

THE EMBRACE FRAMEWORK FOR TRAUMA-INFORMED CARE

Bobby's 2nd Class teacher had recently completed a foundational course in trauma-informed care, and it changed the way she viewed his behaviour. She began to recognize that Bobby's distress and actions were likely symptoms of deeper emotional wounds rather than simple misbehaviour. Instead of labelling him as disruptive, she grew curious about what might be triggering his emotional responses. This shift allowed her to approach Bobby with greater compassion and patience, focusing on understanding his needs rather than just managing his actions.

To support Bobby more effectively, the teacher and special needs assistant considered attachment-based strategies and co-regulation techniques, aimed at helping him feel secure and reducing his stress. They worked on building consistent, predictable relationships with Bobby. For instance, they introduced a daily routine where Bobby was greeted warmly each morning and given time to settle in before the school day started. When Bobby was calm they explored ideas for how they could help. With his input, they created a 'Den' in a corner of the classroom with a small, soft-fabric tent filled with cushions and blankets, books and sensory materials (such as stress balls, and fidget toys) offering a quiet, enclosed retreat for when Bobby needed a break.

These efforts provided Bobby with the stability he so desperately needed. Over time, he began to trust his teacher and special needs assistant a little more, viewing them as a 'secure base', and small but meaningful progress followed—he could remain in the classroom for longer periods and showed fewer signs of agitation. The safety of the Den together with the warm, responsive and predictable relationships being formed, helped soothe Bobby's stress-response system, giving him the emotional foundation to start engaging more positively with school life.

The EMBRACE Framework for trauma-informed care in schools (O'Toole, under submission) is illustrated in Figure 1. As shown, it is represented by concentric circles - the inner circle symbolises the practice-level, emphasising the changes that individual practitioners can make to embed trauma-informed ways of working into their own individual practice. The outer circle represents systemic or organisational-level change, which is about infusing trauma-informed principles within the school as a whole. The example above that focuses on the actions taken by Bobby's second-class teacher serves as an illustration of practice-level changes (the inner circle). A further vignette below illustrates the actions taken by Bobby's school at organisations level (outer circle).

In the EMBRACE Framework, trauma-informed practice is symbolised as a flower—delicate yet beautiful, requiring the right conditions to grow and flourish. Like a flower, it can be fragile, thriving only when nurtured in a supportive environment. The conditions (barriers and facilitators) to the implementation and sustainment of trauma-informed practice in schools is an important consideration from the start.

Figure 1. The EMBRACE Framework for Trauma-informed Care in Schools

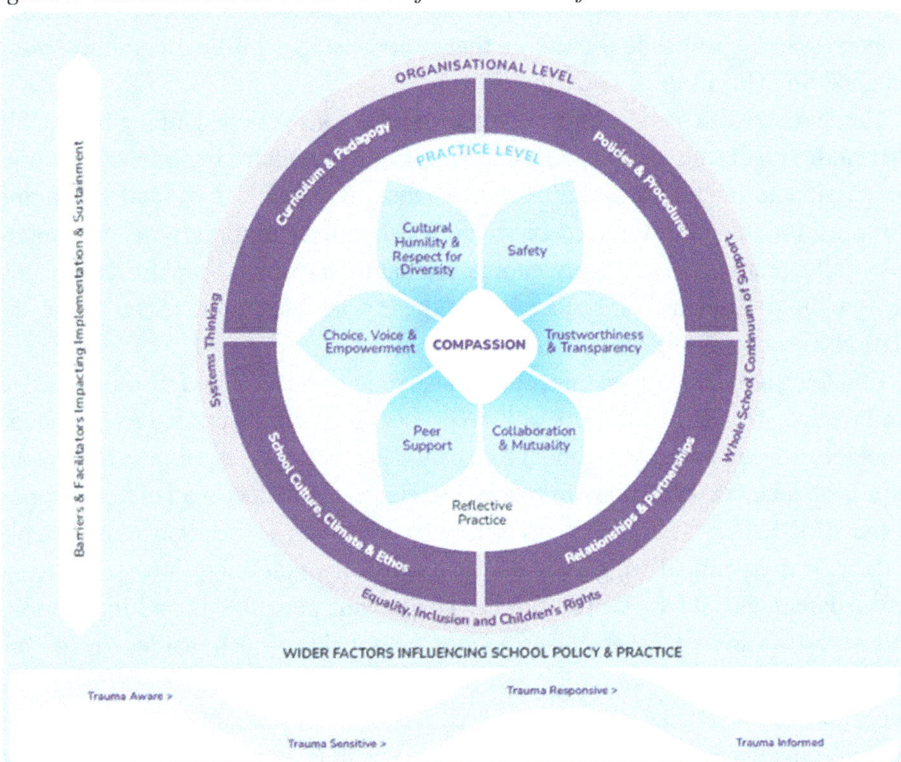

At the heart of the Framework is compassion. This is because compassion helps us to stay present with pain—our own and others'—without turning away. For teachers, this means being able to sit with the distress that children like Bobby may bring into the classroom, and respond with care rather than fear or frustration. Cultivating self-compassion is an important part of this process. When teachers show self-compassion, they are more likely to embrace trauma-informed approaches and are better protected against burnout and emotional exhaustion (O'Toole & Dobutowitsch, 2022). Working with students affected by trauma can stir up strong emotions—frustration, sadness, even helplessness. If teachers don't have space to reflect on these feelings, they often push them down, which can eventually lead to compassion fatigue: a state of emotional depletion and disconnection (Keller et al., 2014). In contrast, many educators describe a deep sense of purpose and fulfilment when they feel they're making a difference—this is known as compassion satisfaction (Stamm, 2010). For example, Bobby's teacher shared how, after months of patient effort, Bobby began to make eye contact and reach out for support. That small breakthrough became a source of strength and motivation. A compassion-centred approach supports teachers to find more of these moments, while also recognising that they cannot do this alone. It's not just about personal resilience—it's about creating systems and school cultures that support staff well-being and emotional sustainability (Edwards & Giussios, 2021).

Compassion also has a calming effect on the nervous system, helping both adults and children feel safe and connected. For students who have experienced trauma, compassionate interactions can restore a sense of dignity, trust, and belonging. Without this foundation, the six core principles of trauma-informed practice—safety, trust, collaboration, peer support, choice, and cultural respect—are difficult to genuinely uphold. Compassion is what brings these principles to life in the day-to-day relationships of school communities.

Engaging authentically in this process also requires critical and sustained reflective practice. This helps staff not only to process difficult emotional reactions that inevitably arise in their professional roles, but also to deepen awareness of personal values, beliefs, biases, and assumptions. Reflective practice is a core component of the EMBRACE Framework, as it allows educators to become more attuned to their own emotional triggers while also critically examining how stereotypes, power dynamics, and social positioning shape their perceptions and interactions. This is particularly vital to fostering an intersectional approach that recognises and responds to the diverse identities and experiences of students. Increasingly, it is recognised that staff may benefit from access to professional supervision to support this reflective work and prevent emotional overload (Lawrence, 2020; O'Toole & Dobutowitsch, 2022).

The outer circles in the EMBRACE Framework emphasise organisational level change. Schools are complex, dynamic social systems; a systems perspective facilitates deeper understanding of issues, multi-layered stakeholder analysis, and solutions that are iterative, responsive and co-designed. The Whole School Continuum of Support (NEPS, 2007), similarly referred to as the Multi-Tiered Support System (MTSS, Sugai & Horner, 2009), acknowledges that children and young people have varying needs that can evolve over time. Those facing greater risks or with more complex needs may require specialized, targeted interventions in addition to the general support provided to all students within their class groups. This approach allows schools to respond flexibly to the changing needs of students, adapting support strategies in line with the school's resources and specific context (NEPS, 2007).

The EMBRACE Framework emphasises that becoming trauma-informed at a whole-school level also involved multilevel and integrated adaptations to four intertwined areas of school practice:

- Curriculum and pedagogy
- Policies and procedures
- Relationships & partnerships
- School culture, climate, and ethos.

These areas of practice align with the Irish Department of Education Wellbeing Policy Statement and Framework for Practice (DES, 2019) and with existing research (O'Toole & Darlington, 2021). Together, they help school staff understand how trauma-informed principles can be embedded into everyday practices—shaping how teaching and learning are approached, how school policies are developed and applied (including codes of behaviour and disciplinary measures), and how trauma responses are recognised and appropriately supported. The EMBRACE Framework places strong emphasis on the centrality of relationships at multiple levels—teacher-student relationships, peer interactions, and partnerships with families and communities. These elements are essential in creating a culture of belonging, where every member of the school community feels safe, seen, and supported. For example, a school might review its behaviour policy through a trauma-informed lens, replacing punitive language with restorative approaches and integrating staff training on understanding dysregulated behaviour as a communication of need. Simultaneously, teachers might adapt classroom routines to offer more predictable structures and emotional check-ins, fostering safety and connection for students who struggle with regulation. Small shifts like these, across each area, can collectively transform the school environment into one of healing and inclusion.

From a systems perspective, trauma-informed practice should not be viewed as a stand-alone approach. Instead it needs to be integrated with the wider school improvement efforts, including educational inclusion, children's rights, wellbeing promotion, anti-oppressive and social justice initiatives in education. Efforts in these respects are underway in many jurisdictions, for instance Scotland has integrated trauma-informed and attachment-based approaches with a rights-based framework (Education Scotland, n.d.), In Ireland trauma-informed approaches are explicitly linked to the wellbeing framework and Continuum of Support models (NEPS, 2025).

Similarly, trauma-informed practice has been integrated with principles of Universal Design for Learning (UDL), as both approaches emphasize flexibility, accessibility, and the creation of supportive learning environments that accommodate the diverse needs of all students (Jenkins, 2024; Salvador, 2022).

An increasingly important aspect of these initiatives is the adoption of an intersectional lens, which helps to illuminate and address power imbalances, biases, and stereotypes. As noted above, students from underrepresented or marginalised communities often face additional systemic barriers that compound trauma, including discrimination and socioeconomic disadvantage. A trauma-informed approach must therefore intentionally attend to these intersecting forms of adversity, ensuring that support strategies are equitable, culturally responsive, and attuned to the diverse identities and social positions of all learners. This strengthens the alignment between trauma-informed practice and wider Equity, Diversity, and Inclusion (EDI) goals, helping schools to foster environments that are not only safe but also just and inclusive for all. Similarly by incorporating a Children's Rights lens, trauma-informed practices in schools can align with broader obligations to respect and uphold children's fundamental rights. A rights-based approach mandates that children's voices be heard and respected in all matters affecting them, as emphasized by the United Nations Convention on the Rights of the Child (UNCRC, United Nations, 1989). This is particularly important in the context of trauma-informed practices, where understanding and addressing the specific needs of students requires active participation and input from children themselves. In schools, this means creating spaces where students feel empowered to share their experiences, concerns, and preferences, and where their voices shape policies, supports, and interventions designed to help them thrive.

A practical example of applying a rights-based and equity-oriented mindset is co-design, which involves sharing power, ensuring meaningful participation, and developing responses that are culturally and contextually appropriate (McKernan, 2024). Co-design recognises that individuals are the experts in their own lives and that there is rarely a one-size-fits-all solution. In co-design particular attention must be paid to the inclusion in the decision making of those who may be coming in from the margins, including parents and children themselves. Unless attention is paid to building strong relationships based on trust their involvement may remain tokenistic (McKercher, 2020). So those with more power should create the conditions of safety and hospitality to make it possible for people with less power to speak and have their views listened to (McKernan, 2024).

Beyond the concentric circles, the graphic in Figure 1 illustrates that school systems are shaped and influenced by wider national, international and transnational policies, access to and quality of community network and support services, changing social and environmental conditions, as well as differing ideas on the goals and purposes of education (Ball, 2012; Lingard & Sellar, 2013). All these changing dynamics influence the nature of the trauma-informed innovation and change. The vertical arrow on the left of the Framework represents the barriers and facilitators that influence the implementation and sustainment of trauma-informed approaches in schools. There are several factors that are known to facilitate the uptake of trauma-informed practice in schools, including staff professional development, robust leadership and resourcing (Cruz González, et al., 2021; Wassink – de Stigter, et al., 2022). The path at the foundation of the Framework underscores that trauma-informed practice is an ongoing, evolving process—a journey that progresses from trauma awareness to sensitivity, responsiveness, and ultimately becoming trauma-informed. As with any journey, the road may not always be straightforward; there may be detours and challenges along the way (www.traumainformedoregon.org). Yet, despite the twists and turns, the journey is both meaningful and essential.

Bobby's 2nd Class teacher shared the successes she had witnessed with her school principal and colleagues. She became a passionate advocate for trauma-informed care (TIC) approaches within the school, garnering support from leadership to invest in continuous professional development (CPD) on trauma-informed practices for all teachers. Inspired by this commitment, the school agreed to establish a "nurture room," specifically designed to provide students like Bobby with a permanent safe and secure environment where they could thrive.

In alignment with these trauma-informed principles, the school also forged partnerships with community organisations, enhancing their capacity to connect with families like Bobby's. This collaborative effort opened up new resources and support systems for Bobby's mother, paving the way for healing and growth.

As a result of these systemic actions, Bobby began to experience hopeful and transformative changes. Gradually, he started participating more actively in classroom activities and demonstrated improved social interactions with his peers. The combination of a nurturing school environment and robust community resources significantly contributed to Bobby's emotional well-being and academic engagement, igniting a sense of possibility for his future.

The vignette above demonstrates what can be achieved when a systemic, trauma-informed approach is embraced. It underscores the critical importance of a multi-agency response in supporting children who are struggling. Schools cannot—and should not—do this work alone. As the saying goes, *"it takes a village to raise a child."* Bobby's case illustrates this well: he and his family are connected to a wide range of professionals and services—not only the school, but also the prison service, addiction services, housing supports, social work, and primary health care. When these services work in isolation, progress can be slow or fragmented. But when agencies collaborate in a cohesive, coordinated way, meaningful change becomes possible for children and families.

In the Irish context, the *Children and Young People's Services Committees* (CYPSCs) play a central role in supporting such collaboration. Backed by government, CYPSCs operate in every county and bring together key statutory, community, and voluntary providers of services for children and young people. These committees offer a structured forum for joint planning and coordination, aiming to improve access to services and ensure that families receive the support they need, when they need it. Their overarching goal is to enhance interagency cooperation and help realise the national outcomes outlined in *Young Ireland: National Policy Framework for Children and Young People 2023–2028*. An example of this work in action is the *Trauma-Informed Kildare Working Group*, a subcommittee of the local CYPSC, which includes members from education, social services, health, youth work, and community development sectors. This group has been established to act as a champion for trauma-informed practice across local networks—facilitating knowledge sharing, joint training, and integrated responses to trauma across services. Initiatives like these demonstrate the potential of place-based, multi-agency collaboration to support systemic change. When trauma-informed principles are applied not just within individual schools but across the ecosystem of services surrounding a child, the conditions are created for healing, safety, and long-term wellbeing—not just for the child, but for their family and wider community. Thus, the EMBRACE Framework offers a cohesive guide for both practice-level and organisational-level changes. It is intentionally designed to be non-prescriptive, recognizing that there are no one-size-fits-all solutions. Instead, it invites individual schools or school districts make decisions based on local needs and priorities, within overarching TIC principles and values.

CONCLUSION

This chapter has explored how trauma, particularly when rooted in structural injustice and intergenerational adversity, profoundly shapes the lives of children like Bobby—and the environments in which they learn. It has traced the evolution of trauma theory from the ACE study to more nuanced, intersectional understandings, and it has shown how trauma manifests not just as individual suffering but as relational and systemic disruption that reverberates through classrooms, families, and communities. The EMBRACE Framework offers a hopeful, practical, and compassionate roadmap for transforming how schools understand and respond to trauma. By weaving together theory, practice, and lived experience, the framework invites a shift away from narrow, individualised responses toward whole-school approaches that centre relationships, equity, and systemic accountability. Importantly, this approach demands more than technical adjustments—it requires cultural change, underpinned by deep compassion, sustained reflection, and a commitment to social justice.

Looking ahead, trauma-informed education must continue evolving in response to the complex and overlapping challenges facing children and communities today. This includes not only recognising the impact of trauma, but also addressing the structural conditions—such as poverty, racism, housing instability, and epistemic injustice—that perpetuate harm. The future of trauma-informed practice lies in its ability to integrate with broader movements for Equity, Diversity and Inclusion (EDI), Children's Rights, wellbeing promotion, and educational justice. If schools are to be places where every child feels safe, seen, and supported, then trauma-informed practice must become part of the everyday fabric of school life—not as an add-on or initiative, but as a guiding ethos that shapes all relationships, policies, and decisions. By EMBRACING this vision, educators, leaders, and policymakers can help cultivate learning environments that do more than respond to trauma—they can help break cycles of harm, restore dignity, and open new possibilities for healing, connection, and thriving.

DISCUSSION QUESTIONS

1. How can trauma show up for staff within a school? How can assumptions and experiences from our own upbringings and environments impact the way we communicate values in schools? How could this effect students?
2. How can routines, expectations, and discipline policies unintentionally affect students with trauma histories? What roles do Reflective Practice and Choice, Voice & Empowerment play in reshaping these policies to be more trauma-sensitive?
3. What are some small, achievable changes you could make in your classroom or school environment to support students with trauma histories? How might Children's Rights or Co-Design guide your approach?
4. Think about specific communication strategies that could support a student dealing with trauma-related issues. What words or phrases would foster Collaboration & Mutuality?

REFERENCES

Anda, R. F., Porter, L. E., & Brown, D. W. (2020). Inside the adverse childhood experience score: Strengths, limitations, and misapplications. *American Journal of Preventive Medicine*. PMID: 32222260

Avery, J., Morris, H., Galvin, E., Misso, M., Savaglio, M., & Skouteris, H. (2021). Systematic review of school-wide trauma-informed approaches. *Journal of Child & Adolescent Trauma*, *14*, 381–197. PMID: 34471456

Ball, S. J. (2012). *Global education Inc.: New policy networks and the neo-liberal imaginary*. Routledge.

Bellis, M. A., Hughes, K., Ford, K., Ramos Rodriguez, G., Sethi, D., & Passmore, J. (2019). Life course health consequences and associated annual costs of adverse childhood experiences across Europe and North America: A systematic review and meta-analysis. *Lancet*, 4. PMID: 31492648

Belsky, J. (1984). The determinants of parenting. *Child Development*, *55*(1), 83–96. PMID: 6705636

Blaustein, M. E., & Kinniburgh, K. M. (2019). *Treating traumatic stress in children and adolescents* (2nd ed.). The Guildford Press.

Bloom, S. L. (2013). *Creating sanctuary: Toward the evolution of sane societies* (2nd ed.). Routledge.

Burke, N. J., Hellman, J. L., Scott, B. G., Weems, C. F., & Carrion, V. G. (2011). The impact of adverse childhood experiences on an urban pediatric population. *Child Abuse & Neglect*, *35*, 408–413. PMID: 21652073

Cohen, J. A., Mannarino, A. P., & Deblinger, E. (2006). *Treating trauma and traumatic grief in children*. Guildford Press.

Courtois, C. A., & Ford, J. D. (2009). *Treating complex traumatic stress disorders: An evidence-based guide*. The Guilford Press.

Crenshaw, K. W. (1989). Demarginalizing the intersection of race and sex: A black feminist critique of antidiscrimination doctrine, feminist theory and antiracist politics. *University of Chicago Legal Forum*, *1989*, 139–167.

Cruz González, C., Rodríguez, C. L., & Segovia, J. D. (2021). What are the keys to achieve successful leadership?: Two case studies of private Catholic schools. *The International Journal of Religion and Spirituality in Society*, *11*(2), 181–190.

Dahl, S. K., Tidselbak Larsen, J., Petersen, L., Bonde Ubbesen, M., Bo Mortensen, P., Munk-Olsen, T., & Musliner, K. L. (2017). Early adversity and risk for moderate to severe unipolar depressive disorder in adolescence and adulthood: A register-based study of 978,647 individuals. *Journal of Affective Disorders, 214*, 122–129. PMID: 28288406

Department of Education and Skills (DES). (2019). *Wellbeing policy statement and framework for practice*. Government of Ireland. https://www.gov.ie/en/campaigns/851a8e-wellbeing-in-education/](https://www.gov.ie/en/campaigns/851a8e-wellbeing-in-education/

Dorsey, S., McLaughlin, K. A., Kerns, S. E. U., Harrison, J. P., Lambert, H. K., & Briggs, E. C.. (2017). Evidence base update for psychosocial treatments for children and adolescents exposed to traumatic events. *Journal of Clinical Child and Adolescent Psychology, 46*, 303–330. PMID: 27759442

Falkenburger, E., Arena, O., & Wolin, J. (2018). Trauma-informed community building and engagement. *The Urban Institute*. https://www.urban.org/sites/default/files/publication/98296/trauma-informed_community_building_and_engagement.pdf

Felitti, V. J., Anda, R. F., Nordenberg, D., Williamson, D. F., Spitz, A. M., Edwards, V., Koss, M. P., & Marks, J. S. (1998). Relationship of childhood abuse and household dysfunction to many of the leading causes of death in adults. *American Journal of Preventive Medicine, 14*(4), 245–258. PMID: 9635069

Finkelhor, D. (2018). Screening for adverse childhood experiences (ACEs): Cautions and suggestions. *Child Abuse & Neglect, 85*, 174–179. PMID: 28784309

Frehill, J., & Booker, R. (2025). The intersection of trauma with social, cultural, and historic inequities: Meeting the needs of marginalised students in Irish primary schools. *Educational and Child Psychology, 42*(1).

Freud, S., & Breuer, J. (1955). *Studies in hysteria*. Hogarth Press. (Original work published 1895)

Fricker, M. (2007). *Epistemic injustice: Power and the ethics of knowing*. Oxford University Press.

Fullerton, E. K., Conroy, M. A., & Correa, V. I. (2009). Early childhood teachers' use of specific praise statements with young children at risk for behavioural disorders. *Behavioral Disorders, 34*(3), 118–135.

Grevstad, J. (2007). Adverse childhood experiences in juvenile justice – Pierce County, WA. Paper presented at the Family Policy Council Partners Summit, Seattle, WA.

Harris, M., & Fallot, R. D. (2001). Envisioning a trauma-informed service system: A vital paradigm shift. *New Directions for Mental Health Services, 2001*(89). PMID: 11291260

Henry, K. L., Fulco, C. J., & Merrick, M. T. (2018). The harmful effect of child maltreatment on economic outcomes in adulthood. *American Journal of Public Health, 108*(9), 1134–1141. PMID: 30088994

Herman, J. (2015). *Trauma and recovery: The aftermath of violence – From domestic abuse to political terror* (2nd ed.). Basic Books. (Original work published 1992)

Hughes, K., Bellis, M. A., Sethi, D., Andrew, R., Yon, Y., Wood, S., Ford, K., Baban, A., Boderscova, L., Kachaeva, M., Makaruk, K., Markovic, M., Povilaitis, R., Raleva, M., Terzic, N., Veleminsky, M., Wlodarczyk, J., & Zakhozha, V. (2019). Adverse childhood experiences, childhood relationships and associated substance use and mental health in young Europeans. *European Journal of Public Health, 29*(4), 741–747. PMID: 30897194

Jaycox, L. H., Kataoka, S. H., Stein, B. D., Langley, A. K., & Wong, M. (2012). Cognitive behavioural intervention for trauma in schools. *Journal of Applied School Psychology, 28*, 239–255.

Johnstone, L., & Boyle, M. (2018). *The power threat meaning framework: Towards the identification of patterns in emotional distress, unusual experiences and troubles or troubling behaviour, as an alternative to functional psychiatric diagnosis*. British Psychological Society.

Keller, M. M., Chang, M.-L., Becker, E. S., Goetz, T., & Frenzel, A. C. (2014). Teachers' emotional experiences and exhaustion as predictors of emotional labor in the classroom: An experience sampling study. *Frontiers in Psychology, 5*. DOI: 10.3389/fpsyg.2014.01442

Kelly-Irving, M., & Delpierre, C. (2019). A critique of the adverse childhood experiences framework in epidemiology and public health: Uses and misuses. *Social Policy and Society, 18*(3), 445–456.

Lawrence, N. (2020). Supervision in education – Healthier schools for all. Barnardo's Scotland. https://www.barnardos.org.uk/sites/default/files/uploads/Supervision%20in%20Education%20-%20Healthier%20Schools%20For%20All%20-%20Main%20report_0.pdf

Lingard, B., & Sellar, S. (2013). Globalization, edu-business and network governance: The policy sociology of Stephen J. Ball and rethinking education policy analysis. *London Review of Education, 11*(3).

Maté, G., & Maté, D. (2022). *The myth of normal: Illness, health and healing in a toxic culture*. Penguin Books.

McCutchen, C., Hyland, P., Shevlin, M., & Cloitre, M. (2022). The occurrence and co-occurrence of ACEs and their relationship to mental health in the United States and Ireland. *Journal of Child Abuse and Neglect*. DOI: 10.1016/j.chiabu.2022.105681

McKercher, K. A. (2020). *Beyond sticky notes: Co-design for real: Mindsets, methods and movements*. Beyond Sticky Notes.

McKernan, R. (2024). Co-design as a trauma-informed process for the design of trauma-informed practices in schools. Paper presented at the European Conference on Educational Research, Nicosia, Cyprus.

Merrick, M. T., Ford, D. C., Ports, K. A., & Guinn, A. S. (2018). Prevalence of adverse childhood experiences from the 2011-2014 Behavioral Risk Factor Surveillance System in 23 states. *JAMA Pediatrics*, *172*(11). PMID: 30242348

National Educational Psychological Service (NEPS). (2007). *Behavioural, emotional and social difficulties: A continuum of support*. NEPS. https://www.sess.ie/sites/default/files/neps_special_needs_guidelines.pdf

O'Toole, C. (2022). When trauma comes to school: Toward a socially just trauma-informed praxis. *International Journal of School Social Work*, *6*(2).

O'Toole, C., & Darlington, E. (2021). *Mental health promotion in schools: State of the art*. Schools for Health in Europe.

O'Toole, C., & Dobutowitsch, M. (2022). The courage to care: Teacher compassion predicts more positive attitudes towards trauma-informed practice. *Journal of Child & Adolescent Trauma*, *16*, 123–133. PMID: 36157295

Perry, B., Pollard, R., & Blakely, T. (1995). Childhood trauma, the neurobiology of adaptation, and 'use dependent' development of the brain: How states become traits. *Infant Mental Health Journal*, *16*, 271–291.

Perry, B., & Szalavitz, M. (2017). *The boy who was raised as a dog: What traumatized children can teach us about loss, love and healing*. Basic Books.

Porche, M. V., Costello, D. M., & Rosen-Reynoso, M. (2016). Adverse family experiences, child mental health and educational outcomes for a national sample of students. *School Mental Health*, *8*, 44–60.

Porges, S. (2011). *The poly-vagal theory: Neurophysiological foundations of emotions, attachment, communication and self-regulation*. Norton.

Rutter, M. (1979). Protective factors in children's responses to stress and disadvantage. In Kent, M. W., & Rolf, J. E. (Eds.), *Primary prevention in psychopathology: Social competence in children* (Vol. 8, pp. 49–74). University Press of New England.

Rutter, M. (1981). *Maternal deprivation reassessed* (2nd ed.). Penguin Books.

SAMHSA (Substance Abuse and Mental Health Services Administration). (2014). *SAMHSA's concept of trauma and guidance for a trauma-informed approach.* https://ncsacw.samhsa.gov/userfiles/files/SAMHSA_Trauma.pdf

Shevrin Venet, A. (2021). *Equity-centered trauma-informed education*. Norton.

Siegel, D. J. (1999). *The developing mind: How relationships and the brain interact to shape who we are*. Guildford Press.

Simon, K., Compton, S. E., & Overstreet, S. (2020). The evolution of trauma-informed schools. In Rossen, E. (Ed.), *Supporting and educating traumatized students: A guide for school-based professionals* (2nd ed.). Oxford University Press.

Sroufe, L. A., & Rutter, M. (1984). The domain of developmental psychopathology. *Child Development*, *55*(1), 17–29. PMID: 6705619

Stamm, B. H. (2012). Helping the helpers: Compassion satisfaction and compassion fatigue in self-care, management, and policy. In Kirkwood, A. D., & Stamm, B. H. (Eds.), *Resources for community suicide prevention*. Idaho State University.

Struck, S., Stewart-Tufescu, A., Asmundson, A. J. N., Asmundson, G. G. J., & Afifi, T. O. (2021). Adverse childhood experiences (ACEs) research: A bibliometric analysis of publication trends over the first 20 years. *Child Abuse and Neglect, 112*. DOI: 10.1016/j.chiabu.2020.104895

Sugai, G., & Horner, R. H. (2009). Responsiveness-to-intervention and school-wide positive behavior supports: Integration of multi-tiered system approaches. *Exceptionality*, *17*, 223–237.

Tardieu, A. (1857). Étude medico-légale sur les attentats aux moeurs (1st ed.). Librairie JB Baillière et Fils.

Tardieu, A. (1860). Étude medico-légale sur les sévices et mauvais traitements exercés sur des enfants. *Annales d'Hygiène Publique et de Mèdicine Légale, 13*, 361-398.

Tardieu, A. (1862). Travail des enfants. In *Dictionnaire d'hygiène publique et de salubrité* (2nd ed., Vol. 3, pp. 35-81). Academic Press.

Tedeschi, R. G., & Calhoun, L. G. (1995). *Trauma & transformation: Growing in the aftermath of suffering*. Sage Publications, Inc.

Thomas, G. (2014). Inequality and the next generation. *The Psychologist, 27*, 240–242.

Trauma Informed Oregon. (2024, October 31). Road map to trauma informed care. *Trauma Informed Oregon.* https://traumainformedoregon.org/implementation/implementation-and-accountability-overview/roadmap-to-trauma-informed-care/

United Nations. (1989). *Convention on the rights of the child.* https://www.unicef.org/child-rights-convention/convention-text

Van der Kolk, B. (2014). *The body keeps the score: Mind, brain and body in the transformation of trauma.* Penguin Books.

Wassink-de Stigter, R., Kooijmans, R., Asselman, M. W., Offerman, E. C. P., Nelen, W., & Helmond, P. (2022). Facilitators and barriers in the implementation of trauma-informed approaches in schools: A scoping review. *School Mental Health, 14*, 470–484.

WHO. (2018). Survey of adverse childhood experiences and associated health-harming behaviours among Polish students. *World Health Organization.* https://www.who.int/europe/publications/i/item/WHO-EURO-2018-2984-42742-59621

WHO. (2024). Preventing child maltreatment. *World Health Organization.* https://www.who.int/europe/activities/preventing-child-maltreatment

ADDITIONAL READING

Phillips, S., Melim, D., & Hughes, D. (2020). *Belonging: A Relationship-Based Approach for Trauma-Informed Education.* Rowman and Littlefield.

Shevrin Venet, A. (2021). *Equity-Centered Trauma-Informed Education.* Norton.

Stokes, H., & Brunzell, T. (2024). *Implementing Trauma-Informed Pedagogies for School Change.* Emerald Publishing.

Chapter 9
Supporting Grieving Students

David J. Schonfeld
https://orcid.org/0000-0003-2479-0003
Children's Hospital of Los Angeles, USA

Thomas Patrick Demaria
https://orcid.org/0000-0002-7984-2344
Children's Hospital of Los Angeles, USA

ABSTRACT

Most school-age children experience the death of a close family member or friend. This chapter summarizes the range of common adjustment reactions and the factors that may complicate or prolong children's grief. In addition, this chapter offers practical strategies for school professionals on how to start the conversation with children about primary and secondary losses, adapt academic requirements, develop coping responses when grief responses are activated in the classroom, develop school-based memorial and commemorative activities, conduct outreach to grieving families, and mobilize peer support for the grieving student.

INTRODUCTION

Although adults often choose to view childhood as a carefree time, the reality is that most children experience the death of a close family member or friend. Even prior to the COVID-19 pandemic, roughly 90% of children in the United States reported that they had experienced such a loss prior to 18 years of age; approximately 1 out of 20 children experienced the death of a parent (Schonfeld & Demaria, 2016), with incidence rates of parental death having risen significantly during the pandemic.

DOI: 10.4018/979-8-3693-1293-3.ch009

Although bereavement is a normative lifetime experience, it is still associated with significant distress that can disrupt social and emotional development and at least temporarily impact psychosocial and academic functioning.

Grieving children need to cope not only with the death of an important individual in their life – what is referred to as the primary loss – but they must also adjust to a wide range of secondary losses. These secondary losses may include disruptions in living situations and the need to change schools or distant moves that separate children from friends, loss of financial security or status, the absence of other concrete and less tangible supports that had been provided by the deceased or a member of the extended family that is no longer as involved, or the reduced engagement with a surviving caregiver who may be struggling emotionally or who is less available due to the need to work longer hours. These additional losses compound children's grief and delay adaptation. Many of these secondary losses are not appreciated by children until they are confronted with the losses at a later age. Children may not grieve the lack of parenting advice their mother might have provided until they are faced with challenges in parenting their own newborn. They may first long for more stories of past generations that help them understand their place within the family's culture when they become grandparents themselves. As a result, the work of grief is never finished; attachment and bonds continue throughout a child's life.

It is important to note that some children will experience grief because of significant non-death related interpersonal losses which are often not recognized (Sweetman, & O'Donnell, 2020). This includes children whose caregivers may be unavailable because of mental illness, substance abuse, health problems, work requirements, legal difficulties, family discord or placement in alternative care systems (Kuit & Ryke, 2023). Disenfranchised grief may occur when there is a lack of acknowledgement of a loss by others because the loss is considered to be minor (e.g. loss of a pet, move to a new location) or the relationship of the child with the person who died is not considered significant (Kumar, 2023).

Although grieving individuals of all ages generally benefit from similar acknowledgment of their loss, support, and accommodations from others, there are some unique considerations in supporting grieving children. Furthermore, even among children, grief is a personal experience and will be influenced by

- the quality of the pre-existing relationship with the deceased;
- the circumstances of the death;
- the quality of available support from parents/guardians and other caring adults;
- the child's prior experience with loss;
- the child's typical coping mechanisms and overall resiliency including their own active agency over their grief experience (Russell et al, 2024);

- the developmental stage and level of understanding of the concepts of death.

Identifying Grief in Children

Grief is a common experience of children and adolescents but not always recognized by those working with children (Adeback, et al, 2022). Symptoms of grief including separation anxiety, distress about the impact of the loss on their lives and troubling feelings about how the loved one died are common (Alvis et al, 2022) but often seen as caused by an underlying mental health problem such as anxiety and/or depression (Mosher, 2018). When a child presents for treatment of a traumatic experience, the primary focus is often placed on the processing of the fears related to the perceived life-threat but not the grief for their many losses associated with their traumatic event.

Children may opt not to mention to others, including their school, that a close family member has died and may not appear to be grieving. When asked about a death, they may minimize their distress and decline offers of support and assistance, at least at first. From an early age, children see that their questions or comments about death often cause discomfort in adults. Children's questions about the implications of a recent death of a family member are often evocative and may cause other family members to become tearful or uncomfortable; this may be interpreted by grieving children as a sign that their questions are inappropriate or naughty. They may feel the need to support surviving family members who are also grieving before they are even able to experience their own grief. This often adds to the sense of isolation often experienced by grieving children. Grieving caregivers may be so overwhelmed that they find it difficult, or may even fail, to recognize and address grief in their own children. One of the benefits of school and healthcare professionals is that they may have more emotional distance from the loss; as a result, children may feel it is safer to discuss their grief with them.

Children's Developmental Understanding of Death

There are four major concepts of death that have been described in the literature that serve as the foundation for an understanding of death which is required for successful adaptation (Schonfeld & Quackenbush, 2021; Panagiotaki et al, 2015; Speece, 1984). On average, these concepts are learned between 5 and 7 years of age, although personal experience with loss and education/explanation may accelerate children's understanding. Children with a potentially life-limited illness, for example, tend to have a precocious understanding of these concepts even in the absence of explicit discussion. These concepts also provide a useful foundation upon which to assess what children with neurodevelopmental or intellectual disabilities understand and how best to explain to them what death means after a personal loss has occurred.

Irreversibility: Unlike cartoon characters that die and later return to life, death is irreversible. Children who do not appreciate this may fail to even begin to mourn, waiting instead for the person to return. Statements such as "he went on a long journey" can undermine this understanding. While some have suggested that this concept is not possible for young children to understand, even toddlers can understand "all gone" – it is not a difficult concept to understand, but as with other the concepts of death, it can be difficult to accept in the context of a personal loss.

Finality or nonfunctionality: Very young children initially attribute life to all things; this animism leads children to believe that inanimate objects are alive. Cartoons, children's stories, and comments by adults that the television or car "died" can all further complicate this understanding. As they get older, children may view distinctions between living things and nonliving things that are inaccurate. For example, children may recognize that locomotion is often characteristic of living things and may conclude that a car is alive, but a tree is not. It isn't until children have a more mature understanding of what are living functions that they are likely to assume that these life functions end completely at the time of death. When someone suggests to a pre-school-age child to draw a picture to place in a casket with a deceased parent, the child may assume that the deceased can see the picture and is conscious of being buried. Until children understand this concept, they may unnecessarily worry about the physical suffering of those that have died, concerned that a dead relative is still conscious, in pain, hungry, or upset. They need this understanding to comprehend why the body may be buried or cremated.

Inevitability or universality: After the death of someone close, children often worry that others close to them will die. It therefore would seem counterintuitive to help children understand that all living things eventually die. But if children do not see death as inevitable, they will question why a particular person died. Often, they assume that they have done something wrong (whether it was something they thought, did, or didn't do) that has led to the death of someone they love, resulting in quilt. Or they may assume that the individual was chosen to die for something the person did, resulting in shame of the deceased.

Causality: Children instead need to understand, at a basic level (and without unnecessary or graphic detail) why someone died. This will decrease the likelihood that alternative explanations will increase confusion or contribute to guilt or shame.

It is important to use the word "dead" or "died" and limit euphemisms and explanations that are based on abstract concepts that may be misunderstood by young children. Young children are likely to make literal misinterpretations. They may be told that during a wake, the body is placed in a box called a casket and refuse to attend because they assume that if the body is placed in the casket, the head must be placed somewhere else. Religious concepts may be shared with children by their families at any age but shouldn't be relied upon as the sole explanation of death since they tend to be abstract and often insufficient to help children understand what has happened. For example, a young child told his brother went to Heaven to be with God because he was such a good baby may worry that unless he misbehaves in church (i.e., God's home) he may also be called back to Heaven.

Children with neurodevelopmental and intellectual disabilities may not be able to communicate their understanding verbally and may demonstrate their distress through non-specific behaviours such as an increase in self-soothing behaviors or changes in sleep, toileting, or behaviors. They may become even less tolerant of change in routines or become more oppositional. Explanations should be geared toward their developmental level; for children who are able to communicate their understanding verbally, this explanation can be followed with questions to assess their comprehension and to identify any persisting concerns or misunderstandings. Older neurodivergent children may also benefit from practical suggestions on how to communicate their needs and feelings to others and how to answer questions from peers and ask for and accept support from those in their social network. Children with developmental disabilities are affected by loss and may be at risk of disenfranchised grief (Gaines, 2022). A review of research found that grief reactions of those with neurodevelopmental disorders are often unrecognized and misunderstood because of their neurodivergence (Mair et al, 2024).

Complicated or Prolonged Grief

Grief can become even more complicated for a child due to the circumstances surrounding the death and the developmental phase of a child (Revet et al, 2020; Falala, et al, 2024). This may be due to strong emotions associated with the death, significant changes in the support the child relied on for stability, and/or exposure of the child to traumatic events at the time of the death. The length of time needed to process their loss is then prolonged because of this these complications resulting in the child experiencing "complicated" or "prolonged grief".

Deaths of relatives and peers in potentially traumatizing circumstances may lead to symptoms of prolonged grief and posttraumatic stress (Boelen et al, 2023). Exposure to traumatic events complicates the process of bereavement by shifting the focus from the actual loss of the person who was important to the child to the frightening circumstances surrounding the death (McClatchey al, 2014). Children with traumatic memories associated with the death may remember and reexperience the traumatic aspects of the death when grief is activated including the imagined or real details of the often-violent death or the pain experienced before the person died (Cohen and Mannarino, 2011). This impedes the child's ability to process the many feelings associated with the loss because the traumatic memories may increase the avoidance of thinking and talking about the loss.

Prolonged Grief Disorder (PGD) has been suggested to represent a longer than usual period of bereavement - usually defined as six months after the death (Spuij, 2012). This may be difficult to apply with children whose length of bereavement may be influenced by family and cultural influences. Rosenblatt (2017) challenges the universal application of a prolonged grief diagnosis by commenting that in many cultures it is considered customary for a member of that culture to continue to be grieving and show emotional manifestations of their loss experience well beyond a six-month period.

Guilt and Shame

Due to children's egocentrism and magical thinking, they are likely to assume there was something they did, didn't do, or should have done that caused or substantially contributed to the death. Even when there is no logical, objective reason to suspect the child feels responsible, it is helpful to reassure grieving children – and adults – that they were not at fault. Children can be told that when bad things happen, people often feel badly and may think they did something bad. Thoughts and feelings don't cause people to die, but often children still feel guilty. They can then be asked if they have ever felt that way themselves. Piaget proposed that children as old as 7 years maintain an egocentric viewpoint (Piaget & Inhelder, 1956) but research has found that children after 4 or 5 years are able to successfully take the perspective of another person although components of egocentrism may continue later in a child's development (Choifer, 2021).

In the immediate aftermath of a death, children will often worry that others close to them may die. It may seem (at an unconscious level) preferrable in this context to assume an illusion of control – if they were somehow responsible for the death, then they can ensure they don't make the same "mistake" and thereby decrease the risk of future deaths. Accepting that they had no contribution to the death may leave them feeling helpless to prevent the death of others that are important in their life. But since it is an illusion of control, it isn't effective in reducing future risk of death and it results in guilt that complicates the grieving process. This is seen commonly even among adults.

This guilt is more common when the pre-existing relationship was ambivalent (such as commonly seen during adolescence) or conflicted, such as when a parent is abusive or distant and uninvolved in the child's life. Guilt can also be anticipated when the actions of the child contributed to the death, such as if the child accidentally discharges a firearm that is the cause of death. In this context or when the guilt is persistent or intense, it is helpful to consider professional counseling which may aim to help the person who is grieving appreciate that the death was accidental and to help them get to the point where they can forgive themselves.

Children may also be embarrassed to share that they are grieving (Brinkmann, 2019) or feel shame due to the circumstances of the death, such as when the death occurred from an accident while under the influence of alcohol or drugs, the result of suicide or drug overdose, while the individual was committing a criminal act, or in other situations that are socially stigmatized (Levi-Belz, 2023). In these situations, active outreach to children is often necessary to encourage them to share and help them cope with their grief.

Cultural Sensitivity

While the experience of grief is universal, the individual's expressions of grief and the mourning practices of groups of people differ significantly based on personal, social, cultural, and religious backgrounds (Holte, 2017). Culture indeed plays an important role in shaping youths' mourning rituals, communication about death, and socialization of emotion regulation strategies within families (Alvis et al, 2022). It may be a tradition of one culture not to speak the name of someone who has died for an extended period, whereas another culture may encourage families to name the next child born after the deceased. In one culture, open expressions of emotions may be discouraged at funerals, but in another, the extent and intensity of emotions expressed may be viewed as an indication of the amount of love and respect. Cultural beliefs also help define who is considered a member of the family and guide expectations of who should be grieving and how the grief should be expressed (Schoulte, 2011). Children often find comfort in a family's faith-based beliefs and practices. Religious beliefs and a shared religious faith may help them find some meaning and acceptance despite what would otherwise appear to be an incomprehensible situation (Jerome, 2011). Although grief reactions are experienced consistently across different cultures, differences in their expression may exist across cultures with some groups being more at risk due to the mechanisms of loss such as refugees, migrants, and conflict survivors (Hilberdink, 2023). Members of a racial or ethnic group that have experienced systemic racism, poverty, or marginalization may have more challenges in adapting to a loss due to the intersectionality of their grief with discrimination or inequity (Wilson & O'Connor, 2022; Powell, 2021). Finally, professionals need to be aware of their own cultural assumptions about grief and bereavement (Walter, 2010) and how their perceived cultural identity may influence how children respond to their interventions.

While it is helpful to know some of the different cultural practices among religions and cultures of most children you are likely to support, it is not necessary to be familiar with the practices of every group to provide effective support. What is critical, though, is to know that there are important differences and to have the cultural humility to ask for guidance from the family about what is important to them, and their community related to mourning practices. Assumptions based on what someone assumes is the child's or family's religious, ethnic, or cultural mourning practices may result in stereotypes and cause people to overlook opportunities to be responsive to the individual child's or family's needs or preferences. Children may come from mixed or blended backgrounds with family members representing different races, ethnicities, religions, and cultures. The degree of cultural identification, including the degree of enculturation (learning about a culture) and acculturation (taking on another culture), may differ from that of earlier generations or even among members of the same generation. People should therefore be cautious about assuming they understand the uniqueness of a child's grief experience based on assumptions about their cultural background (Danieli and Nader, 2006). One child may practice their family's faith devoutly whereas another may opt not to. After a very difficult loss, a questioning or even rejection of prior religious beliefs among individuals or families may lead grieving children to seek a different approach or view. For example, a belief in the absence of an afterlife may be held before the death of someone who is deeply loved but may be seen as intolerable afterwards.

SCHOOL STRATEGIES FOR SUPPORTING GRIEVING STUDENTS

Schools can monitor grieving students' adjustment over time, model and teach coping strategies, and provide psychoeducation about grief and bereavement. They should provide academic and other psychosocial supports and recommend school- and community-based children's bereavement support services as well as mental health services when this level of additional support is indicated or requested. Most teachers and other school professionals, however, feel unprepared and apprehensive about reaching out to provide support to grieving students (Reid & Dixon, 1999). Dyregrov et al. (2015) interviewed a sample of teachers from primary and secondary schools and found that, although the school personnel had high levels of empathy and commitment towards grieving students, they expressed limited knowledge about how child bereavement affects school performance, concentration, and learning. They also expressed guilt for not doing more for bereaved children at their school. The school community and school systems must endorse the importance of their schools becoming both grief-sensitive and supportive. Teachers and school administrators may feel pressured to view attention to social and emotional needs as inappropriate or at least as secondary to their primary role of promoting academic achievement.

Talking with Grieving Students

Grief is a personal experience that occurs within both a developmental and social context (Jones et al, 2015, Sabagh et al, 2025). The overwhelming and intense emotions often feel uniquely personal and intimate and are difficult to express even for adults. This may prompt grieving children to withdraw from peers and well-intentioned adults, furthering the isolation often felt by those who are grieving. Grieving children and their families are likely unaware of the resources available to support grieving children within schools, pediatric practices, and the broader community (Assadi, 2023).

Peers and adults also feel uncomfortable and often unqualified to assist grieving children and may worry that they will say or do the wrong thing and just make matters worse. Often, the safest action may feel like remaining silent or offering only vague references to the loss or offers of general support. But saying nothing communicates a lot to grieving children – that others are unaware, unconcerned, do not feel that the child is able to cope even with their support, or simply unable or unwilling to be of assistance.

Table 1. Steps to take in initiating conversation with a grieving student

Initiating the Conversation -- These steps can help get the conversation started.
Express concern. Let students know you've heard about their loss and are available to listen and offer support.
Be genuine. Children can tell when adults are authentic in their communications. For example, don't tell a child you will miss her uncle if you did not know the man. Do tell the child you are sad she has experienced this loss.
Invite the conversation. Use simple, direct, open-ended questions. For example, ask, "How are you and your family doing?"
Listen and observe. Listen more and talk less. Share observations about students' behavior or responses in a nonjudgmental manner.
Limit personal sharing. You can draw on personal experiences to help you better understand students, but do not need to share this with them. Keep the focus on the student.
Offer practical advice. For example, discuss ways to respond to questions from peers or adults about the death.

(Coalition to Support Grieving Students, 2015)

Child-serving professionals often find children's expressions of grief as unfiltered and evocative. They may be reminded of their own personal losses or worry that children in their own life will experience grief as well (since chances are they will). They may care about the children they are supporting and find themselves becoming tearful or choked up. It is fine to express such genuine emotions in front of grieving children, if professionals do not become so overwhelmed that grieving children feel the need to support them or at least to protect them from further expressions of their grief. Children need to learn effective coping mechanisms for the strong feelings associated with grief (Venkatesan, 2022). It is therefore helpful to see genuine expressions of sadness – and effective strategies to cope with these feelings – modelled by trusted adults.

Academic Supports for Grieving Students

Following the death of a close friend or family member most children will experience at least temporarily academic challenges with some children demonstrating an actual improvement in this academic functioning. Teachers often observe that grieving children struggle in the classroom and have reduced test scores and learning setbacks (Dyregrov, 2015). Difficulty concentrating and distractibility, anxiety, depressed mood, and sleep difficulties may limit a student's learning capacity. Children with learning problems that predated the loss may experience a marked worsening in their academic performance. These learning difficulties because of their loss may appear immediately or may be seen weeks or months after the death of the family member or close friend. The impact on a child's academic development may be extensive and intermittent support may be needed throughout a child's academic career (Abdelnoor & Hollins, 2004; Dyregrov et al, 2022). If interventions are not provided many of these bereaved children will experience a reduction in school grades or even drop out of school (Broberg et al, 2005; Liu et al, 2022; Kazemi et al, 2023).

Given that many if not most grieving students will experience at least temporary challenges with learning after the death of a close family member or friend, it is important to offer academic supports pro-actively, prior to when children first demonstrate academic difficulties and certainly well before signs of academic failure. Schools should be a source of support for grieving students, but if academic expectations even temporarily exceed current abilities, schools become a source of additional distress. The aim is to achieve a balance between maintaining reasonable academic expectations to maintain grieving children's interest in school and preparing them as well as possible for future academic demands, with making accommodations to provide work that feels achievable and appropriate at the time. This will likely change from day-to-day and across subjects and extracurricular activities. It is helpful for someone (such as a school counselor, social worker, or psychologist) to help maintain this balance (e.g., so that the student is excused from an athletic practice if more preparation for an important academic project is necessary or vice versa). Often, one person may serve as the point of contact with the student and another (or the same person) serving as the point of contact for the family. In this way, students in middle or high school settings are not required to talk daily about their grief and coping with upwards of ten school professionals and try on their own to negotiate how best to access academic supports.

Teachers may also wish to consider accommodations to assignments, such as allowing a student who has difficulty sustaining attention to replace a term paper with a project done with a partner or allowing students who are uncomfortable working with others to substitute an individual assignment for a group project. Teachers should apply the principles of differentiated learning to the unique and at times shifting learning challenges of grieving students. Grieving students may be excused from tests immediately after the death or grades prior to the death may be weighted more in determining final class grades. There should also be consideration to modifying the curriculum for the entire class whenever lessons may highlight circumstances like the death experienced by one of the students. For example, books where one of the characters died in a similar manner may be substituted; a lesson on substance abuse prevention may be postponed if a student recently experienced the death of a family members by an overdose.

Management of Grief Triggers and Anniversary Reactions

Grief triggers involve sudden reminders of someone who died that can cause temporary, but still powerful, emotional responses. Anything that reminds grieving children of the person that died can activate these feelings – a song that is played that the deceased used to sing; mention of a place where the family recently went on vacation; a poem that speaks to the special bond between siblings. Even a routine request that children discuss something with their parents can acutely remind grieving children of their loss. These triggers are most likely to occur in the first months after a death. Although the intensity of grief triggers generally lessons over time, they can still occur even years later.

Educators should let grieving students know that grief triggers may occur and establish a plan of how to address them in the classroom setting, so that grieving students know that they can leave the classroom briefly if they are worried that they will start crying or otherwise become overwhelmed by their emotions. The student may be given permission to go to the nurse's office, speak with the school counselor or social worker, or simply sit quietly in the library and practice self-regulatory strategies such as journaling or relaxation techniques. It is helpful to establish a discreet cue from the student to the teacher that will not draw the attention of classmates, such as taking a tissue from a tissue box placed near the doorway as the student exits the room. If children know that they can exit if they need to, they are less likely to feel the need to leave the classroom and more likely to remain in class and engaged in the lesson.

Some likely triggers can be anticipated by teachers, such as an activity focused on Father's or Mother's Day, a father-daughter dance, or high school graduation. Such activities and events should be introduced to students with suggestions on how they can still participate even if their parent is no longer alive, living with them, or actively engaged in their lives (e.g., they can focus on their memories of their father or select another important man in their lives for a Father's Day activity). Other triggers may be anticipated by the children or family, such as the date of when the death occurred or the birthday of the individual who died and shared with school staff.

Engaging Peers

Children generally want and can provide support to grieving peers, but much like adults, they may lack confidence in their ability to provide meaningful support or worry that they may make matters worse by saying or doing the wrong thing. Children have even less experience in providing support than do adults. Children's first exposure to the death of a parent may be through losses experienced by friends; this may cause a sense of personal vulnerability which may lead them to distance themselves rather than reach out to help their grieving peer. This may worsen the sense of isolation felt by grieving children.

When children are unprepared and uninformed, they are more likely to ask repetitive or intrusive questions about the means of death or even tease grieving peers about their loss or how they express their grief. In a study of 35 parentally bereavement children 6-15 years of age, Cain and Lafreniere (2015) reported that 1 of 5 "experienced direct, raw taunting about their loss." This is less likely to occur when teachers talk with classmates about their questions and concerns and prepare them to be better able to support grieving students.

Classroom discussions may help peers understand, at a basic level, what happened so that many children have less need to ask directly of the grieving student. Practical strategies for how to reach out to and support a grieving peer can be reviewed, including effective ways to start a conversation (with suggestions on what to say and what not to say) and offer support (such as sharing class notes or offering to partner on assignments); how to offer companionship while honoring when grieving children are in need of privacy; and helping grieving children advocate for necessary academic accommodations and support (and similar assistance for extracurricular activities).

During these discussions, children can learn more about what impact the death of a parent or other close relative, or friend is likely to have on them and where they can turn to supports in the school, home, and community. Schools can also share print resources on how parents and other caring adults can talk to and support grieving children such as "After a Loved One Dies: How Children Grieve and How Parents and Other Adults Can Support Them" which can be freely downloaded in nine languages and ordered for free in hard copy in English or Spanish at www.grievingstudents.org.

Social media is often used to express and share thoughts and feelings about those who have died. Social media can offer opportunities for social connection, self-expression, and mental health support but can also expose a vulnerable child to significant risks, including compulsive social media use, cyberbullying, unrealistic body image standards, and exposure to substance-related content (Masri-Zada, et al 2025). Students should be encouraged to bring to the school's attention any comments that are worrisome (e.g., suicidal ideation or homicidal comments) or destructive (e.g., comments that are highly critical about the person who died or the reactions of those grieving the loss) (Schonfeld & Quackenbush, 2021).

Coordinating With Families

The main protective factor for children is social support (Lai et al, 2017). How caregivers cope and manage their distress is a consistent predictor of how well children and youth do emotionally after traumatic and stressful experiences (Khamis, 2016; Samuelson et al, 2017). By helping the family, children are helped in turn. When adults are struggling to cope, their children often feel the need to provide them assistance; parents who are not coping well with their own grief are more likely to overlook their own children's needs for grief support.

Schools should actively reach out to the family to inquire about their assessment of how the grieving student is doing, to ask about strategies that family members are using at home to offer support, to identify any perceived needs, and to plan for the student's transition back to school. This is also a time to gently ask about how other family members are doing and let them know that the school can help them identify community resources. Some families will not yet be ready to accept such support. By maintaining contact over time, they may become more aware of their needs and more willing to accept assistance.

Providing Long-Term Support

Over a third of adults who experienced a death during childhood report that they never fully recovered (Koblenz, 2016). The death of a parent early in life is associated with suicidal behavior, depression, and other mortality risks in adulthood (Hollingshaus & Smith, 2015; Berg et al, 2016). The death of an important family member or friend is a life-changing experience and therefore has life-long impact.

Yet most grieving children (and adults) only receive substantial assistance during the initial months after the death. By the second year, support, and accommodations – and even recognition of the death – may have waned or ended almost completely.

Many people find that the second year of bereavement is in some ways more difficult than the initial year, in part because of the withdrawal of support from others. Grieving individuals may have very low expectations for the first major holidays after the death – but not anticipate, for example, how difficult the second Thanksgiving may be when the absence of the bereaved is still strongly felt. They may wonder if they will ever experience joy again. It is therefore helpful to continue the follow-up of grieving students for more than a year after the death.

Transitions between schools can provide exciting new opportunities and challenges for all students, but also be particularly stressful for grieving students. During these times, the loss of a parent/guardian, sibling, or close friend may be acutely felt. With the student's and family's permission, school professionals can share effective strategies and persisting needs with the new school. In a similar manner, communication between teachers is helpful when a child is promoted to a new grade even within the same school.

Graduation from high school and the transition to college, the military, or a career can be especially challenging. It is often associated with a move out of town or state, and the grieving student may lose much of the support of family and peers and the familiarity of their home and community. They may find it difficult to make new friends and adapt to markedly new academic/work expectations. Their sense of isolation and persistent sadness makes it difficult to form new friendships. Doing this in a setting where they have no privacy (even in their own bedroom or bathroom) and when the rest of their peers seem to be happy and excited adds further challenges. Youth may also feel guilty for pursing their own goals at a time when their family is still struggling with their grief; they may worry about not being around to offer support to them. School professionals can help them identify where they can seek support in their new setting and offer to communicate with counseling staff on the student's behalf. It is also much appreciated when school professionals from high school send a brief email or note to let the student know they are still in their thoughts. (Schonfeld & Quackenbush, 2021)

Commemoration and Memorialisation

When the death impacts many children in a school setting (such as after the death of a member of the school community), commemoration and memorialization allow students to recognize that they are not alone in their grief and provide a context and mechanism for them to draw on the support of others. The activities may help them express and adjust to difficult feelings that might otherwise seem overwhelming and learn the coping strategies of others while they in turn share what has worked for them. It may help them connect with shaken beliefs that may have been challenged by the death and begin to find some meaning in the loss. It is important, though, to consider the timing and intent of commemorative and memorial experiences and to ensure that the process is based on student input so that what is done is meaningful to the children. (Schonfeld & Quackenbush, 2021)

In the immediate aftermath of the crisis, the goal of commemorative activities is to create a shared experience that provides mutual support, rather than to establish an enduring legacy of the person or people that died. This will allow students to start to identify, understand, express and cope with their feelings, without creating a sense that the school is attempting to reach premature closure. The process by which the planning is conducted is more important that what specifically is done for the memorial or commemorative event. It is critical to actively include students in a central role so that their needs drive the process and what is done is ultimately aligned with their preferences. Indeed, the planning process often allows them to process within their community what they wish and hope to preserve as a memory and foster collective meaning-making.

In planning permanent memorials, it is important to remember that the goal is preserve the memory of what was lost or altered, rather than to preserve memories of the moment or method of the loss. Careful consideration should also be given to avoid creating precedents for future commemoration and memorialization that are either difficult to sustain (i.e., creating a scholarship named after a student that died using money donated by the students' family – which may not be possible for children of families of lesser financial means or may not be appropriate if a subsequent student dies by suicide). In lieu of formal and permanent memorials (such as plaques or markers), thoughtful activities such as inviting students to provide community service after the death of a school community member are often more meaningful to students and therefore helpful in their adaptation to the loss. (Schonfeld & Quackenbush, 2021)

Grief Support in Contemporary Education

Although bereavement is very common among school-age children and can have a significant impact on their learning, emotional adjustment, and developmental trajectory, educators typically feel uncomfortable and unprepared to provide basic support to grieving students. Educators report limited to no training on how to support grieving students and perceive this to be the main barrier to their providing outreach and support. The COVID-19 pandemic starkly illustrated the need for schools to become more grief-informed, resulting in an increasing interest among educators in practice about this topic (Lively-Endicott et al, 2023). Future training of educators of all disciplines, including school mental health professionals, should incorporate opportunities to enhance educators' knowledge and skills in this important area to remedy this long-standing gap.

CONCLUSION

This chapter examined how children experienced grief following the death of a close family member or friend, and how school professionals could support them through the grieving process. Grief was identified as a common experience in childhood, though often unrecognised or misunderstood by adults, including educators. Children were affected by both primary losses (the death itself) and secondary losses, such as changes in living arrangements, routines, or emotional support. Their grief responses varied depending on developmental stage, relationship with the deceased, prior experiences with loss, and the support available to them. Many children struggled to grasp core concepts of death (e.g., irreversibility, non-functionality, inevitability, and causality) leading to confusion, guilt, fear, or magical thinking. Grief could be further complicated by traumatic circumstances, sudden deaths, or minimal emotional support. In such cases, children often experienced prolonged grief or post-traumatic stress. Neurodivergent children, in particular, were at risk of having their grief overlooked, as they frequently expressed distress through changes in behaviour rather than words. Cultural and religious beliefs played a major role in shaping mourning practices and emotional expression. The chapter emphasised the importance of cultural humility, encouraging educators to ask families about their traditions and preferences, rather than making assumptions based on perceived background. Schools were seen as key environments for supporting grieving children. Educators were encouraged to express concern, initiate open conversations, provide emotional validation, and adjust academic expectations where needed. Support also included helping children manage grief triggers, such as holidays or anniversaries, and teaching peers how to respond with sensitivity and respect. Proactive communication with families and coordination among school staff were highlighted as essential strategies for long-term support. Memorialisation, particularly following a death that affected the broader school community, was most effective when students were actively involved in the planning and when the focus remained on healing and shared meaning rather than permanence.

DISCUSSION POINTS

1. How can you prepare an educator to provide basic support for a grieving student?
2. What can schools do to support the recovery of grieving students?
3. How do you explain the needs of a grieving child to their families and peers?
4. What potential barriers can be avoided in the memorialization and commemoration process following the death of a child or member of the school community?

REFERENCES

Abdelnoor, A., & Hollins, S. (2004). The effect of childhood bereavement on secondary school performance. *Educational Psychology in Practice*, *20*(1), 43–54.

Adebäck, P., Lundh, L., & Nilsson, D. (2022). Children or adolescents who lost someone close during the Southeast Asia tsunami 2004 - The life as young. *Brain and Behavior*, *12*(5), e2563. DOI: 10.1002/brb3.2563 PMID: 35333453

Alvis, L., Zhang, N., Sandler, I. N., & Kaplow, J. B. (2022). Developmental Manifestations of Grief in Children and Adolescents: Caregivers as Key Grief Facilitators. *Journal of Child & Adolescent Trauma*, *16*(2), 447–457. DOI: 10.1007/s40653-021-00435-0 PMID: 35106114

Assadi, F. (2023). Understanding the Childhood Grief: What Should We Tell the Children? *International Journal of Preventive Medicine*, *14*, 96. DOI: 10.4103/ijpvm.ijpvm_371_22 PMID: 37855003

Berg, L., Rostila, M., & Hjern, A. (2016). Parental death during childhood and depression in young adults - a national cohort study. *Journal of Child Psychology and Psychiatry, and Allied Disciplines*, *57*(9), 1092–1098. DOI: 10.1111/jcpp.12560 PMID: 27058980

Blad, E. (2015). Educators often overlook student grief, experts say. *Education Week*, *34*(18), 1, 12–13.

Boelen, P. A., Giannopoulou, I., & Papadatou, D. (2023). Patterns and predictive value of acute prolonged grief and posttraumatic stress in youngsters confronted with traumatic loss: A latent class analysis. *Psychiatry Research*, *319*, 114961. DOI: 10.1016/j.psychres.2022.114961 PMID: 36446220

Brinkmann, S. (2019). Learning to grieve: A preliminary analysis. *Culture and Psychology*, *26*(3), 469–483. DOI: 10.1177/1354067x19877918

Broberg, A., Dyregrov, A., & Lilled, L. (2005). The Göteborg discotheque fire: Posttraumatic stress, and school adjustment as reported by the primary victims 18 months later. *Journal of Child Psychology and Psychiatry, and Allied Disciplines*, *46*(12), 1279–1286. PMID: 16313428

Cain, A., & LaFreniere, L. (2015). The taunting of parentally bereaved children: An exploratory study. *Death Studies*, *39*(4), 219–225. PMID: 25581438

Choifer, A. (2021). Interpretational Complexities in Developmental Research and a Piagetian Reading of the False-Belief Task. *Review of Philosophy and Psychology*, *12*, 923–952. DOI: 10.1007/s13164-020-00519-0

Coalition to Support Grieving Students. (2015). Table 1: Initiating the conversation. In NYL-1A-Talking-With-Children.pdf. Retrieved June 1, 2024 from http://www.grievingstudents.org

Cohen, J. A., & Mannarino, A. P. (2011). Supporting children with traumatic grief: What educators need to know. *School Psychology International*, *32*(2), 117–131. DOI: 10.1177/0143034311400827

Danieli, Y., & Nader, K. (2006). Respecting cultural, religious, and ethnic differences in the prevention and treatment of psychological sequelae. In Schein, L. A., Spitz, H. I., Burlingame, G. M., Muskin, P. R., & Vargo, S. (Eds.), *Psychological effects of catastrophic disasters: Group approaches to treatment* (pp. 203–234). Haworth Press.

Dyregrov, A., Dyregrov, K., Endsjø, M., & Idsoe, T. (2015). Teachers' perception of bereaved children's academic performance. *Advances in School Mental Health Promotion*, *8*(3), 187–198.

Falala, A., Lannes, A., Bui, E., & Revet, A. (2024). Prevalence of prolonged grief disorder in bereaved children and adolescents: A systematic review. *L'Encéphale*, *50*(5), 557–565. DOI: 10.1016/j.encep.2023.11.016 PMID: 38413249

Flavell, J. H., Everett, B. A., Croft, K., & Flavell, E. R. (1981). Young children's knowledge about visual perception: Further evidence for the Level 1–Level 2 distinction. *Developmental Psychology*, *17*, 99–103.

Gaines, A. G. (2022). The Grief Experiences of Children with Developmental Disabilities: A Narrative Literature Review. *Omega*. Advance online publication. DOI: 10.1177/00302228221124520 PMID: 36138512

Hilberdink, C. E., & Ghainder, K., Alexandre Dubanchet, Hinton, D., Manik, A., Hall, B. J., & Bui, E. (2023). Bereavement Issues and Prolonged Grief Disorder: A Global Perspective. *Global Mental Health (Cambridge, England)*, *10*, 1–37. DOI: 10.1017/gmh.2023.28 PMID: 37854407

Hollingshaus, M. S., & Smith, K. R. (2015). Life and death in the family: Early parental death, parental remarriage, and offspring suicide risk in adulthood. *Social Science & Medicine*, *131*, 181–189. DOI: 10.1016/j.socscimed.2015.02.008 PMID: 25704222

Holte Kofod, E. (2017). From morality to pathology: A brief historization of contemporary Western grief practices and understandings. *Nordic Psychology*, *69*(1), 47–60. DOI: 10.1080/19012276.2016.1267914

J. (2011). Bereavement Among African Americans and Latino/a Americans. *Journal of Mental Health Counseling*, 33(1), 11–20. DOI: 10.17744/mehc.33.1.r4971657p7176307

Jerome, A. (2011). Comforting children and families who grieve: Incorporating spiritual support. *School Psychology International*, *32*(2), 194–209.

Jones, A., Deane, C., & Keegan, O. (2015). The development of a framework to support bereaved children and young people: The Irish Childhood Bereavement Care Pyramid. *Bereavement Care*, *34*, 43–51. DOI: 10.1080/02682621.2015.1063857

Khamis, V. (2016). Does parent's psychological distress mediate the relationship between war trauma and psychosocial adjustment in children? *Journal of Health Psychology*, *21*(7), 1361–1370. DOI: 10.1177/1359105314553962 PMID: 27357922

Koblenz, J. (2016). Growing From Grief. *Omega*, *73*(3), 203–230. DOI: 10.1177/0030222815576123

Kuit, N., & Ryke, E. H. (2023). A Rapid Review of Non-death Bereavement Interventions for Children in Alternative Care. *Child & Adolescent Social Work Journal*, *40*, 29–41. DOI: 10.1007/s10560-021-00757-w

Kumar, R. M. (2023). The Many Faces of Grief: A Systematic Literature Review of Grief During the COVID-19 Pandemic. *Illness, Crises, and Loss*, *31*(1), 100–119. DOI: 10.1177/10541373211038084 PMID: 36605776

Lai, B. S., Lewis, R., Livings, M. S., La Greca, A. M., & Esnard, A.-M. (2017). Posttraumatic Stress Symptom Trajectories Among Children After Disaster Exposure: A Review. *Journal of Traumatic Stress*, *30*(6), 571–582. DOI: 10.1002/jts.22242 PMID: 29193316

Levi-Belz, Y. (2023). Interpersonal facilitators of complicated grief and depression in the aftermath of suicide loss: The mediated roles of suicide-related shame and guilt. *Suicide & Life-Threatening Behavior*, *53*(4), 680–691. DOI: 10.1111/sltb.12973 PMID: 37439284

Lively-Endicott, H. R., Naimi, K., Hudson, S. M., & Schonfeld, D. J. (2023). Educator perspectives on grief-sensitive training during the COVID-19 pandemic in US public schools. *The Journal of School Health*. Advance online publication. PMID: 37879312

Mair, A. P. A., Nimbley, E., McConachie, D., Goodall, K., & Gillespie-Smith, K. (2024). Understanding the Neurodiversity of Grief: A Systematic Literature Review of Experiences of Grief and Loss in the Context of Neurodevelopmental Disorders. *Review Journal of Autism and Developmental Disorders (Online)*. DOI: 10.1007/s40489-024-00447-0

Masri-Zada, T., Martirosyan, S., Abdou, A., Barbar, R., Kades, S., Makki, H., Haley, G., & Agrawal, D. K. (2025). The Impact of Social Media & Technology on Child and Adolescent Mental Health. *Journal of Psychiatry and Psychiatric Disorders*, *9*(2), 111–130. PMID: 40520349

McClatchey, I. S., Vonk, M. E., Lee, J., & Bride, B. (2014). Traumatic and Complicated Grief Among Children: One or Two Constructs? *Death Studies*, *38*(2), 69–78. DOI: 10.1080/07481187.2012.725571 PMID: 24517704

Mosher, P. J. (2018). Everywhere and Nowhere: Grief in Child and Adolescent Psychiatry and Pediatric Clinical Populations. *Child and Adolescent Psychiatric Clinics of North America*, *27*(1), 109–124. DOI: 10.1016/j.chc.2017.08.009 PMID: 29157497

Panagiotaki, G., Nobes, G., Ashraf, A., & Aubby, H. (2015). British and Pakistani children's understanding of death: Cultural and developmental influences. *British Journal of Developmental Psychology*, *33*(1), 31–44. PMID: 25262770

Piaget, J., & Inhelder, B. (1956). *The child's conception of space*. Routledge & Kegan Paul.

Reid, J. K., & Dixon, W. A. (1999). Teacher attitudes on coping with grief in the public school classroom. *Psychology in the Schools*, *36*(3), 219–229. DOI: 10.1002/(sici)1520-6807(199905)36:3%3C219:aid-pits5%3E3.0.co;2-0

Revet, A., Bui, E., Benvegnu, G., Suc, A., Mesquida, L., & Raynaud, J. P. (2020). Bereavement and reactions of grief among children and adolescents: Present data and perspectives. *L'Encéphale*, *46*(5), 356–363. DOI: 10.1016/j.encep.2020.05.007 PMID: 32921494

Rosenblatt, P. C. (2017). Researching Grief: Cultural, Relational, and Individual Possibilities. *Journal of Loss and Trauma*, *22*(8), 617–630. DOI: 10.1080/15325024.2017.1388347

Russell, C. E., Chin, M., Bollig, G., Cait, C.-A., Carnevale, F. A., Chrastek, J., Lavorgna, B., Macpherson, C., Remke, S. S., Scaut, L., Skeen, J., Szylit, R., van Breemen, C., & Shalev, R. (2024). Re-Imagining Childhood Grief: Children as Active Agents in a Transactional Process. *Omega, 0*(0). Advance online publication. DOI: 10.1177/00302228241310264 PMID: 39688324

Sabagh, K., Abdollahi Nodeh, M. H., & Naderifar, M. (2025). Loss and Bereavement: In Children. Inn J Pediatr., 35(2), e150107.DOI: 10.5812/ijp-150107

Samuelson, K. W., Wilson, C. K., Padrón, E., Lee, S., & Gavron, L. (2017). Maternal PTSD and Children's Adjustment: Parenting Stress and Emotional Availability as Proposed Mediators. *Journal of Clinical Psychology, 73*(6), 693–706. DOI: 10.1002/jclp.22369 PMID: 27487248

Schonfeld, D. J., & Demaria, T. (2016). Committee on Psychosocial Aspects of Child and Family Health, & Disaster Preparedness Advisory Council. Supporting the Grieving Child and Family. *Pediatrics, 138*(3), e20162147–e20162147. DOI: 10.1542/peds.2016-2147 PMID: 27573086

Schonfeld, D. J., & Quackenbush, M. (2021). *The Grieving Student.* Paul H Brookes Publishing.

Speece, M. W., & Brent, S. B. (1984). Children's understanding of death: A review of three components of a death concept. *Child Development, 55*(5), 1671–1686. PMID: 6510050

Spuij, M., Reitz, E., Prinzie, P., Stikkelbroek, Y., de Roos, C., & Boelen, P. A. (2012). Distinctiveness of symptoms of prolonged grief, depression, and post-traumatic stress in bereaved children and adolescents. *European Child & Adolescent Psychiatry, 21*(12), 673–679. DOI: 10.1007/s00787-012-0307-4 PMID: 22791348

Sweetman, A. & O'Donnell (2020). Non-Death Loss and Grief. Irish Association for Counselling & Psychotherapy, 20(3).

Venkatesan, S. (2022). LOSS, Grief, Bereavement, and Mourning in Children. *International Journal of Recent Scientific Research, 13*(03), 619–624. DOI: 10.24327/ijrsr.2022.1303.0129

Walter, T. (2010). Grief and culture. *Bereavement Care, 29*(2), 5–9. DOI: 10.1080/02682621003707431

Wilson, D. T., & O'Connor, M.-F. (2022). From Grief to Grievance: Combined Axes of Personal and Collective Grief Among Black Americans. *Frontiers in Psychiatry, 13.* Advance online publication. PMID: 35573332

ADDITIONAL READING

Alvis, L., Zhang, N., Sandler, I. N., & Kaplow, J. B. (2022). Developmental Manifestations of Grief in Children and Adolescents: Caregivers as Key Grief Facilitators. *Journal of Child & Adolescent Trauma*, *16*(2), 447–457. DOI: 10.1007/s40653-021-00435-0 PMID: 35106114

Chapter 10
Mainstream Education for Children and Young People With Acquired Brain Injury:
Enabling a Supportive Return to Education

Lorraine M. Duffy
https://orcid.org/0009-0006-8613-3956
Royal College of Surgeons in Ireland, Dublin, Ireland

ABSTRACT

Acquired brain injury (ABI) is a significant cause of childhood disability globally. Returning to education (RtE) can be a challenging, stressful experience for children and young people (CYP) and their families. This chapter will explore research that provides evidence of how to create an ABI aware school for CYP RtE following ABI. Specific focus will be placed on the gaps in provision that currently exist, such as the lack of evidence-based specialised ABI training for educators. The importance of taking a collaborative interdisciplinary approach towards the creation of an ABI aware school will be discussed, which should include CYP, parents/carers, peers, educators, and healthcare professionals (HCPs). Giving time to preparation is an essential first step in creating an ABI aware school. Acknowledging and accepting the new version of a CYP with ABI and remembering who they were pre-ABI are integral parts of the process.

DOI: 10.4018/979-8-3693-1293-3.ch010

INTRODUCTION

There are several variations of the definition of acquired brain injury (ABI) with all stating that ABI is a type of brain damage that occurs after birth which can be traumatic or non-traumatic. For this chapter, an acquired brain injury is defined "as an injury to the brain that is not hereditary, congenital, degenerative or induced by birth trauma. Essentially, this type of brain injury has occurred after birth" (Brain Injury Association of America, n.d.). Traumatic brain inury (TBI) is caused by an external force resulting in altered brain function and can occur because of situations such as car accidents or sports injuries. Non-traumatic brain injury (nTBI) results in damage to brain tissue and function as a result of internal factors caused by stroke and aneurysm for example (Brain Injury Association of America, n.d.). ABI is a global public health issue as it is the main cause of mortality and acquired disability in children and young people (CYP). The majority of brain injuries are mild, however a small number are classified as severe (5%). Despite this, all brain injuries regardless of the level of severity can lead to long-term educational, psychological and cognitive difficulties for CYP (Palanivel & Burrough, 2021).

Thousands of CYP acquire a brain injury annually worldwide. For example, The Children's Trust in the United Kingdom (2024) reports that around 40,000 CYP acquire a brain injury every year. This is an indicator that one child in every classroom will have consequences from ABI by the time they finish school. In the United States, approximately 895,000 CYP (age 0-19 years) acquire a TBI every year which leads to hospitalisation or emergency treatment (Children's Safety Network, 2023). Recent evidence in the United States indicates an increase in the number of CYP suffering from concussions, with school-aged CYP having the highest incidence of ABI (Centers for Disease Control and Prevention, 2023). According to Myers et al. (2017), there is an immediate need for innovative programs, policies, and practices to support CYP with ABI, particularly in terms of academic support and return to education (RtE).

ABI is known to have long-term consequences, the impact of which will vary according to the level of severity of the injury, i.e. mild, moderate or severe. The effect of the consequences for CYP may not be apparent immediately following an ABI. The consequences can be determined by the age and developmental stage of CYP at the time of the injury and may evolve as the brain develops (N-ABLES, 2021; Mayo Clinic, n.d.). Most of our understanding of paediatric ABI has been taken from adult experiences, for example, Child's systematic review (2024) of research that considered the lived experience of adolescents and young people with brain injury highlighted a clear lack of research which focusses on the perspectives of adolescents and young people. As a result much of the adult and child recommendations and interventions are not appropriate for the high number of adolescents globally whose lives are impacted by the consequences of brain injuries (Kakonge et al., 2022; Wales et al., 2013). The consequences and related outcomes of ABI vary for each CYP as they may experience one or more of the consequences, exhibit outcomes at varying levels of severity, may recover in some or all areas, or have lifelong or long-term difficulties. Such consequences can be visible or invisible (The Children's Trust, n.d.; Hammill, Bennett & White, 2019):

Table 1. Key Consequences of Acquired Brain Injury

Cognitive	Physical	Emotional	Behavioural	Social
• Difficulties with memory, attention, speech, processing speed, executive functioning • Lack of self- awareness Cognitive fatigue	• Weakness or paralysis • Fine motor skills, e.g. affecting writing ability • Dizziness, imbalance • Limb weakness • Poor mobility • Vision/hearing difficulties • Dyspraxia • Headaches • Incontinence • Seizures, epilepsy • Hormonal effects such as sexual disinhibition • Sensory difficulties related to eyes, ears, nose • Sleep disruption that can lead to problems with behaviour, concentration or irritability • Physical fatigue	• Anxiety • Low self-esteem • Low mood • Irritability • Anger • Emotional fatigue	• Impulsivity • Easily distracted • Lack of ability to focus • Poor ability to follow instructions • Irritability • Verbal outburts • Withdrawl from activities • Behavioural fatigue	• Poor communication • Reduced participation/ interaction with others

Article 28 of *The United Nations Convention on the Rights of the Child (UNCRC)* (1989) states that all children have a right to education. Article 24 of the *UN Convention on the Rights of Persons with Disabilities* (UNCRPD) (2006) states that individuals with a disability have a right to an inclusive education without discrimination, and should have equitable access to quality education from early childhood and all stages of education throughout their life. Education is a right and should be available for everyone to access in an equitable way; including people with ABI. The education setting is increasingly viewed as a pivotal aspect of CYP's post-brain injury rehabilitation; "The school system is generally viewed as the most natural environment for a child to meet their educational, social and often behavioral needs. However, successful transition to school requires educational interventions which are appropriately developed and delivered." (Linden, Glang, & McKinlay, 2018, p. 312). When we talk of transitions to school this can mean transition from hospital/ rehabilitation to school, from early childhood settings to primary school, from primary school to secondary school and from secondary school to higher education. These are transition periods where all children, including children with ABI and other disabilities must be supported to reach their full potential in an equitable, inclusive way through the implementation of equitable inclusive systems and policies.

This chapter will outline current themes in international research and evidence-based practice that guides schools and families on how best to support CYP aged 5-18 years to make and maintain a successful return to mainstream education after an ABI. The chapter aims to serve as a guide for a variety of readers, such as pyschologists, health professionals, researchers and educators. Academic studies, practical resources and best practice examples are discussed that outline approaches and interventions which may be adopted within the school setting to support a CYP with ABI make a successful RtE. To begin the foundations of the development of an ABI aware school will be outlined, namely individualised, person-centred planning, adopting an interdisciplinary, collaborative approach, adult and peer support, addressing consequences and wellbeing and providing parent support. The following section will explore training and resources for educators through the lens of identifying gaps, providing in-depth examples of best practice training programs and the signposting of useful resources. Preparing in-school supports and the school environment will then be discussed with a focus on existing gaps, assistive technology and classroom and school adjustments. Finally, the effect that a new version of oneself can have on CYP will be explored. In addition, gaps in research and practice will be highlighted throughout, and best practice examples will be outlined with a focus on the United Kingdom, Canada, the United States and Australia. Links to available resources for teachers and school communities will be included where relevant.

CREATING AN ABI AWARE SCHOOL: A COLLABORATIVE, INTERDISCIPLINARY APPROACH

Individualised, Person-Centred Planning

Preparing and creating an ABI aware school is essential in welcoming CYP with ABI return to school. Childhood ABI is generally a sudden event that happens, therefore education settings need to respond in an active and timely way to be appropriately equipped to meet the new needs of children with ABI (Bennett, Fletcher, Talbot, & Robinson, 2023). Medical advancements mean that an increasing number of CYP are surviving incidences that cause brain injury, and are returning to mainstream school with significant cognitive, communication and physical impairments, many of which can have life-long effects (Hayes, Shaw, Pearce, & Forsyth, 2017). Thus, Bennett et al.'s research (2023) and the former demonstrate the need for an interdisciplinary approach to be taken in the care and education of CYP with ABI. Every brain injury is different, which means every RtE plan must be individualised, person-centred and age appropriate to address the acquired needs of CYP, their family and the type of educational provision required (N-ABLES, 2021).

This individualised, person-centred approach is evident in the research of Bate, Turner and Fricke (2021), who state that RtE for CYP with ABI generally involves the inclusion of many people, including, parents or carers, educators, hospital and community-based healthcare professionals, and education support from other sources outside of the school.

Interdisciplinary, Collaborative Approach

The Educational Psychology Service is a key player in the RtE journey for CYP and their families and this service and the school should work collaboratively with one another (Hammill, Bennett, & White, 2019). Support must be provided in an interdisciplinary way with CYP given an opportunity to share their voice and be listened to. Additional school supports can be accessed from different agencies, for example, in Ireland *The National Council for Special Education (NCSE)* can provide further support (https://ncse.ie/), while in the UK, *The National Association for Special Educational Needs (NASEN)* can provide support to schools (https://ncse.ie/). There is growing evidence internationally, specifically within the United States, Australia and Canada that highlights the need for greater collaboration and communication between all stakeholders involved in the RtE of CYP with ABI. The evidence suggests that a greater emphasis needs to be placed on the inclusion of CYP and their parents. However, as discussed previously it is instrumental that the voice and perspectives of CYP is included in initial research as this data can form the foundation for effective, sustainable interventions and educational supports to be implemented (Childs, 2024). In addition, there is a pressing need to address the barriers that prevent professionals, including educators and healthcare professionals from collaborating, such as putting in place processes that allow for them to be released from their normal duties to meet one another (Andersson, Bellon, & Walker, 2016; Hartman, Duncanson, Farahat, & Lindsay, 2015). The following section will examine the role of supporting adults and peers in an ABI Aware School.

Adult and Peer Support

Adults within a school and peers of CYP should be prepared in different ways before the CYP returns to school. All adults at school should be given information about how the CYP acquired their injury, their new needs and the response that is required by the adults in the school. The CYP and their family must have full control over what information is shared with other adults in the school; this would be a crucial first step for the school principal to take when communicating with parents/

carers about the CYP's return to school. The organisation of training for all staff is a key element in developing an effective plan for the CYP's return (Hammill, Bennett, & White, 2019). Hammill, Bennett & White (2019, p. 9) suggest several ways in which schools can support friends and peers of CYP with an ABI RtE:

- Schools should check with the CYP and their parents/carers about what information they consent to be shared. This communication is essential to develop an open and trusting relationship between the school, CYP and family.
- Peers should be given time to ask any questions they may have about their friend or ABI in general.
- ABI specialists, such as HCPs from the hospital or community can meet with peers to give information and answer questions. They can also act as a contact point for any follow-up queries peers, families or teachers may have.
- Finally, the school can encourage the CYP to maintain contact with their friend while they are absent from school, for example, making and sending cards or messages.

The following section will focus on how the consequences of brain injury not just impact the CYP's educational development but also their social and emotional development, their sense of identity and their relationships.

Consequences and Wellbeing

The creation of an ABI aware school can help to reduce stigma for the CYP returning to school and can limit the feeling of isolation through the implementation of inclusive methods that focus on an individualised, interdisciplinary approach. CYP want to return to their family, school and community lives to participate among their uninjured peers, which can be achieved by creating an environment that promotes wellness and inclusivity (McCarron, Watson, & Gracey, 2019).

Social and Emotional Consequences

In Bennett et al's Study (2023) parents noted changes in the level of their child's participation in school. The social and emotional effects were highlighted as parents felt a need for the school and other parents to facilitate friendships as part of an ABI aware school. School participation includes academic and non-academic activities as well as extracurricular tasks (Case-Smith, O'Brien, 2009) and provides purpose and structure for CYP (Case-Smith, 2015). Barriers to school participation include teachers' inability to address the CYPs' needs, negative reactions from peers, poor application of reasonable accommodations and the level to which the CYP could adapt and accept their personal losses, such as friendships, loss of abilities and their future goals (Sharp et al., 2006). In addition, the physical, mental and social consequences have been found to be a barrier to a CYP's academic ability and their transition from primary to secondary school (Jacobs-Nzuzi Khuabi et al., 2202). Research shows that CYP want to be in a school where they feel understood and their individual needs, whether social, emotional, physical or otherwise are respected and addressed: "I'd like to go to a school where they understand me and study ... just that really where they actually understand how hard things are for me" (Buckeridge, Clarke & Sellers, 2019, p.8).

Identity

Brain injury can change a person's sense of identity – the injury not only changes the person's brain in the physical sense but it can also change how a person sees themselves post injury and the realisation of having a disability. This conflict with self-identity is often only understood by the person with the brain injury, for example, one of the six adolescents interviewed in Buckeridge, Clarke and Seller's study (2019, p. 6) stated that he felt other people didn't understand how difficult it is for him to do every day things: "I still need help with stuff ...they (people) just need to know how hard it is ... all of this stuff". In comparison two adolescents who had their brain injury in early childhood viewed their identity in a different unaltered way as they spoke about "my needs" and "my difficulties" which they viewed as having always been part of their personality (Buckeridge, Clarke & Sellers, 2019, p. 6). Thus, the age at which a CYP has their brain injury can have an impact on their own sense of self in later life.

Relationships

The social aspects of school are a key factor in enabling the CYP feel a sense of belonging and acceptance (Sharpe, Bye, Llewellyn & Cusick, 2006). Relationship dynamics can change post brain injury both within a family and outside families, such as with friends. For example, one adolescent in Di Battista et al.'s study (2014, p. 980) indicated that his identity and role in his family had changed: "when that incident happened [my parents] thought aw he's a goner he's dead he's brain-dead ... so I dunno it always plays in their mind aw we could have had a disabled or dead son". Relationships between siblings and friends can be altered for the better and can become more supportive relationships benefitting everyone involved, for example: "My brother helps me with my homework", "Some of my friends help me with my work at school" (Jacobs-Nzuzi Khuabi et al., 2202, p. 40). As noted earlier a teacher's lack of appropriate provision is a barrier to school participation, whereas CYP's learning can be optimised when supportive teachers allow learners to ask questions as needed or who adapt classroom environments (Jacobs-Nzuzi Khuabi et al., 2202). Gauvin-Lepage's case study (2019, p. 3) with an adolescent with a severe TBI and her family highlighted the importance of friends as supportive relationships. The adolescent in this study stated that her difficulties would have been even worse for her had it not been for "the help of my family and friends". Jacobs-Nzuzi Khuabi et al. (2022) found that personal support structures, such as friends and family and external supports can also help facilitate a positive transition from primary to secondary school, emphasising the value and importance of building social capital in childhood and throughout the life course. This links to Linden, Glang, & McKinlay's research (2018) on the importance of supporting CYP transition to school which was cited in the chapter introduction. Similarly, Di Battista et al.'s study (2014) highlighted friends and family as being instrumental in a CYP's recovery and sense of self (2014).

Parent Support

ABI is a sudden event and therefore parents do not have time to prepare for the consequences of the injury and the effects that it will have on the CYP or their family as a whole. Parental support is an integral component of a successful RtE journey for CYP (Bennett et al., 2023; Sedlac ova & Kantor, 2022; Hammill, Bennett, & White, 2019; McCart, Todis, Gomez, & Glang, 2023). Bennett et al. (2023) conducted a study involving parents of CYP (n=59) who had been treated for an ABI. A major theme in the study highlighted the role of parent advocacy in the factors involved in CYP's RtE. Thirty-one parents/carers completed the survey with 29 reporting a high number of changes in their child's ability and need post-ABI, for example, fatigue was the highest change at 86%, changes in behaviour were reported by 76% and changes in thinking and learning were reported by 72%. Their child's level of happiness in school was also reported to have lowered significantly post-ABI. These changes led to parents having to take on a new mindset and role, a similar finding in other research as parents try to practice self-kindness as they learn how to parent the new version of their child (Tyerman, Eccles, & Gray, 2017). The study revealed a need for a multi-system approach between health and education professionals in supporting CYP and their families in their RtE and addressing their needs (Bennett, Fletcher, Talbot, & Robinson, 2023); a similar finding to previous studies (Andersson, Bellon, & Walker, 2016; Hartman, Duncanson, Farahat, & Lindsay, 2015). Parents also highlighted the need for specialist support and information by building collaborative networks with health and education professionals, as found in other research (Bates, Turner & Fricke, 2011). Parents cited a need for additional school support and individualised provision for their children, open strong communication and space to talk and share. Finally, they felt that the challenges of the hidden needs of ABI should be understood by school staff by learning how to understand their behaviour which is linked to the need for training (Hartman, Tibbles, Paniccia, & Lindsay, 2015; Kahn, Linden, McKinlay, Gomez, & Glang, 2018; Todis, McCart, & Glang, 2018; Ball & Howe, 2013).

Maximising parents' participation in their child's RtE is essential, however, parents and teachers can have conflicting ideas about the CYP's needs post-ABI (McCart, Todis, Gomez, & Glang, 2023). Once again a link can be made between the need for training educators and addressing the needs of CYP with ABI. Training educators could help to bridge the gap between educator views and parent views (Kahn, Linden, McKinlay, Gomez, & Glang, 2018), and it may result in educators being more capable of providing appropriate accommodations for CYP (Glang, et al., 2019), and it could lead to better tracking of CYP with ABI by increasing their level of awareness (McCart, Todis, Gomez, & Glang, 2023). It is important to remember that parents of CYP who have sustained an ABI have themselves been through a traumatic experience which may have involved them fearing their child would not live. Some may find it difficult to accept their child's injury, and as a result, they may feel frustrated, particularly as many of the consequences of ABI are invisible (Brock University and Ontario Brain Injury Association, 2014). For these reasons, parents need educators who are trained to support CYP with ABI and their families/carers.

Bennett et al.'s study (2023) highlights the importance and value of including parents/carers in ABI research who have lived experience of having CYP with ABI, in a similar way to other studies (Sedlac ova & Kantor, 2022). Equally, CYP with lived experience have the potential to help improve service delivery and school intervention models. After all, the CYP with ABI and their parents/carers are the true experts on what works best to enable them to have a successful RtE.

In summary, when preparing for an RtE for a CYP with ABI by creating an ABI Aware School "the CYP and family should be at the heart of all RtE planning, with communication and collaboration being essential to success" as evident in N-ABLES best practice guidance below (N-ABLES, 2021, p.9).

Figure 1. N-ABLES ABI RETURN Best Practice Guidance

For more information about ABI RETURN and case studies, please read the booklet or visit www.ukabif.org.uk/ABIRETURN

Preparing the school for the RtE of a CYP with ABI is equally as important as actually returning to school. Time must be given to both phases if schools are to address the academic, social, and personal needs of CYP in an inclusive, participatory way (Sharp, Bye, Llewellyn, & Cusick, 2006). The next section will focus on the need for preparing educators or educating the educators.

TRAINING AND RESOURCES FOR EDUCATORS

Training for Educators: What is Happening?

A significant recurring theme throughout the literature identifies a call for enhanced and improved training for educators (Hartman, Tibbles, Paniccia, & Lindsay, 2015; Kahn, Linden, McKinlay, Gomez, & Glang, 2018; Todis, McCart, & Glang, 2018; Ball & Howe, 2013; Sharp, Bye, Llewellyn, & Cusick, 2006). As such, identifying the type of training most appropriate to enable educators to support CYP with ABI, and filling this gap in provision is in its infancy internationally (Kahn, Linden, McKinlay, Gomez, & Glang, 2018). International research shows that there is a significant lack of awareness by educational professionals about ABI (Linden, Braiden, & Miller, 2013; Norman, et al., 2020), and how best to support CYP when they return to education (Hartman, Duncanson, Farahat, & Lindsay, 2015). This presents an urgent need for this gap in awareness and knowledge to be addressed within education settings globally. According to Wlodarczyck (2012), educators who have knowledge about ABI can influence academic and social domains for students, thus awareness building is vital if CYP with ABI are to be supported to reach their full potential in school. Teachers often feel that they have a lack of training about ABI, with very few initial teacher education programs including training on ABI (Glang, et al., 2018). This can lead to experimentation in the classroom around the use of effective strategies (Bate, Turner, & Fricke, 2021), a lack of understanding about a student with ABI, and the consequences they experience (Andersson, Bellon, & Walker, 2016). This lack of awareness and professional formal training demonstrates the need for a greater focus to be placed on the development of supportive school environments for the successful reintegration of CYP with ABI (Stevens, et al., 2021; Norman, et al., 2020; Heads Together for ABI, 2020).

Best Practice Training Programs

There is a gap internationally in the availability of comprehensive training for in-service and pre-service teachers about how best to support CYP with ABI (Stevens et al., 2021; Norman et al., 2020). Despite this, there are some good evidence-based examples of emerging training programs which aim to train educators and school communities about supporting CYP RtE after ABI. These training examples vary in their approaches with some linking research to practice and others adopting a collaborative approach between state agencies and schools, all of which have the potential to address the outcomes of CYP of school-going age with ABI. The following parts of the chapter will outline four programs which focus specifically on providing training for educators to enhance the academic, social, and behavioural outcomes of

CYP with ABI upon their RtE. The first program was developed by *The Centre for Brain Injury Research and Training (CBIRT)* and has been evaluated twice in the United States. Secondly, a brief outline will be given of the methods that are being used to evaluate a community-based consultancy and training program that is being evaluated at present as part of a four-year study (https://returntoschoolproject.com/). The third program has been studied and is currently undergoing evaluation in the United States, and the final program has been researched to assess the usability and satisfaction of the program by elementary school teachers in Canada.

The Centre for Brain Injury Research and Training (CBIRT)

This center is under the Department of Psychology at the University of Oregon which provides research and training to improve the lives of children and adults with TBI. The center's training promotes the use of best practices among educators and other professionals who have responsibility for people with TBI in their care (Center on Brain Injury Research and Training, n.d.). An evidence-based TBI professional development online program has been developed; *In the Classroom After Concussion: Best Practices for Student Success (Centre on Brain Injury Research and Training, n.d.)*. The course consists of 8 interactive modules targeted at classroom teachers, for example, Return to School and Managing Behaviour. The program was developed in a collaborative way with the CBIRT Advisory Board and State Department of Education partners. The Advisory Board is inclusive of all stakeholders; educators from across the country, youth with TBI and family members.

The inclusion of CYP with lived experience of TBI and families in the development of this program is an example of public patient involvement (PPI) in practice, which gives merit and value to the development and implementation of the program, even before an evaluation was conducted. Patient involvement in research generally involves the inclusion of patients as storytellers or resources for researchers (Cullen, et al., 2022; Gordon, et al., 2020), while public involvement focuses on patient-centred care and acknowledges the expertise of patients and families as people with lived experience, and is therefore an extension of patient involvement (Cullen, et al., 2022; Regan de Bere & Nunn, 2016). Combining both approaches leads to the pedagogy of public patient involvement, which enables members of the public to actively engage in research, with organisations or other activities such as policy to make decisions about issues that affect their lives and communities (Baumann & Brütt, 2021). Ideally PPI should occur in non-tokenistic ways and should involve meaningful engagement and participation. People can give ideas and perspectives in various ways as demonstrated in People's Hub *Spectrum of Participation* which leads to co-design and co-production to better inform policy and practice (https://www.peoplehub.org.uk/co-production/).

The CBIRT program has been evaluated twice and has demonstrated significant changes in educators' knowledge, application, and self-efficacy during both evaluations (Glang, et al., 2018; McCart, et al., 2020). In addition, educators showed an increasing awareness of signs of potential post-injury learning and behavioural challenges, as well as an understanding of parental apprehensions and viewpoints. The intervention proved that the *In the Classroom* training provided educators with improved skills for implementing successful strategies for CYP with TBI (Glang, et al., 2018). Finally, the effectiveness of the program demonstrates the value and accessibility of delivering educator programs through the means of interactive online instruction (Bragg, Walsh, & Heyeres, 2021). It also provides an evidence-based example of how future educator, CYP or family ABI training programs could be delivered by adopting a similar approach designed specifically for a target group.

The Central Oregon TBI (COR-TBI) Model

This is an in-depth RtE model for students with TBI which is funded by the Oregon Department of Education (ODE) and has been in operation since 1994 (Anderson, et al., 2021). The model includes a team of trained professionals, including school counsellors, school nurses and school psychologists whose role is to identify, assess and provide support to students with concussion and more severe TBI from birth to 21 years. It is coordinated through the High Desert Education Service District (HDESD). The model gives state-wide TBI training and resources by taking a multisectoral approach with the inclusion of medical and educational professionals. It is underpinned by a theory of change (See Fig. 1), for example, there are monthly conference calls, open, consistent communication between all professionals and families, tracking CYP's progress after they return to school, professional development for school personnel and provides evidence-informed face to face training, resources and tools in various ways (https://www.hdesd.org/services/traumatic-brain-injury/) for school staff, which help them to create individualised support plans for students (Anderson, et al., 2021).

Figure 2. COR-TBI Logic Model

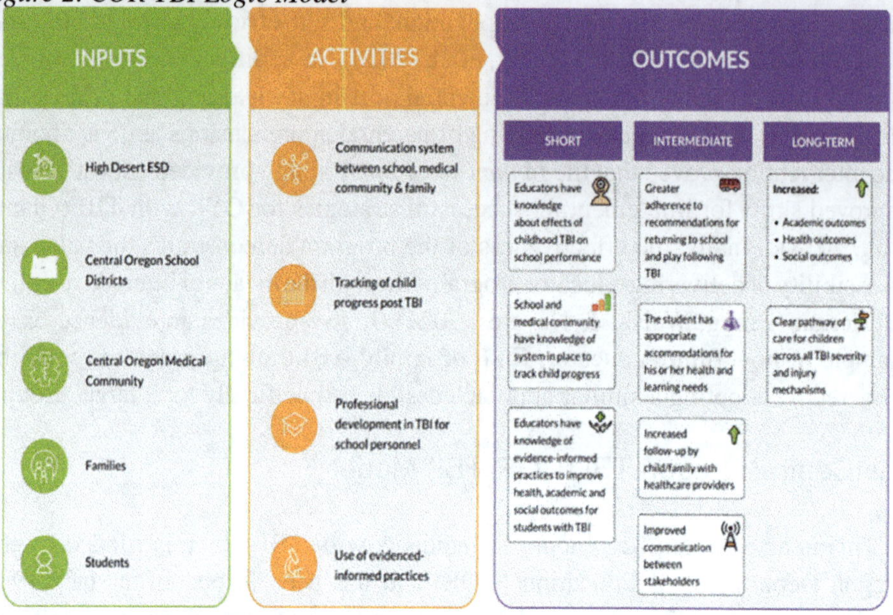

(Anderson, et al., 2021, p. 2)

Anderson et al.'s (2021) project to evaluate the effectiveness of the COR-TBI model has three research questions:

1. Does the COR-TBI model result in improved outcomes for CYP RtE after a TBI in comparison to the treatment as usual group (TAU)?
2. Does the rate at which educators implement the components of the COR-TBI model affect the outcomes for CYP, for example, do higher rates of implementation result in improved health, educational and social outcomes?
3. Since its introduction has the COR-TBI model been changed and sustained over time and if so what components and procedures make it a sustainable model?

It includes a sample of 600 CYP in Central Oregon school districts that are part of the COR-TBI program, and 600 CYP in comparison school districts. The CYP are in elementary, middle, or high school who experience a TBI which is mild, moderate, or severe. The study uses a quasi-experimental design with quantitative measures that have been validated and are reliable to assess the child outcomes and the assessment schedule of all participants, program implementation and TAU implementation. The measures are true indicators of school, social and health outcomes. In addition, parents will complete a Back to School survey and a grade book review will be completed on all participants quarterly which will indicate any changes in academic performance since the CYP returned to school post-injury. Qualitative methods will be used in the form of focus groups and interviews with key stakeholders: (1) students who experience TBI (2) parents of students with TBI (3) educators (e.g., counsellors, classroom teachers, school psychologists) (4) health care professionals (e.g., school nurses, physicians). The researchers believe that this study will "inform provision for students who experience TBI and provide a blueprint for broad dissemination of the COR-TBI model" (Anderson, et al., 2021, p. 9). In summary, the findings of this study and the evaluation methods should provide rigorous evidence-based research, which may be replicated or adapted within different demographic groups or environments in the future.

BrainSTEPS

This program was established in 2007 by the Pennsylvania Department of Health. The RtE program provides brain injury-related consultation and training to schools, students and parents, the aim of which is to improve the quality of education being provided to students in all Pennsylvania public schools (https://brainsteps.net/home/). The program has since been expanded to all Colorado schools (https://colorado.brainsteps.net/). A study of the program by Myers et al. (2017) examined the characteristics of the students (n=3493) enrolled in the BrainSTEPS program from January 2008 to June 2016 and described the program's support activities. Most students (70%) had suffered a mild TBI/concussion, and most of whom acquired the injuries from recreational incidences (59%). Students who experienced moderate/severe TBI had commonly been involved in road traffic accidents (48%). The study found that the program addressed communication and coordination needs for educators, families, and medical professionals through a variety of consultation activities of team members. Communication with educators involved activities such as providing teachers with checklists to complete to identify student's strengths and needs as well as providing training and resources and securing past and present educational records. Communication with families included activities such as organising records and providing training and resources, consulting with students by observing them in classroom settings and assisting them with study skills. Finally, consultation with medical professionals involves communicating with them about medical records. The study provided merit for the completion of an evaluation of the program by recommending opportunities for enhancement of its utlisation. In addition, it proposed opportunities for future research, such as examining parent, youth and educator-reported outcomes which could enable the measurement of successes of the program across different domains.

The efficacy of the program is currently being evaluated through the *School Transition After Traumatic Brain Injury (STATBI) Project*, which is a four-year longitudinal study funded by The Centers for Disease Control and Prevention. Dr. Angela Ciccia, lead investigator states that the aim of the project is to "understand the best way for kids to succeed as they return to school after their TBI" (Case Western University, 2021). The research is taking a collaborative approach as it involves researchers from Case Western Reserve University, Ohio State University, Nationwide Children's Hospital and The Brain Injury Association of Pennsylvania. The participants are children from kindergarten to 12th grade who have had a TBI of any kind from mild to severe (Case Western University, 2021). Project updates are released regularly through the project's social media channels, for example, at the end of the 23-24 school year the study found that understanding the severity of the injury is acutely related to different social, behavioural and health outcomes for students with TBI (Statbi Lab, 2024). The study participants are divided into three groups; 63% have a history of mild/concussion with ongoing symptoms, 15% with moderate injury and 22% with severe injury (Statbi Lab, 2024). The findings from this study will provide in-depth analysis using the lived experience of CYP with TBI, which will provide an evidence-based evaluation of an intervention aimed at helping CYP make a successful RtE following a TBI, which it is hoped will provide evidence of best practice.

Teach-ABI

Finally, Teach-ABI is an online professional development module aimed at elementary school teachers in Canada, which was created to enhance educators' awareness and knowledge about paediatric ABI and the specific needs of these students in a classroom setting (Saly, et al., 2023). The module development involved 6 phases: (1) problem identification; (2) curriculum development; (3) usability testing; (4) pilot testing; (5) efficacy testing, pre-implementation, and planning; (6) sustainability planning and generalization (Saly, et al., 2023). To date, phases 1-3 have been studied with phases 4-6 being planned as future work. The initial problem was identified because of the responses from educators who took part in a needs assessment by completing a survey and participating in a workshop. Educators reported that they had minimal, inadequate support for students returning to education after ABI and that they felt unprepared to assist students as they transitioned back to education. In addition, they reported that they felt families were unprepared for their child to reintegrate into school (Stevens, et al., 2021). The curriculum was developed as part of phase 2 which involved the creation of specific, measurable learning objectives and development of appropriate educational strategies, for example, defining ABI and taking an individualised approach to support students with ABI. The module content was developed by a classroom teacher who had specialised knowledge of paediatric ABI and the format of the module was developed by an e-learning specialist, a knowledge-translation specialist, a graphic designer, and a videographer (Saly, et al., 2023).

Usability testing formed phase 3 which was conducted by Saly et al. (2023) with a sample of educators (n=8). Overall, educators indicated a high level of satisfaction with the content, design and navigation of the program and revealed strong usability and satisfaction. For example, 7 participants found the content to be useful, while 7 participants also liked the fact that the program was divided into two sections: (1) ABI education, and (2) supportive strategies (n=7). Participants suggested several improvements which may be used to adapt the program for the pilot phase. For example, three participants suggested that a read-aloud function could meet educators' different learning styles and would make completing the module more enjoyable. Two participants shared that they would like more information about teaching strategies, such as links to videos or resources that would provide additional information about the strategies listed (Saly, et al., 2023). It was also suggested that the module would be of interest to pre-service teachers which links to research cited earlier outlining this as a gap in training. The participants in this study actively engaged with the module and were given opportunities to question, reflect and share their experience and knowledge about the module content. Overall, Saly et al.'s study (2023) demonstrated the importance of usability testing in the building of online professional development modules and suggests that the in-depth approach used in this study may be applied to the evaluation of future online training modules relating to educator ABI training or relating to other topics.

In summary, a multisectoral, collaborative approach is needed within countries across community, health, and education to promote research with CYP with ABI for CYP with ABI, their families, and teachers. Finally, the urgent need to provide pre-service and in-service training for teachers of CYP with ABI is evident and could be addressed through the implementation of evidence-based tools and interventions to educate educators about ABI, such as CBIRT's *In the Classroom* and *BrainSTEPS* (McCart & DaSalvo, 2024).

ABI Resources

There are many brain injury organisations and charities that provide free ABI resources for everyone to access including teachers and schools, who aim to educate, support, create awareness and advocate for people living with ABI, and promote the sharing of lived experience among the brain injury community around the world:

- ABI Ireland (https://www.abiireland.ie/)
- Brain Injury Association of America (https://www.biausa.org/)
- Brain Injury Canada (https://braininjurycanada.ca/en/)

- Same You, UK (https://www.sameyou.org/)
- Synapse Australia (https://synapse.org.au/)

Although these resources are very relevant and provide general information about brain injury, some of which are directed at educators, they generally require 'buy-in' from teachers and schools, and a willingness by a school staff member to 'search and find' them. Useful resources are available online and through organisations, such as such as manuals and training that are designed specifically for schools which are accessible, and can benefit educators, CYP and families, for example, table 2 provides information on some of the resources available in the UK, USA and Canada.

Table 2. School Specific ABI Resources

Organisation	Country	Description	Link
Brock University and Ontario Brain Injury Association	Canada	*'Educating the Educators'* A handbook for anyone who is involved in the education of CYP living with the consequences of ABI	https://obia.ca/wp-content/uploads/2021/04/Educating-Educators-for-website-2021.pdf
Child Brain Injury Trust	United Kingdom	A guide to for schools: Understanding and supporting children with ABI	https://childbraininjurytrust.org.uk/wp-content/uploads/2018/11/ABI-Mini-Guide.pdf
The Children's Trust	United Kingdom	An ABI RtE guide for families, educators, and other professionals. It provides information on ABI, classroom strategies for teachers and an online programme for school staff to increase awareness and understanding of ABI	https://www.thechildrenstrust.org.uk/brain-injury-information/info-and-advice/return-to-education
N-ABLES	United Kingdom	*'ABI Return – Children and Young People with Acquired Brain Injury – Guiding their Return to Education'* Best practice guidance for educators and families	https://ukabif.org.uk/page/ABIRETURN
Get Schooled on Concussions	United States	A website which provides support to teachers of students with TBI	https://www.getschooledonconcussions.com/

The next section will provide practical guidance on preparing in school supports and school environments for CYP's RtE.

PREPARING IN-SCHOOL SUPPORTS AND THE ENVIRONMENT

Making an RtE can be different for every CYP because recovery time can vary depending on the severity of the injury. Research shows that putting in place personalised accommodations, which address the specific consequences of a CYP's injury, such as fatigue, is a necessary factor in facilitating a successful RtE (Stubberud, et al., 2022). Sharp et al.'s study (2006, p. 771-772) highlights a number of factors which families themselves viewed as essential in organising the return to school. These include having a mandatory period of preparation for the school return, teaching teachers about the adolescents' injuries and what to expect in the classroom by "making sure the teachers are aware". In addition they felt focus should be placed on organising school accommodations such as enrolment status, subject load and special arrangements for assessments, educating peers, personal preparation of the adolescent, for example having visits from friends, and making decisions about the level of parent involvement.

Existing Gaps

Evidence-Based Research

A gap in research is evident which seeks to identify policies and practices that support CYP to improve their outcomes following RtE after TBI. Specific supports are needed upon RtE, however much more evidence-based research and evaluation is needed to identify key supports and best practice models that may be adapted and replicated to suit individual school environments and address the individual needs of CYP globally (Linden, Glang, & McKinlay, 2018). A gap also exists in the variety of ethnicities of participants in CYP research to date; according to Childs (2024) the majority of studies which represent the lived experience of CYP include all or a high proportion of Caucasian participants, leaving the global majority absent from research which could inform best practice implementation of inclusive interventions and supports. For example, Di Battista et al. (2014) and Glennon et al. (2022) include white/Caucasian participants only with Di Battista et al. citing a lack of variety in gender as a limitation in their study also. Studies show that race and gender identity can impact the outcomes and experiences of CYP with brain injuries (Haarbauer-Krupa et al., 2021; Matney, Bowman & Berwick, 2022). Thus, to fill this gap brain injury research with CYP needs to include a wide variety of participant profiles to ensure true representation of the brain injury community, for example age, gender, culture, ethnicity, socio-economic backgrounds and geographical location. Child's research (2024) highlighted the need for the inclusion of the voice of a variety of identities in brain injury research with CYP which would in turn provide an explanation on how CYP understand their ABI and navigate the experience. This wide sampling approach should be approached for CYP, families and carers. Exceptions will always apply, for example, when researching a specific age group or ethnic group as outlined in the study aims.

Additional School Support

CYP's additional educational, physical, cognitive, social, emotional and behavioural needs must be planned in consultation with appropriate support agencies and the CYP's family/carer as part of organising the return to school phase. Entitlement to additional education provision should be researched and arranged with the relevant Department of Education support services, and part-time timetabling must be considered for some CYP as they may RtE on a phased basis (Hammill, Bennett, & White, 2019). Research shows that supportive environments are an integral part of improving cognitive, behavioural and emotional outcomes for CYP with ABI (Linden, Braiden, & Miller, 2013; Jimenez, Virtue, Segar, Stoep, & Rivara, 2019). Stevens et al. (2021) conducted a study in Ontario in which they examined educators' ABI knowledge to assess the supports they identified as important for supporting CYP RtE following an ABI. Educators highlighted the need for specific training courses both in-person and online, integrating the courses into professional development modules for educators and "continuing to create an integrated and inclusive classroom environment that considers the whole student within a growth mindset" (Stevens, et al., 2021, p. 290).

In summary, significant gaps exist in relation to the support provided in mainstream schools for CYP RtE. There has been a slow but steady move towards the inclusion of the voice of CYP in research, however this needs more work and is a vital foundation for any school support, policy or intervention to be effective.

Assistive Technology

Digital interventions, such as assistive technology can enhance the functional independence of a CYP with ABI. Assistive devices are tools that can help the CYP reach their goals and enable them to participate inclusively upon their RtE. Many of the consequences of ABI are invisible, such as poor emotional/behavioural control, executive functioning skill deficits, attention and memory difficulties, language difficulties or challenges with organisation (Wherfel & Bakken, 2023). Assistive devices can support the CYP's abilities and address the consequences of ABI by enabling them to communicate, learn or socialise (Brain Injury Center, 2021). Examples of assistive technologies that can be used to alleviate some of the consequences of ABI dysfunctions include electronic reminders, electronic calendars, mobile applications, and alarms (Wherfel & Bakken, 2023). Speech-to-text software allows a CYP to dictate their words, for example, for an essay, while cameras allow the CYP to take photos of information in the classroom, such as on a whiteboard which can be included in their digital notes to help them recall information (Senelmis, 2022-present). AI also holds potential to be used in an effective way to support CYP with ABI with their functional independence. Jamieson et al. (2020) state that technology should be social, persuasive, and adaptable to individual needs and should support professionals, such as educators or neuropsychologists to plan meaningful activities and supports.

Classroom and School Adjustments

Barriers

Sharp et. al.'s study (2006, p. 773) revealed a number of challenges which adolescents faced after they returned to school, for example teacher responses were an important factor; parents felt some teachers demonstrated a lack of understanding and knowledge for example because children can 'look fine' teachers can often forget or lack understanding about the invisible consequences of ABI. One parent in this study stated that her daughter's ''big problem was that because she looked so great when she went back to school . . . everybody expected a lot more out of her''. Barriers for CYP transitioning from primary to secondary school can include changes in function and enjoyment of the learner, a lack of support from an interdisciplinary team approach, a lack of time for the CYP to prepare mentally for RtE, a lack of reasonable accommodations being implemented by teachers and a poor level of involvement by the CYP themselves in decisions that affected their transition (Jacob-Nzuzi-Khuabi et al., 2022). It is clear that the main barriers relate to teacher training, time given to preparation of the school environment and by all stakeholders, and the poor involvement of the CYP in decision making about things that affect their development as a whole.

Enablers

Hammill, Bennet and White (2019, p. 13-14) outline several ways in which adjustments can be made to the school environment to address a CYP's individual needs. The following questions could be considered:

- Is the environment accessible?
- Can the CYP manage their belongings? Will they need additional support during the school day?
- Will they need additional support/adjustments during lesson/classroom transitions?
- How will personal needs be addressed, such as hygiene?
- Where will the school seek out help/support? Which outside agencies can help?

Some solutions may include:

- Flexible timetables
- Encouraging and nurturing social connections

- Managing academic expectations
- Assessment of progress and monitoring of skills
- All staff within the school should be made aware of adaptations, e.g. permitted to leave early or having homework accommodations
- Giving the CYP an inconspicuous 'out' from a school activity if they are feeling fatigued, such as holding up a card
- Allocating a restful space in school for a 'time out' if needed. Some schools have sensory rooms or similar spaces in place already which may be used

Bennett et al.'s study (2023) found that parents highlighted the need for good school support during transition periods in education, for example, when transitioning from primary school to secondary school. Similarly, Jacob-Nzuzi-Khuabi et al. (2022) found that implementing support structures was one of the key enablers for CYP during this transition period, as well as the learner using personal resources and personal coping strategies. Other bespoke provision supports have also been found to be enablers (Bennett et al., 2023; Hammill, Bennet and White 2019 & Stevens et al. 2021). These provisions included having rest periods, managing expectations, having one-to-one support, enabling adjustments to manage behavioural consequences, including visual aids and having as holistic approach to managing the day. Other adjustments may include providing checklists for daily tasks to keep CYP on track and using visual prompts to help with organisation and planning, for example, notes and checklists. In addition, regular routines are an essential part of a day at school for CYP with ABI so they know what to expect (Senelmis, 2022-present). Finally, as stated throughout this chapter the voice of the CYP is central to all support. As with other supports and provisions additional in-school support and adjustments must be made in consultation with all stakeholders to give the CYP as much support and opportunities to improve their outcomes as possible

'A NEW VERSION OF ME'

A CYP with ABI often has to struggle with becoming a new version of themselves, accepting their new and lost abilities (Sharp et al., 2006), and dealing with the emotional impact of their experience, regardless of whether the injury is mild, moderate or severe and having a fear of losing friends or not being able to make new friends (Sharp et al., 2006). Parents in studies have reported new challenges that their CYP faced following ABI (Bennett et al., 2023; Sharp et al., 2006). These included inappropriate behaviour, anxiety, low mood, memory and concentration difficulties, headaches, learning to pace themselves, fatigue, having a lack of confidence and psychosocial issues. It is evident from the research outlined in this chapter that an interdisciplinary approach that includes parents/carers, teachers, peers, and HCPs such as psychologists (both educational and neuro) can support the CYP accept the new version of themselves. The key to this acceptance lies in the CYP being supported in a context-sensitive way that focuses on their individual needs, within their specific environment to maximise their level of participation in all aspects of their lives (McCarron, Watson, & Gracey, 2019). For example, research shows that parents value maximising their child's participation in social activities post-ABI (Sedlac ova & Kantor, 2022). By recognising the 'new me' in CYP educators must look beyond the consequences of the injury, consider how the CYP feels and recognise the things that are important to them. Additionally, the 'new me' does not eradicate the interests, likes, dislikes and social networks they had before their injury; Remember the 'new me' is simply a new 'version' of the CYP. Child's research (2024) highlighted a gap in research investigating how CYP understand themselves in relation to their TBI over time. Further research in this area could influence intervention design and implementation. Child's states that "initial noticing and acknowledgement of differences pre-post injury does appear to be one of the initial steps in how adolescents have understood life following on from a brain injury" (Childs, 2024, p.76) indicating the importance of giving children and enabling them within their environments to understand and accept their post injury self, without losing sight of their pre injury self. This chapter has highlighted the value of friends and family in the recovery and RtE for a CYP with a brain injury. When it comes to acceptance of a new version of one self and reflecting on their pre and post brain injury abilities friends can have an empowering effect on their sense of identity and self-worth, "... every single one of my friends in my before life are still here in this life now ... they haven't left me, and they never would" (ID 5) (Di Battista et al., 2019, p. 980). Finally, the inclusion of the CYP in their RtE must include listening to their voice and seeking their feedback (N-ABLES, 2021). This 'new version of me' should not prevent a CYP with ABI from achieving their goals and reaching their full potential; an interdisciplinary, collaborative approach can support the CYP in making this a reality.

CONCLUSION

The most significant recurring theme throughout this chapter is the urgent need to support educators of CYP with ABI by providing them with appropriate evidence-based training. A highly effective means to support CYP to achieve better outcomes is through training programmes; this too is currently the greatest gap in supporting CYP RtE following ABI. Further research is needed globally to identify best practice training models and supports that take an interdisciplinary approach in the design, implementation, and evaluation of such training. All stakeholders, for example, educators, psychologists, parents, and crucially the CYP themselves should be included as equal participants in developing supports that aim to enable the CYP RtE.

Mainstream education settings should be inclusive environments that support CYP to reach their full potential, as well as places where CYP feel acknowledged and accepted as the new version of themselves following their ABI. There is a greater need for the inclusion of the lived experience of parents, carers and most significantly CYP in research that explores the most effective ways to support CYP RtE following an ABI and to improve their outcomes. Open, honest communication between all stakeholders is a key part of supporting CYP RtE. CYP must be enabled to participate fully both academically and socially in a way that considers their context and individual needs in a meaningful, active way. Finally collaborative preparation, time and patience are essential when supporting a CYP RtE following ABI. These three goals should not be underestimated as they are pivotal in shaping an inclusive, needs-driven environment for CYP. It is through collaborative preparation, time, and patience that schools can enable CYP with ABI reach their full potential and learn to accept the new version of themselves.

REFERENCES

Anderson, D., Gau, J., Beck, L., Unruh, D., Gioia, G., McCart, M., & Glang, A. (2021). Management of return to school following brain injury: An evaluation model. *International Journal of Educational Research*, 108. PMID: 33927471

Andersson, K., Bellon, M., & Walker, R. (2016). Parents' experiences of their child's return to school following acquired brain injury (ABI): A systematic review of qualitative studies. *Brain Injury : [BI]*, *30*(7), 829–838. PMID: 27057776

Ball, H., & Howe, J. (2013). How can educational psychologists support the re-integration of children with an acquired brain injury upon their return to school? *Educational Psychology in Practice*, *29*(1), 69–78.

Bate, C., Turner, K., & Fricke, S. (2021). Return to school after acquired brain injury in the UK: The educators' perspectives. *Journal of Research in Special Educational Needs*, *21*(3), 242–253.

Baumann, L., & Brütt, A. (2021). Public and patient involvement (PPI) in health policy decisionmaking on the health system-level: Protocol for a systematic scoping review. *BMJ Open*, *11*(5). PMID: 34011588

Bennett, E., Fletcher, A., Talbot, E., & Robinson, L. (2023). Returning to education after childhood acquired brain injury: Learning from lived parental experience. *NeuroRehabilitation*, *52*, 625–640. PMID: 37125567

Bragg, L., Walsh, C., & Heyeres, M. (2021). Successful design and delivery of online professional development for teachers: A systematic review of the literature. *Computers & Education*, *166*(6).

Brain Injury Association of America. (n.d.). *What is the difference between an acquired brain injury and a traumatic brain injury?* Retrieved from https://www.biausa.org/brain-injury/about-brain-injury/nbiic/what-is-the-difference-between-an-acquired-brain-injury-and-a-traumatic-brain-injury

Brain Injury Center. (2021, July 18). *Brain Injury Center*. Retrieved from Choosing the Right ssistive Technology for Children: https://www.braininjurycenter.org/blog/?article=81

Brock University and Ontario Brain Injury Association. (2014). *Educating Educators about ABI* (5th ed.). Brock University and Ontario Brain Injury Association.

Buckeridge, K., Clarke, C., & Sellers, D. (2019). Research Report: Adolescents' experiences of communication following acquired brain injury. *International Journal of Language & Communication Disorders, 00*(0), 1–13.

Case-Smith, J. (2015). An overview of occupational therapy for children. In *Occupational Therapy for Children and Adolescents*. Elsevier.

Case-Smith, J., & O'Brien, J. (2009). *Occupational Therapy for Children* (6th ed.). Elsevier.

Case Western University. (2021, June 14). STATBI Introvideo Titles.

Center on Brain Injury Research and Training. (n.d.). *About us*. Retrieved from https://cbirt.org/about-us

Centers for Disease Control and Prevention. (2023). QuickStats: Percentage of Children and Adolescents Aged ≤17 Years Who Had Ever Received a Diagnosis of Concussion or Brain Injury, by Sex and Age Group — National Health Interview Survey, United States, 2022. *Morbidity and Mortality Weekly Report, 72*(33), 899–899. https://www.cdc.gov/mmwr/volumes/72/wr/pdfs/mm7233-H.pdf PMID: 37590270

Centre on Brain Injury Research and Training. (n.d.). *In the Classroom: Supporting Students with TBI*. Retrieved from Centre on Brain Injury Research and Training: https://cbirt.org/research/completed-projects/classroom-supporting-students-tbi

Children's Safety Network. (2023, February). *Non-fatal traumatic brain injury-related visits to the emergency department, U.S. infants, children, and adolescents ages through 19*. Retrieved from https://www.childrenssafetynetwork.org/sites/default/files/TBI_Factsheet_2023_0.pdf

Childs, A. (2024). The lived experience of adolescents and youths with brain injury: navigating new landscapes. *DClinPscych Thesis Salomons Institute of Applied Psychology*.

Cullen, M., Cadogan, C., George, S., Murphy, S., Freeney, S., Fitzpatrick, R., & Strawbridge, J. (2022). Key stakeholders' views, experiences and expectations of patient and public involvement in healthcare professions' education: A qualitative study. *BMC Medical Education*. PMID: 35449105

Di Battista, A., Godfrey, C., Soo, C., Catroppa, C., & Anderson, V. (2014). In my Before Life': Relationships, Coping an Post-Traumatic Growth in Adolescent Survivors of a Traumatic Brain Injury. *Journal of Rehabilitation Medicine, 46*, 975–983. PMID: 25188467

Gauvin-Lepage, J. (2019). Traumatic brain injury in adolescence and the family resilience process: A case study. *Open Nursing*, *5*, 1–5. PMID: 33415241

Glang, A., McCart, M., Slocumb, J., Gau, J., Davies, S., Gomez, D., & Beck, L. (2018). Preliminary Efficacy of Online Traumatic Brain Injury Professional Development for Educators: An Exploratory Randomized Clinical Trial. *The Journal of Head Trauma Rehabilitation*, *34*(2), 77–86. PMID: 30499929

Glennon, C., Watson, S., Fisher, P., & Gracey, F. (2022). The process of identity change following ABI from the perspectives of adolescents and their mothers: A relational grounded theory approach. *Neuropsychological Rehabilitation*, *32*(8), 1904–1927. PMID: 35857657

Gordon, M., Gupta, S., Thornton, D., Reid, M., Mallen, E., & Melling, A. (2020). Patient/service user involvement in medical education: a best evidence medical education (BEME) systematic review: BEME Guide No. 58. *Medical Teacher*, *42*(1), 4–16. PMID: 31518544

Haarbauer-Krupa, J., Pugh, M. J., Prager, E. M., Harmon, N., Wolfe, J., & Yaffe, K. (2021). Epidemiology of Chronic Effects of Traumatic Brain Injury. *Journal of Neurotrauma*, *38*(23), 3235–3247. PMID: 33947273

Hammill, D., Bennett, D. E., & White, P. (2019). *Making a successful return to education for children and young people with Acquired Brain Injuries* (2nd ed.). Nottinghanshire.

Hartman, L., Duncanson, M., Farahat, S., & Lindsay, S. (2015). Clinician and educator experiences of facilitating students' transition back to school following acquired brain injury: A qualitative systematic review. *Brain Injury*, *29*(12), 1387–1399. PMID: 26362526

Hartman, L., Tibbles, A., Paniccia, A., & Lindsay, S. (2015). *A qualitative synthesis of families' and students' hospital-to- school transition experiences following acquired brain injury*. Global Qualtative Nursing Research.

Hayes, L., Shaw, S., Pearce, M., & Forsyth, R. (2017). Requirements for and current provision of rehabilitation services for children after severe acquired brain injury in the UK: A population-based study. *Archives of Disease in Childhood*, *102*(9), 813–820. PMID: 28416561

Heads Together for ABI. (2020). *Submission to the Department of Education, Skills & Employment Disability Standards for Education Review 2020*. Heads Together for ABI Limited.

Jacob-Nzuzi-Khuabi, L.-A., Ally, K., Khan, S., Moolman, M., Mustapha, A. B., & Parker, M. (2022). Primary to secondary school transition of learners with traumatic brain injuries in the Cape metropolitan area: A learner perspective. *South African Journal of Occupational Therapy*, *52*(2).

Jamieson, M., Jack, R., O'Neill, B., Cullen, B., Lennon, M., Brewster, S., & Evans, J. (2020). Technology to encourage meaningful activities following brain injury. *Disability and Rehabilitation. Assistive Technology*, *15*(4), 453–466. PMID: 30985193

Jimenez, N., Virtue, A., Segar, K., Stoep, A., & Rivara, F. (2019). Effect of school services on academic performance after traumatic brain injury in hispanic and non-hispanic students. *The Journal of School Health*, *89*(7), 519–526. PMID: 31016747

Kahn, L., Linden, M., McKinlay, A., Gomez, D., & Glang, A. (2018). An international perspective on educators' perceptions of children with Traumatic Brain Injury. *NeuroRehabilitation*, *42*(3), 229–309. PMID: 29660961

Kakonge, L., Charron, V. P., Vedder, J., Wormald, K., & Turkstra, L. S. (2022). A mapping review of adolescent identity after TBI: What clinicians need to know. *Neuropsychological Rehabilitation*, *32*(8), 1868–1903. PMID: 35604405

Linden, M. (2018). *How can we help children with brain injuries transition back to school?* Science Daily.

Linden, M., Braiden, H., & Miller, S. (2013). Educational professionals' understanding of childhood traumatic brain injury. *Brain Injury*, *27*(1), 92–102. PMID: 23252440

Linden, M., Glang, A., & McKinlay, A. (2018). A systematic review and meta-analysis of educational interventions for children and adolescents with acquired brain injury. *NeurorRehabiliation*, *42*, 311–323. PMID: 29660957

Matney, C., Bowman, K., & Berwick, D. (Eds.). (2022). *Traumatic Brain Injury: A Roadmap for Accelerating Progress*. National Academies of Sciences, Engineering, and Medicine; Health and Medicine Division; Board on Health Care Services; Board on Health Sciences Policy; Committee on Accelerating Progress in Traumatic Brain Injury Research and Care.

McCarron, R., Watson, S., & Gracey, F. (2019). What do kids with acquired brain injury want? Mapping neuropsychological rehabilitation goals to the international classification of functioning, disability and health. *Jourfnal of international Neuropsychological Society, 25*, 403-412.

McCart, M., & DaSalvo, G. (2024). Educating the educators: Education for schools and teachers. *Brain Injury : [BI]*, *21*(1), 20–22.

McCart, M., Glang, A., Slocumb, J., Gau, J., Becker, L., & Gomez, D. (2020). A quasi-experimental study examining the effects of online traumatic brain injury professional development on educator knowledge, application, and efficacy in a practitioner setting. *Disability and Rehabilitation*, *42*(17), 2430–2436. PMID: 30978108

McCart, M., Todis, B., Gomez, D., & Glang, A. (2023). School experiences following traumatic brain injury: A longitudinal qualitative study. *NeuroRehabilitation*, *52*, 529–537. PMID: 37125570

Myers, R., Egan-Brown, B., Conway, A., Nagele, D., Vaccaro, M., Kendi, S., & Zonfrillo, M. (2017). Examining a Statewide Educational Consulting Program for Pediatric Brain Injury. *Clinical Pediatrics*, *57*(6), 645–655. PMID: 28933193

N-ABLES. (2021). *ABI Return – Children and Young People with Acquired Brain Injury - guiding their return to education.* Retrieved from https://cdn.ymaws.com/ukabif.org.uk/resource/resmgr/return_to_education/return_to_education12_05_2021/abi_return_booklet.pdf

Norman, A., Holloway, M., Odumuyiwa, T., Kennedy, M., Forrest, H., Suffield, F., & Dicks, H. (2020). Accepting what we do not know: A need to improve professional understanding of brain Injury in the UK. *Health & Social Care in the Community*, *28*, 2027–2049. PMID: 32364294

Palanivel, V., & Burrough, M. (2021). Acquired brain injury in children, and their rehabilitation: Where we are now? *Paediatrics & Child Health*, *31*(5), 176–180.

Regan de Bere, S., & Nunn, S. (2016). Towards a pedagogy for patient and public involvement in medical education. *Medical Education*, *50*(1), 79–92. PMID: 26695468

Saly, L., Provvidenza, C., Al-Hakeem, H., Hickling, A., Stevens, S., Kakonge, L., & Scratch, S. (2023). The Teach-ABI Professional Development Module for Educators About Pediatric Acquired Brain Injury: Mixed Method Usability Study. *Human Factors*, 10. PMID: 37184920

Sedlac ova, D., & Kantor, J. (2022). Traumatic Brain injury Identified on the basis of the lived experience of his mother. *Education Research International.*

Senelmis, S. (2022-present). Classroom adjustments: Acquired Brain Injury (ABI). NCCD.

Sharp, N. L., Bye, R., Llewellyn, G., & Cusick, A. (2006). Fitting back in: Adolescents returning to school after severe acquired brain injury. *Disability and Rehabilitation*, *28*(12), 767–778. PMID: 16754574

Statbi Lab. (2024, May 22). *Facebook*. Retrieved from https://www.facebook.com/labstatbi

Stevens, S., Provvidenza, C., Zheng, S., Agnihotri, S., Hunt, A., & Scratch, S. (2021). Understanding the Needs of Ontario Educators in Supporting Students With Acquired Brain Injury in the Classroom. *The Journal of School Health, 91*(4), 285–290. PMID: 33655540

Stubberud, J., Hypher, R., Brandt, A. E., Finnanger, T. G., Skovlund, E., Andersson, S., Risnes, K., & Rø, T. B. (2022). Predictors of Functional School Outcome in Children With Pediatric Acquired Brain Injury. *Frontiers in Neurology*, 13. PMID: 35493829

The Children's Trust. (2024). Retrieved October 2024, from https://www.thechildrenstrust.org.uk/about

The Children's Trust. (n.d.). *Brain Injury Hub: Teacher's Strategies for the Classroom*. Retrieved from The Children's Trust: https://www.thechildrenstrust.org.uk/brain-injury-information/info-and-advice/return-to-education/teachers-strategies-for-the-classroom

The Children's Trust. (n.d.). *The effects of acquired brain injury: An introduction*. Retrieved from https://www.thechildrenstrust.org.uk/brain-injury-information/info-and-advice/living-with-abi/the-effects-of-abi

Todis, B., McCart, M., & Glang, A. (2018). Hospital to school transition following traumatic brain injury: A qualitative longitudinal study. *NeuroRehabilitation, 42*(3), 269–276. PMID: 29660964

Tyerman, E., Eccles, F., & Gray, V. (2017). The experiences of parenting a child with an acquired brain injury: A metasynthesis of the qualitative literature. *Brain Injury : [BI], 31*(12), 1553–1563. PMID: 28750173

United Nations (1989). Convention on the Rights of the Child. *Treaty Series, 1577*,3.

United Nations (2006). *Convention on the Rights of Persons with Disabilities*. Treaty Series 2515.

Wales, L., Hawley, C., & Sidebotham, P. (2013). How an occupational therapist should conceptualise self-awareness following traumatic brain injury in childhood- A literature review. *British Journal of Occupational Therapy*, *76*(7), 325–332.

Wherfel, Q., & Bakken, J. (2023). Using technology to enhance learning for students with traumatic brain injuries. *Using Technology to Enhance Special Education*, *37*, 143–158.

Wlodarczyk, K. (2012). *Educator evaluation of academic and social competence in students with acquired brain injury (ABI) relative to assessed performance and sense of belonging*. Retrieved from https://dr.library.brocku.ca/bitstream/handle/10464/ 4100/Brock_Wlodarczyk_Kathy_2012.pdf?sequence=1&isAllowed=y

Chapter 11
Climate Emotions and Climate Change Education

Anne Marie Kavanagh
https://orcid.org/0000-0002-6962-452X
Dublin City University, Ireland

Ashling Bourke
https://orcid.org/0000-0002-3997-895X
Dublin City University, Ireland

ABSTRACT

It is widely acknowledged that humans are embedded within complex interconnected systems—psychological, social, political, and ecological—and that human and planetary wellbeing are inseparable from one another. For the planet to "be well", the root causes of climate change must be addressed. This chapter examines this interplay between human and planetary wellbeing from psychological and sociological perspectives and argues for an interdisciplinary approach to Climate Change Education (CCE) that addresses individual, structural, and systemic responses to the climate crisis. It critically examines the relationship between the psychological concepts of resilience, positive affect, and hope and climate engagement and action. The authors argue that transformative approaches to CCE should address both cognitive and affective components and the individual and structural dimensions of the climate crisis.

DOI: 10.4018/979-8-3693-1293-3.ch011

INTRODUCTION

It is increasingly apparent that climate change is *the* existential threat of our time. Analysis of global daily temperatures, for example, shows that July 22nd, 2024, was officially the Earth's hottest date on record (NASA, 2024). The three warmest years on record for Europe have all occurred since 2020, and the ten warmest since 2007 (Copernicus Climate Change Service, 2024). This trend of rising global temperatures is accompanied by a host of other cascading effects including intense wildfires, extreme weather patterns (e.g., droughts, flooding), ocean acidification, marine heatwaves, ice-melting, biodiversity loss and species extinction (United Nations, n.d.). These impacts have profound effects on ecosystems and on human societies and individuals, particularly on their rights and wellbeing (Intergovernmental Panel on Climate Change [IPCC], 2023; Stern et al., 2021). People with marginalised identities, including people of colour, indigenous groups, women and girls, those living in under-resourced communities and communities in the Global South all face higher vulnerability to climate change (Klinenberg et al., 2020). The IPCC, the world's most authoritative expert group on climate, cautions that the wellbeing of all living things will continue to deteriorate as the window of opportunity "to secure a liveable future" continues to close (2022, p. 3). It is widely accepted that arresting climate change's advance requires scientific, political *and* educational interventions. For example, the UN Framework Convention on Climate Change (UNFCCC) assigns responsibility to Parties of the Convention to undertake educational and public awareness campaigns on climate change. Climate Change Education (CCE), which recognises the climate crisis as an individual and collective problem that requires individual and collective responses has emerged as the dominant education intervention to climate change; although, the recommended pedagogical approaches within this approach and their underpinning logics vary significantly across educational systems.

This chapter offers an interdisciplinary (psychological and sociological) consideration of the logic underpinning approaches to CCE. While the study of psychology is concerned with the individual - their behaviour, cognition, and affect - at the centre of wider social structures, and the mechanisms through which such social factors affect the individual, sociologists are more interested in the social and structural contexts that influence the individual (Thoits, 1995). Thus, there is an overlap between the two disciplines, and both disciplines have significant influence on educational policy and practice (e.g., O'Brien, 2008). For example, possibly the most frequently cited psychological theory on the interplay between the reciprocal relationships between the individual and their social ecologies is Bronfenbrenner's Bioecological Systems Theory (1979, 1989) which is frequently also employed in the sociological educational literature. Nonetheless, tensions exist both in education and in the understanding of the climate crisis, particularly, the emphasis given to the individual actor versus wider social structures and institutions. Hampton and Whitmarsh (2023) have argued that much of the individual vs systems debate in climate change is a consequence of the broader philosophical lens of the disciplines' perspectives on systemic and individual agency 'as old as social science itself' that risks confusion and deterrence to those outside of the disciplines. Similarly, there are tensions between the disciplines in the education context and the oft cited interdisciplinarity is frequently lacking as proponents erroneously dichotomise disciplines and interdisciplines, confuse specialisation and synthesis, and misconstrue integration (Graff, 2016).

The IPCC (2014) explicitly states that climate change is unequivocally caused by human activity. This encompasses both the everyday routinised actions of individual actors (citizens & consumers) and the collective actions of more powerful institutional actors (e.g., global corporations, industry, international and multinational governance institutions, national governments) (Bryan, 2023). While the sociological focus has been on the micro-, meso- and macro-drivers of climate change including the interplay of power and politics in policy structures and the corporate sector, and their implications for social and climate justice (Dietz et al., 2020), the psychological focus has been on the interaction between these systems and the individual and how these interrelationships impact on attitudes and behaviours (e.g., Bourke et al., 2024), as well as, inter alia, the impacts climate change on mental health and psychosocial support interventions, advocacy, behavioural change. In their seminal work on understanding psychology's contribution to climate change, Swim et al., (2011) argue that consideration must be given to how cognitive, affective, motivational, and interpersonal responses and processes impact on human causes and consequences of climate change and related responses (adaptation and mitigation). This means that CCE influenced by this perspective would look to integrate affective, cognitive, and relational components in exploring the complexities of the issues.

While acknowledging from the outset that responses to the climate crisis must be structural and systemic *as well as individual*, for the purposes of this chapter we will focus on and engage critically with psychology's contribution to understanding the individual's relationship to the climate crisis. In addition, we will critically examine how psychological concepts including wellbeing, resilience and positive/negative affect, are considered within CCE discourses. Before this analysis, we will explore the relationship between human and planetary wellbeing.

HUMAN AND PLANETARY WELLBEING AS INSEPARABLE

The idea that human beings are *always* embedded within complex interconnected psychological, social, political and ecological systems is increasingly acknowledged in theory and practice (Shackleton & Cocks, 2021; Common Worlds Research Collective, 2020). It is also increasingly acknowledged that human and planetary wellbeing are inseparable from one another. As is argued by the Common Worlds Research Collective (2020), they are "one in the same thing" (p. 2). Human beings cannot live well or be well together unless the planet is well and vice versa. Climate change can have considerable detrimental impacts on human's psychological wellbeing and mental health. Climate change can cause psychological distress through a range of direct and indirect pathways, including the psychological impact, such as depression, anxiety and trauma, from direct exposure to extreme weather events (Cruz et al., 2020; Charlson et al., 2021; Rataj et al., 2018); the impact that displacement and the breaking up of communities and social networks, and the loss of cultural practices and identities that are closely tied to the natural environment (Clayton, 2020; Lawrance et al., 2022; Ash & Obradovich, 2020; ; Lebel et al., 2022). The mental health effects of these events will primarily impact those with pre-existing vulnerabilities and those in positions of disadvantage due to geography, socio-economic disparities, gender, age, mobility, ability, existing mental health challenges or ethnic or cultural group (Bourque & Cunsolo Willox, 2014; Hrabok et al., 2020; Swim et al., 2011). Children are particularly vulnerable to the impacts of climate change given their biological sensitivity, immature physiology, their dependence within their environment, and lifelong exposure (Burke et al., 2018). There also exists significant mental health impacts that result from the existential threat that awareness and knowledge of the ecological crisis brings as well as the vicarious experiences of climate change impacts. These include fears about the future of the planet, PTSD, depression, anxiety, phobias, sleep disorders, attachment disorders, and substance abuse (Burke et al., 2018). In particular 'eco-anxiety' has been widely studied to represent the anxiety and uncertainty about the unprecedented scale of current and future risks (Doherty & Clayton, 2011; Swim et al., 2022; Coffey et al., 2021).

For the planet to "be well", the root causes of climate change must be addressed. This necessitates approaches that take account of the complex interplay between individual behaviour and consumption patterns and wider social forces and macro-structures (e.g., Consumer Capitalism, international trade agreements, subsidies paid by government to the fossil fuel industry) (Bryan, 2024). Bryan's (2022) Social Ecology of Responsibility Framework (SERF), drawing on Bronfenbrenner's Bioecological Systems Theory, argues for the exploration of the symbiotic relationship that exists between the everyday taken-for-granted habits of individuals and the climate-related injustices driven by powerful institutions (e.g., governments; transnational corporations). She maintains that various processes and conditions at different levels interact and inform one another in relation to the global climate crisis. Consequently, a multi-systems approach is necessary if CCE is to realise its transformative goals. Societal and structural (e.g. economic, social) as well as individual responses to climate change are required. However, Monroe and colleagues note in their systematic review of effective CCE strategies that very few educational programmes "intentionally approached climate change from both social and science disciplines (multidisciplinary, interdisciplinary, or transdisciplinary)."

CLIMATE CHANGE EDUCATION

While climate change education is in its relative infancy, there is nonetheless a spectrum of approaches in evidence (Monroe et al., 2019). Approaches vary significantly from learning about climate science in order to increase climate literacy to engaging in deliberative discussion to support students' understanding of their own and others' viewpoints and knowledge about climate change (Kumar et al., 2023). Other approaches focus on developing problem-solving skills and action competence and engaging in political advocacy including designing and implementing school and/or community projects (Kumar et al., 2023; Monroe et al. 2019). These approaches are shaped by different lenses from the scientific, geographical and environmental to the social, cultural, economic, historical, affective/emotional, ethical, and political (Hawkey, 2023; Oberman & Sainz, 2021). As far back as the 1990s Jensen and Schnack (1997) argued that CCE should support young people to become capable of acting to address the impacts of climate change at both at personal and societal levels. However, how exactly individuals and collectives should respond remains ambiguous, subjective and controversial (Oberman & Sainz, 2021). Recent systematic reviews of CCE found a disproportionate focus on science-based education (Rousell & Cutter-Mackenzie-Knowles, 2020; Monroe et al., 2019), where the focus has been on knowledge of the scientific processes underlying climate change. While scientific and geographical lenses are essential, empirical research has consistently shown that the provision of factual information about climate change alone fails to change perspectives (Carmichael & Bruelle, 2020). Thus, it is increasingly acknowledged that CCE must also address affective dimensions particularly if CCE is to change perspectives and motivate action (Ojala, 2012; 2015). This conceptualisation recognises that knowledge about climate change is by itself an "insufficient precondition for successful [climate] action" (Frick et al., 2004, p. 1598).

As such, CCE approaches can draw from those other curricular areas that have a significant focus on affective dimensions of learning such as wellbeing and social and personal education. In particular, CCE education and Relationships and Sexuality Education (RSE) have similar underpinnings in this domain as they both may be viewed as 'controversial' topics of education and require significant values and attitudes reflections on the part of teachers. The ability and willingness of teachers to reflect on their own attitudes and social norms is an important prerequisite to teaching sexuality education and sexual attitudes reassessment or values clarification has been an integral part of sexuality education and training since the 1990s (Sitron and Dyson 2009). This type of input and the development of critical consciousness would be valuable for CCE. Consequently, teacher education and teacher preparation are key sites for good quality CCE.

While the focus on the affective and cognitive dimensions is not unique within an educational context, the additional behavioural focus on climate action suggests that CCE occupies a unique and challenging space in education. Rousell and Cutter-Mackenzie-Knowles (2020) recommend approaches to CCE that are participatory, interdisciplinary, creative, and affect-driven. The type of CCE that students experience has significant implications for how they see, think about and act (or not) in response to the climate crisis (Mochizuki & Bryan, 2024). How CCE and the disciplines which inform it frame the nature of and solutions to the problem matter.

Climate change frequently falls under the banner of GCE. Although GCE has a significant action component, research suggests that teachers' rate their skills in this area as relatively low (Barry et al., 2023). Applying psychological research, Katzarska-Miller and Reysen (2019) propose a two-factor model for the development of GCE. This model proposes the "why" of GCE and the "how" of GCE. The how encompasses "global awareness" and "normative environment". Global awareness refers to the learners' knowledge of the world and their feelings of interconnectedness with others whereas the normative environment is the extent to which valued others endorse a global citizen identity

The integration of these three components is also a challenge for the development and assessment across the three domains. Bloom's Taxonomy may be beneficial as it can be used to classify cognitive learning outcomes in conjunction with the use of affective and psychomotor dimensions. Some of the concerns they had at the time of development might still apply today - that of national priorities leading schools to concentrate more on grade attainment, the fear of indoctrination through persuasion and coercion, scepticism about grading learners on affective outcomes, and the perception that affective domain objective are private matters (Krathwohl, Bloom & Masia, 1964; Kuboja, & Ngussa, (2015).

THE MOTIVATIONAL VALUE OF EMOTIONS IN CLIMATE CHANGE EDUCATION

For the remainder of this chapter, we will focus on the affective or emotional dimensions of CC and CCE, taking a sociological and psychological perspective. The motivational value of emotions is particularly relevant to the education context where emotions impact on teaching, motivation, and learning (Schutz & DeCuir, 2002). While there are differences and nuances between scholars' interpretations of climate emotions, broadly speaking, they are understood to be "emotions, feelings, affect, and moods" related to climate or ecological issues (Pihkala, 2020, n.p.). For example, climate emotion may be understood as an affective response which is connected to, and shaped by, climate change and climate injustices (Galway & Beary, 2022). Research demonstrates that both positive and negative emotions are important drivers of environmental decision-making and behaviour (Brosch, 2021; Kovács et al., 2024; Lerner et al., 2015; Ojala et al., 2021; Whitmarsh et al., 2022). This means that CCE must deal with a range of uncomfortable emotions, requiring particular skills and attributes for teachers to allow learners to express such emotions in the classroom.

Climate Emotions and the Influence of Positive Psychology on Approaches to CCE

The influence of positive psychology in global education is increasingly visible in the publications of major international organisations like the OECD and UNESCO (Bryan, 2023, 2024; Mochizuki & Bryan, 2024) and in national educational curricula (NCCA, 2021). Its influence is evident in the focus on concepts associated with subjective well-being (e.g., hope, optimism) and socio-emotional competencies. However, it is argued that this focus may pose a challenge for the effective pedagogical use of the affective domain in CCE (Kalwak & Weihgold, 2022; Mochizuki & Bryan, 2024). Positive psychology is a branch of psychology that focuses on enhancing the positive qualities that enable individuals and communities to thrive and flourish. These include, for example, happiness, well-being, resilience, and personal strengths. While well-being is differentially defined within the discipline, for the most part, conceptualisations have encompassed experiences of positive (including pleasure) and negative affect and more cognitive elements such as striving, growth and cognitive evaluations of life satisfaction. Since the initial expansion of psychological theories of well-being, research has highlighted the empirical complexity and nuance in these elements. For example, human emotions are extremely complex, and unlikely to follow the simple dichotomy of positive and negative affect that initial hedonic theories of well-being espouse (Diener et al., 2009; Seligman, 2018; Silton et al., 2020). While research does indicate that experiencing relatively high levels of positive and relatively low levels of negative emotions predicts wellbeing (Fredrickson & Joiner, 2002; Lyubomirsky, King, & Diener, 2005), more recent empirical evidence suggests we should also consider fluctuations and dynamics of emotions across time rather than just strength and valence (Houben et al., 2015). Houben et al. (2015), in their meta-analysis of the relationships between patterns of short-term emotion dynamics and psychological well-being, found that lower levels of psychological well-being was associated with more variable, more unstable, but also more inert emotions (how well the intensity of an emotional state can be predicted from the emotional state at a previous moment) and these associations were stronger for negative than positive emotions (i.e., the dynamic patterns of negative emotions were more predictive of psychological well-being). The authors suggest that despite the importance of the message of positive psychology, a large part of the emotional flourishing encountered in different forms of high psychological well-being is reflected in the dynamics of negative emotions, rather than positive emotions. Reflecting these findings, more recent CCE research suggests that negative emotions such as anxiety, guilt, frustration, anger and worry are associated with higher engagement in pro-environmental behaviour (Brosch, 2021; Clayton & Karazsia, 2020; Kovcás et al., 2024). For example, research indicates that the intensity of frustration related to the climate crisis motivates individuals to engage in pro-environmental action, including in the form of activism and policy support (Fritsche et al., 2018; Gregerson et al., 2023; Stanley et al., 2021). As such the CCE classroom should be a place that allows for the expression of the continuum of emotion and policy and practice should be updated from this simplistic dichotomy of emotions.

Given that positive and negative emotions do not occupy opposite end of a dichotomy (Russell & Carroll, 1999), a more nuanced consideration of emotional responses, and the potential of such emotions in mobilising climate action is required (Ojala 2012; Pihkala, 2020). Scholars also caution against the pathologisation and medicalisation of climate emotions and the eco- and climate-anxiety to which they are related (Clayton, 2020). The terminology used in the literature is illustrative - *eco-anxiety*, *environmental grief*, and *climate depression.* In the first instance, it may suggest that these emotional responses are abnormal, inappropriate, and irrational rather than normal, rational and legitimate responses to an existential crisis (Silva & Coburn, 2022). When framed in this way, these legitimate responses to the climate crisis are constructed as individual pathologies which require psychological intervention. This psychopathological framing directs attention away from the socio-political causes of the climate crisis and related responses (Clayton, 2020) and from engagement with more politically oriented emotions (such as moral outrage and anger) which could mobilise students to take action (Bryan and Mochizuki,

2024). Thus, it is important that a balance be struck in CCE between supporting the learner's psychological needs while also acknowledging the appropriateness of these emotions within the context of ecological breakdown.

The pedagogical possibilities of engaging emotions as a way of motivating engagement and action in CCE education may be undermined by narrow understandings of well-being. That is those which centre the cultivation of positive emotions. This simplistic approach negates the many places in education where difficult knowledge challenges the ultimate focus on happiness; knowledge which is affectively rather than cognitively challenging. Britzman (1998) defines difficult knowledge as a concept meant to signify both representations of social traumas in curriculum and the individual's encounters with them in pedagogy. The type of pedagogical engagement is foregrounded in more justice-oriented approaches to CCE.

Climate Change Education as Necessarily Transformative?

The type of pedagogical engagement in justice-oriented CCE necessitates a disruption of constricting and harmful habitual individual behaviours and perspectives– what Fromm terms the "pathology of normalcy" (2011), and interrogation of the role of structural and institutional forces (e.g., political-economic structures, socio-cultural norms, international corporations, governments, industry) in perpetrating climate harms (Bryan, 2024). It therefore leads to encounters with "ecological forms of difficult knowledge" (Bryan, 2023, p. 100) as students (in carbon-intensive societies) grapple with their own implication in climate harms. It also leads to a questioning of the stories that we live by – "those fundamental stories that industrialised societies are based on" (e.g., stories of human superiority, stories of the other-than-human world as mere resources to be exploited, stories of unlimited economic growth as the main goal of society) (Stibbe, 2021, p. 3.). These encounters can cause significant pedagogical discomfort. Although this is arguably required for the "paradigm shift" that is advocated for by the Common Worlds Research Collective's (2020, p. 3) position paper (commissioned for the UNESCO Futures of Education report):

> *education must play a pivotal role in radically reconfiguring the ways we think about our place and agency within this interdependent world, and therefore the ways we act. This requires a complete paradigm shift, from learning about the world in order to act upon it, to learning to become with the world around us. Our future survival depends on our capacity to make this shift (emphasis added).*

CCE is therefore necessarily transformative and needs to address the cognitive *and* affective, individual *and* structural dimensions of the climate crisis (Mochizuki & Bryan, 2024; Rousell & Cutter-Mackenzi-Knowles; Reid, 2019).

Foregrounding Resilience in CCE?

There is an increased emphasis on personal agency, individual responsibility and action, and building adaptive skills in the form of resilience in the policies of the OECD and UNESCO (Bryan, 2023, 2024; Mochizuki & Bryan, 2024). Kalwak and Weihgold (2022) refer to this as the "individualization and responsibilization of individuals against the global and systemic threat of the climate crisis" (p. 2). Resilience is increasingly noted within the context of climate change education (Baker et al., 2021); although its foregrounding is contested. Within the psychological literature, cultivating resilience to the mental health and wellbeing impacts of climate change is argued to be critical to sustaining human cultures as the climate crisis intensifies (Adams et al., 2021; Longman et al., 2023; Ma et al., 2022). Within the sociological literature, it is argued that a focus on resilience fails to engage with the triggers of climate emotions and fails to address the socio-political and political-economic causes of the climate crisis (Bryan & Mochizuki, 2024). Resilience is a complex and multidimensional concept that can be understood as the dynamic process of multiple biological, psychological, social and ecological systems that interact to support individuals to regain, sustain or improve their mental wellbeing within the context of exposure to significant adversity (Ungar & Theron, 2020). The evolution of developmental research on resilience has moved through several waves from its initial narrow focus on individual traits, to the current understanding of resilience as the social-ecological processes that are co-facilitated by individuals and their physical and social ecologies. Such conceptualisations are sensitive to the nuances of the contextual realities and cultural norms in which resilience occurs (Ungar, 2013; Ungar & Theron, 2020). Given the significant and multifaceted impact of climate change on mental health, and the differential vulnerabilities of varying demographics and geographies, it is imperative that we look at psychological adaptations to climate change and understand how best to support individuals in contexts of atypically high levels of stress exposure such as catastrophic climate events and forced migration. Therefore, CCE must integrate the socio-ecological understanding of resilience rather than the outdated individual trait resilience that has understandably been criticised for potentially inadvertently leading to the message that if individuals are not doing enough to combat climate change, it is because they are not trying hard enough or are not sufficiently resilient (Mochizuki & Bryan, 2024). Therefore, a sociological framing which positions climate emotions as socio-political phenomena (Kalwak & Weihgold, 2022) such as "political feelings that circulate within wider cultural, social, political, and material structures" (Mochizuki & Bryan, 2024, p. 10) as well as a psychological perspective on the motivating role of emotions for action and the need to support those most vulnerable is required for the individual and collective action required to mitigate and adapt to the effects of the crisis.

The Need for Empathy and Solidarity?

While individual affective components such as empathy are promoted in mainstream approaches to CCE, more justice-oriented approaches tend to focus more on solidarity. This is because more justice-oriented approaches move the focus of climate change from the suffering of relatable individuals to the systemic factors that create (climate) injustices and marginalise entire communities of people (Varna, 2020). The focus thus shifts from the personal to the political (Varna, 2020). We argue that both empathy *and* solidarity are necessary components of effective CCE. Empathy is a multidimensional construct the requires cognitive perspective taking, an emotional response to the plight of others and a tendency or drive to respond to another's emotions and feelings. It is an important concept in the context of CC where there is a significant temporal and geographical lag between individual's behaviours and the impacts of climate change. However, on its own, it is insufficient as it does not recognise the political dimensions of the crisis and the necessity for collective action. In her critique of empathy, Nussbaum's (1996) argues that empathy is limiting because it "binds us to our own immediate sphere of life, to what has affected us, to what we see before us or can easily imagine ... [which] distorts the world" (p. 43). Similarly, Andreotti (2011) argues that due to our own contexts and identities, we can never truly experience or understand what others experience or feel. Solidarity, on the other hand, is "a commitment to social justice that translates into action when social justice is defined as dignity for everyone in a society" (Varna, 2020, p. 1706). When taken together, there is scope for the individual response to expand to the collective, and recognition of the need for individual and structural change for effective climate change mitigation.

Hope and Climate Change

Given the focus on the emotional aspects of CCE and the levels of climate related anxiety that is experienced, hope has been argued to be an emotion that should be integrated within CCE. It is increasingly visible in policies relating to CCE. The empirical literature suggests that the hope that can emerge from collective climate action has been associated with higher engagement in pro-environmental behaviour (Brosch, 2021; Ojala, 2012; 2015). Ojala (2015), draws on Lazarus' (1991) definition of hope, as an emotion related to a cognitive appraisal pattern of wishing for a desired state to come true even though the odds are not greatly in favour of it. She argues that individual pathways are not enough to feel hope; one must also have faith that other, more powerful, societal actors will do their part in reaching the desired goal (Ojala, 2012, 2015). However, hope has been critiqued as a barrier to environmental behaviour or leading to an optimistic bias that undermines the seriousness of the issue

(Mochizuki & Bryan, 2024; Gifford, 2011). To address such critiques Ojala (2012; 2015) has differentiated between "constructive hope," which has been positively associated with pro-environmental engagement, and "hope based on denial of the seriousness of climate change," which is negatively related to engagement (Ojala, 2012). Ojala (2012; 2015) found that hope based on positive reappraisal and trust in laypersons and other societal actors' capability was a motivational force, while hope based on denial of the seriousness of climate change had a negative association with environmental engagement. Ojala (2015) found that students' perception of how their teachers communicate about emotions in relation to societal problems predicted whether the students feel constructive hope and whether they base their hope on denial. She argues that if teachers want to promote constructive hope about climate change, they should recognise and take seriously the negative emotions evoked by climate change information (Ojala, 2013). Feelings of hopelessness signal an unsupportive socio-political environment which leaves climate mitigation to individuals. Rather than seeking to replace hopelessness with hope and optimism, students need to be supported to engage critically with and unpack the social reasons for their feelings, rather than just the individual feelings. Put another way, they need to be supported to critically engage with the root causes of the climate crisis, wider political-economic practice ideologies and systems and the socio-cultural norms they create. While not discounting the importance of constructive hope, what the climate crisis demands is political courage and urgent action.

The Imperative of Individual and Structural Change

While we have emphasised the affective components of CCE, we also note the critical importance of climate science literacy which is not particularly strong in the wider population (O'Mahoney et al., 2024). Interacting with scientists and addressing misconceptions are two of the four themes identified as relevant to CCE by Monroe et al. (2019) in their systematic review. This multidisciplinary approach to CCE should utilise a multiple systems approach to climate action which focuses on varying individual and systemic layers of influence. While psychology has been critiqued for an overly individualised response with a limited acknowledgement of the systems that embed consumptive behaviour that rely on fossil fuels (e.g., Clayton et al., 2017; Doherty, 2018; Mochizuki & Bryan, 2024), for the most part psychology's response has taken on a social-ecological approach (e.g. Bourke et al., 2023). There is no doubt that considerable changes in individual behaviour and lifestyles are required to meet the ambitious carbon zero targets (e.g., the European Green Deal). Hampton and Whitmarsh (2023) suggest a cross-cutting perspective to understand various pro-environmental behaviour including individual actions as well as the broader ecologies and systems that limit individual choice and pro-environmental behaviour. Drawing on empirical support from psychology, sociology, geography, and interdisciplinary climate research, Hampton and Whitmarsh (2023) identify six domains of individual choice for climate action - including consumption domains (travel, diet, shopping, energy choices) as well as social (community involvement, influencing family and peers) and civic domains (protesting, direct action, voting) while recognising the layers of individual, social, physical, and political factors that combine to influence and constrain low-carbon choices in each domain. CCE that is co-constructed and multidisciplinary should consider both the domains of action, including consumptive behaviours - which are still critical given that household consumption accounts for more than 60% of global GHG emissions (Ivanova et al., 2016) - as well as social influence and civic behaviours, influencing these domains. Focusing on different domains of influence may result in different emotional responses such that an emphasis on personal impacts may engender feelings of guilt and powerlessness, while influence and climate citizenship framing may foster more constructive, empowering associations with climate change (Hampton & Whitmarsh, 2023).

CONCLUSION

Addressing the climate crisis requires individual and collective engagement and action at local, national, and global levels. s. The emphasis on individual agency alone can lead to a focus on personal behaviour change without also addressing wider socio-cultural norms and practices, and the institutional, ideological, and political-economic systems that are driving climate and ecological breakdown. A more multi-disciplinary approach to CCE calls for a social-justice approach to pedagogy and content recognising the difficult knowledge encountered and the disproportional vulnerabilities of some populations. Indeed, children and young people, a group who are recognised are being disproportionately affected but with little voice in the crisis, will be a key demographic in receipt of CCE (not negating the importance of lifelong CCE). It is critical that a multidisciplinary approach to CCE considers the individual, systematic and structural impacts of climate change and the need for all scaled solutions and urgent action at all levels of response. It is also critical that 'negative' emotions are not sidelined given the focus of wellbeing in educational curricula. Such emotions provide possibilities for critical engagement with self as an implicated subject and potentially elicit climate action. A critical approach to CCE needs to be underpinned by environmental justice and equity that critically engages with the individual, economic, social and political factors as the causes of the climate crisis. Such an approach should recognise the role of the wide continuum of emotional responses on collective and individual action. Ultimately this CCE should be envisioned as a route towards individual, collective, other-than-human, and planetary wellbeing.

DISCUSSION QUESTIONS

1. Does the planet have intrinsic value (valuable in and of itself) or instrumental value (valuable in how it can best serve human interests)?
2. What obligations or moral duties do humans have for protecting the planet?
3. In what ways might you be implicated in the climate crisis?
4. Young people and future generations are disproportionately impacted by climate change, do people in the future have the same rights as people of today?
5. Should the countries with the highest carbon emissions have more responsibilities in combating the climate crisis than countries with lower emissions?
6. In what ways might exploring the more difficult components of the climate crisis be challenging for teachers?
7. What roles can school play?
8. What action would you like to see national governments taking?
9. How can psychology contribute to our responses to the climate crisis?
10. What role does climate change education have in our mitigation and adaptation efforts?

    What are the limitations to the focus on hope and resilience in climate change education?
11. Why is CCE a challenging curricular are for both teachers and learners?
12. How can we bring balance to the debate between individual and systemic causes and responses to the climate crisis within climate change education?

REFERENCES

Adams, H., Blackburn, S., & Mantovani, N. (2021). Psychological resilience for climate change transformation: Relational, differentiated and situated perspectives. *Current Opinion in Environmental Sustainability*, *50*, 303–309. DOI: 10.1016/j.cosust.2021.06.011

Ash, K., & Obradovich, N. (2020). Climatic stress, internal migration, and Syrian civil war onset. *The Journal of Conflict Resolution*, *64*(1), 3–31. DOI: 10.1177/0022002719864140

Baker, C., Clayton, S., & Bragg, E. (2021). Educating for resilience: Parent and teacher perceptions of children's emotional needs in response to climate change. *Environmental Education Research*, *27*(5), 687–705. DOI: 10.1080/13504622.2020.1828288

Barry, M., Mallon, B., Bourke, A., Usher, J., & Daly, A. (2023). *Teachers and Global Citizenship Education: Values, Attitudes and Practices A Research Report on a National Survey of Irish Primary Teachers and Global Citizenship Education*. Global Village.

Boluda-Verdu, I., Senent-Valero, M., Casas-Escolano, M., Matijasevich, A., & Pastor-Valero, M. (2022). Fear for the future: Eco-anxiety and health implications, a systematic review. *Journal of Environmental Psychology*, *84*, 101904. DOI: 10.1016/j.jenvp.2022.101904

Bourke, A., Jabbour, S., Martin, A., Walsh, L., & Hadfield, K. (2024). A Review of Climate Change Attitudes Using a Person-Centred Framework. EPA Research Report.

Bourque, F., & Cunsolo Willox, A. (2014). Climate change: The next challenge for public mental health? *International Review of Psychiatry (Abingdon, England)*, *26*(4), 415–422. DOI: 10.3109/09540261.2014.925851

Britzman, D. P. (1998). *Lost subjects, contested objects: Toward a psychoanalytic inquiry of learning*. State University of New York Press.

Bronfe Brenner, U. (1989). Ecological systems theory. In R. Vasta (Ed.), Annals of child development (Vol. 6, pp. 187–249). JAI Press.

Bronfenbrenner, U. (1979). *The ecology of human development: Experiments by nature and design*. Harvard University Press.

Brosch, T. (2021). Affect and emotions as drivers of climate change perception and action: A review. *Current Opinion in Behavioral Sciences*, *42*, 15–21. DOI: 10.1016/j.cobeha.2021.02.001

Bryan, A. (2023). Pedagogy of the implicated (subject): Slantwise pedagogical encounters with difficult ecological knowledge. In B. Mallon, F. Waldron & C. Ní Cassaithe (Eds.), *Pushing the boundaries of human rights education: Concepts, challenges and contexts* (pp. 98-115). Routledge.

Bryan, A., & Mochizuki, Y. (2024). Rethinking agency, affect, and education: Towards new childhood and youth studies in the Anthropocene. In Wyn, J., Cahill, H., & Cuervo, H. (Eds.), *Springer Handbook of Children and Youth Studies.*

Burke, S. E., Sanson, A. V., & Van Hoorn, J. (2018). The psychological effects of climate change on children. *Current Psychiatry Reports*, *20*, 1–8. DOI: 10.1007/s11920-018-0896-9

Carmichael, J. T., & Brulle, R. J. (2017). Elite cues, media coverage, and public concern: An integrated path analysis of public opinion on climate change, 2001–2013. *Environmental Politics*, *26*(2), 232–252. DOI: 10.1080/09644016.2016.1263433

Charlson, F., Ali, S., Benmarhnia, T., Pearl, M., Massazza, A., Augustinavicius, J., & Scott, J. G. (2021). Climate change and mental health: A scoping review. *International Journal of Environmental Research and Public Health*, *18*(9), 4486. DOI: 10.3390/ijerph18094486

Clayton, S. (2020). Climate anxiety: Psychological responses to climate change. *Journal of Anxiety Disorders*, *74*. Advance online publication. DOI: 10.1016/j.janxdis.2020.102263

Clayton, S., & Karazsia, B. (2020). Development and validation of a measure of climate change anxiety. *Journal of Environmental Psychology*, *69*, 101434. DOI: 10.1016/j.jenvp.2020.101434

Clayton, S., Manning, C. M., Krygsman, K., & Speiser, M. (2017). *Mental health and our changing climate: Impacts, implications, and guidance*. American Psychological Association, and ecoAmerica. Retrieved from https://www.apa.org/news/press/releases/2017/03/mental-health-climate.pdf

Coffey, Y., Bhullar, N., Durkin, J., Islam, M. S., & Usher, K. (2021). Understanding eco-anxiety: A systematic scoping review of current literature and identified knowledge gaps. *The Journal of Climate Change and Health*, *3*, 100047. DOI: 10.1016/j.joclim.2021.100047

Common Worlds Research Collective. (2020). Learning to become with the world: Education for future survival. Background paper for the futures of education initiative. Retrieved from https://unesdoc.unesco.org/ark:/48223/pf0000374032

Copernicus Climate Change Service. (C3S) (2024). European State of the Climate 2023, Summary. DOI: 10.24381/bs9v-8c66

Cruz, J., White, P. C., Bell, A., & Coventry, P. A. (2020). Effect of extreme weather events on mental health: A narrative synthesis and meta-analysis for the UK. *International Journal of Environmental Research and Public Health, 17*(22), 8581. DOI: 10.3390/ijerph17228581

Diener, E., Lucas, R. E., & Scollon, C. N. (2009). Beyond the hedonic treadmill: Revising the adaptation theory of well-being. The Science of Well-being: The Collected Works of Ed Diener, 103-118. DOI: 10.1037/0003-066X.61.4.305

Dietz, T., Shwom, R. L., & Whitley, C. T. (2020). Climate change and society. *Annual Review of Sociology, 46*, 135–158. DOI: 10.1146/annurev-soc-121919-054614

Doherty, T. J., & Clayton, S. (2011). The psychological impacts of global climate change. *The American Psychologist, 66*(4), 265–276. DOI: 10.1037/a0023141

Fredrickson, B. L., & Joiner, T. (2002). Positive emotions trigger upward spirals toward emotional well-being. *Psychological Science, 13*(2), 172–175. DOI: 10.1111/1467-9280.00431

Fritsche, I., Barth, M., Jugert, P., Masson, T., & Reese, G. (2018). A social identity model of pro-environmental action (SIMPEA). *Psychological Review, 125*(2), 245–269. DOI: 10.1037/rev0000090

Fromm, E. (2011). *The pathology of normalcy.* American Mental Health Foundation Books. DOI: 10.3389/fpsyg.2022.920313

Graff, H. J. (2016). The "problem" of interdisciplinarity in theory, practice, and history. *Social Science History, 40*(4), 775–803. DOI: 10.1017/ssh.2016.31

Gregersen, T., Andersen, G., & Tvinnereim, E. (2023). The strength and content of climate anger. *Global Environmental Change, 82*, 102738. DOI: 10.1016/j.gloenvcha.2023.102738

Hampton, S., & Whitmarsh, L. (2023). Choices for climate action: A review of the multiple roles individuals play. *One Earth, 6*(9), 1157–1172. DOI: 10.1016/j.oneear.2023.08.006

Hawkey, K. (2023). *History and the climate crisis.* UCL Press.

Houben, M., Van Den Noortgate, W., & Kuppens, P. (2015). The relation between short-term emotion dynamics and psychological well-being: A meta-analysis. *Psychological Bulletin, 141*(4), 901–930. DOI: 10.1037/a0038822

Hrabok, M., Delorme, A., & Agyapong, V. I. (2020). Threats to mental health and well-being associated with climate change. *Journal of Anxiety Disorders*, *76*, 102295. DOI: 10.1016/j.janxdis.2020.102295

IPCC. (2014). *Climate Change 2014: Synthesis Report*. Contribution of Working Groups I, II and III to the Fifth Assessment Report of the Intergovernmental Panel on Climate Change. IPCC. https://www.ipcc.ch/site/assets/uploads/2018/05/SYR_AR5_FINAL_full_wcover.pdf

IPCC. (2022). Climate change 2022: Impacts, adaptation, and vulnerability. Contribution of Working Group II to the Sixth Assessment Report of the Intergovernmental Panel on Climate Change. Cambridge University Press. DOI: 10.1017/9781009325844

IPCC. (2023). *Climate Change 2023: Synthesis report*. Contribution of Working Groups I, II and III to the Sixth Assessment Report of the Intergovernmental Panel on Climate Change. IPCC. DOI: 10.59327/IPCC/AR6-9789291691647

Ivanova, D., Stadler, K., Steen-Olsen, K., Wood, R., Vita, G., Tukker, A., & Hertwich, E. G. (2016). Environmental impact assessment of household consumption. *Journal of Industrial Ecology*, *20*(3), 526–536. DOI: 10.1111/jiec.12371

Jensen, B. B., & Schnack, K. (2006). The action competence approach in environmental education: Reprinted from Environmental Education Research (1997) 3 (2), pp. 163–178. *Environmental Education Research*, *12*(3-4), 471–486. DOI: 10.1080/1350462970030205

Kalwak, W., & Weihgold, V. (2022). The relationality of ecological emotions: An interdisciplinary critique of individual resilience as psychology's response to the climate crisis. *Frontiers in Psychology*, *22*, 823620. DOI: 10.3389/fpsyg.2022.823620

Katzarska-Miller, I., & Reysen, S. (2019). Educating for global citizenship: Lessons from psychology. *Childhood*, *95*(6), 24–33. DOI: 10.1080/00094056.2019.1689055

Klinenberg, E., Araos, M., & Koslov, L. (2020). Sociology and the climate crisis. *Annual Review of Sociology*, *46*(1), 649–669. DOI: 10.1146/annurev-soc-121919-054750

Kovács, L. N., Jordan, G., Berglund, F., Holden, B., Niehoff, E., Pohl, F., Younssi, M., Zevallos, I., Ágoston, C., Varga, A., & Kökönyei, G.. (2024). Acting as we feel: Which emotional responses to the climate crisis motivate climate action. *Journal of Environmental Psychology*, *96*. Advance online publication. DOI: 10.1016/j.jenvp.2024.102327

Krathwohl, D. R., Bloom, B. S., & Masia, B. B. (1964). Taxonomy of educational objectives: The classification of educational goals, Hand book II: Affective domain. New York: David Mckay Company Incorporated.

Kuboja, J. M., & Ngussa, B. M. (2015). Affective learning and cognitive skills improvement: Experience of selected schools in Arusha, Tanzania. *International Journal of Academic Research in Progressive Education and Development, 4*(2), 38–53. DOI: 10.6007/IJARPED/v4-i2/1727

Kumar, P., Sahani, J., Rawat, N., Debele, S., Tiwari, A., Emygdio, A. P. M., Abhijith, K. V., Kudadia, V., Holmes, K., & Pfautsch, S. (2023). Using empirical science education in schools to improve climate change literacy. *Renewable & Sustainable Energy Reviews, 17*, 113232. DOI: 10.1016/j.rser.2023.113232

Lawrance, E., Thompson, R., Fontana, G., & Jennings, N. (2021). The impact of climate change on mental health and emotional wellbeing: current evidence and implications for policy and practice. Grantham Institute briefing paper, 36, 1-36. DOI: 10.1080/09540261.2022.2128725

Lebel, L., Paquin, V., Kenny, T. A., Fletcher, C., Nadeau, L., Chachamovich, E., & Lemire, M. (2022). Climate change and Indigenous mental health in the Circumpolar North: A systematic review to inform clinical practice. *Transcultural Psychiatry, 59*(3), 312–336. DOI: 10.1177/13634615211066698

Lerner, J. S., Li, Y., Valdesolo, P., & Kassam, K. S. (2015). Emotion and decision making. *Annual Review of Psychology, 66*, 799–823. DOI: 10.1146/annurev-psych-010213-115043

Longman, J., Braddon, M., Verlie, B., Schlosberg, D., Hampshire, L., Hawke, C., & Saurman, E. (2023). Building resilience to the mental health impacts of climate change in rural Australia. *The Journal of Climate Change and Health, 12*, 100240. DOI: 10.1016/j.joclim.2023.100240

Lyubomirsky, S., King, L., & Diener, E. (2005). The benefits of frequent positive affect: Does happiness lead to success? *Psychological Bulletin, 131*(6), 803. DOI: 10.1037/0033-2909.131.6.803

Ma, T., Moore, J., & Cleary, A. (2022). Climate change impacts on the mental health and wellbeing of young people: A scoping review of risk and protective factors. *Social Science & Medicine, 301*, 114888. DOI: 10.1016/j.socscimed.2022.114888

Mochizuki, Y., & Bryan, A. (2024). Victims or vanguards? The discursive construction of the anthropocene generation and climate change education's hopeful, resilient, post-political subject. In Wyn, J., Cahill, H., & Cuervo, H. (Eds.), *Springer Handbook of Children and Youth Studies*.

Monroe, M. C., Plate, R. R., Oxarart, A., Bowers, A., & Chaves, W. A. (2019). Identifying effective climate change education strategies: A systematic review of the research. *Environmental Education Research*, *25*(6), 791–812. DOI: 10.1080/13504622.2017.1360842

NASA. (2024, July). *NASA data July 22 was Earth's hottest day on record*. Retrieved from, https://www.nasa.gov/earth/nasa-data-shows-july-22-was-earths-hottest-day-on-record/#:~:text=July%2022%2C%202024%2C%20was%20the,record%2C%20set%20in%20July%202023

NCCA. (2021). *Draft primary curriculum framework*. Retrieved from https://ncca.ie/media/4456/ncca-primary- curriculum-framework-2020.pdf

Nohilly, M., & Tynan, F. (2022). The evolution of wellbeing in educational policy in Ireland: Towards an interdisciplinary approach. *International Journal of Wellbeing*, *12*(1), 42–53. DOI: 10.5502/ijw.v12i1.1663

Nussbaum, M. (1996). Compassion: The basic social emotion. *Social Philosophy & Policy*, *13*(1), 27–58. DOI: 10.1017/S0265052500001515

O'Brien, M. (2008). Well-being and post-primary schooling. Dublin: NCCA.

O'Mahony, D., Quinlan, C., Cotter, D., Rochford, M. F., Leiserowitz, A., Regan, A., Carman, J., & Rosenthal, S. (2024). *Climate Change in the Irish Mind: Wave 2, Report 1*. Environmental Protection Agency.

Oberman, R., & Sainz, G. M. (2021). Critical thinking, critical pedagogy and climate change education. In A. M. Kavanagh, F. Waldron & B. Mallon (Eds.), *Teaching for social justice and sustainable development across the primary curriculum* (pp. 69-83). Routledge.

Obradovich, N., Migliorini, R., Paulus, M. P., & Rahwan, I. (2018). Empirical evidence of mental health risks posed by climate change. *Proceedings of the National Academy of Sciences of the United States of America*, *115*(43), 10953–10958. DOI: 10.1073/pnas.1801528115

Ojala, M. (2012). How do children cope with global climate change? Coping strategies, engagement, and well-being. *Journal of Environmental Psychology*, *32*(3), 225–233. DOI: 10.1016/j.jenvp.2012.02.004

Ojala, M. (2015). Hope in the face of climate change: Associations with environmental engagement and student perceptions of teachers' emotion communication style and future orientation. *The Journal of Environmental Education, 46*(3), 133–148. DOI: 10.1080/00958964.2015.1021662

Ojala, M., Cunsolo, A., Ogunbode, C. A., & Middleton, J. (2021). Anxiety, worry, and grief in a time of environmental and climate crisis: A narrative review. *Annual Review of Environment and Resources, 46*(1), 35-58. DOI: 10.1146/annurev-environ-012220-022716

Pihkala, P. (2020). Anxiety and the ecological crisis: An analysis of eco-anxiety and climate anxiety. *Sustainability, 12*, 7836. DOI: 10.3390/su12197836

Rataj, E., Kunzweiler, K., & Garthus-Niegel, S. (2016). Extreme weather events in developing countries and related injuries and mental health disorders-a systematic review. *BMC Public Health, 16*, 1–12.

Reid, A. (2019). Climate change education and research: Possibilities and potentials versus problems and perils? *Environmental Education Research, 25*(6), 767–790. DOI: 10.1080/13504622.2019.1664075

Rousell, D., & Cutter-Mackenzie-Knowles, A. (2020). A systematic review of climate change education: Giving children and young people a 'voice' and a 'hand' in redressing climate change. *Children's Geographies, 18*(2), 191–208. DOI: 10.1080/14733285.2019.1614532

Russell, J. A., & Carroll, J. M. (1999). On the bipolarity of positive and negative affect. *Psychological Bulletin, 125*(1), 3–30. DOI: 10.1037/0033-2909.125.1.3

Schutz, P. A., & DeCuir, J. T. (2002). Inquiry on emotions in education. *Educational Psychologist, 37*(2), 125–134. DOI: 10.1207/S15326985EP3702_7

Seligman, M. (2018). PERMA and the building blocks of well-being. *The Journal of Positive Psychology, 13*(4), 333–335. DOI: 10.1080/17439760.2018.1437466

Shackleton, C. M., & Cocks, M. L. (2021). Urban nature and biocultural realities. In Cocks, M. L., & Shackleton, C. M. (Eds.), *Diversities of nature in cities: enriching belonging, wellbeing and bioculture* (pp. 1–24). Earthscan/Routledge.

Sheffield, P. E., & Landrigan, P. J. (2011). Global climate change and children's health: Threats and strategies for prevention. *Environmental Health Perspectives, 119*(3), 291–298. DOI: 10.1289/ehp.1002233

Silton, R. L., Kahrilas, I. J., Skymba, H. V., Smith, J., Bryant, F. B., & Heller, W. (2020). Regulating positive emotions: Implications for promoting well-being in individuals with depression. *Emotion (Washington, D.C.)*, *20*(1), 93–97. DOI: 10.1037/emo0000675

Silva, J. F. B., & Coburn, J. (2022). Therapists' experience of climate change: A dialectic between personal and professional. *Counselling & Psychotherapy Research*, *23*(2), 417–431. DOI: 10.1002/capr.12515

Stanley, S. K., Hogg, T. L., Leviston, Z., & Walker, I. (2021). From anger to action: Differential impacts of eco-anxiety, eco-depression, and eco-anger on climate action and wellbeing. *The Journal of Climate Change and Health*, *1*, 100003. DOI: 10.1016/j.joclim.2021.100003

Stern, N., Patel, I., & Ward, B. (2021). Covid-19, climate change, and the environment: A sustainable, inclusive, and resilient global recovery. *BMJ (Clinical Research Ed.)*, (2405). Advance online publication. DOI: 10.1136/bmj.n2405

Stibbe, A. (2021). *Ecolinguistics: Language, ecology and the stories we live by*. Routledge.

Swim, J. K., Aviste, R., Lengieza, M. L., & Fasano, C. J. (2022). OK Boomer: A decade of generational differences in feelings about climate change. *Global Environmental Change*, *73*, 102479. DOI: 10.1016/j.gloenvcha.2022.102479

Swim, J. K., Clayton, S., & Howard, G. S. (2011). Human behavioral contributions to climate change: Psychological and contextual drivers. *The American Psychologist*, *66*(4), 251–265. DOI: 10.1037/a0023472

Thoits, P. A. (1995). Social psychology: The interplay between sociology and psychology. *Social Forces*, *73*(4), 1231–1243. DOI: 10.1093/sf/73.4.1231

Ungar, M. (2013). Resilience, trauma, context, and culture. *Trauma, Violence & Abuse*, *14*(3), 255–266. DOI: 10.1177/1524838013487805

Ungar, M., & Theron, L. (2020). Resilience and mental health: How multisystemic processes contribute to positive outcomes. *The Lancet. Psychiatry*, *7*(5), 441–448. DOI: 10.1016/S2215-0366(19)30434-1

Varma, A. (2020). Evoking empathy or enacting solidarity with marginalized communities?: A case study of journalistic humanizing techniques in the San Francisco Homeless Project. *Journalism Studies*, *21*(12), 1705–1723. DOI: 10.1080/1461670X.2020.1789495

Whitmarsh, L., Player, L., Jiongco, A., James, M., Williams, M., Marks, E., & Kennedy-Williams, P. (2022). Climate anxiety: What predicts it and how is it related to climate action? *Journal of Environmental Psychology*, *83*, 101866.

ADDITIONAL READING

Bryan, A., & Mochizuki, Y. (2024). Rethinking agency, affect, and education: Towards new childhood and youth studies in the Anthropocene. In Wyn, J., Cahill, H., & Cuervo, H. (Eds.), *Springer Handbook of Children and Youth Studies.*

Oberman, R., & Sainz, G. M. (2021). Critical thinking, critical pedagogy and climate change education. In Kavanagh, A. M., Waldron, F., & Mallon, B. (Eds.), *Teaching for social justice and sustainable development across the primary curriculum* (pp. 69–83). Routledge.

Whitmarsh, L., Player, L., Jiongco, A., James, M., Williams, M., Marks, E., & Kennedy-Williams, P. (2022). Climate anxiety: What predicts it and how is it related to climate action? *Journal of Environmental Psychology*, *83*, 101866. DOI: 10.1016/j.jenvp.2022.101866

Chapter 12
Embracing the Digital Age in Contemporary Classrooms

Keith Young
Mary Immaculate College, Ireland

ABSTRACT

This chapter examines the psychological dimensions of educational technology, framing digital transformation not merely as a technical shift but as a developmental, cognitive, and ethical one. Drawing on foundational theories from educational psychology, it explores how technology mediates not only how students learn, but how they experience autonomy, construct identity, and navigate emotion and motivation in increasingly digital environments. The discussion traces how these experiences are shaped by deeper systemic factors such as inequitable access, ethical tensions around data use and surveillance, and the emergence of generative AI. Throughout, the chapter argues for a move beyond either enthusiasm or resistance, advocating instead for a human-centred, augmentation-oriented approach to technology, one that respects learners' psychological needs, supports equity, and prepares students for critically engaged digital citizenship in a rapidly changing world.

INTRODUCTION

The pace of technological development has, in many ways, outstripped our ability to respond meaningfully and adapt in a timely manner. While change has always been a feature of human progress, the digital age has enabled rapid advances in devices, platforms, and software that now permeate nearly every sector of society. From AI-powered tools to algorithmically curated content, these technologies have

DOI: 10.4018/979-8-3693-1293-3.ch012

not only accelerated the rate of adoption but have also embedded themselves into the everyday rhythms of life, reshaping how we communicate, work, and learn. Education has been deeply affected by this transformation, with digital technologies altering how knowledge is accessed, delivered, and experienced.

These developments can offer significant benefits. Digital platforms can expand access to learning, especially for students who face geographic, economic, or physical barriers (UNESCO 2023; Taggart & Roulston 2024; Song et al. 2024). Online and blended learning environments allow for increased personalisation and flexibility, supporting greater engagement and self-directed learning (Major, Francis & Tspali 2021; Bond et al. 2024). When thoughtfully implemented, such tools can also foster learners' self-efficacy and autonomy (Bandura 1994; Prifti 2022).

Yet these same technologies also introduce new risks. Inequities in access and digital literacy persist (Jin et al. 2020), while concerns about sustained attention, shallow engagement, and reduced critical thinking are increasingly raised (Selwyn 2021; Cladis 2020; Ashour 2020; Henderson et al. 2015). Digital tools can introduce extraneous cognitive load that hinders learning if not carefully managed (Sweller 1994; Skulmowski & Xu 2022). Moreover, as educational experiences move online, questions around data privacy, surveillance, and the ethics of algorithmic influence become more urgent (Lupton & Williamson 2017).

The digital shift isn't just about tools or systems, it's also about minds and emotions. Online spaces shape learners' identities, emotional development, and sense of self, often in ways that are complex, contradictory, and still poorly understood. The same technologies that connect and empower can also isolate, compare, and fragment. For educators, the demands of navigating these shifts, pedagogically, emotionally, and ethically, add to already significant workloads and pressures. As digital ecosystems evolve faster than policy or pedagogy can keep pace, the task of integrating technology in ways that genuinely support human learning becomes both more urgent and more difficult.

This chapter examines the psychological dimensions of digital transformation in education. Drawing on contemporary research in educational psychology, it explores how technologies influence learning, motivation, identity, and wellbeing, while also attending to broader issues such as equity, access, and responsible digital citizenship. It argues for an approach to educational technology that is grounded in human development, one that seeks to augment rather than replace the relationships, skills, and experiences that make learning meaningful. In doing so, the chapter is structured around six key themes: cognition and learning in the digital age; motivation, autonomy, and self-efficacy; identity, social media, and emotional development; equity, access, and the digital divide; ethics, citizenship, and responsible technology use; and the future of educational technology as a tool for augmentation, not substitution.

Cognition and Learning in the Digital Age

The integration of digital tools into education, ranging from Learning Management Systems (LMS) like Moodle and Google Classroom to generative AI platforms and adaptive software, has impacted how students access content, receive feedback, and engage with learning. These technologies offer considerable potential to enhance educational outcomes when used with purpose, providing real-time feedback, individualized instruction, and flexible access to learning resources (Turnbull, Chugh & Luck, 2020; Furqon et al., 2023). However, their integration in education has elicited mixed findings regarding its overall impact on teaching and learning outcomes (Timotheu et al. 2023). This variation is largely due to the complexity of classroom environments, where the effectiveness of technological tools can be influenced by multiple variables, including the specific subject matter, the context in which they are used, and the pedagogical strategies employed by teachers (UNESCO 2023). It's also possible that some tools are simply not effective and simply introducing them to educational contexts does not mean they will positively impact on learning outcomes (Cristia et al., 2017).

Platforms and Pedagogy

LMS function as centralized platforms where students can track progress, interact with resources, and communicate with teachers. When embedded within coherent pedagogical frameworks, these systems can support student autonomy and self-efficacy (Bandura, 1994; Prifti, 2022). They also enable ongoing formative assessment and feedback, both of which are associated with improved learning outcomes (Faulconer, Griffith & Gruss, 2022). In addition, computer-assisted learning programs, especially those used for repeated practice in areas such as mathematics or language, have shown promise in reinforcing foundational skills (Outhwaite et al., 2022). Adaptive technologies further individualize learning by adjusting content difficulty in response to student performance (Murphy et al., 2022; Wang et al., 2023).

Case Study: Adaptive Learning with TALP in Taiwan (Liu, 2022)

In a Taiwanese elementary school, researchers studied the use of the Taiwan Adaptive Learning Platform (TALP), a government-developed system designed to support precision education. TALP identifies students' learning deficits, delivers varied learning materials, and provides timely feedback. Involving 76 fifth-grade students, the study combined testing data with teacher interviews. While quantitative test results showed no significant gains, teachers reported that TALP helped them better understand students' needs and adjust instruction.

The findings suggest that adaptive platforms like TALP may enhance teaching by supporting early identification of learning challenges and providing tailored feedback to guide student progress.

The rapid expansion of online and blended learning models, particularly after the COVID-19 pandemic, has further shaped how educational technologies are used in practice. In blended learning, students alternate between in-person instruction and online components. This structure offers flexibility and can accommodate a wider range of learning pathways. Similarly, fully online learning environments enable remote access to instruction and materials, which has increased educational reach and scalability. A related development is the rise of flipped classrooms, where students engage with instructional content, such as lectures or readings, before class, reserving in-person time for discussion, problem-solving, or applied activities (Latorre-Cosculluela, 2021). These models shift more responsibility onto students to manage their own time, stay organized, and engage meaningfully with asynchronous content, requiring stronger self-regulation and motivation.

While these models offer new opportunities for personalisation and access, they also introduce challenges related to focus, self-management, and cognitive load. Without the structure and cues of a traditional classroom, some students may struggle to maintain consistent engagement, leading to superficial or fragmented learning experiences. This is especially true when digital tools are poorly integrated into course design or used in ways that overwhelm rather than support learners.

Cognitive Load in Digital Learning Environments: Attention and Distraction

Cognitive Load Theory (Sweller, 1994) provides a useful framework for understanding how digital environments can sometimes impede learning. Working memory has limited capacity, and when students are confronted with poorly designed interfaces, excessive information, or non-essential features, their cognitive resources may be consumed by navigating the system itself rather than engaging with the material. This extraneous load can interfere with the deeper processing required for long-term retention and understanding (Skulmowski & Xu, 2022).

In addition to platform design, the broader digital environment contributes to cognitive challenges. With the rise of smartphones, tablets, and social media, students are increasingly exposed to distractions that compete with academic tasks (McGarr, 2024; McGarr & McDonagh, 2021). Even tools intended for learning can become vehicles for multitasking and off-task behaviour, as students toggle between educational materials and entertainment. This digital distraction has been linked to negative effects on learning outcomes, particularly in the development of critical and analytical thinking skills (Cladis, 2020). As students grow accustomed to fast-paced, bite-sized content, such as what they encounter on social platforms, they may find it harder to sustain the attention and cognitive effort required for more complex academic tasks (Selwyn, 2021).

These concerns are especially pronounced among younger learners, whose executive functions are still developing. Research suggests that increased screen time and frequent task-switching are associated with reduced attention spans, greater impulsivity, and cognitive fatigue. When these patterns become habitual, they may undermine students' ability to concentrate, retain information, and engage in goal-directed learning (Rosen, Carrier, and Cheever, 2013; Gazzaley & Rosen, 2016).

Generative AI: Cognitive Tool or Shortcut?

The rise of generative AI tools, such as ChatGPT, adds another layer to these dynamics. While AI has the potential to support learning by offering explanations, clarifying content, or guiding students through tasks, it also enables a form of cognitive outsourcing. Students may be tempted to use AI to complete assignments without engaging in the necessary mental processes themselves, which risks undercutting critical thinking, reflection, and knowledge construction (Bastani et al., 2024; Lodge et al. 2023). Over-reliance on AI can shift the focus from learning to task completion, reinforcing surface-level engagement.

However, these tools need not be counterproductive. When integrated thoughtfully, such as by encouraging students to evaluate, revise, or critique AI-generated responses, they can support inquiry and metacognition (ElSayary, 2024). While there is also evidence to suggest that they could foster metacognitive laziness (Fan et al., 2025) it appears the key lies in how such tools are introduced and framed within instructional design.

Ultimately, digital technologies and flexible learning models such as online and blended learning are not inherently cognitively beneficial or harmful. Their effectiveness depends on how well they are aligned with instructional goals, how thoughtfully they are implemented, and how carefully they are designed to support cognitive processes. Educators must consider not only the functionality of tools, but also their cognitive demands and the potential for distraction or disengagement.

As technology continues to reshape the educational landscape, its role must be seen as part of a larger pedagogical ecosystem. Thoughtful integration, grounded in research and responsive to students' developmental needs, is essential if we are to ensure that technology enhances rather than diminishes the quality of learning.

MOTIVATION, AUTONOMY, AND SELF-EFFICACY

Digital technologies can shape student motivation in both positive and negative ways. According to Self-Determination Theory (Deci & Ryan, 2013), optimal learning environments support three basic psychological needs: autonomy, competence, and relatedness. When these needs are met, students are more likely to experience intrinsic motivation, the drive to engage in learning for its own sake. In the digital age, technologies can support these needs by offering students choice, adaptive challenges, and collaborative opportunities. However, these same tools can also create distractions, increase cognitive load, or reinforce extrinsic motivations in ways that undermine sustained engagement.

Motivation

One of the most commonly reported benefits of digital tools in education is increased student engagement. Interactive media, gamified elements, and visually rich content often capture attention in ways traditional materials do not. For instance, platforms that use rewards, badges, or progress tracking have been shown to increase short-term motivation (Gaonkar et al, 2022). Similarly, approaches that integrate team-based, technology-mediated tasks can stimulate students' intrinsic interest by providing a sense of purpose and active involvement (Lawlor, Marshall & Tangney, 2016).

However, the nature of this motivation is important to consider. While gamification can initially boost engagement, overreliance on points or rewards may lead students to focus on outcomes rather than the learning process itself. This extrinsically motivated behaviour can, over time, reduce deeper forms of engagement if not connected to meaningful learning goals (Calderón, Merono & MacPhail, 2020; Gaonkar et al., 2022). Moreover, students accustomed to rapid feedback and bite-sized information, common in digital environments, may struggle with tasks that require sustained effort or critical thinking (Cladis, 2020; Selwyn, 2021).

The presence of digital distractions also complicates the relationship between technology and motivation. With easy access to entertainment, messaging, and social media within the same devices used for learning, students may find it difficult to maintain focus. Research suggests that digital distractions can negatively affect not only attention spans but also learners' capacity for self-regulation and deep engagement (Wang et al., 2022). Thus, while digital tools can boost motivation, they must be carefully integrated to avoid undermining concentration and long-term commitment to learning.

Autonomy

Autonomy, the perception of control over one's learning, is a crucial component of motivation and academic persistence. Digital platforms offer new opportunities for learners to make choices about what, how, and when they learn. Blended and online environments, in particular, allow students to engage with content at their own pace and often on their own schedule, which supports a greater sense of independence (Rasheed, Kamsin & Abdullah, 2020; Moireira & Lima, 2024).

Adaptive learning technologies further support autonomy by personalizing content to students' needs. By adjusting challenge levels based on prior responses, such systems allow learners to progress through material in ways that align with their skill level and learning pace (Murphy et al., 2022; Wang et al., 2023). These platforms can reduce frustration and boost persistence, especially for students who might otherwise disengage due to feelings of incompetence or lack of control.

Nevertheless, autonomy without adequate support can be counterproductive. Students with lower digital literacy or limited experience navigating online tools may feel overwhelmed when expected to work independently. For these learners, autonomy may translate into confusion or disengagement.

Self-Efficacy

Self-efficacy, as defined by Bandura (1994), refers to a student's belief in their capacity to succeed in specific learning tasks. This belief plays a central role in shaping academic outcomes: students with high self-efficacy are more likely to take on challenges, persist through setbacks, and regulate their learning behaviours. Digital platforms, when thoughtfully designed, can support these beliefs by facilitating mastery experiences, offering immediate feedback, and modelling successful strategies.

LMS can help cultivate self-efficacy by providing consistent feedback and making progress visible (Faulconer, Griffith & Gruss, 2022). Students can track their assignments, view teacher comments, and observe their improvements over time. These experiences reinforce their sense of competence and control over learning outcomes. Furthermore, online tools that promote formative feedback, rather than just summative assessments, give students multiple opportunities to revise and grow, reinforcing their belief in their own ability to learn (Prifti, 2022).

Digital self-efficacy, a more specific construct, refers to a learner's confidence in using digital tools effectively. As Ulfert-Blank & Schmidt (2022) note, digital self-efficacy influences not only whether students are willing to engage with technology but also how persistently they use it when confronted with obstacles. Students with high digital self-efficacy are more likely to explore new tools, seek help, and recover from failure. In contrast, those with lower confidence may avoid digital tasks altogether or give up quickly when faced with technical difficulties. In order for students to navigate these environments effectively they need to be digitally literate (Tang & Chaw 2016; Rasheed, Kamsin & Abdullah 2020).

This divide is particularly significant for students from disadvantaged backgrounds, who may lack prior exposure or access to reliable digital infrastructure. Simply providing devices or internet connections is not sufficient; students must also be supported in building the skills and confidence needed to navigate these systems effectively. Without this foundation, the potential motivational and self-efficacy benefits of digital tools remain out of reach.

Case Study: Self-Efficacy and Motivation in Blended Learning (Liwanag & Galicia, 2023)

A study of 351 senior high school students across six campuses of the University of Perpetual Help System (Philippines) examined how technological self-efficacy and learning motivation relate to self-directed learning in a blended environment. Using standardized survey instruments, the researchers found that students generally reported high levels of self-efficacy with educational technology, strong learning motivation (both intrinsic and extrinsic), and high self-directed learning capacity.

Statistical analysis revealed significant positive relationships between all three constructs. Technological self-efficacy and learning motivation together explained 67% of the variance in students' self-directed learning. Control of learning beliefs, task value, and teacher support were among the strongest predictors. The findings suggest that when students feel confident in using technology and see value in what they are learning, they are more likely to take initiative and ownership of their learning process.

Educators play a pivotal role in developing students' self-efficacy, both generally and in digital contexts. Teachers who model effective digital tool use, provide structured guidance, and create low-risk opportunities for experimentation help students build confidence gradually. Scaffolded tasks, peer collaboration, and positive reinforcement all contribute to an environment in which students feel capable and supported in their learning journeys.

Motivation and self-efficacy do not exist in isolation, they are closely linked to how students understand themselves. As learners engage with digital tools, these technologies also become spaces where identity, emotion, and social connection are shaped, often in complex and contradictory ways.

IDENTITY, SOCIAL MEDIA, AND EMOTIONAL DEVELOPMENT

Digital Identity and Adolescence

Technology plays a central role in shaping identity, particularly during adolescence, a critical period for self-discovery and psychosocial development (Avci et al., 2024). Social media platforms and algorithmically curated content increasingly influence how young people perceive themselves and others. These digital environments can function as arenas for self-expression and identity exploration, yet they also carry risks such as negative social comparisons, identity diffusion, and diminished psychological wellbeing (Castellví et al., 2020; Pötzsch, 2019).

Psychosocial theories, such as Erikson's (1968) stages of development, highlight the adolescent quest for a coherent and stable sense of self. Digital spaces can both support and disrupt this developmental task. Maslin et al. (2023) suggest online environments provide young people with new avenues for autonomy and creativity, however, they also expose them to commercial pressures, pervasive surveillance, and social norms that may constrain authentic identity formation (Livingstone & Stoilova, 2021). As young people navigate their digital worlds, they may find opportunities to express diverse aspects of themselves but also experience pressures to conform to curated and often unrealistic ideals (Livingstone 2008).

The Mental Health Debate

In recent years, growing concerns have emerged about the impact of social media and digital technologies on mental health and emotional development. Haidt (2024), in *The Anxious Generation*, draws attention to rising rates of anxiety and depression, particularly among adolescent girls, which he links to overexposure to screens, diminished real-world interaction, social comparison, and sleep disruption. His argument has resonated with a wider public anxious about the effects of screen-based culture, especially in relation to adolescent wellbeing.

However, Haidt's claims are not without criticism. Peter Gray (2024), for instance, offers an alternative lens by cautioning against overly deterministic interpretations of screen time effects. Gray emphasizes the importance of autonomy, unstructured play, and broader societal conditions in shaping youth development. He critiques narrow interpretations that blame technology alone for rising mental health issues, arguing instead that such problems are better understood in light of reduced opportunities for independence, self-directed activity, and meaningful social engagement. His work invites a more holistic understanding of mental health, one that situates digital environments within a broader developmental and societal context.

Complex Evidence and Nuanced Impacts

Recent research reviews have further complicated the narrative by showing that the evidence linking digital technology use to mental health outcomes is, at best, mixed. Valkenburg, Meier, and Beyens (2022) argue that the evidence for direct causal relationships between social media use and wellbeing is weak or inconsistent. Similarly, Dienlin and Johannes (2020) conclude that the general effects of digital technology on mental health skew slightly negative but are small in magnitude. They stress that outcomes depend largely on how technology is used: passive, habitual, or avoidant behaviours tend to correlate with negative emotional states, while active, social, and purposeful uses can be associated with more positive experiences.

Even so, this active/passive distinction has itself come under scrutiny. Valkenburg, van Driel, and Beyens (2022) suggest that this binary is too coarse to capture the complexity of digital engagement. They argue for more granular analyses that examine the type of content consumed, the social and emotional context, and individual differences in susceptibility. Such findings suggest that broad generalisations about "screen time" are unhelpful and that any discussion of mental health impacts must consider context, intent, and user agency.

Case Study: Media Use and Adolescent Identity Processing (Sebre & Miltuze, 2021)

A study of 359 adolescents aged 11–18 examined how different styles of identity development relate to digital media use and associated beliefs. Using the Identity Style Inventory and the Media Activity Form, researchers found that adolescents who adopted an informational identity processing style, characterized by active self-exploration, were less likely to spend time gaming or constantly communicating online, and more likely to endorse adaptive beliefs about media use, such as its benefits for schoolwork.

In contrast, those with a diffuse-avoidant style, marked by procrastination and uncertainty, spent significantly more time gaming and were more likely to feel preoccupied with being online. Adolescents with a normative style, focused on conformity and external expectations, used media less for schoolwork or communication.

The findings suggest that adolescents' patterns of digital engagement are closely linked to how they approach questions of identity, autonomy, and purpose. For educators and counsellors, this highlights the need to support media literacy and self-reflection as part of students' psychological development, not just their academic progress.

Education, Fatigue, and the Always-On Culture

As digital tools become more embedded in educational settings, the concern is no longer limited to personal or recreational use. Extending beyond the Covid-19, students are increasingly expected to engage with school through digital devices and online platforms (Yates et al., 2020; Parveen & Ramzan, 2024). This "always-on" culture can lead to stress, burnout, and a sense of social isolation, particularly among younger students still developing emotional regulation and self-discipline (Braghieri et al., 2022).

Moreover, prolonged digital engagement can blur the boundaries between academic and personal life. Research has identified forms of digital and "Zoom" fatigue that diminish focus, reduce motivation, and compromise wellbeing (Deniz et al., 2022; Gregerson et al., 2023; Romero-Rodríguez et al., 2023). These effects can be exacerbated by the lack of clear routines and the emotional labour required to manage constant online interactions.

Building Digital Resilience and Wellbeing

This convergence of identity formation, mental health, and digital engagement raises urgent questions for educators and policymakers. As students navigate increasingly immersive online worlds, schools and parents must take a proactive role in helping them build digital self-efficacy, the ability to critically reflect on their digital lives, manage online risks, and develop emotional resilience (Soyoof et al., 2024). This involves moving beyond simplistic notions of screen time and instead promoting intentional and balanced digital use.

Integrating digital wellbeing into personal and social education curricula is one concrete step. Such initiatives can help students explore how their digital habits intersect with their emotional health and sense of self (Feerrar, 2022). At the same time, schools should adopt policies that support balanced technology use: structured screen breaks, limited non-essential device usage, and encouragement of offline activities and face-to-face socialisation.

Educators also have an important role in modelling healthy digital behaviours. By creating space for reflective conversations about online life, what causes joy, stress, connection, or anxiety, teachers can foster emotional literacy and critical awareness (Sun et al., 2022). This supports not only mental health but also a more grounded and authentic sense of identity in digital contexts.

Identity and emotional wellbeing in digital spaces are deeply influenced by students' access to technology, support, and digital literacy. For many, the ability to explore and express themselves online is shaped, and often constrained, by broader inequalities in infrastructure, guidance, and opportunity.

EQUITY, ACCESS, AND THE DIGITAL DIVIDE

The digital divide refers to the gap between individuals who have access to digital technologies and those who do not, but in education, this concept has evolved beyond infrastructure alone. Today, the divide includes disparities in digital literacy, student support systems, and the learning conditions that shape how technology is used. Access is only the first step; equally important is whether students can use technology effectively, confidently, and in ways that support their learning. These differences carry significant implications for students' engagement, motivation, and sense of academic capability (Hill & Reimer, 2022; UNESCO, 2023).

Students from wealthier households or urban areas often enjoy consistent access to high-speed internet, personal devices, and digitally literate support systems. In contrast, students from low-income or rural communities frequently face not only technological but also instructional and emotional barriers. During the COVID-19 pandemic, these gaps became particularly clear, as millions of students without reliable infrastructure or digital fluency struggled to participate fully in remote learning (Mohan et al., 2020). These challenges often undermined students' academic confidence and sense of belonging, setting back progress toward educational equity.

Digital Literacy and Student Confidence

The divide is no longer just about having access to devices. A more pressing issue is whether students can use technology in ways that help them succeed. Digital literacy now includes critical thinking, responsible use, and the ability to manage time and attention in online environments (Audrin & Audrin, 2022). Students who lack these skills may quickly feel overwhelmed, leading to reduced motivation and lower academic self-efficacy, the belief in their own ability to succeed in digital learning tasks (Getenet et al., 2024).

Self-directed use of technology requires a degree of independence and discipline that many students are still developing. This is especially true when digital learning takes place outside structured classroom settings. When students lack support or modelling from teachers or caregivers, they may struggle to stay organized, persist through challenges, or use digital tools for more than just passive consumption. Without these supports, students can become disengaged and discouraged.

The Role of Families and Home Support

Support at home plays a vital role in shaping how students experience technology. Research by Helsper, Veltri & Livingstone (2024) emphasizes the importance of parental mediation, the ways families discuss, guide, and model digital behaviour.

This can influence how children use digital tools, how safe they feel online, and how likely they are to approach technology with confidence rather than fear (Livingstone et al., 2017).

However, many parents, particularly in lower-income or less digitally connected households, may not feel equipped to provide this guidance. When caregivers lack digital literacy themselves, they may be unable to help with technical problems or model effective online learning behaviours. This can deepen existing gaps and leave students feeling isolated or unsupported.

Schools can help by offering digital literacy workshops for families and encouraging stronger home-school communication about technology use. Equipping parents and caregivers with even basic tools and understanding can strengthen the learning environment well beyond the classroom.

Infrastructure, Curriculum, and Global Disparities

Access to reliable internet and up-to-date devices remains a major issue, especially in low-income countries, rural areas, and marginalized communities (Lythreatis, Singh & El-Kassar, 2022). Without investment in infrastructure, students in these regions face structural disadvantages that limit their ability to participate fully in modern education.

But even where devices and connectivity are widespread, students often lack opportunities to build meaningful digital skills. A UNESCO (2023) report found that in many countries, including those with strong infrastructure, students still make limited educational use of digital tools. This suggests a need not only for access, but also for intentional curriculum design that helps students develop confidence and competence in digital learning.

Digital literacy should be treated as a foundational skill, taught explicitly and systematically across year levels and subjects. When systems fail to do this, students may rely on trial-and-error learning or carry over poor digital habits, such as skimming, multitasking, or over-reliance on search engines, which can limit their deeper learning and critical engagement.

Case Study: Children's Experiences of the Digital Divide (Law et al., 2023)

A child-centred study across Brazil, Kenya, Pakistan, South Africa, and Turkey explored how the digital divide affected children's education during the COVID-

19 pandemic. Using diaries, drawings, and focus groups, researchers gathered insights from 73 children and 76 parents and professionals.

Findings highlighted that many children lacked access to reliable technology or internet, limiting their ability to engage with remote learning. Children reported frustration and a sense of exclusion when unable to participate fully. Parents struggled to support their children's learning due to limited digital skills and resources. Professionals noted the digital divide exacerbated existing inequalities and called for structural changes, such as device access, improved infrastructure and digital literacy support to ensure inclusive and equitable education.

Supporting Teachers to Lead the Way

Teachers play a key role in how technology is introduced and used in classrooms. When educators have the training and confidence to use digital tools well, they are more likely to create engaging, inclusive learning experiences. Without adequate support, however, technology can become a source of frustration, both for teachers and their students leading to degree of technostress (Akram et al., 2022; Özgür, 2020).

Professional development should help teachers understand not only how to use tools, but how to integrate them in ways that support attention, motivation, and critical thinking. Teachers need time and resources to explore best practices, reflect on what works in their context, and adapt as technologies evolve. This is especially important in under-resourced schools, where teachers may face more challenges in adopting new tools.

Creating Inclusive and Supportive Digital Learning Environments

Equity in digital education means more than providing a device or internet connection. It means ensuring that all students, regardless of income, location, language, or ability, can participate meaningfully in digital learning. This includes designing accessible platforms, offering multilingual support, and creating lessons that are culturally responsive and adaptable to different learning needs (McNicholl et al., 2021).

It also means fostering a sense of safety, confidence, and curiosity. Students need environments where it's okay to make mistakes, where questions are welcomed, and where they feel encouraged to explore and grow. These elements, so fundamental to good teaching, are just as essential in digital settings as they are in physical classrooms.

As digital tools continue to impact on education, addressing the divide is not just about keeping up with technology. It's about creating learning environments that empower all students to thrive, technically, academically, and personally.

ETHICS, CITIZENSHIP, AND RESPONSIBLE TECHNOLOGY USE

As digital technologies become increasingly embedded in educational practice, the ethical dimensions of this shift demand serious and sustained attention. While these tools offer opportunities for personalised learning, streamlined assessment, and improved access, they also raise critical concerns around privacy, surveillance, autonomy, and mental health. Moreover, ethical use is not simply a matter of how technology is implemented pedagogically, but how it is situated within broader social, economic, and environmental contexts (Fawns, 2022). Teachers, schools, and policymakers must engage critically with these issues to ensure that digital education supports, rather than undermines, the psychological wellbeing and holistic development of learners.

Privacy, Surveillance, and Psychological Safety

Among the most pressing ethical concerns is the collection and use of student data. Educational platforms routinely gather vast quantities of information about learners, including academic performance, behavioural patterns, and social interactions, often with limited transparency or oversight (Pangrazio & Selwyn, 2021; Lupton & Williamson, 2017). While such data can enhance teaching and support interventions, it can also generate a sense of constant surveillance that impacts how students behave, feel, and engage in digital environments.

From a psychological perspective, this raises concerns about psychological safety, the feeling that one can learn, ask questions, and make mistakes without fear of being judged, penalised, or monitored inappropriately. When students are aware that their actions are being tracked and evaluated by opaque systems, it can lead to stress, self-censorship, and reduced trust in the learning environment. Teachers must therefore advocate for transparent data practices, select tools with robust security measures, and engage students in conversations about digital privacy and agency. Legal frameworks like GDPR provide important safeguards, but ethical use goes beyond compliance, it must actively prioritise the rights and dignity of learners.

Datafication, Platformisation, and Algorithmic Judgement

The increasing platformisation and commercialisation of education introduces additional ethical complexities. As educational activities become more reliant on large-scale digital platforms, the line between public good and corporate interest becomes blurred (Pangrazio, Selwyn & Cumbo, 2023; Kerssens & van Dijk, 2023). These platforms not only mediate learning but shape it, through algorithmic recommendations, behavioural nudges, and data-driven feedback systems. While such features can personalise learning experiences, they also risk reducing education to quantifiable metrics, neglecting dimensions like creativity, collaboration, and critical thinking.

From a psychological standpoint, environments that prioritize data-driven performance can undermine learning in subtle but significant ways. Excessive emphasis on measurable outcomes may shift students' focus away from intrinsic goals, reducing deep engagement and creativity (Deci & Ryan, 2013; Pangrazio & Selwyn, 2021). These systems can also contribute to heightened self-monitoring and anxiety, particularly when students feel constantly evaluated or compared through algorithmic profiling (Lupton & Williamson, 2017; Pangrazio, Selwyn & Cumbo, 2023). Such dynamics can affect motivation, emotional safety, and identity development, core components of psychological wellbeing in education (Erikson, 1968; Bandura, 1994; Avci et al., 2024). Rather than reducing students to data points, educators should aim to use learning analytics as tools for support and reflection, while maintaining a commitment to holistic, relational, and developmentally informed teaching practices.

Digital Citizenship and Critical Digital Literacy

In response to these concerns, the concept of digital citizenship offers a constructive framework. Developing digital citizenship involves more than teaching students how to use technology, it's about equipping them with the critical skills and ethical awareness to navigate digital spaces responsibly and reflectively (Öztürk, 2021). This includes understanding privacy settings, recognising algorithmic bias, interrogating digital footprints, and fostering respectful online communication. As Castellví et al. (2020) and Pötzsch (2019) argue, critical digital literacy must be central to this work, enabling learners to question not just how technology functions, but whose interests it serves and what values it embeds.

Importantly, digital citizenship should be based on individuals' ability to think and act independently, rather than on reliance or dependence on digital systems or others. Students need opportunities to make informed choices about when, how, and why they engage with digital tools or environments. Teachers play a crucial role here, modelling ethical technology use and creating classroom environments where students feel safe to explore, critique, and challenge the digital systems that shape their educational experiences.

Environmental Ethics and Sustainable Technology Use

Finally, ethical engagement with educational technology must also account for its environmental footprint. The production of digital devices relies on extractive processes and global supply chains that raise serious ecological and human rights concerns (McGarr, 2023). The operation of educational platforms, particularly data centres, consumes vast amounts of energy, contributing to carbon emissions and climate change.

Educators can promote sustainability by choosing durable devices, advocating for green procurement policies, and encouraging students to consider the environmental impacts of their digital habits. Ethical technology use thus extends beyond the immediate classroom to encompass planetary responsibility, reinforcing the importance of embedding ecological awareness into digital citizenship education.

Ethical concerns about data, agency, and environmental impact point to a deeper question: what kind of future are we building through educational technology? As new tools like AI and immersive platforms emerge, the challenge is not just adoption, but intentional design that aligns with human values and developmental needs.

THE FUTURE OF EDUCATIONAL TECHNOLOGY: AUGMENTATION, NOT REPLACEMENT

The next frontier in education will be shaped by artificial intelligence tutors and immersive technologies such as virtual and augmented reality (Al-Ansi et al., 2023; Holmes & Miao, 2023). These innovations are not just new tools, they represent a reimagining of how students engage with knowledge, how teachers scaffold learning, and how schools operate. The promise is considerable: real-time personalisation, scalable feedback, and richer, more interactive learning experiences. Yet the rapid pace of technological development also surfaces deep pedagogical and psychological questions. How can we leverage these technologies to support learning without undermining the human elements that make education meaningful?

AI Tutoring Systems and Generative Technologies

Among the most transformative developments are intelligent tutoring systems (ITS) and generative AI models. These systems offer personalised instruction, real-time feedback, and adaptive pathways for learners based on ongoing assessment of their strengths and struggles. Platforms like ChatGPT already serve as informal tutors for many students, helping with writing, problem-solving, and conceptual explanation.

These technologies promise to democratise access to personalised support, allowing learners to work at their own pace and receive immediate guidance. For instance, an ITS could recognise when a student is stuck on a concept in algebra and dynamically provide scaffolded activities or alternative explanations until understanding is achieved. Such systems could, in theory, replicate the one-on-one support of expert teachers at scale.

But as Lodge et al. (2023) and Hamilton, Wiliam, and Hattie (2023) caution, the rise of generative AI also raises foundational questions about what constitutes meaningful learning. If students are routinely using AI to produce essays, solve equations, or simulate lab work, what intellectual and creative processes are at risk of being bypassed?

Psychologically, these developments touch on the concept of desirable difficulties, learning experiences that are effortful but lead to deeper understanding and long-term retention (de Bruin et al., 2023; Nihalani & Robinson, 2022). Generative AI, while efficient, it may bypass the cognitive struggle that builds metacognition, transferable knowledge, and resilience. When students are offered instant solutions, they may lose opportunities for sustained problem-solving and reflection, which are central to durable learning.

Co-Intelligence and the Ethics of Offloading

To navigate the opportunities and risks of AI in education, some scholars advocate a paradigm of co-intelligence, a collaborative approach in which learners partner with AI tools to extend, rather than replace, their cognitive capabilities. As Mollick and Mollick (2023) argue, the most productive use of AI in learning environments involves treating it not as an oracle that delivers answers, but as a thinking partner that supports exploration and iteration. In this model, students might brainstorm with AI, simulate different perspectives, test hypotheses, or co-develop drafts, all while retaining human judgement and agency.

Co-intelligence reframes learning as an interactive, iterative process rather than a transactional one. It invites students to actively engage with AI systems while maintaining ownership of the learning journey. However, this approach depends on intentional pedagogy. Educators must design activities that go beyond surface-level use of AI, requiring students to evaluate, synthesise, and reflect on the information AI provides. Without this scaffolding, there is a real risk that students will offload too much cognitive effort, bypassing essential skills like critical thinking, problem-solving, and creativity.

This raises important questions about what learners should be expected to do independently, and what can be done in collaboration with AI (Lodge et al., 2023). Miao and Holmes (2021) emphasise the importance of AI literacy, which includes not only technical fluency, but also ethical reasoning, epistemic awareness, and an understanding of bias and limitations in algorithmic systems. Students must learn not just how to use AI, but when, why, and whether to do so.

Educators will need to help students strike a careful balance between productive offloading and the development of core competencies. While AI can support certain forms of analysis or generation, over-reliance risks turning learners into passive recipients of questionable machine output rather than active constructors of meaning. Future curricula must therefore cultivate both collaboration with AI and the critical distance needed to assess its role.

These shifts also necessitate a rethinking of assessment. If generative AI can produce fluent and persuasive responses, traditional tasks may no longer reflect authentic student learning. Performance must be measured not only by outcomes, but by the depth of student reasoning, the ability to explain choices, and the capacity to iterate and improve over time. In a co-intelligent classroom, how a student arrives at an idea may be as important as the idea itself.

Immersive Technologies and the Psychology of Presence

Beyond AI, virtual and augmented reality technologies are rapidly expanding the possibilities of how students engage with content (Al-Ansi et al., 2023). These tools can allow learners for example to inhabit detailed environments, explore ecosystems, conduct virtual chemistry experiments, or step into historical moments. The result can be increased engagement and deeper conceptual understanding, particularly for abstract or spatially complex subjects (Villena-Taranilla et al., 2022), though findings are mixed and can be mediated by education level (Yu & Xu, 2022).

Psychological research supports the potential of embodied cognition in these contexts (Mejia-Puig; 2023; Mansour et al., 2024). Yet immersive technologies are not without risks. Excessive use can lead to screen fatigue, motion sickness, emotional overstimulation or extraneous cognitive load (Parong & Meyer, 2020). Young learners may have difficulty regulating their responses to high-intensity environments, and poorly designed simulations may lead to misconceptions rather than clarity. Moreover, the novelty effect, initial engagement driven by excitement rather than learning value, may mask deeper pedagogical shortcomings (Jiang & Fryer, 2024). However there is some evidence to suggest this is only the case in the short-term (Lee, Chen & Basu, 2025).

Holmes (2023) warns that without clear instructional goals, immersive tools may become distractions. As with AI, their successful integration depends on thoughtful design, clear learning outcomes, and ongoing evaluation. Teachers also require training and support to use these tools effectively, not as digital gimmicks, but as meaningful learning instruments.

Technology With Intention

The future of educational technology isn't just about whether we use it, but how we use it well. The tools are already here, the challenge is in applying them with purpose, wisdom, and care. While AI, VR, and AR offer powerful affordances for personalisation, engagement, and access, they also carry risks of over-reliance, cognitive passivity, and reduced human interaction.

The key insight, echoed across the literature, is that technology should augment, not replace the essential human dimensions of education, effort, curiosity, creativity, empathy, and social connection. If deployed intentionally, these tools can elevate learning. But if used indiscriminately, they may erode the very qualities that education exists to develop.

The most powerful classrooms of the future will be defined not by the sophistication of their tools, but by their commitment to a pedagogy of collaborative, reflective, and ethical learning, where students learn not only with technology, but through it, about themselves and the world around them.

CONCLUSION

The digital transformation of education holds enormous promise, but also profound risk. As we integrate increasingly sophisticated technologies into classrooms, learning environments, and assessment systems, we are reshaping not just how students learn, but what it means to learn in the first place. This moment demands critical reflection. Are our digital tools truly enhancing educational experiences, or are they fragmenting attention, narrowing engagement, and displacing the human relationships that make learning meaningful?

This chapter has argued that psychological science must play a central role in answering these questions. Insights from cognitive, developmental, and educational psychology offer powerful tools to understand how digital technologies affect attention, motivation, identity formation, and wellbeing. By drawing on this evidence, educators and policymakers can make more informed, ethically grounded choices about when and how to use technology, and, just as importantly, when not to.

Innovation must not come at the expense of equity, inclusion, or psychological health. While digital platforms can expand access and personalize learning, they also risk reinforcing social divides, amplifying distractions, and encouraging over-reliance on automated systems that undermine critical thinking and independent problem-solving. Technology should support learners' autonomy, curiosity, and agency, not diminish them. Achieving this requires more than access to devices; it demands digital literacy, ethical awareness, and the cultivation of reflective, discerning users.

The role of educators remains central in this evolving landscape. Teachers are not just facilitators of content but mediators of meaning, connection, and care. Their professional judgment, creativity and emotional attunement are irreplaceable. Meaningful integration of technology requires investment in teacher training and support systems that empower educators to navigate the digital terrain with confidence and sensitivity. We must resist narratives that position technology as a neutral or superior replacement for human expertise. Instead, we should embrace tools that augment human potential while keeping pedagogical and relational integrity at the core.

Reclaiming a human-centred approach means reasserting education's fundamental purpose: to nurture capable, connected, and critically aware human beings. It means embracing innovation without losing sight of the essential ingredients of learning, curiosity, collaboration, and compassion. It means grounding our decisions not in the novelty of tools, but in the enduring needs of learners and teachers alike.

As we chart the path forward, we must commit to thoughtful, inclusive, and evidence-informed digital integration. Technology must remain the servant, never the master, of educational aims. As UNESCO (2023) so aptly reminds us:

> *It is essential to learn to live both with and without digital technology; to take what is needed from an abundance of information but ignore what is not necessary; to let technology support, but never supplant, the human connection on which teaching and learning are based. (p. 24)*

DISCUSSION QUESTIONS

1. How can educators balance the use of technology with the need to foster critical thinking, creativity, and independent problem-solving in students, considering the psychological impact of digital engagement on cognitive development?
2. What steps can schools and governments take to address the growing digital divide, both in terms of access to technology and the skills needed to use it effectively, while considering the psychological effects of unequal access on student self-esteem and academic self-efficacy?
3. What ethical considerations should be prioritized when integrating AI and data-driven platforms into education, particularly concerning student privacy, data security, and inclusivity, from a psychological perspective on student trust and well-being?

4. In what ways can educators be better supported in developing their own digital literacy and competence, ensuring that they can effectively integrate technology into their teaching practices?
5. How should the education system adapt its assessment methods in response to the increasing influence of generative AI, virtual reality, and other advanced technologies, particularly in light of the psychological need for students to feel ownership and authenticity in their work?

REFERENCES

Akram, H., Abdelrady, A. H., Al-Adwan, A. S., & Ramzan, M. (2022). Teachers' perceptions of technology integration in teaching-learning practices: A systematic review. *Frontiers in Psychology*, *13*, 920317.

Al-Ansi, A. M., Jaboob, M., Garad, A., & Al-Ansi, A. (2023). Analyzing augmented reality (AR) and virtual reality (VR) recent development in education. *Social Sciences & Humanities Open*, *8*(1), 100532.

Ashour, S. (2020). How technology has shaped university students' perceptions and expectations around higher education: An exploratory study of the United Arab Emirates. *Studies in Higher Education*, *45*(12), 2513–2525.

Audrin, C., & Audrin, B. (2022). Key factors in digital literacy in learning and education: A systematic literature review using text mining. *Education and Information Technologies*, *27*(6), 7395–7419.

Avci, H., Baams, L., & Kretschmer, T. (2024). A systematic review of social media use and adolescent identity development. *Adolescent Research Review*, 1–18.

Bandura, A. (1994). Self-efficacy. Encyclopedia of human behavior, 4(4), 71-81.

Bastani, H., Bastani, O., Sungu, A., Ge, H., Kabakcı, O., & Mariman, R. 2024. Generative ai can harm learning. Available at *SSRN*, 4895486.

Bond, M., Buntins, K., Bedenlier, S., Zawacki-Richter, O., & Kerres, M. (2020). Mapping research in student engagement and educational technology in higher education: A systematic evidence map. *International Journal of Educational Technology in Higher Education*, *17*, 1–30.

Braghieri, L., Levy, R. E., & Makarin, A. (2022). Social media and mental health. *The American Economic Review*, *112*(11), 3660–3693.

Calderón, A., Merono, L., & MacPhail, A. (2020). A student-centred digital technology approach: The relationship between intrinsic motivation, learning climate and academic achievement of physical education pre-service teachers. *European Physical Education Review*, *26*(1), 241–262.

Castellví, J., Díez-Bedmar, M. C., & Santisteban, A. (2020). Pre-service teachers' critical digital literacy skills and attitudes to address social problems. *Social Sciences*, *9*(8), 134.

Cladis, A. E. (2020). A shifting paradigm: An evaluation of the pervasive effects of digital technologies on language expression, creativity, critical thinking, political discourse, and interactive processes of human communications. *E-Learning and Digital Media, 17*(5), 341–364.

Cristia, J., Ibarrarán, P., Cueto, S., Santiago, A., & Severín, E. (2017). Technology and child development: Evidence from the one laptop per child program. *American Economic Journal. Applied Economics, 9*(3), 295–320.

de Bruin, A. B., Biwer, F., Hui, L., Onan, E., David, L., & Wiradhany, W. (2023). Worth the effort: The start and stick to desirable difficulties (S2D2) framework. *Educational Psychology Review, 35*(2), 41.

Deci, E. L., & Ryan, R. M. (2013). *Intrinsic motivation and self-determination in human behavior*. Springer Science & Business Media.

Deniz, M. E., Satici, S. A., Doenyas, C., & Griffiths, M. D. (2022). Zoom fatigue, psychological distress, life satisfaction, and academic well-being. *Cyberpsychology, Behavior, and Social Networking, 25*(5), 270–277.

Dienlin, T., & Johannes, N. (2020). The impact of digital technology use on adolescent well-being. *Dialogues in Clinical Neuroscience, 22*(2), 135–142.

ElSayary, A. (2024). Integrating generative AI in active learning environments: Enhancing metacognition and technological skills. *Journal of Systemics, Cybernetics and Informatics, 22*(3), 34–37.

Erikson, E. H. (1968). *Identity: Youth and crisis*. W. W. Norton & Company.

Fan, Y., Tang, L., Le, H., Shen, K., Tan, S., Zhao, Y., & Gašević, D. (2025). Beware of metacognitive laziness: Effects of generative artificial intelligence on learning motivation, processes, and performance. *British Journal of Educational Technology, 56*(2), 489–530.

Faulconer, E., Griffith, J., & Gruss, A. (2022). The impact of positive feedback on student outcomes and perceptions. *Assessment & Evaluation in Higher Education, 47*(2), 259–268.

Fawns, T. (2022). An entangled pedagogy: Looking beyond the pedagogy—technology dichotomy. *Postdigital Science and Education, 4*(3), 711–728.

Feerrar, J. (2022). Bringing digital well-being into the heart of digital media literacies. *The Journal of Media Literacy Education, 14*(2), 72–77.

Furqon, M., Sinaga, P., Liliasari, L., & Riza, L. S. (2023). The Impact of Learning Management System (LMS) Usage on Students. TEM Journal, 12(2).

Gaonkar, S., Khan, D., & Manisha, A. S. (2022). Impact of Gamification on Learning and Development. *Journal of Advances in Education and Philosophy*, *6*(2), 63–70.

Gazzaley, A., & Rosen, L. D. (2016). *The distracted mind: Ancient brains in a high-tech world*. Mit Press.

Getenet, S., Cantle, R., Redmond, P., & Albion, P. (2024). Students' digital technology attitude, literacy and self-efficacy and their effect on online learning engagement. *International Journal of Educational Technology in Higher Education*, *21*(1), 3.

Gray, P. (2024, June 30). The importance of critical analyses in examining social science evidence (#45). Play Makes Us Human. Substack. https://petergray.substack.com/p/45-the-importance-of-critical-analyses

Gregersen, E. M., Astrupgaard, S. L., Jespersen, M. H., Gårdhus, T. P., & Albris, K. (2023). Digital dependence: Online fatigue and coping strategies during the COVID-19 lockdown. *Media Culture & Society*, *45*(5), 967–984.

Haidt, J. (2024). *The anxious generation: How the great rewiring of childhood is causing an epidemic of mental illness*. Penguin Press.

Hamilton, A., Wiliam, D., & Hattie, J. (2023). The Future of AI in Education: 13 things we can do to minimize the damage. Academic Press.

Helsper, E. J., Veltri, G. A., & Livingstone, S. (2024). Parental mediation of children's online risks: The role of parental risk perception, digital skills and risk experiences. New Media & Society.

Henderson, M., Selwyn, N., Finger, G., & Aston, R. (2015). Students' everyday engagement with digital technology in university: Exploring patterns of use and 'usefulness'. *Journal of Higher Education Policy and Management*, *37*(3), 308–319.

Hill, J., & Reimer, T. (2022). Crossing the digital divide and the equity expanse: Reaching and teaching all students during the pandemic. Journal of Leadership, Equity, and Research.

Holmes, W. (2023). The unintended consequences of artificial intelligence and education. Academic Press.

Holmes, W., & Miao, F. (2023). *Guidance for generative AI in education and research*. UNESCO Publishing.

Jin, K. Y., Reichert, F., Cagasan, L. P.Jr, de La Torre, J., & Law, N. (2020). Measuring digital literacy across three age cohorts: Exploring test dimensionality and performance differences. *Computers & Education*, *157*, 103968.

Kerssens, N., & van Dijck, J. (2023). How platformisation affects pedagogical autonomy in primary schools. In *World Yearbook of Education 2024* (pp. 89–105). Routledge.

Korte, M. (2020). The impact of the digital revolution on human brain and behavior: Where do we stand? *Dialogues in Clinical Neuroscience*, *22*(2), 101–111.

Latorre-Cosculluela, C., Suárez, C., Quiroga, S., Sobradiel-Sierra, N., Lozano-Blasco, R., & Rodríguez-Martínez, A. (2021). Flipped Classroom model before and during COVID-19: Using technology to develop 21st century skills. *Interactive Technology and Smart Education*, *18*(2), 189–204.

Law, E. L. C., Vostanis, P., & O'Reilly, M. J. (2023). Insights from impacts of the digital divide on children in five majority world countries during the COVID-19 pandemic. *Behaviour & Information Technology*, *42*(15), 2696–2715.

Lawlor, J., Marshall, K., & Tangney, B. (2016). Bridge21–exploring the potential to foster intrinsic student motivation through a team-based, technology-mediated learning model. *Technology, Pedagogy and Education*, *25*(2), 187–206.

Lee, J., Chen, C., & Basu, A. (2025). From Novelty to Knowledge: A Longitudinal Investigation of the Novelty Effect on Learning Outcomes in Virtual Reality. *IEEE Transactions on Visualization and Computer Graphics*.

Liu, T. C. (2022). A case study of the adaptive learning platform in a Taiwanese elementary school: Precision education from teachers' perspectives. *Education and Information Technologies*, *27*(5), 6295–6316.

Livingstone, S. (2008). Taking risky opportunities in youthful content creation: Teenagers' use of social networking sites for intimacy, privacy and self-expression. *New Media & Society*, *10*(3), 393–411.

Livingstone, S., Ólafsson, K., Helsper, E. J., Lupiáñez-Villanueva, F., Veltri, G. A., & Folkvord, F. (2017). Maximizing opportunities and minimizing risks for children online: The role of digital skills in emerging strategies of parental mediation. *Journal of Communication*, *67*(1), 82–105.

Livingstone, S., & Stoilova, M. (2021). The 4Cs: Classifying online risk to children. Academic Press.

Liwanag, M. F., & Galicia, L. S. (2023). Technological self-efficacy, learning motivation, and self-directed learning of selected senior high school students in a blended learning environment. *Technium Soc. Sci. J.*, *44*, 534.

Lodge, J. M., Yang, S., Furze, L., & Dawson, P. (2023). It's not like a calculator, so what is the relationship between learners and generative artificial intelligence? Learning. *Research and Practice*, *9*(2), 117–124.

Lupton, D., & Williamson, B. (2017). The datafied child: The dataveillance of children and implications for their rights. *New Media & Society*, *19*(5), 780–794.

Lythreatis, S., Singh, S. K., & El-Kassar, A. N. (2022). The digital divide: A review and future research agenda. *Technological Forecasting and Social Change*, *175*, 121359.

Major, L., Francis, G. A., & Tsapali, M. (2021). The effectiveness of technology-supported personalised learning in low-and middle-income countries: A meta-analysis. *British Journal of Educational Technology*, *52*(5), 1935–1964.

Mansour, N., Aras, C., Staarman, J. K., & Alotaibi, S. B. M. (2024). Embodied learning of science concepts through augmented reality technology. *Education and Information Technologies*, 1–31.

Maslin, K., Murcia, K., Blackley, S., & Lowe, G. (2023). Fostering young children's creativity in online learning environments: A systematic literature review. *Thinking Skills and Creativity*, *47*, 101249.

McGarr, O. (2023). Investigating student teachers' responses to including sustainable development as part of their professional digital competence development. *Technology, Pedagogy and Education*, *32*(5), 653–665.

McGarr, O. (2024). Teacher educators' views and responses to digital distraction in pre-service teacher education. *Teaching and Teacher Education*, *148*, 104701.

McGarr, O., & McDonagh, A. (2021). Exploring the digital competence of pre-service teachers on entry onto an initial teacher education programme in Ireland. *Irish Educational Studies*, *40*(1), 115–128.

McNicholl, A., Casey, H., Desmond, D., & Gallagher, P. (2021). The impact of assistive technology use for students with disabilities in higher education: A systematic review. *Disability and Rehabilitation. Assistive Technology*, *16*(2), 130–143.

Mejia-Puig, L., & Chandrasekera, T. (2023). The virtual body in a design exercise: A conceptual framework for embodied cognition. *International Journal of Technology and Design Education*, *33*(5), 1861–1882.

Miao, F., & Holmes, W. (2021). International Forum on AI and the Futures of Education, developing competencies for the AI Era, 7-8 December 2020: synthesis report.

Mohan, G., McCoy, S., Carroll, E., Mihut, G., Lyons, S., & Mac Domhnaill, C. (2020). Learning for all? Second-level education in Ireland during COVID-19. ESRI Survey and Statistical Report Series 92 June 2020.

Mollick, E., & Mollick, E. (2024). *Co-Intelligence*. Random House UK.

Moreira, F. P., & Lima, D. A. (2024). Systematic literature review on the impact of Blended Learning in promoting student engagement and autonomy: Findings and recommendations. *Revista Brasileira de Informática na Educação*, *32*, 242–269.

Murphy, R., Roschelle, J., Feng, M., & Mason, C. A. (2020). Investigating efficacy, moderators and mediators for an online mathematics homework intervention. *Journal of Research on Educational Effectiveness*, *13*(2), 235–270.

Nihalani, P. K., & Robinson, D. H. (2022). Balancing collaboration and cognitive load to optimize individual and group desirable difficulties. *Journal of Educational Computing Research*, *60*(2), 433–454.

Outhwaite, L., Early, E., Herodotou, C., & Van Herwegen, J. (2022). Can Maths apps add value to young children's learning? A systematic review and content analysis. Academic Press.

Özgür, H. (2020). Relationships between teachers' technostress, technological pedagogical content knowledge (TPACK), school support and demographic variables: A structural equation modeling. *Computers in Human Behavior*, *112*, 106468.

Öztürk, G. (2021). Digital citizenship and its teaching: A literature review. *Journal of Educational Technology and Online Learning*, *4*(1), 31–45.

Pangrazio, L., & Selwyn, N. (2021). Towards a school-based 'critical data education'. *Pedagogy, Culture & Society*, *29*(3), 431–448.

Pangrazio, L., Selwyn, N., & Cumbo, B. (2023). Tracking technology: Exploring student experiences of school datafication. *Cambridge Journal of Education*, *53*(6), 847–862.

Parong, J., & Mayer, R. E. (2021). Cognitive and affective processes for learning science in immersive virtual reality. *Journal of Computer Assisted Learning*, *37*(1), 226–241.

Parveen, D. S., & Ramzan, S. I. (2024). The role of digital technologies in education: Benefits and challenges. *Int. Res. J. Adv. Eng. Manag*, *2*(06), 2029–2037.

Pötzsch, H. (2019). Critical digital literacy: Technology in education beyond issues of user competence and labour-market qualifications. TripleC: Communication, Capitalism & Critique. *Open Access Journal for a Global Sustainable Information Society*, *17*(2), 221–240.

Prifti, R. (2022). Self–efficacy and student satisfaction in the context of blended learning courses. *Open Learning*, *37*(2), 111–125.

Rasheed, R. A., Kamsin, A., & Abdullah, N. A. (2020). Challenges in the online component of blended learning: A systematic review. *Computers & Education*, *144*, 103701.

Romero-Rodríguez, J. M., Hinojo-Lucena, F. J., Kopecký, K., & García-González, A. (2023). Digital fatigue in university students as a consequence of online learning during the Covid-19 pandemic. *Educación XX1*, *26*(2), 141-164.

Rosen, L. D., Carrier, L. M., & Cheever, N. A. (2013). Facebook and texting made me do it: Media-induced task-switching while studying. *Computers in Human Behavior*, *29*(3), 948–958.

Sebre, S. B., & Miltuze, A. (2021). Digital media as a medium for adolescent identity development. Technology. *Knowledge and Learning*, *26*(4), 867–881.

Selwyn, N. (2021). *Education and technology: Key issues and debates*. Bloomsbury Publishing.

Skulmowski, A., & Xu, K. M. (2022). Understanding cognitive load in digital and online learning: A new perspective on extraneous cognitive load. *Educational Psychology Review*, *34*(1), 171–196.

Song, Y., Weisberg, L. R., Zhang, S., Tian, X., Boyer, K. E., & Israel, M. (2024). A framework for inclusive AI learning design for diverse learners. Computers and Education: Artificial Intelligence, 100212.

Soyoof, A., Reynolds, B. L., Neumann, M., Scull, J., Tour, E., & McLay, K. (2024). The impact of parent mediation on young children's home digital literacy practices and learning: A narrative review. *Journal of Computer Assisted Learning*, *40*(1), 65–88.

Sun, H., Yuan, C., Qian, Q., He, S., & Luo, Q. (2022). Digital resilience among individuals in school education settings: A concept analysis based on a scoping review. *Frontiers in Psychiatry*, *13*, 858515.

Sweller, J. (1994). Cognitive load theory, learning difficulty, and instructional design. *Learning and Instruction*, *4*(4), 295–312.

Taggart, S., & Roulston, S. (2024). Educational technologies in schools in Northern Ireland: Teachers' digital competences in the Goldilocks zone. *Journal of Digital Learning in Teacher Education*, 1–19. DOI: 10.1080/21532974.2024.2393575

Tang, C. M., & Chaw, L. Y. (2016). Digital Literacy: A Prerequisite for Effective Learning in a Blended Learning Environment? *Electronic Journal of e-Learning*, *14*(1), 54–65.

Timotheou, S., Miliou, O., Dimitriadis, Y., Sobrino, S. V., Giannoutsou, N., Cachia, R., & Ioannou, A. (2023). Impacts of digital technologies on education and factors influencing schools' digital capacity and transformation: A literature review. *Education and Information Technologies*, *28*(6), 6695–6726.

Turnbull, D., Chugh, R., & Luck, J. (2020). Learning management systems, an overview. Encyclopedia of education and information technologies, 1052-1058.

Ulfert-Blank, A. S., & Schmidt, I. (2022). Assessing digital self-efficacy: Review and scale development. *Computers & Education*, *191*, 104626.

UNESCO. (2023) *Technology in Schools – A tool on whose terms*? https://unesdoc.unesco.org/ark:/48223/pf0000385723

Valkenburg, P. M., Meier, A., & Beyens, I. (2022). Social media use and its impact on adolescent mental health: An umbrella review of the evidence. *Current Opinion in Psychology*, *44*, 58–68.

Valkenburg, P. M., van Driel, I. I., & Beyens, I. (2022). The associations of active and passive social media use with well-being: A critical scoping review. *New Media & Society*, *24*(2), 530–549.

Villena-Taranilla, R., Tirado-Olivares, S., Cózar-Gutiérrez, R., & González-Calero, J. A. (2022). Effects of virtual reality on learning outcomes in K-6 education: A meta-analysis. *Educational Research Review*, *35*, 100434.

Wang, C. H., Salisbury-Glennon, J. D., Dai, Y., Lee, S., & Dong, J. (2022). Empowering College Students to Decrease Digital Distraction through the Use of Self-Regulated Learning Strategies. *Contemporary Educational Technology*, *14*(4).

Wang, S., Christensen, C., Cui, W., Tong, R., Yarnall, L., Shear, L., & Feng, M. (2023). When adaptive learning is effective learning: Comparison of an adaptive learning system to teacher-led instruction. *Interactive Learning Environments*, *31*(2), 793–803.

Yates, A., Starkey, L., Egerton, B., & Flueggen, F. (2021). High school students' experience of online learning during Covid-19: The influence of technology and pedagogy. *Technology, Pedagogy and Education, 30*(1), 59–73.

Yu, Z., & Xu, W. (2022). A meta-analysis and systematic review of the effect of virtual reality technology on users' learning outcomes. *Computer Applications in Engineering Education, 30*(5), 1470–1484.

Chapter 13
Educational Policy:
A Complex Landscape

Daniel Muijs
https://orcid.org/0000-0002-0131-8921
Queen's University Belfast, UK

ABSTRACT

Educational policymaking has always been complex and contested but has become even more so in recent years. Education policy faces a range of challenges, many of which have heightened since the pandemic. These include growing and more complex needs of children and young people, especially in relation to SEN and mental health; increasing contestation and politicisation of education among a variety of stakeholders; growing international competition; and growing societal inequality in many countries. This chapter provides an overview of these developments and how they may shape and be shaped by educational psychologists.

INTRODUCTION

Educational policy has always been complex, as it is shaped by a range of actors, systems, and stakeholders. There is a long history of contestation in education policy, going back to the development of universal primary education in the 19th and 20th centuries in the Global North, where the role of religious institutions such as the Catholic church was a source of dispute in many countries (Herbsts, 2002). Similar disputes have been present on issues such as academic selection (Cantley, 2024) and school age (Woodin et al., 2013). Pedagogies have also long been contested, with discourse around progressive and traditional education arguably dating back to Voltaire's critique of extant education methods in the 18th century, over debates between John Dewey and Walter Lippmann in the US in the early 20th century (Re-

DOI: 10.4018/979-8-3693-1293-3.ch013

ese, 2001), to current social media spats between 'traditionalist' and 'progressive' teachers (Watson, 2020). Educational psychology has long been pivotal in these discussions, be it in theorising and researching learning or the role of diagnostics and testing in assessing educational potential for example (Muijs & Reynolds, 2017). It has therefore long been the case that educational psychology has informed, and has been informed by, debates in educational policy.

Complexity has, however, grown in recent decades, as education systems grapple with increased inequality, increased diversity, and a burgeoning mental health crisis among children and young people. At the same time, educational policy has become an increasingly contested domain. The past years have seen education become embroiled in so-called 'culture wars', around such areas as gender and racial equality (Zimmerman, 2022). Education has not escaped the increasing polarisation evident in society, in which often heated debates in social media spill over into the public sphere. This is most obvious in the US, where elected school boards and school board meeting have been the focus of highly contested debates around issues such of curriculum and culture (Zimmerman, 2022).

In this chapter we will look at the complex and developing policy area through five main lenses: the growing needs of children and young people, the growing role of technology, the multiplicity of stakeholders, the internationalisation of policy debates, and the continuing issues around equity and quality in education. In this we will discuss the role of educational psychology and its practitioners.

The main findings suggest that in all these areas we are seeing a growing complexity, which is both heightening the demands on educational psychologists. One would in theory expect this to lead to a greater role for the educational psychology community in policymaking and policy-influencing, but this is not the case in most countries. Reasons for this include financial constraints and a retreat towards the certainty of simplicity among some policymakers, and a reticence and lack of tools to engage with policy among some in the profession.

GROWING AND MORE COMPLEX NEEDS OF CHILDREN AND YOUNG PEOPLE

A major development in recent years has been the growing needs of children and young people. This has manifested itself in increased demand for psychological and educational services, as more students have been diagnosed as having special educational needs, which challenges both inclusive provision in mainstream schools and support for children in the special schools sector and is therefore a major issue for educational psychology. This is very much an international phenomenon, with steep increases in diagnosis in, for example, Northern Ireland (Irish News, 2024),

Belgium (Opgroeien.be, 2024), and the US (Education Week, 2023). At the same time many needs have become more complex, requiring more extensive support and more expensive treatment (Currigan, 2019; Van Herwegen, 2022). These developing needs have seen the demand for SEN provision far outstrip supply and finances in many jurisdictions. This has increasingly led to dissatisfaction with the SEN system among a range of stakeholders, with psychological services and schools feeling overwhelmed, teachers feeling they are being asked to deal with issues they are not prepared for, parents feeling their children are not able to access the support they require, and policymakers concerned about the ever-rising costs of the system. Parental dissatisfaction with support available in mainstream schools has in many cases led to an increased demand for diagnosis. This is especially acute in countries where the disconnect between need and provision is seen by parents as requiring that their children receive an official diagnosis that alone is seen as giving them access to the support required. This need for diagnosis in turn feeds the pressure on schools and psychological services, as well as on government finances (Van Herwegen, 2022).

These issues have been exacerbated by the COVID-19 pandemic. We have seen a significant increase in the mental health needs of children and young people, which again is evidenced internationally, as well as issues caused by learning loss (Donnelly & Patrinos, 2022; Panchal et al., 2023). The closure of early years provision during the height of the pandemic in many jurisdictions has led to delays in socialisation of young children and resulting issues when they join educational settings (Gelir, 2023). As a result, there is a lot of policy discourse around both SEN and mental health in schools. In relation to SEN, policymakers are struggling with the balance of meeting demand and sustainable financing of the system, while in relation to mental health there is a growing emphasis on the need for provision and approaches. The latter has led to much discussion on the precise role of schools and education in relation to children and young people's mental health. There have been calls for wellbeing to be at the heart of the aims of schools and education, and for schools to be mental-health aware (World Health Organisation, 2023). These initiatives often receive government support, for example through training grants for mental health leads in England (Department for Education 2021) but have in turn been criticised as lacking impact (Schools Week, 2023). These discussions have in some cases become a part of the educational 'culture wars' between so-called progressive and traditional voices (Moore et al., 2022), with the latter questioning the emphasis on mental health in schools. This argument includes disagreement on whether school structures can themselves harm students' mental health. Some claim that more regimented environments (sometimes known as zero-tolerance schools) cause mental harm through their strict regimentation, and are unsuited to neurodiverse students, while others see a calm and very ordered environment as by contrast fostering mental health (Boylan et al., 2023; Dutil, 2020; Harrison, 2023; Reid, 2022). In policy wellbeing and mental health are seen as increasingly important, with many governments promoting mental health interventions, even in countries where more 'traditional' approaches to education have dominated other areas of policymaking (such as England).

A particularly interesting development in this regard is the growth of trauma-informed approaches in schools, which are premised on the importance of addressing Adverse Childhood Experiences (ACE's) through an understanding of how trauma can affect the life and behaviour of students. Approaches typically focus on understanding trauma, creating safe environments, building positive relationships, promoting emotional regulation, and supporting health and resilience (Boylan et al., 2023). There are a range of initiatives around this, not just in mainstream education, but also in second-chance education in, for example, Austria, Malta, Ireland, and Italy (Spiteri et al., 2021). In some countries, such as Northern Ireland, trauma-based approaches are part of the national policy framework and are meant to inform policy across areas from education to health and criminal justice (Mooney et al., 2024). While there is evidence these programmes have positive impacts, they have been subject to criticism, with commentators claiming an overuse of trauma in explaining behaviour, and being used as an 'excuse' to allow poor behaviour in schools, a problem that is reported to have increased since the pandemic (e.g. in Scotland), and is concerning many educators (Boylan et al., 2023, Caffaro et al., 2023; Collier et al., 2022).

Evidence suggests that a system that answers to the complex needs of students must be built on multi-agency work in which education, health, social and psychological services work together to support children and young people in a networked governance approach (Collier et al., 2022). As a result, the past twenty years has seen an increase in initiatives which aim to provide integrated services to children and young people with different levels of ambition and focus, from the school-focussed, such as for example in the Integrated Schools programme in Northern Ireland (Department of Education, 2024 to full-service family centres such as those in Finland which aim to integrate local government services for families children with services provided by non-governmental organizations and parishes (Joronen et al., 2022).

Such services have shown significant promise and impact. A recent analysis of the impact of Sure Start, a programme providing integrated early years services in England which was set up under a Labour Party government, found that the centres had provided significant benefits, including improved secondary school attainment for children who had attended the centres up to age 5. The impact was especially positive for pupils from low SES background and those with SEN (Carneiro et al., 2024). It is noteworthy in this regard that funding for the programme was cut by two thirds under the Conservative governments from 2010 onwards (Mudie, 2020).

It is important that in attempting to address these issues we don't lose sight of the social factors that play an important role in causing and exacerbating them. Poverty and disadvantage are major causes of mental ill-health. This relationship can be seen at the micro-level, where conditions such as poor housing and malnutrition are major contributors, at the meso-level where we see the impact of neighbourhood poverty, and at the macro-level where societal inequality is sometimes posited as contributing to mental ill-health (Marbin et al., 2022). In disadvantaged areas we also see a greater prevalence of issues such as intergenerational trauma, such as in Northern Ireland where the legacy of the civil war known as 'The Troubles' has been found to affect children and young people through family and neighbourhood (Mooney et al., 2025).

TOO MANY COOKS? THE COMPLEXITY OF MULTIPLE STAKEHOLDERS AND INFLUENCERS

Another of the complexities of educational policy is the range of stakeholders involved. Education has multiple goals, for example gaining individual educational credentials, cognitive and non-cognitive development of children and young people as healthy, happy, and democratic citizens, development of knowledge and skills in the workforce, and/or fostering social justice and equality at community, state, and individual levels. Education as a policy area is therefore characterised by the interests of a wide range of actors. These include producers in the form of schools and educators, private service providers and external organisations as well as a range of consumers, in the form of students and parents, but also communities and society as a whole. Both producers and consumers are situated at a range of levels, from the individual to the global with local and national levels in between. These different actors have a range of interests, which sometimes compete. Examples of this are replete in education policymaking. National and local government may have different priorities, such as in the case of England where national government has progressively weakened the role of local government in education provision (Gill & Janmaat, 2019). Parents and schools may disagree on the teaching of contentious topics. In the US, for example, a recent survey suggests that 54% of parents believe their children should be able to opt out of learning about sexual orientation and gender identity, while teachers disagree (Pew Research Centre, 2024). This is a challenge for practitioners, not least educational psychologists, who can find themselves squeezed between different demands, for example from parents and local authorities, and buffeted by policy changes which may lead to rapidly changing priorities and funding.

Policymakers deal with this complexity of voices in several different ways. In many European countries a consensual approach is used, whereby a joint position is sought through co-construction of policy with a range of representative bodies such as unions, professional organisations, and representative bodies. In other countries, such as some US states and England, a majoritarian approach is used, whereby the ruling government largely overrides the views of other actors by dint of their elected mandate (Cairney & Widtfelt, 2015). From a policymaking perspective both approaches have advantages and disadvantages. The consensual approach can lead to policies that have broad support, have been reality-tested with stakeholders, and therefore can be long-lasting. But this approach can also lead to delay or an inability to take difficult decisions. The majoritarian approach can lead to more rapid and decisive decision-making, but also to polices that do not have the broad support of those tasked with implementing them, that lack realism, or that are based on limited ideological perspectives. They are also prone to being overturned as the majority changes, as was evident when the emergence of the Conservative-Liberal Democrat coalition government in England led to the rapid dismantling of extended schools services and the 'Every Child Matters' programme, which changed the role of educational psychologists within the English education system (Hill, 2013).

One group of stakeholders who have traditionally not had a strong voice in policy are students. Education policy is frequently made for and about, but without, them. This is, however, slowly starting to change, with an increased emphasis on children's rights. This is by no means a universal development, with some countries moving a lot faster than others, but nevertheless the direction of travel is clear, and welcome. The UN Convention on the Rights of the Child (United Nations, 1989) detailed children's right to be heard in any decision involving them, and though this principle has been somewhat slow to percolate the education system, it has potentially profound consequences for it (Lansdown et al., 2014; Ziemes & Gutzwiller-Helfenfinger, 2019). An interesting example of a policy initiative that was specifically designed with children and young people is California's Children and Youth Behavioral Health Initiative (CYBHI). In developing the initiative CYBHI established youth advisory councils composed of children and young people who had lived experience with mental health challenges, conducted focus groups and surveys with children and young people, organized co-creation workshops where children and young people worked alongside mental health professionals, policymakers, and other stakeholders, supported Youth-led initiatives, and established feedback mechanisms to gather ongoing feedback from children and young people (CYBHI, 2024). It is to be expected that the call to involve children in co-constructing provision is one that will be increasingly influential in the development of educational psychology in many countries over the coming decade.

Policymaking in most countries happens either primarily at the national, regional, or local authority levels. Countries differ significantly in the extent to which they centralise or decentralise education policymaking, but local communities as opposed to local government tend to have limited input in many education systems. Again, there is some movement on this, with the emergence of place-based education policies providing a greater voice to communities in setting up their own education policies. The work of Queen's Communities and Places in Northern Ireland, where the university is working with local communities to develop bottom-up education policy and provision in collaboration (and sometimes opposition) to established educational actors, is an interesting example (Higgins et al., 2023).

A recent development in educational policymaking is the growing influence of social media. This influence is three-fold. Firstly, there is a growing democratisation of debates around education and education policy. A positive effect of social media is a flattening of hierarchy, whereby practitioners can develop wide reach, and engage directly with academics and policymakers through social media. This is evident, for example, in the popularity of Facebook groups such as 'We are Teachers', a community of more than 3 million teachers, or the so-called 'EduTwitter' which is a forum for much educational debate. Such social media channels are often influential on policymakers, as a venue easily accessible to civil servants and politicians. Both individuals and initiatives emerging from social media (such as ResearchEd) have had considerable influence over the past decade (Omar et al., 2017; McGill, 2020).

Social media can also influence policy through direct campaigns reaching the public and policymakers. An example of this is the popular podcast 'Sold a Story', in which the journalist Emily Hanford criticised US policy and practice on teaching reading, and which has had a major influence on policy in many US states (Winter, 2022). This is also true in Psychology, where social media has played a major role in bringing prominence and influence to psychologists like Dr Jessica Taylor whose approaches may lie outside of the mainstream of practice (Taylor, 2022). On a more negative note, social media are widely seen to have led to a coarsening and polarisation of educational policy debates, just as they have in other public spheres, and have contributed to the (re)- emergence of the educational culture wars described above (Watson, 2020).

An issue that affects education policy more than most areas is the curse of the experiential expert. Because almost everyone has experienced schooling, everyone is an expert and has an opinion. This means that policymaking too often occurs through personal anecdote rather than evidence. This is evident in academic selection, where evidence overwhelmingly shows negative consequences for social mobility and equality, but politicians and commentators frequently refer to the individuals they know who have attended selective schools and overcome disadvantage (Cantley, 2024). While those individual cases are certainly valid, basing policy arguments on them is rather like basing health policy on the apocryphal example of the 100-year-old who smokes a packet of cigarettes a day. Expertise matters to effective policymaking, and, as we will see below, this is where educational psychologists can play an important role.

THE COMPLEX INFLUENCE OF TECHNOLOGY ON EDUCATION AND PSYCHOLOGY

One of the key changes occurring in the field (as in the world around us) is the growing influence of technologies such as digital tools and most recently artificial intelligence.

This influence takes a number of different forms. There is firstly the influence of technology on (the mental health of) children and young people themselves. That technology has changed the way children and young people interact with their environment, for example through the use of social media, is undeniable. What is far less clear is the extent to which this is influencing their development and (mental) health, though a lot of ink has been spilled writing about this issue. That new technologies raise questions of this nature is not surprising. There is a long history of 'moral panics' around the introduction thereof, staring with books, and going on through the invention of cinema, radio, television and computer games (Roe, 1983; Roe & Muijs, 1998). Nevertheless, links have been made between the growth of mental health problems described above and the emergence of the smartphone, which have co-occurred. Jonathan Haidt, for example, has suggested that social media are the cause of mental health difficulties in young people, and in particular girls (Haidt, 2024). Research provides some support for this view. Social media use appears linked with adverse mental health outcomes in children and young people. One meta-analysis noted correlation coefficients between 0.10 and 0.15 (Gabrielle et al., 2024), and another between 0.27 and 0.35 (Shannon et al., 2022), in measures of depressive symptoms, anxiety, and loneliness. Mediating factors include sleep disruption, social comparison, and cyberbullying. In contrast, some reports indicate that active use and interaction with real-life friends may relate to enhanced well-being. Not all studies report negative correlations however (Cingel et al., 2022), while the conflation of correlation and causation has also been criticised. Clearly, it is of importance tfor educational psychologists to know as much as is possible what is causing the increase in mental health issues in children and young people, but at this point the results point to a range of possible factors rather than any one in particular, be it covid or social media use.

Of course, these technological developments don't just influence children and young people. In the section on stakeholders we have pointed to the role of social media in political polarisation, but it is also the case that the interface between research and policy increasingly runs through social media, with social media activists/influencers rising to positions of political influence by becoming known on social media (Watson, 2020).

Technology is significantly influencing education policy debates across areas such as access, use of digital devices for student learning and assessment, and safeguarding. As became very evident during the Covid pandemic the digital divide remains a central concern: access to devices and internet is unequal across socioeconomic lines. Governments have tried to address this through a range of polices, typically aimed at providing internet access in poorly served areas or by providing devices to pupils from disadvantaged households. The Baharatnet Project in India is an example of the former, having to date connected over half a million rural villages to broadband internet (Ministry of Communication, 2024), while the Polish government is supplying laptops to all grade 4 pupils (Notes from Poland, 2025). These initiatives at first sight look sensible in light of the increased importance of digital technology, but while providing broadband infrastructure may provide some lasting benefits this. Is less clear for digital devices, which can rapidly become outdated and thus require expensive replacement and upkeep. Furthermore, an increasing body of research points to some disadvantages of digital devices for learning. More of the brain appears activated when writing with a pen than when typing, for example (van der Meer & Van Der Weel, 2017), while a recent study suggests that use of AI assistant while writing leads to low levels of cognitive activation (Kosmyna et al., 2025).

This brings us to one of the key developments in recent years, which is the flowering of Large-Language Models which have led to an explosion of the use of AI in many fields. This is influencing policy and practice in a range of areas, with the potential to have further influence in future. This is already having a profound impact in the area of assessment, where the impact of AI is bringing the continued validity of essay-based assessment into question. AI-powered grading is rapidly emerging in policy discussions. Governments and educators see benefits in automated scoring as well as other uses of AI in education, and are increasingly drawing up guidelines and policies in this area (Funa & Gabay, 2025). We are only at the start of the development of the use of AI as we write this book chapter, so further changes will undoubtedly have occurred as you read this. AI has been posited by various commentators as likely to take a range of jobs, with some suggesting Psychologists may be among those (Abrams, 2023). This seems unlikely, though it does seem more than likely that AI will become incorporated in assessment, administration and even forms of counselling in future.

There is understandable excitement about the potential of AI in these areas, but we need to be cognitive of the possible pitfalls with its use as well, especially when going beyond the lightening of administrative tasks. If using AI in assessing for example, we need to be cognisant of the fact that AI models have been found tom discriminate against people based on their race and disability status (ACLU, 2022). There is also the tendency of models to 'hallucinate' and fabricate information where clear answers are not forthcoming in their datasets. It is also clear that AI models are sensitive to the parameters introduced by their developers, such as chatbots providing answers that please their users, even where these are clearly wrong and/or racist in nature (Hagen et al., 2025). We have already discussed the potential cognitive impacts above. All these issues mean that one of the roles of educational psychologist must be to maintain a critical perspective towards the use of technology in practice, and must hold up a mirror to policy in this regard.

THE COMPLEXITY OF INTERNATIONAL COMPARISON AND COMPETITION

Recent decades have been characterised by a growing internationalisation of education policy (Lingard, 2020). Large-Scale International Studies of Achievements, such as the OECD-run Programme for International Student Assessment (PISA), and the Progress in International Reading Literacy Study/Trends in Mathematics and Science (PIRLS/TIMSS) studies run by the International Education Association (IEA) have heightened a tendency towards comparison between countries, creating competition to top the academic attainment charts. The results of these international studies are hotly anticipated, and have led to policy responses, particularly in countries where results have declined. A well-known example of this is the so-called 'PISA-Shock' in Germany following the 2000 PISA tests. Disappointing performance levels in the tests led to extensive policy reforms, including the introduction of national education standards, investment in school leadership, a softening of the streaming system, increased school autonomy, introduction of central examinations, and investment in pre-school education (Davoli & Entorf, 2018).

Other countries too have responded to perceived poor performance in these tests by introducing reforms to their education systems. In many cases, these take the form of policy-borrowing from high performing or strongly improving countries, with Finland and Singapore being frequently cited and studied. While clearly learning from the international picture is valuable, the examples of Finland and Singapore also point to the limitations of this approach. Firstly, there is the issue of cultural specificity. Education policy does not occur within a vacuum, but results from socio-political and cultural configurations, which may not be easily replicable elsewhere. Heller-Sahlgren (2015), for example, points to the cultural esteem in which teaching, and the teaching profession are held in Finnish society as a result of specific historical conditions to explain that country's performance. Other cultural factors, such as societal attitudes to education and familiarity with test-taking, may also affect outcomes and be hard to replicate. Country performance on international tests is also not entirely stable, Finland, for example, has seen significant decreases in performance on the PISA tests recently.

Another criticism of the international studies is that they lead to an overemphasis on attainment compared to other valuable outcomes for children and young people, such as health and happiness (Zhao, 2020). This has clear dangers in an environment in which we are seeing major issues around children and young people's mental health, as it may direct attention (and therefore investment) away from the vital psychological services these children need towards am emphasis on improving test performance. In recent years, the international studies have started to go beyond cognitive tests by including measures of motivation and well-being. These can show very different results to the cognitive tests, with the most recent PIRLS study showing a totally different ranking for attitudes to reading than for the reading tests (IEA, 2022), and the PISA 2018 tests showing a negative correlation between reading performance and life satisfaction at the country level (OECD, 2018). These results have received rather less attention from policymakers, though it must be pointed out here that factors such as well-being tend to be harder to measure reliably (Rappleye et al., 2020).

There are also technical limitations to the international tests. Countries differ in their definitions and inclusion criteria for students, for example, meaning that the proportion of students included can vary significantly between countries. PISA allows up to 5% of the target population not to be included in the sample (based on a number of criteria such as disability or accessibility of school), but while in many countries the actual percentage excluded is as low as 0.5%, in the last PISA round 16 countries did not meet the 5% target, with Denmark excluding as much as 11,6% of students (OECD, 2023). Test equating across countries is also challenging, and though the technical teams that design the tests make strenuous efforts to neutralise this issue, there is evidence that even within countries language in which the test is taken can influence outcomes, with Welsh language test takers underperforming English language test takers in Wales, for example (Jerrim & Lopez-Agudo, 2021).

The above points to the limitations of using such international tests as a basis for policy, but nevertheless they remain useful, provided the rich evidence that is present in the tests (and which includes surveys of students, teachers and principals on e.g. intercultural competencies, wellbeing and pedagogical practices, for example) is used to interrogate strengths and weaknesses of the system rather than to engage in a rather unhelpful league-table competition. While learning from practice elsewhere is helpful, simply transporting policies from one context to another is unlikely to be productive.

EQUITY AND QUALITY: ENDURING COMPLEXITIES

One of the main issues education grapples with is that of equity. This of course is a broad topic, and one that has long been a subject of both policymaking and research in education, going back to the introduction of universal primary education in the global North which at least in part was aimed at improving opportunities for children from the working classes which had not heretofore been able to access education (Zinkina et al., 2016).

As a concept equity is multifaceted, and at times controversial, but in this chapter, we will define it as the principle of ensuring that all students, regardless of their background, circumstances, or abilities, have access to the resources, opportunities, and support they need to succeed academically. Equity in this definition involves addressing disparities and injustices in education to ensure that every student has an equal chance to reach their full potential. This includes factors such as providing adequate funding for schools serving disadvantaged communities, offering support services for students with diverse needs, promoting inclusive teaching practices, and actively working to eliminate barriers to learning and achievement.

This key aim of educational policy is obviously interwoven with societal and global inequities, and therefore in many ways the definition of a complex problem. Initiatives that focus solely on improving education itself without addressing barriers to learning due to children and young people's circumstances can only address equity to a limited degree. Making schools as effective as possible is important and will disproportionally help the most disadvantaged as the effect of schooling is up to three times greater for students from disadvantaged backgrounds than for those from advantaged backgrounds. But even if all schools were optimally effective very significant disparities would remain according to social background, as statistical simulations have shown (Muijs & Reynolds, 2017). Addressing barriers to learning thus requires integrated whole-community policies, that work with and are co-constructed by the local community. Support services are crucial to this, and the ecology that is needed to address the broader health issues of children and young people is also needed to address educational inequality. However, if, as has been the case over recent decades in many countries, societal inequality increases, one cannot expect education to be immune to this, even less inoculate against it (Robertson, 2016). Rising inequality itself is therefore a factor that adds to the complexity of achieving desirable policy goals in education, not least as well as affecting attainment inequality has been shown to have strong negative impacts on physical and mental health (Yu, 2018).

Most policymakers would of course espouse the value of equity, but this enthusiasm wanes when it is perceived as a threat to perceptions of quality. This can be the case in debates around academic selection, for example, where attempts at comprehensivisation are sometimes seen as reducing quality. It is, however, incorrect to state that there is a discrepancy between equity and quality, and in fact many studies suggest that greater equity is correlated with higher quality of education (Kyriakides& Creemers, 2018). Education policies can therefore fruitfully pursue both.

That is not to say that there are never policies which aim to enhance equity that can come at a cost to quality. An example of this are policies to enhance access to education in resource-constrained countries. The UN's Millennium Development Goals led to a sustained effort in many cases to provide universal access to primary education (MDG 2) and to improve access to post-primary education. This has in many ways been a resounding success. From 2000 to 2021 the global attendance rate went from less than 80% to 87%, and about four out of five children attending primary education completed it. The number of out-of-school children reduced by over 35 per cent (UNICEF, 2022). Unfortunately, however, in many countries severe resource constraints have meant that increased access was not accompanied by sufficient resourcing to ensure the supply of well-educated teachers and effective classroom and school resources, which has led to major quality issues, with many children who attend schools unable to reach basic levels of literacy and numeracy (Mugendawala & Muijs, 2020). In response to this the UN's Sustainable Development Goals have reformulated the core educational aim as 'Ensure inclusive and equitable quality education' (SDG 4), but progress on this has been slow due to the aforementioned resource constraints (UNESCO, 2023).

Of course, what policies do enhance equity and quality is a controversial issue, and one that has increasingly become part of the political debate. While in the past education was rarely at the centre of politics, and issues such as pedagogy were primarily left to teachers, teacher educators and experts, this has changed significantly. In countries as diverse as the Netherlands, Belgium, England, the US, Poland and Portugal, policy and debate have moved into the arena of both curriculum and pedagogy (Wille & Bovens, 2019). England provides an early and clear example of this, where, from the advent of the National Curriculum in 1993, over the National Literacy and Numeracy strategies in 1997, through to the curriculum reforms of the Conservative-Liberal Democrat coalition government, policy has prescribed both content and forms of teaching. This has been the case for both Labour and Conservative-led governments, and has at times led to highly prescriptive policies, such as the 'Literacy Hour' under the government of Tony Blair which went as far as to set out how many minutes should be spent on different teaching activities (such as the whole-class plenary) every lesson (Muijs & Reynolds, 2017). Curriculum too has become ever more the subject of political debate and therefore policy, with moral panics around the content of curricula being particularly prevalent in the more conservative parts of the US, leading to the banning of teaching of concepts such as Critical Race Theory in Florida, for example (Ali, 2021). This overt politicisation of the educational realm is not necessarily conducive to effective policymaking, as it will tend to envelop education in ideological battles and lead to rapid policy changes as power changes.

Both equity and quality are hindered by two key issues affecting education across countries: staff shortages and lack of funding. The issue of teacher shortages is one that is exercising educational policy across countries and appears somewhat independent from the specific education policies individual countries pursue (Ovenden-Hope & Passy, 2020). To make matters worse, teacher shortages are accompanied by staff shortages across the services that engage with children and young people, for example social workers (Astvik et al., 2020). These shortages must be seen in the context of broader tightness of the labour market but are also related to pay structures that have seen pay in teaching and social services, for example, fall behind and become increasingly uncompetitive (See et al., 2020). It is important to note in this context that there is inevitably a limit to what education alone can achieve in terms of equity, without addressing the broader social conditions and social and emotional needs of children and young people.

EDUCATIONAL PSYCHOLOGY: MAKING OR UNDERGOING POLICY?

What then is the role of educational psychologists in this complex policy landscape? It is clear looking at the issues described above that there should be such as role. And in many countries, there is a clear expectation that the role of educational psychologists includes the influencing of policy, at local, regional, and/or national level (Wolfendale et al., 1992). This is evident, for example, in role descriptions of Educational Psychologists, which may for example describe the role as involving system leadership, which can occur at a national, regional or local level, supporting policy and strategic development (EPS, 2024).

In practice, however, this policy influence might be limited, with psychologists seldom being at the centre of educational policy debates. There are several reasons why this may be the case, including a disconnect between the scientific identity of the field and the rather unscientific nature of policymaking and a lack of strong representative bodies that can directly influence policies, such as the teacher unions (DeCuir-Gunby, 2023). There has also been some criticism of the extent to which

Educational {psychology research engages with policy issues. Nichols (2023) suggests several reasons for this lack of interest, including a lack of relevance of policy to researchers' individual research agendas and interests, a perception that policy-based research could negatively affect the objectivity and rigour of research, a perception that policymakers are only interested in RCT's, and a scepticism over whether policy is actually research-informed. While there is validity to these arguments, it is also the case that if researchers don't engage with policy they cannot be surprised if policy isn't research-informed, thus creating an element of circularity in the argument. Nicholls & Herrick (2023) point to a lack of guidance and training of psychologists on how they might contribute to the educational policy arena. This is indeed not part of academic training, but there are several relatively straightforward recommendations that may be helpful, taken from my own experience of working as a civil servant.

Firstly, it is important to develop networks and collaborations. These do not have to be with politicians. It is an error to assume that politicians are the only or main actors in the education space. Civil servants, unions, advisory bodies, and non-governmental organisations all influence education policy and are often more open to practitioners and researchers. As Siegel et al., (2021) point out, policymaking is a "complex system with multiple individual and organizational stakeholders". Engagement with policymakers needs to be sustained. Policymaking is dynamic and ever-changing, so continued engagement with the process is necessary (Siegel et al., 2021). Secondly, arrive with solutions, not problems. Policymakers are often already aware of the problems but, in part due to the complexity mentioned above, may struggle with solutions and are often open to the latter. Merely pointing out the issues is unlikely to lead them to act.

A constructive and collaborative approach is important. Policymakers are equally prone to emotion as anyone else and will not quickly engage with those they perceive as implacably hostile to them. Policymakers do not as a rule read academic papers. Short, snappy summaries with clear policy recommendations are much more likely to succeed. Clarity is prized. It is helpful to try and find a 'hook' into policy, for example a topical issue, or a link with known priorities and interests of policymakers. Policy can also be influenced in a more indirect way. Traditional media remain influential, and often set the agenda for social media. Social media have become increasingly so (see above), so engagement with one or both is a useful way to come to the attention of policymakers (Kaplan, 2023).

CONCLUSION

While predicting the future is hard, there are some clear trendlines that we can hypothesise will influence policy in the coming years. The first of these is a continuation of the growth in concern for the non-cognitive sides of education. While learning and attainment remain drivers of policy, there is a growing concern with the well-being and mental health of children and young people, and their role in them becoming healthy and happy adults. This concern will be linked to a growing movement for inclusion that will include students across the range of neurodiversity and sexualities, as well as those from various backgrounds. Schools in many countries have not adapted particularly well to the growing diversity of the student population in terms of ethnic and linguistic background, but this diversity is only going to increase, so it is imperative that policymakers, educators, and indeed educational psychologists learn from those countries, regions, schools, and communities that have created inclusive environments in which all students can thrive.

The education sector is likely to face some significant challenges and tensions in the coming decade. The funding situation in most countries is likely to be tight and get tighter as treasuries run up against the limitations of the borrowing done during and after the covid-19m pandemic, and this will bump up against the growing demands made of the sector in terms of the needs of children and young people. Issues of equity and inclusion will remain to the fore and will do so in a landscape in which inequality in society may increase if policy does not compensate for tightening finances through redistribution and reform. The rapid developments in technology such as AI are likely to present both challenges and opportunities to educational psychologists and service users alike.

An interesting question is to what extent technological developments will impact on educational policy in the coming decade. To date, while education has incorporated various technical innovations, these have not fundamentally changed the nature of education. However, the advent of new technologies such as artificial intelligence and virtual reality have the potential to be far more disruptive to the system, in ways good and bad. Examples of the former include the ability of AI to support educators and psychologists in work such as developing lesson plan and diagnosis, the ability of AI to provide tailored and bespoke learning pathways for students, and the ability of VR to provide virtual training spaces. Examples of the latter include the ability to use AI to cheat on assessment, ability to easily manufacture information, and new avenues for bullying and harassment. In the coming years much policy debate will undoubtedly ensure over how to enhance the former and reduce the latter.

Education policy will remain a political football, with competing demands from different actors making it increasingly hard to find solutions that satisfy all. This can seem problematic, but it needn't be. Fundamentally, policy is about making choices. And while those choices need to be made in a consultative and cooperative manner, they still need to be made. The lodestar in making them must be to develop healthy, happy, inclusive, and economically thriving communities, children, and young people. If we keep this in mind, much can be achieved.

QUESTIONS FOR DISCUSSION AND REFLECTION

1. In what ways can educational policy address the growing complexity of supporting students with special educational needs (SEN) and mental health challenges, while ensuring that school systems and practitioners are not overburdened?
2. How has the increasing politicisation of education influenced curriculum and pedagogical policy decisions, and what strategies might educational psychologists employ to effectively contribute to policymaking in such a contested environment?
3. What should be the role of schools in promoting students' mental health and well-being, and how can trauma-informed educational approaches be implemented without compromising academic standards and student outcomes?
4. How does the trend towards international comparisons in education policy, such as (e.g., PISA rankings) influence national education priorities?
5. What are the potential risks of relying on such assessments in shaping policies related to equity and well-being?

REFERENCES

Abrams, Z. (2023). AI is changing every aspect of psychology. Here's what to watch for. *Monitor on Psychology*, *54*(4), 46.

ACLU. (2022). *Algorithms Are Making Decisions About Health Care, Which May Only Worsen Medical Racism.* https://www.aclu.org/news/privacy-technology/algorithms-in-health-care-may-worsen-medical-racism.

Ali, S. S. (2021). Florida Board of Education passes rule banning critical race theory in classrooms. NBC News, 10/6/2021. https://www.nbcnews.com/news/us-news/florida-board-education-passes-rule-banning-critical-race-theory-classrooms-n1270363

Astvik, W., Welander, J., & Larsson, R. (2020). Reasons for staying: A longitudinal study of work conditions predicting social workers' willingness to stay in their organisation. *British Journal of Social Work*, *50*(5), 1382–1400.

Boylan, M., Truelove, L., Pearse, S., O'Brien, S., Sheehan, H., Cowell, T., & Long, E. (2023). Developing trauma-informed teacher education in England. *London Review of Education*, *21*(1), 29. Advance online publication. DOI: 10.14324/LRE.21.1.29

Cafaro, C. L., Gonzalez Molina, E., Patton, E., McMahon, S. D., & Brown, M. (2023). Meta-analyses of teacher-delivered trauma-based and trauma-informed care interventions. *Psychological Trauma: Theory, Research, Practice, and Policy*, *15*(7), 1177–1187. DOI: 10.1037/tra0001515

Cairney, P., & Widfeldt, A. (2015). Is Scotland a Westminster-style Majoritarian Democracy or a Scandinavian-style Consensus Democracy? A Comparison of Scotland, the UK and Sweden. *Regional & Federal Studies*, *25*(1), 1–18. DOI: 10.1080/13597566.2014.958818

Cantley, I. (2024). The Philosophical Limitations of Educational Assessment: Implications for Academic Selection.

Carneiro, P., Cattan, S., & Ridpath, N. (2024). The short- and medium-term impacts of Sure Start on educational outcomes. *Institute for Fiscal Studies.* https://ifs.org.uk/publications/short-and-medium-term-impacts-sure-start-educational-outcomes

Children and Youth Behavioral Health Initiative. (2024). Putting our kids first. https://cybhi.chhs.ca.gov

Cingel, D., Carter, M. C., & Krause, H.-V. (2022). Social media and self-esteem. *Current Opinion in Psychology, 45*. Advance online publication. DOI: 10.1016/j.copsyc.2022.101304

Collier, S., Bryce, I., Trimmer, K., & Krishnamoorthy, G. (2022). Validating the barriers and enablers for teachers accessing professional development of trauma informed pedagogy. *Social Sciences & Humanities Open, 6*(1), 1–7. DOI: 10.1016/j.ssaho.2022.100332

Currigan, S. (2019). Special Needs Pupils in Schools: Why Numbers Are Rising. https://beaconschoolsupport.co.uk/newsletters/why-are-there-more-children-with-complex-special-needs-than-ever-before

Davoli, M., & Entorf, H. (2018). The PISA Shock, Socioeconomic Inequality, and School Reforms in Germany. *IZA Institute of Labor Economics*. https://docs.iza.org/pp140.pdf

DeCuir-Gunby, J. T. (2023). Advancing the debate: The need for policy-oriented activism research in educational psychology. *Educational Psychologist, 58*(4), 284–289. DOI: 10.1080/00461520.2023.2252070

Department for Education. (2021). Promoting and supporting mental health and wellbeing in schools and colleges. https://www.gov.uk/guidance/mental-health-and-wellbeing-support-in-schools-and-colleges

Department of Education. (2024). Extended schools programme. https://www.education-ni.gov.uk/articles/extended-schools-programme

Donnelly, R., & Patrinos, H. A. (2022). Learning loss during Covid-19: An early systematic review. *Prospects, 51*, 601–609. DOI: 10.1007/s11125-021-09582-6

Dutil, S. (2020). Dismantling the School-to-Prison Pipeline: A Trauma-Informed, Critical Race Perspective on School Discipline. *Children & Schools, 42*(3), 171–178. DOI: 10.1093/cs/cdaa016

Enfield Psychological Services. (2024). The role of an educational psychologist. https://www.enfield.gov.uk/educationalpsychologyservice/the-role-of-an-educational-psychologist)

Funa, A. A., & Gabay, A. E. (2025). Policy guidelines and recommendations on AI use in teaching and learning: A meta-synthesis study. *Social Sciences & Humanities Open, 11*. Advance online publication. DOI: 10.1016/j.ssaho.2024.101221

Gabrielle, T., Sonne, M., & Indolo, N. N. (2024). The Impact of Social Media on Adolescent Mental Health: A Meta-Analysis. *Scientia Psychiatrica, 5*(3), 551–564. DOI: 10.37275/scipsy.v5i3.175

Gelir, I. (2023). The effects of the COVID-19 pandemic on preschool children's learning and development. *SN Social Sciences, 3*, 143. DOI: 10.1007/s43545-023-00736-1

Gill, O., & Janmaat, J. G. (2019). The 'schools revolution' in England: A configurational comparative analysis of academisation across local authorities. *Cambridge Journal of Education, 49*(5), 575–604. DOI: 10.1080/0305764X.2019.1581135

Hagen, L., Jingnan, L., & Nguyen, A. (2025). *Elon Musk's AI chatbot, Grok, started calling itself 'MechaHitler'* NPR, July 9 2025. https://www.npr.org/2025/07/09/nx-s1-5462609/grok-elon-musk-antisemitic-racist-content

Haidt, J. (2024). *The anxious generation: how the great rewiring of childhood is causing an epidemic of mental illness*. Penguin Press.

Harrison, M. H. (2023). Nuance in "No Excuses": Unexpected Progressive Pedagogy and Policy. *Education and Urban Society, 55*(3), 342–370. DOI: 10.1177/00131245221076096

Heller-Sahlgren, G. (2015). *Real Finnish Lessons: The true story of an education superpower*. Centre for Policy Studies. https://cps.org.uk/wp-content/uploads/2021/07/150410115444-RealFinnishLessonsFULLDRAFTCOVER.pdf

Herbst, J. (2002). Nineteenth-Century Schools between Community and State: The Cases of Prussia and the United States. *History of Education Quarterly, 42*(3), 317–341. DOI: 10.1111/j.1748-5959.2002.tb00001.x

Higgins, K., Murtagh, B., Gallagher, T., Grounds, A., Robinson, G., Loudon, E., & Doherty, M. (2023). Queen's Communities and Place: towards the alignment of higher education place-based strategy with local need. *Research for All, 7*(1). https://pure.qub.ac.uk/en/publications/queens-communities-and-place-towards-the-alignment-of-higher-educ

Hill, V. (2013). Working across diverse contexts with wider populations: The developing role of the educational psychologist. In Arnold, C., & Hardy, J. (Eds.), *British educational psychology: The first hundred years* (pp. 128–140). The British Psychological Society.

IEA. (2022). PIRLS 2021. International results in reading. https://pirls2021.org

Irish News. (2024, April 8). Paul Givan: System struggling to keep pace with increased demand for SEN places. https://www.irishnews.com/news/northern-ireland/system-struggling-to-keep-pace-with-increased-demand-for-sen-places-givan-YGIWHYERZ5FSRDESBKML6ZEGCI/#:~:text=The%20Education%20Minister%20said%20more,to%20be%20found%20by%20September.&text=5%3A09PM%20BST-,The%20education%20system%20is%20struggling%20to%20keep%20pace%20with%20the,%20),%20Paul%20Givan%20has%20said

Jerrim, J., & Lopez-Agudo, L. A. (2021). The impact of test language on PISA scores: New evidence from Wales. *British Educational Research Journal*, *48*(3), 420–445. DOI: 10.1002/berj.3774

Joronen, K., Hastrup, A., Nieminen, S., Rantanen, A., & Pelkonen, M. (2022). Family centres in Finland – a new integrated service model for families with children and adolescents. *International Journal of Integrated Care*, *22*, 113. DOI: 10.5334/ijic.ICIC21141

Kaplan, A. (2023). A framework for approaching policy-oriented educational psychology research. *Educational Psychologist*, *58*(4), 229–243. DOI: 10.1080/00461520.2023.2253301

Kosmyna, N., Hauptman, E., Yuan, Y. T., Situ, J., Liao, X.-H., Beresnitsky, A. V., Braunstein, I., & Maes, P. (2025). Your Brain on ChatGPT: Accumulation of Cognitive Debt when Using an AI Assistant for Essay Writing Task. https://arxiv.org/abs/2506.08872

Kyriakides, L., & Creemers, B. P. (2018). Investigating the quality and equity dimensions of educational effectiveness. *Studies in Educational Evaluation*, *57*, 1–5.

Lansdown, G., Jimerson, S. R., & Shahroozi, R. (2014). Children's rights and school psychology: Children's right to participation. *Journal of School Psychology*, *52*(1), 3–12. DOI: 10.1016/j.jsp.2013.12.006

Lingard, B. (2020). *Globalisation and education: theorising and researching changing imbrications in education policy*. Routledge.

Marbin, D., Gutwinski, S., Schreiter, S., & Heinz, A. (2022). Perspectives in Poverty and Mental Health. *Frontiers in Public Health*, *10*, 975482.

McGill, R. M. (2020). *How has Twitter influenced education politics in England?* Wlfson College, Cambridge University. https://www.researchgate.net/publication/341793032_How_has_Twitter_influenced_education_politics_in_England

Ministry of Communication. (2024). *Bharatnet Project*. https://usof.gov.in/en/bharatnet-project

Mooney, S., Fargas, M., MacDonald, M., O'Neill, D., Walsh, C., Hayes, D., & Montgomery, L. (2024). *'We are on a journey': implementing trauma informed approaches in Northern Ireland - Executive summary report*. Queen's University Belfast. https://pureadmin.qub.ac.uk/ws/portalfiles/portal/558170230/Implementing_TIAs_NI._Executive_Report._QUB_2024.pdf

Moore, A., Stapley, E., Hayes, D., Town, R., & Deighton, J. (2022). Barriers and Facilitators to Sustaining School-Based Mental Health and Wellbeing Interventions: A Systematic Review. *International Journal of Environmental Research and Public Health, 19*(6), 3587. DOI: 10.3390/ijerph19063587

Mudie, K. (2020, February 15). Tories have closed 1,300 family centres in last 10 years, figures reveal. *mirror*. https://www.mirror.co.uk/news/politics/tories-closed-1300-family-centres-21506487

Mugendawala, H., & Muijs, D. (2020). Educational process factors for effective education in resource-constrained countries: A multilevel analysis. *School Effectiveness and School Improvement, 31*(3), 445–467. DOI: 10.1080/09243453.2019.1702562

Muijs, D., & Reynolds, D. (2017). *Effective teaching: evidence and practice*. Sage.

Nichols, S. L. (2023). Educational psychology and educational policy: Intersections and new directions. In Schutz, P., & Muis, K. (Eds.), *Handbook of educational psychology* (4th ed.). Routledge.

Nichols, S. L., & Herrick, I. R. (2023). Introduction to the special issue on policy-oriented research: Enhancing the relevancy of educational psychology to policy. *Educational Psychologist, 58*(4), 205–213. DOI: 10.1080/00461520.2023.2252074

Notes from Poland. (22025). *Poland begins to give free laptops to all Fourth-Graders*. https://notesfrompoland.com/2023/09/04/poland-begins-giving-free-laptops-to-all-fourth-graders/

OECD. (2018). *PISA 2018 Results (Volume III): What School Life Means for Students' Lives*. https://www.oecd-ilibrary.org/sites/c414e291-en/index.html?itemId=/content/component/c414e291-en#:~:text=PISA%20findings%20also%20show%20that,those%20in%20the%20top%20quarter

Omar, M. S., Njeru, A., & Yi, S. (2017). The influence of Twitter on education policy making. In *2017 18th IEEE/ACIS International Conference on Software Engineering, Artificial Intelligence, Networking and Parallel/Distributed Computing (SNPD)* (pp. 133-136). DOI: 10.1109/SNPD.2017.8022712

Opgroeien.be. (2024). Cijferrapprt. https://www.opgroeien.be/kennis/cijfers-en-onderzoek/groeipakket#

Ovenden-Hope, T., & Passy, R. (2020). *Exploring teacher recruitment and retention. Contextual challenges from international perspectives*. Routledge.

Panchal, U., Salazar de Pablo, G., & Franco, M. (2023). The impact of COVID-19 lockdown on child and adolescent mental health: Systematic review. *European Child & Adolescent Psychiatry*, *32*, 1151–1177. DOI: 10.1007/s00787-021-01856-w

Pew Research Centre. (2014). Race and LGBTQ Issues in K-12 Schools. https://www.pewresearch.org/social-trends/2024/02/22/race-and-lgbtq-issues-in-k-12-schools/

Rappleye, J., Komatsu, H., Uchida, Y., Krys, K., & Markus, H. (2020). 'Better policies for better lives'?: Constructive critique of the OECD's (mis)measure of student well-being. *Journal of Education Policy*, *35*(2), 258–282. DOI: 10.1080/02680939.2019.1576923

Reese, W. J. (2001). The Origins of Progressive Education. *History of Education Quarterly*, *41*(1), 1–24. DOI: 10.1111/j.1748-5959.2001.tb00072.x

Reid, A. (2022). *Leading Mindfully for Healthy and Successful Schools*. Taylor and Francis.

Robertson, S. L. (2016). Piketty, capital and education: A solution to, or problem in, rising social inequalities? *British Journal of Sociology of Education*, *37*(6), 823–835.

Roe, K. (1983). *Mass Media and Adolescent Schooling: Conflict or Co-existence?* Almqvist and Wiksell International.

Roe, K., & Muijs, D. (1998). Children and Computer Games: A Profile of the Heavy User. *European Journal of Communication*, *13*(2), 181–200. DOI: 10.1177/0267323198013002002

Schools Week. (2023, May 18). Mental health leads struggle to find time for the job. Author.

See, B. H., Morris, R., Gorard, S., Kokotsaki, D., & Abdi, S. (2020). Teacher Recruitment and Retention: A Critical Review of International Evidence of Most Promising Interventions. *Education Sciences*, *10*(10), 262. DOI: 10.3390/educsci10100262

Shannon, H., Bush, K., Villeneuve, P. J., Hellemans, K. G., & Guimond, S. (2022). Problematic Social Media Use in Adolescents and Young Adults: Systematic Review and Meta-analysis. *JMIR Mental Health*, *9*(4), e33450. DOI: 10.2196/33450

Siegel, J., Arenson, M., Mikytuck, A., & Woolard, J. (2021). Engaging public policy with psychological science. *Translational Issues in Psychological Science*, *7*(1), 1–8. DOI: 10.1037/tps0000284

Spiteri, R., O'Riordan, M. R., Cefai, C., Hickey, G., & Smith, S. (2023). Early school leaving and trauma-based education: A study in four European countries. *Pastoral Care in Education*, *41*(1), 26–41. DOI: 10.1080/02643944.2022.2032812

Taylor, J. (2022). *Sexy But Psycho: Uncovering the psychiatric labelling of women and girl*. Little Brown Publications.

UNESCO. (2023). 2023 SDG4 scorecard on progress towards national SDG 4 benchmarks: key findings. https://unesdoc.unesco.org/ark:/48223/pf0000384273

UNICEF. (2022). Unicef data: monitoring the situation of children and women: primary education. https://data.unicef.org/topic/education/primary-education/

United Nations. (1989). *The United Nations convention on the rights of the child*. https://www.unicef.org.uk/wp-content/uploads/2016/08/unicef-convention-rights-child-uncrc.pdf

van der Meer, A. L., & Van der Weel, F. R. (2017). Only three fingers write, but the whole brain works: A high-density EEG study showing advantages of drawing over typing for learning. *Frontiers in Psychology*, *8*, 706.

Van Herwegen, J. (2022). Why has there been a rise in number of SEN children, especially in the early years? *UCL Centre for Educational Neuroscience*. http://www.educationalneuroscience.org.uk/2022/04/01/why-has-there-been-a-rise-in-number-of-sen-children-especially-in-the-early-years/

Watson, S. (2020). New Right 2.0: Teacher populism on social media in England. *British Educational Research Journal*, *47*(2), 299–345. DOI: 10.1002/berj.3664

Wille, A., & Bovens, M. (2019). Education as a Cleavage. In *Diploma Democracy: The Rise of Political Meritocracy*. Oxford: Oxford University Press. https://ssrn.com/abstract=3370399or http://dx.doi.org/DOI: 10.2139/ssrn.3370399

Winter, J. (2022, January 9). The rise and fall of vibes-based literacy. *The New Yorker*. https://www.newyorker.com/news/annals-of-education/the-rise-and-fall-of-vibes-based-literacy

Wolfendale, S., Bryans, T., Fox, M., Labram, A., & Sigston, A. (Eds.). (1992). *The profession and practice of educational psychology: Future directions*. Cassell Educational.

Woodin, T., McCulloch, G., & Cowan, S. (2013). The School-Leaving Age in International Perspective. In *Secondary Education and the Raising of the School-Leaving Age* (Secondary Education in a Changing World). Palgrave Macmillan. DOI: 10.1057/9781137065216_2

World Health Organization. (2023). How school systems can improve health and well-being: topic brief: mental health. https://www.who.int/publications/i/item/9789240064751

Yu, S. (2018). Uncovering the hidden impacts of inequality on mental health: A global study. *Translational Psychiatry*, *8*(1), 98. DOI: 10.1038/s41398-018-0148-0

Zhao, Y. (2020). Two decades of havoc: A synthesis of criticism against PISA. *Journal of Educational Change*, *21*(2), 245–266. DOI: 10.1007/s10833-019-09367-x

Zieme, J., & Gutwiller-Helfenfinger, E. (2019). Children's Rights and Educational Psychology. *European Psychologist*, *24*(2). Advance online publication. DOI: 10.1027/1016-9040/a000373

Zimmerman, J. (2022). *Whose America? Culture Wars in the Public Schools*. University of Chicago Press.

Zinkina, J., Korotayev, A., & Andreev, A. (2016). Mass primary education in the nineteenth century. In *Globalistics and Globalization Studies* (pp. 63–70). Global Transformations and Global Future.

Chapter 14
Promoting Wellbeing and Coping Skills in Higher Education

Chris Gibbons
https://orcid.org/0000-0001-6631-721X
Queen's University Belfast, UK

ABSTRACT

Throughout this book, a range of factors have been explored that impact on educators and on students. Chapter 7 puts the spotlight on the student experience of stress. What is critical, of course, is how well one copes and this is the focus of this final chapter. In trying to create a structure to see the key influences that relate to student stress, the author separated the sources of stress from their effects and from how students cope. This is an over-simplification of course. The sources and effects of stress and how students cope are all inter-related and bi-directional. The significance of a source of stress depends on one's current wellbeing, and this is affected by how well one has and is coping. It was mentioned in Chapter 7, for example, that responses to stress can become new stressors, such as loneliness as a response to stress and this response interacts with other stressors, such as the student's experience of academic stress leading to a greater impact on academic outcome. Moreover, students with an earlier history of childhood trauma were more likely to experience more adverse outcomes on wellbeing, health, and academic performance compared with students who did not report earlier trauma. This illustrates how sources of stress and their effects and coping are all inter-connected.

DOI: 10.4018/979-8-3693-1293-3.ch014

INTRODUCTION

This chapter offers a grounding in what stress is, its prevalence in students and its effects. The chapter outlines its huge impact on student mental health and academic performance. This chapter focuses on coping in students. It explores key ingredients, such as a range personality attributes; along with control, support, and a number of cognitive, and emotional focused strategies. In trying to create a structure to see the key influences that relate to student stress, I have separated the sources of stress from their effects, in Chapter 7, from how students cope, Chapter 14. This is an over-simplification of course, the sources and effects of stress and how students cope are all inter-related and bi-directional. The significance of a source of stress depends on one's current wellbeing and this is affected by how well one has and is coping. It was mentioned in Chapter 7, for example, that responses to stress can become new stressors, such as loneliness as a response to stress (McIntyre et al., 2018) and this response interacts with other stressors, such as the student's experience of academic stress, to lead to a greater impact on academic outcome. Moreover, students with an earlier history of childhood trauma were more likely to experience more adverse outcomes on wellbeing, health and academic performance compared to students who did not report earlier trauma. This illustrates how sources of stress, and their effects and coping are all inter-connected.

Intelligence is one of the strongest predictors of academic achievement. It is as strong as any personality ingredient (Schneider & Preckel, 2017). However, it is not covered in this analysis because academic achievement is just one outcome and personality and other influences on coping have a stronger influence than intelligence on wellbeing (Schneider & Preckel, 2017). Proxies for intelligence are the qualification students enter university with and as this is set by university admissions criteria, it means that intelligence, compared to personality, is more similar across any given cohort. Personality and the influences on coping are more variable and the evidence offered suggests they are more adaptable or at least the cognitive processes that underlie them are, in relation to their influence on wellbeing, mood, motivation, satisfaction and health. In covering these influences on how students cope, please try to be aware of how you could incorporate some of these insights into the work you do with your students.

PERSONALITY AND COPING

McCrae and Costa, (2004) developed one of the most widely used measures of personality. Their scale measures five core traits – openness, conscientiousness, extraversion, agreeableness and neuroticism, often abbreviated to OCEAN or the

Big Five. It is research exploring this measure of personality that will be one of the main focuses when considering the influence of personality on student coping.

Neuroticism and Openness

Neuroticism or levels of emotional stability and openness, in most studies, are found to be predictors of student anxiety (Vollrath & Torgersen, 2000, Gibbons, 2022). In education contexts, openness is important if learning is to expand. It represents a willingness to grow and to get things wrong and to allow oneself to feel vulnerable. Gibbons (2022) found that openness was associated with adverse mental health in students. That is not necessarily bad – feeling vulnerable and accepting that one might make mistakes, for example, through disappointing results and critical feedback, are inevitable if skills and understanding currently outside one's comfort zone are to be mastered and to later fall within it. They are the growing pains of a growth mindset (Dweck, 2015). A growth mindset is one that avoids putting labels on what one can achieve and puts the focus instead on one's learning potential. In the face of difficulty in understanding and in some poor results, it is easy to slip into a fixed mindset and believe you have reached the limit of what you can do. We all flit between both fixed and growth mindsets. The challenge is to learn to re-interpret experiences where it feels too difficult, and to reframe these experiences instead as the growing pains not of what one is unable to do, but what one is unable to do yet.

Students who achieve, do, to varying degrees, adopt a growth mindset. This is supported by the finding that feelings of vulnerability, doubt and disappointment are common among the large number of students who eventually succeed, if not shine, in their performance but who experience imposter syndrome at different points during their learning (Parkman, 2016). Imposter syndrome is where one feels unqualified and out of one's depth, that one is an 'imposter' and does not deserve one's place! It may not be pleasant, but students should be comforted by the fact that it is the norm to experience this at times. Being open-minded is integral if one is to effectively master new learning, and so too is its association with heightened stress.

In terms of neuroticism, Lipson and Eisenberg (2018) found, from a survey of 4280 students in the US, that a tendency to be worry-prone was associated with a higher rumination over academic demands and over the cost and effort required in going to university and this rumination was associated with adverse mental health. Mackaskill (2018) replicated the same findings with second year students in the UK.

In a series of studies exploring stress and coping in second year psychology students, Gibbons (2022, 2023a, 2024) found neuroticism to be a predictor of student anxiety. Of all the Big five traits (McCrae & Costa, 2004), scores on neuroticism, which is, at its simplest, a tendency to be worry-prone, was the strongest predictor of anxiety in a study on 162 psychology students during the pandemic (Gibbons,

2022). It was the second largest predictor, after lack of motivation, of adverse mental health in a study with a different cohort (n=175) and in this same analysis, it was found to act as a mediator between the ratings given to support and anxiety (Gibbons, 2023a). Where participants rated the support from family and friends as, while well intentioned, a hassle, it was associated with anxiety, but this relationship was no longer significant when neuroticism was added. To explain, being high on neuroticism acts as an adaptive trait. It means one more readily tunes into potential threats and this can be pre-emptive in helping avoid threats where a fight or flight response is appropriate (Seligman, 1971). While adaptive and useful in responding to the stresses humans faced in their distant past, it comes at a cost to the individual where the stressor is recurring or omni-present, such as financial worries, relationship issues, assignment deadlines and exams. Those who are worry-prone more readily inflate the threat stress demands pose. In Gibbons' (2023b) mediation finding, the advice and support from well-intentioned family and friends becomes just another stressor if it is not helpful and for those already anxious, this may leave them struggling to cope and this can impact on their capacity to concentrate, problem-solve and study effectively (Eysenck et al, 2007). Letting your students know that almost all students do and, to grow, should, experience some anxiety, and that, for some, this will be higher, because of their personality tendency, will help. As will some of the evidence-based suggestions offered later in this chapter on how to cope better.

Ergene (2003), concluded from a meta-analysis of 77 studies (n=2,482), that students test anxiety was the second strongest predictor (after conscientiousness) of academic achievement and those high in neuroticism are more likely to experience this type of anxiety. In the same review, Ergene (2003) found that 4–6-hour anxiety reduction programmes reduced test anxiety with an effect size of d=-0.68 between pre and post programme test anxiety measures. This suggests that, for those anxious prone, there are ways in which this can be managed. It is also possible to manage this through other cognitive strategies, such as, through hardiness and defensive pessimism and both are outlined below.

Agreeableness and Conscientiousness

In Neves and Hewitt (2020) UK Student Academic Experience Survey (SAES), key predictors of course satisfaction pre-pandemic in 2019 (n=14,072) and during the pandemic in 2020 (n=10,227) were the level of challenge on the course, course organisation, the opportunity to interact with others, and student effort invested. The opportunity to interact may reflect the value of agreeableness and Gibbons (2023a) found it was associated with lower anxiety. While few studies that measure personality in students, find it a predictor of wellbeing, where it is, it may reflect the value of being non-confrontational, of fitting in, of being diplomatic. These are qualities that make it likely one can avoid or can diffuse interpersonal conflict, and they are attributes high in social desirability. We like more people who show these qualities, and this has dividends to self-esteem and mood.

This last finding, on student effort, reflects the importance of conscientiousness. In a learning context, conscientiousness refers to the tendency to be organized, disciplined, hard-working and achievement focused. In the same study, it was found to be the strongest predictor of course satisfaction (Gibbons, 2023a). In a separate analysis, Gibbons (2022) found that levels of conscientiousness buffered the impact of course-related stress on learning motivation. Using the hassle and uplifting scale outlined earlier, the more students rated teaching experience as a hassle, the more learning motivation declined, but for those high in conscientiousness, they reported the highest mean on learning motivation and the decline in motivation was negligible as hassle ratings increased. This was, in contrast, to those low in conscientiousness. For them, their learning motivation was lower and decline was steeper, as their experience of course-related hassles increased. Gibbons (2022) argued, it was unlikely to be conscientiousness alone that was at work. Rather, those students high in this trait were likely to be more responsive to the messages on how to study effectively. They honed their study skills, and this gave their conscientiousness teeth. Ergene (2003), concluded from a meta-analysis of 77 studies (n=2,482), that conscientiousness was the strongest predictor of academic achievement. In a systematic review of 38 meta-analyses, exploring the influence of 105 variables with a combined sample of almost two million students, conscientiousness had the largest absolute effect size on academic achievement (Schneider & Preckel, 2017). This was as strong an influence as intelligence was on students' academic achievement.

Context Control and Hardiness

Most research exploring the role of control, measures dispositional control, such as Rotter's (1966) locus of control. Context control is not dispositional control. It is a sense of control that is acquired by developing the skills needed in a particular context and for students this is done by honing their higher education study skills. It has been found, in several studies, to be a robust predictor of student mental health, motivation, and course satisfaction (e.g., Gibbons 2010, 2022, 2023a, 2024; Maddi, 2002, Maddi, Harvey, Khoshaba, Fazel & Resurreccion, 2009). Context control is similar to one of the key elements of hardiness. This concept was developed by Maddi (2002), and it contains three elements – control, commitment and challenge (the 3 Cs). These are qualities that can be adapted. They help buffer against the adverse effects of stress, and they help one adapt to change.

In a learning context, those high in commitment become more engaged in any activity they think might enhance their learning and understanding. They invest effort and are proactive and eager to expand their understanding. This supports Neves and Hewitt's (2020) SAES findings. Students high in commitment are proactive in learning and harnessing the skills or techniques or knowledge needed to learn. Those high in control make it a priority to identify the skills they need to master a learning situation and they do not avoid but faceup to the inevitable challenges in learning. Those high in challenge acknowledge that change and, with it, feelings of difficulty and some insecurity, are necessary to improve. They reframe the change the challenge poses, not as a 'threat' but as a necessary step to learning (Maddi, et al., 2009).

Academic hardiness is an adapted version of the original scale (Creed, Conlon & Dhaliwal, 2013). It measures how students react to academic demands and challenges. Maddi et al., (2009) offer evidence that those high in the 3Cs are more motivated in their learning and are higher in courage. This manifests, for example, in better stress management, social skills, diplomacy and conflict resolution and Maddi et al., (2009) see this as the basis for resilience and its effectiveness is supported by other research into academic hardiness in university students (Creed et al., 2013; Daneshamooz and Alamolhodaei, 2012; Spiridon & Evangelia, 2015).

In a survey of 184 second year psychology students, Gibbons (2024) found that hardiness-control was associated with low anxiety and hardiness-commitment was positively associated with high learning motivation. Such results suggest it is an effective coping strategy. One of the items on the scale states: 'If I get behind, I panic and feel ill'. This suggests it is a coping mechanism adopted as a compensation measure to manage the anxiety associated with feeling out of control when, for example, one falls behind in one's studies. It also measures a student's ability to bounce back from academic mistakes and to remain motivated in the face of disappointing results.

Hardiness-control is associated with higher class attendance, being diligent and pro-active in notetaking, in engaging with learning material and with an increased effort to try and master one's learning. It is reflected in not being held back by learning disappointments but instead, homing-in on what one can learn from feedback to improve in the next assessment (Creed et al., 2013; Daneshamooz & Alamolhodaei, 2012; Spiridon & Evangelia, 2015).

Gibbons' (2024) results point to the value for students in harnessing control, irrespective of where one would score on dispositional control i.e., hardiness-control measures a type of coping one can improve in. Indeed, it seems that those high on this type of control often develop it as a compensation to the anxiety triggered by feeling out of control. It should come as a consolation to students that experiences of feeling overwhelmed and out of control can trigger better coping.

EXTRAVERSION

Extraversion refers to a tendency to be sociable, outgoing and to have a preference for social interaction. It has been associated with elevated mood and lower anxiety (Kuijpers *et al.*, 2021). A meta-analysis review exploring the relationship between extraversion and wellbeing and positive affect, reported a substantial effect size of r=.44 (Steel, Schmidt & Shultz, 2008). Interestingly, Hudson and Fraley (2017) reported within-person correlations between extraversion and wellbeing i.e., repeated testing over time, and found that those who acted more extraverted reported improved wellbeing. As well as illustrating that extraverted behaviour is common in those who cope well, it suggests that it is an aspect of personality that is adaptable.

Several studies have attempted to get participants to act or fake being extraverted or introverted. McNiel, Lowman and Fleeson (2010) replicated earlier findings by Fleeson, Malanos and Achille, (2002) and McNiel and Fleeson (2006), with participant students asked to act extraverted or introverted in a ten-minute conversation. All those acting extraverted reported higher positive affect and, interestingly, this was irrespective of their baseline scores on trait extraversion. Jacques-Hamilton, Sun and Smillie, (2019) replicated the positive affect findings but with participants asked to act in a more extraverted way across a week, although they found the variance in positive affect was smaller when trait extraversion was controlled for.

Margolis and Lyubomirsky (2020) randomly assigned participants to fake being more extraverted over one week and more introverted over the next or vice versa They picked extraverted and introverted behaviours to fake that were similar in social desire-ability i.e., to fake being more talkative, assertive and spontaneous (extraversion) or deliberate, quiet and reserved (introversion) and they were given realistic scenarios in which they could do this, for example: 'When my friends are discussing something important to me, I will [will not] express my opinion'. They operationalized wellbeing as positive and negative affect, flow or performing optimally, competence, autonomy and connectedness. Significant main effects were found with positive affect, flow and connectedness for those faking extraversion and, like Jacques-Hamilton et al., (2019), this was most pronounced for those high in trait extraversion, i.e., where the behaviours they were asked to do matched or were similar to their existing personality, *but* there was a boost to wellbeing for all.

There are several factors that explain why extraverts cope better. They may physiologically have a higher threshold for change and for stress stimuli in general compared to introverts (Eysenck & Eysenck, 2013; Gray, 1970). They are more people-oriented and this means they tend to benefit more from support as a coping resource and because they cope better, they tend to interpret new stress demands, such as, for students, a disappointing teaching experience or a disappointing assignment result or a poor interactions with peers, as less threatening compared to those coping less well; and extraverted traits – being outgoing, sociable, people-orientated etc., tend to be seen, in the West at least, as more socially desirable and this boosts self-esteem.

When students give a presentation, they are faking extraversion. When they are asked to introduce themselves to their neighbour in class inductions, they are faking extraversion. With a little creativity, educators could introduce activities, taking just a few minutes, that require students to exhibit extraversion. A couple I use include asking all students to find someone they do not know in class and to tell them two things about themselves. One is true and one a lie, but they have to pass both off as true. Their partner must try and spot the lie. They then swap. Another is where I will get students to stand in two circles of equal size (it could be two lines depending on your teaching space). An inner circle facing out and outer circle facing in. Those in the outer circle 'interview' the person facing them, using the questions I show on the screen (what's your name, where are you from, what's your interests, are you working, where was your last holiday, where's your next? etc. And I ask them to close, saying something positive that they like about the one being interviewed). The interviewers are faking extraversion. I only give them a couple of minutes and will show them a two-minute gif clock on my PowerPoint. Then the inner circle moves one spot to the left and the exercise repeated. These activities get students networking in fun ways. Many will be being more extraverted than they would normally be but they know everyone is doing it so any awkwardness is shared and, in fact, dissipates almost instantly and the 'interviewers' are being extraverted just to one other person at a time.

SUPPORT

The value of support in coping is well established. One of the most cited models of stress is the Job-Demand-Control-Support model (Karasek & Theorell, 1990). It was originally called the Job-Demand-Control model (Karasek, 1979) and support was added because of the weight of evidence that it effectively reduced and buffered the individual against stress (Johnson & Hall,1988). Several types of support have been identified, each with particular benefits, including social support or the support that increases self-esteem; information and instrumental support or the support that can help one better understand and better solve a task or problem; and emotional support, where the need for validation and empathy are high. A common criticism across many studies measuring support is that they fail to distinguish the type of support being measured (Griva & Joekes, 2003). Karasek (1979) and Schachter (1959) argue that support is beneficial because humans are social animals and affiliation or the desire to be with others, is a basic human need i.e., support works, in part, because its absence is a source of distress for most, and it works because of those different goals support can help with, in terms of emotional needs, self-esteem, social comparison and information on how to cope.

Social support has been shown to buffer against stressful life events in students (Dollete & Phillips, 2004). Its absence is associated with depression in students (Alsubaie, Stain, Webster & Wadman, 2019; Bukhari & Afzal, 2017) and with poor quality of life (Dafaalla et al., 2016) and these findings have been supported by several systematic reviews, especially in terms of the buffering effect social support has on mental health (e.g. Chu, Saucier, & Hafner, 2010; Rueger, Malecki, Pyun, Aycock, & Coyle, 2016). University students satisfied with their levels of support report a more stable mood; report less stress and are more likely to be well-adjusted compared to those reporting lower support (Friedlander, Reid, Shupak, & Cribbie, 2007).

Measuring not just the different types of support but the different sources of support and measuring support as both a hassle, or where it acts as another stressor, and again as a uplift – where it helps, allows one to capture its more nuanced influence. Gibbons (2023) found, from a survey of 187 psychology students, that tutor support rated as a hassle predicted student anxiety. This replicated an earlier finding with 162 psychology students studying during the pandemic. However, in this analysis, this relationship was mediated by context control and by optimism. Those high in either of these mediators scored lower on hassle ratings towards tutor support and scored lower on anxiety. Both optimism and context control tend to be associated with good coping and are therefore associated with lower anxiety and when coping well disappointing experiences in support, for example, are reframed as less threatening. So, if support is limited or experienced as unhelpful, there are other strategies one can adopt. It is also possible that the support rated as a hassle was still good support and merely reflected the students' expectation and this may be misplaced if they are new to higher education or still adjusting to the demands of being an independent learner where tutor and lecturer support is typically more guidance oriented compared to the more directive approach more common from teachers in schools.

Similarly, in a survey of 187 psychology students, post pandemic, peer support rated as a hassle was associated with anxiety but this finding was mediated by measures on extraversion and neuroticism. Higher scores on extraversion were associated with lower hassle ratings for peer support. It is likely that those, more extraverted, coped better. They had a larger pool of support on which to draw and not just more support but more diverse support. So, if some peers were not particularly helpful, there were others one could turn to and, when coping well, new stress demands are perceived as less threatening. This may explain the negative relationship between extraversion and peer support rated as a hassle and extraversion and anxiety and the positive relationship when the mediator was neuroticism not extraversion.

Some studies identify both family and friends as important sources of support, as well as peer support. Support from family and friends tends to remain high in students in collectivist-oriented cultures. Awang et al., (2014), reported this finding in students studying in Malaysia but in both collectivist and especially in individualistic cultures, peer support is key and even more important than the support from lecturers, tutors and the wider university support structures (Bukhari & Afzal, 2017; Gibbons, 2009, Gibbons, 2010, 2022; Rueger, et al., 2016). This is likely to reflect the importance of peer influence during adolescence and this is the age cohort characteristic of most students tested. It is also the case that turning to one's peers may be easier than approaching lecturers. It may be that peers can offer an understanding or guidance that is simpler and easier to follow and chatting to student peers might be a means of resolving a learning issue before it has to be consciously recognised as particularly problematic and needing the help of tutors or lecturers.

Gibbons (2022, 2024) found that where students rated peer support as an uplift it was associated with higher learning motivation and wellbeing. Gibbons (2010) found, in a survey of nursing students (n=171), that the more peer support was rated as uplifting, the lower were scores on emotional exhaustion and where support was rated as a hassle it was a predictor of depersonalization. Interestingly, the same study found an interaction effect between support rated as a hassle and one's preference for support and personal achievement. It was not the case that support was good for you and its absence bad for you – which is the general message in the health psychology literature. Rather, if you had a strong *preference* for support and your experience of support was disappointing, this led to a steep decline in levels of personal achievement, but if you had a low preference for support, a disappointing support experience made no change in the levels of personal achievement. This highlights the importance of considering *individual factors* in how one copes – what might work for most students, support in this case, might not for all because some might have a preference for other ways of coping.

OPTIMISM AND PESSIMISM

Optimism refers to a cognitive bias in the expectation of success and in a tendency to reframe events and to recall them more positively. Optimists construe stress demands in a way that makes success more likely. They tend to perceive change and stress demands as opportunities to grow and achieve and good copers more frequently score stress demands as higher on uplifts and lower on hassles (Gibbons, 2010). They are biased to attend more to positive events over negative ones, especially when faced with circumstances outside their control (called defensive optimism), and they are more active in learning from their coping mistakes (Lazarus & Folkman, 1987).

Much has been made of the adverse impact social media use has on mental health, especially among adolescents (e.g. Twenge et al., 2022). Murray-Gibbons and Gibbons (2023) explored the role of optimism as a coping strategy. Others' lives on social media platforms are often illusionary – a highlight reel of what their real life is like. This is associated with lower self-esteem and higher anxiety for many users of social media. Murray-Gibbons and Gibbons (2023) found this was less so for optimists. They found that optimists tended to be on social media less and they tended to use more active commenting compared to the norm of scrolling and passive engagement. Just as optimists in real life, avoid toxic relationships and seek meaningful connections, so, too, do they on social media.

Optimism in students has been associated with motivation, performance and wellbeing (Cabras & Mondo, 2018; Seligman, 2008; Sharot, 2011). However, the research evidence is mixed. Some of the research evidence for optimism may mistake the effect for the cause – if one is successful, optimistic thinking will follow (the effect). Being optimistic is not a bias if it merely reflects past successes. This is called 'realistic optimism' and the cause of that success might relate to those cognitive biases and reframing tendencies characteristic of optimists and it could relate to any number of ingredients, such as the earlier evidence on control, confidence, and extraversion, all qualities which optimists tend to score higher on, and optimists, like extraverts, exhibit attributes that most people tend to like and they tend to have a great support network and it may be these factors that are critical to their success (Gibbons, 2023a).

There are negatives to optimism too – if one overestimates the likelihood of positive outcomes, disappointment will be experienced more and when positive outcomes occur, because they were expected, they will be enjoyed less (Bell, 1985). Pessimists do not experience this downside. For them, good outcomes are more enjoyable because they are unexpected and bad outcomes less disappointing because they were anticipated. There is a risk that low expectations may reinforce under-achievement, but Norem and Cantor (1986) offer evidence of circumstances where pessimism helps. They argue, for those anxious-prone and who have tended to do well, a more effective strategy, is defensive pessimism. This involves setting unrealistically low expectations in situations that cause you anxiety. Setting a high expectation of success could add to already heightened anxiety and inhibit performance, tipping you past the peak (B) to (C) in Figure 1.

Figure 1. The curvilinear relationship between anxiety and performance

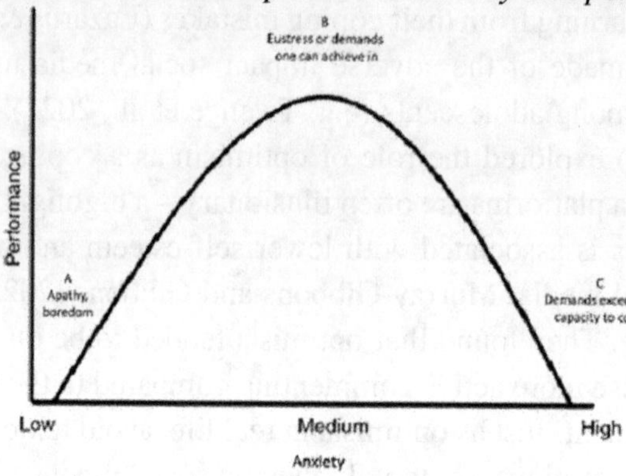

Gibbons (2023a) found, for example, that students high (in the upper quartile) on defensive pessimism *and* in anxiety and who had tended to achieve, were just as high in learning motivation compared to those high (in the upper quartile) on optimism and in a later replication, those high on defensive pessimism, compared to those high in optimism, were lower on anxiety, higher on course satisfaction and motivation (Gibbons, 2023b). Telling your students who have tended to do well but who are anxious and especially burdened by the stress of expecting success, to set the bar low may seem counter-intuitive but it is likely to help them optimise their performance.

COPING AND COGNITIVE STRATEGIES

Both optimists and extraverts tend to use other cognitive and emotional strategies. Those high in these traits tend to be more emotionally expressive and have higher self-confidence and there is efficacy for both of these attributes (Pennebaker, 2004; Gibbons & Morgan, 2015). Optimists tend to reframe threats as challenges and reframe failure or mistakes as opportunities to learn. They are higher in growth mindset, that ingredient mentioned earlier (Dweck, 2015; Lazarus & Folkman, 1987; Seligman, 2008).

In a survey on stress and coping in students, Gibbons (2024) found no support for optimism (remember, I said earlier that there tends to be a mixed picture on its efficacy in students) but scores on extraversion predicted lower anxiety and higher support. Those high (in the upper quartile) in extraversion were coping better and yet there was no difference in their learning motivation compared with those in the upper quartile on defensive pessimism.

In supporting the effectiveness of defensive pessimism, the study showed that those high in defensive pessimism were much higher in anxiety than those high in extraversion but there was no difference between these groups on learning motivation and defensive pessimism can be construed as a cognitive strategy – a way of reframing the threat posed by learning demands.

Rather than interpret personality qualities as dispositional attributes that cannot be changed, Seligman (2002) argues, for optimism for example, that it should be interpreted as an 'explanatory style' or a way of interpreting or reframing the challenges or stressors one faces. Similarly, Gibbons (2023a, 2024) argues that the success of those who cope well may have less to do with given personality qualities and more to do with underlying coping and cognitive strategies that tend to be used more by those high in extraversion or optimism or other traits. Gibbons (2024) compared those in the upper quartile on extraversion, against those in the lowest quartile (the introverts) and found that the extraverts were more likely to rate peer support as an uplift, more likely to practise self-forgiveness when they made mistakes; to employ defensive optimism, to reframe disappointments and mistakes, to be more emotionally expressive and to score higher on growth mindset. These are all *strategies* not traits. That is, they can be learnt and developed, and there is good evidence too that traits that we tend to think of as largely fixed, such as extraversion, can be adapted and even faked, to good effect.

SUGGESTIONS ON HELPING YOUR STUDENTS COPE BETTER

Levels of neuroticism among students is a strong predictor of anxiety but if one is to be open-minded and to grow, to go out of one's comfort zone and develop a deeper and fuller understanding, one has to face change and be willing to get it wrong. So, all students who want to grow will experience anxiety and some doubts over their competence. This may be especially challenging for those who start with a tendency to be worry-prone. Interestingly, the evidence suggests that those experiencing anxiety and helplessness are often motivated, precisely by that anxiety, to cope better. This could be done through a number of coping strategies, including developing hardiness and defensive pessimism and review evidence suggests that short anxiety reduction programmes are highly effective for students too and many students will develop their own mastery to manage their anxiety. Even just letting your students know at the start of their studies that varying experiences of doubt and uncertainty and anxiety is part of the journey in adjusting to becoming a student in higher education will help. It seems counterintuitive but to become a successful student it is the norm to go through periods where one feels unsuccessful.

Of all the attributes associated with success, including in academic achievement, motivation and general coping, conscientiousness is key. Those high in conscientiousness tend to be organized, disciplined, hard-working and achievement focused. It can also act as a buffer against stress demands on motivation. However, it is unlikely to drive these positive outcomes on its own. Those high in conscientiousness tend to be on the front foot in learning and mastering the study and time management skills needed to succeed in higher education. They tend to score higher in academic hardiness, in terms of commitment to the task, in embracing change as a challenge and in harnessing control in a learning context.

Students who exhibit extraverted tendencies tend to do well too, at least in terms of positive mood and lower anxiety. Conscientiousness tends to be the stronger influence on academic achievement, and extraversion on wellbeing and positive affect. The good news is that even faking extraversion in small and subtle ways, irrespective of one's trait measure on extraversion, has positive effects.

Acting in extraverted ways lowers anxiety and builds support. While those high in trait extraversion are likely to find this easier, it is relatively straightforward for all students to fake extraversion in small and subtle ways – to be proactive in saying hello to someone new, to make a point of saying three things in a group discussion, to thank someone for their help, to offer help, to set up a study buddy group or WhatsApp study group etc. and, as was illustrated earlier, educators should maximise ways to encourage students to feign being more extraverted in warm-up exercises and class activities.

Most students benefit from having a support network. However, some do not feel the need for a strong support network and still succeed. This is because they adopt some of the other qualities associated with good coping, but most students feel more connected, have a higher self-esteem and feel they benefit from the emotional and information support offered by other students. And it is peer support that is key. Family and friends and the university infrastructure of support is important and often more important for students from collectivist cultures, but even among these groups, peer support is important. Students with peer support have a better mood, lower depression and burn-out, better mental health, better quality of life and report lower attrition. Most programmes have students work in groups to utilise peer support. This can range from peer mentoring schemes, breakfast clubs, subject societies and socials, along with tutor-led and tutor absent, student-led tutorials. The degree to which students engage with peers is likely to play an important role in their success and wellbeing.

The picture is mixed on the benefits of levels of optimism in students. There is growing evidence of its efficacy in non-students but where we see evidence that it is a predictor, it may relate more to measures of realistic optimism (one's optimism merely reflects an accurate description of past success) and there is a downside in being or trying to be optimistic – expecting to do well in an assignment might just be adding pressure and that is not good if one is already feeling the pressure of study demands. If you have tended to do well in the past and you are feeling anxious, then setting the bar low on your expectations is unlikely to lead you to invest less effort but it will relieve you of that added stress that could push you passed that level of anxiety associated with optimal performance (the peak of our inverted U in Figure 1).

Arguably, key to student success is a set of cognitive and coping strategies that tend to be used more by students who are conscientiousness and often optimistic and often extraverted, but which are strategies that any student could adopt. These include making it a habit to reframe stressors – to reframe disappointments and critical feedback as learning steps towards success – you must get it wrong before you can get it right. This is the growth mindset. To use defensive pessimism, it is just another type of reframing; practice self-forgiveness or, more simply, be less hard on yourself when you do get a disappointing result. This self-compassion or self-forgiveness is characteristic in students who cope well. Allow the associated emotion with an assignment disappointment to be expressed and then focus on the one or two things you can learn from that feedback for the next assignment. If you are facing situations outside your control as a student, whether it is to do with your university experience or in your life outside university, then home-in on the small positives, the value of the positive relationships in your life, or the parts of the course you enjoy or the positives in your social life. We call this defensive optimism, and it works well when faced with circumstances outside our control. Students who cope well tend to be more emotionally expressive too. This can be outwardly, or it can be expressed privately in a journal or through some mix of the two. Students and educators, who invest 15-20 minutes in what Pennebaker (2004) calls expressive writing, which is essentially describing and then reframing emotional issues in one's life, report better psychological and physical health.

We are none of us that good that we cannot still improve, and the good news is that one need only make a few small changes in how you cope for that to reap large dividends in performance and wellbeing. This chapter offers a range of evidence-based strategies to improve coping and, while the focus of the chapter has been on student coping, the same ways of coping apply to educators too.

DISCUSSION QUESTIONS

1. What evidence-based strategies can educators implement to facilitate the development of effective coping mechanisms among students, particularly in relation to academic demands and the broader challenges of university life?
2. How does the bi-directional relationship between stressors, coping mechanisms, and well-being challenge traditional models of stress management, and what implications does this have for interventions aimed at supporting student mental health?
3. In what ways do personality traits, such as neuroticism, conscientiousness, extraversion or optimism, influence the effectiveness of student coping strategies, and how can educators tailor their support to accommodate individual differences in personality?
4. How does the concept of a growth mindset interact with feelings of vulnerability and imposter syndrome in students, and what pedagogical approaches can help mitigate these challenges while promoting resilience and achievement?
5. Given that peer support can function as both a source of stress and a critical coping resource, how can educational institutions design peer-based support systems that maximize positive outcomes for student well-being and academic performance?
6. How can educators incorporate cognitive strategies like defensive pessimism and reframing into academic curricula and classroom practices to foster more effective stress management and improve student performance and engagement?

RECOMMENDED READING

1. Michael Schneider and Franzis Preckel offer one of the most exhaustive reviews I have come across reviewing the key variables associated with success and academic achievement. It does not include in its review other important outcomes, like student mood, mental health or wellbeing, but pooling together the reviews and studies from across two decades and involving over two million students is impressive. The nature of such in-depth reviews, involving complex analyses, can make them hard to follow in places, but the take aways are clear and far more is offered in their paper than I was able to offer in this chapter. The paper if not open access but it can be requested from the authors through Research Gate: Schneider, M., & Preckel, F. (2017). Variables associated with achievement in higher education: A systematic review of meta-analyses. *Psychological bulletin, 143*(6), 565.

2. Stella Cottrell's Study skills handbook ranks as one of the best guides for supporting students as they transition and develop their higher education skill set. It covers preparing for university. Identifying and develop generic (such as e-learning and research skills) and more specific study skills (such as working with numbers and writing reports), along with important tips on developing critical thinking. Books, like this, that are often regularly updated, help students and educators keep abreast of key skills needed to succeed in higher education: Cottrell, S. (2024). *The study skills handbook*. Bloomsbury Publishing.
3. I have made a point of drawing attention to the paucity of research that adopts a positive psychology perspective towards stress and coping in higher education. There have been more extensive attempts to integrate positive psychology into schools and Martin Seligman and colleagues offer a review in its effectiveness in: Seligman, M. E., Ernst, R. M., Gillham, J., Reivich, K., & Linkins, M. (2009). Positive education: Positive psychology and classroom interventions. *Oxford review of education*, *35*(3), 293-311.
4. Lindsey Oades and colleagues show how this can be extended to the experience in university in: Oades, L. G., Robinson, P., Green, S., & Spence, G. B. (2014). Towards a positive university. In *Positive psychology in higher education* (pp. 5-12). Routledge.
5. Finally, as educators, we need to emphasise the importance of critical thinking in our students and we must apply this to our own efforts to understand theory and research. For that reason, I want to close with a counterbalance to the focus positive psychologists puts on optimistic thinking and recommend Julie Norem's work. There are several papers you could choose from. The following is just one and all the recommendations here are available through open access sources: Norem, J. K. (2008). Defensive pessimism, anxiety, and the complexity of evaluating self-regulation. *Social and Personality Psychology Compass*, *2*(1), 121-134.

This chapter complements Chapter 7 in this text. If you are interested in coping with stress, you should read Chapter 7 to give you the foundation on what stress is, its sources and the effects of stress in students.

REFERENCES

Alsubaie, M. M., Stain, H. J., Webster, L. A. D., & Wadman, R. (2019). The role of sources of social support on depression and quality of life for university students. *International Journal of Adolescence and Youth, 24*(4), 484–496.

Awang, M. M., Kutty, F. M., & Ahmad, A. R. (2014). Perceived social support and well-being: First-year student experience in university. *International Education Studies*, *7*(13). Advance online publication. DOI: 10.5539/ies.v7n13p261

Bell, D. E. (1985). Disappointment in decision making under uncertainty. *Operations Research, 33*, 1–27.

Bukhari, S. R., & Afzal, F. (2017). Perceived social support predicts psychological problems among university students. *International Journal of Indian Psychology, 4*(2), 2349–3429.

Cabras, C., & Mondo, M. (2018). Coping strategies, optimism, and life satisfaction among first-year university students in Italy: Gender and age differences. *Higher Education*, *75*, 643–654.

Chu, P. S., Saucier, D. A., & Hafner, E. (2010). Meta-analysis of the relationships between social support and wellbeing in children and adolescents. *Journal of Social and Clinical Psychology*, *29*(6), 624–645.

Creed, P. A., Conlon, E. G., & Dhaliwal, K. (2013). Revisiting the academic hardiness scale: Revision and revalidation. *Journal of Career Assessment*, *21*(4), 537–554.

Dafaalla, M., Farah, A., Bashir, S., Khalil, A., Abdulhamid, R., Mokhtar, M., & Abdalrahman, I. (2016). Depression, anxiety, and stress in Sudanese medical students: A cross-sectional study on role of quality of life and social support. *American Journal of Educational Research*, *4*(13). https://pubs.sciepub.com/education/4/13/4

Daneshamooz, S., & Alamolhodaei, H. (2012). Cooperative learning and academic hardiness on students' mathematical performance with different levels of mathematics anxiety. *Educational Research*, *3*(3), 270–276.

Dollete, S., & Phillips, M. (2004). Understanding girls' circle as an intervention on perceived social support, body image, self-efficacy, locus of control and self-esteem. *The Journal of Psychology*, *90*(2), 204–215.

Dweck, C. (2015). Carol Dweck revisits the growth mindset. *Education Week*, *35*(5), 20–24.

Ergene, T. (2003). Effective interventions on test anxiety reduction: A meta-analysis. *School Psychology International, 24*, 313–328. DOI: 10.1177/01430343030243004

Eysenck, H. J., & Eysenck, S. B. (2013). The biological basis of personality. In *Personality Structure and Measurement (Psychology Revivals)* (pp. 49-62). Routledge.

Eysenck, M. W., Derakshan, N., Santos, R., & Calvo, M. G. (2007). Anxiety and cognitive performance: Attentional control theory. *Emotion (Washington, D.C.), 7*(2), 336. DOI: 10.1037/1528-3542.7.2.336 PMID: 17516812

Fleeson, W., Malanos, A. B., & Achille, N. M. (2002). An intraindividual process approach to the relationship between extraversion and positive affect: Is acting extraverted as "good" as being extraverted? *Journal of Personality and Social Psychology, 83*, 1409–1422. PMID: 12500821

Friedlander, L. J., Reid, G. J., Shupak, N., & Cribbie, R. (2007). Social support, self-esteem, and stress as predictors of adjustment to university among first-year undergraduates. *Journal of College Student Development, 48*(3), 259–274.

Gibbons, C. (2009). The two sides of stress. *Nursing Standard, 23*(44), 61.

Gibbons, C. (2010). Stress, coping and burn-out in nursing students. *International Journal of Nursing Studies*, (47), 1299–1309. PMID: 20359710

Gibbons, C. (2022). Understanding the role of stress, personality and coping on learning motivation and mental health in university students during a pandemic. *BMC Psychology, 10*(1), 261. DOI: 10.1186/s40359-022-00971-w PMID: 36357950

Gibbons, C. (2023a). Untangling the role of optimism, pessimism and coping influences on student mood, motivation and satisfaction. *Innovations in Education and Teaching International*. Advance online publication. DOI: 10.1080/14703297.2023.2260780

Gibbons, C. (2023b). Surviving a pandemic - Understanding the role of student stress, personality and coping on course satisfaction and anxiety during lockdown. *Innovations in Education and Teaching International, 60*, 463–475. https://www.tandfonline.com/doi/full/10.1080/14703297.2022.2064326

Gibbons, C. (2024). Not just surviving, but flourishing – insights into student coping, anxiety and motivation. DOI: 10.21203/rs.3.rs-4177097/v1

Gibbons, C. & Morgan, H. (2015) Mindfulness - As a coping strategy, *Eisteach - The Irish Journal of Counselling and Psychotherapy, 15*(2), 14-18.

Gray, J. A. (1970). The psychophysiological basis of introversion-extraversion. *Behaviour Research and Therapy, 8*(3), 249–266. PMID: 5470377

Griva, K., & Joekes, K. (2003). UK Teachers Under Stress: Can we predict wellness on the basis of characteristics of the teaching job? *Psychology & Health, 18*, 457–471.

Hudson, N. W., & Fraley, R. C. (2017). Volitional personality change. In Specht, J. (Ed.), *Personality development across the lifespan* (pp. 555–571). Elsevier.

Jacques-Hamilton, R., Sun, J., & Smillie, L. D. (2019). Costs and benefits of acting extraverted: A randomized controlled trial. *Journal of Experimental Psychology. General, 148*(9), 1538. PMID: 30489119

Johnson, J. V., & Hall, E. M. (1988). Job strain, work place social support, and cardiovascular disease: A cross-sectional study of a random sample of the Swedish working population. *American Journal of Public Health, 78*, 1336–1342. PMID: 3421392

Karasek, R., & Theorell, T. (1990). *Healthy Work: Stress, Productivity, and the Reconstruction of Working Life*. Basic Books.

Karasek, R. A. (1979). Job demands, job decision latitude and mental strain: Implications for job redesign. *Administrative Science Quarterly, 24*, 285–308.

Kuijpers, E., Pickett, J., Wille, B., & Hofmans, J. (2021). Do you feel better when you behave more extraverted than you are? The relationship between cumulative counterdispositional extraversion and positive feelings. *Personality and Social Psychology Bulletin*. Advance online publication. PMID: 34056978

Lazarus, R. S., & Folkman, S. (1987). Transactional theory and research on emotions and coping. *European Journal of Personality, 1*(3), 141–169. DOI: 10.1002/per.2410010304

Lipson, S., & Eisenberg, D. (2018). Mental health and academic attitudes and expectations in university populations: Results from the healthy minds study. *Journal of Mental Health (Abingdon, England), 27*(3), 205–213. DOI: 10.1080/09638237.2017.1417567 PMID: 29265935

Mackaskill, A. (2018). Undergraduate mental health issues: The challenge of the second year of study. *Journal of Mental Health (Abingdon, England)*. Advance online publication. DOI: 10.1080/09638237.2018.1437611 PMID: 29429365

Maddi, S. R. (2002). The story of hardiness: Twenty years of theorizing, research, and practice. *Consulting Psychology Journal, 54*(3), 173–185.

Maddi, S. R., Harvey, R. H., Khoshaba, D. M., Fazel, M., & Resurreccion, N. (2009). Hardiness training facilitates performance in college. *The Journal of Positive Psychology, 4*(6), 566–577.

Margolis, S., & Lyubomirsky, S. (2020). Experimental manipulation of extraverted and introverted behavior and its effects on wellbeing. *Journal of Experimental Psychology. General, 149*(4), 719. PMID: 31368759

McCrae, R. R., & Costa, P. T. (2004). A contemplated revision of the Neo Five-Factor inventory. *Personality and Individual Differences, 36*(3), 587–596.

McIntyre, , Worsley, Corcoran, Woods, & Bentall. (2018). Academic and Non-Academic Predictors of Student Psychological Distress: The Role of Social Identity and Loneliness. *Journal of Mental Health (Abingdon, England), 27*(3), 230–239. DOI: 10.1080/09638237.2018.1437608 PMID: 29436883

McNiel, J. M., & Fleeson, W. (2006). The causal effects of extraversion on positive affect and neuroticism on negative affect: Manipulating state extraversion and state neuroticism in an experimental approach. *Journal of Research in Personality, 40*, 529–550.

McNiel, J. M., Lowman, J. C., & Fleeson, W. (2010). The effect of state extraversion on four types of affect. *European Journal of Personality, 24*, 18–35.

Murray-Gibbons, , SGibbons, , C. (2023). Revealing the Complex Relationship between Social Media use, Social Comparison Orientation and Optimism on Health Outcomes. *Psychology & Behavioral Sciences International Journal 21*(2): 556057. DOI: 10.19080/PBSIJ.2023.20.556057

Neves, J., & Hewitt, R. (2020). *Student academic experience survey*. Higher Education Policy Institute.

Norem, J., & Cantor, N. (1986). Defensive pessimism: Harnessing anxiety as motivation. *Journal of Personality and Social Psychology, 51*(6), 1208. PMID: 3806357

Parkman, A. (2016). The imposter phenomenon in higher education: Incidence and impact. *Journal of Higher Education Theory and Practice, 16*(1).

Pennebaker, J. W. (2004). Theories, therapies, and taxpayers: On the complexities of the expressive writing paradigm. *Clinical Psychology : a Publication of the Division of Clinical Psychology of the American Psychological Association, 11*(2), 138–142.

Rotter, J. B. (1966). Generalized expectancies for internal versus external control of reinforcement. *Psychological Monographs, 80*(1), 1. PMID: 5340840

Rueger, S. Y., Malecki, C. K., Pyun, Y., Aycock, C., & Coyle, S. (2016). A meta-analytic review of the association between perceived social support and depression in childhood and adolescence. *Psychological Bulletin, 142*(10), 1017–1067. PMID: 27504934

Schachter, S. (1959). The psychology of affiliation: Experimental studies of the sources of gregariousness. Academic Press.

Schneider, M., & Preckel, F. (2017). Variables associated with achievement in higher education: A systematic review of meta-analyses. *Psychological Bulletin, 143*(6), 565. PMID: 28333495

Seligman, M. E. (1971). Phobias and preparedness. *Behavior Therapy*, 2(3), 307–320. PMID: 27816071

Seligman, M. E. (2002). Positive psychology, positive prevention, and positive therapy. *Handbook of positive psychology,* 2(2002), 3-12.

Seligman, M. E. (2008). Positive health. *Applied Psychology, 57*(s1), 3–18. .1464-0597.2008.00351.xDOI: 10.1111/j

Sharot, T. (2011). The optimism bias. *Current Biology*, *21*, R941–R945. PMID: 22153158

Spiridon, K., & Evangelia, K. (2015). Exploring relationships between academic hardiness, academic stressors and achievement in university undergraduates. *Journal of Applied Educational and Policy Research*, *1*(1), 53–73. DOI: 10.7897/2277-4343.04135

Steel, P., Schmidt, J., & Shultz, J. (2008). Refining the relationship between personality and subjective wellbeing. *Psychological Bulletin*, *134*(1), 138. PMID: 18193998

Twenge, J. M., Haidt, J., Lozano, J., & Cummins, K. M. (2022). Specification curve analysis shows that social media use is linked to poor mental health, especially among girls. *Acta psychologica, 224*, 103512.

Vollrath, M., & Torgersen, S. (2000). Personality types and coping. *Personality and Individual Differences*, *29*(2), 367–378.

Compilation of References

Abdelnoor, A., & Hollins, S. (2004). The effect of childhood bereavement on secondary school performance. *Educational Psychology in Practice*, *20*(1), 43–54.

Abrams, Z. (2023). AI is changing every aspect of psychology. Here's what to watch for. *Monitor on Psychology*, *54*(4), 46.

ACLU. (2022). *Algorithms Are Making Decisions About Health Care, Which May Only Worsen Medical Racism.* https://www.aclu.org/news/privacy-technology/algorithms-in-health-care-may-worsen-medical-racism.

Adams, H., Blackburn, S., & Mantovani, N. (2021). Psychological resilience for climate change transformation: Relational, differentiated and situated perspectives. *Current Opinion in Environmental Sustainability*, *50*, 303–309. DOI: 10.1016/j.cosust.2021.06.011

Adebäck, P., Lundh, L., & Nilsson, D. (2022). Children or adolescents who lost someone close during the Southeast Asia tsunami 2004 - The life as young. *Brain and Behavior*, *12*(5), e2563. DOI: 10.1002/brb3.2563 PMID: 35333453

Adlaf, E. M., Demers, A., & Gliksman, L. (2000). *Canadian campus survey 2004.* Centre for Addiction and Mental Health.

Akram, H., Abdelrady, A. H., Al-Adwan, A. S., & Ramzan, M. (2022). Teachers' perceptions of technology integration in teaching-learning practices: A systematic review. *Frontiers in Psychology*, *13*, 920317.

Al-Ansi, A. M., Jaboob, M., Garad, A., & Al-Ansi, A. (2023). Analyzing augmented reality (AR) and virtual reality (VR) recent development in education. *Social Sciences & Humanities Open*, *8*(1), 100532.

Ali, S. S. (2021). Florida Board of Education passes rule banning critical race theory in classrooms. NBC News, 10/6/2021. https://www.nbcnews.com/news/us-news/florida-board-education-passes-rule-banning-critical-race-theory-classrooms-n1270363

Alsubaie, M. M., Stain, H. J., Webster, L. A. D., & Wadman, R. (2019). The role of sources of social support on depression and quality of life for university students. *International Journal of Adolescence and Youth, 24*(4), 484–496.

Alvis, L., Zhang, N., Sandler, I. N., & Kaplow, J. B. (2022). Developmental Manifestations of Grief in Children and Adolescents: Caregivers as Key Grief Facilitators. *Journal of Child & Adolescent Trauma, 16*(2), 447–457. DOI: 10.1007/s40653-021-00435-0 PMID: 35106114

American Psychiatric Association. (2000). Diagnostic and statistical manual of mental disorders (4th ed., text rev.; DSM-IV-TR). American Psychiatric Publishing.

American Psychological Association. (2022). Definition of Psychology. https://dictionary.apa.org/psychology

Amri, A., Bird, D. K., Ronan, K., Haynes, K., & Towers, B. (2017). Disaster risk reduction education in Indonesia: Challenges and recommendations for scaling up. *Natural Hazards and Earth System Sciences, 17*(4), 595–612. DOI: 10.5194/nhess-17-595-2017

Anda, R. F., Porter, L. E., & Brown, D. W. (2020). Inside the adverse childhood experience score: Strengths, limitations, and misapplications. *American Journal of Preventive Medicine*. PMID: 32222260

Anderson, D., Gau, J., Beck, L., Unruh, D., Gioia, G., McCart, M., & Glang, A. (2021). Management of return to school following brain injury: An evaluation model. *International Journal of Educational Research*, 108. PMID: 33927471

Andersson, K., Bellon, M., & Walker, R. (2016). Parents' experiences of their child's return to school following acquired brain injury (ABI): A systematic review of qualitative studies. *Brain Injury : [BI], 30*(7), 829–838. PMID: 27057776

Andrews, B., & Wilding, J. M. (2004). The relation of depression and anxiety to life-stress and achievement in students. *British Journal of Psychology, 95*(Pt 4), 509–521.

Armstrong, D. (2018). Addressing the wicked problem of behaviour in schools. *International Journal of Inclusive Education, 22*(9), 997–1013. DOI: 10.1080/13603116.2017.1413732

Aronson, B. A. (2017). The White Savior Industrial Complex: A Cultural Studies Analysis of a Teacher Educator, Savior Film, and Future Teachers. *Journal of Critical Thought and Praxis, 6*(3).

Artino, A. R. (2012). Academic self-efficacy: From educational theory to instructional practice. *Perspectives on Medical Education, 1*, 76–85. DOI: 10.1007/s40037-012-0012-5

Ash, K., & Obradovich, N. (2020). Climatic stress, internal migration, and Syrian civil war onset. *The Journal of Conflict Resolution, 64*(1), 3–31. DOI: 10.1177/0022002719864140

Ashour, S. (2020). How technology has shaped university students' perceptions and expectations around higher education: An exploratory study of the United Arab Emirates. *Studies in Higher Education, 45*(12), 2513–2525.

Aslan, C. (2017). Examining Epistemological Beliefs of Teacher Candidates According to Various Variables'. *Eurasian Journal of Educational Research, 17*(67), 37–50. DOI: 10.14689/ejer.2017.67.3

Assadi, F. (2023). Understanding the Childhood Grief: What Should We Tell the Children? *International Journal of Preventive Medicine, 14*, 96. DOI: 10.4103/ijpvm.ijpvm_371_22 PMID: 37855003

Astvik, W., Welander, J., & Larsson, R. (2020). Reasons for staying: A longitudinal study of work conditions predicting social workers' willingness to stay in their organisation. *British Journal of Social Work, 50*(5), 1382–1400.

Audrin, C., & Audrin, B. (2022). Key factors in digital literacy in learning and education: A systematic literature review using text mining. *Education and Information Technologies, 27*(6), 7395–7419.

Avci, H., Baams, L., & Kretschmer, T. (2024). A systematic review of social media use and adolescent identity development. *Adolescent Research Review*, 1–18.

Avery, J., Morris, H., Galvin, E., Misso, M., Savaglio, M., & Skouteris, H. (2021). Systematic review of school-wide trauma-informed approaches. *Journal of Child & Adolescent Trauma, 14*, 381–197. PMID: 34471456

Awang, M. M., Kutty, F. M., & Ahmad, A. R. (2014). Perceived social support and well-being: First-year student experience in university. *International Education Studies, 7*(13). Advance online publication. DOI: 10.5539/ies.v7n13p261

Azorín, C., & Ainscow, M. (2020). Guiding Schools on Their Journey Towards Inclusion. *International Journal of Inclusive Education, 24*(1), 58–76.

Back, L., Bennett, A., Edles, L. D., Gibson, M., Inglis, D., Jacobs, R., & Woodward, I. (2012). *Cultural sociology: an introduction*. Wiley-Blackwell.

Baik, C., Naylor, R., & Arkoudis, S. (2015). *The first year experience in Australian universities: Findings from two decades*. Melbourne Centre for the Study of Education.

Baker, C., Clayton, S., & Bragg, E. (2021). Educating for resilience: Parent and teacher perceptions of children's emotional needs in response to climate change. *Environmental Education Research, 27*(5), 687–705. DOI: 10.1080/13504622.2020.1828288

Ball, H., & Howe, J. (2013). How can educational psychologists support the reintegration of children with an acquired brain injury upon their return to school? *Educational Psychology in Practice, 29*(1), 69–78.

Ball, S. J. (2012). *Global education Inc.: New policy networks and the neo-liberal imaginary*. Routledge.

Bandura, A. (1994). Self-efficacy. Encyclopedia of human behavior, 4(4), 71-81.

Bandura, A. (1977). *Social learning theory*. Prentice Hall.

Bandura, A. (1986). *Social foundations of thought and action: A social cognitive theory*. Prentice Hall.

Bandura, A. (1997). *Self-efficacy: The exercise of control*. Freeman.

Barnes, C. (2018). Theories of disability and the origins of the oppression of disabled people in western society. In *Disability and society* (pp. 43–60). Routledge.

Barry, M., Mallon, B., Bourke, A., Usher, J., & Daly, A. (2023). *Teachers and Global Citizenship Education: Values, Attitudes and Practices A Research Report on a National Survey of Irish Primary Teachers and Global Citizenship Education*. Global Village.

Bartholomew, K. J., Ntoumanis, N., Cuevas, R., & Lonsdale, C. (2014). Job pressure and ill-health in physical education teachers: The mediating role of psychological need thwarting. *Teaching and Teacher Education, 37*, 101–107. DOI: 10.1016/j.tate.2013.10.006

Barton, L. (1996). Sociology and disability: some emerging issues. In Barton, L. (Ed.), *Disability and Society: emerging issues and insights*. Longman.

Barton, L. (2002). Inclusive Education and the Management of Change in Britain. *Exceptionality Education Canada, 12*, 169–185.

Bastani, H., Bastani, O., Sungu, A., Ge, H., Kabakcı, O., & Mariman, R. 2024. Generative ai can harm learning. Available at *SSRN*, 4895486.

Bate, C., Turner, K., & Fricke, S. (2021). Return to school after acquired brain injury in the UK: The educators' perspectives. *Journal of Research in Special Educational Needs, 21*(3), 242–253.

Baumann, L., & Brütt, A. (2021). Public and patient involvement (PPI) in health policy decisionmaking on the health system-level: Protocol for a systematic scoping review. *BMJ Open, 11*(5). PMID: 34011588

Bayram, N., & Bilgel, N. (2008). The prevalence and socio-demographic correlations of depression, anxiety and stress among a group of university students. *Social Psychiatry and Psychiatric Epidemiology, 43*(8), 667–672. PMID: 18398558

Bell, D. E. (1985). Disappointment in decision making under uncertainty. *Operations Research, 33*, 1–27.

Bellis, M. A., Hughes, K., Ford, K., Ramos Rodriguez, G., Sethi, D., & Passmore, J. (2019). Life course health consequences and associated annual costs of adverse childhood experiences across Europe and North America: A systematic review and meta-analysis. *Lancet*, 4. PMID: 31492648

Belsky, J. (1984). The determinants of parenting. *Child Development, 55*(1), 83–96. PMID: 6705636

Bennett, E., Fletcher, A., Talbot, E., & Robinson, L. (2023). Returning to education after childhood acquired brain injury: Learning from lived parental experience. *NeuroRehabilitation, 52*, 625–640. PMID: 37125567

Berger, P. L., & Luckmann, T. (1966). The Social Construction of Reality: A Treatise in the Sociology of Knowledge. Academic Press.

Berg, L., Rostila, M., & Hjern, A. (2016). Parental death during childhood and depression in young adults - a national cohort study. *Journal of Child Psychology and Psychiatry, and Allied Disciplines, 57*(9), 1092–1098. DOI: 10.1111/jcpp.12560 PMID: 27058980

Blad, E. (2015). Educators often overlook student grief, experts say. *Education Week, 34*(18), 1, 12–13.

Blanco, C., Okuda, M., Wright, C., Hasin, D. S., Grant, B. F., Liu, S. M., & Olfson, M. (2008). Mental health of college students and their non–college-attending peers: Results from the national epidemiologic study on alcohol and related conditions. *Archives of General Psychiatry, 65*(12), 1429–1437. DOI: 10.1001/archpsyc.65.12.1429 PMID: 19047530

Blaustein, M. E., & Kinniburgh, K. M. (2019). *Treating traumatic stress in children and adolescents* (2nd ed.). The Guildford Press.

Bloom, S. L. (2013). *Creating sanctuary: Toward the evolution of sane societies* (2nd ed.). Routledge.

Boelen, P. A., Giannopoulou, I., & Papadatou, D. (2023). Patterns and predictive value of acute prolonged grief and posttraumatic stress in youngsters confronted with traumatic loss: A latent class analysis. *Psychiatry Research, 319*, 114961. DOI: 10.1016/j.psychres.2022.114961 PMID: 36446220

Boluda-Verdu, I., Senent-Valero, M., Casas-Escolano, M., Matijasevich, A., & Pastor-Valero, M. (2022). Fear for the future: Eco-anxiety and health implications, a systematic review. *Journal of Environmental Psychology, 84*, 101904. DOI: 10.1016/j.jenvp.2022.101904

Bombèr, L. M. (2007). *Inside I'm hurting: practical strategies for supporting children with attachment difficulties in schools*. Worth.

Bond, M., Buntins, K., Bedenlier, S., Zawacki-Richter, O., & Kerres, M. (2020). Mapping research in student engagement and educational technology in higher education: A systematic evidence map. *International Journal of Educational Technology in Higher Education, 17*, 1–30.

Borsay, A. (2006). Personal trouble or public issue? Towards a model of policy for people with physical and mental disabilities. In Barton, L. (Ed.), *Overcoming disabling barriers: 18 years of Disability & society*. Routledge.

Bourke, A., Jabbour, S., Martin, A., Walsh, L., & Hadfield, K. (2024). A Review of Climate Change Attitudes Using a Person-Centred Framework. EPA Research Report.

Bourque, F., & Cunsolo Willox, A. (2014). Climate change: The next challenge for public mental health? *International Review of Psychiatry (Abingdon, England), 26*(4), 415–422. DOI: 10.3109/09540261.2014.925851

Bowlby, J. (1977). The making and breaking of affectional bonds: I. Aetiology and psychopathology in the light of attachment theory. *The British Journal of Psychiatry, 130*(3), 201–210. DOI: 10.1192/bjp.130.3.201

Bowles, A., Fisher, R., McPhail, R., Rosenstreich, D., & Dobson, A. (2014). Staying the Distance: Students' Perceptions of Enablers of Transition to Higher Education. *Higher Education Research & Development, 33*(2), 212–225. DOI: 10.1080/07294360.2013.832157

Boylan, M., Truelove, L., Pearse, S., O'Brien, S., Sheehan, H., Cowell, T., & Long, E. (2023). Developing trauma-informed teacher education in England. *London Review of Education, 21*(1), 29. Advance online publication. DOI: 10.14324/LRE.21.1.29

Bragg, L., Walsh, C., & Heyeres, M. (2021). Successful design and delivery of online professional development for teachers: A systematic review of the literature. *Computers & Education, 166*(6).

Braghieri, L., Levy, R. E., & Makarin, A. (2022). Social media and mental health. *The American Economic Review, 112*(11), 3660–3693.

Brain Injury Association of America. (n.d.). *What is the difference between an acquired brain injury and a traumatic brain injury?* Retrieved from https://www.biausa.org/brain-injury/about-brain-injury/nbiic/what-is-the-difference-between-an-acquired-brain-injury-and-a-traumatic-brain-injury

Brain Injury Center. (2021, July 18). *Brain Injury Center.* Retrieved from Choosing the Right ssistive Technology for Children: https://www.braininjurycenter.org/blog/?article=81

Brame, C. J. (2016). Effective educational videos: Principles and guidelines for maximizing student learning from video content. *CBE Life Sciences Education, 15*(4), es6. Advance online publication. DOI: 10.1187/cbe.16-03-0125

Brewer, M. B., & Roccas, S. (2015). Individual values, social identity, and optimal distinctiveness. In *Individual self, relational self, collective self* (pp. 219–237). Psychology Press.

Brewster, L., Jones, E., Priestley, M., Wilbraham, S. J., Spanner, L., & Hughes, G. (2022). 'Look after the staff and they would look after the students' cultures of wellbeing and mental health in the university setting. *Journal of Further and Higher Education, 46*(4), 548–560. DOI: 10.1080/0309877X.2021.1986473

Brighouse, T., & Waters, M. (2022). *About Our Schools: Improving on Previous Best.* Crown House Publishing.

Brinkmann, S. (2019). Learning to grieve: A preliminary analysis. *Culture and Psychology, 26*(3), 469–483. DOI: 10.1177/1354067x19877918

Britzman, D. P. (1998). *Lost subjects, contested objects: Toward a psychoanalytic inquiry of learning.* State University of New York Press.

Broberg, A., Dyregrov, A., & Lilled, L. (2005). The Göteborg discotheque fire: Posttraumatic stress, and school adjustment as reported by the primary victims 18 months later. *Journal of Child Psychology and Psychiatry, and Allied Disciplines*, *46*(12), 1279–1286. PMID: 16313428

Brock University and Ontario Brain Injury Association. (2014). *Educating Educators about ABI* (5th ed.). Brock University and Ontario Brain Injury Association.

Broglia, E., Millings, A., & Barkham, M. (2017). Challenges to Addressing Student Mental Health in Embedded Counselling Services: A Survey of UK Higher and Further Education Institutions. *British Journal of Guidance & Counselling*, *46*(4), 441–445. DOI: 10.1080/03069885.2017.1370695

Bronfe Brenner, U. (1989). Ecological systems theory. In R. Vasta (Ed.), Annals of child development (Vol. 6, pp. 187–249). JAI Press.

Bronfenbrenner, U. (1979). *The ecology of human development*. Harvard university press.

Bronfenbrenner, U. (1979). *The ecology of human development: Experiments by nature and design*. Harvard University Press.

Bronfenbrenner, U. (2005). Making human beings human: Bioecological perspectives on human development. *Sage (Atlanta, Ga.)*.

Brosch, T. (2021). Affect and emotions as drivers of climate change perception and action: A review. *Current Opinion in Behavioral Sciences*, *42*, 15–21. DOI: 10.1016/j.cobeha.2021.02.001

Brown, A. (2013). Waiting for Superwoman: White female teachers and the construction of the" neoliberal savior"" in a New York City public school. *The Journal for Critical Education Policy Studies*, *11*(2).

Brown, J. S. (2018). Student mental health: Some answers and more questions. *Journal of Mental Health (Abingdon, England)*, *27*(3), 193–196. DOI: 10.1080/09638237.2018.1470319 PMID: 29768071

Brownlee, J., Schraw, G., & Berthelsen, D. (2012). *Personal epistemology and teacher education*. Routledge.

Bruner, J. S. (1966). *Toward a theory of instruction*. Norton.

Bryan, A. (2023). Pedagogy of the implicated (subject): Slantwise pedagogical encounters with difficult ecological knowledge. In B. Mallon, F. Waldron & C. Ní Cassaithe (Eds.), *Pushing the boundaries of human rights education: Concepts, challenges and contexts* (pp. 98-115). Routledge.

Bryan, A., & Mochizuki, Y. (2024). Rethinking agency, affect, and education: Towards new childhood and youth studies in the Anthropocene. In Wyn, J., Cahill, H., & Cuervo, H. (Eds.), *Springer Handbook of Children and Youth Studies.*

Buckeridge, K., Clarke, C., & Sellers, D. (2019). Research Report: Adolescents' experiences of communication following acquired brain injury. *International Journal of Language & Communication Disorders, 00*(0), 1–13.

Budiyanto, , Sheehy, K., Kaye, H., & Rofiah, K. (2017). Developing Signalong Indonesia: Issues of happiness and pedagogy, training and stigmatisation. *International Journal of Inclusive Education.* Advance online publication. DOI: 10.1080/13603116.2017.1390000

Buehl, M. M., & Alexander, P. A. (2005). 'Motivation and Performance Differences in Students' Domain-Specific Epistemological Belief Profiles'. *American Educational Research Journal, 42*(4), 697–726. DOI: 10.3102/00028312042004697

Bukhari, S. R., & Afzal, F. (2017). Perceived social support predicts psychological problems among university students. *International Journal of Indian Psychology, 4*(2), 2349–3429.

Bureau, J. S., Howard, J. L., Chong, J. X. Y., & Guay, F. (2022). Pathways to student motivation: A meta-analysis of antecedents of autonomous and controlled motivations. *Review of Educational Research, 92*(1), 46–72. DOI: 10.3102/00346543211042426

Burgstahler, S. (2007). Who needs an accessible classroom? *Academe, 93*(3), 37–39. Retrieved September 24, 2024, from https://www.jstor.org/stable/40253051

Burke, N. J., Hellman, J. L., Scott, B. G., Weems, C. F., & Carrion, V. G. (2011). The impact of adverse childhood experiences on an urban pediatric population. *Child Abuse & Neglect, 35*, 408–413. PMID: 21652073

Burke, S. E., Sanson, A. V., & Van Hoorn, J. (2018). The psychological effects of climate change on children. *Current Psychiatry Reports, 20*, 1–8. DOI: 10.1007/s11920-018-0896-9

Burner, Nodeland, & Aamaas. (2018). Critical Perspectives on Perceptions and Practices of Diversity in Education. Academic Press.

Byrne, A. (2022). Care and Capitalism: Why Affective Equality Matters for Social Justice. *Journal of Political Power, 15*(3), 572–576. DOI: 10.1080/2158379X.2022.2105496

Cabras, C., & Mondo, M. (2018). Coping strategies, optimism, and life satisfaction among first-year university students in Italy: Gender and age differences. *Higher Education, 75*, 643–654.

Cafaro, C. L., Gonzalez Molina, E., Patton, E., McMahon, S. D., & Brown, M. (2023). Meta-analyses of teacher-delivered trauma-based and trauma-informed care interventions. *Psychological Trauma: Theory, Research, Practice, and Policy, 15*(7), 1177–1187. DOI: 10.1037/tra0001515

Cain, A., & LaFreniere, L. (2015). The taunting of parentally bereaved children: An exploratory study. *Death Studies, 39*(4), 219–225. PMID: 25581438

Cairney, P., & Widfeldt, A. (2015). Is Scotland a Westminster-style Majoritarian Democracy or a Scandinavian-style Consensus Democracy? A Comparison of Scotland, the UK and Sweden. *Regional & Federal Studies, 25*(1), 1–18. DOI: 10.1080/13597566.2014.958818

Calderón, A., Merono, L., & MacPhail, A. (2020). A student-centred digital technology approach: The relationship between intrinsic motivation, learning climate and academic achievement of physical education pre-service teachers. *European Physical Education Review, 26*(1), 241–262.

Callaghan, J. (1976). Ruskin College Speech. https://education- uk.org/documents/speeches/1976ruskin.html

Cannon, W. B. (1932). *The Wisdom of the Body*. Norton.

Cann, R., Sinnema, C., & Rodway, J. (2024). What do we know about interventions to improve educator wellbeing? A systematic literature review. *Journal of Educational Change, 25*, 231–270. DOI: 10.1007/s10833-023-09490-w

Cantillon, S., & Lynch, K. (2017). Affective equality: Love matters. *Hypatia, 32*(1), 169–186.

Cantley, I. (2024). The Philosophical Limitations of Educational Assessment: Implications for Academic Selection.

Carmichael, J. T., & Brulle, R. J. (2017). Elite cues, media coverage, and public concern: An integrated path analysis of public opinion on climate change, 2001–2013. *Environmental Politics, 26*(2), 232–252. DOI: 10.1080/09644016.2016.1263433

Carneiro, P., Cattan, S., & Ridpath, N. (2024). The short- and medium-term impacts of Sure Start on educational outcomes. *Institute for Fiscal Studies.* https://ifs.org.uk/publications/short-and-medium-term-impacts-sure-start-educational-outcomes

Carroll, E., & McCoy, S. (2021). All in This Together? New and enduring forms of inequality post-pandemic. Ireland's Education Yearbook 2021. https://irelandseducationyearbook.ie/downloads/IEYB2021/YB2021-Second-Level-08.pdf

Carroll, E., McCoy, S., & Mihut, G. (2022, December). Exploring cumulative disadvantage in early school leaving and planned post-school pathways among those identified with special educational needs in Irish primary schools. *British Educational Research Journal, 48*(6), 1065–1082. DOI: 10.1002/berj.3815

Carroll, E., McCoy, S., & Ye, K. (2024). *'Embracing diversity in all its forms': The voluntary secondary sector in Irish education, ESRI Research Series 182*. ESRI. DOI: 10.26504/rs182

Carroll, E., Ye, K., & McCoy, S. (2022). Educationally maintained inequality? The role of risk factors and resilience at 9, 13 and 17 in disabled young people's post-school pathways at 20. *Irish Educational Studies, 41*(3), 573–594. DOI: 10.1080/03323315.2022.2093257

Case Western University. (2021, June 14). STATBI Introvideo Titles.

Case-Smith, J. (2015). An overview of occupational therapy for children. In *Occupational Therapy for Children and Adolescents*. Elsevier.

Case-Smith, J., & O'Brien, J. (2009). *Occupational Therapy for Children* (6th ed.). Elsevier.

Caspersen, Buland, Hermstad, & Røe. (2020). På vei mot Inkludering? Sluttrapport fra evalueringen av modellutprøvingen Inkludering på alvor. Trondheim: NTNU Samfunnsforskning Mangfold og inkludering.

Castellví, J., Díez-Bedmar, M. C., & Santisteban, A. (2020). Pre-service teachers' critical digital literacy skills and attitudes to address social problems. *Social Sciences, 9*(8), 134.

Center on Brain Injury Research and Training. (n.d.). *About us*. Retrieved from https://cbirt.org/about-us

Center on the Developing Child at Harvard University. (2015). *Supportive relationships and active skill building strengthen the foundations of resilience* (Working Paper No. 13). https://developingchild.harvard.edu/wp-content/uploads/2024/10/The-Science-of-Resilience2.pdf

Centers for Disease Control and Prevention. (2023). QuickStats: Percentage of Children and Adolescents Aged ≤17 Years Who Had Ever Received a Diagnosis of Concussion or Brain Injury, by Sex and Age Group — National Health Interview Survey, United States, 2022. *Morbidity and Mortality Weekly Report, 72*(33), 899–899. https://www.cdc.gov/mmwr/volumes/72/wr/pdfs/mm7233-H.pdf PMID: 37590270

Centre on Brain Injury Research and Training. (n.d.). *In the Classroom: Supporting Students with TBI.* Retrieved from Centre on Brain Injury Research and Training: https://cbirt.org/research/completed-projects/classroom-supporting-students-tbi

Charlson, F., Ali, S., Benmarhnia, T., Pearl, M., Massazza, A., Augustinavicius, J., & Scott, J. G. (2021). Climate change and mental health: A scoping review. *International Journal of Environmental Research and Public Health, 18*(9), 4486. DOI: 10.3390/ijerph18094486

Chemers, M. M., Hu, L. T., & Garcia, B. F. (2001). Academic self-efficacy and first year college student performance and adjustment. *Journal of Educational Psychology, 93*(1), 55.

Chikoko, V. (2021). Re-visiting the decolonising of South African higher education question: A systematic literature review. *South African Journal of Higher Education, 35*(1), 21–36.

Children and Youth Behavioral Health Initiative. (2024). Putting our kids first. https://cybhi.chhs.ca.gov

Children's Disability Network Team (CDNT). (2022). Policy framework for service delivery of children's disability network teams. https://www.hse.ie/eng/services/list/4/disability/progressing-disability/pds-programme/documents/policy-framework-for-children-s-disability-network-teams.pdf

Children's Safety Network. (2023, February). *Non-fatal traumatic brain injury-related visits to the emergency department, U.S. infants, children, and adolescents ages through 19.* Retrieved from https://www.childrenssafetynetwork.org/sites/default/files/TBI_Factsheet_2023_0.pdf

Childs, A. (2024). The lived experience of adolescents and youths with brain injury: navigating new landscapes. *DClinPscych Thesis Salomons Institute of Applied Psychology.*

Choifer, A. (2021). Interpretational Complexities in Developmental Research and a Piagetian Reading of the False-Belief Task. *Review of Philosophy and Psychology, 12*, 923–952. DOI: 10.1007/s13164-020-00519-0

Chow, S. J., & Yong, B. C. S. (2013). Secondary school students' motivation and achievement in combined science. *US-China Education Review B*, *3*(4), 213–228.

Chu, P. S., Saucier, D. A., & Hafner, E. (2010). Meta-analysis of the relationships between social support and wellbeing in children and adolescents. *Journal of Social and Clinical Psychology*, *29*(6), 624–645.

Churchland, A., & Savatolhagh, F. (2024). Women are systematically under-cited in neuroscience. New tools can change that. https://www.thetransmitter.org/publishing/women-are-systematically-under-cited-in-neuroscience-new-tools-can-change-that/

Cingel, D., Carter, M. C., & Krause, H.-V. (2022). Social media and self-esteem. *Current Opinion in Psychology*, *45*. Advance online publication. DOI: 10.1016/j.copsyc.2022.101304

Cladis, A. E. (2020). A shifting paradigm: An evaluation of the pervasive effects of digital technologies on language expression, creativity, critical thinking, political discourse, and interactive processes of human communications. *E-Learning and Digital Media*, *17*(5), 341–364.

Clayton, S., Manning, C. M., Krygsman, K., & Speiser, M. (2017). *Mental health and our changing climate: Impacts, implications, and guidance*. American Psychological Association, and ecoAmerica. Retrieved from https://www.apa.org/news/press/releases/2017/03/mental-health-climate.pdf

Clayton, S. (2020). Climate anxiety: Psychological responses to climate change. *Journal of Anxiety Disorders*, *74*. Advance online publication. DOI: 10.1016/j.janxdis.2020.102263

Clayton, S., & Karazsia, B. (2020). Development and validation of a measure of climate change anxiety. *Journal of Environmental Psychology*, *69*, 101434. DOI: 10.1016/j.jenvp.2020.101434

Coalition to Support Grieving Students. (2015). Table 1: Initiating the conversation. In NYL-1A-Talking-With-Children.pdf. Retrieved June 1, 2024 from http://www.grievingstudents.org

Coffey, Y., Bhullar, N., Durkin, J., Islam, M. S., & Usher, K. (2021). Understanding eco-anxiety: A systematic scoping review of current literature and identified knowledge gaps. *The Journal of Climate Change and Health*, *3*, 100047. DOI: 10.1016/j.joclim.2021.100047

Cohen Kadosh, R., Levy, N., & O'Shea, J. (2012). The neuroethics of non-invasive brain stimulation. *Current Biology*, *22*(4), R108–R111.

Cohen, J. A., & Mannarino, A. P. (2011). Supporting children with traumatic grief: What educators need to know. *School Psychology International*, *32*(2), 117–131. DOI: 10.1177/0143034311400827

Cohen, J. A., Mannarino, A. P., & Deblinger, E. (2006). *Treating trauma and traumatic grief in children*. Guildford Press.

Cole, T. (2012). The white savior industrial complex. *The Atlantic (Boston, Mass.)*, *21*(March). https://www.theatlantic.com/international/archive/2012/03/the-white-savior-

Collie, R. J. (2023). Teachers' work motivation: Examining perceived leadership practices and salient outcomes. *Teaching and Teacher Education*, *135*, 104348. DOI: 10.1016/j.tate.2023.104348

Collie, R. J., & Martin, A. J. (2017). Teachers' sense of adaptability: Examining links with perceived autonomy support, teachers' psychological functioning, and students' numeracy achievement. *Learning and Individual Differences*, *55*, 29–39. DOI: 10.1016/j.lindif.2017.03.003

Collie, R. J., Shapka, J. D., Perry, N. E., & Martin, A. J. (2016). Teachers' psychological functioning in the workplace: Exploring the roles of contextual beliefs, need satisfaction, and personal characteristics. *Journal of Educational Psychology*, *108*, 788–799. DOI: 10.1037/edu0000088

Collier, S., Bryce, I., Trimmer, K., & Krishnamoorthy, G. (2022). Validating the barriers and enablers for teachers accessing professional development of trauma informed pedagogy. *Social Sciences & Humanities Open*, *6*(1), 1–7. DOI: 10.1016/j.ssaho.2022.100332

Common Worlds Research Collective. (2020). Learning to become with the world: Education for future survival. Background paper for the futures of education initiative. Retrieved from https://unesdoc.unesco.org/ark:/48223/pf0000374032

Coombes, L., Chan, G., Allen, D., & Foxcroft, D. R. (2016). Mixed-methods evaluation of the good behaviour game in English primary schools. *Journal of Community & Applied Social Psychology*, *26*(5), 369–387. DOI: 10.1002/casp.2268

Cooper, P., & Jacobs, B. (2011). *Evidence of best practice models and outcomes in the education of children with emotional disturbance/behavioural difficulties. An International Review*. NCSE.

Copernicus Climate Change Service. (C3S) (2024). European State of the Climate 2023, Summary. DOI: 10.24381/bs9v-8c66

Cortese, S., Ferrin, M., Brandeis, D., Buitelaar, J., Daley, D., & Dittmann, R. W.European ADHD Guidelines Group. (2015). Cognitive training for attention-deficit/hyperactivity disorder: Meta-analysis of clinical and neuropsychological outcomes from randomized controlled trials. *Journal of the American Academy of Child and Adolescent Psychiatry, 54*(3), 164–174. DOI: 10.1016/j.jaac.2014.12.010

Courtois, C. A., & Ford, J. D. (2009). *Treating complex traumatic stress disorders: An evidence-based guide*. The Guilford Press.

Creed, P. A., Conlon, E. G., & Dhaliwal, K. (2013). Revisiting the academic hardiness scale: Revision and revalidation. *Journal of Career Assessment, 21*(4), 537–554.

Crenshaw, K. W. (1989). Demarginalizing the intersection of race and sex: A black feminist critique of antidiscrimination doctrine, feminist theory and antiracist politics. *University of Chicago Legal Forum, 1989*, 139–167.

Crenshaw, K. W. (1995). Mapping the margins: Intersectionality, identity politics, and violence against women of color. In Crenshaw, K., Gotanda, N., Peller, G., & Thomas, K. (Eds.), *Critical race theory: The key writings that formed the movement* (pp. 357–383). The New Press.

Cristia, J., Ibarrarán, P., Cueto, S., Santiago, A., & Severín, E. (2017). Technology and child development: Evidence from the one laptop per child program. *American Economic Journal. Applied Economics, 9*(3), 295–320.

Cronholm, P. F., Forke, C. M., Wade, R., Bair-Merritt, M. H., Davis, M., Harkins-Schwarz, M., & Fein, J. A. (2015). Adverse childhood experiences: Expanding the concept of adversity. *American Journal of Preventive Medicine, 49*(3), 354–361. DOI: 10.1016/j.amepre.2015.02.001

Crow, L. (2014). Scroungers and superhumans: Images of disability from the summer of 2012: A visual inquiry. *Journal of Visual Culture, 13*(2), 168–181. DOI: 10.1177/1470412914534812

Cruz González, C., Rodríguez, C. L., & Segovia, J. D. (2021). What are the keys to achieve successful leadership?: Two case studies of private Catholic schools. *The International Journal of Religion and Spirituality in Society, 11*(2), 181–190.

Cruz, J., White, P. C., Bell, A., & Coventry, P. A. (2020). Effect of extreme weather events on mental health: A narrative synthesis and meta-analysis for the UK. *International Journal of Environmental Research and Public Health, 17*(22), 8581. DOI: 10.3390/ijerph17228581

Cullen, M., Cadogan, C., George, S., Murphy, S., Freeney, S., Fitzpatrick, R., & Strawbridge, J. (2022). Key stakeholders' views, experiences and expectations of patient and public involvement in healthcare professions' education: A qualitative study. *BMC Medical Education*. PMID: 35449105

Curcio, G., Ferrara, M., & De Gennaro, L. (2006). Sleep loss, learning capacity and academic performance. *Sleep Medicine Reviews, 10*(5), 323-337. .DOI: 10.1016/j.smrv.2005.11.001

Currigan, S. (2019). Special Needs Pupils in Schools: Why Numbers Are Rising. https://beaconschoolsupport.co.uk/newsletters/why-are-there-more-children-with-complex-special-needs-than-ever-before

Dafaalla, M., Farah, A., Bashir, S., Khalil, A., Abdulhamid, R., Mokhtar, M., & Abdalrahman, I. (2016). Depression, anxiety, and stress in Sudanese medical students: A cross-sectional study on role of quality of life and social support. *American Journal of Educational Research*, *4*(13). https://pubs.sciepub.com/education/4/13/4

Dahl, S. K., Tidselbak Larsen, J., Petersen, L., Bonde Ubbesen, M., Bo Mortensen, P., Munk-Olsen, T., & Musliner, K. L. (2017). Early adversity and risk for moderate to severe unipolar depressive disorder in adolescence and adulthood: A register-based study of 978,647 individuals. *Journal of Affective Disorders*, *214*, 122–129. PMID: 28288406

Daneshamooz, S., & Alamolhodaei, H. (2012). Cooperative learning and academic hardiness on students' mathematical performance with different levels of mathematics anxiety. *Educational Research*, *3*(3), 270–276.

Danieli, Y., & Nader, K. (2006). Respecting cultural, religious, and ethnic differences in the prevention and treatment of psychological sequelae. In Schein, L. A., Spitz, H. I., Burlingame, G. M., Muskin, P. R., & Vargo, S. (Eds.), *Psychological effects of catastrophic disasters: Group approaches to treatment* (pp. 203–234). Haworth Press.

Davoli, M., & Entorf, H. (2018). The PISA Shock, Socioeconomic Inequality, and School Reforms in Germany. *IZA Institute of Labor Economics*. https://docs.iza.org/pp140.pdf

de Bruin, A. B., Biwer, F., Hui, L., Onan, E., David, L., & Wiradhany, W. (2023). Worth the effort: The start and stick to desirable difficulties (S2D2) framework. *Educational Psychology Review*, *35*(2), 41.

Deci, E. L., & Ryan, R. M. (1985). *Intrinsic motivation and self-determination in human behavior*. Plenum Press.

Deci, E. L., & Ryan, R. M. (2000). The "what" and "why" of goal pursuits: Human needs and the self-determination of behavior. *Psychological Inquiry, 11*(4), 227–268.

Deci, E. L., & Ryan, R. M. (2002). The paradox of achievement: The harder you push, the worse it gets. In Aronson, J. (Ed.), *Improving academic achievement: Impact of psychology factors on education* (pp. 61–87). Academic Press.

DeCuir-Gunby, J. T. (2023). Advancing the debate: The need for policy-oriented activism research in educational psychology. *Educational Psychologist, 58*(4), 284–289. DOI: 10.1080/00461520.2023.2252070

Degener, T. (2016). A human rights model of disability. In *Routledge handbook of disability law and human rights* (pp. 31–49). Routledge.

DeLongis, A., Coyne, J. C., Dakof, G., Folkman, S., & Lazarus, R. S. (1982). Relationship of daily hassles, uplifts, and major life events to health status. *Health Psychology, 1*, 119–136.

Dempsey, C., S. McCoy. (forthcoming). Literature Review on Wellbeing Promotion in Schools. Dublin: Economic and Social Research Institute.

Dempsey, C., Farrell, E., & McCoy, S. (2025). Understanding the role of school experiences in the wellbeing of girls, SEN and low SES students: A self-determination theory approach. *Studies in Educational Evaluation, 86*, 101489. DOI: 10.1016/j.stueduc.2025.101489

Dempsey, C., & McCoy, S. (2025). The role of academic self-concepts, parent expectations, and teacher-student interactions in socio-economic gaps in attainment. *The British Journal of Educational Psychology*. PMID: 40913327

Deniz, M. E., Satici, S. A., Doenyas, C., & Griffiths, M. D. (2022). Zoom fatigue, psychological distress, life satisfaction, and academic well-being. *Cyberpsychology, Behavior, and Social Networking, 25*(5), 270–277.

Denovan, A., Dagnall, N., Dhingra, K., & Grogan, S. (2019). Evaluating the Perceived Stress Scale among UK university students: Implications for stress measurement and management. *Studies in Higher Education, 44*(1), 120–133.

Denovan, A., & Macaskill, A. (2017). Stress and subjective wellbeing among first year UK undergraduate students. *Journal of Happiness Studies, 18*(2), 505–525. DOI: 10.1007/s10902-016-9736-y

Department for Education. (2021). Promoting and supporting mental health and wellbeing in schools and colleges. https://www.gov.uk/guidance/mental-health-and-wellbeing-support-in-schools-and-colleges

Department of Education and Skills (DES). (2019). *Wellbeing policy statement and framework for practice*. Government of Ireland. https://www.gov.ie/en/campaigns/851a8e-wellbeing-in-education/](https://www.gov.ie/en/campaigns/851a8e-wellbeing-in-education/

Department of Education and Skills. (2017a). DEIS plan 2017: Delivering Equality of Opportunity in Schools. Retrieved from https://www.gov.ie/en/publication/0fea7-deis-plan-2017/

Department of Education and Skills. (2017b). Guidelines for Primary Schools Supporting Pupils with Special Educational Needs in Mainstream Schools. https://www.education.ie/en/The-Education-System/Special-Education/Guidelines-for-Primary-Schools-Supporting-Pupils-with-Special-Educational-Needs-in-Mainstream-Schools.pdf

Department of Education and Youth. (2025). Review of The Education for Persons with Special Educational Needs (EPSEN) Act 2004, Dublin: Department of Education and Youth. https://assets.gov.ie/static/documents/Report_on_the_Review_of_Education_for_Persons_with_Special_Educational_Needs_EPSEN_Act.pdf

Department of Education. (2015) Framework for Junior Cycle. www.education.ie/en/Publications/Policy-reports/Framework-for-Junior-Cycle-2015.pdf

Department of Education. (2019). *Wellbeing Policy Statement and Framework for Practice*. Government of Ireland.

Department of Education. (2022) *Cineáltas Action Plan on Bullying*. Department of Education (Ireland). https://www.gov.ie/en/publication/52aaf-cinealtas-action-plan-on-bullying/

Department of Education. (2023a) Counselling in Primary Schools-Pilot (CPS-P) 2023-2025, Dublin: Department of Education. https://www.gov.ie/en/department-of-education/publications/counselling-in-primary-schools-pilot-cps-p-2023-2025/

Department of Education. (2023b). Initial Teacher Education Policy Statement, Dublin Department of Education. https://www.gov.ie/en/publication/926b4-ite-policy-statement/

Department of Education. (2024). Extended schools programme. https://www.education-ni.gov.uk/articles/extended-schools-programme

Department of Education. (2024a). The Quality of Education for Children and Young People from Ukraine, Dublin: Department of Education. https://assets.gov.ie/static/documents/quality-of-education-for-children-and-young-people-from-ukraine.pdf

Department of Education. (2024b). *Additional Language Needs – Whole-school and Classroom Approaches for Inclusive Language Learning: Findings from Primary and Post-primary school inspections of English as an Additional Language*. Department of Education.

Devine, D. (2017). Migrant children in urban schools in Ireland. In Pink, W. T., & Noblit, G. W. (Eds.), *Second International Handbook of Urban Education* (pp. 1103–1124). Springer. DOI: 10.1007/978-3-319-40317-5

Dewey, J. (1938/1963). *Experience and education*. Collier Books.

Di Battista, A., Godfrey, C., Soo, C., Catroppa, C., & Anderson, V. (2014). In my Before Life': Relationships, Coping an Post-Traumatic Growth in Adolescent Survivors of a Traumatic Brain Injury. *Journal of Rehabilitation Medicine*, *46*, 975–983. PMID: 25188467

Diener, E., Lucas, R. E., & Scollon, C. N. (2009). Beyond the hedonic treadmill: Revising the adaptation theory of well-being. The Science of Well-being: The Collected Works of Ed Diener, 103-118. DOI: 10.1037/0003-066X.61.4.305

Dienlin, T., & Johannes, N. (2020). The impact of digital technology use on adolescent well-being. *Dialogues in Clinical Neuroscience*, *22*(2), 135–142.

Dietz, T., Shwom, R. L., & Whitley, C. T. (2020). Climate change and society. *Annual Review of Sociology*, *46*, 135–158. DOI: 10.1146/annurev-soc-121919-054614

Dille, B., & Mezack, M. (1991). Identifying predictors of high risk among community college telecourse students. *American Journal of Distance Education*, *5*(1), 24–35.

Doherty, T. J., & Clayton, S. (2011). The psychological impacts of global climate change. *The American Psychologist*, *66*(4), 265–276. DOI: 10.1037/a0023141

Dollete, S., & Phillips, M. (2004). Understanding girls' circle as an intervention on perceived social support, body image, self-efficacy, locus of control and self-esteem. *The Journal of Psychology*, *90*(2), 204–215.

Domitrovich, C. E., Durlak, J. A., Staley, K. C., & Weissberg, R. P. (2017). Social-emotional competence: An essential factor for promoting positive adjustment and reducing risk in school children. *Child Development*, *88*(2), 408–416. DOI: 10.1111/cdev.12739

Donnelly, R., & Patrinos, H. A. (2022). Learning loss during Covid-19: An early systematic review. *Prospects*, *51*, 601–609. DOI: 10.1007/s11125-021-09582-6

Donoghue, C. (2003). Challenging the Authority of the Medical Definition of Disability: An analysis of the resistance to the social constructionist paradigm. *Disability & Society*, *18*(2), 199–208. DOI: 10.1080/0968759032000052833

Dorsey, S., McLaughlin, K. A., Kerns, S. E. U., Harrison, J. P., Lambert, H. K., & Briggs, E. C.. (2017). Evidence base update for psychosocial treatments for children and adolescents exposed to traumatic events. *Journal of Clinical Child and Adolescent Psychology*, *46*, 303–330. PMID: 27759442

Droubi, S., Galamba, A., Fernandes, F. L., de Mendonça, A. A., & Heffron, R. J. (2023). Transforming education for the just transition. *Energy Research & Social Science*, *100*, 103090.

Duckworth, A. L., & Seligman, M. E. (2005). Self-discipline outdoes IQ in predicting academic performance of adolescents. *Psychological Science*, *16*(12), 939–944. DOI: 10.1111/j.1467-9280.2005.0164

Duggan, C., & Byrne, M. (2013). *What works in the provision of higher, further and continuing education, training and rehabilitation for adults with disabilities. A Review of the Literature. Trim, IRL.* National Council for Special Education.

Durkheim, E. (1952). *Suicide: a study in sociology* [Le suicide: étude de sociologie]. Routledge & Kegan Paul. (Original publication 1897)

Durlak, J. A., Weissberg, R. P., Dymnicki, A. B., Taylor, R. D., & Schellinger, K. B. (2011). The impact of enhancing students' social and emotional learning: A meta-analysis of school-based universal interventions. *Child Development*, *82*(1), 405–432. DOI: 10.1111/j.1467-8624.2010.01564.x

Dutil, S. (2020). Dismantling the School-to-Prison Pipeline: A Trauma-Informed, Critical Race Perspective on School Discipline. *Children & Schools*, *42*(3), 171–178. DOI: 10.1093/cs/cdaa016

Dweck, C. (2015). Carol Dweck revisits the growth mindset. *Education Week*, *35*(5), 20–24.

Dweck, C. S. (2006). *Mindset: The new psychology of success.* Random House.

Dyrbye, L. N., Thomas, M. R., & Shanafelt, T. D. (2006). Systematic review of Depression, anxiety, and other indicators of psychological distress among U.S. and Canadian medical students. *Academic Medicine*, *81*(4), 354–373. PMID: 16565188

Dyregrov, A., Dyregrov, K., Endsjø, M., & Idsoe, T. (2015). Teachers' perception of bereaved children's academic performance. *Advances in School Mental Health Promotion*, *8*(3), 187–198.

Eisenberg, D., Hunt, J., & Speer, N. (2013). Mental health in American colleges and universities: Variation across student subgroups and across campuses. *The Journal of Nervous and Mental Disease, 201*(1), 60–67. PMID: 23274298

El Ansari, W., Oskrochi, R., & Haghgoo, G. (2014). Are students' symptoms and health complaints associated with perceived stress at university? Perspectives from the United Kingdom and Egypt. *International Journal of Environmental Research and Public Health, 11*(10), 9981–10002. PMID: 25264677

Elias, M. J. (2019). What if the doors of every schoolhouse opened to social-emotional learning tomorrow: Reflections on how to feasibly scale up high-quality SEL. *Educational Psychologist, 54*(3), 233–245. DOI: 10.1080/00461520.2019.1636655

Elias, M. J., Leverett, L., Duffell, J. C., Humphrey, N., Stepney, C., & Ferrito, J. (2015). Integrating SEL with related prevention and youth development approaches. In Durlak, J. A., Domitrovich, C. E., Weissberg, R. P., & Gullotta, T. P. (Eds.), *Handbook of social and emotional learning: Research and practice* (pp. 33–49). Guilford Press.

Elliott, A., McGregor, H., & Thrash, T. (2004). The need for competence. In Deci, E., & Ryan, R. (Eds.), *Handbook of self-determination research* (pp. 361–388). University of Rochester Press.

ElSayary, A. (2024). Integrating generative AI in active learning environments: Enhancing metacognition and technological skills. *Journal of Systemics, Cybernetics and Informatics, 22*(3), 34–37.

Enfield Psychological Services. (2024). The role of an educational psychologist. https://www.enfield.gov.uk/educationalpsychologyservice/the-role-of-an-educational-psychologist)

Engel, G. L. (1977). The need for a new medical model: A challenge for biomedicine. *Science, 196*(4286), 129–136. DOI: 10.1126/science.847460

Ergene, T. (2003). Effective interventions on test anxiety reduction: A meta-analysis. *School Psychology International, 24*, 313–328. DOI: 10.1177/01430343030243004

Erikson, E. H. (1968). *Identity: Youth and crisis*. W. W. Norton & Company.

European Agency for Development in Special Needs Education (EADSNE). (2003). *Thematic Education.*

European Agency for Development in Special Needs Education (EADSNE). (2018). Financing Policies for Inclusive Education Systems. Resourcing Levers to Reduce Disparity in Education. Brussels: EASNIE. https://www.european-agency.org/sites/default/files/fpies-synthesis-report.pdf

European Commission Directorate-General for Education Youth Sport and Culture. (2022). Investing in our future: Quality investment in education and training. Publications Office of the European Union. Retrieved from https://data.europa.eu/doi/10.2766/45896

Ewe, L. P., & Galvin, T. (2023). Universal Design for Learning across Formal School Structures in Europe—A Systematic Review. *Education Sciences*, *13*(9), 867. DOI: 10.3390/educsci13090867

Eysenck, H. J., & Eysenck, S. B. (2013). The biological basis of personality. In *Personality Structure and Measurement (Psychology Revivals)* (pp. 49-62). Routledge.

Eysenck, M. W., Derakshan, N., Santos, R., & Calvo, M. G. (2007). Anxiety and cognitive performance: Attentional control theory. *Emotion (Washington, D.C.)*, *7*(2), 336. DOI: 10.1037/1528-3542.7.2.336 PMID: 17516812

Fabbrini, F., Bokhorst, D., Sabato, S., Theodoropoulou, S., Spasova, S., Marenco, M., Debusscher, P., Atanasova, A., Rasnača, Z., Vanhercke, B., & Moja, F. (2023). Social Policy in the European Union: State of Play 2022. Brussels: ETUI: European Trade Union Institute Belgium.

Fahmy, M. N. (2020). The Need for a Collective Social Conscience. *Global Perspectives*, *1*(1), 17641. DOI: 10.1525/gp.2020.17641

Falala, A., Lannes, A., Bui, E., & Revet, A. (2024). Prevalence of prolonged grief disorder in bereaved children and adolescents: A systematic review. *L'Encéphale*, *50*(5), 557–565. DOI: 10.1016/j.encep.2023.11.016 PMID: 38413249

Falkenburger, E., Arena, O., & Wolin, J. (2018). Trauma-informed community building and engagement. *The Urban Institute*. https://www.urban.org/sites/default/files/publication/98296/trauma-informed_community_building_and_engagement.pdf

Fani, T., & Ghaemi, F. (2011). Implications of Vygotsky's zone of proximal development (ZPD) in teacher education: ZPTD and self-scaffolding. *Procedia: Social and Behavioral Sciences*, *29*, 1549–1554.

Fan, Y., Tang, L., Le, H., Shen, K., Tan, S., Zhao, Y., & Gašević, D. (2025). Beware of metacognitive laziness: Effects of generative artificial intelligence on learning motivation, processes, and performance. *British Journal of Educational Technology*, *56*(2), 489–530.

Farley, S. B., Yoon, H. J., & Padilla, C. (2021). What Values Will Define and Guide OD in the Future? *Inspirations for the Future of OD & the Reality of Our Work*, 27.

Faulconer, E., Griffith, J., & Gruss, A. (2022). The impact of positive feedback on student outcomes and perceptions. *Assessment & Evaluation in Higher Education, 47*(2), 259–268.

Fawns, T. (2022). An entangled pedagogy: Looking beyond the pedagogy—technology dichotomy. *Postdigital Science and Education, 4*(3), 711–728.

Feerrar, J. (2022). Bringing digital well-being into the heart of digital media literacies. *The Journal of Media Literacy Education, 14*(2), 72–77.

Felitti, V. J., Anda, R. F., Nordenberg, D., Williamson, D. F., Spitz, A. M., Edwards, V., Koss, M. P., & Marks, J. S. (1998). Relationship of childhood abuse and household dysfunction to many of the leading causes of death in adults. *American Journal of Preventive Medicine, 14*(4), 245–258. PMID: 9635069

Felitti, V. J., Anda, R. F., Nordenberg, D., Williamson, D. F., Spitz, A. M., Edwards, V., & Marks, J. S. (1998). Relationship of childhood abuse and household dysfunction to many of the leading causes of death in adults: The Adverse Childhood Experiences (ACE) Study. *American Journal of Preventive Medicine, 14*(4), 245–258. DOI: 10.1016/S0749-3797(98)00017-8

Fielding, M. (2012). Education as if people matter: John MacMurray, community and the struggle for democracy. *Oxford Review of Education, 38*(6), 675–692. DOI: 10.1080/03054985.2012.745044

Finkelhor, D. (2018). Screening for adverse childhood experiences (ACEs): Cautions and suggestions. *Child Abuse & Neglect, 85*, 174–179. PMID: 28784309

Fitzpatrick, C., Loader, R., McCartney, S., McConnell, B., McMullen, J., Murray, C., Orr, K., Purdy, N., & Simms, V. (2023). *The Consequences of the Cuts to Education for Children and Young People in Northern Ireland*. Ulster University, Stranmillis University College, Queen's University, Belfast, Newcastle University.

Flavell, J. H., Everett, B. A., Croft, K., & Flavell, E. R. (1981). Young children's knowledge about visual perception: Further evidence for the Level 1–Level 2 distinction. *Developmental Psychology, 17*, 99–103.

Fleeson, W., Malanos, A. B., & Achille, N. M. (2002). An intraindividual process approach to the relationship between extraversion and positive affect: Is acting extraverted as "good" as being extraverted? *Journal of Personality and Social Psychology, 83*, 1409–1422. PMID: 12500821

Flood, M. (2021). An Introduction to Universal Design for Learning (UDL). Ireland's Education Yearbook 2021. https://irelandseducationyearbook.ie/downloads/IEYB2021/YB2021-Second-Level-05.pdf

Florian, L., & Rouse, M. (2009). The inclusive practice project in Scotland: Teacher education for inclusive education. [Online]. *Teaching and Teacher Education*, *25*(4), 594–601.

Ford, D. Y. (2021). Intelligence testing and cultural diversity: The need for alternative instruments, policies, and procedures. In *Alternative assessments with gifted and talented students* (pp. 107–128). Routledge.

Frederick, A., & Shifrer, D. (2019). Race and disability: From analogy to intersectionality. *Sociology of Race and Ethnicity (Thousand Oaks, Calif.)*, *5*(2), 200–214. DOI: 10.1177/2332649218783

Fredrickson, B. L., & Joiner, T. (2002). Positive emotions trigger upward spirals toward emotional well-being. *Psychological Science*, *13*(2), 172–175. DOI: 10.1111/1467-9280.00431

Fredrickson, B. L., & Losada, M. F. (2005). Positive affect and the complex dynamics of human flourishing. *The American Psychologist*, *60*(7), 678. DOI: 10.1037/0003-066X.60.7.678

Frehill, J., & Booker, R. (2025). The intersection of trauma with social, cultural, and historic inequities: Meeting the needs of marginalised students in Irish primary schools. *Educational and Child Psychology*, *42*(1).

Frenzel, A. C., Goetz, T., Lüdtke, O., Pekrun, R., & Sutton, R. E. (2009). Emotional transmission in the classroom: Exploring the relationship between teacher and student enjoyment. *Journal of Educational Psychology*, *101*(3), 707–719. DOI: 10.1037/a0014695

Freud, S., & Breuer, J. (1955). *Studies in hysteria*. Hogarth Press. (Original work published 1895)

Fricker, M. (2007). *Epistemic injustice: Power and the ethics of knowing*. Oxford University Press.

Friedlander, L. J., Reid, G. J., Shupak, N., & Cribbie, R. (2007). Social support, self-esteem, and stress as predictors of adjustment to university among first-year undergraduates. *Journal of College Student Development*, *48*(3), 259–274.

Friedman, H. S., & Martin, L. R. (2011). Does childhood personality predict longevity? *Journal of Personality and Social Psychology, 101*(1), 1–18. DOI: 10.1037//0022-3514.65.1.176

Friere, P. (1972). *Pedagogy of the Oppressed.* Penguin.

Fritsche, I., Barth, M., Jugert, P., Masson, T., & Reese, G. (2018). A social identity model of pro-environmental action (SIMPEA). *Psychological Review, 125*(2), 245–269. DOI: 10.1037/rev0000090

Fromm, E. (2011). *The pathology of normalcy.* American Mental Health Foundation Books. DOI: 10.3389/fpsyg.2022.920313

Fullerton, E. K., Conroy, M. A., & Correa, V. I. (2009). Early childhood teachers' use of specific praise statements with young children at risk for behavioural disorders. *Behavioral Disorders, 34*(3), 118–135.

Funa, A. A., & Gabay, A. E. (2025). Policy guidelines and recommendations on AI use in teaching and learning: A meta-synthesis study. *Social Sciences & Humanities Open, 11.* Advance online publication. DOI: 10.1016/j.ssaho.2024.101221

Furqon, M., Sinaga, P., Liliasari, L., & Riza, L. S. (2023). The Impact of Learning Management System (LMS) Usage on Students. TEM Journal, 12(2).

Gable, S. L., & Haidt, J. (2005). What (and why) is positive psychology? *Review of General Psychology, 9*(2), 103–110. DOI: 10.1037/1089-2680.9.2.103

Gabrielle, T., Sonne, M., & Indolo, N. N. (2024). The Impact of Social Media on Adolescent Mental Health: A Meta-Analysis. *Scientia Psychiatrica, 5*(3), 551–564. DOI: 10.37275/scipsy.v5i3.175

Gaines, A. G. (2022). The Grief Experiences of Children with Developmental Disabilities: A Narrative Literature Review. *Omega.* Advance online publication. DOI: 10.1177/00302228221124520 PMID: 36138512

Gaonkar, S., Khan, D., & Manisha, A. S. (2022). Impact of Gamification on Learning and Development. *Journal of Advances in Education and Philosophy, 6*(2), 63–70.

Gauvin-Lepage, J. (2019). Traumatic brain injury in adolescence and the family resilience process: A case study. *Open Nursing, 5,* 1–5. PMID: 33415241

Gazzaley, A., & Rosen, L. D. (2016). *The distracted mind: Ancient brains in a high-tech world.* Mit Press.

Gelir, I. (2023). The effects of the COVID-19 pandemic on preschool children's learning and development. *SN Social Sciences, 3,* 143. DOI: 10.1007/s43545-023-00736-1

Gergen, K. J. (2009). *Relational being: Beyond self and community*. Oxford University Press.

Getenet, S., Cantle, R., Redmond, P., & Albion, P. (2024). Students' digital technology attitude, literacy and self-efficacy and their effect on online learning engagement. *International Journal of Educational Technology in Higher Education, 21*(1), 3.

Gibbons, C. & Morgan, H. (2015) Mindfulness - As a coping strategy, *Eisteach - The Irish Journal of Counselling and Psychotherapy, 15*(2), 14-18.

Gibbons, C. (2008). *Measuring Stress and Eustress in Nursing Students* (Doctoral dissertation, Queen's University Belfast). https://ethos.bl.uk/OrderDetails.do?uin=uk.bl.ethos.501265

Gibbons, C. (2009). The two sides of stress. *Nursing Standard, 23*(44), 61.

Gibbons, C. (2015) Stress, eustress and the National Student Survey, *Psychology Teaching Review, 21*(2), 86-92. https://eric.ed.gov/?id=EJ1146635

Gibbons, C. (2010). Stress, coping and burn-out in nursing students. *International Journal of Nursing Studies*, (47), 1299–1309. PMID: 20359710

Gibbons, C. (2022). Understanding the role of stress, personality and coping on learning motivation and mental health in university students during a pandemic. *BMC Psychology, 10*(1), 261. DOI: 10.1186/s40359-022-00971-w PMID: 36357950

Gibbons, C. (2023a). Untangling the role of optimism, pessimism and coping influences on student mood, motivation and satisfaction. *Innovations in Education and Teaching International*. Advance online publication. DOI: 10.1080/14703297.2023.2260780

Gibbons, C. (2023b). Surviving a pandemic - Understanding the role of student stress, personality and coping on course satisfaction and anxiety during lockdown. *Innovations in Education and Teaching International, 60*, 463–475. https://www.tandfonline.com/doi/full/10.1080/14703297.2022.2064326

Gibbons, C. (2024). Not just surviving, but flourishing – insights into student coping, anxiety and motivation. *Research Square*. DOI: 10.21203/rs.3.rs-4177097/v1

Gibbons, C., Dempster, M., & Moutray, M. (2009). Surveying nursing students on their sources of stress: A validation study. *Nurse Education Today, 29*(8), 867–872. PMID: 19501429

Gibson-Graham, J. K., Cameron, J., & Healy, S. (2016). Commoning as a postcapitalist politics. In Amin, A., & Howell, P. (Eds.), *Releasing the Commons: Rethinking the futures of the commons* (pp. 205–225). Routledge.

Gilleece, L., A. Clerkin, D. Flannery. (2025). Reducing educational disadvantage across post-primary schools: Evidence from the first decade of the DEIS plan in Ireland, Studies in Educational Evaluation, 86. DOI: 10.1016/j.stueduc.2025.101466

Gill, O., & Janmaat, J. G. (2019). The 'schools revolution' in England: A configurational comparative analysis of academisation across local authorities. *Cambridge Journal of Education, 49*(5), 575–604. DOI: 10.1080/0305764X.2019.1581135

Glang, A., McCart, M., Slocumb, J., Gau, J., Davies, S., Gomez, D., & Beck, L. (2018). Preliminary Efficacy of Online Traumatic Brain Injury Professional Development for Educators: An Exploratory Randomized Clinical Trial. *The Journal of Head Trauma Rehabilitation, 34*(2), 77–86. PMID: 30499929

Glennon, C., Watson, S., Fisher, P., & Gracey, F. (2022). The process of identity change following ABI from the perspectives of adolescents and their mothers: A relational grounded theory approach. *Neuropsychological Rehabilitation, 32*(8), 1904–1927. PMID: 35857657

Goffman, E. (1990). *Stigma: notes on the management of spoiled identity*. Penguin.

Goodley, D., & Tregaskis, C. (2006). Storying disability and impairment: Retrospective accounts of disabled family life. *Qualitative Health Research, 16*(5), 630–646. DOI: 10.1177/1049732305285840

Gordon, M., Gupta, S., Thornton, D., Reid, M., Mallen, E., & Melling, A. (2020). Patient/service user involvement in medical education: a best evidence medical education (BEME) systematic review: BEME Guide No. 58. *Medical Teacher, 42*(1), 4–16. PMID: 31518544

Government of Ireland. (2019). Healthy Ireland Framework 2019–2025. Dublin: Government publications. www.gov.ie/en/publication/e8f9b1-healthy-ireland framework-2019-2025/

Government of Ireland. (2020). Migrant Integration Strategy. Dublin: Government publications. www.gov.ie/en/publication/5a86da-the-migrant-integration-strategy -2017-2020/

Graff, H. J. (2016). The "problem" of interdisciplinarity in theory, practice, and history. *Social Science History, 40*(4), 775–803. DOI: 10.1017/ssh.2016.31

Gran, B. K. (2017). An International Framework of Children's Rights. *Annual Review of Law and Social Science, 13*, 79–100. DOI: 10.1146/annurev-lawsocsci-110615-084638

Gray, P. (2024, June 30). The importance of critical analyses in examining social science evidence (#45). Play Makes Us Human. Substack. https://petergray.substack.com/p/45-the-importance-of-critical-analyses

Gray, J. A. (1970). The psychophysiological basis of introversion-extraversion. *Behaviour Research and Therapy*, *8*(3), 249–266. PMID: 5470377

Greenfield, P. M. (1997). You can't take it with you: Why ability assessments don't cross cultures. *The American Psychologist*, *52*(10), 11–15. DOI: 10.1037/0003-066X.52.10.1115

Gregersen, E. M., Astrupgaard, S. L., Jespersen, M. H., Gårdhus, T. P., & Albris, K. (2023). Digital dependence: Online fatigue and coping strategies during the COVID-19 lockdown. *Media Culture & Society*, *45*(5), 967–984.

Gregersen, T., Andersen, G., & Tvinnereim, E. (2023). The strength and content of climate anger. *Global Environmental Change*, *82*, 102738. DOI: 10.1016/j.gloenvcha.2023.102738

Grevstad, J. (2007). Adverse childhood experiences in juvenile justice – Pierce County, WA. Paper presented at the Family Policy Council Partners Summit, Seattle, WA.

Griva, K., & Joekes, K. (2003). UK Teachers Under Stress: Can we predict wellness on the basis of characteristics of the teaching job? *Psychology & Health*, *18*, 457–471.

Gubric, N., Badovinac, S., & Johri, A. M. (2020). Student Mental Health in the Midst of the COVID-19 Pandemic: A Call for Further Research and Immediate Solutions. *The International Journal of Social Psychiatry*, *66*(5), 517–518. DOI: 10.1177/0020764020925108 PMID: 32364039

Haarbauer-Krupa, J., Pugh, M. J., Prager, E. M., Harmon, N., Wolfe, J., & Yaffe, K. (2021). Epidemiology of Chronic Effects of Traumatic Brain Injury. *Journal of Neurotrauma*, *38*(23), 3235–3247. PMID: 33947273

Hagen, L., Jingnan, L., & Nguyen, A. (2025). *Elon Musk's AI chatbot, Grok, started calling itself 'MechaHitler'* NPR, July 9 2025. https://www.npr.org/2025/07/09/nx-s1-5462609/grok-elon-musk-antisemitic-racist-content

Haidt, J. (2024). *The anxious generation: how the great rewiring of childhood is causing an epidemic of mental illness*. Penguin Press.

Haidt, J. (2024). *The anxious generation: How the great rewiring of childhood is causing an epidemic of mental illness*. Penguin Press.

Hallam, S. (2005). *Enhancing motivation and learning throughout the lifespan*. Institute of Education.

Hamblin, D. (1978). *The Teacher and Pastoral Care*. Basil Blackwell.

Hamilton, A., Wiliam, D., & Hattie, J. (2023). The Future of AI in Education: 13 things we can do to minimize the damage. Academic Press.

Hammill, D., Bennett, D. E., & White, P. (2019). *Making a successful return to education for children and young people with Acquired Brain Injuries* (2nd ed.). Nottinghanshire.

Hampton, S., & Whitmarsh, L. (2023). Choices for climate action: A review of the multiple roles individuals play. *One Earth*, *6*(9), 1157–1172. DOI: 10.1016/j.oneear.2023.08.006

Harris, M., & Fallot, R. D. (2001). Envisioning a trauma-informed service system: A vital paradigm shift. *New Directions for Mental Health Services*, *2001*(89). PMID: 11291260

Harrison, M. H. (2023). Nuance in "No Excuses": Unexpected Progressive Pedagogy and Policy. *Education and Urban Society*, *55*(3), 342–370. DOI: 10.1177/00131245221076096

Hartman, L., Duncanson, M., Farahat, S., & Lindsay, S. (2015). Clinician and educator experiences of facilitating students' transition back to school following acquired brain injury: A qualitative systematic review. *Brain Injury*, *29*(12), 1387–1399. PMID: 26362526

Hartman, L., Tibbles, A., Paniccia, A., & Lindsay, S. (2015). *A qualitative synthesis of families' and students' hospital-to- school transition experiences following acquired brain injury*. Global Qualtative Nursing Research.

Hartnup, B., Dong, L., & Eisingerich, A. B. (2018). How an environment of stress and social risk shapes student engagement with social media as potential digital learning platforms: Qualitative study. *JMIR Medical Education*, *4*(2), e10069. PMID: 30006324

Hart, S. (2004). *Learning without limits*. Open University Press.

Hascher, T., & Waber, J. (2021). Teacher well-being: A systematic review of the research literature from the year 2000–2019. *Educational Research Review*, *34*, 100411. DOI: 10.1016/j.edurev.2021.100411

Hattie, J. (2003). Teachers Make a Difference What is the research evidence ? *Lloydia Cincinnati*, 12(2002), 1–17. DOI: 10.1177/002221949002300106

Hawkey, K. (2023). *History and the climate crisis*. UCL Press.

Hayes, L., Shaw, S., Pearce, M., & Forsyth, R. (2017). Requirements for and current provision of rehabilitation services for children after severe acquired brain injury in the UK: A population-based study. *Archives of Disease in Childhood, 102*(9), 813–820. PMID: 28416561

Heads Together for ABI. (2020). *Submission to the Department of Education, Skills & Employment Disability Standards for Education Review 2020*. Heads Together for ABI Limited.

Hefner, J. L., & Eisenberg, D. (2009). Social support and mental health among college students. *The American Journal of Orthopsychiatry*, *79*, 491–499. PMID: 20099940

Heller-Sahlgren, G. (2015). *Real Finnish Lessons: The true story of an education superpower*. Centre for Policy Studies. https://cps.org.uk/wp-content/uploads/2021/07/150410115444-RealFinnishLessonsFULLDRAFTCOVER.pdf

Helsper, E. J., Veltri, G. A., & Livingstone, S. (2024). Parental mediation of children's online risks: The role of parental risk perception, digital skills and risk experiences. New Media & Society.

Henderson, M., Selwyn, N., Finger, G., & Aston, R. (2015). Students' everyday engagement with digital technology in university: Exploring patterns of use and 'usefulness'. *Journal of Higher Education Policy and Management*, *37*(3), 308–319.

Henry, K. L., Fulco, C. J., & Merrick, M. T. (2018). The harmful effect of child maltreatment on economic outcomes in adulthood. *American Journal of Public Health, 108*(9), 1134–1141. PMID: 30088994

Herbst, J. (2002). Nineteenth-Century Schools between Community and State: The Cases of Prussia and the United States. *History of Education Quarterly*, *42*(3), 317–341. DOI: 10.1111/j.1748-5959.2002.tb00001.x

Hergenhahn, B. R., & Olson, M. H. (1999). *An introduction to theories of personality*. Prentice-Hall, Inc.

Herman, J. (2015). *Trauma and recovery: The aftermath of violence – From domestic abuse to political terror* (2nd ed.). Basic Books. (Original work published 1992)

Hernández-Torrano, D., Somerton, M., & Helmer, J. (2020). Mapping Research on Inclusive Education Since Salamanca Statement: A Bibliometric Review of the Literature Over 25 Years. *International Journal of Inclusive Education*, 1–20. DOI: 10.1080/13603116.2020.1747555

Herpen, , Hofman, & Severiens. (2020). A Head Start in Higher Education: The Effect of A Transition Intervention on Interaction, Sense of Belonging, and Academic Performance. *Studies in Higher Education, 45*(4), 862–877. DOI: 10.1080/03075079.2019.1572088

Heung, V., & Grossman, D. (2007). Inclusive Education as a Strategy for Achieving Education for All: Perspectives from Three Asian Societies. In *International Perspectives on Education and Society* (Vol. 8, Issue 6, pp. 155–180). DOI: 10.1016/S1479-3679(06)08005-4

Hickman, C. E., Pihkala, P., Clayton, S., Lewandowski, E., Mayall, E. E., Wray, B., Mellor, C., & Van Susteren, L. (2021). Climate anxiety in children and young people and their beliefs about government responses to climate change: a global survey. In *Articles Lancet Planet Health* (Vol. 5). www.thelancet.com/

Higgins, K., Murtagh, B., Gallagher, T., Grounds, A., Robinson, G., Loudon, E., & Doherty, M. (2023). Queen's Communities and Place: towards the alignment of higher education place-based strategy with local need. *Research for All, 7*(1). https://pure.qub.ac.uk/en/publications/queens-communities-and-place-towards-the-alignment-of-higher-educ

Higher Education Authority (HEA). (2022). *National Access Plan: A Strategic Action Plan for Equity of Access, Participation and Success in Higher Education 2022-2028*. HEA.

Hilberdink, C. E., & Ghainder, K., Alexandre Dubanchet, Hinton, D., Manik, A., Hall, B. J., & Bui, E. (2023). Bereavement Issues and Prolonged Grief Disorder: A Global Perspective. *Global Mental Health (Cambridge, England), 10*, 1–37. DOI: 10.1017/gmh.2023.28 PMID: 37854407

Hill, J., & Reimer, T. (2022). Crossing the digital divide and the equity expanse: Reaching and teaching all students during the pandemic. Journal of Leadership, Equity, and Research.

Hill, V. (2013). Working across diverse contexts with wider populations: The developing role of the educational psychologist. In Arnold, C., & Hardy, J. (Eds.), *British educational psychology: The first hundred years* (pp. 128–140). The British Psychological Society.

Hobfoll, S. E., Watson, P., Bell, C. C., Bryant, R. A., Brymer, M. J., Friedman, M. J., & Ursano, R. J. (2007). Five essential elements of immediate and mid–term mass trauma intervention: Empirical evidence. *Psychiatry, 70*(4), 283–315. DOI: 10.1521/psyc.2007.70.4.283

Hofer, B. K., & Pintrich, P. R. (1997). *The Development of Epistemological Theories: Beliefs About Knowledge and Knowing and Their Relation to Learning. Review of Educational Research*, *67*(1), 88–140. DOI: 10.3102/00346543067001088

Hofer, B. K. (2010). Personal Epistemology in Asia: Burgeoning Research and Future Directions. *The Asia-Pacific Education Researcher*, *19*(1), 179–184. DOI: 10.3860/taper.v19i1.1516

Hollingshaus, M. S., & Smith, K. R. (2015). Life and death in the family: Early parental death, parental remarriage, and offspring suicide risk in adulthood. *Social Science & Medicine*, *131*, 181–189. DOI: 10.1016/j.socscimed.2015.02.008 PMID: 25704222

Holmes, W. (2023). The unintended consequences of artificial intelligence and education. Academic Press.

Holmes, T. H., & Rahe, R. H. (1967). The social readjustment rating scale. *Psychosomatic Medicine*, *11*, 213–218. PMID: 6059863

Holmes, W., & Miao, F. (2023). *Guidance for generative AI in education and research*. UNESCO Publishing.

Holte Kofod, E. (2017). From morality to pathology: A brief historization of contemporary Western grief practices and understandings. *Nordic Psychology*, *69*(1), 47–60. DOI: 10.1080/19012276.2016.1267914

Horgan, D., Martin, S., O'Riordan, J., & Maier, R. (2022). Supporting languages: The socio-educational integration of migrant and refugee children and young people. *Children & Society*, *36*(3), 369–385. DOI: 10.1111/chso.12525

Houben, M., Van Den Noortgate, W., & Kuppens, P. (2015). The relation between short-term emotion dynamics and psychological well-being: A meta-analysis. *Psychological Bulletin*, *141*(4), 901–930. DOI: 10.1037/a0038822

Howard, J. L., Bureau, J. S., Guay, F., Chong, J. X. Y., & Ryan, R. M. (2021). Student Motivation and Associated Outcomes: A Meta-Analysis From Self-Determination Theory. *Perspectives on Psychological Science*, *16*(6), 1300–1323. DOI: 10.1177/1745691620966789

Howard, J. L., Gagné, M., & Bureau, J. S. (2017). Testing a continuum structure of self-determined motivation: A meta-analysis. *Psychological Bulletin*, *143*(12), 1346–1377. DOI: 10.1037/bul0000125

Howard-Jones, P. (2014). Neuroscience and education: Myths and messages. *Nature Reviews. Neuroscience*, *15*(12), 817–824. DOI: 10.1038/nrn3817

Howe, C., & Mercer, N. (2007). Children's social development, peer interaction and classroom learning. *Primary* Review Research Survey.

Hrabok, M., Delorme, A., & Agyapong, V. I. (2020). Threats to mental health and well-being associated with climate change. *Journal of Anxiety Disorders, 76*, 102295. DOI: 10.1016/j.janxdis.2020.102295

Hudson, N. W., & Fraley, R. C. (2017). Volitional personality change. In Specht, J. (Ed.), *Personality development across the lifespan* (pp. 555–571). Elsevier.

Hughes, G., & Spanner, L. (2019). *The University Mental Health Charter*. Student Minds.

Hughes, K., Bellis, M. A., Sethi, D., Andrew, R., Yon, Y., Wood, S., Ford, K., Baban, A., Boderscova, L., Kachaeva, M., Makaruk, K., Markovic, M., Povilaitis, R., Raleva, M., Terzic, N., Veleminsky, M., Wlodarczyk, J., & Zakhozha, V. (2019). Adverse childhood experiences, childhood relationships and associated substance use and mental health in young Europeans. *European Journal of Public Health, 29*(4), 741–747. PMID: 30897194

Hughes, T. (1993). *Tom Brown's Schooldays and Tom Brown at Oxford*. Wordsworth Classics. (Original work published 1857)

Ibrahim, A. K., Kelly, S. J., Adams, C. E., & Glazebrook, C. (2013). A systematic review of studies of depression prevalence in university students. *Journal of Psychiatric Research, 47*(3), 391–400. PMID: 23260171

IEA. (2022). PIRLS 2021. International results in reading. https://pirls2021.org

Indriasari, F. N., Widyarani, L., & Kusuma, P. D. (2018). Emergency Preparedness for Children with Autism Spectrum Disorder (ASD) in Yogyakarta. *Jurnal Keperawatan Soedirman, 13*(3), 155. DOI: 10.20884/1.jks.2018.13.3.747

IPCC. (2014). C*limate Change 2014: Synthesis Report*. Contribution of Working Groups I, II and III to the Fifth Assessment Report of the Intergovernmental Panel on Climate Change. IPCC. https://www.ipcc.ch/site/assets/uploads/2018/05/SYR_AR5_FINAL_full_wcover.pdf

IPCC. (2022). Climate change 2022: Impacts, adaptation, and vulnerability. Contribution of Working Group II to the Sixth Assessment Report of the Intergovernmental Panel on Climate Change. Cambridge University Press. DOI: 10.1017/9781009325844

IPCC. (2023). *Climate Change 2023: Synthesis repor*t. Contribution of Working Groups I, II and III to the Sixth Assessment Report of the Intergovernmental Panel on Climate Change. IPCC. DOI: 10.59327/IPCC/AR6-9789291691647

Irish News. (2024, April 8). Paul Givan: System struggling to keep pace with increased demand for SEN places. https://www.irishnews.com/news/northern-ireland/system-struggling-to-keep-pace-with-increased-demand-for-sen-places-givan-YGIWHYERZ5FSRDESBKML6ZEGCI/#:~:text=The%20Education%20Minister%20said%20more,to%20be%20found%20by%20September.&text=5%3A09PM%20BST-,The%20education%20system%20is%20struggling%20to%20keep%20pace%20with%20the,%20),%20Paul%20Givan%20has%20said

Ivancheva, M., Lynch, K., & Keating, K. (2019). Precarity, gender and care in the neoliberal academy. *Gender, Work and Organization*, *26*(4), 448–462.

Ivanova, D., Stadler, K., Steen-Olsen, K., Wood, R., Vita, G., Tukker, A., & Hertwich, E. G. (2016). Environmental impact assessment of household consumption. *Journal of Industrial Ecology*, *20*(3), 526–536. DOI: 10.1111/jiec.12371

J. (2011). Bereavement Among African Americans and Latino/a Americans. *Journal of Mental Health Counseling*, 33(1), 11–20. DOI: 10.17744/mehc.33.1.r4971657p7176307

Jacob-Nzuzi-Khuabi, L.-A., Ally, K., Khan, S., Moolman, M., Mustapha, A. B., & Parker, M. (2022). Primary to secondary school transition of learners with traumatic brain injuries in the Cape metropolitan area: A learner perspective. *South African Journal of Occupational Therapy*, *52*(2).

Jacques-Hamilton, R., Sun, J., & Smillie, L. D. (2019). Costs and benefits of acting extraverted: A randomized controlled trial. *Journal of Experimental Psychology. General*, *148*(9), 1538. PMID: 30489119

James, D., Yates, J., & Ferguson, E. (2013). Can the 12-item general health questionnaire be used to identify medical students who might 'struggle'on the medical course? A prospective study on two cohorts. *BMC Medical Education*, *13*, 1–8. PMID: 23548161

Jamieson, M., Jack, R., O'Neill, B., Cullen, B., Lennon, M., Brewster, S., & Evans, J. (2020). Technology to encourage meaningful activities following brain injury. *Disability and Rehabilitation. Assistive Technology*, *15*(4), 453–466. PMID: 30985193

Jaycox, L. H., Kataoka, S. H., Stein, B. D., Langley, A. K., & Wong, M. (2012). Cognitive behavioural intervention for trauma in schools. *Journal of Applied School Psychology*, *28*, 239–255.

Jensen, B. B., & Schnack, K. (2006). The action competence approach in environmental education: Reprinted from Environmental Education Research (1997) 3 (2), pp. 163–178. *Environmental Education Research, 12*(3-4), 471–486. DOI: 10.1080/13504620600942998

Jerome, A. (2011). Comforting children and families who grieve: Incorporating spiritual support. *School Psychology International, 32*(2), 194–209.

Jerrim, J., & Lopez-Agudo, L. A. (2021). The impact of test language on PISA scores: New evidence from Wales. *British Educational Research Journal, 48*(3), 420–445. DOI: 10.1002/berj.3774

Jerrim, J., Morgan, A., & Sims, S. (2023). (in press). Teacher autonomy: Good for pupils? Good for teachers? *British Educational Research Journal.* Advance online publication. DOI: 10.1002/berj.3892

Jimenez, N., Virtue, A., Segar, K., Stoep, A., & Rivara, F. (2019). Effect of school services on academic performance after traumatic brain injury in hispanic and non-hispanic students. *The Journal of School Health, 89*(7), 519–526. PMID: 31016747

Jin, K. Y., Reichert, F., Cagasan, L. P.Jr, de La Torre, J., & Law, N. (2020). Measuring digital literacy across three age cohorts: Exploring test dimensionality and performance differences. *Computers & Education, 157*, 103968.

Johansen, M. O., Elissen, S., & Jeno, L. M. (2023). The bright and dark side of autonomy: How autonomy support and thwarting relate to student motivation and academic functioning. *Frontiers in Education, 8*, 1153647. DOI: 10.3389/feduc.2023.1153647

Johnson, D. W., & Johnson, R. T. (2002). *Learning together and alone: Cooperative, competitive, and individualistic learning*. Pearson.

Johnson, J. V., & Hall, E. M. (1988). Job strain, work place social support, and cardiovascular disease: A cross-sectional study of a random sample of the Swedish working population. *American Journal of Public Health, 78*, 1336–1342. PMID: 3421392

Johnstone, L., & Boyle, M. (2018). *The power threat meaning framework: Towards the identification of patterns in emotional distress, unusual experiences and troubles or troubling behaviour, as an alternative to functional psychiatric diagnosis*. British Psychological Society.

Jones, A., Deane, C., & Keegan, O. (2015). The development of a framework to support bereaved children and young people: The Irish Childhood Bereavement Care Pyramid. *Bereavement Care, 34*, 43–51. DOI: 10.1080/02682621.2015.1063857

Jones, E., Priestley, M., Brewster, E., Wilbraham, S. J., Hughes, G., & Spanner, L. (2021). Student wellbeing and assessment in higher education: The balancing act. *Assessment & Evaluation in Higher Education*, *46*(3), 438–450. DOI: 10.1080/02602938.2020.1782344

Jordan, A., Glenn, C., & McGhie-Richmond, D. (2010). The Supporting Effective Teaching (SET) project: The relationship of inclusive teaching practices to teachers' beliefs about disability and ability, and about their roles as teachers. *Teaching and Teacher Education*, *26*(2), 259–266. DOI: 10.1016/j.tate.2009.03.005

Jordan, A., & Stanovich, P. (2003). Teachers' personal epistemological beliefs about students with disabilities as indicators of effective teaching practices. *Journal of Research in Special Educational Needs*, *3*(1), 1–14. DOI: 10.1111/j.1471-3802.2003.00184.x

Joronen, K., Hastrup, A., Nieminen, S., Rantanen, A., & Pelkonen, M. (2022). Family centres in Finland – a new integrated service model for families with children and adolescents. *International Journal of Integrated Care*, *22*, 113. DOI: 10.5334/ijic.ICIC21141

Kagan, D. M. (1992). Implications of Research on Teacher Belief. *Educational Psychologist*, *27*(1), 65–90.

Kahn, L., Linden, M., McKinlay, A., Gomez, D., & Glang, A. (2018). An international perspective on educators' perceptions of children with Traumatic Brain Injury. *NeuroRehabilitation*, *42*(3), 229–309. PMID: 29660961

Kakonge, L., Charron, V. P., Vedder, J., Wormald, K., & Turkstra, L. S. (2022). A mapping review of adolescent identity after TBI: What clinicians need to know. *Neuropsychological Rehabilitation*, *32*(8), 1868–1903. PMID: 35604405

Kalwak, W., & Weihgold, V. (2022). The relationality of ecological emotions: An interdisciplinary critique of individual resilience as psychology's response to the climate crisis. *Frontiers in Psychology*, *22*, 823620. DOI: 10.3389/fpsyg.2022.823620

Kane, M., & Engle, R. (2002). The role of prefrontal cortex in working-memory capacity, executive attention, and general fluid intelligence: An individual difference perspective. *Psychonomic Bulletin & Review*, *9*(4), 637–671. DOI: 10.3758/BF03196323

Kangas-Dick, K., & O'Shaughnessy, E. (2020). Interventions that promote resilience among teachers: A systematic review of the literature. *International Journal of School & Educational Psychology*, *8*(2), 131–146. DOI: 10.1080/21683603.2020.1734125

Kanner, A. D., Coyne, J. C., Schaefer, C., & Lazarus, R. S. (1981). Comparison of two modes of stress measurement: Daily hassles and uplifts versus major life events. *Journal of Behavioral Medicine*, *4*, 1–25. PMID: 7288876

Kaplan, A. (2023). A framework for approaching policy-oriented educational psychology research. *Educational Psychologist*, *58*(4), 229–243. DOI: 10.1080/00461520.2023.2253301

Karasek, R. A. (1979). Job demands, job decision latitude and mental strain: Implications for job redesign. *Administrative Science Quarterly*, *24*, 285–308.

Karasek, R., & Theorell, T. (1990). *Healthy Work: Stress, Productivity, and the Reconstruction of Working Life*. Basic Books.

Katzarska-Miller, I., & Reysen, S. (2019). Educating for global citizenship: Lessons from psychology. *Childhood*, *95*(6), 24–33. DOI: 10.1080/00094056.2019.1689055

Keller, M. M., Chang, M.-L., Becker, E. S., Goetz, T., & Frenzel, A. C. (2014). Teachers' emotional experiences and exhaustion as predictors of emotional labor in the classroom: An experience sampling study. *Frontiers in Psychology*, *5*. DOI: 10.3389/fpsyg.2014.01442

Kelly-Irving, M., & Delpierre, C. (2019). A critique of the adverse childhood experiences framework in epidemiology and public health: Uses and misuses. *Social Policy and Society*, *18*(3), 445–456.

Kenny, N., McCoy, S., & Mihut, G. (2020, September). Special Education Reforms in Ireland: Changing Systems, Changing Schools, International Journal of Inclusive Education. *Online (Bergheim)*, *23*. https://www.tandfonline.com/doi/full/10.1080/13603116.2020.1821447

Kenny, N., McCoy, S., & O'Higgins Noman, J. (2023). A Whole Education Approach to Inclusive Education: An Integrated Model to Guide Planning, Policy, and Provision. *Education Sciences*, *13*(9). Advance online publication. DOI: 10.3390/educsci13090959

Kerr, H. (2013). Mental distress survey overview. *MRS Evidence Matters*: United Kingdom. Retrieved from https://www.nus.org.uk/Global/Campaigns/20130517%20Mental%20Distress%20Survey%20%20Overview.pdf

Kerssens, N., & van Dijck, J. (2023). How platformisation affects pedagogical autonomy in primary schools. In *World Yearbook of Education 2024* (pp. 89–105). Routledge.

Kessler, R. C., Green, J. G., Gruber, M. J., Sampson, N. A., Bromet, E., Cuitan, M., Furukawa, T. A., Gureje, O., Hinkov, H., Hu, C.-Y., Lara, C., Lee, S., Mneimneh, Z., Myer, L., Oakley-Browne, M., Posada-Villa, J., Sagar, R., Viana, M. C., & Zaslavsky, A. M. (2010). Screening for serious mental illness in the general population with the K6 screening scale: Results from the WHO World Mental Health (WMH) survey initiative. *International Journal of Methods in Psychiatric Research, 19*(Suppl 1), 4–22. PMID: 20527002

Khamis, V. (2016). Does parent's psychological distress mediate the relationship between war trauma and psychosocial adjustment in children? *Journal of Health Psychology, 21*(7), 1361–1370. DOI: 10.1177/1359105314553962 PMID: 27357922

King-Sears, M. E. (2009). Universal design for learning: Technology and pedagogy. *Learning Disability Quarterly, 32*(4), 199–201. DOI: 10.2307/27740372

Kittay, E. F. (1999). *Love's Labor*. Routledge.

Klinenberg, E., Araos, M., & Koslov, L. (2020). Sociology and the climate crisis. *Annual Review of Sociology, 46*(1), 649–669. DOI: 10.1146/annurev-soc-121919-054750

Koblenz, J. (2016). Growing From Grief. *Omega, 73*(3), 203–230. DOI: 10.1177/0030222815576123

Korpershoek, H., Canrinus, E. T., Fokkens-Bruinsma, M., & de Boer, H. (2020). The relationships between school belonging and students' motivational, social-emotional, behavioural, and academic outcomes in secondary education: A meta-analytic review. *Research Papers in Education, 35*(6), 641–680. DOI: 10.1080/02671522.2019.1615116

Korte, M. (2020). The impact of the digital revolution on human brain and behavior: Where do we stand? *Dialogues in Clinical Neuroscience, 22*(2), 101–111.

Kosmyna, N., Hauptman, E., Yuan, Y. T., Situ, J., Liao, X.-H., Beresnitsky, A. V., Braunstein, I., & Maes, P. (2025). Your Brain on ChatGPT: Accumulation of Cognitive Debt when Using an AI Assistant for Essay Writing Task. https://arxiv.org/abs/2506.08872

Kovács, L. N., Jordan, G., Berglund, F., Holden, B., Niehoff, E., Pohl, F., Younssi, M., Zevallos, I., Ágoston, C., Varga, A., & Kökönyei, G.. (2024). Acting as we feel: Which emotional responses to the climate crisis motivate climate action. *Journal of Environmental Psychology, 96*. Advance online publication. DOI: 10.1016/j.jenvp.2024.102327

Krathwohl, D. R., Bloom, B. S., & Masia, B. B. (1964). Taxonomy of educational objectives: The classification of educational goals, Hand book II: Affective domain. New York: David Mckay Company Incorporated.

Kuboja, J. M., & Ngussa, B. M. (2015). Affective learning and cognitive skills improvement: Experience of selected schools in Arusha, Tanzania. *International Journal of Academic Research in Progressive Education and Development, 4*(2), 38–53. DOI: 10.6007/IJARPED/v4-i2/1727

Kuijpers, E., Pickett, J., Wille, B., & Hofmans, J. (2021). Do you feel better when you behave more extraverted than you are? The relationship between cumulative counterdispositional extraversion and positive feelings. *Personality and Social Psychology Bulletin*. Advance online publication. PMID: 34056978

Kuit, N., & Ryke, E. H. (2023). A Rapid Review of Non-death Bereavement Interventions for Children in Alternative Care. *Child & Adolescent Social Work Journal, 40*, 29–41. DOI: 10.1007/s10560-021-00757-w

Kumar, P., Sahani, J., Rawat, N., Debele, S., Tiwari, A., Emygdio, A. P. M., Abhijith, K. V., Kudadia, V., Holmes, K., & Pfautsch, S. (2023). Using empirical science education in schools to improve climate change literacy. *Renewable & Sustainable Energy Reviews, 17*, 113232. DOI: 10.1016/j.rser.2023.113232

Kumar, R. M. (2023). The Many Faces of Grief: A Systematic Literature Review of Grief During the COVID-19 Pandemic. *Illness, Crises, and Loss, 31*(1), 100–119. DOI: 10.1177/10541373211038084 PMID: 36605776

Kyriacou, C. (2015). Teacher stress and burnout: Methodological perspectives. In Wright, J. D. (Ed.), *International Encyclopedia of the Social & Behavioral Sciences* (pp. 72–74). Elsevier. DOI: 10.1016/B978-0-08-097086-8.92087-7

Kyriakides, L., & Creemers, B. P. (2018). Investigating the quality and equity dimensions of educational effectiveness. *Studies in Educational Evaluation, 57*, 1–5.

Lai, B. S., Lewis, R., Livings, M. S., La Greca, A. M., & Esnard, A.-M. (2017). Posttraumatic Stress Symptom Trajectories Among Children After Disaster Exposure: A Review. *Journal of Traumatic Stress, 30*(6), 571–582. DOI: 10.1002/jts.22242 PMID: 29193316

Lambert, N. M., Gwinn, A. M., Baumeister, R. F., Strachman, A., Washburn, I. J., Gable, S. L., & Fincham, F. D. (2013). A boost of positive affect: The perks of sharing positive experiences. *Journal of Social and Personal Relationships, 30*(1), 24–43. DOI: 10.1177/026540751244940

Lansdown, G., Jimerson, S. R., & Shahroozi, R. (2014). Children's rights and school psychology: Children's right to participation. *Journal of School Psychology*, *52*(1), 3–12. DOI: 10.1016/j.jsp.2013.12.006

Larcombe, W., Finch, S., Sore, R., Murray, C. M., Kentish, S., Mulder, R. A., & Williams, D. (2016). Prevalence and socio-demographic correlates of psychological distress among students at an Australian university. *Studies in Higher Education*, *41*, 1074–1091.

Latorre-Cosculluela, C., Suárez, C., Quiroga, S., Sobradiel-Sierra, N., Lozano-Blasco, R., & Rodríguez-Martínez, A. (2021). Flipped Classroom model before and during COVID-19: Using technology to develop 21st century skills. *Interactive Technology and Smart Education*, *18*(2), 189–204.

Laurence, J., & McGinnity, F. (2025). F. and K. Murphy. (2025). Community-level drivers of attitudes towards immigration in Ireland. *Journal of Ethnic and Migration Studies*, *51*(11). Advance online publication. DOI: 10.1080/1369183X.2025.2487198

Law, E. L. C., Vostanis, P., & O'Reilly, M. J. (2023). Insights from impacts of the digital divide on children in five majority world countries during the COVID-19 pandemic. *Behaviour & Information Technology*, *42*(15), 2696–2715.

Lawlor, J., Marshall, K., & Tangney, B. (2016). Bridge21–exploring the potential to foster intrinsic student motivation through a team-based, technology-mediated learning model. *Technology, Pedagogy and Education*, *25*(2), 187–206.

Lawrance, E., Thompson, R., Fontana, G., & Jennings, N. (2021). The impact of climate change on mental health and emotional wellbeing: current evidence and implications for policy and practice. Grantham Institute briefing paper, 36, 1-36. DOI: 10.1080/09540261.2022.2128725

Lawrence, N. (2020). Supervision in education – Healthier schools for all. Barnardo's Scotland. https://www.barnardos.org.uk/sites/default/files/uploads/Supervision%20in%20Education%20-%20Healthier%20Schools%20For%20All%20-%20Main%20report_0.pdf

Lazarus, R. S., & Folkman, S. (1987). Transactional theory and research on emotions and coping. *European Journal of Personality*, *1*(3), 141–169. DOI: 10.1002/per.2410010304

Leaper, C. (2011). Research in developmental psychology on gender and relationships: Reflections on the past and looking into the future. *British Journal of Developmental Psychology*, *29*(2), 347–356. DOI: 10.1111/j.2044-835X.2011.02035.x

Lebel, L., Paquin, V., Kenny, T. A., Fletcher, C., Nadeau, L., Chachamovich, E., & Lemire, M. (2022). Climate change and Indigenous mental health in the Circumpolar North: A systematic review to inform clinical practice. *Transcultural Psychiatry*, *59*(3), 312–336. DOI: 10.1177/13634615211066698

Lee, J., Chen, C., & Basu, A. (2025). From Novelty to Knowledge: A Longitudinal Investigation of the Novelty Effect on Learning Outcomes in Virtual Reality. *IEEE Transactions on Visualization and Computer Graphics*.

Lee, J., Zhang, Z., Song, H., & Huang, X. (2013). Effects of Epistemological and Pedagogical Beliefs on the Instructional Practices of Teachers: A Chinese Perspective. *The Australian Journal of Teacher Education*, *38*(12), 119–146. https://ro.ecu.edu.au/ajte/vol38/iss12/8/

Lemalu-Sankale, N. (2023, November 21). *Beyond the 'White Saviour': A grateful African's view on Mr. Beast's wells.* Medium. https://medium.com/@gratefulafrican/beyond-the-white-savior-a-grateful-african-s-view-on-mr-beast-s-wells-19935aa7e648

Lenz, B. (2001). The transition from adolescence to young adulthood: A theoretical perspective. The Journal of School Meehan, C., and K. Howells. 2018. "What Really Matters to Freshers?": Evaluation of First Year Student Experience of Transition into University. *Journal of Further and Higher Education*, *42*(7), 893–907. DOI: 10.1080/0309877X.2017.1323194

Lerner, J. S., Li, Y., Valdesolo, P., & Kassam, K. S. (2015). Emotion and decision making. *Annual Review of Psychology*, *66*, 799–823. DOI: 10.1146/annurev-psych-010213-115043

Levi-Belz, Y. (2023). Interpersonal facilitators of complicated grief and depression in the aftermath of suicide loss: The mediated roles of suicide-related shame and guilt. *Suicide & Life-Threatening Behavior*, *53*(4), 680–691. DOI: 10.1111/sltb.12973 PMID: 37439284

Lewinsohn, P. M., Allen, N. B., Seeley, J. R., & Gotlib, I. H. (1999). First onset versus recurrence of depression: Differential processes of psychosocial risk. *Journal of Abnormal Psychology*, *108*, 483–489. PMID: 10466272

Lewis, S. J., Arseneault, L., Caspi, A., Fisher, H. L., Matthews, T., Moffitt, T. E., & Danese, A. (2019). The epidemiology of trauma and post-traumatic stress disorder in a representative cohort of young people in England and Wales. *The Lancet. Psychiatry*, *6*(3), 247–256. https://www.thelancet.com/action/showPdf?pii=S2215-0366%2819%2930031-8

Lindahl, R. (2006). The Right to Education in a Globalized World. *Journal of Studies in International Education, 10*(1), 5–26. DOI: 10.1177/1028315305283308

Linden, M. (2018). *How can we help children with brain injuries transition back to school?* Science Daily.

Linden, M., Braiden, H., & Miller, S. (2013). Educational professionals' understanding of childhood traumatic brain injury. *Brain Injury, 27*(1), 92–102. PMID: 23252440

Linden, M., Glang, A., & McKinlay, A. (2018). A systematic review and meta-analysis of educational interventions for children and adolescents with acquired brain injury. *NeurorRehabiliation, 42*, 311–323. PMID: 29660957

Lingard, B. (2020). *Globalisation and education: theorising and researching changing imbrications in education policy*. Routledge.

Lingard, B., & Sellar, S. (2013). Globalization, edu-business and network governance: The policy sociology of Stephen J. Ball and rethinking education policy analysis. *London Review of Education, 11*(3).

Lipson, S., & Eisenberg, D. (2018). Mental health and academic attitudes and expectations in university populations: Results from the healthy minds study. *Journal of Mental Health (Abingdon, England), 27*(3), 205–213. DOI: 10.1080/09638237.2017.1417567 PMID: 29265935

Liu, T. C. (2022). A case study of the adaptive learning platform in a Taiwanese elementary school: Precision education from teachers' perspectives. *Education and Information Technologies, 27*(5), 6295–6316.

Lively-Endicott, H. R., Naimi, K., Hudson, S. M., & Schonfeld, D. J. (2023). Educator perspectives on grief-sensitive training during the COVID-19 pandemic in US public schools. *The Journal of School Health*. Advance online publication. PMID: 37879312

Livingstone, S., & Stoilova, M. (2021). The 4Cs: Classifying online risk to children. Academic Press.

Livingstone, S. (2008). Taking risky opportunities in youthful content creation: Teenagers' use of social networking sites for intimacy, privacy and self-expression. *New Media & Society, 10*(3), 393–411.

Livingstone, S., & Blum-Ross, A. (2020). *Parenting for a Digital Future: How Hopes and Fears about Technology Shape Children's Lives*. Oxford University Press.

Livingstone, S., Ólafsson, K., Helsper, E. J., Lupiáñez-Villanueva, F., Veltri, G. A., & Folkvord, F. (2017). Maximizing opportunities and minimizing risks for children online: The role of digital skills in emerging strategies of parental mediation. *Journal of Communication*, *67*(1), 82–105.

Liwanag, M. F., & Galicia, L. S. (2023). Technological self-efficacy, learning motivation, and self-directed learning of selected senior high school students in a blended learning environment. *Technium Soc. Sci. J.*, *44*, 534.

Lodge, J. M., Yang, S., Furze, L., & Dawson, P. (2023). It's not like a calculator, so what is the relationship between learners and generative artificial intelligence? Learning. *Research and Practice*, *9*(2), 117–124.

Lolich, L., & Lynch, K. (2016). The affective imaginary: Students as affective consumers of risk. *Higher Education Research & Development*, *35*(1), 17–30.

Lolich, L., & Lynch, K. (2017). No choice without care: Palliative care as a relational matter, the case of Ireland. *Soundings: An Interdisciplinary Journal*, *100*(4), 353–374.

Longman, J., Braddon, M., Verlie, B., Schlosberg, D., Hampshire, L., Hawke, C., & Saurman, E. (2023). Building resilience to the mental health impacts of climate change in rural Australia. *The Journal of Climate Change and Health*, *12*, 100240. DOI: 10.1016/j.joclim.2023.100240

Lopes Cardozo, M.T. (2012). Transforming pre-service teacher education in Bolivia: From indigenous denial to decolonisation? *Compare: A Journal of Comparative and International Education*, *42*(5), 751-772.

Luhmann, N., & Rasch, W. (2002). *Theories of Distinction: Redescribing the Descriptions of Modernity*. Stanford University Press.

Lundahl, L. (2016). Equality, Inclusion and Marketization of Nordic Education: Introductory Notes. Research in Comparative and International Education, 11, 3–12. doi:.DOI: 10.1177/1745499916631059

Lundy, L. (2007). 'Voice' is not enough: Conceptualising Article 12 of the United Nations Convention on the Rights of the Child. *British Educational Research Journal*, *33*(6), 927–942. DOI: 10.1080/01411920701657033

Lupton, D., & Williamson, B. (2017). The datafied child: The dataveillance of children and implications for their rights. *New Media & Society*, *19*(5), 780–794.

Lynch, K. (2010). Carelessness: A hidden doxa of higher education. *Arts and Humanities in Higher Education*, *9*(1), 54–67.

Lynch, K. (2010). Carelessness: A Hidden Doxa of Higher Education. *Arts and Humanities in Higher Education*, *9*(1), 54–67. DOI: 10.1177/1474022209350104

Lynch, K. (2020). Affective Equality and Social Justice. In Celentano, D., & Caranti, L. (Eds.), *Paradigms of Justice: Redistribution, Recognition, and Beyond* (pp. 118–139). Routledge.

Lynch, K. (2021). *Care and Capitalism*. Polity Press.

Lynch, K., Baker, J., & Lyons, M. (Eds.). (2009). *Affective equality: Love, care, and injustice*. Palgrave Macmillan.

Lynch, K., & Kalaitzake, M. (2020). Affective and calculative solidarity: The impact of individualism and neoliberal capitalism. *European Journal of Social Theory*, *23*(2), 238–257.

Lythreatis, S., Singh, S. K., & El-Kassar, A. N. (2022). The digital divide: A review and future research agenda. *Technological Forecasting and Social Change*, *175*, 121359.

Lyubomirsky, S., King, L., & Diener, E. (2005). The benefits of frequent positive affect: Does happiness lead to success? *Psychological Bulletin*, *131*(6), 803. DOI: 10.1037/0033-2909.131.6.803

Mac Domhnaill, C., Lyons, S., & McCoy, S. (2020). *Specialist support for persons with disabilities living in the community: Review of international practice*. ESRI. www.esri.ie/system/files/publications/SUSTAT97_0.pdf

MacDonald, K. (2006). Psychology and white ethnocentrism. *The Occidental Quarterly*, *6*(4), 2007.

Mace, R. (1985). Universal design: Barrier-free environments for everyone. In Stein, B. S., & Shoemaker, R. H. (Eds.), *Designing for accessibility: An architectural agenda for the 80's*. Van Nostrand Reinhold.

Mace, R. (1997). Universal Design: A collaborative approach. *Journal of Design and Technology Education*, *2*(2), 86–94.

Mackaskill, A. (2018). Undergraduate mental health issues: The challenge of the second year of study. *Journal of Mental Health (Abingdon, England)*. Advance online publication. DOI: 10.1080/09638237.2018.1437611 PMID: 29429365

Macmurray, J. (2012). Learning to be Human. *Oxford Review of Education*, *38*(6), 661–674.

Maddi, S. R. (2002). The story of hardiness: Twenty years of theorizing, research, and practice. *Consulting Psychology Journal, 54*(3), 173–185.

Maddi, S. R., Harvey, R. H., Khoshaba, D. M., Fazel, M., & Resurreccion, N. (2009). Hardiness training facilitates performance in college. *The Journal of Positive Psychology, 4*(6), 566–577.

Maftei, A., Dumitriu, A., & Holman, A. C. (2021). They will discover I'm a fraud!" The Imposter Syndrome Among Psychology Students. *Studia Psychologica, 63*(4), 337–351.

Maguire, M., Ball, S., & Braun, A. (2010). Behaviour, classroom management and student 'control': Enacting policy in the English secondary school. *International Studies in Sociology of Education, 20*(2), 153–170. DOI: 10.1080/09620214.2010.503066

Mair, A. P. A., Nimbley, E., McConachie, D., Goodall, K., & Gillespie-Smith, K. (2024). Understanding the Neurodiversity of Grief: A Systematic Literature Review of Experiences of Grief and Loss in the Context of Neurodevelopmental Disorders. *Review Journal of Autism and Developmental Disorders (Online).* DOI: 10.1007/s40489-024-00447-0

Major, L., Francis, G. A., & Tsapali, M. (2021). The effectiveness of technology-supported personalised learning in low-and middle-income countries: A meta-analysis. *British Journal of Educational Technology, 52*(5), 1935–1964.

Malle, B. F., & Korman, J. (2013). *Attribution theory.* Oxford University Press.

Manathunga, C. (2020). Decolonising higher education: Creating space for Southern knowledge systems. *Scholarship of Teaching and Learning in the South, 4*(1), 4–25.

Mansour, N., Aras, C., Staarman, J. K., & Alotaibi, S. B. M. (2024). Embodied learning of science concepts through augmented reality technology. *Education and Information Technologies*, 1–31.

Marbin, D., Gutwinski, S., Schreiter, S., & Heinz, A. (2022). Perspectives in Poverty and Mental Health. *Frontiers in Public Health, 10*, 975482.

Margolis, S., & Lyubomirsky, S. (2020). Experimental manipulation of extraverted and introverted behavior and its effects on wellbeing. *Journal of Experimental Psychology. General, 149*(4), 719. PMID: 31368759

Marin, M. F., Lord, C., Andrews, J., Juster, R. P., Sindi, S., Arsenault-Lapierre, G., & Lupien, S. J. (2011). Chronic stress, cognitive functioning and mental health. *Neurobiology of Learning and Memory, 96*(4), 583–595. PMID: 21376129

Markic, S., & Eilks, I. (2013). 'Potential changes in prospective chemistry teachers beliefs about teaching and learning a cross level study. *International Journal of Science and Mathematics Education, 11*(4), 979–998. DOI: 10.1007/s10763-013-9417-9

Marland, M. (1974). *Pastoral Care*. Heinemann Educational Books.

Martin, A. J. (2007). Examining a multidimensional model of student motivation and engagement using a construct validation approach. *The British Journal of Educational Psychology, 77*, 413–440.

Martin, A. J. (2013). Motivation to learn. In Holliman, A. J. (Ed.), *The Routledge International Companion to Educational Psychology*. Routledge.

Maslach, C., & Jackson, S. E. (1986). *Maslach Burnout Inventory manual* (2nd ed.). Consulting Psychologists Press.

Maslach, C., Schaufeli, W. B., & Leiter, M. P. (2001). Job burnout. *Annual Review of Psychology, 52*(1), 397–422. PMID: 11148311

Maslin, K., Murcia, K., Blackley, S., & Lowe, G. (2023). Fostering young children's creativity in online learning environments: A systematic literature review. *Thinking Skills and Creativity, 47*, 101249.

Masri-Zada, T., Martirosyan, S., Abdou, A., Barbar, R., Kades, S., Makki, H., Haley, G., & Agrawal, D. K. (2025). The Impact of Social Media & Technology on Child and Adolescent Mental Health. *Journal of Psychiatry and Psychiatric Disorders, 9*(2), 111–130. PMID: 40520349

Masten, A. S. (2014). *Ordinary magic: Resilience in development*. Guilford Press.

Ma, T., Moore, J., & Cleary, A. (2022). Climate change impacts on the mental health and wellbeing of young people: A scoping review of risk and protective factors. *Social Science & Medicine, 301*, 114888. DOI: 10.1016/j.socscimed.2022.114888

Maté, G., & Maté, D. (2022). *The myth of normal: Illness, health and healing in a toxic culture*. Penguin Books.

Matney, C., Bowman, K., & Berwick, D. (Eds.). (2022). *Traumatic Brain Injury: A Roadmap for Accelerating Progress*. National Academies of Sciences, Engineering, and Medicine; Health and Medicine Division; Board on Health Care Services; Board on Health Sciences Policy; Committee on Accelerating Progress in Traumatic Brain Injury Research and Care.

Maybery, D., Maybery, M., Bresnan, R., Croft, B., Graham, R., Macaulay, J., & Szakacs, E. (2002). Responding to daily event questionnaires: The influence of the order of hassle and uplift scales. *Stress and Health, 18*(1), 19–26. DOI: 10.1002/smi.915

McAnelly, K., & Gaffney, M. (2019). Rights, Inclusion and Citizenship: A Good News Story About Learning in the Early Years. *International Journal of Inclusive Education, 23*(10), 1081–1094.

McCarron, R., Watson, S., & Gracey, F. (2019). What do kids with acquired brain injury want? Mapping neuropsychological rehabilitation goals to the international classification of functioning, disability and health. *Jourfnal of international Neuropsychological Society, 25*, 403-412.

McCarthy, P. (2013) Expectations You Encounter: The Educational Experiences and Transition Choices/Opportunities of Blind/Vision Impaired People in the Republic of Ireland [Unpublished PhD thesis]. Trinity College Dublin.

McCart, M., & DaSalvo, G. (2024). Educating the educators: Education for schools and teachers. *Brain Injury : [BI], 21*(1), 20–22.

McCart, M., Glang, A., Slocumb, J., Gau, J., Becker, L., & Gomez, D. (2020). A quasi-experimental study examining the effects of online traumatic brain injury professional development on educator knowledge, application, and efficacy in a practitioner setting. *Disability and Rehabilitation, 42*(17), 2430–2436. PMID: 30978108

McCart, M., Todis, B., Gomez, D., & Glang, A. (2023). School experiences following traumatic brain injury: A longitudinal qualitative study. *NeuroRehabilitation, 52*, 529–537. PMID: 37125570

McClatchey, I. S., Vonk, M. E., Lee, J., & Bride, B. (2014). Traumatic and Complicated Grief Among Children: One or Two Constructs? *Death Studies, 38*(2), 69–78. DOI: 10.1080/07481187.2012.725571 PMID: 24517704

McCloud, T., & Bann, D. (2019). Financial stress and mental health among higher education students in the UK up to 2018: Rapid review of evidence. *Journal of Epidemiology and Community Health, 73*(10), 977–984. PMID: 31406015

McCluskey, G., Lloyd, G., Kane, J., Riddell, S., Stead, J., & Weedon, E. (2008). Can restorative practices in schools make a difference? *Educational Review, 60*(4), 405–417. DOI: 10.1080/00131910802393456

McCoy, S., Ye, K., & Carroll, E. (2025) Paths, Tracks, Gaps and Cliffs: Tracking the post-school pathways of students with special education needs. Dublin: NCSE. https://www.esri.ie/publications/paths-tracks-gaps-and-cliffs-the-post-school-transitions-of-students-with-special

McCoy, S., Banks, J., Frawley, D., Watson, D., & Shevlin, M. (2014). *Understanding Special Class Provision in Ireland: Findings from a National Survey of Schools*. ESRI and National Council for Special Education. https://www.esri.ie/publications/understanding-special-class-provision-in-ireland-findings-from-a-national-survey-of

McCoy, S., & Marcus-Quinn, A. (2025). Navigating youth, smartphones, and policy: A balanced perspective on digital wellbeing. *Pediatric Research*. Advance online publication. DOI: 10.1038/s41390-025-04288-3 PMID: 40731095

McCrae, R. R., & Costa, P. T. (2004). A contemplated revision of the Neo Five-Factor inventory. *Personality and Individual Differences*, *36*(3), 587–596.

McCutchen, C., Hyland, P., Shevlin, M., & Cloitre, M. (2022). The occurrence and co-occurrence of ACEs and their relationship to mental health in the United States and Ireland. *Journal of Child Abuse and Neglect*. DOI: 10.1016/j.chiabu.2022.105681

McGarr, O. (2023). Investigating student teachers' responses to including sustainable development as part of their professional digital competence development. *Technology, Pedagogy and Education*, *32*(5), 653–665.

McGarr, O. (2024). Teacher educators' views and responses to digital distraction in pre-service teacher education. *Teaching and Teacher Education*, *148*, 104701.

McGarr, O., & McDonagh, A. (2021). Exploring the digital competence of pre-service teachers on entry onto an initial teacher education programme in Ireland. *Irish Educational Studies*, *40*(1), 115–128.

McGill, R. M. (2020). *How has Twitter influenced education politics in England?* Wlfson College, Cambridge University. https://www.researchgate.net/publication/341793032_How_has_Twitter_influenced_education_politics_in_England

McGinnity, F., Laurence, J., & Cunniffe, E. (2023). *Comparing Migrant Integration in Ireland and Northern Ireland, ESRI Research Series 158*. Economic and Social Research Institute.

McIntyre, , Worsley, Corcoran, Woods, & Bentall. (2018). Academic and Non-Academic Predictors of Student Psychological Distress: The Role of Social Identity and Loneliness. *Journal of Mental Health (Abingdon, England)*, *27*(3), 230–239. DOI: 10.1080/09638237.2018.1437608 PMID: 29436883

McKercher, K. A. (2020). *Beyond sticky notes: Co-design for real: Mindsets, methods and movements*. Beyond Sticky Notes.

McKernan, R. (2024). Co-design as a trauma-informed process for the design of trauma-informed practices in schools. Paper presented at the European Conference on Educational Research, Nicosia, Cyprus.

McNicholl, A., Casey, H., Desmond, D., & Gallagher, P. (2021). The impact of assistive technology use for students with disabilities in higher education: A systematic review. *Disability and Rehabilitation. Assistive Technology*, *16*(2), 130–143.

McNiel, J. M., & Fleeson, W. (2006). The causal effects of extraversion on positive affect and neuroticism on negative affect: Manipulating state extraversion and state neuroticism in an experimental approach. *Journal of Research in Personality*, *40*, 529–550.

McNiel, J. M., Lowman, J. C., & Fleeson, W. (2010). The effect of state extraversion on four types of affect. *European Journal of Personality*, *24*, 18–35.

Meehan, C., & Howells, K. (2018). 'What really matters to freshers?': Evaluation of first year student experience of transition into university. *Journal of Further and Higher Education*, *42*(7), 893–907.

Mejia-Puig, L., & Chandrasekera, T. (2023). The virtual body in a design exercise: A conceptual framework for embodied cognition. *International Journal of Technology and Design Education*, *33*(5), 1861–1882.

Mercy Corps. (2020). *The facts: Indonesia earthquakes, tsunamis and other natural disasters*. Mercy Corps. https://reliefweb.int/report/indonesia/facts-indonesia-earthquakes-tsunamis-and-other-natural-disasters

Merrick, M. T., Ford, D. C., Ports, K. A., & Guinn, A. S. (2018). Prevalence of adverse childhood experiences from the 2011-2014 Behavioral Risk Factor Surveillance System in 23 states. *JAMA Pediatrics*, *172*(11). PMID: 30242348

Meyer, A., & Rose, D. (1998). Learning to read in the computer age. In *From reading research to practice*. Cambridge, MA: Brookline Books.

Meyer, A., & Rose, D. H. (2000). The universality of universal design: Educational implications of principles of universal design. *Journal of Learning Disabilities*, *33*(6), 505–515.

Meyer, J. W. (2010). World Society, Institutional Theories, and the Actor. *Annual Review of Sociology*, *36*, 1–20.

Miao, F., & Holmes, W. (2021). International Forum on AI and the Futures of Education, developing competencies for the AI Era, 7-8 December 2020: synthesis report.

Michalko, R. (2009). The excessive appearance of disability. *International Journal of Qualitative Studies in Education : QSE*, *22*(1), 65–74. DOI: 10.1080/09518390802581885

Miller, K. K., Brown, C. R., Shramko, M., & Svetaz, M. V. (2019). Applying trauma-informed practices to the care of refugee and immigrant youth: 10 clinical pearls. *Children (Basel, Switzerland)*, *6*(8), 94. DOI: 10.3390/children6080094 PMID: 31434278

Miltimore, J. (2023, November 15). *Why Mr. Beast is under fire for bringing clean water to 500,000 Africans*. American Institute for Economic Research. https://aier.org/article/why-mr-beast-is-under-fire-for-bringing-clean-water-to-500000-africans/

Ministry of Communication. (2024). *Bharatnet Project.* https://usof.gov.in/en/bharatnet-project

Mitchell, G., Murphy, E., Bojarcz, S., & Cohen, S. (2023) Is an EU-Wide Approach to the Mental Health Crisis Necessary? Dublin: FEPS Policy Study. https://feps-europe.eu/wp-content/uploads/2023/03/PS-Is-an-EU-wide-approach-to-the-mental-health-crisis-necessary.pdf

Mohan, G., McCoy, S., Carroll, E., Mihut, G., Lyons, S., & Mac Domhnaill, C. (2020). Learning for all? Second-level education in Ireland during COVID-19. ESRI Survey and Statistical Report Series 92 June 2020.

Mohan, G., Carroll, E., McCoy, S., Mac Domhnaill, C., & Mihut, G. (2021). Magnifying inequality? Home learning environments and social reproduction during school closures in Ireland. *Irish Educational Studies*, *40*(2), 265–274. www.tandfonline.com/doi/full/10.1080/03323315.2021.1915841

Mok, Y. F. (2002). Teacher growth: The formation and pursuit of personal values. *Interchange*, *33*, 115–138.

Mollick, E., & Mollick, E. (2024). *Co-Intelligence*. Random House UK.

Moncrieffe, M., Race, R., Harris, R., Chetty, D., Riaz, N., Ayling, P., & Steinburg, S. (2020). Decolonising the curriculum. *Research Intelligence*, *142*(9).

Monroe, M. C., Plate, R. R., Oxarart, A., Bowers, A., & Chaves, W. A. (2019). Identifying effective climate change education strategies: A systematic review of the research. *Environmental Education Research*, *25*(6), 791–812. DOI: 10.1080/13504622.2017.1360842

Mooney, S., Fargas, M., MacDonald, M., O'Neill, D., Walsh, C., Hayes, D., & Montgomery, L. (2024). *'We are on a journey': implementing trauma informed approaches in Northern Ireland - Executive summary report.* Queen's University Belfast. https://pureadmin.qub.ac.uk/ws/portalfiles/portal/558170230/Implementing_TIAs_NI._Executive_Report._QUB_2024.pdf

Moore, A., Stapley, E., Hayes, D., Town, R., & Deighton, J. (2022). Barriers and Facilitators to Sustaining School-Based Mental Health and Wellbeing Interventions: A Systematic Review. *International Journal of Environmental Research and Public Health, 19*(6), 3587. DOI: 10.3390/ijerph19063587

Moran, E. F. (2016). *People and nature: an introduction to Human Ecological Relations.* John Wiley & Sons.

Moreira, F. P., & Lima, D. A. (2024). Systematic literature review on the impact of Blended Learning in promoting student engagement and autonomy: Findings and recommendations. *Revista Brasileira de Informática na Educação, 32*, 242–269.

Morris, S., Earl, K., & Neave, A. (2017). Health survey for England 2016 well-being and mental health. *Health and Social Care Information Centre.*

Mosher, P. J. (2018). Everywhere and Nowhere: Grief in Child and Adolescent Psychiatry and Pediatric Clinical Populations. *Child and Adolescent Psychiatric Clinics of North America, 27*(1), 109–124. DOI: 10.1016/j.chc.2017.08.009 PMID: 29157497

Mudie, K. (2020, February 15). Tories have closed 1,300 family centres in last 10 years, figures reveal. *mirror.* https://www.mirror.co.uk/news/politics/tories-closed-1300-family-centres-21506487

Mugendawala, H., & Muijs, D. (2020). Educational process factors for effective education in resource-constrained countries: A multilevel analysis. *School Effectiveness and School Improvement, 31*(3), 445–467. DOI: 10.1080/09243453.2019.1702562

Muijs, D., & Reynolds, D. (2017). *Effective teaching: evidence and practice.* Sage.

Murphy, R., Roschelle, J., Feng, M., & Mason, C. A. (2020). Investigating efficacy, moderators and mediators for an online mathematics homework intervention. *Journal of Research on Educational Effectiveness, 13*(2), 235–270.

Murray-Gibbons, , SGibbons, , C. (2023). Revealing the Complex Relationship between Social Media use, Social Comparison Orientation and Optimism on Health Outcomes. *Psychology & Behavioral Sciences International Journal 21*(2): 556057. DOI: 10.19080/PBSIJ.2023.20.556057

Murray-Gibbons, S., & Gibbons, C. (2023). Revealing the Complex Relationship between Social Media use, Social Comparison Orientation and Optimism on Health Outcomes. *Psychology & Behavioral Sciences International Journal, 21*(2), 556057. DOI: 10.19080/PBSIJ.2023.20.556057

Myers, R., Egan-Brown, B., Conway, A., Nagele, D., Vaccaro, M., Kendi, S., & Zonfrillo, M. (2017). Examining a Statewide Educational Consulting Program for Pediatric Brain Injury. *Clinical Pediatrics, 57*(6), 645–655. PMID: 28933193

N-ABLES. (2021). *ABI Return – Children and Young People with Acquired Brain Injury - guiding their return to education.* Retrieved from https://cdn.ymaws.com/ukabif.org.uk/resource/resmgr/return_to_education/return_to_education12_05_2021/abi_return_booklet.pdf

Nalipay, M. J. N., King, R. B., & Cai, Y. (2020). Autonomy is equally important across East and West: Testing the cross-cultural universality of self-determination theory. *Journal of Adolescence, 78*, 67–72. DOI: 10.1016/j.adolescence.2019.12.009

NASA. (2024, July). *NASA data July 22 was Earth's hottest day on record.* Retrieved from, https://www.nasa.gov/earth/nasa-data-shows-july-22-was-earths-hottest-day-on-record/#:~:text=July%2022%2C%202024%2C%20was%20the,record%2C%20set%20in%20July%202023

National Council for Curriculum and Assessment (NCCA). (2015). Framework for Junior Cycle 2015. Dublin: NCCA. https://ncca.ie/media/3249/framework-for-junior-cycle-2015-en.pdf

National Council for Special Education. (2017). NCSE Press Release 18th January 2017 NCSE Welcomes a Better and More Equitable Way of Allocating Teaching Resources for Special Needs. Trim: NCSE. https://www.sess.ie/sites/default/files/inline-files/NCSE_Press_Release_New%20Model_18.01.17.pdf

National Council for Special Education. (2025). NCSE Relate Framework, Trim: NCSE. https://ncse.ie/relate

National Educational Psychological Service (NEPS). (2007). *Behavioural, emotional and social difficulties: A continuum of support.* NEPS. https://www.sess.ie/sites/default/files/neps_special_needs_guidelines.pdf

National Scientific Council on the Developing Child. (2015*). Supportive Relationships and Active Skill-Building Strengthen the Foundations of Resilience: Working Paper No. 13*. Retrieved from www.developingchild.harvard.edu

NCCA. (2021). *Draft primary curriculum framework.* Retrieved from https://ncca.ie/media/4456/ncca-primary- curriculum-framework-2020.pdf

Neves, J., & Hewitt, R. (2020). *Student academic experience survey*. Higher Education Policy Institute.

Neville, C. (2023). Developing critical decolonial awareness and reflection in language teachers at post-primary level: Empowering student language teachers as agents of change. *Irish Educational Studies*, 1–21.

Nicaise, I., Vandevoort, L., & Verelst, S. (2024). The effectiveness of equity funding in schools. In Downes, P., Li, G., Van Praag, L., & Lamb, S. (Eds.), *The Routledge international handbook of equity and inclusion in education* (1st ed., pp. 103–124). Routledge. DOI: 10.4324/9781003282921

Nichols, S. L. (2023). Educational psychology and educational policy: Intersections and new directions. In Schutz, P., & Muis, K. (Eds.), *Handbook of educational psychology* (4th ed.). Routledge.

Nichols, S. L., & Herrick, I. R. (2023). Introduction to the special issue on policy-oriented research: Enhancing the relevancy of educational psychology to policy. *Educational Psychologist*, *58*(4), 205–213. DOI: 10.1080/00461520.2023.2252074

Nickerson, C. A. (2018). There is no empirical evidence for critical positivity ratios: Comment on Fredrickson (2013). *Journal of Humanistic Psychology*, *58*(3), 284–312. DOI: 10.1177/0022167817740468

Nihalani, P. K., & Robinson, D. H. (2022). Balancing collaboration and cognitive load to optimize individual and group desirable difficulties. *Journal of Educational Computing Research*, *60*(2), 433–454.

Nilholm, C., & Göransson, K. (2017). What is Meant by Inclusion? An Analysis of European and North American Journal Articles with High Impact. *European Journal of Special Needs Education*, *32*(3), 437–451.

Nind, M., Wearmouth, J., Collins, J., Hall, K., Rix, J., & Sheehy, K. (2004). *A systematic review of pedagogical approaches that can effectively include children with special educational needs in mainstream classrooms*. https://oro.open.ac.uk/15231/

Noble, T., & McGrath, H. (2016). *Bounce back! A wellbeing & resilience program* (3rd ed.). Pearson Australia.

Nohilly, M., & Tynan, F. (2022). The evolution of wellbeing in educational policy in Ireland: Towards an interdisciplinary approach. *International Journal of Wellbeing*, *12*(1), 42–53. DOI: 10.5502/ijw.v12i1.1663

Norem, J., & Cantor, N. (1986). Defensive pessimism: Harnessing anxiety as motivation. *Journal of Personality and Social Psychology*, *51*(6), 1208. PMID: 3806357

Norman, A., Holloway, M., Odumuyiwa, T., Kennedy, M., Forrest, H., Suffield, F., & Dicks, H. (2020). Accepting what we do not know: A need to improve professional understanding of brain Injury in the UK. *Health & Social Care in the Community, 28*, 2027–2049. PMID: 32364294

Notes from Poland. (22025). *Poland begins to give free laptops to all Fourth-Graders.* https://notesfrompoland.com/2023/09/04/poland-begins-giving-free-laptops-to-all-fourth-graders/

Ntoumanis, N., Ng, J. Y. Y., Prestwich, A., Quested, E., Hancox, J. E., Thøgersen-Ntoumani, C., Deci, E. L., Ryan, R. M., Lonsdale, C., & Williams, G. C. (2020). A meta-analysis of self-determination theory-informed intervention studies in the health domain: Effects on motivation, health behavior, physical, and psychological health. *Health Psychology Review, 15*(2), 214–244. DOI: 10.1080/17437199.2020.1718529

Nussbaum, M. (1996). Compassion: The basic social emotion. *Social Philosophy & Policy, 13*(1), 27–58. DOI: 10.1017/S0265052500001515

O'Brien, M. (2008). Well-being and post-primary schooling. Dublin: NCCA.

O'Brien, C. (2025, March). Schools in poorest areas to get extra support under 'Deis-plus' scheme. *The Irish Times, 3.* https://www.irishtimes.com/ireland/education/2025/03/03/schools-in-poorest-areas-to-get-extra-support-under-deis-plus-scheme/

O'Mahony, D., Quinlan, C., Cotter, D., Rochford, M. F., Leiserowitz, A., Regan, A., Carman, J., & Rosenthal, S. (2024). *Climate Change in the Irish Mind: Wave 2, Report 1*. Environmental Protection Agency.

O'Neill, S. (2024). *Decolonising politics curricula: Exploring the experiences and views of racially minoritised students*. Learning and Teaching in Politics and International Studies. DOI: 10.1177/02633957241276065

O'Siochru, C., & Norton, L. (2014). Epistemic match: A pedagogical concept for understanding how students fit into the chosen subject. *Innovations in Education and Teaching International, 51*(2), 195–206.

O'Toole, C. (2022). When trauma comes to school: Toward a socially just trauma-informed praxis. *International Journal of School Social Work, 6*(2).

O'Toole, C., & Darlington, E. (2021). *Mental health promotion in schools: State of the art*. Schools for Health in Europe.

O'Toole, C., & Dobutowitsch, M. (2022). The courage to care: Teacher compassion predicts more positive attitudes towards trauma-informed practice. *Journal of Child & Adolescent Trauma, 16*, 123–133. PMID: 36157295

Oberman, R., & Sainz, G. M. (2021). Critical thinking, critical pedagogy and climate change education. In A. M. Kavanagh, F. Waldron & B. Mallon (Eds.), *Teaching for social justice and sustainable development across the primary curriculum* (pp. 69-83). Routledge.

Obradovich, N., Migliorini, R., Paulus, M. P., & Rahwan, I. (2018). Empirical evidence of mental health risks posed by climate change. *Proceedings of the National Academy of Sciences of the United States of America, 115*(43), 10953–10958. DOI: 10.1073/pnas.1801528115

OECD. (2017). *PISA 2015 Results* (Volume III). OECD.

OECD. (2018). *PISA 2018 Results (Volume III): What School Life Means for Students' Lives.* https://www.oecd-ilibrary.org/sites/c414e291-en/index.html?itemId=/content/component/c414e291-en#:~:text=PISA%20findings%20also%20show%20that,those%20in%20the%20top%20quarter

OECD. (2024). Review of Resourcing Schools to Address Educational Disadvantage in Ireland. Paris: OECD. https://www.oecd.org/en/publications/oecd-review-of-resourcing-schools-to-address-educational-disadvantage-in-ireland_3433784c-en.html

Ojala, M., Cunsolo, A., Ogunbode, C. A., & Middleton, J. (2021). Anxiety, worry, and grief in a time of environmental and climate crisis: A narrative review. *Annual Review of Environment and Resources, 46*(1), 35-58. DOI: 10.1146/annurev-environ-012220-022716

Ojala, M. (2012). How do children cope with global climate change? Coping strategies, engagement, and well-being. *Journal of Environmental Psychology, 32*(3), 225–233. DOI: 10.1016/j.jenvp.2012.02.004

Ojala, M. (2015). Hope in the face of climate change: Associations with environmental engagement and student perceptions of teachers' emotion communication style and future orientation. *The Journal of Environmental Education, 46*(3), 133–148. DOI: 10.1080/00958964.2015.1021662

Oliver, M. (1990). *Politics of disablement.* Macmillan International Higher Education.

Omar, M. S., Njeru, A., & Yi, S. (2017). The influence of Twitter on education policy making. In *2017 18th IEEE/ACIS International Conference on Software Engineering, Artificial Intelligence, Networking and Parallel/Distributed Computing (SNPD)* (pp. 133-136). DOI: 10.1109/SNPD.2017.8022712

Opgroeien.be. (2024). Cijferrapprt. https://www.opgroeien.be/kennis/cijfers-en - onderzoek/groeipakket#

Organisation for Economic Cooperation and Development (OECD). (2009). OECD Teaching and Learning International Survey (TALIS) Teacher Questionnaire Main Study Version (MS-12-01). In *OECD Teaching and Learning International Survey* (TALIS). DOI: 10.1111/j.1469-7610.1984.tb00150.x

Outhwaite, L., Early, E., Herodotou, C., & Van Herwegen, J. (2022). Can Maths apps add value to young children's learning? A systematic review and content analysis. Academic Press.

Ovenden-Hope, T., & Passy, R. (2020). *Exploring teacher recruitment and retention. Contextual challenges from international perspectives*. Routledge.

Owens, J., & de St Croix, T. (2020). Engines of Social Mobility? Navigating Meritocratic Education Discourse in an Unequal Society. *British Journal of Educational Studies*, *68*(4), 403–424. DOI: 10.1080/00071005.2019.1708863

Oxfam. (2021). *5 natural disasters that beg for climate action*. Oxfam International. https://www.oxfam.org/en/5-natural-disasters-beg-climate-action

Özgür, H. (2020). Relationships between teachers' technostress, technological pedagogical content knowledge (TPACK), school support and demographic variables: A structural equation modeling. *Computers in Human Behavior*, *112*, 106468.

Öztürk, G. (2021). Digital citizenship and its teaching: A literature review. *Journal of Educational Technology and Online Learning*, *4*(1), 31–45.

Pajares, M. F. (1992). Teachers' Beliefs and Educational Research: Cleaning up a Messy Construct. *Review of Educational Research*, *62*(3), 307–332.

Palanivel, V., & Burrough, M. (2021). Acquired brain injury in children, and their rehabilitation: Where we are now? *Paediatrics & Child Health*, *31*(5), 176–180.

Panagiotaki, G., Nobes, G., Ashraf, A., & Aubby, H. (2015). British and Pakistani children's understanding of death: Cultural and developmental influences. *British Journal of Developmental Psychology*, *33*(1), 31–44. PMID: 25262770

Panchal, U., Salazar de Pablo, G., & Franco, M. (2023). The impact of COVID-19 lockdown on child and adolescent mental health: Systematic review. *European Child & Adolescent Psychiatry*, *32*, 1151–1177. DOI: 10.1007/s00787-021-01856-w

Pangrazio, L., & Selwyn, N. (2021). Towards a school-based 'critical data education'. *Pedagogy, Culture & Society*, *29*(3), 431–448.

Pangrazio, L., Selwyn, N., & Cumbo, B. (2023). Tracking technology: Exploring student experiences of school datafication. *Cambridge Journal of Education*, *53*(6), 847–862.

Parker, I. (2007). Critical psychology: What it is and what it is not. *Social and Personality Psychology Compass*, *1*(1), 1–15. DOI: 10.1111/j.1751-9004.2007.00008.x

Parkman, A. (2016). The imposter phenomenon in higher education: Incidence and impact. *Journal of Higher Education Theory and Practice*, *16*(1).

Parong, J., & Mayer, R. E. (2021). Cognitive and affective processes for learning science in immersive virtual reality. *Journal of Computer Assisted Learning*, *37*(1), 226–241.

Parveen, D. S., & Ramzan, S. I. (2024). The role of digital technologies in education: Benefits and challenges. *Int. Res. J. Adv. Eng. Manag*, *2*(06), 2029–2037.

Pascoe, M., Hetrick, S., & Parker, A. (2019). The Impact of Stress on Students in Secondary School and Higher Education. *International Journal of Adolescence and Youth*, *25*(1), 104–112. DOI: 10.1080/02673843.2019.1596823

Patall, E. A., Cooper, H., & Robinson, J. C. (2008). The effects of choice on intrinsic motivation and related outcomes: A meta-analysis of research findings. *Psychological Bulletin*, *134*(2), 270–300. DOI: 10.1037/0033-2909.134.2.270

Peace-Hughes, T. (2021). Exploring how performativity influences the culture of secondary schooling in Scotland. *British Journal of Educational Studies*, *69*(3), 267–286. DOI: 10.1080/00071005.2020.1801986

Pekrun, R., Goetz, T., Titz, W., & Perry, R. P. (2002). Academic emotions in students' self- regulated learning and achievement: A program of qualitative and quantitative research. *Educational Psychologist*, *37*(2), 91–105. DOI: 10.1207/S15326985EP3702_4

Pelling, M., O'Brien, K., & Matyas, D. (2015). Adaptation and transformation. *Climatic Change*, *133*, 113–127. DOI: 10.1007/s10584-014-1303-0

Pennebaker, J. W. (2004). Theories, therapies, and taxpayers: On the complexities of the expressive writing paradigm. *Clinical Psychology : a Publication of the Division of Clinical Psychology of the American Psychological Association*, *11*(2), 138–142.

Perry, B., Pollard, R., & Blakely, T. (1995). Childhood trauma, the neurobiology of adaptation, and 'use dependent' development of the brain: How states become traits. *Infant Mental Health Journal*, *16*, 271–291.

Perry, B., & Szalavitz, M. (2017). *The boy who was raised as a dog: What traumatized children can teach us about loss, love and healing*. Basic Books.

Peters, M. A. (2015). Why is my curriculum white? *Educational Philosophy and Theory*, *47*(7), 641–646.

Peters, S. J., & Engerrand, K. G. (2016). Equity and excellence: Proactive efforts in the identification of underrepresented students for gifted and talented services. *Gifted Child Quarterly*, *60*, 159–171. DOI: 10.1177/0016986216643165

Pew Research Centre. (2014). Race and LGBTQ Issues in K-12 Schools. https://www.pewresearch.org/social-trends/2024/02/22/race-and-lgbtq-issues-in-k-12-schools/

Phiri, P., Sajid, S., & Delanerolle, G. (2023). Decolonising the psychology curriculum: A perspective. *Frontiers in Psychology*, *14*, 1–6. DOI: 10.3389/fpsyg.2023.1193241 PMID: 37388662

Piaget, J. (1952). Jean Piaget. In Boring, E. G., Werner, H., Langfeld, H. S., & Yerkes, R. M. (Eds.), *A History of Psychology in Autobiography* (Vol. 4, pp. 237–256). Clark University Press. DOI: 10.1037/11154-011

Piaget, J. (1952). *The origins of intelligence in children* (Cook, M., Trans.). International Universities Press.

Piaget, J. (1972). *The psychology of the child* (Weaver, H., Trans.). Basic Books.

Piaget, J. (2001). *The child's conception of the world* (2nd ed.). (Grieve, J. B., Trans.). Routledge.

Piaget, J., & Inhelder, B. (1956). *The child's conception of space*. Routledge & Kegan Paul.

Pihkala, P. (2020). Anxiety and the ecological crisis: An analysis of eco-anxiety and climate anxiety. *Sustainability*, *12*, 7836. DOI: 10.3390/su12197836

Pinar, W. F. (1975) *The method of currere*. Paper presented at the annual meeting of the American Educational Research Association, Washington, DC.

Pinar, W. F. (2011). *The Character of Curriculum Studies: Bildung, Currere, and the Recurring Question of the Subject*. Palgrave Macmillan.

Porche, M. V., Costello, D. M., & Rosen-Reynoso, M. (2016). Adverse family experiences, child mental health and educational outcomes for a national sample of students. *School Mental Health*, *8*, 44–60.

Porges, S. (2011). *The poly-vagal theory: Neurophysiological foundations of emotions, attachment, communication and self-regulation*. Norton.

Postman, N. (2011). *Technopoly: The surrender of culture to technology*. Vintage.

Pötzsch, H. (2019). Critical digital literacy: Technology in education beyond issues of user competence and labour-market qualifications. TripleC: Communication, Capitalism & Critique. *Open Access Journal for a Global Sustainable Information Society*, *17*(2), 221–240.

Priestley, M. (1998). Constructions and creations: Idealism, materialism and disability theory. *Disability & Society*, *13*(1), 75–94.

Prifti, R. (2022). Self–efficacy and student satisfaction in the context of blended learning courses. *Open Learning*, *37*(2), 111–125.

Prime Minister's Office. (2025). Downing Street opens doors to Adolescence creators for vital discussion on protecting our children. Press Release. https://www.gov.uk/government/news/downing-street-opens-doors-to-adolescence-creators-for-vital-discussion-on-protecting-our-children#:~:text=Jack%20Thorne%2C%20Adolescence%20Co%2DWriter,schools%20is%20beyond%20our%20expectations

Pring, R. (2023). Pastoral Care in Education: On Being and Developing as a Person. In D. Trotman, P. Jones, N. Purdy & S. Tucker (Eds.), *Pastoral Care in Education: New Directions for New Times* (pp.32-39). Cambridge Scholars.

Purdy, N., Ballentine, M., Lyle, H., Orr, K., Symington, E., Webster, D., & York, L. (2023). *Growing up Online: Children's online activities, harm and safety in Northern Ireland – an Evidence Report*. Stranmillis University College/Safeguarding Board for Northern Ireland. Available at https://www.stran.ac.uk/growing-up-online-in-ni/

Purdy, N., Logue, J., Montgomery, M., O'Hare, K., & Redpath, J. (2021). *A Fair Start: Final Report and Action Plan*. Department of Education for Northern Ireland.

Purdy, N., & Spears, B. (2020). Co-participatory approaches to research with children and young people. *Pastoral Care in Education*, *38*(3), 187–190. DOI: 10.1080/02643944.2020.1788816

Purdy, N., & Spears, B. (2023). Co-participatory Research Methods in Pastoral Care: Lessons from two case studies. In Trotman, D., Purdy, N., & Jones, P. (Eds.), *Pastoral Care in Education: Time for Change*. Cambridge Scholars.

Purdy, N., Symington, E., Ballentine, M., Orr, K., Walsh, G., & Tate, K. (2025). *Effective School Leadership in Disadvantaged Communities*. Centre for Research in Educational Underachievement, Stranmillis University College.

Quintero, J., Baldiris, S., Rubira, R., Cerón, J., & Velez, G. (2019). Augmented reality in educational inclusion. A systematic review on the last decade. In *Frontiers in Psychology* (Vol. 10, Issue AUG, pp. 0–14). DOI: 10.3389/fpsyg.2019.01835

Quirke, M. C. (2024). *There Has to be More Than One Way-How the Learning Experience of People with Disabilities Can Inform Career Guidance* (Doctoral dissertation, University of Dublin).

Quirke, M., Mc Guckin, C., & Mc Carthy, P. (2023). *Adopting a UDL attitude within academia: Understanding and practicing inclusion across higher education*. Routledge.

Quirke, M., Mc Guckin, C., & McCarthy, P. (2022). How to adopt an "inclusion as process" approach and navigate ethical challenges in research. In *SAGE Research Methods Cases*. SAGE Publications, Ltd. DOI: 10.4135/9781529605341

Quirke, M., Mc Guckin, C., & McCarthy, P. (2023). *Adopting a UDL Attitude Within Academia: Understanding and Practicing Inclusion Across Higher Education*. Routledge. DOI: 10.4324/9781003137672

Quirke, M., & McCarthy, P. (2020). *A Conceptual Framework of Universal Design for Learning (UDL) for the Irish Further Education and Training Sector Where Inclusion is Everybody's Business*. SOLAS.

Ramakrishnan, J. L., & Masten, A. S. (2020). Mastery motivation and school readiness among young children experiencing homelessness. *The American Journal of Orthopsychiatry*, *90*(2), 223–235. DOI: 10.1037/ort0000428

Rapp, A. C., & Corral-Granados, A. (2021). Understanding inclusive education – a theoretical contribution from system theory and the constructionist perspective. *International Journal of Inclusive Education*, *28*(4), 423–439. DOI: 10.1080/13603116.2021.1946725

Rappleye, J., Komatsu, H., Uchida, Y., Krys, K., & Markus, H. (2020). 'Better policies for better lives'?: Constructive critique of the OECD's (mis)measure of student well-being. *Journal of Education Policy*, *35*(2), 258–282. DOI: 10.1080/02680939.2019.1576923

Rasheed, R. A., Kamsin, A., & Abdullah, N. A. (2020). Challenges in the online component of blended learning: A systematic review. *Computers & Education*, *144*, 103701.

Rataj, E., Kunzweiler, K., & Garthus-Niegel, S. (2016). Extreme weather events in developing countries and related injuries and mental health disorders-a systematic review. *BMC Public Health*, *16*, 1–12.

Rawls, J. (1971). *A Theory of Justice*. Harvard University Press.

Reese, W. J. (2001). The Origins of Progressive Education. *History of Education Quarterly*, *41*(1), 1–24. DOI: 10.1111/j.1748-5959.2001.tb00072.x

Reeve, J., & Cheon, S. H. (2021). Autonomy-supportive teaching: Its malleability, benefits, and potential to improve educational practice. *Educational Psychologist*, *56*(1), 54–77. DOI: 10.1080/00461520.2020.1862657

Regan de Bere, S., & Nunn, S. (2016). Towards a pedagogy for patient and public involvement in medical education. *Medical Education*, *50*(1), 79–92. PMID: 26695468

Reid, A. (2019). Climate change education and research: Possibilities and potentials versus problems and perils? *Environmental Education Research*, *25*(6), 767–790. DOI: 10.1080/13504622.2019.1664075

Reid, A. (2022). *Leading Mindfully for Healthy and Successful Schools*. Taylor and Francis.

Reid, J. K., & Dixon, W. A. (1999). Teacher attitudes on coping with grief in the public school classroom. *Psychology in the Schools*, *36*(3), 219–229. DOI: 10.1002/(sici)1520-6807(199905)36:3%3C219:aid-pits5%3E3.0.co;2-0

Revet, A., Bui, E., Benvegnu, G., Suc, A., Mesquida, L., & Raynaud, J. P. (2020). Bereavement and reactions of grief among children and adolescents: Present data and perspectives. *L'Encéphale*, *46*(5), 356–363. DOI: 10.1016/j.encep.2020.05.007 PMID: 32921494

Ribeiro, I., Pereira, R., Freire, I., de Oliveira, B., Casotti, C., & Boery, E. (2018). Stress and Quality of Life among University Students: A Systematic Literature Review. *Health Profession Education*, *4*(2), 70–77. DOI: 10.1016/j.hpe.2017.03.002

Richards, M., & Huppert, F. A. (2011). Do positive children become positive adults? Evidence from a longitudinal birth cohort study. *The Journal of Positive Psychology*, *6*(1), 75–87. DOI: 10.1080/17439760.2011.536655

Richardson, T., Elliott, P., & Roberts, R. (2017). Relationship between loneliness and mental health in students. *Journal of Public Mental Health*, *16*, 48–54.

Richter, A., Sjunnestrand, M., Romare Strandh, M., & Hasson, H. (2022). Implementing school-based mental health services: A scoping review of the literature summarizing the factors that affect implementation. *International Journal of Environmental Research and Public Health*, *19*(6), 3489. DOI: 10.3390/ijerph19063489 PMID: 35329175

Rieser, R. (2014). What's Happening with Inclusive Education Around the World. World of Inclusion. http://worldofinclusion.com/whats-happening-with-inclusive-education-around-the-world/

Rix, J. (2015). Must inclusion be special? Rethinking educational support within a community of provision. Routledge. DOI: 10.4324/9781315713748

Rix, J. (2013). *Continuum of Education Provision for Children with Special Educational Needs: Review of International Policies and Practices*. National Council for Special Education.

Robertson, S. L. (2016). Piketty, capital and education: A solution to, or problem in, rising social inequalities? *British Journal of Sociology of Education, 37*(6), 823–835.

Rodger, S., Thomas, Y., Greber, C., Broadbridge, J., Edwards, A., Newton, J., & Lyons, M. (2014). Attributes of excellence in practice educators: The perspectives of Australian occupational therapy. *Australian Occupational Therapy Journal, 61*(3), 159–167.

Roe, K. (1983). *Mass Media and Adolescent Schooling: Conflict or Co-existence?* Almqvist and Wiksell International.

Roe, K., & Muijs, D. (1998). Children and Computer Games: A Profile of the Heavy User. *European Journal of Communication, 13*(2), 181–200. DOI: 10.1177/0267323198013002002

Rogers, C. R. (1951). *Client-Centred Therapy: It's Current Practice, Implications and Theory*. Houghton Mifflin.

Rokeach, M. (1967). *Rokeach Value Survey*. DOI: 10.1037/t01381-000

Rokeach, M. (1973). *The Nature of Human Values*. Free Press.

Rokeach, M., & Regan, J. F. (1980). The Role of Values in the Counselling Situation. *The Personnel and Guidance Journal, 58*, 576–582. DOI: 10.1002/j.2164-4918.1980.tb00454.x

Romero-Rodríguez, J. M., Hinojo-Lucena, F. J., Kopecký, K., & García-González, A. (2023). Digital fatigue in university students as a consequence of online learning during the Covid-19 pandemic. *Educación XX1, 26*(2), 141-164.

Rose, D. H., & Meyer, A. (2002). Teaching Every Student in the Digital Age: Universal Design for Learning. Alexandria, VA: Association for Supervision and Curriculum Development (ASCD).

Rosenblatt, P. C. (2017). Researching Grief: Cultural, Relational, and Individual Possibilities. *Journal of Loss and Trauma, 22*(8), 617–630. DOI: 10.1080/15325024.2017.1388347

Rosen, L. D., Carrier, L. M., & Cheever, N. A. (2013). Facebook and texting made me do it: Media-induced task-switching while studying. *Computers in Human Behavior, 29*(3), 948–958.

Ross, C., Kennedy, M., & Devitt, A. (2021). Home School Community Liaison Coordinators (HSCL) perspectives on supporting family wellbeing and learning during the COVID-19 school closures: Critical needs and lessons learned. *Irish Educational Studies, 40*(2), 311–318. DOI: 10.1080/03323315.2021.1915842

Roth, G., Assor, A., Kanat-Maymon, Y., & Kaplan, H. (2007). Autonomous motivation for teaching: How self- determined teaching may lead to self-determined learning. *Journal of Educational Psychology, 99*(4), 761–774. DOI: 10.1037/0022-0663.99.4.761

Rotter, J. B. (1966). Generalized expectancies for internal versus external control of reinforcement. *Psychological Monographs, 80*(1), 1. PMID: 5340840

Rousell, D., & Cutter-Mackenzie-Knowles, A. (2020). A systematic review of climate change education: Giving children and young people a 'voice' and a 'hand' in redressing climate change. *Children's Geographies, 18*(2), 191–208. DOI: 10.1080/14733285.2019.1614532

Royal College of Psychiatrists. (2011). *Mental health of students in higher education. (College report CR166).* Author.

Rueger, S. Y., Malecki, C. K., Pyun, Y., Aycock, C., & Coyle, S. (2016). A meta-analytic review of the association between perceived social support and depression in childhood and adolescence. *Psychological Bulletin, 142*(10), 1017–1067. PMID: 27504934

Russell, C. E., Chin, M., Bollig, G., Cait, C.-A., Carnevale, F. A., Chrastek, J., Lavorgna, B., Macpherson, C., Remke, S. S., Scaut, L., Skeen, J., Szylit, R., van Breemen, C., & Shalev, R. (2024). Re-Imagining Childhood Grief: Children as Active Agents in a Transactional Process. *Omega, 0*(0). Advance online publication. DOI: 10.1177/00302228241310264 PMID: 39688324

Russell, J. A., & Carroll, J. M. (1999). On the bipolarity of positive and negative affect. *Psychological Bulletin, 125*(1), 3–30. DOI: 10.1037/0033-2909.125.1.3

Rutter, M. (1979). Protective factors in children's responses to stress and disadvantage. In Kent, M. W., & Rolf, J. E. (Eds.), *Primary prevention in psychopathology: Social competence in children* (Vol. 8, pp. 49–74). University Press of New England.

Rutter, M. (1981). *Maternal deprivation reassessed* (2nd ed.). Penguin Books.

Ryan, R. M., & Deci, E. L. (2017). *Self-determination theory: Basic psychological needs in motivation, development, and wellness*. Guilford Publications.

Ryan, R. M., & Deci, E. L. (2020). Intrinsic and extrinsic motivation from a self-determination theory perspective: Definitions, theory, practices, and future directions. *Contemporary Educational Psychology*, *61*, 1–11.

Sabagh, K., Abdollahi Nodeh, M. H., & Naderifar, M. (2025). Loss and Bereavement: In Children. Inn J Pediatr., 35(2), e150107.DOI: 10.5812/ijp-150107

Sabnis, S. V., & Proctor, S. L. (2021). Use of critical theory to develop a conceptual framework for critical school psychology. *School Psychology Review*. Advance online publication. DOI: 10.1080/2372966X.2021.1949248

Sagiv, L., Roccas, S., Cieciuch, J., & Schwartz, S. H. (2017). Personal values in human life. *Nature Human Behaviour*, *1*(9), 630–639. PMID: 31024134

Saito, M. (2003). Amartya Sen's Capability Approach to Education: A Critical Exploration. *Journal of Philosophy of Education*, *37*(1), 17–33. DOI: 10.1111/1467-9752.3701002

Sala, G., & Gobet, F. (2019). Cognitive training does not enhance general cognition. *Trends in Cognitive Sciences*, *23*(1), 9–20. DOI: 10.1016/j.tics.2018.10.004

Saly, L., Provvidenza, C., Al-Hakeem, H., Hickling, A., Stevens, S., Kakonge, L., & Scratch, S. (2023). The Teach-ABI Professional Development Module for Educators About Pediatric Acquired Brain Injury: Mixed Method Usability Study. *Human Factors*, 10. PMID: 37184920

SAMHSA (Substance Abuse and Mental Health Services Administration). (2014). *SAMHSA's concept of trauma and guidance for a trauma-informed approach*. https://ncsacw.samhsa.gov/userfiles/files/SAMHSA_Trauma.pdf

Samuelson, K. W., Wilson, C. K., Padrón, E., Lee, S., & Gavron, L. (2017). Maternal PTSD and Children's Adjustment: Parenting Stress and Emotional Availability as Proposed Mediators. *Journal of Clinical Psychology*, *73*(6), 693–706. DOI: 10.1002/jclp.22369 PMID: 27487248

Sarkar, S., Gupta, R., & Menon, V. (2017). A systematic review of depression, anxiety, and stress among medical students in India. *Journal of Mental Health and Human Behaviour, 22*(2), 88–96.

Scalabrino, C., Navarrete Salvador, A., & Oliva Martínez, J. M. (2022). A theoretical framework to address education for sustainability for an earlier transition to a just, low carbon and circular economy. *Environmental Education Research, 28*(5), 735–766.

Scanlon, D. L., Rowling, L., & Weber, Z. (2007). "You Don't Have like an Identity . . . You are Just Lost in a Crowd": Forming a Student Identity in the First-Year Transition to University. *Journal of Youth Studies, 10*(2), 223–241. DOI: 10.1080/13676260600983684

Scanlon, G., Barnes-Holmes, Y., Shevlin, M., & McGuckin, C. (2020). *Transition for pupils with special educational needs.* Peter Lang Ltd.

Scanlon, G., & Doyle, A. (2021). Transition Stories: Voices of School Leavers with Intellectual Disabilities. *Special Issue: Education as a Catalyst for the Social Inclusion of People with Learning Disabilities, 49*, 4. DOI: 10.1111/bld.12433

Schachter, S. (1959). The psychology of affiliation: Experimental studies of the sources of gregariousness. Academic Press.

Schafer, W. (1992). *Stress management for wellness* (2nd ed.). Harcourt Brace Janovich.

Scheithauer, H., Schultze-Krumbholz, A., Pfetsch, J., & Hess, M. (2021). Types of Cyberbullying. In *The Wiley Blackwell Handbook of Bullying: A Comprehensive and International Review of Research and Intervention.* Wiley Blackwell.

Schneider, M., & Preckel, F. (2017). Variables associated with achievement in higher education: A systematic review of meta-analyses. *Psychological Bulletin, 143*(6), 565. PMID: 28333495

Schonfeld, D. J., & Demaria, T. (2016). Committee on Psychosocial Aspects of Child and Family Health, & Disaster Preparedness Advisory Council. Supporting the Grieving Child and Family. *Pediatrics, 138*(3), e20162147–e20162147. DOI: 10.1542/peds.2016-2147 PMID: 27573086

Schonfeld, D. J., & Quackenbush, M. (2021). *The Grieving Student.* Paul H Brookes Publishing.

Schools Week. (2023, May 18). Mental health leads struggle to find time for the job. Author.

Schutz, P. A., & DeCuir, J. T. (2002). Inquiry on emotions in education. *Educational Psychologist, 37*(2), 125–134. DOI: 10.1207/S15326985EP3702_7

Schwartz, B. (2004). *The paradox of choice: Why more is less.* Ecco/Harper Collins.

Schwartz, E., & Jordan, A. (2011). Teachers epistemological beliefs and practices with students with disabilities and at-risk in Inclusive classrooms. Implications for teacher development. In Brownlee, J., Schraw, G., & Berthelsen, D. (Eds.), *Personal Epistemology and Teacher Education* (pp. 210–226). Routledge.

Schwartz, S. H. (1992). Universals in the content and structure of values: Theoretical advances and empirical tests in 20 countries. In Zanna, M. P. (Ed.), (pp. 1–65). Advances in experimental social psychology. Academic Press.

Sebre, S. B., & Miltuze, A. (2021). Digital media as a medium for adolescent identity development. Technology. *Knowledge and Learning, 26*(4), 867–881.

Sedlac ova, D., & Kantor, J. (2022). Traumatic Brain injury Identified on the basis of the lived experience of his mother. *Education Research International.*

See, B. H., Morris, R., Gorard, S., Kokotsaki, D., & Abdi, S. (2020). Teacher Recruitment and Retention: A Critical Review of International Evidence of Most Promising Interventions. *Education Sciences, 10*(10), 262. DOI: 10.3390/educsci10100262

Seligman, M. E. (2002). Positive psychology, positive prevention, and positive therapy. *Handbook of positive psychology, 2*(2002), 3-12.

Seligman, M. E. (2008). Positive health. *Applied Psychology, 57*(s1), 3–18. .1464-0597.2008.00351.xDOI: 10.1111/j

Seligman, M. (2011). *Flourish.* Random House.

Seligman, M. (2018). PERMA and the building blocks of well-being. *The Journal of Positive Psychology, 13*(4), 333–335. DOI: 10.1080/17439760.2018.1437466

Seligman, M. E. (1971). Phobias and preparedness. *Behavior Therapy, 2*(3), 307–320. PMID: 27816071

Seligman, M. E. P., & Maier, S. F. (1967). Failure to escape traumatic shock. *Journal of Experimental Psychology, 74*(1), 1–9. DOI: 10.1037/h0024514

Seligman, M. E., Ernst, R. M., Gillham, J., Reivich, K., & Linkins, M. (2009). Positive education: Positive psychology and classroom interventions. *Oxford Review of Education, 35*(3), 293–311. DOI: 10.1080/03054980902934563

Selwyn, N. (2021). *Education and technology: Key issues and debates.* Bloomsbury Publishing.

Selye, H. (1956). *The Stress of Life*. McGraw-Hill.

Sen, A. (2001). *Development as Freedom*. Oxford University Press.

Senelmis, S. (2022-present). Classroom adjustments: Acquired Brain Injury (ABI). NCCD.

Shackleton, C. M., & Cocks, M. L. (2021). Urban nature and biocultural realities. In Cocks, M. L., & Shackleton, C. M. (Eds.), *Diversities of nature in cities: enriching belonging, wellbeing and bioculture* (pp. 1–24). Earthscan/Routledge.

Shaeffer, S. (2019). Inclusive Education: A Prerequisite for Equity and Social Justice. *Asia Pacific Education Review*, *20*(2), 181–192.

Shahjahan, R. A., Estera, A. L., Surla, K. L., & Edwards, K. T. (2022). "Decolonizing" curriculum and pedagogy: A comparative review across disciplines and global higher education contexts. *Review of Educational Research*, *92*(1), 73–113.

Shain, F., Yıldız, Ü. K., Poku, V., & Gokay, B. (2021). From silence to 'strategic advancement': Institutional responses to 'decolonising' in higher education in England. *Teaching in Higher Education*, *26*(7–8), 920–936. https://doi-org.elib.tcd.ie/10.1080/13562517.2021.1976749

Shakespeare, T., & Watson, N. (1998). Theoretical Perspectives on Research. *Growing up with disability, 34*, 13.

Shannon, H., Bush, K., Villeneuve, P. J., Hellemans, K. G., & Guimond, S. (2022). Problematic Social Media Use in Adolescents and Young Adults: Systematic Review and Meta-analysis. *JMIR Mental Health*, *9*(4), e33450. DOI: 10.2196/33450

Sharot, T. (2011). The optimism bias. *Current Biology*, *21*, R941–R945. PMID: 22153158

Sharp, N. L., Bye, R., Llewellyn, G., & Cusick, A. (2006). Fitting back in: Adolescents returning to school after severe acquired brain injury. *Disability and Rehabilitation*, *28*(12), 767–778. PMID: 16754574

Sheehy, K., Budiyanto, & Rofiah, K. (2023). *Inclusive disaster-risk reduction education*, Best poster award: Relevant global challenge to be explored in education. Green Forum Network International Conference March, Milton Keynes, UK.

Sheehy, K., Rix, J., Collins, J., Hall, K., Nind, M., & Wearmouth, J. (2009). *A systematic review of whole class, subject- based pedagogies with reported outcomes for the academic and social inclusion of pupils with special educational needs.* https://oro.open.ac.uk/10735/

Sheehy, K. (2017). Ethics, epistemologies, and inclusive pedagogy. *International Perspectives on Inclusive Education*, *9*, 59–78. DOI: 10.1108/S1479-363620170000009003

Sheehy, K., & Budiyanto. (2015). The Pedagogic Beliefs of Indonesian Teachers in Inclusive Schools. *International Journal of Disability Development and Education*, *62*(5), 469–485. DOI: 10.1080/1034912X.2015.1061109

Sheehy, K., Budiyanto, Kaye, H., & Rofiah, K. (2017). Indonesian teachers' epistemological beliefs and inclusive education. *Journal of Intellectual Disabilities*. Advance online publication. DOI: 10.1177/1744629517717613

Sheehy, K., Garcia-Carrizosa, H., Rix, J., Seale, J., & Hayhoe, S. (2019). Inclusive museums and augmented reality: Affordances, participation, ethics, and fun. *The International Journal of the Inclusive Museum*, *12*(4). Advance online publication. DOI: 10.18848/1835-2014/CGP/v12i04/67-85

Sheehy, K., Vackova, P., van Manen, S., Saragih Turnip, S., Rofiah, K., & Twiner, A. (2022). Inclusive disaster risk reduction education for Indonesian children. *International Journal of Inclusive Education*. Advance online publication. DOI: 10.1080/13603116.2022.2115156

Sheffield, P. E., & Landrigan, P. J. (2011). Global climate change and children's health: Threats and strategies for prevention. *Environmental Health Perspectives*, *119*(3), 291–298. DOI: 10.1289/ehp.1002233

Shevrin Venet, A. (2021). *Equity-centered trauma-informed education*. Norton.

Siegel, D. J. (1999). *The developing mind: How relationships and the brain interact to shape who we are*. Guildford Press.

Siegel, J., Arenson, M., Mikytuck, A., & Woolard, J. (2021). Engaging public policy with psychological science. *Translational Issues in Psychological Science*, *7*(1), 1–8. DOI: 10.1037/tps0000284

Silton, R. L., Kahrilas, I. J., Skymba, H. V., Smith, J., Bryant, F. B., & Heller, W. (2020). Regulating positive emotions: Implications for promoting well-being in individuals with depression. *Emotion (Washington, D.C.)*, *20*(1), 93–97. DOI: 10.1037/emo0000675

Silva, J. F. B., & Coburn, J. (2022). Therapists' experience of climate change: A dialectic between personal and professional. *Counselling & Psychotherapy Research*, *23*(2), 417–431. DOI: 10.1002/capr.12515

Silverwood, J., & Wolstencroft, P. (2023). The Ruskin Speech and Great Debate in English education, 1976–1979: A study of motivation. *British Educational Research Journal*, *49*(4), 766–781.

Simic, N., & Manenica, I. (2012). Exam Experience and Some Reactions to Exam Stress. *Human Physiology*, *38*(1), 67–72. DOI: 10.1134/S0362119712010161 PMID: 22567840

Simon, K., Compton, S. E., & Overstreet, S. (2020). The evolution of trauma-informed schools. In Rossen, E. (Ed.), *Supporting and educating traumatized students: A guide for school-based professionals* (2nd ed.). Oxford University Press.

Skinner, B. F. (2019). *The behavior of organisms: An experimental analysis*. BF Skinner Foundation.

Skinner, E. A., & Belmont, M. J. (1993). Motivation in the classroom: Reciprocal effects of teacher behavior and student engagement across the school year. *Journal of Educational Psychology*, *85*(3), 571–581. DOI: 10.1037/0022-0663.85.4.571

Skulmowski, A., & Xu, K. M. (2022). Understanding cognitive load in digital and online learning: A new perspective on extraneous cognitive load. *Educational Psychology Review*, *34*(1), 171–196.

Sloane, E. (2024). Trinity College Dublin renames former Berkeley Library after poet Eavan Boland. https://www.irishtimes.com/ireland/education/2024/10/09/trinity-college-dublin-renames-former-berkeley-library-after-poet-eavan-boland/

Söder, M. (2009). Tensions, perspectives and themes in disability studies. *Scandinavian Journal of Disability Research*, *11*(2), 67–81. DOI: 10.1080/15017410902830496

Song, Y., Weisberg, L. R., Zhang, S., Tian, X., Boyer, K. E., & Israel, M. (2024). A framework for inclusive AI learning design for diverse learners. Computers and Education: Artificial Intelligence, 100212.

Soyoof, A., Reynolds, B. L., Neumann, M., Scull, J., Tour, E., & McLay, K. (2024). The impact of parent mediation on young children's home digital literacy practices and learning: A narrative review. *Journal of Computer Assisted Learning*, *40*(1), 65–88.

Speece, M. W., & Brent, S. B. (1984). Children's understanding of death: A review of three components of a death concept. *Child Development*, *55*(5), 1671–1686. PMID: 6510050

Spencer, M. B. (2006). Phenomenology and ecological systems theory: Development of diverse groups. In Damon, W., & Lerner, R. (Eds.), Handbook of child psychology: Vol. 1. *Theoretical models of human development* (6th ed., pp. 829–893). Wiley.

Spiridon, K., & Evangelia, K. (2015). Exploring relationships between academic hardiness, academic stressors and achievement in university undergraduates. *Journal of Applied Educational and Policy Research, 1*(1), 53–73. DOI: 10.7897/2277-4343.04135

Spiteri, R., O'Riordan, M. R., Cefai, C., Hickey, G., & Smith, S. (2023). Early school leaving and trauma-based education: A study in four European countries. *Pastoral Care in Education, 41*(1), 26–41. DOI: 10.1080/02643944.2022.2032812

Spuij, M., Reitz, E., Prinzie, P., Stikkelbroek, Y., de Roos, C., & Boelen, P. A. (2012). Distinctiveness of symptoms of prolonged grief, depression, and post-traumatic stress in bereaved children and adolescents. *European Child & Adolescent Psychiatry, 21*(12), 673–679. DOI: 10.1007/s00787-012-0307-4 PMID: 22791348

Sroufe, L. A., & Rutter, M. (1984). The domain of developmental psychopathology. *Child Development, 55*(1), 17–29. PMID: 6705619

Stallman, H. M. (2010). Psychological distress in university students: A comparison with general population data. *Australian Psychologist, 45*(4), 249–257.

Stamm, B. H. (2012). Helping the helpers: Compassion satisfaction and compassion fatigue in self-care, management, and policy. In Kirkwood, A. D., & Stamm, B. H. (Eds.), *Resources for community suicide prevention*. Idaho State University.

Stanley, S. K., Hogg, T. L., Leviston, Z., & Walker, I. (2021). From anger to action: Differential impacts of eco-anxiety, eco-depression, and eco-anger on climate action and wellbeing. *The Journal of Climate Change and Health, 1*, 100003. DOI: 10.1016/j.joclim.2021.100003

Statbi Lab. (2024, May 22). *Facebook*. Retrieved from https://www.facebook.com/labstatbi

Steel, P., Schmidt, J., & Shultz, J. (2008). Refining the relationship between personality and subjective wellbeing. *Psychological Bulletin, 134*(1), 138. PMID: 18193998

Stein, M., Federspiel, A., Koenig, T., Wirth, M., Strik, W., Wiest, R., & Dierks, T. (2012). Structural plasticity in the language system related to increased second language proficiency. *Cortex, 48*(4), 458–465. DOI: 10.1016/j.cortex.2010.10.007

Steptoe, A., Tsuda, A., & Tanaka, Y. (2007). Depressive symptoms, socio-economic background, sense of control, and cultural factors in university students from 23 countries. *International Journal of Behavioral Medicine, 14*, 97–107. PMID: 17926438

Stern, N., Patel, I., & Ward, B. (2021). Covid-19, climate change, and the environment: A sustainable, inclusive, and resilient global recovery. *BMJ (Clinical Research Ed.)*, (2405). Advance online publication. DOI: 10.1136/bmj.n2405

Stevens, S., Provvidenza, C., Zheng, S., Agnihotri, S., Hunt, A., & Scratch, S. (2021). Understanding the Needs of Ontario Educators in Supporting Students With Acquired Brain Injury in the Classroom. *The Journal of School Health, 91*(4), 285–290. PMID: 33655540

Stibbe, A. (2021). *Ecolinguistics: Language, ecology and the stories we live by*. Routledge.

Storrie, K., Ahern, K., & Tuckett, A. (2010). A Systematic Review: Students with Mental Health Problems -A Growing Problem. *International Journal of Nursing Practice, 16*(1), 1–6. DOI: 10.1111/j.1440-172X.2009.01813.x PMID: 20158541

Struck, S., Stewart-Tufescu, A., Asmundson, A. J. N., Asmundson, G. G. J., & Afifi, T. O. (2021). Adverse childhood experiences (ACEs) research: A bibliometric analysis of publication trends over the first 20 years. *Child Abuse and Neglect, 112*. DOI: 10.1016/j.chiabu.2020.104895

Stubberud, J., Hypher, R., Brandt, A. E., Finnanger, T. G., Skovlund, E., Andersson, S., Risnes, K., & Rø, T. B. (2022). Predictors of Functional School Outcome in Children With Pediatric Acquired Brain Injury. *Frontiers in Neurology*, 13. PMID: 35493829

Stults-Kolehmainen, M. A., & Sinha, R. (2014). The effects of stress on physical activity and exercise. *Sports Medicine (Auckland, N.Z.)*, *44*, 81–121. PMID: 24030837

Sturm, T. (2019). "Constructing and Addressing Differences in Inclusive Schooling–Comparing Cases from Germany." Norway and the United States. *International Journal of Inclusive Education, 23*(6), 656–669.

Sugai, G., & Horner, R. H. (2009). Responsiveness-to-intervention and school-wide positive behavior supports: Integration of multi-tiered system approaches. *Exceptionality, 17*, 223–237.

Sun, H., Yuan, C., Qian, Q., He, S., & Luo, Q. (2022). Digital resilience among individuals in school education settings: A concept analysis based on a scoping review. *Frontiers in Psychiatry, 13*, 858515.

Suto, I., & Oates, T. (2021). High-Stakes Testing after Basic Secondary Education: How and Why Is It Done in *High- Performing Education Systems? Research Report*. http://www.cambridgeassessment.org.uk

Sweetman, A. & O'Donnell (2020). Non-Death Loss and Grief. Irish Association for Counselling & Psychotherapy, 20(3).

Sweller, J. (1994). Cognitive load theory, learning difficulty, and instructional design. *Learning and Instruction, 4*(4), 295–312.

Swim, J. K., Aviste, R., Lengieza, M. L., & Fasano, C. J. (2022). OK Boomer: A decade of generational differences in feelings about climate change. *Global Environmental Change, 73*, 102479. DOI: 10.1016/j.gloenvcha.2022.102479

Swim, J. K., Clayton, S., & Howard, G. S. (2011). Human behavioral contributions to climate change: Psychological and contextual drivers. *The American Psychologist, 66*(4), 251–265. DOI: 10.1037/a0023472

Taggart, S., & Roulston, S. (2024). Educational technologies in schools in Northern Ireland: Teachers' digital competences in the Goldilocks zone. *Journal of Digital Learning in Teacher Education*, 1–19. DOI: 10.1080/21532974.2024.2393575

Tang, C. M., & Chaw, L. Y. (2016). Digital Literacy: A Prerequisite for Effective Learning in a Blended Learning Environment? *Electronic Journal of e-Learning, 14*(1), 54–65.

Tardieu, A. (1857). Étude medico-légale sur les attentats aux moeurs (1st ed.). Librairie JB Baillière et Fils.

Tardieu, A. (1862). Travail des enfants. In *Dictionnaire d'hygiène publique et de salubrité* (2nd ed., Vol. 3, pp. 35-81). Academic Press.

Tardieu, A. (1860). Étude medico-légale sur les sévices et mauvais traitements exercés sur des enfants. *Annales d'Hygiène Publique et de Mèdicine Légale, 13*, 361-398.

Taylor, J. (2022). *Sexy But Psycho: Uncovering the psychiatric labelling of women and girl.* Little Brown Publications.

Teaching Council. (2020). Céim: Standards for Initial Teacher Education. https://www.teachingcouncil.ie/assets/uploads/2023/08/ceim-standards-for-initial-teacher-education.pdf

Tedeschi, R. G., & Calhoun, L. G. (1995). *Trauma & transformation: Growing in the aftermath of suffering*. Sage Publications, Inc.

Tembo, S., & Bateson, S. (2024). Before race: A literature review on de/colonial habits in play within early childhood. *Journal of Early Childhood Research, 0*(0). Advance online publication. DOI: 10.1177/1476718X241241142

Tenenbaum, H. R., & Ruck, M. D. (2007). Are teachers' expectations different for racial minority than for European American students? A meta-analysis. *Journal of Educational Psychology, 99*(2), 253. DOI: 10.1037/0022-0663.99.2.253

Tesfagiorgis, M., Tsegai, S., Mengesha, T., Craft, J., & Tessema, M. (2020). The correlation between parental socioeconomic status (SES) and children's academic achievement: The case of Eritrea. *Children and Youth Services Review, 116*, 105242. DOI: 10.1016/j.childyouth.2020.105242

Tett, L., Cree, V. E., & Christie, H. (2017). From further to higher education: Transition as an on-going process. *Higher Education, 73*, 389–406. DOI: 10.1007/s10734-016-0101-1

The Children's Trust. (2024). Retrieved October 2024, from https://www.thechildrenstrust.org.uk/about

The Children's Trust. (n.d.). *Brain Injury Hub: Teacher's Strategies for the Classroom.* Retrieved from The Children's Trust: https://www.thechildrenstrust.org.uk/brain-injury-information/info-and-advice/return-to-education/teachers-strategies-for-the-classroom

The Children's Trust. (n.d.). *The effects of acquired brain injury: An introduction.* Retrieved from https://www.thechildrenstrust.org.uk/brain-injury-information/info-and-advice/living-with-abi/the-effects-of-abi

Thoits, P. A. (1995). Social psychology: The interplay between sociology and psychology. *Social Forces, 73*(4), 1231–1243. DOI: 10.1093/sf/73.4.1231

Thomas, L. (2016). Chapter 9 - Developing Inclusive Learning to Improve the Engagement, Belonging, Retention, and Success of Students from Diverse Groups. In *Widening Higher Education Participation A Global Perspective.* Chandos Publishing.

Thomas, C. (2004). Disability and Impairment. In Swain, J., French, S., Barnes, C., & Thomas, C. (Eds.), *Disabling barriers - enabling environments.* SAGE.

Thomas, G. (2014). Inequality and the next generation. *The Psychologist, 27*, 240–242.

Thomas, L. (2012). Building Student Engagement and Belonging in Higher Education at a Time of Change. *Paul Hamlyn Foundation, 100*, 1–99.

Thomas, M. S., Crosby, S., & Vanderhaar, J. (2019). Trauma-informed practices in schools across two decades: An interdisciplinary review of research. *Review of Research in Education, 43*(1), 422–452. DOI: 10.3102/0091732X1882112

Thorley, C. (2017). Not By Degrees: Not by degrees: Improving student mental health in the UK's universities. IPPR. www.ippr.org/publications/not-by-degrees

Timberlake, M. T., Thomas, A. B., & Barrett, B. (2017). The allure of simplicity: Scripted curricula and equity. *Teaching and Teacher Education*, *67*, 46–52.

Timotheou, S., Miliou, O., Dimitriadis, Y., Sobrino, S. V., Giannoutsou, N., Cachia, R., & Ioannou, A. (2023). Impacts of digital technologies on education and factors influencing schools' digital capacity and transformation: A literature review. *Education and Information Technologies*, *28*(6), 6695–6726.

Todis, B., McCart, M., & Glang, A. (2018). Hospital to school transition following traumatic brain injury: A qualitative longitudinal study. *NeuroRehabilitation*, *42*(3), 269–276. PMID: 29660964

Toyama, M., & Sakurai, S. (1999). Daily hassles and uplifts, and college students' health: Focusing on daily uplifts. *Japanese Journal of Educational Psychology*. Advance online publication. DOI: 10.5926/jjep1953.47.3_374

Trauma Informed Oregon. (2024, October 31). Road map to trauma informed care. *Trauma Informed Oregon*. https://traumainformedoregon.org/implementation/implementation-and-accountability-overview/roadmap-to-trauma-informed-care/

Trotman, D., Jones, P., Purdy, N., & Tucker, S. (2023). Concluding Remarks. In D. Trotman, P. Jones, N. Purdy & S. Tucker (Eds.), *Pastoral Care in Education: New Directions for New Times* (pp. 336-338). Cambridge Scholars.

Turnbull, D., Chugh, R., & Luck, J. (2020). Learning management systems, an overview. Encyclopedia of education and information technologies, 1052-1058.

Turner, J., Bartlett, D., Andiappan, M., & Cabot, L. (2015). Students' perceived stress and perception of barriers to effective study: Impact on academic performance in examinations. *British Dental Journal*, *219*(9), 453–458. DOI: 10.1038/sj.bdj.2015.850 PMID: 26564362

Twenge, J. M., Haidt, J., Lozano, J., & Cummins, K. M. (2022). Specification curve analysis shows that social media use is linked to poor mental health, especially among girls. *Acta psychologica, 224*, 103512.

Tyerman, E., Eccles, F., & Gray, V. (2017). The experiences of parenting a child with an acquired brain injury: A metasynthesis of the qualitative literature. *Brain Injury : [BI]*, *31*(12), 1553–1563. PMID: 28750173

Ulfert-Blank, A. S., & Schmidt, I. (2022). Assessing digital self-efficacy: Review and scale development. *Computers & Education*, *191*, 104626.

UNESCO. (1994). The Salamanca Statement and Framework for action on special needs education: Adopted by the World Congress on Special Needs Education, Access and Quality. Salamanca, Spain.

UNESCO. (2023) *Technology in Schools – A tool on whose terms*? https://unesdoc.unesco.org/ark:/48223/pf0000385723

UNESCO. (2023). 2023 SDG4 scorecard on progress towards national SDG 4 benchmarks: key findings. https://unesdoc.unesco.org/ark:/48223/pf0000384273

Ungar, M. (2013). Resilience, trauma, context, and culture. *Trauma, Violence & Abuse*, *14*(3), 255–266. DOI: 10.1177/1524838013487805

Ungar, M., & Theron, L. (2020). Resilience and mental health: How multisystemic processes contribute to positive outcomes. *The Lancet. Psychiatry*, *7*(5), 441–448. DOI: 10.1016/S2215-0366(19)30434-1

UNICEF. (2022). Unicef data: monitoring the situation of children and women: primary education. https://data.unicef.org/topic/education/primary-education/

UNICEF. (2023). Inclusive education. Every Child Has the Right to Quality Education and Learning. https://www.unicef.org/education/inclusive-education

United Nations (1989). Convention on the Rights of the Child. *Treaty Series*, *1577*,3.

United Nations (2006). *Convention on the Rights of Persons with Disabilities*. Treaty Series 2515.

United Nations Children's Fund (UNICEF). (2020). *Towards an equal future: Reimagining girls' education through STEM*. UNICEF.

United Nations Educational Scientific Cultural Organisation. (1994). *The Salamanca statement and framework for action on special needs education*. UNESCO.

United Nations. (1989). *Convention on the rights of the child*. https://www.unicef.org/child-rights-convention/convention-text

United Nations. (1989). Convention on the Rights of the Child. Treaty no. 27531. United Nations Treaty Series. Available at: https://treaties.un.org/doc/Treaties/1990/09/19900902%2003-14%20AM/Ch_IV_11p.pdf

United Nations. (1989). *The United Nations convention on the rights of the child*. https://www.unicef.org.uk/wp-content/uploads/2016/08/unicef-convention-rights-child-uncrc.pdf

United Nations. (2015). *Transforming our world: The 2030 Agenda for Sustainable Development*. A/RES/70/1.

Uslu, F., & Gizir, S. (2017). School belonging of adolescents: The role of teacher–student relationships, peer relationships and family involvement. *Educational Sciences: Theory & Practice*, *17*(1), 63–82.

Uztemur, S. (2020). 'The Relationships between Middle School Teachers' Epistemological Beliefs and Learner Autonomy Support Behaviours: The Role of Teaching-Learning Conceptions as the Mediating Variable'. *Egitim ve Bilim*, *45*(202), 211–239. DOI: 10.15390/EB.2020.8272

Vaez, M., Kristenson, M., & Laflamme, L. (2004). Perceived quality of life and self-rated health among first-year university students. *Social Indicators Research*, *68*, 221–234.

Valkenburg, P. M., Meier, A., & Beyens, I. (2022). Social media use and its impact on adolescent mental health: An umbrella review of the evidence. *Current Opinion in Psychology*, *44*, 58–68.

Valkenburg, P. M., van Driel, I. I., & Beyens, I. (2022). The associations of active and passive social media use with well-being: A critical scoping review. *New Media & Society*, *24*(2), 530–549.

Van der Kolk, B. (2014). *The body keeps the score: Mind, brain and body in the transformation of trauma*. Penguin Books.

Van der Kolk, B. A. (2014). *The body keeps the score: Brain, mind, and body in the healing of trauma*. Viking.

van der Meer, A. L., & Van der Weel, F. R. (2017). Only three fingers write, but the whole brain works: A high-density EEG study showing advantages of drawing over typing for learning. *Frontiers in Psychology*, *8*, 706.

Van Herwegen, J. (2022). Why has there been a rise in number of SEN children, especially in the early years? *UCL Centre for Educational Neuroscience*. http://www.educationalneuroscience.org.uk/2022/04/01/why-has-there-been-a-rise-in-number-of-sen-children-especially-in-the-early-years/

Varma, A. (2020). Evoking empathy or enacting solidarity with marginalized communities?: A case study of journalistic humanizing techniques in the San Francisco Homeless Project. *Journalism Studies*, *21*(12), 1705–1723. DOI: 10.1080/1461670X.2020.1789495

Vasilic, B. (2022). Behaviour as relational process: Linking theory to practice. *Educational Psychology in Practice*, *38*(4), 379–391. DOI: 10.1080/02667363.2022.2098257

Venkatesan, S. (2022). LOSS, Grief, Bereavement, and Mourning in Children. *International Journal of Recent Scientific Research, 13*(03), 619–624. DOI: 10.24327/ijrsr.2022.1303.0129

Villena-Taranilla, R., Tirado-Olivares, S., Cózar-Gutiérrez, R., & González-Calero, J. A. (2022). Effects of virtual reality on learning outcomes in K-6 education: A meta-analysis. *Educational Research Review, 35*, 100434.

Vollrath, M., & Torgersen, S. (2000). Personality types and coping. *Personality and Individual Differences, 29*(2), 367–378.

Vrikki, M., Wheatley, L., Howe, C., Hennessy, S., & Mercer, N. (2019). Dialogic practices in primary school classrooms. *Language and Education, 33*(1), 85–100. DOI: 10.1080/09500782.2018.1509988

Vujnovic, M. (2017). *Hypercapitalism.* The Wiley-Blackwell Encyclopaedia of Globalization. DOI: 10.1002/9780470670590.wbeog278.pub2

Vygotsky, L. S. (1978). *Mind in society: The development of higher psychological processes* (Cole, M., John-Steiner, V., Scribner, S., & Souberman, E., Eds.). Harvard University Press.

Wales, L., Hawley, C., & Sidebotham, P. (2013). How an occupational therapist should conceptualise self-awareness following traumatic brain injury in childhood- A literature review. *British Journal of Occupational Therapy, 76*(7), 325–332.

Walter, T. (2010). Grief and culture. *Bereavement Care, 29*(2), 5–9. DOI: 10.1080/02682621003707431

Walton, E. (2018). Decolonising (Through) Inclusive Education? *Educational Research for Social Change, 7*(0), 31–45. DOI: 10.17159/2221-4070/2018/v7i0a3

Wang, C. H., Salisbury-Glennon, J. D., Dai, Y., Lee, S., & Dong, J. (2022). Empowering College Students to Decrease Digital Distraction through the Use of Self-Regulated Learning Strategies. *Contemporary Educational Technology, 14*(4).

Wang, S., Christensen, C., Cui, W., Tong, R., Yarnall, L., Shear, L., & Feng, M. (2023). When adaptive learning is effective learning: Comparison of an adaptive learning system to teacher-led instruction. *Interactive Learning Environments, 31*(2), 793–803.

Wassink-de Stigter, R., Kooijmans, R., Asselman, M. W., Offerman, E. C. P., Nelen, W., & Helmond, P. (2022). Facilitators and barriers in the implementation of trauma-informed approaches in schools: A scoping review. *School Mental Health, 14*, 470–484.

Waters, L. (2011). A review of school-based positive psychology interventions. *The Australian Educational and Developmental Psychologist, 28*(2), 75-90.

Watson, S. (2020). New Right 2.0: Teacher populism on social media in England. *British Educational Research Journal, 47*(2), 299–345. DOI: 10.1002/berj.3664

Welsh, R. O., & Little, S. (2018). The school discipline dilemma: A comprehensive review of disparities and alternative approaches. *Review of Educational Research, 88*(5), 752–794. DOI: 10.3102/0034654318791582

Wherfel, Q., & Bakken, J. (2023). Using technology to enhance learning for students with traumatic brain injuries. *Using Technology to Enhance Special Education, 37*, 143–158.

Whitmarsh, L., Player, L., Jiongco, A., James, M., Williams, M., Marks, E., & Kennedy-Williams, P. (2022). Climate anxiety: What predicts it and how is it related to climate action? *Journal of Environmental Psychology, 83*, 101866.

WHO. (2018). Survey of adverse childhood experiences and associated health-harming behaviours among Polish students. *World Health Organization*. https://www.who.int/europe/publications/i/item/WHO-EURO-2018-2984-42742-59621

WHO. (2024). Preventing child maltreatment. *World Health Organization*. https://www.who.int/europe/activities/preventing-child-maltreatment

Wille, A., & Bovens, M. (2019). Education as a Cleavage. In *Diploma Democracy: The Rise of Political Meritocracy.* Oxford: Oxford University Press. https://ssrn.com/abstract=3370399or http://dx.doi.org/DOI: 10.2139/ssrn.3370399

Wilson, D. T., & O'Connor, M.-F. (2022). From Grief to Grievance: Combined Axes of Personal and Collective Grief Among Black Americans. *Frontiers in Psychiatry, 13*. Advance online publication. PMID: 35573332

Winter, J. (2022, January 9). The rise and fall of vibes-based literacy. *The New Yorker.* https://www.newyorker.com/news/annals-of-education/the-rise-and-fall-of-vibes-based-literacy

Wise, S. L., & DeMars, C. E. (2005). Low examinee effort in low-stakes assessment: Problems and potential solutions. *Educational Assessment, 10*(1), 1–17.

Witt, C., & Ulmer, J. (2010). The impact of inquiry-based learning on the academic achievement of middle school students. In *Proceedings of the 29th Annual Western Region AAAE Research Conference* (Vol. 269, p. 282).

Wlodarczyk, K. (2012). *Educator evaluation of academic and social competence in students with acquired brain injury (ABI) relative to assessed performance and sense of belonging.* Retrieved from https://dr.library.brocku.ca/bitstream/handle/10464/ 4100/Brock_Wlodarczyk_Kathy_2012.pdf?sequence=1&isAllowed=y

Wolfendale, S., Bryans, T., Fox, M., Labram, A., & Sigston, A. (Eds.). (1992). *The profession and practice of educational psychology: Future directions.* Cassell Educational.

Wolf, K., & Schmitz, J. (2023, April 21). Scoping review: Longitudinal effects of the COVID-19 pandemic on child and adolescent mental health. *European Child & Adolescent Psychiatry*, 1–56. DOI: 10.1007/s00787-023-02206-8 PMID: 37081139

Wolf, T. M., Elston, R. C., & Kissling, G. E. (1989). Relationship of Hassles, Uplifts, and Life Events to Psychological Weil-Being of Freshman Medical Students. *Behavioral Medicine (Washington, D.C.)*, *15*(1), 37–45. DOI: 10.1080/08964289.1989.9935150 PMID: 2923991

Woodin, T., McCulloch, G., & Cowan, S. (2013). The School-Leaving Age in International Perspective. In *Secondary Education and the Raising of the School-Leaving Age* (Secondary Education in a Changing World). Palgrave Macmillan. DOI: 10.1057/9781137065216_2

Woollard, J. (2010). *Psychology for the classroom: Behaviourism.* Routledge.

World Health Organization. (2006). A state of complete physical mental and social wellbeing and not merely the absence of disease or infirmity. *Constitution of the World Health Organization basic documents, 45*, 1-20.

World Health Organization. (2022). *Mental health.* Retrieved from: https://www .who.int/news-room/fact- sheets/detail/mental-health-strengthening-our-response

World Health Organization. (2023). How school systems can improve health and well-being: topic brief: mental health. https://www.who.int/publications/i/item/ 9789240064751

Wrench, A., Garrett, R., & King, S. (2014). Managing health and well-being: Student experiences in transitioning to higher education. *Asia-Pacific Journal of Health, Sport and Physical Education*, *5*(2), 151–166.

Wright, B. A., & Lopez, S. J. (2009). Widening the diagnostic focus: A case for including human strengths and environmental resources. In Lopez, S. J., & Snyder, C. R. (Eds.), *Oxford handbook of positive psychology* (pp. 71–87). Oxford University Press.

Wu, S., & Rao, N. (2011). Chinese and German teachers' conceptions of play and learning and children's play behaviour. *European Early Childhood Education Research, 19*(4), 469–481. DOI: 10.1080/1350293X.2011.623511

Yates, A., Starkey, L., Egerton, B., & Flueggen, F. (2021). High school students' experience of online learning during Covid-19: The influence of technology and pedagogy. *Technology, Pedagogy and Education, 30*(1), 59–73.

Young, C. B., Wu, S. S., & Menon, V. (2012). The neurodevelopmental basis of math anxiety. *Psychological Science, 23*(5), 492–501. DOI: 10.1177/095679761142913

Yu, S. (2018). Uncovering the hidden impacts of inequality on mental health: A global study. *Translational Psychiatry, 8*(1), 98. DOI: 10.1038/s41398-018-0148-0

Yu, Z., & Xu, W. (2022). A meta-analysis and systematic review of the effect of virtual reality technology on users' learning outcomes. *Computer Applications in Engineering Education, 30*(5), 1470–1484.

Zembylas, M. (2018). Reinventing critical pedagogy as decolonizing pedagogy: The educationof empathy. *Review of Education, Pedagogy & Cultural Studies, 40*(5), 404–421.

Zhang, Y., Qu, B., Lun, S., Wang, D., Guo, Y., & Liu, J. (2012). Quality of life of medical students in China: A study using the WHOQOL-BREF. *PLoS One, 7*(11), e49714. PMID: 23209595

Zhao, Y. (2020). Two decades of havoc: A synthesis of criticism against PISA. *Journal of Educational Change, 21*(2), 245–266. DOI: 10.1007/s10833-019-09367-x

Zheng, B., Lynam, A., & McGuckin, C. (2024) Creating Inclusive Schools: Enhancing Educational Opportunities for Migrant and Refugee Children in Ireland, Ireland's Education Yearbook 2024. https://irelandseducationyearbook.ie/downloads/IEYB2024/Irelands-Yearbook-of-Education-2024-Research-9.pdf

Zieme, J., & Gutwiller-Helfenfinger, E. (2019). Children's Rights and Educational Psychology. *European Psychologist, 24*(2). Advance online publication. DOI: 10.1027/1016-9040/a000373

Zimmerman, J. (2022). *Whose America? Culture Wars in the Public Schools*. University of Chicago Press.

Zinkina, J., Korotayev, A., & Andreev, A. (2016). Mass primary education in the nineteenth century. In *Globalistics and Globalization Studies* (pp. 63–70). Global Transformations and Global Future.

About the Contributors

Aoife M. Lynam is Assistant Professor in Psychology of Education, Trinity College Dublin. Aoife has received the Trinity Gold Medal (2009), a Trinity College Dublin (TCD) Faculty Scholarship (2012-15), and an Irish Research Council for the Humanities and the Social Sciences Scholarship (2013-2015). Her Ph.D research explored the experiences of bereaved young people in Irish primary and post-primary schools. Aoife lectures in Psychology of Education and Social, Personal, and Health Education (SPHE) and has supervised pre-service teachers on school placement and for their research dissertations at Masters and Doctoral level. Aoife is an Advisory Board Member of the Irish Childhood Bereavement Network (ICBN), part of the Management Board for Trinity Research in Childhood Centre (TRiCC), and a Board Director on the Vision Ireland Services Board. Aoife has published and presented her research both nationally and internationally.

Conor Mc Guckin graduated from the University of Ulster with a B.Sc. (Hons.: First Class) in Psychology and Organizational Science, and from the Open University with a B.Sc. (Open) degree. He gained his Ph.D. in Psychology for his research exploring bully/victim problems among school pupils across Northern Ireland. Conor is a Chartered Psychologist (CPsychol) with The British Psychological Society), a Chartered Psychologist (C.Psychol.Ps.S.I.) with The Psychological Society of Ireland, and a Chartered Scientist (CSci) with The British Science Council. Conor is also an Associate Fellow of both The British Psychological Society (AFBPsS) and The Psychological Society of Ireland (A.F.Ps.S.I.). Conor has a long history of involvement in, and leadership of, national and international research and applied practice projects.

* * *

Ashling Bourke is an Associate Professor in Psychology and Human Development at the Institute of Education. Her research and teaching interests include the processes that impact on child and adolescent wellbeing and children's rights. Ashling has experience in a wide range of research topics and research methodologies and she has an active research profile the intersection of Psychology, Rights, and Education. She teaches modules on social psychology, wellbeing, learning, research methods, and developmental psychology.

Kate Carr Fanning is an Assistant Professor at University College Dublin (UCD), where she serves as Director of Inclusive Education and Programmes Director. She has over a decade of experience in lecturing and programme leadership across universities in Ireland and England, specialising in inclusive education, educational psychology, teacher education, and childhood studies. Kate's research focuses on the experiences and needs of students with social, emotional, and mental health difficulties, including ADHD and other forms of neurodivergence. She is a Director of ADHD Ireland, serves on the Professional Advisory Board of ADHD Europe, and collaborates internationally on the development of educational and mental health supports. Her consultancy spans work with families, schools, and organisations, including projects in New York and the development of digital interventions for ADHD.

Thomas Demaria, Ph.D., is a Clinical Psychologist and a Fellow in both the Trauma and Clinical Divisions of the American Psychological Association. Dr. Demaria has earned numerous awards for his participation in several hundred local and national community and school crisis responses including school shootings. He is a two-time recipient of the prestigious New York State Liberty Award for community service following the World Trade Center terrorist attacks and in the Gulf Coast following Hurricane Katrina. Dr. Demaria was honored with a Humanitarian Award from the Center for Christian & Jewish studies for his work with Holocaust survivors and earned special recognition from the International Society for Traumatic Stress for both Clinical Excellence in Service Delivery and Distinguished Mentorship of Students.

Lorraine M. Duffy is a senior postdoctoral researcher at the Royal College of Surgeons in Ireland. She is an accredited health promotion practitioner with the International Union for Health Promotion and Education (IUHPE). Her Ph.D. explored cultural diversity and intercultural education in the early childhood classroom. Lorraine has researched and published articles on health and education topics including brain injury, youth mentoring, primary education, initial teacher education, the needs of children and families and disability support. Her research interests include brain injury, brain health, qualitative research methods, public and patient involvement (PPI), lived experience of health conditions and the participation of children and young people in health, education and social research. Lorraine advocates for the rights of people with brain injury and other neurological conditions through her research, and through her collaboration with organisations in Ireland and internationally.

Lucie Ehiwe is a qualified humanistic integrative psychotherapist with a background in Psychology as a lecturer and researcher. She specialised in developmental psychology and research on the psychology of school bullying and cyberbullying. Lucie's lecturing work has focused on developmental psychology (which examines physical, cognitive, and emotional change from birth to death) and research methods, which has been helpful in both viewing change/transition in the context of life stages, and in considering the complexities of psychological diagnoses, treatments, and interventions.

Geraldine Fitzgerald is Subject Librarian for the School of Education and the School of Psychology in Trinity College Dublin. Prior to working in TCD, Geraldine worked in a number of special, corporate and academic libraries in Ireland and Sweden. Geraldine is passionate about improving user experience in the Library and has been involved in a number of initiatives and interdepartmental research projects to improve the Library's sensory environment.

Conor Galvin is Director of the Doctorate in Education (PhD Education) at UCD School of Education, where he also lectures on education, sustainability, public policy, and research methods. His research explores professional knowledge, sustainability education, development policy in the Global South, innovation transfer, and the impact of emerging technologies on learning and society. He leads UCD's involvement in major European projects and has served as evaluator, assessor, and advisor on numerous EU and OECD initiatives in education and technology. Prof. Galvin also contributes to international development and peace support education, advises on Ireland's participation in PISA and TIMSS, and has held visiting and leadership roles at institutions including Cambridge University and UCD College of Human Sciences. Recipient of UCD's President's Award for Teaching, he is a frequent invited speaker and guest lecturer in Ireland and across Europe.

Chris Gibbons, PhD., is Associate Professor at Queen's University Belfast. He is a visiting professor at Trinity College Dublin and also teaches at Dublin Business School. He has two distinct research interests. The first is health psychology - principally stress and coping, with a positive psychology focus on how stress can help one achieve, and the role of personality and cognitive factors associated with achievement. The second is in promoting the quality of teaching and learning in education at all levels. He is interested in pursuing all avenues to make the learning experience an effective and enriching one for students. He has been a Fellow of the Higher Education Academy and an HE Practitioner since August 2002 and he is a qualified school teacher and member of the General Teachers' Council in Northern Ireland. He is passionate about promoting the understanding of psychology and about spreading excellence in teaching. This led him to found the Association for Psychology Teachers (APT www.associationforpsychologyteachers.com) in 1995, a body that organises annual student conferences and teacher and lecturer CPD events. The success of the event was celebrated by 'The Psychologist' in 2018. Dr Gibbons has received multiple teaching awards, most recently (in 2022) a National Teaching Hero Award from the National Forum for the Enhancement of Teaching in Higher Education in Ireland.

Andrew J. Holliman is Associate Professor (Teaching) at UCL Institute of Education, UK. He currently serves as Chair of the Psychology of Education Section at the British Psychological Society, and is recognized as a Chartered Psychologist and Scientist, Fellow of the British Psychological Society, and Senior Fellow of the Higher Education Academy. His research interests include the psychology of education, teaching and learning in higher education, and the development of children's literacy.

Anne Marie Kavanagh (PhD) is Assistant Professor in Ethical and Intercultural Education in the School of Human Development, Dublin City University, Ireland. She teaches and researches in the areas of intercultural education, social justice education, climate justice education, ethical education, and human rights education. She is a member of the steering committee of the DCU Centre for Human Rights and Citizenship Education (CHRCE) and a member of the DCU Anti-Bullying Centre. In 2021, her first co-edited book (with Prof Fionnuala Waldron & Dr Benjamin Mallon) 'Teaching for Social Justice and Sustainable Development Across the Primary Curriculum' was published by Routledge.

Patricia McCarthy is a Visiting Research Fellow in the School of Education, Trinity College Dublin where she is an active member of the teaching and research community. Having graduated with a PhD from Trinity College Dublin in 2014 focused on the educational experiences and transition opportunities of vision impaired/blind young people, Dr McCarthy continues to advocate and research actively. A key component of her research to date focuses on UD, UDL, inclusion and participation of marginalised groups; Patricia's ontological position as a disabled researcher has been instrumental in the development of her research and recent publications. She is a published expert in disability in relation to student/learner experiences of participation in education and society. As a registered blind person, Patricia is an active advocate for people with disabilities, advising various governmental and civic society organisations.

Selina McCoy is Head of Education Research at the Economic and Social Research Institute and is Adjunct Professor of Sociology at Trinity College Dublin. She has over 25 years' experience with responsibility for pioneering research and evaluation projects in the fields of educational inequality, inclusion, academic achievement and student development. For the last 14 years, Selina has been the Irish national expert at the European Commission Independent Experts in Education and Training. Selina was also a member of the 15-member European Commission Expert Group on Quality Investment in Education and Training. She is a regular contributor on policy debate in education and has delivered many keynotes at academic, policy and stakeholder events nationally and across Europe.

Ruth McKernan is employed as a Team Manager with the National Council for Special Education. She is also an accredited psychotherapist with a small private practice working with adult survivors of trauma, as well as being a graduate member of the Psychological Society of Ireland and secretary to the Trauma and Adversity Special Interest Group. She is a PhD candidate in Maynooth University, carrying out research in the area of trauma informed education.

Daniel Muijs is Head of the School of Social Sciences, Education and Social Work and Professor of Education at Queen's University Belfast. He is an acknowledged expert in the fields of educational and teacher effectiveness, school improvement and research methods and has published widely in these areas. He is co-editor of the journal 'School Effectiveness and School Improvement', and Executive Editor of 'Education Sciences'. He has held advisory posts in a range of academic, policy and professional organisations. He previously held professorial and leadership positions at a range of universities in England, the Netherlands and Belgium, and was Head of Research and Evaluation at Ofsted. Daniel holds a PhD in Social Sciences from the Catholic University of Leuven (Belgium), an MSc in Managerial Economic (Catholic University of Leuven) and a BA in Communication Sciences (Catholic University of Leuven).

Catriona O'Toole is a Chartered Psychologist and Associate Professor at Maynooth University, specialising in trauma-informed education, school engagement, and well-being. Known for her EMBRACE Framework for Trauma-Informed Care in Schools, she collaborates with global and national bodies like UNESCO MGIEP and Alcohol Action Ireland, advancing research-driven, inclusive educational practices.

Catriona serves on the Executive Committee of the International Network for School Attendance and holds leadership roles in both the European Educational Research Association and Ireland's Trauma and Adversity Special Interest Group.

Noel Purdy is a Professor of Teacher Education and Director of Research and Scholarship and Director of the Centre for Research in Educational Underachievement at Stranmillis University College, Belfast. His research interests are in educational underachievement, special educational needs and pastoral care, and addressing on- and offline bullying in schools. He chaired the Expert Panel on Educational Underachievement in Northern Ireland (*A Fair Start*, 2021), and the DE Steering Committee in the Republic of Ireland (*Cineáltas*, 2022). He is Editor of the journal Pastoral Care in Education and is a parent governor of a special school. In 2024, he was awarded an OBE for services to education in the King's Birthday Honours List.

Mary Quirke is a researcher, educator, and advocate dedicated to inclusive education, Universal Design for Learning (UDL), and equitable career and work transitions. She holds a PhD from Trinity College Dublin (TCD), where her research explores learner voice, inclusive learning, career transitions, and pathways into employment, particularly for individuals with disabilities. With extensive experience across policy, practice, and research, Dr. Quirke has worked in Further and Higher Education, vocational training, and workplace inclusion and has also contributed to national and European projects promoting inclusive learning and employment strategies. She has most recently led national research studies, exploring different learning environments and experiences while ensuring learner voices are central and continues to collaborate with educators, policymakers, and advocacy groups to advance evidence-based, learner-centred approaches. As the champion of Universal Design for Guidance (UDG), Dr. Quirke emphasises designing for diversity from the outset and aligning UDL thinking with different theories and professional practice.

David J. Schonfeld, MD, is a developmental-behavioral pediatrician and director of the National Center for School Crisis and Bereavement (www.schoolcrisiscenter.org), Children's Hospital Los Angeles. He has provided consultation after numerous school crisis events and disasters and has presented more than 1,000 times on the topics of crisis and loss and authored more than 150 scholarly articles, book chapters, and books. Dr. Schonfeld is a member of the Executive Committee of the American Academy of Pediatrics Council on Children and Disasters and Chair of the National Advisory Committee on Children and Disasters; he served as a Commissioner for the National Commission on Children and Disasters and the Sandy Hook Advisory Commission.

Kieron Sheehy is Professor of Education (Innovation Pedagogies) at The Open University, UK. He has a particular interest in addressing issues for those who might be stigmatized and excluded within educational systems. This has encompassed examining developing practical pedagogies for inclusive classrooms and researching the relationship between epistemological beliefs and educational practice. He is currently working on projects developing inclusive disaster risk reduction education and understanding fun in learning.

Keith Young is an Assistant Professor in ICT/Digital Learning in Mary Immaculate College, Ireland. He holds a BTech. (Ed) in Materials and Engineering Technology from the University of Limerick, a PhD in Education from the University of Limerick and a MSc in Software Design with Artificial Intelligence from the Technological University of the Shannon: Midlands Midwest. His main interests include developing student teachers capacity to meaningfully and critically engage with the use of digital technologies as part of their practice.

Index

P

Q

R

S

T

U

V

www.ingramcontent.com/pod-product-compliance
Lightning Source LLC
LaVergne TN
LVHW062331300926
849161LV00007B/1647